New Frontiers of the Capability Approach

For over three decades, the capability approach (CA) proposed and developed by Amartya Sen and Martha Nussbaum has had a distinct impact on development theories and approaches. Going beyond a merely economic conception of development, it engages more widely with its normative aspects. This book explores the new frontiers of the CA and its links to human development in three main areas. First, it delves into the philosophical foundations of the approach, re-examining its links to concepts of common good, collective agency and epistemic diversity. Second, it addresses its 'operational frontier', aiming to give inclusive explanations of some of the most advanced methods available for capability researchers. Third, it discusses the wide range of applications for which this approach can be used, as carried out both by renowned capability scholars and by researchers from different disciplines. This broad interdisciplinary range includes the areas of human and sustainable development, inequalities, labour markets, education, special needs, cities, urban planning, housing, social capital and happiness studies, among others.

FLAVIO COMIM is an associate professor at the University Ramon Llull/IQS in Spain and an affiliated lecturer at the Centre of Development Studies, University of Cambridge. He has been a consultant for UNESCO, UNEP, FAO, WHO and UNDP. He co-edited the books *The Capability Approach: Concepts, Measures and Applications* (Cambridge, 2008), with Mozaffar Qizilbash and Sabina Alkire, and *Capabilities, Gender, Equality* (Cambridge, 2014), with Martha Nussbaum.

SHAILAJA FENNELL is Senior Lecturer in Development Studies at the University of Cambridge. Her previous publications include *Rules, Rubrics and Riches: The Interrelations between Legal Reform and International Development* (2010) and *Gender Education and Equality in a Global Context: Conceptual Frameworks and Policy Perspectives* (edited with M. Arnot, 2008).

P. B. ANAND is a reader in environmental economics and public policy at the University of Bradford where he has been teaching since 1998. His previous works include his book *Scarcity, Entitlements and the Economics of Water in Developing Countries* (2007) and papers on applying the capability approach to issues related to access to water and sustainability.

New Frontiers of the Capability Approach

Edited by

FLAVIO COMIM
IQS/Universitat Ramon Llull

SHAILAJA FENNELL
University of Cambridge

P. B. ANAND
University of Bradford

CAMBRIDGE
UNIVERSITY PRESS

CAMBRIDGE
UNIVERSITY PRESS

University Printing House, Cambridge CB2 8BS, United Kingdom

One Liberty Plaza, 20th Floor, New York, NY 10006, USA

477 Williamstown Road, Port Melbourne, VIC 3207, Australia

314–321, 3rd Floor, Plot 3, Splendor Forum, Jasola District Centre, New Delhi – 110025, India

79 Anson Road, #06-04/06, Singapore 079906

Cambridge University Press is part of the University of Cambridge.

It furthers the University's mission by disseminating knowledge in the pursuit of education, learning, and research at the highest international levels of excellence.

www.cambridge.org
Information on this title: www.cambridge.org/9781108427807
DOI: 10.1017/9781108559881

First published 2018

Printed and bound in Great Britain by Clays Ltd, Elcograf S.p.A.

A catalogue record for this publication is available from the British Library.

Library of Congress Cataloging-in-Publication data

Names: Comim, Flavio, editor. | Fennell, Shailaja, 1964- editor. | Anand, P. B., editor.
Title: New frontiers of the capability approach / edited by Flavio Comim, Shailaja Fennell, P. B. Anand.
Description: Cambridge, UK ; New York, NY : Cambridge University Press, 2018. | Large print. | Includes bibliographic references.
Identifiers: LCCN 2018009332 | ISBN 9781108427807 (hardback : alk. paper)
Subjects: LCSH: Capabilities approach (Social sciences) | Economic development—Sociological aspects. | Human behavior.
Classification: LCC HD75 .N479 2018 | DDC 330.15/56—dc23
LC record available at https://lccn.loc.gov/2018009332

ISBN 978-1-108-42780-7 Hardback

Contents

List of Figures   *page* viii

List of Tables   x

List of Contributors   xii

Preface and Acknowledgements   xiv

1 Introduction   1
   FLAVIO COMIM, SHAILAJA FENNELL AND P. B. ANAND

2 On Sen on the Capability of Capabilities:
   The Story of a Not-For-Profit Enterprise   12
   GAY MEEKS

   Part I   The Need for New Foundations

3 Capabilities and the Common Good   53
   JONATHAN WARNER

4 Measuring the Meta-Capability of Agency: *A Theoretical*
   Basis for Creating a Responsibility Indicator   82
   MATHIAS NEBEL AND MA. TERESA HERRERA RENDÓN NEBEL

5 Equal Liberty, Reflective Equilibrium and Education:
   Defending Rawls from Sen's Criticisms   116
   CAROLINE SOUZA AND GABRIEL GOLDMEIER

6 On Epistemic Diversity, Ontologies and Assumptions in
   Capability Approaches   139
   JOSH PLATZKY MILLER

7 Collective Agency Capability: *How Capabilities Can*
   Emerge in a Social Moment   153
   RAZIA SHARIFF

Part II   The Operationalisation Frontier

8   Sen's Capability Approach, Social Choice Theory
     and the Use of Rankings   179
     FLAVIO COMIM

9   Selecting Capabilities for Development: *An Evaluation
     of Proposed Methods*   198
     MORTEN F. BYSKOV

10   From Resources to Functioning: *Rethinking and Measuring
     Conversion Rates*   232
     ENRICA CHIAPPERO, PAOLA SALARDI
     AND FRANCESCO SCERVINI

11   Demystifying the Use of Simultaneous Equation Models
     for Operationalising the Capability Approach   246
     JAYA KRISHNAKUMAR AND RICARDO NOGALES

Part III   The Application Frontier

12   Human Development in India: *Comparing Sen and his
     Competitors*   273
     DES GASPER

13   Sustainable Human Development Measurement Issues:
     A New Proposal   314
     MARIO BIGGERI AND VINCENZO MAURO

14   Inequality and Capabilities: *A Multidimensional Empirical
     Exploration in Chile*   329
     MACARENA ORCHARD AND MARTINA YOPO

15   Living Wages in International Supply Chains and the
     Capability Approach: *Towards a Conceptual Framework*   351
     STEPHANIE SCHRAGE AND KRISTIN HUBER

16   For a Happy Human Development   384
     TADASHI HIRAI

17   Capability of Capabilities and Aspirations of the
     Middle Classes in India   411
     MEERA TIWARI

18   The Value of Individual and Community Social Resources   436
     PAUL ANAND AND IRIS MANTOVANI

     Part IV   The Housing and Urban Frontier

19   Tracking the Transition From 'Basic Needs' to 'Capabilities'
     for Human-Centred Development: *The Role of Housing
     in Urban Inclusion*   475
     SHAILAJA FENNELL, JAIME ROYO-OLID AND MATTHEW BARAC

20   Building Regulations through the Capability Lens:
     A Safer and Inclusive Built Environment?   505
     PRACHI ACHARYA

21   Cities and the Capability Approach   519
     P. B. ANAND

     Part V   The Education Frontier

22   Formal Education, Well-Being and Aspirations:
     *A Capability-Based Analysis on High School Pupils
     from France*   549
     ROBIN VOS AND JÉRÔME BALLET

23   Other People's Adaptations: *Teaching Children with
     Special Educational Needs to Adapt and to Aspire*   571
     CRISTINA DEVECCHI AND MICHAEL WATTS

24   Expanding Children's Capabilities at the Writers'
     Workshop   597
     HELENA KIFF

25   Education, Capabilities and Sustainable Development   617
     CAROLINE SAROJINI HART

Author Index   643

Subject Index   652

Figures

7.1 Instrumental freedom changes needed for collective
     agency capability to emerge   166
8.1 From non-comparability to full-comparability   187
11.1 The capability approach in a diagrammatic form   257
14.1 Histogram of the General Capabilities Index   340
15.1 Anker and Anker's living wage calculation methodology
     for ISEAL   357
15.2 The role of work and remuneration in the model
     of the capability approach   362
15.3 The systemic dimension of too low wages in the
     international garment industry – challenges on
     three levels   367
15.4 A model to compare and analyse accountability
     standards   370
15.5 A framework to compare and analyse living wage
     approaches   374
17.1 NMC capability expansion   424
17.2 NMC Doxa, habitus and the upward aspiration spiral   425
19.1 Key relationships of power   482
19.2 Left: Social anthropologist Margot Ehrlich consults
     tsunami victim about life and housing preferences.
     Right: Architect Tiago Vier informs and collects choices
     of end users about different choices of house types   484
19.3 Incremental post-tsunami houses by *Architecture &*
     Développement in Tamil Nadu, India   489
19.4 Capabilities informed hypothetical design guidelines
     for bonded-labourers low-cost housing in Alang Ship
     breaking yards, Gujarat, India   494
19.5 Collage of conventional vs incremental low-cost houses
     in Gujarat   495

19.6 Woman sitting in semi-public verandah in Ahmedabad,
      India   498
20.1 Capabilities framework for building standards   513
21.1 Urbanisation and living longer? (a) Change in life
      expectancy 1961–2011, (b) Cities and long life   531
21.2 Urbanisation but not living longer? (a) Urban population
      as per cent total: 1961 to 2011 in countries where life
      expectancy did not change much, (b) Countries where life
      expectancy in 2011 is almost the same as 1961   532
21.3 Social gradient in Bradford's mortality rates?   533
21.4 Urbanisation and urban poverty: (a) Guinea and
      Honduras, (b) Ethiopia and Paraguay (c) Ecuador,
      Malawi, Thailand and Kazakhstan   536
21.5 Urbanisation and gender inequality in wage employment
      (a) in 2000 and (b) in 2010   540
21.6 Urbanisation and proportion of people living in slums
      2014   541
22.1 Frequency of response per modality in module 3:
      value and quality of education   559
22.2 Frequency of response per modality in module 4:
      well-being in school   560
22.3 Frequency of response per modality in module 5:
      aspirations, with regard to education   561
25.1 Multi-stage process of converting commodities and
      capitals to capabilities and functionings   624
25.2 Illustration of the trade-off between an individual's
      capabilities and functionings and those of others   635

Tables

9.1 Overview of methods for the selection of capabilities
     and functionings proposed within the human development
     and capability literature   202
12.1 Word choices in Narendra Modi's speeches   301
12.2 Sen and Drèze in comparison to five other analyses of
     India. Patterns of attention and lack of attention to
     topics in human development   307
13.1 HDI components and new dimensions and proxy variable
     normalized for selected countries, year 2005   323
13.2 A comparison between arithmetic mean, geometric
     mean and MHDI   323
14.1 List of 11 capabilities   335
14.2 Means of the 11 capabilities indexes in the population
     and their distribution according to sex, age and
     socioeconomic status   338
14.3 Means of the General Capabilities Index by gender,
     age and socioeconomic status   341
14.4 Capabilities quintile ratio of the General Capabilities
     Index and the 11 capabilities indexes   343
14.5 F statistics of Capabilities' Indexes and wellbeing
     measurements in the different clusters structures   345
14.6 Means of Capabilities' Indexes and wellbeing in the
     structure of four clusters   346
14.7 Distribution of the clusters according to sex, age and
     socioeconomic status   348
17.1 NMC aspiration–agency–capability mapping   426
17.2 Selected SDGs, agency, instrumental and constitutive
     freedoms   429
18.1 Measures of experienced utility   445
18.2 Measures of social resources   447

18.3 Determinants of life satisfaction   450
18.4 Happiness equations: Instrumental variables   456
18.5 Experience-based methods of valuation in the literature   457
18.6 Happiness equations: linear specification   462
18.7 Happiness equations: diminishing marginal utility   464
18.8 Happiness and social resources in the US and UK   466
19.1 Housing capabilities identified by the Equalities
      Commission, UK   492
22.1 Distribution of modalities per variable in the
      hierarchical cluster analysis groups   564
25.1 Extract from SDG 4, UN, 2015, pp. 17/35   619

Contributors

Prachi Acharya, University of Cambridge

P. B. Anand, University of Bradford

Paul Anand, Open University

Jérôme Ballet, University of Bordeaux and GREThA

Matthew Barac, London Metropolitan University

Mario Biggeri, University of Florence

Morten F. Byskov, University of Warwick

Enrica Chiappero, University of Pavia and CRHED University of Free State

Flavio Comim, IQS/Universitat Ramon Llull and University of Cambridge

Cristina Devecchi, University of Northampton

Shailaja Fennell, University of Cambridge

Des Gasper, International Institute of Social Studies (The Hague), Erasmus University Rotterdam, Netherlands

Gabriel Goldmeier, UCL Institute of Education

Caroline Sarojini Hart, University of Sheffield

Ma. Teresa Herrera Rendón Nebel, Universidad Popular Autonoma del Estado de Puebla

Tadashi Hirai, University of Cambridge

Kristin Huber, Universität

Helena Kiff, University of East Anglia

Jaya Krishnakumar, University of Geneva

Iris Mantovani, London Economics

Vincenzo Mauro, University of Pisa

Gay Meeks, University of Cambridge

Josh Platzky Miller, University of Cambridge

Mathias Nebel, Universidad Popular Autonoma del Estado de Puebla

Ricardo Nogales, University of Oxford and Universidad Privada Boliviana

Macarena Orchard, University of Nottingham

Jaime Royo-Olid, University of Cambridge

Paola Salardi, University of Toronto

Francesco Scervini, University of Pavia

Stephanie Schrage, Universität Hamburg

Razia Shariff, Canterbury Christ Church University

Caroline Souza, University of Cambridge

Meera Tiwari, University of East London

Robin Vos, University of Bordeaux and GREThA

Jonathan Warner, Quest University Canada

Michael Watts, Education Consultant

Martina Yopo, University of Cambridge

Preface and Acknowledgements

This book is a result of the first Cambridge Capability Conference (CCC) held in June 2016. It is a testimony to the vitality of the approach to tackle emerging human development challenges. This conference was the start of a new phase of capability conferences in Cambridge. From the early Cambridge and Pavia Capability Conferences in the first half of the 2000s and the creation of the Human Development and Capability Association, the literature on the capability approach (CA) has seen a prolific expansion. While the impressive intellectual stature of the founding figures of the CA, Amartya Sen and Martha Nussbaum, has been a decisive factor in the multi-dimensional and interdisciplinary expansion of the approach, it is important to acknowledge that much of the proliferation has also been due to the development of a large community of capability scholars spread all over the world.

Cambridge, both the University and the city, is home to many people working on the CA and has been an integral part of this history. It has provided a vibrant and stimulating environment for the delivery of lectures, convening of conferences, writing of PhD theses and undertaking of research on human development from a capability perspective. In fact, one of the best-kept Cambridge secrets is that for more than thirty-five years, the University has benefited from lectures on the CA offered by Gay Meeks. Gentle and reserved, she does not like to talk about her own achievements, a rare virtue nowadays, some might say. Yet, she is extremely influential not only due to the elegance of her writing, but also because of her generosity in lecturing to generations of students. It is not an exaggeration to suggest that many of us would not have learnt to understand and value the CA if we had not had the opportunity to sit in on her authoritative and stimulating lectures.

This book is first and foremost a record of our gratitude and admiration for Meeks who was invited to be the first keynote speaker of this conference series where we try to recreate the intellectually challenging environment of her lectures and the intimate intellectual atmosphere of the early Capability Conferences.

Meeks started her academic life getting a first in her BA at 'the other place' (the University of Oxford) in philosophy, politics and economics in 1971, followed by her PhD at the University of Edinburgh in 1975. During her PhD days she worked as a tutor in philosophy at the University of Glasgow. When she finished, she became an ESRC post-doctoral fellow at the Faculty of Economics and a Calouste Gulbenkian research fellow at Lucy Cavendish College in Cambridge. From 1978 to 1980 she was a lecturer in economics for St Anne's College, Oxford (yes, that college of Michael Sandel's 50p story!), a junior dean and joint warden of St Anne's-Balliol Graduate Centre. From 1985 to 1994 she was a fellow and director of studies in economics for Robinson College, in Cambridge. That overlapped with her appointment as a research associate from 1984 to 2001 at the Department of Applied Economics, Cambridge. During the twenty-two years, from 1986 to 2008, she was an affiliated lecturer at the Faculty of Economics in Cambridge. In 2001, she resumed her fellowship at Robinson College that continued until 2009. Since 2001, she has been appointed senior research associate, first in the Faculty of Economics, now in POLIS.

For so many of us, Meeks was the lecturer of an intriguing and challenging paper called 'Philosophical Issues in Economics'. This paper was given as part of the MPhil in economics until 2008 and from then on in the MPhil in development studies in Cambridge. This paper introduced the CA and provided a critical view of normative economics, a different kind of development based on principles broader than utilitarianism can offer, at least in its narrower forms.

The paper has also been an exemplar in academic excellence: from her meticulous notes, usually revised and amended, Meeks would not simply offer the key concepts to understand complex methodological debates, but also provide an impressive list of scholars who had already discussed the topics, accompanied by questions through which her students could develop their own thinking. If one felt intimidated by reading the 'giants' of economics and philosophy, Meeks would offer sets of tailored questions that would induce and empower her students to think critically about core issues for the understanding of economics as a moral science. This is not a minor achievement. One did not simply read Sen's 'Rational Fools'. One was invited to think about it. One was also invited to consider others' arguments and points of view (the mark of a good essay!), never forgetting, of course, as she would repeat two to three times during the academic year, that 'Sen was the hero' of the paper.

One would 'learn by doing' that in order to be a good academic one would have to confront opposing views, stimulating values of tolerance and sympathy in the training of future generations of lecturers and professionals in other fields. But that was only half of the story: Meeks has always been an extremely gentle and kind teacher, offering generous office hours for seeing students, who would bring their ideas, hypotheses, misunderstandings and, yes, delusions (not always in comprehensible English) to her and receive kind and wise ministering.

We are delighted to be able to express our gratitude to Dr Meeks, as well as to all other participants of our first CCC and to the Centre of Development Studies in Cambridge that provided an interdisciplinary home for this forum. Our thanks also go to Doreen Woolfrey, because without her help the conference would not have been possible. We are also very grateful to our editor, Phil Good, who believed in this project when it was only an incipient idea.

1 | Introduction

FLAVIO COMIM, SHAILAJA
FENNELL AND P. B. ANAND

The Capability Approach is an evaluative framework for assessing people's advantage. It focuses on distributive issues; in particular, those concerned with justice and equality. It shares a research agenda with the Human Development perspective, tackling issues of poverty, inequality, health and education, labour and human rights, among so many others still to be explored. The capability approach has become an important framework for thinking about development and quality of life because it changes the analytical locus of attention from resources and subjective views into objective 'doings and beings' (called functionings) and their corresponding freedoms (called capabilities) in evaluating how well people are living. As such, it broadens different informational spaces in carrying out inter-subjective comparisons of individuals' well-being and agency. Despite the considerable progress that has been achieved by this approach in the last three decades, it continues to offer new perspectives to be explored.

This book starts with a chapter based on Gay Meeks's keynote speech paper, 'On Sen on the Capability of Capabilities: The story of a not-for-profit enterprise', where she offers a historical reconstruction of Sen's capability approach, metaphorically seeing it in terms of growth phases of a successful company. By doing so, Meeks offers a rich, authoritative and unique narrative of the creation of the approach in which its different parts are seen as stages of a coherent strategy. Her paper is an essential call to see the capability approach as part of Sen's long-term intellectual enterprise. Indeed, it is remarkable to note how he laid out the foundations of the Capability Approach back in his early social choice writings in the early 1970s, pursing the same research agenda for almost fifty years.

The book is then divided into five parts, namely, (i) foundations, (ii) operationalisation, (iii) from concepts to applications, (iv) capabilities, cities and institutions and (v) capabilities and education. These parts were chosen to represent some of the 'new frontiers of the capability approach' addressed by this book.

The first group of chapters examines the foundations of the capability approach, critically delving into its individualistic nature and putting forward a range of alternatives to overcome what several authors consider as a key limitation of the approach. Jonathan Warner raises the point that human flourishing should be seen as a coordination exercise. The problem, as he sees it, is related to a certain overemphasis on the notion of agency sponsored by the approach. But what happens, he asks, when agency clashes with other values? This seems to be a question that has been hanging for some time in the literature and that can allow us to see its shortcomings and expand its frontiers by developing new analytical structures. Warner puts forward the concept of a 'flourishing community' and 'the common good' as strategic orientating principles to advance the notion of public interest. He follows an Aristotelian root, expanding on a now well-established debate on the capability literature.

A core concept for Warner is the notion of 'virtue'. This is a point also discussed by Caroline Souza and Gabriel Goldmeier within the context of political science. The authors, however, follow a different route from Warner's, addressing the debate in terms of the social contractarian tradition followed by the approach rather than in terms of its individualistic nature. In particular, they examine a debate between hypothetical contracts versus social contracts, exploring the ideas of Gauthier as a way of discussing the roots of cooperative behaviour. They address the same set of issues raised by Warner. However, instead of talking about individualist agency as he does, they address the issue of the limits of self-interest and its links with social choice theory, a theme also explored in this book by Comim. At the end, Souza and Goldmeier share Warner's proposal that 'common civic values' have a role to play in examining social arrangements

Mathias Nebel and Ma. Teresa Herrera Rendón Nebel also focus on the concept of agency as the *locus* to investigate critically the shortcomings of the Capability Approach. But instead of proceeding in the direction of Warner and Souza and Goldmeier, they prefer to put forward the notion of meta-capability of agency (that they define as the ability that people have of exercising their freedoms) establishing a link with the concept of responsibility (that they argue has been neglected by the approach). They choose the meta-capability of agency as a way of embedding agency within social relations, what analytically speaking is in the same direction suggested by the other papers. But they choose a different theoretical foundation to complement the approach based on the work by Ricoeur and Lèvinas. Their chapter moves beyond the philosophical frontier by examining possible empirical indicators for levels of responsibility, using as an example labour processes.

Josh Platzky Miller tackles the same question about the individualistic nature of the capability approach. But the way that he chooses to explore alternative conceptions of intersubjective personhood, as he puts it, is by considering a co-existence between different alternatives. In particular, he concentrates on 'assemblage theory' and 'communities'. The first characterises irreducible properties of social structures and how interrelations between parts cannot be fully captured by the capability approach; the second raises the political dimension of mobilisation that it is necessary for characterising communities and people's humanity in their social complexity. The merge with different theories is also the strategy chosen by Razia Shariff. Her way to build these new foundational frontiers entails the use of critical theory (in particular by using Foucault and Bordieu). Her argument is that critical theory can offer a broader ontology of social change than the one provided by Rawlsian theory, which, to a large extent, is a theme shared with Souza and Goldmeier. However, her emphasis is on understanding social transformation and for this reason she advocates that the concept of power needs to be taken more seriously. These critical thoughts are applied constructively to Sen's notions of instrumental freedoms, showing how they can be seen in a historical case (the Shahbag Movement).

These chapters, when taken together, not only question the individualistic nature of the capability approach, but also propose a rich range of alternatives, or 'new frontiers', as we say in this book, of the capability approach. Thus, they move beyond this well-established debate by suggesting concrete candidates as complementary concepts (in no particular order) such as 'common civic values', 'the common good', 'the meta-capability of agency', 'assemblage theory' or 'critical theory'.

The next group of chapters offers new perspectives on issues related to the operationalisation of the approach. Flavio Comim investigates the social choice roots of Sen's capability approach, putting forward its main implications for examining human development issues. He suggests that the principles of pluralism, comparative analysis and reasoned scrutiny can take us a long way in using the approach and that 'capabilities' per se will not do all the methodological work that needs to be done in applying the approach to human development issues, in line with Meeks's concluding remarks. Rather than attempting a taxonomy of different methods, such as the one offered by Byskov, he focuses on the field of rankings and meta-rankings that he argues are more compatible with Sen's approach. One can pay lip-service to any of the principles mentioned above; the real issue is about how to engage with them. On the other hand, Morten Byskov examines different methods for selecting capabilities. He classifies current methodologies into four groups, namely, ad hoc methods, foundational methods, procedural methods and multi-staged methods including the so-called synthesising method that promotes a dialectical dialogue between normative theory and the democratic decision-making process.

Another chapter that explores a potential empirical strategy for operationalising the capability approach is that written by Enrica Chiappero, Paola Salardi and Francesco Scervini. The focus of their attention is on the concept of 'conversion rate' and how the existing literature, as they argue, has often imprecisely defined and estimated this rate. Within this context, they put forward a conceptual framework for defining conversion factors and conversion rates. Similar to Comim, who focuses on the notion of rankings, and to Byskov, who puts forward the synthesising method, they concentrate on a key concept and explore its potential policy implications. Their paper, however, moves beyond measurement to discuss estimation challenges, such as endogeneity. By doing so, they engage with an empirical agenda similar to the one suggested by Jaya Krishnakumar and Ricardo Nogales.

In what has been named 'the operationalisation frontier', it is indeed important to distinguish between measurement, applications and estimation. Whereas measurement is about working with variables that can be described within capabilities spaces, applications could explore different aspects of the approach and estimation tackles the most suitable techniques to work with capability data. Krishnakumar and Nogales discuss one of the most promising frontiers in the operationalisation of the capability approach by analysing the potential role of simultaneous equation models. These models allow for a complete description of human development from a multidimensional and interconnected perspective, taking into account social, economic, political and institutional factors, that are key for the conversion issues as explored by Chiappero, Salardi and Scervini. In estimation exercises, it is essential for a human development agenda to compare between different groups of individuals and Krishnakumar and Nogales demonstrate in their chapter with two empirical applications how this can be achieved.

The operationalisation frontier remains one of the most challenging aspects of the capability approach because the translation of its theoretical richness into practical and concrete contexts faces several empirical hurdles. Taken together, however, these chapters provide some alternatives to handling these difficulties. They are not the only chapters in the book to engage with empirical issues but they are distinguished in the sense that they chose to structure their analyses with an emphasis on general instruments.

Nevertheless, one can also appreciate the relevance of history and political context in understanding the potential application of the approach. In this sense, Gasper's chapter provides a unique account of Sen's influence on the contemporary development arena in India by contrasting the impact of his and Jean Drèze's book, *India: Uncertain Glory* against the impact of other books that convey different visions of India. Des Gasper shows that, historically speaking, Drèze and Sen operate at the reasoned level of universalistic humanists, focusing on what happens to the poorest and most excluded groups in Indian society. Their vision, motivated by the capability approach, contrasts with visions of 'dreaming engineers, nationalist leaders and chauvinistic crowds', as Gasper puts it. Without anticipating Gasper's main conclusions, is it interesting to see that the application of the capability approach has a social context that needs to be appreciated. As such, Gasper's chapter nicely complements Meeks's discussion, seeing Sen's work on India as part of a wider political and social context. Gasper also invites the reader to think about development as a vision and as a set of practices with political significance.

Another important direction in which the application of the capability approach spreads is in tackling technical issues related to the elaboration of composite indicators. Mario Biggeri and Vincenzo Mauro face the challenge of exploring new frontiers of the Human Development Index (HDI) by applying the Multidimensional Synthesis of Indicators (MSI) approach to the traditional HDI. This allows them to expand the scope of informational spaces considered by the HDI in order to include other freedoms such as political, civil and environmental freedoms. Their paper discusses the differences in using arithmetic vis-à-vis geometric means in elaborating composite capability indicators. Whereas Biggeri and Mauro offer a discussion that it is *prima facie* very different from Gasper's narrative, both chapters explore new frontiers in which the capability approach can engage with civil society and promote public reason, competing with visions or with alternative indicators in order to guide public policy.

This discussion would not be complete without a proper account of the role of inequality in thinking about human development policies. Macarena Orchard and Martina Yopo face this challenging issue, expanding the capability framework to the literature on empirical measurements of multidimensional inequality. They do not limit their discussion to a simple review of the debate but rather, by using cluster analysis and a pluralist context-specific approach, they put forward a methodology for considering bi-dimensional capabilities (including objective functionings and subjective evaluations). Indeed, their technical work illustrates Meeks's discussion about the scope of the application of the approach. It is very interesting to note how they move from a direct principle that 'some capabilities are more unequally distributed than others' towards a discussion of intersectionality of capabilities, using Chilean data for empirical discussions.

The intersectionality of capabilities is also a theme (although it does not appear with this name) of Stephanie Schrage and Kristin Huber's chapter. They start from a series of empirical questions concerning what is a living wage and how to define a minimum level of well-being (a central question that the capability approach inherited from John Rawls's concern with primary goods as a pre-condition for social justice). The problem, as they discuss, is that the international garment industry has seen the emergency of multiple and overlapping standards with considerable variation. For them, changing the focus from the means of living to people's actual opportunities and real freedoms is the way forward. They ground their analysis on normative theory, as Byskov would put it, and put forward a conceptual framework that they call 'the living wages approach' that takes into account several features of the capability approach. Similarly to Orchard and Yopo, they also face the tensions between objective and subjective informational spaces.

Indeed, the issues about the use of subjective information and the difficulties in achieving intersubjective comparability in normative evaluations have given rise to a wide range of debates, such as the one on adaptive preferences. A new frontier of the capability approach, explored in this book in the chapter by Tadashi Hirai, delves into different interpretations of 'happiness' by Nussbaum and Sen. These are not issues that are relevant for merely theoretical reasons but that have deep practical importance to empirical work. As a matter of fact, what counts or not for normative evaluations are often at the core of public policy discussions. Hirai suggests that the big divide with regard to subjective information between Nussbaum and Sen is that whereas Sen considers that 'happiness' can have evidential value for evaluations, Nussbaum goes beyond this, arguing that happiness, as general subjective information, can be important to explain people's motivations and can be, for this reason, used in an eudaimonic perspective, such as the one, put forward by self-determination theory (SDT).

The theme of motivations as the theme of aspirations is usually discussed in capability literature from an individual perspective. However, in this book Meera Tiwari examines the influence of middle classes' aspirations, mobility and values in India on policy-making, a topic that engages with Gasper's analysis of interpretations of India. To such an extent, Tiwari works with categories of analysis that emerge from Bourdieu's writings (such as 'habitus' and 'doxa') that overlap with Shariff's defence of critical theory as a way of providing a broader social ontology to the capability approach. As a result, Tiwari sees how middle classes' aspirations shape from residential patterns in cities (an issue also discussed by Shailaja Fennell, Jaime Royo-Olid and Matthew Barac) to a promotion of lifestyles and how they strongly influence policy-making in India. She suggests an aspiration-agency-capability mapping as a way of examining these socially embedded links. An alternative approach to social links is put forward by Paul Anand, who explores the value of social capital as a social resource. His approach raises theoretical, conceptual and methodological questions about how capability research can or should engage with the literature on social resources.

The book continues to explore new frontiers of the capability approach and the following chapters could have been a straightforward continuation of the sequence just described. However, they constitute key clusters of ideas about 'cities and the urban space' and 'education capabilities' and, in order to appreciate more what they are collectively arguing, they were grouped into different sections. Indeed,

Fennell, Royo-Olid and Barac introduce key conceptual distinctions, for instance between 'habitation' and 'habitare', that are essential for evaluating housing and habitation programmes from a capability perspective. By doing so, they not only demonstrate how the approach can be used but also compare it with alternatives, such as the basic needs, participatory and affordable housing approaches. They argue that a capability-imbued housing approach is demand-driven because it respects people's agency and goes beyond a conception of housing as merely shelter by expanding into people's positive freedoms. It is also process-sensitive, allowing incremental self-building.

Prachi Acharya applies the capability approach to examine building regulatory frameworks. The problem addressed by all these chapters in this section is that often housing, building and urban policies do not take into account what people value and how living in cities shapes and is shaped by their capabilities. Acharya shows how the approach can be applied to very specific issues, such as to certain aspects of construction methods and materials. Her argument for taking more seriously the issue of building codes for low-income housing in the global south echoes the message from the initial chapters of this book that collective alternatives must be considered for a more inclusive human development. The chapter also contrasts the capability alternative against basic needs and participatory approaches and highlights the importance of agency in building more inclusive and equitable construction standards.

The scope of the discussion is widened with P. B. Anand, who critiques the literature on cities and capabilities and then identifies potential 'new frontiers' for applying the capability approach to cities, examining, in particular, the criteria needed for inclusive and sustainable cities. He also focuses on the notion of agency embedded in different social contexts. He engages in a literature review in order to select key elements for building a capability grounded framework for urban issues. Once the framework is established, he uses it to examine empirical evidence about cities and a wide range of freedoms, from life expectancy to safety. The issue of housing, raised by Fennell, Royo-Olid and Barac, also appears in his chapter, linking resources to functionings and capabilities in an integrated way, also discussed by Orchard and Yopo. The empirical contribution of this chapter highlights that cities do not automatically lead to enhanced capabilities. The issue of life expectancy is a case in point – while increasing the share of urban population led to significant gain in life expectancy in some countries, the relationship is quite complex. Likewise, increasing urbanisation does not always lead to reduction in extreme poverty. Anand identifies issues for further development of both theoretical and operational aspects of the capability approach in relation to cities.

Altogether these chapters provide a framework for thinking about cities and urban development from a capability perspective. Whereas it is true that they contribute specifically to the substantive issues that they discuss (housing, building regulations, development planning), they also put forward, based on the contributions of Arjun Appadurai and Alexandre Apsan Frediani, among others, a new set of conceptual and analytical tools that take the frontier of the approach further.

Finally, the last section of the book tackles the challenging prospects of education. The first chapter by Robin Vos and Jérôme Ballet examines the process formation of youth aspirations in France related to education systems. More concretely, they investigate the impact of formal education on students' aspirations in France. They put forward a dynamic view of capabilities, taking account of the results of the SDT literature, as evidenced by Hirai. By using factorial analysis and hierarchical cluster analysis, they isolate the impact of objective and subjective measures of students attending the lycée. Their conclusions raise concerns about the impact of formal education on students, namely, promoting a reduction on students' well-being and decreasing their capacity of aspiration (when one should expect just the opposite). Their results bring to the fore earlier results by Unterhalter on the ambiguous role of schools on children's development and raise the need for further scrutiny about how schools influence youth's aspirations.

Similar to Vos and Ballet, Cristina Devecchi and Michael Watts also investigate the impact of schools on children's capacity of adaptation and aspirations. In particular, they explore the impact of schools on children with special educational needs (SEN) and disabilities. These two chapters raise a critical similar point: education has the potential to empower, to raise expectations and reduce adaptive preferences. But the way in which it has been carried out has been, as Devecchi and Watts put it, a 'considerable disservice' to these causes. Moreover, in the case of children with SEN and disabilities, there are several barriers raised by education systems such as the nature of curricula, the structure of schooling, the assessment procedures used and the adaptation processes that they trigger. It is interesting to note that these authors are facing some of the complexities of working with agency and social structures, proposed by some initial chapters. Devecchi and Watts, however, expand the frontiers of the debate by introducing new conceptual and narrative tools for tackling the problem of adaptive preferences.

But it is not all doom and gloom. The remaining two chapters of this section offer narratives about how certain interventions can be successful in expanding children's capabilities. Helena Kiff analyses the impact of 'the Writers' Workshop' on children's capabilities. It is important to note how a planned intervention can bring together many desired outcomes, such as allowing children to 'find a voice' or providing an environment for nurturing them or developing in them a sense of affiliation. The chapter then uses Nussbaum's capability perspective to code and classify the results from a twelve-month ethnographic study. The rich array of conclusions is impossible to present in this introduction but it is worth mentioning how the author explores the impacts of 'therapeutic writing'.

Caroline Sarojini Hart investigates how educational processes can contribute to the seventeen Sustainable Development Goals. She raises a similar caveat regarding how educational opportunities might not be sufficient to produce just outcomes. But, she asks, can the individual pursuit of freedom overshadow the pursuit of collective values? There are key trade-offs between valuable capabilities that are difficult to sort. This discussion links with Comim's proposal for taking social choice more seriously as one of the engines of the capability approach. It also relates to the need to define concrete visions of development, as raised by Gasper. Hart, however, appeals to a richer ontology from critical theory, along the lines discussed by the Part I of this volume, by employing Bourdieu's diverse notions of capital related to education and pushing the frontier of the approach to consider a multi-stage process of converting, through the education process, commodities and different forms of capitals into functionings and capabilities. There is natural overlap with Chiappero, Salandi and Scervini's chapter on the conversion issue. Hart also discusses the importance of discussing trade-offs for public policy.

To conclude, this introduction provides a brief presentation of the chapters of the book, highlighting their main contributions and points of intersection. The division of the book into five parts aims to call attention first to the importance of discussing the foundations of the capability approach before applying it. In so doing, we acknowledge that the operationalisation of the approach is still an unfinished agenda and that the range of alternatives and instruments offered by this book is part of a much wider movement of scholars who are using and transforming the approach. Moreover, the other parts of the book all push the boundaries of the approach by introducing and examining new conceptual issues embedded in concrete issues and empirical work. At the same time, the chapters illuminate and add practical guidance to a wide range of empirical issues, such as housing, cities and education, that deserve a separate section. Altogether the chapters of this book provide a long-term perspective of the capability approach, not only in terms of what Sen and Nussbaum have put forward but also in all its richness produced by a diverse group of scholars and practitioners who have transformed it and expanded its frontiers to face the new human development challenges that lie ahead.

2 | On Sen on the Capability of Capabilities

The Story of a Not-For-Profit Enterprise

GAY MEEKS

This is a revised version of my keynote paper for the inaugural Cambridge Capabilities Conference (CCC)[1] in June 2016. Consulting 'keynote' definitions (as new to the role) yielded the disconcerting proposition that amongst other things the talk might be expected to make an important 'revelation'. Ten days before the Brexit referendum, conference participants hoping for revelation might have looked, if from the UK, for decisive guidance on how they should vote; but I could not claim Sen's concern for capabilities was capable of determining that answer for us, capable though it would be of pointing towards considerations on which we might well set store. The 'other things' mentioned besides expectation of revelation included, scarcely less dauntingly, the lofty aim of indicating the marrow, the pith, the heart, the central theme, the core of all the learned papers to follow, whose variety and degree of scholarship however seemed to render any such attempt inappropriate, beyond picking up on the thread running through them that the capabilities concept is alive and well, that it matters, and that approaches using it give rise to very interesting questions (these however defying a general summing up – they are not exhausted by the questions where it may matter most, how best to use it in different contexts, whether it needs supplementation, stiffening or amendment, how far its application can chime in with or must diverge from other approaches, and what it can – or sometimes can't – help us to do). Nor could I presume as suggested to 'set the tone' for others. So instead, I set out merely to set the scene, by telling the story, in somewhat novel terms and from my own perspective,[2] of the evolution of Amartya Sen's approach to viewing advantage in terms

---

[1] Hopefully not at risk of confusion with CCC standing for Computational Complexity Conference, Civilian Conservation Corp, Committee on Climate Change, Copyright Clearance Centre or Chaos Communication Congress.
[2] While the framing of the story was freshly created for the conference and this book, a good deal of the material has been drawn from what was then

of capability – the real, not just formal, opportunity to flourish and to choose the life you have reason to value – and to viewing development as the enhancement of freedom.

Getting down to business then, I decided to bring some business language into the framing of the story I am telling. This was because I had been struck by apparent parallels between, on the one hand, the rapid development of capability promoting endeavour and, on the other, the phases of growth of a successful company.[3] But to have any chance of offering an illuminating – if metaphorical – frame for the story at hand, the stages of company growth held in mind must be those of a not-for-profit enterprise that does not seek gains for its owner: when comparing Sen's work on capabilities to that of an entrepreneur developing a unique product, I see him as engaged in this enterprise for its own sake. It would be ironic if the tale told risked giving an impression that the prime present-day challenger to the economics of exclusive self-interest was anything other than an archetypal academic, dedicated – one might say, committed – to pursuing scholarship not for profit but for its intrinsic value and for the contribution it can make to the human condition.

Of course, no-one is as well informed on this tale as Sen himself: accordingly, I draw heavily on his own accounts, especially relying on them as the story opens.[4]

Phase One

The Entrepreneur's Apprenticeship

How did Sen's academic training equip him to develop his ideas on capability?

His was certainly a broad apprenticeship – in economics, development, philosophy and the theory of social choice.

---

my newly written chapter on Sen for *The Palgrave Companion to Cambridge Economics*, edited by Robert Cord, subsequently published in 2017.

[3] Perhaps there may be some slight precedent in Sen's own introduction of the term 'brand name' (applied to Rational Choice Theory) into the title of his Comment in Peter and Schmid (2007).

[4] Leaning heavily on his Nobel Laureate biographical note (1998) and drawing also on his 'Conversation' with Klamer (1989). Unattributed quotations in this section come from the autobiographical note.

He took his first degree (economics major, mathematics minor, first class honours) at the University of Calcutta and writes that he found the academic ethos of his college (Presidency) "captivating". He enjoyed the excellent teaching and the mathematical approach to economics, and was bowled over by reading Arrow's newly published book, *Social Choice and Individual Values*. At the same time, his thinking was being influenced by the political situation in India: this made him acutely aware of "foundational disputes" between pursuit of distributional equity on the one hand and tolerance of plurality on the other. His awareness in his early student days of this inbuilt tension seems already to prime him for exploring ways of addressing it in his work on capabilities.

On coming to Cambridge in the mid-1950s, he was obliged to complete a second BA in pure economics on top of his first-class Indian degree before being entered for the PhD; and although saying this was "fair enough" in view of his young age, he also commented wryly[5] that there was actually "quite a drop" in the sophistication of the subject after the teaching he had benefitted from in Calcutta.[6] Moreover, he describes how – in contrast with the atmosphere of friendly debate among the economists in his college (Trinity) – he encountered in the Cambridge faculty not a stimulating forum for constructive discussion (such as this conference aims to achieve) but rather a "desert of constant feuding" between "contending armies" (passionate proponents of Keynesian macroeconomics and neoclassical economists who were unconvinced). This was an awkward battleground to traverse for someone with "close relations with economists on both sides", who keenly felt the absence of the spirit of tolerance in which more constructive interchange might have been possible. However, the difficult balancing act required to find a considerate course through the civil war situation prevailing in the faculty may have been another importantly formative experience. Many of Sen's subsequent arguments seek to steer what, in the Aristotelian mould, may be seen as a middle way, preferring the golden mean to extremes at either pole – an approach that may also be at home in Confucian and Buddhist philosophy but that for all its distinguished antecedents tends to be hard to put across – one might say, hard to *sell* – on account of being open to fierce attacks from two opposing directions.

---

[5] In the conversation with Klamer.
[6] He topped the list in the Economics Tripos with his further first.

Sen would have chosen to write his doctorate on the theory of social choice but, extraordinary as this may seem in retrospect, could find no supervisor in Cambridge willing to countenance taking that topic on. However, Joan Robinson agreed to supervise him, not on social choice theory (which she slammed as "ethical rubbish") but on a topic in development economics,[7] this feeding another element into the early academic experience. Sen found Joan Robinson "totally brilliant but vigorously intolerant", his views often meeting with "stern reproach ... for not being quite true to neo-Keynesianism". She tried to talk him out of his continuing interest in social choice theory and welfare economics but, fortunately we may say, did not succeed.

Where next then in this 'apprenticeship'? It is just as well that Sen says, "the peripatetic life seems to suit me", for – the doctoral thesis essentially complete but not yet due to be examined – he escaped the acrimony within the faculty by heading back to India (and, as it happened, straight into a professorship at a new university) – before returning to Cambridge to take up a prize fellowship at Trinity, and then a college lectureship there (visiting MIT and Stanford also during a year's leave).

The Trinity prize fellowship was again surely strategic in the formation of his later thinking. He writes that it gave him several "years of freedom to do anything I liked (no questions asked)", a delicious prospect it is easy to understand him relishing. What he 'liked to do' was to branch out from economics and development into philosophical analysis, which he enjoyed for its own sake as well as for its bearing on the logic of social choice and on the related issues of equity and democracy that had already captured his attention in his first student days. My sense that this research time in philosophy had strategic significance for Sen's subsequent work is buttressed by the Nobel prize committee's judgment that: "By combining tools from economics and philosophy, [Sen] has restored an ethical dimension to the discussion of vital economic problems". Whether that restoration was needed is questioned by Dasgupta, who does not think economics ever lost its ethical dimension – in the broad sense of its shared concern with betterment of the human lot.[8] Yet readers of Graaff's classic 1957 study of

---

[7] A Maurice Dobb inspired topic concerning choice of technique.

[8] Arguing that economists tend to focus on the facts because they care about the "determinants" of well-being, taking the broad ethical foundations of their subject as read: see his 2005 paper, "What do economists analyse and why: Values or facts?", followed up by Dasgupta (2007, 2009).

Theoretical Welfare Economics would not readily escape concluding that this vehicle of economic thought had driven itself into a dead-end: it is from this blockage that Sen has so successfully piloted us away.

Sen punctuated his prize fellowship time with a visiting spell at MIT ("an inspiring place") and then before long returned to India, to a professorship in Delhi where he savoured the "dynamic ... intellectual atmosphere" and was able at last properly to indulge his passion for working on social choice. There were more visits to the United States, this time to Berkeley and Harvard, and it was at Harvard that he started teaching a renowned joint course with Arrow and Rawls on social justice.[9] Phase One now complete, this brings us to Phase Two.

Phase Two

Engagement in R&D

Sen was now deeply involved in path-breaking research on social choice – as it turned out perhaps not so much engaged in as driving its, so to speak, R&D department. In 1970, his masterful text *Collective Choice and Social Welfare* was published. As Flavio Comim will argue in Chapter 8, and as the 2017 publication of a new expanded edition testifies, this classic book, both inspired and provoked by the problem Arrow had uncovered, embodies crucial rethinking on social choice that not only set a new and constructive course for that body of theory but would turn out also to underlie much of the subsequent development of Sen's ideas on capability and justice. Many seeds of his later approach to capabilities can be found in this book and in papers published at a similar time. Themes already well apparent are the importance of gaining a better understanding of the role of reasoned scrutiny in individual and social choice, concern with its informational

---

[9] If it seems odd to dub so long a spell as 'apprenticeship', especially when the later part was already so prestigious, I would plead, first, that these years may justly be singled out as being formative in the development of Sen's later concern for capabilities, and secondly, in mitigation, that the renown he might indeed have been owed at this time was not yet reliably vouchsafed, as we know from his own anecdote – telling of a fellow plane passenger who, on learning that he was visiting Harvard from Delhi and was exploring the theory of justice, recommended a particularly interesting course to attend, "taught by two very famous people, John Rawls and Kenneth Arrow, and some other guy" (Sen speaking at the London School of Economics, January 2017).

base, and recognition that in the absence of ideal decision conditions appropriate ways forward will often still exist.

Sen's research led him to conclude *Collective Choice and Social Welfare* with the comment that it may be more useful to work not with 'pure' systems of social choice, however theoretically appealing, but rather with the 'impurities' of "partial interpersonal comparability ... partial cardinality ... restricted domains ... intransitive social indifference ... incomplete social preference ... and so on ... while purity is an uncomplicated virtue for olive oil, sea air and heroines of folk tales, it is not so for systems of collective choice" (1970a: 200, 2017: 265). For instance, progress can be made in reaching welfare judgments without access to full information on exact interpersonal comparisons, once it is seen that there is room for "partial comparability", occupying the extensive space between "full comparability and no comparability at all". Sen memorably illustrates the point through reference to Nero fiddling happily while Rome burnt and "all other Romans were plunged into misery". Here merely *some* comparability may be quite enough to do the trick, for as Sen argues it can be entirely reasonable to conclude "that the sum total of welfare went down ... while Nero played his fiddle" even if we do not know the precise "one-to-one correspondence" of every Roman's welfare units with every other Roman. And similarly, says Sen, it can be reasonable notwithstanding our incomplete knowledge of interpersonal comparatives to assert that the sum total of welfare under the existing distribution of money income "is less than what could happen with a more equal distribution" (1970a: 99–100, 2017: 153–4). This opening up of possibilities for decision in spite of incomplete information is a current which flows strongly through his later discussions of how a capability approach might be applied.

A further seed from which an extensive branch of Sen's later thinking would grow – planted in 1967 and nurtured in the 1970 text – was his case to show that what he calls "nonbasic" value judgments are not purely subjective but are rather premised on an understanding of underlying analytical assumptions and relevant factual information,[10]

---

[10] One might perhaps write of 'objective' information here, but 'factual' may more readily allow for the theory-laden and, it can be argued (as by Myrdal, Carr, Putnam and others), the value-laden nature of facts themselves (see Putnam (2002) but also Dasgupta (2007)). On the other hand, Sen himself does not shy away from using the term 'objectivity' when he speaks of domains of impartiality (and in 'Description as Choice', while eloquent on description

and are thus subject to revision in the light of shifts in that understanding, for example on new information becoming available. In the 1970 text, he illustrated the point with a person making the value judgment that: "A rise in national income measured both at base and final-year prices indicates a better economic situation". This only qualifies as a basic judgment in that individual's value system if it is held "to apply under all conceivable circumstances"; so the classification depends on whether there are any circumstances – one such might be "if the poor were much poorer" – in which he would revise it. Value judgments that may be revised according to circumstance are categorised as nonbasic; and the significance of this for Sen's wider argument is that this class of value judgments can be the subject of reasoned discussion.

But how extensive is this class? Very extensive, contends Sen. He holds that "many of the value judgments we habitually express are not basic", and suggests that judgments of this kind encompass most if not all value judgments. It is hinted that the complementary set of basic value judgments – those not amenable to reasoned discussion – might be empty. Sen points out that even where situations liable to change a person's value judgment are improbable, this allows the possibility of change – along with inviting *factual* assessment of its (admittedly small) likelihood – and renders the judgment nonbasic; and he argues that while "some value judgments are demonstrably nonbasic ... no value judgment is demonstrably basic". On the other hand, it may be "establish[ed]" that [a] judgment is not nonbasic in any *obviously* relevant way" (my emphasis), and Sen does not explicitly assert that it is impossible to reach a point where there can be no further "rational disputation" of the basis of a value judgment. But he insists on there being an inescapable problem – that "there is no sure-fire test which tells us that this ultimate point has in fact arrived" (1970a: 59–64, 2017: 109–14). (This unconventional view on the extensive reach of the nonbasic might perhaps be buttressed in respect of moral value judgments by the contention that moral evaluation necessarily depends on facts about the human condition and human well-being, a philosophical position attractively presented by Foot and defended by Warnock.)[11]

---

involving selection, he also asks, "Why must every factual statement involve values?" [1980b: 364]).

[11] Foot maintains that "The grounding of a moral argument is ultimately in facts about human life" (2001: 24), and that "a man cannot make his own personal decision about the considerations which are to count as evidence in morals"

Sen's general conclusion is that "it seems impossible to rule out the possibility of fruitful scientific discussion on value judgments" (1970a: 64, 2017: 114). This is a factor crucial to his later accounts of the scope for reasoned scrutiny of individual and social evaluations. And it presages the role he goes on to champion for the Impartial Spectator in *The Idea of Justice* in furthering "objectivity [of] ethical and political convictions", where the witness of "others who are far as well as near" is celebrated for contributing fresh perspectives to discussion, introducing new observations into processes of both private and public reasoning (2009a,: 45, 126).

Phase Three

Identifying a Gap in the Market

To the development of these constructive arguments on enhancing the possibility of social choice in the absence of complete interpersonal comparability in utility and in the presence of differing value judgments, Sen added in the early 1970s a forthright series of analyses of limitations in the moral, economic and political philosophies then prevailing in policy discussions, indicating – in the metaphorical framework of this chapter – that existing products did not fully satisfy market needs.[12]

First, *Collective Choice and Social Welfare* spearheaded another form of informational broadening, exposing shortfalls in utility-focused preference data by introducing us to the would-be Paretian Liberal and diagnosing the cause of his discomfiture, and indeed collapse. The aspiring Paretian Liberal, new to the scene in 1970, is now a familiar if chimerical figure, yearning to square the circle. Sen obliged him to confront the impossibility he faces by presenting him with two memorable characters with rhyming appellations, the Prude and the

---

(1978), these books amplifying her arguments from the 1950s onwards (illustrated in 1958 by her claim that the assertion it is good to clasp your hands three times an hour is unintelligible unless a plausible background can be filled in); and Warnock urges that we cannot form any conception of how Martians suddenly landing in London would morally evaluate what they found there as we have no way of knowing what *their* needs and wants would be (1967). In other works, Sen refers to support he can draw from Scanlon, Nagel and Putnam for questioning the purely subjectivist position.

[12] See Meeks (1985).

Lewd.[13] Suppose that the Prude would prefer that an available copy of some distinctly risqué book[14] is not read by anyone, including him, but nevertheless would prefer reading it himself to opting for this access to depravity to be given to an individual whom he regards as already all too lewd. And suppose that the Lewd person, very keen that the opportunity to peruse the available copy of the book should not be left untaken, and eager to read it himself, would nevertheless prefer that the Prude be given what the Lewd expects to be an eye-opening experience for him. Then it is apparent that if the book is to be read by one of them, both individuals share a preference for this being the Prude, making that outcome Pareto superior to the Lewd reading it. Yet on liberal principles, as commonly understood, what a person reads, there being no harm to others, is a matter for that individual's own choice only, and then the book would indeed be read – but by the Lewd person who relishes the prospect, not the Prude who emphatically does not. In these circumstances and on the apparently very mild demands made in the given assumptions and definitions, it is impossible simultaneously to meet both Paretian and liberal requirements.

There has been a wealth of discussion both of the strength of this argument and of ways in which the problem it poses might be dealt with. One suggested way out of the impasse could be to side with the parties' mutual preference that the reading be done by the Prude, perhaps even through them contracting so (but as the Prude's first preference was that the book be left unread, why should he agree to the scheme; and if he does, what is to stop him cheating the spirit of the contract by turning the pages without absorbing the text?). An alternative escape route might be to disallow in Paretian calculation the anti-liberal preferences each is entertaining – 'meddlesome' preferences over what the other does in what should be a private domain. Numerous other solutions and challenges have been proposed in a substantial literature on the issue. Sen discusses various possibilities himself but concludes that the potential for conflict between personal liberty and overall desire fulfilment should be recognised, with acknowledgement of the importance, but not the unqualified importance, of each. An "evaluative view of the acceptable priorities" between the competing

---

[13] Originally, the Lascivious.

[14] The 1970 example was *Lady Chatterley's Lover* following a 1960's court case over its alleged obscenity; but decades later the set-up may seem more powerful if this is updated – say (from hearsay, of course), to *Fifty Shades of Grey*?

principles will be needed, and it must be "sensitive to the trade-offs on this that the persons may themselves endorse" in the light of their relative valuations of liberal principles and utility-based Paretian ones (1999a[15]). And he draws the general moral that social choice theory should be enriched by taking non-utility information into account.[16]

A paper later on in the decade took further Sen's critique of informational shortcomings in the standard preference approach, introducing us this time to the Rational Fool, who obscures the richness of human agency as he frequents microeconomic models "decked in the glory of ... *one* all-purpose preference ordering" (1977: 335–36). The single ordering conceals the "distinctions between quite different concepts" that may motivate choice. It may invite the simplistic assumption, fostered by ambiguity of the term 'prefer', that choices always reflect self-interest (in the sense of increasing the chooser's utility, either directly or through sympathy with someone else). But, Sen argues, a significant class of actions is performed from 'commitment', not for utility gain: there is a risk of being blind to this if we are distracted by the Rational Fool who, for all his cleverness in other ways, does not recognise the distinction.

And Sen found classical Benthamite utilitarianism wanting with respect to issues of income distribution. Back in England from 1971 in a professorship at the LSE, it was in his 1972 Radcliffe lectures at the University of Warwick and the subsequent book *On Economic Inequality* (1973, expanded edition 1997) that he drew attention to the share of a given income 'cake' that an individual at a marginal utility disadvantage would be liable to receive in a simple utilitarian model. Needing more resources than a second individual to achieve the same level of utility, an equal division of income between them would leave the first person worse off in utility terms; yet, regarding him in relation to the goal of maximising the utilitarian sum as a less efficient generator of utility from income, this model would compound that utility deprivation by giving him less income too. Under this account of the utilitarian approach then, such individuals face

---

[15] P. 94 in the reprint in Sen (2002).

[16] Information that however John Stuart Mill, the champion of liberty, might want to claim would fit under his particularly generous utilitarian umbrella (its generosity being indeed so wide as to lead Sandel and others to doubt his utilitarian credentials (Sandel, 2009: 49–52); but see Mill, *On Liberty*, and also Glover's assessment (Glover, 1990: 39)).

a double disadvantage, their lower quantum of utility from a given income being compounded by receipt of a less-than-equal income share, with more income directed at those better placed to boost utility overall. Sen motivated the discussion by considering a person with disabilities who might happen to be in such a position and presented utilitarianism as being "fundamentally ... very far from an egalitarian approach" (1973: 18).[17]

However, Sen acknowledged merits in the utilitarian distribution criterion as well as shortcomings. This even-handedness in critique was apparent in his 1974 paper which brought Rawls's approach to distribution into play: the paper, 'Rawls versus Bentham: An Axiomatic Examination of the Pure Distribution Problem', showed that, while each of the systems compared[18] did capture an important aspect of distribution, neither Benthamite sum-ranking nor the Rawlsian 'maximin' criterion could fulfil a seemingly modest and reasonable set of axioms. Consequently Sen judged each of these systems to be "essentially incomplete", classical utilitarianism neglecting the significance Rawls perceived in relative welfare levels between different people, and Rawlsian maximin being blind to the significance Bentham recognised in the magnitude of gains and losses in aggregate welfare. Sen concludes: "It is not surprising that the utilitarian approach and the maximin approach both run into some fairly straightforward difficulties since each leaves out completely one of the two parts of the total picture ... [A] more complete theory is yet to emerge" (1974: 309).

In these various ways Sen's analysis of the leading 'products' of the day led him to conclude they were not adequate in themselves (or indeed together) to meet the extensive range of market needs.

---

[17] This "far-from-egalitarian" argument confronted the common belief that because of the diminishing marginal utility of income to each individual, utility maximisation would equate with an equal distribution of income, a belief premised on assuming identical utility functions. A utilitarian policy maker might perhaps try to reclaim this ground by making that assumption as a working hypothesis when more detailed information is lacking. And on a broader conception of utilitarianism such as that of John Stuart Mill, the model's assumption that each person's utility depends only on his own income might be replaced with one allowing utility also to be derived from seeing benefit to those less favoured than oneself.

[18] The paper does not cover Mill's variety of utilitarianism or Rawls's maximin applied to 'primary goods'.

Phase Four

Launching the Product: The USP

What might fill or at any rate narrow the market gap? Sen's now prominent but then unfamiliar proposal was an approach based on capabilities.[19] It is tempting to say that Sen created the capability approach; but he firmly rejects that contention, modestly stressing the long tradition of concern for human flourishing which stretches back through Karl Marx and Adam Smith to Aristotle. To pursue the metaphor of this chapter, the capability 'product' proudly bears an Aristotelian hallmark and adopts principles of revered designer Smith: yet, while not wholly new, it was new to the twentieth-century post-war market. For generations, this focus on flourishing had been overshadowed by the ubiquitous and towering presence of utilitarianism, not to be repositioned in the light until Sen – in company it might be said with some reflective basic needs theorists – took it up again.[20]

The restoration of this approach was not without the risk typical of the launch phase of a new enterprise, an especially hazardous endeavour when the market is effectively commanded by acclaimed established business. Entrepreneurial courage is to be detected in Sen's investment of time and effort in essentially interdisciplinary work on capabilities, when a conventional and prestigious academic career with more reliable rewards was energetically beckoning: he could easily have opted for a comfortable life in economics by staying within the orthodox club standing ready to embrace him. In the terms of Leijonhuvud's entertaining and tongue-in-cheek report on mainstream economists' tribal practices in 1973 – 'Life among the Econ' – Sen had already risked the wrath of the higher Econ castes by breaking the taboo against associating with other tribes (thus "endangering … moral fibre") and by mingling with the lowly "Devlops" caste (who are

---

[19] There might be other contenders for filling the gap, or narrowing it, including a richer version of Rawls, or Mill's capacious version of utilitarianism. Sen's subsequent work has tended to pay great (appreciative but critical) attention to Rawls, perhaps rather less to Mill; but in his 1970 classic and expanded 2017 edition the latter is admired for his essay on liberty, and in the 2017 edition accorded a starring role for his work on representative democracy (comment by Sen in his January 2017 talk at the LSE).

[20] Soon to be joined by Nussbaum who, as Sen acknowledges, pointed out the connection to Aristotle.

"suspect[ed] ... of relinquishing modl-making") (1973: 329). But at this point, having earned immense respect from 'high caste' colleagues for his seminal work on social choice and his pronounced facility with the techniques of formal proof, he could surely have overcome the supposed stigma of those early indiscretions and settled down to be feted by the highest "priestly" caste – the Math-Econ – as one of their own. Nobel Prize notwithstanding, his reception within some quarters of the tribe might yet be warmer had he chosen a less adventurous career path.

Instead in 1979 (now in an Oxford professorship) he made the 'pitch' for being concerned with equality in "basic capabilities" in his Tanner lecture, 'Equality of What?', which set the frame for much of the enterprise to come.[21] Referring again to the possible case of a person with special needs who is at a marginal utility disadvantage, Sen expands his argument into the thesis that neither utilitarian nor other 'welfarist' (i.e. solely utility-reliant) nor Rawlsian approaches, nor any combination of the three, are sufficient templates for social arrangements. The charge against traditional sum-maximising utilitarianism on grounds of the diminished share of the cake accorded to the disadvantaged person is as before.[22] However, this charge does not hold against all welfarist approaches: for instance, on the assumptions of the model so far, the principle of equalising individuals' levels of total utility would entail his receipt of a more than equal income distribution share. But Sen now modifies the model and points to a new difficulty (1980a: 217). What if the person with disabilities is so buoyant (as Sen puts it, has such a "jolly disposition") or alternatively has come to expect so little (has such a "low aspiration level") that in spite of severe practical difficulties in achieving, say, basic mobility in

---

[21] Delivered at Stanford in 1979; published text Sen (1980a). In *Inequality Reexamined* he argues that it is "a common characteristic of virtually all approaches to the ethics of social arrangements that have stood the test of time ... to want equality of *something*" for all concerned, without which the approaches would "tend to ... lack social plausibility" (1992: ix, see also 2009a: 291–5).

[22] Although he charges utilitarianism with being non-egalitarian with respect to income distribution, he also notes its insistence on a "special type of equality" (1980a: 199) which makes it egalitarian in a different respect – in giving "exactly the same importance to the utilities of all people in the objective function" (1992: 14, see also 2009a: 292). A unit gain in the utility of a Dalit is to count just as much as a unit gain in utility for a billionaire.

a poor community, his utility level at the initial income distribution is not low? This will pose no worry to an ardent welfarist, to whom utility is what counts, no matter what the source – a happiness pill, or what you will: if a cheerful nature can hold its own in hard times, this is simply good news. But others might want to recognise a special need for resources, in spite of the admirably buoyant temperament.[23] When J. K. Rowling's sage Dumbledore offers comfort to Harry by saying, "Happiness can be found even in the darkest of times, if one only remembers to turn on the light"[24] this does not mean the dark times themselves do not matter.

Sen reasons then that, although welfarism's utility focus has the welcome attribute of directing attention to people rather than resting with resources, it accords no direct attention to their needs and therefore falls short. Whether those needs gain attention indirectly through the service of utility concerns will depend not only on the decision rule used but also on the influence of both mental and physical factors on 'efficiency' in utility generation. As there can be no guarantee under either rule that special needs for resources will be met, welfarism is judged insufficiently robust.

As to Rawls's alternative to utilitarianism, Sen detected "an element of 'fetishism'"[25] in Rawls's own metric of "primary social goods" – described by Rawls as "things that every rational man is presumed to want", including "rights, liberties and opportunities, income and wealth, and the social bases of self-respect" (1971: 62). Sen accepts that this list is "broad and inclusive" but protests that, although the disabled person on this goods-focused basis would not be penalised in the distribution of these well-specified resources, no special provision would be made for his needs.

So if the contention was that such provision should be made, "despite there being no marginal utility argument (because it is expensive), despite there being no total utility argument (because he is so contented), and despite there being no primary goods deprivation (because

---

[23] Similarly one might want to *dis*allow claims for extra resources of the Fortnum and Mason variety arising from those who "have to be deluged in champagne and buried in caviar to bring them to a normal level of utility, which you and I get from a sandwich and a beer" (1980a: 214–15), even if one might suspect here some need for support in terms of mental health.

[24] Taking it that one can.

[25] Echoing Marx's concept of 'commodity fetishism'.

he has the goods that others have), the case must rest on something else". That "something else" is, Sen believes, "the interpretation of needs in the form of basic capabilities", "a person being able to do certain basic things [including] the ability to move about ... to meet one's nutritional requirements ... to be clothed and sheltered ... to participate in the social life of the community" (1980a: 218) – where what is necessary to meet these needs will vary among individuals and between communities (all these considerations deeply relevant as Schrage and Huber argue in Chapter 15 to suitably defining the 'living wage').

Sen acknowledges technical complexities in indexing capability bundles, including culture-dependence in how different capabilities are weighted, and also notes that equalising basic capabilities is not the only way in which capability considerations might be utilised. Nor does he bill the "constructive thesis" he advances alongside his central critique as more than a "partial ... guide to the moral good" or as rendering other approaches entirely redundant (1980a: 219–20): the 'brochure' takes care not to overreach. But though the publicity is suitably balanced and restrained, the launch here of a capabilities 'product' – or at least its prototype – proved pivotal.

Sen's selection of a special needs case as an effective example for the purpose of his "case-implication critique" accords with his deep concern for the well-being of persons with disabilities. In his 2004 keynote speech, "Disability and Justice", to the World Bank's second international conference on disability, he stressed that, while the vast numbers of people with disabilities living in developing countries (more than 400 million) were often "the poorest of the poor in terms of income", their restricted income was "reinforced and much magnified by ... the difficulty in converting income and resources into good living" (2004: 6).[26] The value of a capabilities approach to addressing disability issues is evident (as will be reflected in Chapter 23 in relation to Special Educational Needs).

But as Sen also explains in 'Equality of What?', the significance of diverse needs runs across the board: "people ... have very different needs varying with health, longevity, climatic conditions, location, work conditions, temperament, and even body size (affecting food and clothing requirements)". How resources affect what different people can achieve will depend on personal, social and environmental

---

[26] See also Sen 2009a: 258–60.

conversion factors, and the "evidence [is] that conversion of goods to capabilities varies from person to person substantially". Sen allows that the established 'products' might work well enough with respect to addressing needs fairly if people "were basically very similar". It is because they are not that Sen claims there is indeed a "gap [that] can be narrowed by the idea of basic capability equality ... [This] has virtues that the other characterisations of equality do not possess" (1980a: 215–16, 219–20). A key virtue lies in taking due account of how these individual human differences, in a variety of social and environmental settings, impact on what people are able to be and do. This can be seen as the Unique Selling Point – the USP – of the capabilities 'brand'.[27]

By the mid-1980s product design and testing had advanced a good deal further. Important philosophical papers by Sen in this period probed and developed the conceptual framework with respect to, *inter alia,* interpretations of liberty, consequence-sensitivity of rights, positional valuations, partial orderings, the nature of well-being, identity and goals, and many key aspects of agency, the insights notably drawn together in the Dewey lectures on 'Well-being, Agency and Freedom' delivered at Columbia University in 1984.[28] And in a very succinct yet remarkably comprehensive handbook, including what might be seen as an early 'instruction manual' for product operation and use, Sen's monograph, *Commodities and Capabilities* (based on his 1982 Hennipman lecture at the University of Amsterdam, first published in 1985) combined more precise specification of the capabilities 'product' with explicit extension and generalisation, supplying also reports on some initial applications.[29]

In *Commodities and Capabilities* all the expected components remain in place – emphasis on the role of partial orderings ("many economic and social relations are inherently partial and incomplete ... evaluation of well-being can plausibly be seen as belonging to that category"); faith in the potential but not unbridled reach of objectivity ("I do

---

[27] The merely metaphorical framing of Sen as entrepreneur needs particular emphasis in relation to this branding aspect, for he recounts that he came up with the 'capabilities' label ("not an awfully attractive word") rather casually and only incidentally – on the prompting of a philosopher colleague at Oxford who felt the approach needed a name (see also note 62).

[28] See e.g. Sen 1982b, 1983, 1985b, 1985c.

[29] In the account of the monograph below, specific page references are not given to its short text.

believe that the 'limits' of objectivity extend well into the assessment of well-being"); recognition of the plurality of considerations in judging whether a person is doing well ("each has an importance of its own"); expression of caution about "the scope for uncontroversial assessment of well-being" when people's well-being rankings vary; positivity in showing this does not eliminate scope for some agreement; reference to the restrictiveness of assuming pursuit of self-interest as the sole motivation behind choice ("a very narrow view of human beings"); insistence on the deficiencies of purely resource-based approaches to well-being ("confounding ... the *state* of a person with the extent of his or her *possessions*") while giving the role of commodities due importance; stress on the ("serious") limitations of utility-based approaches, as well as acknowledgement of happiness as a contributor to well-being (to be "included in the list of some important ... [and] relevant ... functionings"), with desire fulfilment also serving an "important role" in offering evidence – albeit indirect and "tentative" – on a person's valuations ("we must not spurn the insights we get from utilitarian moral philosophy, even as we reject utilitarianism"); and presentation of a capability approach to assessing interest, well-being and advantage not as providing a single measure "superior to all others and applicable in all contexts" but rather as "fill[ing] in what may well be important gaps in the [existing] conceptual apparatus".

But much was added. Functionings are defined as the "achievement[s] of a person: what he or she manages to do or be". Capabilities are defined as "the freedom that a person has in terms of choice of functionings, given her personal features (conversion of [commodity] characteristics into functionings) and her command over commodities ('entitlements')". In as it were 'technical' passages of the 'handbook', issues of relevant data are discussed; and the mechanics are spelt out, linking the person's (constrained) choice of commodity vector (with its implied commodity characteristics) to her available set of "utilisation functions", each of which reflects "one pattern of use of commodities that [the person] can actually make", patterns which she then values in terms of her well-being. Her selected utilisation function – where the choice need not be utility or self-interest based – generates a functioning vector from the vector of commodity characteristics, where the achieved functions "can be thought to be the person's *being* (e.g. whether well-nourished, well-clothed, mobile, taking part in the life of the community)". There is detailed illustration of how "the conversion

of commodity-characteristics into personal achievements of functionings depends on a variety of factors – personal and social": in the
case of the nutritional and social-related characteristics of bread, Sen
suggests at least thirteen, ranging from metabolic rates, parasitic diseases and climate to familial situation, social convention and presence
of seasonal festivals. The handbook rounds off with two appendices
showing the capability 'product' in action: the first gives an illustrative
and revealing application, so far as limited data allowed, of its trac-
tion in international comparisons of five developing countries (India,
China, Sri Lanka, Brazil and Mexico) – demonstrating, in the business
metaphor, 'proof of concept', while the second explores its potential in
relation to investigating well-being in India, where a gendered aspect
becomes apparent, the evidence "seem[ing] to confirm ... the inferior
position of Indian women in terms of some of the most elementary
functionings and capabilities".

The formal and general statement of definitions and relationships
brings out the contrast between what a person is achieving – her actual
functionings – and the 'real', i.e. constrained, opportunities ('functioning bundles') from which she is able to choose – the extent of her
capability set. This calls attention to the concept of capabilities being
"a 'freedom' type notion"; and the 'handbook' already points up some
resultant complexities, occasioning what might perhaps be called
product safety warnings. One concerns the degree of freedom experienced by different members within a single household. Another relates
to freedoms (e.g. from being free from an infectious disease) which can
only be achieved by collective action (e.g. "through anti-epidemic public policy"). A third is the difficulty that the evidence of what has been
chosen does not show what might have been, yet evidence on breadth
of choice matters (compelled outcomes, whether through compulsion
or lack of options, lack freedom even if achieving a desired functioning): Sen suggests it may be a good move, though not a simplifying
one, to "incorporate[e] aspects of freedom *among* the functionings".

In this monograph, Sen does not claim to have solved all the difficulties: "the approach needs to be pursued a good deal more ... many
issues remain unclear ... [this] somewhat different perspective ... [on]
well-being and advantage ... from the ones typically used ... is ... no
more than a beginning". But there is much in this central 'manual' (and
the contemporaneous batch of philosophical articles) that foreshadows future development, arguably defusing some later tensions.

A Digression: Taking Stock

The narrative of Phases One to Four has shown the historic build-up to the capability endeavour becoming a going concern in 1979 and, in the 1980s, an established enterprise with a distinctive product, meeting a market need. The next three decades see spectacular expansion. Sen is at the heart of this but very many others join in the business of consolidation, refinement, application, extension, partnership and spinoff. And there are challenges from competitors and analysts. With these subsequent phases crowding in thick and fast, doing full justice to them would require a whole book (and in the keynote speech would sorely have tried the patience of participants). Instead, much of the rest of this chapter stands back from a detailed account of the subsequent phases of the enterprise, often only sketching the outlines of their succession and interrelations.[30]

Phase Five

Product Differentiation

Scherer and Ross's authoritative text, *Industrial Market Structure and Economic Performance,* notes several forms that product differentiation can take. Perhaps the most straightforward is to provide a product with truly different attributes. Sen had taken pains to spell out what I am dubbing the USP of the capability approach to well-being assessment – its sensitivity to the diversity of individuals and their context of life. A key way in which his reintroduction of concern for individual human flourishing differentiates the 'product' is by giving prominence to the impact that the varying personal, social and environmental conversion factors will have on translating means for well-being into realisable options of well-being achievement. In this way the capability product is seen as contributing to filling a market gap.

But is the product really so different? 'Image differentiation' is another form of product differentiation, in which the strategy is to create and reinforce in consumers' minds the subjective image of a uniquely desirable product. This opens the possibility that the

---

[30] With some reference to the (vast) literature from which the reader may fill the outlines in.

product might be more distinct in its advertised appeal than in reality. Suggestions have been made that the capability approach is only superficially distinctive from orthodox welfare economics, with doubt whether capability sets amount to anything more than conventional opportunity sets – 'old wine in new bottles'. Perhaps the reply might be, see the 'handbook' for functionings, conversion factors, comments on valuation, and so on – can you really have tasted this wine?

Taking note of Sen's own description in 'Equality of What?' of his focus on capabilities as a "natural extension of Rawls's concern with primary goods", Rawlsians might wonder if the distance from Rawls's non-welfarist approach has been overstated. True, the extension is to be in a "non-fetishist direction", "shifting attention from goods to what goods do to human beings" (1980a: 218–19), and is driven by giving due consideration to "hard cases" – Rawls earlier having admitted he felt "hard cases" can "distract our moral perception" (1975: 96). But there was considerable further interchange between the two authors, each appreciative of the other – their exchange of view facilitated by Sen taking up a Harvard post in 1987 (where he has principally been based since then, holding Philosophy, Economics and Thomas W. Lamont University professorships, with a six-year interlude in England as Master of Trinity College, Cambridge, from 1998–2004).[31] Sen had already noted in his Tanner lecture that Rawls "motivate[d] judging advantage in terms of primary goods by referring to capabilities", although then – the fetishism complaint – "focussing on goods as such" (1980a: 219). By 2001, Rawls was saying that his "framework does recognise the fundamental relation between primary goods and persons' basic capabilities" (2001: 169); and in 2009 Sen wrote of Rawls's "underlying concern for capabilities" – still holding, though, that he "does not give [it] enough room" (2009a: 262),[32] so that a degree of product differentiation remains. What Sen regarded by that stage as a deeper characterisation of his fundamental divergence in approach (while still paying tribute to Rawls' formative influence on questions of liberty and reason) was between Rawls's idealised

---

[31] It must be admitted that Sen's Mastership of Trinity was serendipitous for Cambridge since 1998 happened also to be the year in which he was awarded the Nobel Prize in economic sciences.

[32] With provision for 'special needs' relegated to a secondary 'legislative' stage and, Sen feels, still inadequate recognition of the wider issue of general diversity in conversion factors.

"transcendental institutionalism ... aiming only at the characterization of perfectly just societies" and his own concentration on "a theory of justice that can serve as the basis of practical reasoning", with "ways of judging how to reduce injustice and advance justice" in the world in which we live (2009a: ix, 7–8).

More closely allied to capabilities was the basic needs approach, which in some versions might even be held to have occupied to some extent the gap in the market that Sen was seeking to fill. Stewart puts up a forceful defence against the fetishism charge that he again lodges, holding that there is more concern with human flourishing and individual achievement in the basic needs approach than Sen has realised. But there are genuine product differences. Sen had extended his approach beyond basic capabilities to capabilities in general whereas the basic needs approach, though starting from a wide concern with human needs, had tended to become squarely focussed on the poor. Stewart acknowledges the greater generality of Sen's approach and also allows that it is simultaneously less "broad-brush", paying greater attention to variation in individual needs and to "the special needs of certain groups". And she gives generous praise to its "much more elegant philosophical foundation" (2006: 18).

Phase Six

Building the Brand in Different Markets

The aggressive for-profit entrepreneur with a premium product, intent on quickly expanding his business further and entrenching brand image, might be expected to invest heavily in marketing of various kinds in order to bolster market share and construct barriers to entry.[33] But – to refer back to the qualification with which the framing metaphor was introduced – this was far from the purpose of the capability 'enterprise' and Sen's *modus operandi* is very different. Yet his considered case for viewing well-being and development through the capability lens was soon influential in a wide range of 'markets'. An unusual factor was his ability to convey his arguments on capabilities with equal facility to mathematical economists, applied economists, mainstream or heterodox economists, moral philosophers, political

---

[33] I am grateful to Carla Francini for helpful insights into marketing strategies.

philosophers, development economists and other development studies academics, development practitioners, global institutions, feminist thinkers and educationalists – and this is not an exhaustive list. With its mention in many of his books, articles and speeches and in associated comment and review, the term 'capabilities' began to come into common currency.

A possible role for more deliberate 'product promotion and presentation' strategies for scholarly work with important policy implications may be one of the morals of Gasper's revealing comparison of alternative analyses of the state of Indian development in Chapter 12, including the most recent of Dreze and Sen's thoughtful studies of India, *An Uncertain Glory – India and its Contradictions* (2013). With rival and sharply divergent policy diagnoses on offer for that country, a degree of 'marketing' and customer focus could have its place in capturing political attention.

Phase Seven

Customer Complaints and Trading Standards Issues; Design Modifications

It would be unlikely for a new product with such impact on the market to have a wholly smooth run. The complaints outlined below are a selection from the range of potential difficulties raised (arranged by content rather than listed in priority or chronological order). Some challenges seemed mistaken, some could readily be met, some related to admitted limitations on the product's scope, yet others raised 'product performance' issues that were addressed by means of developments in design to increase power and allow the introduction of more sophisticated features.[34] The sketch below does not detail the

---

[34] Gasper (2007) gives a helpful four-fold taxonomy of "possible limitations or failings in an intellectual system" – the four categories with their contrasting implications being, overlooked strengths; interim gaps; structural gaps, which may be "innocuous, unfortunate, or chronic"; and "unfortunate treatment, resulting in minor, substantial but remediable, or chronic damage" – then discussing critiques of Sen's capability framework in these terms (see also notes 41 and 56). In a fine compact summary of the capability approach, Clark had earlier given a different slant on unrecognised strengths when he remarked that "in many cases key strengths are reconstrued as potential weaknesses by critics" (2006a: 36).

sequencing of modifications, treating them instead as if embodied in a single new model from Sen, dubbed 'Mark II'.[35]

Complaint 1: the product is not usable in practice – it doesn't work.

The complaint that the capability approach was not "operational" (Sugden, 1993) seemed more substantial in the product's early days, when on first acquaintance some obstacles did appear daunting. As several commentators have remarked, it is hard to sustain in the light of ongoing use (to be illustrated in this conference, with a notable sequence of papers on applying the approach scheduled to start when I stop). Sen acknowledged from the first that putting the approach to use involved significant challenges: experience has shown they can be overcome more than enough to dismiss any claim it is 'unusable'. The literature has grown rich in examples of empirical studies, as well as in constructive discussions of ways of using the approach in different contexts. Aspects of measurement and empirical application have been explored in substantial projects. Major international statistical comparisons increasingly draw on the approach.[36]

One aspect of sometimes unfavourable review of the product's ability to deliver in practice may relate to heightened expectation of what it is designed to do – perhaps based on misconception of what was offered for delivery, perhaps on a more exacting opinion of what *should* be offered. This may be relevant to Dasgupta's harsh comments that "discussions on capabilities end nowhere", the approach being "altogether too flabby" (2009: 624). Sen himself says in effect that some discussions on weightings and valuation trade-offs – it could be a fair proportion – will "end nowhere"; but the case he makes is that this does not rule out enough of them ending somewhere to make capabilities sufficiently fit for use. Key limitations, qualifications and stratagems in the approach were already flagged up in *Commodities and*

---

[35] The 'shorthand' Mark II designation might also be somewhat misleading if it suggested that the design features in question were entirely new, when they are rather being further developed and given more prominence.

[36] See as illustrative of usage the lists in Clark (2006a) and Sen (2009a: xxiv); collections edited by Comim, Qizilbash and Alkire (2008), Basu and Kanbur (2009), Ibrahim and Tiwari (2014); Kuklys (2005); papers relating to the 'capabilities measurement project' (e.g. Anand, Santos and Smith, 2009); papers relating to the 'equality measurement' project (e.g. Burchardt and Vizard, 2011, 2014); the UN's Human Development Index, Gender-related Development Index, Gender Empowerment Measure and Gender Inequality Index.

Capabilities, but perhaps it is still worth emphasising its overall pragmatism. There is no pretence that strategies for reasoned resolution will always succeed on Sen's approach, with its unashamed pluralism in values and its down-to-earth recognition of "the possible plurality of robust and impartial reasons that can emerge from searching scrutiny"[37]; but he holds this is no reason to scorn the array of conclusions that may be feasible: "We go as far as we reasonably can" (2009a: 401). This combines with focus on areas of patent injustice where overlapping evaluation consensus is more likely, and with "the practical need to make do with whatever information we can feasibly obtain ... [taking care to avoid] empirical overambitiousness" (1985a: 32).

A further – and deeper – answer to the 'not operational' complaint came from Atkinson when he wrote: "There is ... more than one way in which an idea of this kind can be operationally effective ... [A] concept is effective if it causes people to think in a different way" (1999: 185–6).

Complaint 2: the product is advertised as superior to the dominant economic product on matters of agency, but it isn't and has been missold.

This persistent complaint goes back to 1977 and the discussion of commitment and self-interest that centred on the Rational Fool. One limited protest concerns an initial example of acting from commitment. One boy offers another the choice of large or small apple, rather than taking the large one himself, the offer evidently being from commitment not sympathy since when left with the small apple he is put out; but mightn't the offer just have been a sneaky strategy to get the large apple for himself without seeming greedy, which would have worked if only the second boy had stuck to the etiquette? Yes; so the 'advertisement' was changed, with less contentious examples and the 1997 introduction of a specific "strategic nobility" category of action (in which apparent commitment could be disguised self-interest).[38]

---

[37] Sen illustrates competing ideas of justice with a favourite example in which the justice claims of three children to possess a home-made flute could each have validity: under competing conceptions, it could be just for the flute to be given to the musical child who will get pleasurable fulfilment from playing it, or the poorest child who lacks other toys, or the child who actually made it, and "it is quite possible that no unanimity may emerge" (Sen, 2009a: 12–15, 57, 201, 399).

[38] Sen's illustrations of committed action do extend to weightier matters than the selection of pieces of fruit and garden party chairs (although fruit selection is curiously common in the literature). He notes that "we do not have to be

A more general 'misselling' complaint, first voiced by Hahn (1991), was that although Sen was right about possible motivations, there was no call for a more complex meta-ranking structure, such as Sen had proposed, since the usual single ordering model of preference already incorporates the result of any motivational trade-offs.[39] But Sen does not deny that the matter can be approached in that way: his argument is that, given the importance of valuation issues which go beyond self-interest, there is an advantage in proceeding differently. The traditional approach is less explanatory, and with information on reasons for the ranking hidden behind the scenes, there is risk of misinterpretation. In favour of the status quo, Hahn just murmurs in passing about relating his view to "a theory of the integrated personality: a man knows what he wants" (1991: 8, see also Sen, 1991a).[40]

Complaint 3: there is a faulty component in the commitment concept.

The component in question had been added to counter suggestions that a person acting considerately to allow for the goals of another, inconveniencing herself, must in some sense have adopted the other's goals as her own. Mark II saw a person, say Sen, complying with a request to lower a plane window blind – shutting out an attractive view of sunlight on the clouds – so that his neighbour could see his computer screen better as he continued to play a silly computer game, when Sen's opinion is that the player would be better off shutting the game down. It would seem odd then to say that Sen has adopted his neighbour's playing of the game as a goal of his own. Indeed, the act of compliance can simply be a case of "let[ting] others be" (Sen, 2009a: 193). But can it? This contention led to a chorus of philosophical

a Gandhi, or a Martin Luther King, or a Nelson Mandela, or a Desmond Tutu, to recognise that we can have aims and priorities that differ from the single-minded pursuit of our own well-being only" (2009a: 18–19), and discusses in several contributions commitment in relation to work motivation in different cultures, responsibility to other species and responsibility to future generations with respect to climate change.

[39] Recently Hausman (2012) has argued in rather similar vein for a single preference ranking reflecting "total comparative evaluation" – preference, all things considered.

[40] Among Hausman's reasons for maintaining it is beneficial to restrict the term 'preference' to indicating the "total subjective ranking" in the single ordering are that this "matches economic practice", while leaving open for separate discussion "what things determine preferences" (a question that he agrees however "should not be left out of economics") (2012: 63–5).

voices demanding as it were a product recall. Mustn't Sen then have had some other goal – why else would he have acted? Other goals can be imagined here; but Sen maintains there is no necessity for a further goal to be involved – unless it is true that if you hold back from what you aimed to do, you must still be doing what you aim. There seems a loss of descriptive richness if self-denying acts of restraint must come under the banner of acting on one's own goals, just as much as acts of gross self-indulgence do. If Sen is right, the component does its job and the product is safe to use (see Sen, 2005, 2007, 2009a).[41]

Complaint 4: in dealing with the adaptation issue, the product is liable to break down and is dangerous in use.

"The view that the utilitarian approach takes of individual well-being ... can be easily swayed by mental conditioning and adaptive attitudes ... Our desires and pleasure-taking abilities adjust to circumstances, especially to make life bearable in adverse situations" (Sen, 1999b: 62). How general a feature this is has been contested;[42] but, accepting that it exists, the complaint is that mental conditioning could sway a person's valuation of functionings in a similar way. If it does, the product 'won't do what it says on the tin'.[43] So Sen's capability approach (as set out in the 'handbook') can't be relied upon to fix the problem.

It might then seem that some paternalist intervention tool would be required in order to combat (what the capability theorist identifies as) entrenched deprivation of a person's objective circumstance accompanied by mental adaptation. This sparks complaint from commentators fearing a dangerous erosion of individual freedom.

---

[41] However, Gasper (2007) suggests that, while Sen's commitment category can fulfil its intended role in exposing the narrowness of the understanding of rationality in orthodox economics, for the purposes of explaining behaviour and guiding policy it needs fertilisation from social psychology.

[42] By, for instance, Helliwell, Huang and Wang, Ch. 2 in Helliwell, Layard and Sachs (eds.), 2017. See also the illuminating discussions in Clark (2012).

[43] The central role of valuation of functionings became clear in *Commodities and Capabilities* and was reinforced in *The Standard of Living* (1987: 108), in Sen's answer to Williams' question, "How do we decide what does count as a significant extension of capabilities?" (Williams led up to the question through the example of the creation of yet another washing powder, 'Bloppo', which on the one hand creates the capability of choosing to buy Bloppo but on the other "takes away the capability (perhaps slightly more substantial) of only having to choose between [a smaller number of] washing powders" (1987: 98)).

But now there is a shift from speaking of the functionings a person values to those she has "reason to value". The modification is not meant to be a matter of instructing her as to what she should value – what it is held to be rational for her to value – but rather of envisaging a process whereby reasoned discussion with the aid of non-parochial – "transpositional" – perspectives and data (such as the Impartial Spectator might bring to bear) creates the opportunity for her to revise her valuation if she wishes, on reviewing it through this wider lens. Similarly, where the deprivation issue relates to public policy, reasoned scrutiny with "open impartiality" can fruitfully inform (but not determine) choice. In this way and after elaboration in several presentations, Mark II is advanced as in this context providing a way for the 'deprived adapted' freely to re-adapt.

Mark II did not quell concern from Sugden that other people's judgment of what it is rational to desire might be allowed to "override individuals' actual desires" (2006: 50); and, while accepting (under fire from Sen (2006a)) that the concept of 'reason to value' is not "paternalistic or elitist", he still felt the theory "does not allow a robust formulation of each individual's freedom to choose how to live her own life" (2008: 305, 308).[44] In a thorough refereeing of this contest, Qizilbash gives Sen a safe win on points but does not award him a knock-out blow and, in closing, hints there was reason for Sugden to mount his fight (2011: 51).

It had to be considered how Mark II might be engaged in widely different cultural contexts, whose relevance Sen had been sensitive to from the outset. He argues that truly "participatory freedom" will require universal availability of education.[45] And an implicit prerequisite of Mark II must be a certain degree of Enlightenment respect for reason (without which Scanlon's criterion of what cannot reasonably be rejected could not well play a part). Sen indicates that in societies where there is "entrenched discrimination", provision of wider information could be very powerful in changing locally based perceptions of feasible functionings (1999b: 32–3, 2009a: 161–3). Exposure to knowledge that opportunities previously believed infeasible are in fact feasible is a key mechanism in the operation of Mark II, as is

---

[44] See Sumner (1996) on issues concerning agent autonomy.

[45] The charity *Survival International* might hope that a so-far-uncontacted Amazonian tribe need not 'participate'.

acquaintance with an expanded range of possible evaluations (Sen's position on the nature of and relation between values and facts is very relevant here).[46] The Impartial Spectator will be busy. She will need access. Even when she has it, not all reasons for valuing that have been influenced by deprived circumstances will necessarily respond: for example, a person deprived of educational opportunities who has adjusted to his lot may have lost the aspiration to go to college (especially if his peers have no such aspiration) and would not necessarily wish to take up a college place if the opportunity did arise, regardless of knowing others valued it.[47] But completeness is not being claimed.

Complaint 5: product capability needs more demarcation.

This heading covers customer queries about how and where to use the product, and perhaps sums to a request for an updated set of instructions, to draw together sometimes scattered existing guidance.

One query is about equality. While "reducing inequality of capabilities ... is a big concern", *The Idea of Justice* spells out several reasons why the capability approach does not demand equality of capabilities. They include aggregative as well as distributional concerns, other possible moral bases for distribution, and the significance of process as well as opportunity freedom[48] (2009a: 232–3, 295–8). Similar qualifications were applied to equality of *basic* capabilities in 'Equality of What?'.[49] Sen does connect seeking "equality of something" with lasting "approaches to the ethics of social arrangements" (1992: ix) but does not view the capability approach as an approach of that sort[50] – it "does not, on its own, propose any specific formula for policy decisions" (2009a: 232).

Is it then left to public reasoning to decide, for example, whether or not public policy should seek to effect the looked-for expansion of at least basic capabilities in cases of special need? Will this give a

---

[46] See Meeks (working paper, 2017).

[47] See Burchardt (2009). Mill had been alert to feelings being "a very tender plant, easily killed, not only by hostile influences, but by mere want of sustenance", and he remarked on "men los[ing] their high aspirations ... because they have not time or opportunity for indulging them" (*Utilitarianism, Chapter II*).

[48] The example given is that equity in process in matters of life and death could reasonably be held to override the equity in opportunity freedom that might result from directing more medical attention to men than women in order to redress a "natural masculine handicap" (2009a: 296). [This leaves it open for redress to win the day in matters that are not life and death.]

[49] See Clark and Meeks (2016).

[50] Except in so far as in relation to justice it demands impartiality, linked to "seeing people as equals" (2009a: 291–5).

secure enough basis for determining provision? We have seen that Sen supports a theory of "justice as practical reason" that tries to "identify manifestly unjust situations that can feasibly be bettered" (2009b: 299); and he is clear that "the prevention and alleviation of disability ... [is] fairly central ... to the removal of manifest injustice" (2009a: 259): requirements for achieving this would seem to include reaching agreement on acceptable policy measures after reasoned scrutiny under principles of open impartiality, non-discrimination and non-rejectability[51] – which are themselves in a sense egalitarian – with the reasoning process involving considerations of feasibility but also of rights claims, where "capability inescapably ... generate[s] obligations", and where social obligation can arise from the "responsibility of effective power" (2009a: 196–200, 205, 206, 271, 272, 292, 293, 379, 387). But this may not sufficiently draw together relevant factors in Sen's writing:[52] perhaps there is scope here for a Mark III?

Another query concerns the interrelationship of the concepts of capability and freedom. Capabilities are defined in *Description as Freedom* as "the substantive freedoms ... to choose a life one has reason to value" (1999b: 74), so on this basis all capabilities are seen as freedoms – although Gasper and van Staveren suggest this overextends the freedom concept. But are all freedoms to be seen as capabilities, or would that overextend the capability concept? Sen suggested in the 'handbook', and subsequently, that achieving something freely could itself be seen as a valued functioning, drawing process aspects into the capability set;[53] but recently he has given more emphasis to keeping process aspects distinct.[54] Is it the position that, while the capability concept is in principle capable of encompassing everything that could possibly factor into a person's ability to be or do, stretching it to its limits may make useful distinctions begin to lose their grip?

Complaint 6: the product needs to be made stronger.

A very interesting series of papers, many appearing in a special issue of *Feminist Economics* in 2003, discuss ways in which Sen's treatment

---

[51] The Scanlon criterion mentioned above of what cannot *reasonably* be rejected.

[52] For another piecing together of the jigsaw, see Gotoh and Dumouchel (2009: 17–18).

[53] See also Sen's Arrow Lectures, 'Freedom and Social Choice', delivered at Stanford University in 1991, published in revised version in 2002 as Part VI of *Rationality and Freedom*.

[54] I am grateful to Javier Gonzalez for discussion on this (see Gonzalez, 2011).

of capabilities might be bolstered by making much more allowance for the social and institutional factors that affect how freely an individual can in fact choose, absent obvious coercion. The issues raised include conflicting aspects of empowerment, the significant role of collective capabilities and the impact of various forms of familial and corporate power.[55] It was not held in the main that these factors need undermine his approach, forceful though they are (a somewhat more pessimistic view can be found in Chapter 6 by Miller): the typical tone is well captured in Evans's closing remark that "Sen's capability approach provides an invaluable analytical and philosophical foundation ... but it is a foundation that must be built on, not just admired" (2002: 60).

Given the opportunity to respond to the 2003 collection, Sen was fully sympathetic to further 'product development' on these lines, but suggested there was rather more inbuilt strength in the specified dimensions than had been realised.[56] *Commodities and Capabilities* had indeed already been sensitive to several of them; concern over restricted capabilities for women had been persistent; and Sen's view of individuals as indivisible from social relations was nearer to that of Marx than to the 'atomised' individual of orthodox economics. In *The Idea of Justice*, Mark II perhaps gives rather more prominence to some of the features highlighted in these discussions, as when Sen insists that "individual human beings with their various plural identities, multiple affiliations and diverse associations are quintessentially social creatures with different types of societal interactions" (2009a: 247).

Phase Eight

Joint Ventures and Mergers

A successful brand can spark joint ventures, attracting other producers to work alongside.

From an early point, the commonalities between the capability approach and the basic needs approach made this a natural pairing,

---

[55] See, for instance, Evans (2002), Agarwal, Humphries and Robeyns (2003), Gasper and van Staveren (2003), Hill (2003).

[56] Qizilbash's 2005 review of the articles in this strand of comment that appeared in the 2003 special issue of *Feminist Economics* seconds this, while also contending that more work, consistent with Sen's framework, is needed: Gasper's response to Qizilbash suggests that need may be quite substantial (Gasper, 2007).

with relevance to answering Complaint 1. Combining forces without abandoning distinct identity, they contributed to the human development approach "pioneered by ... visionary economist ... Mahbub ul Haq" (Sen, 2009a: 226). Streeten and Stewart were among those working with Sen and Haq on the early United Nations Development Reports in which attention was switched from the traditional measure of development through *per capita* GNP to a measure aiming better to reflect well-being. The first Human Development Index was published in 1990, capturing (proxy) data on health, education and the standard of living in a single number. This was, as Sen puts it, a "heroic selection" of factors relevant to well-being (2006b), but he follows Haq in holding that it is the very "boorishness" of the index that allows it to pose a punchy challenge to the already boorish GNP statistics, with the detailed reports on human development painting a fuller picture.

A second joint capabilities venture had involved philosopher Martha Nussbaum. Originally a classicist, she could bring her expertise on Aristotle to bear on questions of capability (as in her paper in 1988). Together they edited *The Quality of Life* (1993). I need not elaborate on how her interest in capabilities grew into what might be billed as a spin-off business, developing a line of argument distinct from Sen's – and sometimes sharply different. It is well-known that she parts company most pointedly from him in her – much debated – assertion of the need to set out a list of central capabilities, with a minimum threshold to be guaranteed by government as a matter of human dignity. This may help to meet one of the twin elements in Complaint 4 – but at the price of exacerbating the other (similarly for the first part of Complaint 5).

One might speculate over whether closer working relationships of some sort will develop between proponents of the capability approach and a recently resurgent welfarism, given their common platform of advocating measures of national well-being that go beyond income – going beyond in ways that might seem more similar now that the primary concept of happiness used in international studies tends to be 'life evaluation'.[57] But with some pronounced disagreement remaining, for instance on the adaptation issue, acquisition bids might seem more

---

[57] It is interesting to compare the analysis and country rankings in the Human Development Report 2016 from UNDP and the World Happiness Report 2017 (presented at the UN). See also the Stiglitz-Sen-Fitoussi *Report by the Commission on the Measurement of Economic Performance and Social Progress*, 2009.

probable than joint ventures. Each side might suppose it should take over the other. On the one hand, as the 'handbook' had indicated early on, happiness has its place in the list of important functionings; and it is appreciated in the capability reckoning for supplying *prima facie* evidence on people's other valued achievements. (This might court previous backers of Bentham.) Psychic adaptation to adverse circumstances is still held to give reason to resist welfarism. On the other hand, Layard wrote in 2005 that the seven factors identified in surveys as most affecting happiness[58] were "similar to the personal 'capabilities' that ... Sen has proposed as the goals of public policy"[59] (2005: 113). (This might court previous backers of Sen.) The "real danger of paternalism" is held to give reason to resist the capability approach. Since neither reason for resistance to the rival approach is above challenge,[60] future dialogue might conceivably open the door to joint enterprise after all, or even friendly merger. But continuing standoff looks at the time of writing a safer bet.

Phase Nine

Could Global Dominance Come to Undermine Performance?

There are risks that a multinational enterprise gaining global dominance may become less robust if it faces substantially weakened competition and may be subject to problems of control and corporate social responsibility if new managers dilute or overlay the aims of the original owner-manager. And it is fair to say that the capability enterprise has become global – witness, for instance, the breadth and size of attendance at the most recent conference of the Human Development and Capability Association (formed in 2004 as a 'global community of academics and practitioners' in this field).

---

[58] These were: family relationships, financial situation, work, community and friends, health, personal freedom and personal values.

[59] He means by this the five instrumental freedoms Sen lists (in 1999b: 10, 38–40).

[60] For instance, Layard might remark that the life evaluation measure is now being favoured, and that this has been shown to track life circumstances closely (in contrast with emotional report measures); and Sen can insist how central it is to his approach that people do make their own (reasoned) evaluations of alternative ways of living available to them in their capability set, with public policy also the subject of democratic and reasoned scrutiny.

However, although interest in an approach through capabilities has mushroomed, competitive perspectives still remain strong – with Pogge on the Rawlsian wing, Layard, Helliwell and Sachs on the happiness front, and the still ubiquitous persistence of preoccupation with measures of *per capita* GDP alone – so there are plenty of issues to keep capability advocates on their toes.

Loss of control of the aims of the original enterprise might be a greater concern. Robeyns argues in a recent paper (2016) that there are already many different strands in the capability approach. To cover the even wider range of capability theories that *could* fit into the approach, she coins the term 'capabilitarianism' – a name that does not trip off the tongue but is an interesting move, in some ways reminiscent of the introduction of 'welfarism' to denote a broader class of utility based systems than utilitarianism alone. That extension of utility ideas might not have gone down well with Bentham: capabilitarianism would not be expected to go down well with Nussbaum, whose more restrictive conception of the capability approach it is designed to oppose. But the flexibility and plurality of the Robeyns design may fit better with Sen's thinking (unless the degree of open-endedness proves too extreme, with resulting 'brand erosion').[61] It could counteract what he has sometimes feared to be the emergence of a cult-like mindset among some capability adherents, putting product reputation at risk. On the other hand, as he says he is not comfortable now with the phrase 'the capability approach', 'capabilitarianism' might be thought too grand. I believe his own preference has been to speak of "having concern for capabilities".[62]

Phase Ten

Appraisal of Future Prospects

The evolution of Sen's capability 'enterprise' since its launch some forty years ago has transformed the study of well-being and the

---

[61] She encapsulates in a cartwheel diagram possible relationships between what she suggests are 'core' characteristics of the capability approach, to be set at the 'hub', and the wide range of considerations that can feed into alternative capability theories, displayed as surrounding modules filling the spaces between 'spokes'.

[62] As declared on a visit to Cambridge's Centre of Development Studies in 2015.

understanding of development in terms of freedom. The course of its development charted above shows it being both stress-tested and enriched. It remains a work-in-progress, still developing, still being modified; and as Sen has stressed from the outset, it is not a panacea, offers a framework for assessing well-being not a formulaic policy decision rule, is compatible with aspects of the production of rival 'firms', and is neither designed to resolve, nor capable of resolving, all value conflicts. But it *is* capable of assisting significantly in the realisation of the UN's Sustainable Development Goals for 2030 (agreed in 2015), with their diversity-conscious mantra: "Leave No-one Behind". I think the audit report can safely say of this not-for-profit business: it is performing well and fulfilling its aims; there is no risk whatsoever of bankruptcy; its reputation stands high; there can be confidence in its long-term survival.

References

Papers reprinted in the following listed collections are marked: * if in Sen's *Choice, Welfare and Measurement* (1982), ** if in his *Rationality and Freedom*, + if in Wood and Wood: Volume I, ++ if in Wood and Wood: Volume II.

++Agarwal, B., Humphreys, J. and Robeyns, I. (2003). 'Exploring the challenges of Amartya Sen's work and ideas: An introduction'. *Feminist Economics*, 9(2–3): 3–12.

Anand, P., Santos, C. and Smith, R. (2009). 'The measurement of capabilities'. Chapter 16 in Basu, K. and Kanbur, R. (eds.). Volume I: 283–310.

Arrow, K. J. (1951). *Social Choice and Individual Values*. New York, NY: Wiley.

++Atkinson, A. B. (1999). 'The contributions of Amartya Sen to welfare economics'. *Scandinavian Journal of Economics*, 101(2): 173–90.

Basu, K. and Kanbur, R. (eds.) (2009). *Arguments for a Better World: Essays in Honour of Amartya Sen*. Volumes I and II. Oxford: Oxford University Press.

Burchardt, T. (2009). 'Agency goals, adaptation and capability sets'. *Journal of Human Development and Capabilities*, 10(1): 3–19.

Burchardt, T. and Vizard, P. (2011). '"Operationalizing" the capability approach as a basis for equality and human rights monitoring in twenty-first-century Britain'. *Journal of Human Development and Capabilities*, 12(1): 91–119.

Clark, D. A. (2006a). 'The capability approach'. In D. A. Clark (ed.) (2006b): 32–45.

(ed.) (2006b). *The Elgar Companion to Development Studies*. Cheltenham, UK, and Northampton, MA: Edward Elgar.

(ed.) (2012). *Adaptation, Poverty and Development: The Dynamics of Subjective Well-Being*. Basingstoke: Palgrave Macmillan.

Clark, D. A. and Meeks, J. G. (2016). 'What of equality?' Working paper.

Comim, F., Qizilbash, M. and Alkire, S. (eds.) (2008). *The Capability Approach: Concepts, Measures and Applications*. Cambridge: Cambridge University Press.

Cord, R. (ed.) (2017). *The Palgrave Companion to Cambridge Economics*. Volume 2. Basingstoke: Palgrave Macmillan.

Dasgupta, P. S. (2005). 'What do economists analyse and why: Values or facts?' *Economics and Philosophy*, 21(02): 221–78.

(2007). 'Reply to Putnam and Walsh'. *Economics and Philosophy*, 23(3): 365–72.

(2009). 'Facts and values in modern economics'. Chapter 22 in H. Kincaid and D. Ross (eds.) *The Oxford Handbook of Philosophy of Economics*. Oxford: Oxford University Press: 580–640.

Drèze, J. and Sen, A. K. (2013). *An Uncertain Glory: India and Its Contradictions*. Princeton, NJ: Princeton University Press.

++Evans, P. (2002). 'Collective capabilities, culture and Amartya Sen's *Development as Freedom*'. *Studies in Comparative International Development*, 37(2): 54–60.

Foot, P. (1958). 'Moral beliefs'. *Proceedings of the Aristotelian Society*, New Series 59: 83–104.

(1978). *Virtues and Vices: and Other Essays in Moral Philosophy*. Berkeley and Los Angeles, CA: University of California Press.

(2001). *Natural Goodness*. Oxford: Oxford University Press.

++Gasper, D. and van Staveren, I. (2003). 'Development as freedom – and what else?' *Feminist Economics*, 9(2–3): 137–61.

Gasper, D. (2007). 'Adding links – Dialogue, adding persons, and adding structures: Using Sen's frameworks'. *Feminist Economics*, 13(1): 67–85.

Glover, J. (1990). *Utilitarianism and Its Critics*. New York, NY: Macmillan.

Gonzalez, J. (2011). 'About freedom and its multiple dimensions'. Mimeo.

Gotoh, R. and Dumouchel, P. (2009). *Against Injustice: The New Economics of Amartya Sen*. Cambridge: Cambridge University Press.

Graaff, J. de V. (1957). *Theoretical Welfare Economics*. Cambridge: Cambridge University Press.

Hahn, F. H. (1991). 'Benevolence'. Chapter 1 in J. G. Meeks (ed.): 7–11.

Hausman, D. M. (2012). *Preference, Value, Choice and Welfare*. Cambridge: Cambridge University Press.

Helliwell, J. F., Huang, H. and Wang, S. (2017). 'Social foundations of world happiness'. Chapter 2 in J. F. Helliwell, R. Layard and J. D. Sachs (eds.).

Helliwell, J. F., Layard, R. and Sachs, J. D. (eds.) (2017). *World Happiness Report 2017*. Sustainable Development Solutions Network. Available at: http://worldhappiness.report/ed/2016/

++Hill, M. T. (2003). 'Development as empowerment'. *Feminist Economics*, 9(2–3): 117–35.

Ibrahim, S. and Tiwari, M. (eds.) (2014). *The Capability Approach: From Theory to Practice*. Basingstoke: Palgrave Macmillan.

++Klamer, A. (1989). 'A conversation with Amartya Sen'. *Journal of Economic Perspectives*, 3(1): 135–50.

Kuklys, W. (2005). *Amartya Sen's Capability Approach: Theoretical Insights and Empirical Applications*. Berlin: Springer-Verlag.

Layard, R. (2005). *Happiness: Lessons from a New Science*. London: Allen Lane.

Leijonhuvud, A. (1973). 'Life among the Econ'. *Western Economic Journal*, 11(3): 327–37.

Meeks, J. G. (1985). 'Utility in economics: A survey of the literature'. Chapter 2 in C. F. Turner and E. Martin (eds.) *Surveying Subjective Phenomena*. Volume 2. US National Science Foundation, New York: Russell Sage Foundation: 41–92.

(ed.) (1991). *Thoughtful Economic Man: Essays on Rationality, Moral Rules and Benevolence*. Cambridge: Cambridge University Press.

(2017). 'Amartya Sen (1933–)'. Chapter 47 in R. Cord (ed.): 1045–78.

Mill, J. S. (1859). *On Liberty*. London: Longman, Roberts & Green.

(1861). *Utilitarianism*. London: Fraser's magazine.

Peter, F. and Schmid, H. B. (eds.) (2007) *Rationality and Commitment*. New York, NY: Oxford University Press.

Putnam, H. (2002). *The Collapse of the Fact/Value Dichotomy and Other Essays*. Cambridge and London: Harvard University Press.

Qizilbash, M. (2005). 'Sen on freedom and gender justice'. *Feminist Economics*, 11(3): 149–64.

(2011). 'Sugden's critique of the capability approach'. *Utilitas*, 23(1): 25–51.

Rawls, J. (1971). *A Theory of Justice*. Oxford: Clarendon Press.

(1975). 'A Kantian concept of equality'. *Cambridge Review*: February.

(2001). *Justice as Fairness: A Restatement*, E. Kelly (ed.). Cambridge MA: Harvard University Press.

Robeyns, I. (2016). 'Capabilitarianism'. *Journal of Human Development and Capabilities*, 17(3): 397–414.

Sandel, M. (2009). *Justice: What's the Right Thing to Do?* London: Allen Lane.

Scanlon, T. (1998). *What We Owe to Each Other*. Cambridge, MA: Harvard University Press.

Scherer, F. M. and Ross, D. (1990). *Industrial Market Structure and Economic Performance*. Third edition. Boston, MA: Houghton Mifflin.

Sen, A. K. (1967). 'The nature and classes of prescriptive judgements'. *The Philosophical Quarterly*, 17(66): 44–62.

(1970a). *Collective Choice and Social Welfare*. San Francisco, CA: Holden-Day.

*Sen, A. K. (1970b). 'The impossibility of a Paretian Liberal'. *Journal of Political Economy*, 78(1): 152–57.

Sen, A. K. (1973). *On Economic Inequality*. (Expanded edition 1997 with substantial annexe by J. E. Foster and A. K. Sen). Oxford: Oxford University Press.

(1974). 'Rawls versus Bentham: An axiomatic examination of the pure distribution problem'. *Theory and Decision*, 4(3–4): 301–9.

*+Sen, A. K. (1977). 'Rational Fools: A critique of the behavioural foundations of economic theory'. [The Herbert Spencer Lecture 1976]. *Philosophy & Public Affairs*, 6(4): 317–44.

*Sen, A. K. (1980a). 'Equality of what?' Chapter 6 in S. M. McMurrin (ed.). *The Tanner Lectures on Human Values*. Volume 1. Salt Lake City: University of Utah Press. Cambridge: Cambridge University Press: 195–220.

*(1980b). 'Description as choice'. *Oxford Economic Papers*, New Series, 32(3): 353–69.

Sen, A. K. (1982a). *Choice, Welfare and Measurement*. Oxford: Blackwell.

(1982b). 'Rights and agency'. *Philosophy and Public Affairs*, 11(1): 3–39.

**+Sen, A. K. (1983). 'Liberty and social choice'. *Journal of Philosophy*, 80(1): 5–28.

Sen, A. K. (1985a). *Commodities and Capabilities*. Amsterdam: North-Holland. Republished Delhi: Oxford University Press.

**+Sen, A. K. (1985b). 'Goals, commitment and identity'. *Journal of Law, Economics and Organization*, 1: 341–5.

+Sen, A. K. (1985c). 'Well-being, freedom and agency: the Dewey Lectures 1984'. *Journal of Philosophy*, 82(4): 169–221.

Sen, A. K. (1987). *The Standard of Living*. (G. Hawthorn (ed.), with comments by J. Muelbauer, R. Kanbur, K. Hart and B. Williams). [The 1985 Tanner Lectures, Clare Hall]. Cambridge: Cambridge University Press.

(1991a). 'Beneconfusion'. Chapter 2 in J. G. Meeks (ed.): 12–16.

(1991b). 'Freedom and social choice', The Arrow Lectures, published in revised version in Sen, A. K. (2002), Part VI.

(1992). *Inequality Reexamined*. New York: Russell Sage Foundation. Cambridge MA: Harvard University Press. Oxford: Clarendon Press.

**+ Sen, A. K. (1997). 'Maximisation and the act of choice'. *Econometrica*, 65(4): 745–79.

Sen, A. K. (1998). 'Amartya Sen – Biographical'. Stockholm: Nobel Foundation. Available at www.nobelprize.org/nobel_prizes/economic-sciences/laureates/1998/sen-bio.html.

**+Sen, A. K. (1999a). 'The possibility of social choice'. *American Economic Review*, 89(3): 349–78. [1998 Nobel Lecture, Stockholm: The Nobel Foundation. Available at www.nobelprize.org/nobel_prizes/economic-sciences/laureates/1998/sen-lecture.html.]

Sen, A. K. (1999b). *Development as Freedom*. New York, NY: Knopf. Oxford and Delhi: Oxford University Press.

(2002). *Rationality and Freedom*. Cambridge MA: Harvard University Press.

(2004). 'Disability and justice'. Keynote speech at the World Bank 2004 conference on 'Disability and Inclusive Development'. Available at http://webcache.googleusercontent.com/search?q=cache:-SdEGXlABL wJ:siteresources.worldbank.org/DISABILITY/Resources/280658-1172 606907476/DisabilityDevelopmentWB.doc+&cd=3&hl=en&ct= clnk&gl=uk.

(2005). 'Why exactly is commitment important for rationality?'. *Economics and Philosophy*, 21(1): 5–14. [Reprinted in F. Peter and H. B. Schmid (eds.).]

(2006a). 'Reason, freedom and well-being'. *Utilitas*, 18(1): 80–96.

(2006b). 'The human development index'. In D. A. Clark (ed.) (2006b): 256–60.

(2007). 'Comment: Rational choice: discipline, brand name, and substance'. In F. Peter and H.B. Schmid (eds.): 339–61.

(2009a). *The Idea of Justice*. London: Allen Lane.

(2009b). 'Response'. Chapter 13 in R. Gotoh and P. Dumouchel (eds.).

(2017). *Collective Choice and Social Welfare*. Expanded edition. London: Penguin.

Stewart, F. (2006). 'Basic Needs Approach'. In D. A. Clark (ed.) (2006b): 14–18.

++Sugden, R. (1993). 'Welfare, resources and capabilities: A review of *Inequality Reexamined* by Amartya Sen'. *Journal of Economic Literature*, 31(4): 1947–62.

Sugden, R. (2006). 'What we desire, what we have reason to desire, whatever we might desire: Mill and Sen on the value of opportunity'. *Utilitas*, 18(1): 33–51.

(2008). 'Capabilities, happiness and opportunity'. Chapter 12 in L. Bruni, F. Comim and M. Pugno (eds.) *Capabilities and Happiness*. Oxford: Oxford University Press: 299–322.

Sumner, L. W. (1996). *Welfare, Happiness and Ethics*. Oxford: Clarendon Press.

Vizard, P. and Burchardt, T. (2014). 'Using the capability approach to evaluate health and care for individuals and groups in England'. In Ibrahim S. and Tiwari M. (eds.) *The Capability Approach from Theory to Practice*. Basingstoke: Palgrave.

Warnock, G. J. (1967). *Contemporary Moral Philosophy*. Basingstoke: Palgrave Macmillan.

Williams, B. (1987). 'The standard of living: interests and capabilities'. In Sen, A. K. (1987, ed. G. Hawthorn).

Wood, J. C. and Wood, R. D. (eds.) (2007). *Amartya Sen: Critical Assessments of Contemporary Economists*. Volumes I and II. Abingdon: Routledge.

PART I

The Need for New Foundations

3 | Capabilities and the Common Good

JONATHAN WARNER

Introduction: Incompleteness of the Capabilities Approach

During the past fifteen years, the capabilities approach (CA), partially facilitated by the first two Cambridge Conferences and the subsequent formation of the Human Development and Capabilities Association, has become an important, even indispensable, framework for thinking about development. At the very least, the CA has helped change the emphasis of development thinking away from a top-down solution to what ought to be done to a new concern to listen to the voices of actual people. The older approach treated underdeveloped areas of the world as lacking something that an authority figure, such as the Great White Father in Washington, or Western consultants, could provide. That, in effect, means seeing people living in countries deemed to be less developed as passive – as patients who need to be treated by Western medicine. Instead, the CA has helped reinforce a move to a perspective that emphasizes the importance of people's own thinking, feeling and ideas about what kind of life they want to live.

Agency has therefore come to be seen as an essential part of any robust and non-neocolonial approach to development. In Sen's formulation of the CA, people need to have (access to) the opportunities that are necessary for them to live a life that they have reason to value. Being able to make the choice of what is valuable is itself valuable; indeed, the ability to choose between (valuable) options is not only important, but perhaps even constitutive of what it means to live a valuable life. For Sen, an agent is 'someone who acts and brings about change, and whose achievements can be judged in terms of her own values and objectives' (Sen, 1999: 19). The ability to act as an agent – agency freedom – is the 'freedom to bring about the achievements one values and which one attempts to produce' (Sen, 1992: 57). While not all agents always act in ways which respect others' freedoms (suggesting that there need to be limits to the free exercise of choice), appropriate agency is presented as a valuable capability.[1] My choosing and being able to live a life that allows me to make choices, is more valuable than one where choices are made for me, even if those choices are the ones which I would have made anyway.

While agency is important and valuable, to idolize it as the supreme good of human existence is going too far: as Amartya Sen has made clear, all choices are to varying extents partial, limited and constrained. The emphasis on choices (and important ones, at that) requires that people are capable of choosing freely and are able to follow through with their choices (so they reflect what their considered judgement informs them is what they want), and that the resulting outcomes are good and valuable. These are high standards to reach, but it is generally thought that rational adult human beings are capable of reaching them, at least most of the time. A further difficulty arises when individual choices are used as the only basis for deciding what constitutes a good and valuable society. The achievement or flourishing of one person or group, when not co-ordinated with that of others, can produce outcomes that are less good than what could have been achieved, even in terms of the metric of value used by the agent. The next section of this chapter defends this claim; I then go on to suggest that the concept of the common good, as an orien-tating principle, might be helpful in providing an extra information basis to help produce a good society – one that flourishes and is populated by flourishing individuals, all living lives they have reason to value.

For liberal political philosophers (such as John Rawls), the burden of transitioning from a set of flourishing individuals to a flourishing society is shouldered by offices and institutions that are democratic in nature. They need to be open to be filled by all qualified applicants, selected by some kind of majority-voting mechanism, with appropri-ate safeguards for minority choices to protect their proponents from the tyranny of the majority. Many social policy disputes, such as gay marriage or, more broadly, the rights of certain groups to oppose the

---

[1] Capabilities include both the negative and positive freedoms of Berlin's (1958, 1969) distinction. The freedom to be and to do requires not only the negative liberty of freedom from interference in certain areas of life, but also the positive liberty of being able to do certain things, for each to be the master of him or herself. Agency of choice, though, as Berlin shows, is subject to conscious and unconscious constraints imposed from outside. This chapter can be seen as an attempt to wrestle with some of the implications of the CA's difficulty in dealing adequately with this problem.

majority's way of doing things, are of this nature. In this chapter, I want to suggest an alternative approach – one which is largely congruent with the liberal tradition, but which provides a normative principle that could, at best, act as arbiter in disputes of the kind mentioned, or, at worst, at least suggest questions worth asking when contemplating a social policy decision. That is the idea of the common good. Although denounced by some as threadbare and in need of renewal (see Welby, 2015, quoting Sacks, 2007: 11) and seen by others as coming with too much historical baggage to be of use today, I want to explore to what extent some plausible account of the common good could be helpful in expanding an account of appropriate agency in producing valuable lives. The aim of this chapter is to establish a framework, to suggest what types of questions a consideration of the common good might lead us to ask, rather than attempting to spell out a full account of the concept. That would take a much longer work.

Living a Life That Is Valuable: Sen and Sour Grapes

It is fairly obvious, as hinted in the previous section, that untrammelled exercise of agency by all will not produce a harmonious society; for example, if my valuable life involves exploiting you (as my slave, perhaps), or if my expensive tastes mean that there are no resources left for you. (The North Korean tyrant, Kim Jong-un, perhaps exemplifies both of these.) Not all chosen lives that the agent has reason to value are good: the recent wave of terrorist attacks are horrifying evidence of this. The perpetrator may well believe that his place in paradise is assured by his actions, or that righting a perceived injustice is required of her, but destroying the valuable lives of others is inconsistent with their flourishing.[2] Therefore, for society to function in a way that allows all to flourish there needs to be some kind of framework that allows for the constraining of such choices and that is able to mediate between competing views when it is necessary to do so. As Martha Nussbaum has pointed out, not all functionings are conducive to appropriate human development, especially in ensuring equal capabilities for women (Nussbaum, 2000, 2003: 44ff).

---

[2] Even institutions that seem to be designed to promote agency can be used to produce unfreedoms – for example, education can be structured to oppress rather than liberate, as the apartheid system in South Africa sought to do.

As a preliminary exploration, though, it is helpful to consider a number of more subtle objections to a strong account of agency. By 'strong' agency, I mean the view that in most cases individual choices will trump other considerations; that is, the onus will be on the person wishing to violate a free choice to provide convincing arguments for this interference with self-mastery.[3] If, for example, it could be shown to be self-defeating (in that the outcomes it produces are less valuable to the agent than the outcomes of some other process), then an all-encompassing embrace of it would be misplaced.

First, choices are often not obviously the choices of the agent. Preferences (which are generally reflected in choices)[4] are subject to adaptation to the circumstances in which one finds oneself: one actually believes, or comes to believe, or, at least, articulates the view that one believes, that the life chosen (or other choice made) is the best available, even when, to an outside observer, it clearly isn't. The problem here is how to square maladaptive preferences with agency. My bad choice is still my choice, even if it is the result of peer pressure, the socio-religious environment in which I live and my lack of knowledge of alternatives that might be open to me. Much has been written on the problem of maladaptive preferences, and what to do about them, starting at least from Berlin (1969) and developed by Elster (1982, 1985), with recent contributions from authors such as Khader (2011).

Second, and related to what has been said earlier, imagination may fail. Henry Ford once said that if he'd asked his customers what they wanted, they would have asked for a better horse, rather than a cleaner, cheaper and more efficient alternative, the horseless carriage. No one knew how much they needed a smart phone, with all the worlds of possibility that it opens up, until Steve Jobs demonstrated that they

---

[3] By contrast, 'weak' agency would see agency as a virtue – but as one virtue among many. One example of the difference would be the contrast between 'salt water' and 'fresh water' economists (Krugman, 2009) on the degree to which markets will maximize welfare. The freshwater/strong agency/'Market fundamentalist' view will be suspicious of any attempt to limit people's choices as expressed by their economic decision-making; the saltwater/weak agency/'Keynesian' view claims that individual choices need to be constrained to rescue the economy from recession.

[4] Sen is, of course, right to point out the differences between preferences, desires, choices and welfare (Sen, 1970, 1992). There are many reasons why a preference might not be reflected in a choice: duty and altruism are just two kinds of reasons that might justify this.

did. If what we consider valuable is subject to being changed by the ideas of others, then agency may lead to worse outcomes than buying into an 'off-the-shelf' valuable life decided upon by a mentor or life coach, for example. Perhaps there are cases where Western experts really do know better.

Third, people may make bizarre choices. What to make of the man who bases his life and perceived well-being on the childhood game of avoiding stepping on cracks in the paving stones? Could a life based on such a proposition be valuable? Certainly the man would say yes, it's actually the only thing that really matters; and how can he be gainsaid? Sen here has a kind of solution: the life must not only be valuable to the person living it, but also there must be reasons given why it is valuable, hence the formulation 'a life which one has reason to value' (Sen, 1999: 18). The man himself doesn't have to be able himself to articulate the reason why a life spent avoiding paving-stone cracks at all costs is valuable; it's enough that there are persuasive reasons that can be given by someone that it actually *is* valuable. However, it is not immediately clear what might constitute a persuasive reason and who it is that decides what counts as persuasive. How is it to be decided that a particular life is, or is not valuable, such that someone (a Smithian impartial observer, a man on the Clapham omnibus, or whoever) can determine, from the outside, whether it is so. Or, what about J. J. C. Smart's pleasure machine (or an infinite period playing a virtual reality game like *Better than Life* from the cult science fiction comedy *Red Dwarf*)?[5] A certain sort of Utilitarian would perhaps agree to be hooked up to the machine; on the (reasonable) ground that it maximizes her lifetime's utility.

Fourth, it might be urged that agency seems sometimes to clash with other values. For example, a contemporary area of dispute in some countries is the compulsory nature of public education. Generally, proponents of the CA argue that mandatory formal education is necessary, to give children the skills and knowledge they need to have the capacity to make informed choices, and to formulate, for themselves, what a valuable life might be. The problem with this is that this runs the risk of opening possibilities and opportunities that the

[5] See Smart and Williams (1973); and https://en.wikipedia.org/wiki/Better_Than_ Life_(Red_Dwarf) for a synopsis of the game; the novel of the same name (Naylor, 1990) also features the 'game'.

person wishes he'd never heard of. Once one has learned something, it's often almost impossible to forget (like swimming or bicycle-riding), to the extent that even thinking about it, or even having thoughts about it coming unbidden cause pain and so make one's life less enjoyable (and so, from certain perspectives at least, less valuable). Contra Mill (1863, chapter 2), it might be better to be a fool satisfied than Socrates dissatisfied. An example is the contemporary dispute between home-schooling parents and the state; the parents want to inculcate their beliefs and lifestyle into their offspring, and are (rightly) concerned that the types of state-provided education available will irrevocably damage their children. (For example, fundamentalist, creationist Christians may opt for home schooling to protect their children from 'misleading, atheistic propaganda' inherent in the theory of evolution taught at state schools.) If there is a compelling state interest in over-riding the parents' wishes, then it would appear that agency is a good only within state-sanctioned limits.[6]

Fifth, agency can result in a prisoners' dilemma or a classical tragedy, where doing what is, or appears to be, best for myself inevitably leads to a situation where I end up with something less than the outcome I would have wished. This doesn't have to be the simple prison-time minimization of the original prisoners' dilemma; Derek Parfit has devised cases where agency, even when the agent is a rational altruist, might be self-defeating. One set of his examples concerns rescuing others, when a team effort is required, but where each agent has the option of rescuing a different (smaller) group of people by going it alone.

I know all of the following. A hundred miners are trapped in a shaft with flood-waters rising. These men can be brought to the surface in a lift raised by weights on long levers. If I and three other people go to stand on some platform, this will provide just enough weight to raise the lift, and will save the lives of these hundred miners. If I do not join the rescue mission, I can go elsewhere and save, single-handedly, the lives of ten other people (Parfit, 1983: 67–68).

Parfit also discusses a number of variations on the theme. The number of lives saved by single-handed action can be varied; he also has a

---

[6] Home-schooling is illegal in Germany; some home-schoolers sought asylum in the USA as a result – see 'Home Schooling German Family Allowed to Stay in US' http://abcnews.go.com/US/home-schooling-german-family-allowed-stay-us/story?id=22788876

case where there is a fifth person, who will take my place in the team if I go solo – because he is concerned with a question of agency – how important is it that I save as many people as I can?[7]

In each of these cases, the introduction of a new basis of information which goes beyond the individual focus of the CA has the potential to produce superior outcomes.[8] The common good is one such analytical framework; others include various forms of government structures (the liberal view of the emphasis on democratic decision-making was mentioned above), or a substantive (and shared) overarching moral theory (such as utilitarianism).

Economists, especially in the field of behavioural economics, are aware of and have also studied cases where a strong attachment to agency is self-defeating, and have produced resolutions to the problems they discuss.[9] For example: time inconsistency, changing one's mind, plans or actions mid-stream, exists where the temptation to renege on a commitment causes a change of heart. Politicians are said to be particularly susceptible to this vice: they promise lots of things to garner votes, but then don't follow through as, having been elected, the costs of doing so are too great. The Greek hero Odysseus exemplifies the problem: he wanted to hear the Sirens' song, but knew that, if he did, he would lose his life as the singers lured him irresistibly onto treacherous rocks. Or, to take a more recent finding: people, especially when young, often have an excessively high discount rate for future benefits. That is, they'll prefer instant gratification over a much bigger reward later. Mischel and Ebbesen (1970) conducted tests on pre-school children: they could take one marshmallow now, or receive

---

[7] An earlier set of examples concerned saving children – if it's important that I save my own children, I'll choose to save three of them, rather than co-operating with someone to save four children, two of his and two of mine (Parfit, 1977). Perhaps Clifford Geetz was right to pillory Oxford philosophers for producing examples that are so unlikely in the real world that they can give us little, if any, guidance (Geetz, 1973).

[8] This is true regardless of whether or not one thinks, like Sen and Nussbaum, that the CA is not trying to produce a complete theory of justice. Other bases of information could be seen as fleshing out a complete theory, or of offering further (perhaps marginal) enhancements to a partial and incomplete theory.

[9] Behavioural economics is now a large and growing field; its motivation was initially to explore how real people actually acted (rather than assuming that everyone always acted so as to maximize their expected utility). Thaler's (1980) pioneering paper and work by authors such as Kahneman and Tversky (1979) established the discipline. Airely (2008) and Thaler and Sunstein (2008) have popularized the insights of the discipline and suggested policies based on them.

two if they left it untouched for ten or fifteen minutes. Surprisingly, those four-year-olds who held out longer became more cognitively and socially competent adolescents (Mischel, Shoda and Rodriguez, 1989). The differences persisted: the study participants who held out the longest even had better mental health as adults (Mischel et al., 2011).

This problem was familiar to St Paul:

What I want to do I do not do, but what I hate I do ... I have the desire to do what is good, but I cannot carry it out. For I do not do the good I want to do, but the evil I do not want to do – this I keep on doing ... For in my inner being I delight in God's law; but I see another law at work in me, waging war against the law of my mind and making me a prisoner of the law of sin at work within me. What a wretched man I am! Who will rescue me from this body that is subject to death? (Romans 7:15–24)

Without the right incentive or motivation, we are prone to make choices that are suboptimal (as the four-years did): we are easily diverted by temptation (as Odysseus feared he would be); and so we need help. Insights from behavioural economics can suggest how to provide the incentives: evidence shows that a viable policy response is to put appropriate nudges in place, 'Libertarian paternalism', as Thaler and Sunstein (2008) call it.[10] Or (as Odysseus did) the same effect can be achieved through irrevocable self-precommitment: having himself tied to his ship's mast to avoid being lured on to the rocks by the sweet songs of the Sirens, and having his crew put wax in their ears so that they couldn't hear either the music or his begging to be untied when he heard it saved the hero from shipwreck. If 'irrevocable' is not possible, 'expensive' might be enough. People can make contracts with themselves to commit (for example) to not smoking, by giving a large sum of money to a friend who will return it only if they don't smoke for the period of the contract. An accountability partner can hold the money, or berate the contractor for reneging, if the latter is concerned that their commitment will waver. Alternatively, StickK can play the role of friend or arbitrator, by making a large donation of the contractor's money to an 'anti-charity' (a charity to whose aims the contractor is implacably opposed, such as Planned Parenthood for

---

[10] This, of course, can be abused. Akerlof and Shiller (2015) entertainingly document such cases.

a pro-life Christian, perhaps) if they fail to carry through with what they said they would do.[11]

Paul's problem is deeper, though: the incentive is there (lead the good life in order to please God); but he is still unable to live as he should. The modern solution is often the use of accountability groups (such as Alcoholics Anonymous) to try to hold people to the course to which they wish to commit.[12]

Severine Deneulin has pointed out another paradox, where moving internationally from a poor country (El Salvador) to increase one's career prospects, and to send money home to one's family seems like an appropriate exercise of agency. It promotes development in the short run, but in the long run it becomes negative: it undermines development by producing structural changes in the sending country that leave it worse off than if the emigrants had stayed at home (Deneulin, 2006).

So: if (inappropriate) use of agency can produce outcomes that are worse, in the agent's view, than some other obtainable outcome, then even appropriate agency without some constraints can be self-defeating. Sen's version of the Capability Approach is particularly susceptible to this criticism; Nussbaum's approach, with its appeal to a thick, vague theory of the good less so (as she has pointed out – Nussbaum, 2003). If there is some orientating principle that transcends agency, or, at least, places constraints on it, then there is a solution to at least some of these issues. The recognition of an underlying substantive (albeit vague) theory of the good, combined with overlapping consensus between reasonable people's theories rules out bizarre views and goes some way to blunt the force of the adaptive preferences argument.

Nussbaum, Virtue and *After Virtue*

Nussbaum's account of the CA develops a more rigid structure than Sen's. Her version of the CA is best known for the list of ten central human functional capabilities, or basic human capabilities (Nussbaum, 2000: 76–8). Her insistence that there are universal values, and that it is, therefore, possible to have a theory of the good (albeit a thick and vague one) finds its roots ultimately in Aristotelian thought.

---

[11] See www.stickk.com/. The site was co-founded by the economist Dean Karlan, and records his own use of self-contracting to lose weight.
[12] The success rate, though, seems to be low – see Dodes and Dodes (2014).

For Aristotle, 'happiness' or 'well-being' (*eudaimonia*) is not merely a state, in that it involves activity, exhibiting *areté* (virtue or excellence) in accordance with reason. *Logos* (reason or rationality) is unique to human beings, and *eudaimonia* comes from the proper (virtuous?) development of one's highest and most human capabilities; *eudaimonia* for a human being is the attainment of *areté* in reason.

The CA at first sight comports well with this framework. Instead of being an almost free-floating system based on the ability of people to make (valuable) choices, it is anchored in an account of the type of environment where there is some positive account of what constitutes the good. In other words, a way has been found to derive an evaluative conclusion from a series of factual statements about the nature of the world and, especially, of its human inhabitants. This is part of a battle between the anthropocentric Enlightenment view of autonomous human agents and the earlier accounts of a discernible final goal (*telos*) of human life.

However, it is not clear that this Aristotelian anchor will hold. As Alasdair MacIntyre (1981) argues, the language of virtue has come adrift from its context and has become a linguistic fossil, rather than a living reality. We know how to use the vocabulary of virtue correctly in sentences, but, he claims, we're unable to give a full account of its meaning.[13] That meaning, he claims, is embedded in the context of heroic Greek literature, or perhaps the *polis* of Plato, Socrates and Aristotle; but not in the modern world of Kantian, utilitarian or emotivist/intuitionist theories of ethics.

Partly as a response to MacIntyre's *After Virtue*, there has been renewed interest in virtue theory in the past few decades.[14] Ethicists within the Roman Catholic tradition had kept the flame tended.[15]

---

[13] A similar point, in a different context, is made by the Old Testament scholar, John Walton, who refers to the presuppositions of a particular civilization or society as its 'cultural river'. Certain conventions are so well known, that the Old Testament writers assume that everyone knows and understands their significance. (See his work in NIV, 2016.)

[14] Of course, MacIntyre is indebted to previous authors, including Anscombe (1958), as he acknowledges (MacIntyre, 1981: 53).

[15] *Putting on Virtue: The Legacy of the Splendid Vices* (Herdt, 2008) is an important recent work in the field. The Jubilee Centre for Character and Virtues at Birmingham University believes, unlike Socrates in Plato's *Meno*, that virtue can be learnt, and has devised curricula for schools in an attempt to demonstrate the truth of this proposition. The evidence so far is that the project can produce more virtuous children.

It remains to be seen if this revival can unseat the theories of twentieth-century ethics, from Moore (1903) to Hare (1963) and beyond. Can ethics be rooted in something more than (to paraphrase John Mackie's 1977 subtitle to his *Ethics*) an invention of right and wrong? If not, then we're left with something akin to Sen's approach, where right and wrong would be relative to what constitutes a valuable life. But if substantive views of at least in what parameters the good must lie, then the types of solutions to many questions in development (including its scope and purpose) become clear.

Nussbaum's account of capabilities hints at the possibility of something greater than choices that individuals value as the *summun bonum*. A thick theory of the good, even if vague, would serve as an additional organizational principle for living a good life. A good life is the kind of life that one should value; and not just any life that one can produce good reasons for valuing. Taking this approach means that there is not a different type of criterion – some *telos*, some claims about the nature of life, perhaps, that reduce the range of valued lives to those that are good.

Adaptive preferences can still exist within a framework of virtue ethics, or within Nussbaum's framework, but their range is reduced: there are now criteria by which they can be judged to be maladaptive – when they reduce the opportunities of the agent to live the good life. One could, perhaps, give reasons why a slave might value a life of enslavement (trading opportunities seen as valueless for security, shelter and food, perhaps) – but such a life would not be good.

The problems of weakness of the will and of responsibility for lapses remain, however. If for some reason my choices are an inappropriate adaptation, am I really responsible for them? Further, what if I can't help myself, if I'm enslaved to some ideology, false god or even my own desires, which seems to have been Paul's problem? He knows what's right; what comprises a good life, but cannot live it. His desire (and preference) don't match his choice; but he is unable to act differently.[16] This suggests that even knowing what a valuable life looks like is insufficient: because of various kinds of weaknesses (the human

---

[16] Sen, in his Arrow lectures (Sen, 2004: Section VI) argues that preferences can be reasoned about, and perhaps changed. Behavioural economics suggests that this is not always the case (Airely, 2008); and Paul's problem is different. He knows what his desire/preference is; but he can't choose it.

condition) we are unable to live as we should, even if we know how we should live and want to live that way.

Paul found the answer in Jesus Christ. Jesus inspired him, loved him, redeemed him and transformed him into a man prepared joyfully to accept many different forms of suffering to get the message about the Christ to as many people as he could. But Paul also realized that he could not do this alone: he needed fellow labourers who would assist him, intercede for him and build the work. With this support, Paul was able to consider the needs of the communities he visited and embedded himself within, and to adapt his message to the people he worked with (1 Corinthians 9: 19–23). Paul's working-in-community suggests another approach, the one I want to consider here.

If the good life, the life one has reason to value, is one which allows for individual flourishing (thus far, the CA), but which needs and is also concerned with participating in a flourishing community[17] then something more is needed, which takes account of the communal nature of the good life.

If a flourishing community is greater than the sum of its parts, then this presupposes that it is possible to have a cluster of people, a group, all of whom are individually flourishing, and all of whom are geographically close to each other, but the group *qua* group fails to flourish. This could be the case for a number of different reasons. For example, power relations within the group mean that unfreedom for many is the norm. Or, the co-ordination problems discussed earlier mean that the community is impoverished in some way. Or because relationships between the members of the set are somehow impaired, or there are no valuable relationships between them. The difference might be illustrated by the difference between a monastery and a set of hermits, who individually flourish (by worshiping and contemplating the divine) but have no communion with their fellows; between a good zoo, where the animals have space to live as they would in the wild, and a functioning ecosystem; between a set of people 'living the dream', but with no interaction with their neighbours (a 'suburb') and a community ('town'); or between individuals-in-markets

---

[17] Often location is part of the definition of a community: to have a (valuable) relationship with one's neighbour requires that the neighbour is nearby. But if the idea of a virtual or internet community makes sense, then geographic proximity might not be essential.

(or the atomized individualized life in the world of Forster's (1909) *The Machine Stops*) and persons-in-community (Cobb, 1994: 13).[18]

In short, a flourishing community requires not only that each of its members flourishes, but that the relationships between them lead to something more. Such community members, when deciding what kinds of lives are valuable, will ask questions not only about the components of individual flourishing and the good life, but also about the types of flourishing that are most likely to build rich relationships and a flourishing community; in other words, questions about the nature of the common good.

The Common Good

A basic definition of the common good seems easy – as a first approximation, the common good is (something which is to) the benefit or interests of all. Perhaps this apparent simplicity is why the concept is often used, but seldom analysed.[19] But getting a useful understanding of the concept risks one of two possible errors – to make the term so broad (as above) that it ceases to have any meaning beyond that of a political slogan, or, conversely, to narrow its focus to, perhaps, just a list of disparate big hairy ideas that do not necessarily comport well together (e.g. combating climate change, reducing poverty, electrification, global free trade, population control and the ability to move freely across international borders). In any case, something is lacking in the simple definition mentioned above.

For many modern writers, such as Deneulin (2006) and Hollenbach (2002) the common good is relational: it is inevitably communal and shared.

> The common good is a good which transcends the human good of each individual life. It does not dwell only in an individual life but in the life of interaction among individuals ... As Hollenbach noted ... the

---

[18] Or, another example: Baylor University's attempt to become a major research University staffed by Christians came unstuck for several reasons; Wood (2004) claims that at root was what he calls 'the heresy of solitary faith'. A set of Christians who are scholars each pursuing his or her own research agenda does not make a (Christian) community.

[19] For example, Cobb (1994) never defines the common good, and the term does not appear in the book's index, but it is fairly clear from context what he has in mind.

shared life of interaction with others is a good in itself ... [The common good] is not the sum total of institutional arrangements which secure the conditions for people to achieve certain levels of human well-being; it is the *whole* of the conditions of social life which enable people to live flourishing human lives (Deneulin, 2006: 53).

The term, 'common good', like 'natural right' or 'public interest' comes with a lot of baggage. It is most at home in the natural law school of thought – Thomas Aquinas's synthesis of Christian and Aristotelian ideas is perhaps the greatest exemplar of this approach. Catholic Social Teaching (CST) builds on this basis, and, since the promulgation of the first CST Encyclical, *Rerum Novarum* in 1891, the trajectory of Papal thought on social and, latterly, environmental issues has had a strong communitarian emphasis, which makes frequent reference to the need to seek the common good.[20] In fact, the number of uses of the phrase 'the common good' in an author's work is generally a good indication of how close s/he is to this tradition.

The Encyclical *Gaudium et Spes* (1965: 26) defines common good as follows, drawing attention to the development of its scope over time:

Every day human interdependence grows more tightly drawn and spreads by degrees over the whole world. As a result the common good, that is, the sum of those conditions of social life which allow social groups and their individual members relatively thorough and ready access to their own fulfilment, today takes on an increasingly universal complexion and consequently involves rights and duties with respect to the whole human race. Every social group must take account of the needs and legitimate aspirations of other groups, and even of the general welfare of the entire human family.

It is the association with natural law that provides much of the baggage that accompanies the concept of the common good. Rooted in a pre-modern tradition, it has been regarded with suspicion by Enlightenment thinkers, who came to prefer terms such as the public interest. This is because the common good was associated historically with a pre-democratic form of governance – that there was a discernible common good that was capable of being achieved, and that it was

---

[20] The documents which collectively form the basis of Catholic Social Teaching are helpfully arranged at www.catholicsocialteaching.org.uk/principles/documents/

the task of those in authority (ultimately, kings and rulers) to determine its content. This sits uneasily with more modern conceptions of political theory, where the public interest could be cashed out in terms of the desires or opinions expressed by the polity, rather than some objectively determinable, and possibly eternal, truth. (See Douglass, 1980 for an historically based account.)

Two further additions to the proposed definition are in order. First, the CST literature talks frequently of solidarity. For a community to function, its members must agree that all need to be enabled to flourish and supported in their flourishing; that is, the community needs to stand together in order to function. Second, the common good can be limited in space and its application to particular communities.[21] The CST doctrine of subsidiarity is important here: the view that (political) decisions should be taken at the lowest applicable level of government, and by government only when the institutions of civil society could not produce the common good by themselves.[22] Thus, decisions about the production of breakfast cereals or the baking of bread are not an appropriate area for government control. The free market, sometimes with some regulation to prevent exploitation, has proven adequate to the task of providing these goods.[23] The routing of footpaths is of greatest concern to people living in the vicinity, and so, in England, it is generally Parish Councils that make decisions about them. Planning matters of largely local significance are made by district councils; library facilities have come to be the preserve of county councils. Matters of national significance require national governments, and, at present, matters affecting Europe are seen as the appropriate sphere of action of the European Union. Global issues, such as combating climate change or ensuring free trade, need to be addressed within a

---

[21] This is potentially problematic. The Mafia is arguably a community; it exhibits solidarity between its members, and perhaps seeks their common good. But its scope is limited to its membership; CST generally sees community in terms of geographic scope, whereas the Mafia doesn't.

[22] This is spelt out most clearly in Mater et Magistra (1961: 53) and the references therein.

[23] There is, of course, a big debate over the appropriate scope and limits of market activity. This debate surfaces in differing understandings of the argument of the Encyclicals (where the Acton Institute [www.acton.org] under its president the Reverend Robert Sirico critiques mainstream interpretations of Papal thinking from a more Libertarian perspective), and, more generally, on the extent to which capitalism can enhance the common good (see Deneulin, 2009).

world-wide framework. Boundaries between their spheres of activity tend to be fluid and are dealt with in different ways in different countries. For example, a confederate system such as Canada's emphasizes the role of the provinces at the expense of the national government (a system taken to an extreme in Switzerland), whereas the centralizing trend of a federal system (such as the United States) has strengthened the federal government at the expense of the states. One vision of Europe is that this centralizing trend should continue, with ever more powers being ceded to the EU, to produce an ever-closer union. The UK's vote in the Brexit referendum is Britain's rejection of that vision and a belief that the common good of the UK could better be served by a re-domesticization of legal and legislative functions.

The constituents of the common good are immediately relevant to political decisions (how will the proposed policy impact the people of the relevant community?); but those kinds of questions are also relevant to thinking about what constitutes a good life; how I should live. How will my living in this way affect others? Do we need to co-ordinate what we do in order to avoid some of the problems raised in the first section, for example? A brief excursion into the history of the idea of the common good is helpful here.

Aquinas, Paul and the Common Good: Flourishing in Society and in the Church

It is hard to think ourselves back into the world of the Middle Ages. Presuppositions about the nature and task of humanity, the ordering of society and what a valuable life would look like are very different from our views on those matters today. As Alistair MacIntyre argues, even the words we hear were birthed in a different context and have nuances that we miss.

The common good has the capacity to provide a framework of analysis of those conditions necessary to produce a society which is flourishing, that is, including those things necessary for the members of the society to flourish. This framework provides a setting for questions about public policy that will complement those concerning the effects on individual liberty, agency and flourishing by seeking to see what policies will enhance the common good as well as individual goods.

When Papal Encyclicals reference the common good, those references are generally to Aquinas and St Isidore of Seville (c. 560–636), the last of the Fathers of the Church and author of the first work in the *Summa* genre (synopses of what is known), and a major source of the work of that great thirteenth-century Summarizer, Thomas Aquinas.

Aquinas' thought is teleological. The natural law – things common from the innate nature of human beings – determines their purpose and end, their *telos*. Human beings find various innate desires, imprinted by God; the final end is *eudaimonia*.[24] Good is to be done, evil avoided, for knowledge of the good, and the inclination to do it, is within us (as Paul claims – Romans 7: 22–4). In any case, evil does not have an independent existence – it is parasitic on good.[25] Aquinas finds other inclinations in human beings – the desire of each to preserve his own being, to procreate (inclinations that are shared with other animals and possibly all life), and, uniquely to people, to do good, to know the truth about God and to live in society. This last is our primary concern, but it is worth noting that knowledge of truth about God, and possessing knowledge of good and evil, also have consequences for what a valuable life looks like. So, for Aquinas and other Christians, the *telos* to which humans are striving is to see Christ in glory (the 'beatific vision'). God will ultimately bring the present age to an end, and His saints will join Him in the manifest Kingdom of Heaven. A life one has reason to value, then, would be a life that is consistent with this trajectory.

What this entails is clear from Scripture. As the prophets told Israel, '[God] has shown you … what is good. And what does the Lord require of you? To act justly and to love mercy and to walk humbly with your God' (Micah 6: 8). 'Take your evil deeds out of my sight! Stop doing wrong, learn to do right! Seek justice, encourage the oppressed. Defend the cause of the fatherless, plead the case of the widow' (Isaiah 1: 16b–17). Or, in the words of the Teacher in Ecclesiastes, 'Fear God, and keep His commandments, for this is the whole duty of man' (12: 13). From the New Testament comes the morality of the Sermon on the Mount (Matthew 5–7) and Jesus's exhortation (John 13: 34–5) to love each other.

---

[24] For Aquinas, were he writing in Greek rather than Latin, 'blessedness', (the Biblical *makarios*) might be a better term. Nussbaum (1986: 330–4) is among modern writers who see *eudaimonia* and *makarios* as near-synonyms. See Miller (2010) for analysis of the meaning and use of the Greek and Latin terms.

[25] *Summa Theologica* Part 1 Question 48:3 and 49:3.

These commandments presuppose community, living with other people, rather than just them. The instructions are on how to do it. A person's *telos* cannot be achieved alone, but only in society, and so community will be a necessary condition for valuable human life.[26] As Aristotle pointed out, man is a political animal. If humankind is inherently social, or political, a person's true end will be found in community. The flourishing of human society will be an end in itself, which transcends any instrumental value it has as a way of ensuring the private good of the members of the community (i.e. their flourishing as individuals). Rather, it is to seek something that Aquinas claims is qualitatively different: the supreme human good, which is the common good. Just as the whole is greater than the part, so the good of the community is greater than individual goods; and also different in kind. It is not, *pace* Mark Murphy (2005), just the sum of individual goods.[27]

Isidore and Aquinas found an application for this approach in their work, and it is this that has provided a vigorous vine on which the fruit of CST has grown and ripened.

If Aquinas is correct, then Nussbaum's affiliation capability would be at the centre of a Thomist account of capabilities. Membership of a flourishing community is a greater good than individual flourishing, just as for Nussbaum membership of an appropriate community is a valuable capability. But for Nussbaum affiliation is ultimately a choice: one doesn't have to participate, although the structure of human society means that most people will actually participate.[28] To Aquinas, though, affiliation isn't a choice – it's not something one can

---

[26] This does not mean that the collective must always trump the individual (nor vice versa), but just that these considerations, perhaps augmented by others, should be part of the information basis for determining the nature of a good society. Constant (1819) gives a trenchant criticism of the contrast between ancient and modern views of liberty, and sides with the 'modern' conception of liberty as primarily individual. But he also points out that both sorts of freedom (individual and political/collective are essential; and implicitly acknowledges that the balance between the two may shift over time.

[27] A set of people attached to Smart's pleasure machine or playing *Better than Life* are all manically happy; and hooking more people up to the machine would increase aggregate delirious happiness; but their happiness is not part of the common good.

[28] Deneulin and Stewart (2002) point out that Sen recognizes the importance of irreducibly social goods and their embeddedness in societal structures, but, they claim, the CA can give such goods only instrumental value, in as far as they contribute to an individually orientated basis of what a valuable life looks like.

opt in to, or out of; it is something one is born to.[29] One can't change one's parents (and other biological relations); similarly, one is born into membership of a number of different communities. Some look as if they are voluntary groups (like sports clubs), but most are not. To leave, or to be compelled to leave, a family or a community is about the most shocking thing that could happen to someone. The most severe of punishments in ancient societies was generally death or permanent exile. Indeed, exile was a form of death, an irrevocable exclusion from society. Just as the dead cannot continue to flourish, nor can the exiled.

There is therefore an important distinction between a community and a group. A group is a purely voluntary association, set up for a particular purpose and defined in terms of that purpose, that people can join and leave at their leisure. There is, as in economists' models of Perfect Competition, freedom of entry and exit. By contrast, a community is more akin to a political or geographic entity: it is harder, or sometimes impossible, to leave or enter. Becoming a member of a family (by adoption) is difficult and often expensive; there are many legal formalities to be observed. Becoming a naturalized citizen of a state, or renouncing one's citizenship, is often difficult and expensive too. Although the United States recognizes the right of its citizens to renounce their status, the process is long, difficult, and expensive, as Canadian 'border babies' have discovered.[30]

While a group will have common aims and will work for the good of the group, there is a distinction between that and the common good. One can talk loosely of the common good of the members of the group; but the common good of a society requires something more as it must apply to all of the community. It needs to produce benefits for everyone, regardless of any private interests they might have; there needs to be a significant degree of solidarity between its members.

If, then, one is inextricably bound to a community, then how the community operates is of supreme importance – what is the *telos* of

---

[29] This, of course, can have a dark side: nepotism, tribalism, xenophobia and racism being just examples. See Sen (2007).

[30] Renunciation must take place before a consular officer, and the number of appointments is severely limited, producing long wait-times to get an appointment. Those renouncing must pay a fee of $2,350, have submitted all required tax forms for the previous six years (and paid any taxes due), must prove they are making the choice of their own free will (so mentally handicapped people cannot apply) and, if they are rich, pay an 'exit tax'.

the community? The answer is clear: the realization of a well-ordered and harmonious society, where each individual was able to live out his particular role or calling. Together, the community would seek the common good. Different people within the community will have different tasks: Aquinas says that.

It belongs to the notion of human law to be ordained to the common good of the state. In this respect human law may be divided according to the different kinds of men who work in a special way for the common good: e.g. priests, by praying to God for the people; princes, by governing the people; soldiers, by fighting for the safety of the people.[31]

Gifts or roles are distributed among the population – with the purpose of securing the common good. The concept, if not the wording, of 'the common good' can be found in the New Testament. Paul writes to the church in Corinth, in the context of the bestowal and use of spiritual gifts. The New International Version translates Chapter 12 as follows:

To each one the manifestation of the Spirit is given for the common good. All these [manifestations] are the work of one and the same Spirit, and he distributes them to each one, just as he determines. Just as a body, though one, has many parts, but all its many parts form one body, so it is with Christ. For we were all baptized by one Spirit so as to form one body – whether Jews or Gentiles, slave or free – and we were all given the one Spirit to drink. Even so the body is not made up of one part but of many. If [all parts of the body] were all [the same], where would the body be? As it is, there are many parts, but one body. The eye cannot say to the hand, 'I don't need you!' And the head cannot say to the feet, 'I don't need you!' ... So there should be no division in the body, but that its parts should have equal concern for each other. If one part suffers, every part suffers with it; if one part is honoured, every part rejoices with it. Now you [collectively] are the body of Christ, and each one of you is a part of it.

Paul's argument here is that the gifts (manifestations) of the Holy Spirit are not for personal benefit, but for the good of the body of Christ, the church. Members of the church will have different gifts, roles and callings (apostles, teachers, etc.); but all are equally part of the body (just as ears and eyes and legs are all parts of the human body, and the body loses its wholeness if one or more parts are missing. The 'common' of common good refers to this wholeness – if one person or part ails, then everyone, the whole body, is sick. The achievement

---

[31] *Summa Theologica* Second part of the second Book, Question 95 Article 4.

of a healthy body is the goal; each part must itself be healthy, and the relationships and interactions between them must be healthy, too.

It is time to link this analysis back to modern society. One important aspect of lives that we consider to be worth living is being involved in a project greater than ourselves. It is this project – perhaps ensuring that my children can live valuable lives (as used in overlapping generations models), or the production of, or addition to, a social good that will in some way benefit posterity. These kinds of transcendent goals may get lost in an analysis of what makes life valuable that stresses individual decision-making. This desire to live what one might call a significant life, rather than one which is (merely) individually valuable is evidence of the importance of both the social nature of human beings and our ability to think beyond our own individual interests. If such meaningfulness can be achieved by the exercise of agency of people joining together to form voluntary associations, then the CA is right to emphasize individual choice. If associations need a stronger glue than this (some constraints on entry and exit, perhaps) then a different approach might be of greater value.

Group or Community? 'Third-Generation' Rights Revisited

It is instructive to note that, when exponents of the Capability Approach talk about the capabilities of people together, the reference is usually to a group rather than a community. Groups are more fluid, and cover a much wider range of affiliation options, from the low-entry, electronic listserv or Facebook group, through high-cost (but low commitment) groups such as golf clubs, to high-stakes life-changing affiliations (marriage; joining a religious order and taking a vow to remain part of it eternally, for example). Or just a collection or cluster of people who happen to be in close geographical proximity. A large group is a crowd, but a crowd is not a community.

In the early days of the CA, John M. Alexander presented a paper on what he called third-generation rights, or community capabilities, stressing that there were some things that could be achieved only by a community, that required acknowledgement beyond the recognition of the individual capabilities of each member of the community (Alexander, 2004).[32] For those working along these lines, the rights

---

[32] Evans (2002) makes a similar point about what he calls 'collective capabilities'.

of First Nations in North America provide a fruitful set of issues to address. How does one become a member of a particular band, tribe or nation? Can one lose this status? Are children of mixed parentage admitted to the community? What special (or different) rights does membership of the community give to its members? And what can the community itself do that its individual members themselves may not? The more collectivist traditional cultures of the Salish coast peoples (who live in the Pacific Northwest of North America) mean that decisions affecting the community require much more talk and discussion than is traditional among the European settler population. The aim is to reach consensus, something like the common good, rather than just securing a majority for some course of action.[33] No one person has the right to speak for the whole community – which means that different leaders may say different things about an issue. (Thus the energy infrastructure construction company, Enbridge, in getting the consent of a leader from each band for its Northern Gateway oil pipeline project was not the same as the band itself committing to the pipeline.)[34]

Frances Stewart has also written on group capabilities (Stewart, 2005). While she argues that groups are a 'critically important category', and not just of instrumental value for enlarging individual capabilities (which is Sen's view (1999: 116)), she still sees them as an exercise of individual agency, rather than something greater. She recognizes that groups can, of course, be for evil as well as good – a mafia family, for example, exists for the benefit of its members – and for the disbenefit for almost everyone else. To Stewart, groups are functional – they are 'instrumental to some wider purpose', perhaps a simple economic one (a food-buying co-operative), or to facilitate a

[33] Consensus, but not unanimity. As seventeenth- and eighteenth-century Poland discovered, requiring unanimity allowed anyone to place his own good higher than the common good, and so veto a consensus decision. This turned out unhappily for Poland; the systemic failure to achieve unanimity led to paralysis and ultimately to partition in 1795. A good history is provided in Davies (1981).

[34] The project was subsequently denied permission by the Canadian government (Tasker, 2016). In Canada, First Nation land is most usually held in common, which allows for the preservation of hunting grounds, sacred sites and other common use areas, and is the traditional way that land was owned. But this is not without its problems: it makes it impossible to have an individual title to a piece of land that could be used as collateral for a mortgage, which has the result that a disproportionate number of First Nation people live in trailers (mobile homes).

shared interest (a football supporters' club).[35] That is, it makes sense to ask what the group is for (which will be most likely mentioned in its constitution, if it is formally organized). The membership confers benefits from the achievement of the functional goal of the group (getting to see football matches; cheaper food) and the success of the group (cheering on the team to a greater number of wins), in addition to efficiency benefits (cheaper food), or empowerment to increase claims-satisfactions (Trades Unions), or the feelings of satisfaction that comes from helping others. All these benefits comport well with the CA. But, says Stewart, groups also influence members' (and perhaps non-members') preferences and behaviour. '[S]ociety – and indeed particular groups within society – shapes *every* individual, influencing preferences and consequent choices' (189).

What Stewart says of groups would apply also to the tighter bonds of communities – what one might call involuntary groups. Leaving a football supporters' club is, generally, not difficult and, beyond the loss of the benefits it confers, does not usually lead to some kind of retribution from those remaining in the group, nor is it (generally) seen as a form of exile. With a community, such as a nation, things are harder, as mentioned above.

There is a similar conundrum for secession. A liberal political theory which emphasized individuals' rights would be committed to allowing provinces or regions where the majority wants it to secede from the parent state. But this conclusion is often resisted: Katanga, Biafra and Eritrea all had to fight for secession. The Canadian Supreme Court has decreed that a positive vote for secession by Quebec is insufficient for the province to leave the confederation; the other provinces would have to give their consent. How easy it will be for Scotland to cease to be part of the United Kingdom remains to be seen.[36]

---

[35] She never uses the word 'community' in the article. Communities do not (necessarily) exist for some purpose – they are not necessarily functional.

[36] The Voice and Exit organization (www.voiceandexit.com/) advocates for a more libertarian approach to government; if individuals can easily move themselves and their property to another jurisdiction if they don't like their own government, then governmental monopoly on power will be weakened, to the benefit of individuals. Moving immobile property across land borders is difficult, and often impossible; but if people lived on boats and could move them to new moorings at will, this problem would be reduced; hence Voice and Exit's interest in 'Seasteading'. Seastead groups could develop into communities if people chose not to leave; but, in the absence of any binding commitment,

The Common Good, Public Goods and the Public Interest

It is easy to confuse the common good with a number of related concepts, and to attempt to make connections between them that do not exist. Therefore, this section looks briefly at how the common good is related to the concept of the public interest, and to the economist's categories of public goods and common resources, and how they differ from the common good.

According to Barry's (1965: 173–206) analysis, something is in x's interests if it enables x to get what s/he wants. So, the public interest could be construed to mean those things that are in the interests of (all) x in their public personae; as members of the public. The private interests of x may, of course, trump his interests as a member of the public. It's in the public interest that drunk driving is punished; but if x often drives drunk (and believes that he is perfectly safe doing so), it is in his private interest to oppose a policy to fine or imprison those with too much alcohol in their bloodstream.

Following this line of reasoning, a public good would be something that is good for x as a member of the public. The public good would be the web of policies that satisfy that criterion. This is a rather different kind of definition from that of the common good in that it neglects the richer relational element that is so important to the idea of the common good.

Economists approach the idea of public goods in a different way. Greg Mankiw is the lead author of a family of introductory and intermediate undergraduate texts on economics.[37] His account of the traditional demarcation lines distinguishes a public good as one which has two features: it is non-rival (my enjoyment of it does not stop your enjoyment of it, such as broadcast television, or a large, uncrowded park); and non-excludable – if the good exists, then I can't be prevented from having access to it. The defence forces protect all of us, whether we pay our taxes or not. Such goods tend to be underprovided by the private sector, because of the difficulty in getting people to pay for them if they can't be excluded. But TV broadcasters (by advertising)

---

the *threat* of leaving introduces an element of uncertainty which is detrimental to flourishing.

[37] His *Principles of Economics* textbook, now in its seventh edition, was first published in 1998, and has been the best-selling introductory text for much of the time since.

and Trinity House lighthouses (by charging harbour-owners) have found ways of raising funds for them. Many public goods also serve the common good (lighthouses, and, arguably, broadcast TV come into this category), but just as some rival and/or excludable goods can serve the common good (such as electrification, cable TV and internet access), not all public goods serve the common good. Roads are always public goods (if they are not toll roads), but too many roads, or roads in the wrong place may be detrimental to the common good.[38]

Conversely, it is quite possible that private goods can serve the common good. A community centre or concert hall could be privately owned, and promoters of events at such a venue may decide to charge an admission fee. The concert, or community event, is then not a public good, as it is excludable, and, if the venue has to limit the number of people who can attend, it is also rival. Nevertheless, if it is good that people have the option to attend concerts and plays periodically, the concert hall serves the common good.

Conclusion: Appropriate Agency and the Common Good

For the provision of some goods and activities, an exclusive focus on agency is inappropriate. We saw earlier that sometimes agency can be counterproductive, leading to worse outcomes in terms of the agent's valuation than an alternative arrangement. A consideration of the good of the community might help resolve some of these questions.[39] But there are also certain irreducibly collective goods for which agency is inappropriate. One example is justice. What matters is that justice is done – that society be tolerably just, with a fair allocation of resources, that a system of redress for wrongs exists and is accessible to everyone. These features are more important than the person of the judge (although her character and ability to understand, interpret and apply the rules might be) – what matters, as I said, is that justice is done,

---

[38] The New York Times (2016), reporting on the problems of Puerto Rico, tells of a new expressway section built to enable better access for exporters in Arecibo to the port at San Juan. But the village of Abra San Francisco has become cut off as a result – there is no access to the new road, and the expressway made it much more difficult for the community to access public transport. The road is a public good, but it doesn't serve the common good.

[39] For example, in Derek Parfit's cases, unless there are good reasons for acting otherwise, saving as many lives as possible would seem a reasonable common good criterion.

not that I do it. Even Robert Nozick (1974) recognizes this: his minimalist state required that agency in administering corrective justice be restricted. A state of vigilante justice isn't a state.

I want to suggest that the same can be true of questions concerning the constitution of a valuable life. That the life I live is one that I have reason to value is too weak a criterion to determine whether or not I should live that life. In addition, it is also necessary to consider how living that life would lead me to participate in, and contribute to, the community or society in which I live. A consideration of the common good raises those types of questions, which need to be asked. Will this way of living, which I have reason to value, assist or hinder the flourishing of others in my community? How will it build (or destroy) relationships with people around me? What kinds of relationships might these be? Further, what community needs to be considered: my immediate neighbours, my town or city, my country or the world? As globalization develops, we become more aware of how our behaviour and choices, and the types of lives we lead, have unintended consequences for the whole planet. My use of carbon-rich fuels, along with that of my society and region, add to the warming of the planet. The latest addition to the CST literature, Pope Francis' Encyclical Laudato Si' (2015) addresses the issue of climate change. 'The climate is a common good, belonging to all and meant for all', as Francis puts it (23). As we bump into planetary limits (Rockström et al., 2009), we can no longer live lives that do not take into account the effects of our flourishing on others. Global issues of this type (Francis also mentions pollution, water supply, loss of biodiversity, societal breakdown and global inequality as issues) require turning attention to more than just individual flourishing. Addressing the questions that a consideration of the common good raises would not be a bad place to start in broadening the conversation about what constitutes a good life, the kind that we ought to have reason to value.

References

Airely, D. (2008) *Predictably Irrational*. New York, NY: HarperCollins.

Akerlof, G. A. and Shiller, R. J. (2015) *Phishing for Phools: The Economics of Manipulation and Deception*. Princeton, NJ and Oxford: Princeton University Press.

Alexander, J. M. (2004) 'Capabilities Human Rights and Moral Pluralism'. *The International Journal of Human Rights* Vol. 8, No. 4, pp. 451–69.

Anscombe, G. E. M. (1958) 'Modern Moral Philosophy'. *Philosophy* Vol. 22, No. 124, pp. 1–19.

Barry, B. (1965) *Political Argument*. London: Routledge & Kegan Paul.

Berlin, I. (1958) *Two Concepts of Liberty* Lecture, Oxford University, 31 October; subsequently published by the Clarendon Press, and in Berlin (1969).

(1969) *Four Essays on Liberty*. Oxford: Oxford University Press.

Cobb, J. (1994) *Sustaining the Common Good*. Cleveland, OH: The Pilgrim Press.

Constant, B. (1819) 'The Liberty of the Ancients Compared with that of the Moderns'. In Biancamaria Fontana ed., *The Political Writings of Benjamin Constant*. Cambridge: Cambridge University Press, 1988, pp. 309–28.

Davies, N. (1981) *God's Playground: A History of Poland*. Oxford: Oxford University Press.

Deneulin, S. (2006) 'Individual well-being, migration remittances and the common good'. *The European Journal of Development Research* Vol. 18, No. 1 (March), pp. 45–58.

(2009) 'Ideas related to human development'. In Séverine Deneulin and Lila Shahni, eds. *An Introduction to the Human Development and Capability Approach*. London: Earthscan.

Deneulin, S. and Stewart, F. (2002) 'Amartya Sen's Contribution to Development Thinking'. *Studies in Comparative International Development* Vol. 37, No. 2, pp. 61–70.

Dodes, L. and Dodes, Z. (2014) *The Sober Truth: Debunking the Bad Science behind 12-step Programs and the Rehab Industry*. Boston, MA: Beacon.

Douglass, B. (1980) 'The Common Good and the Public Interest'. *Political Theory* Vol. 8, No. 1 (February), pp. 103–17.

Elster, J. (1982) 'Sour grapes: Utilitarianism and the genesis of wants'. In Amartya Sen and Bernard Williams, eds. *Utilitarianism and Beyond*. Cambridge: Cambridge University Press, pp. 219–38.

(1985) *Sour Grapes: Studies in the Subversion of Rationality*. Cambridge: Cambridge University Press.

Evans, P. (2002) 'Collective capabilities, culture, and Amartya Sen's development as freedom'. *Studies in Comparative International Development* Vol. 37, No. 2, pp. 54–60.

Forster, E. M. (1909) 'The Machine Stops'. *The Oxford and Cambridge Review* November.

Gaudium et Spes (1965) [Joy and Hope] Encyclical of Pope Paul VI, promulgated December 7.

Geetz, C. (1973) 'Thick Description: Toward an Interpretative Theory of Culture'. In *The Interpretation of Cultures: Selected Essays*. New York, NY: Basic Books, pp. 3–30.

Hare, R. M. (1963) *Freedom and Reason*. Oxford: Oxford University Press.

Herdt, J. (2008) *Putting on Virtue: The Legacy of the Splendid Vices*. Chicago, IL: University of Chicago Press.

Hollenbach, D. (2002) *The Common Good and Christian Ethics*. Cambridge: Cambridge University Press.

Kahneman, D. and Tversky, A. (1979) 'Prospect Theory: An Analysis of Decision under Risk'. *Econometrica* Vol. 47, No. 2, pp. 263–91.

Khader, S. J. (2011) *Adaptive Preferences and Women's Empowerment*. New York, NY: Oxford University Press.

Krugman, P. (2009) How Did Economists Get It So Wrong? *The New York Times*, 2 September.

Laudato Si' (2015) [Praise be to you] Encyclical of Pope Francis, promulgated 24 May.

MacIntyre, A. (1981) *After Virtue*. Notre Dame: University of Notre Dame Press.

Mackie, J. L. (1977) *Ethics: Inventing Right and Wrong*. London: Pelican.

Mankiw, G. N. (1998) *Principles of Economics*. Fort Worth: Harcourt College.

Mater et Magistra (1961) [Mother and Teacher] Encyclical of Pope John XXIII, promulgated 15 May.

Mill, John Stuart (1863) *Utilitarianism* London: Parker, Son and Bourn.

Miller, J. (2010) 'A distinction regarding happiness in ancient philosophy'. *Social Research: An International Quarterly* Vol. 77, No. 2 (Summer), pp. 595–624.

Mischel, W. and Ebbesen, E. B. (1970) 'Attention in delay of gratification'. *Journal of Personality and Social Psychology* Vol. 16, No. 2, pp. 329–337.

Mischel, W., Ayduk, O., Berman, M. G., et al. (2011) '"Willpower" over the life span: Decomposing self-regulation'. *SCAN* Vol. 6, pp. 252–6.

Mischel, W., Shoda, Y. and Rodriguez, M. L. (1989) 'Delay of Gratification in Children'. *Science New Series* Vol. 244, No. 4907, pp. 933–8.

Moore, G. E. (1903) *Principia Ethica*. Cambridge: Cambridge University Press.

Murphy, Mark C. (2005) The common good *The Review of Metaphysics* Vol. 59, No. 1, pp. 133–64.

Naylor, G. (1990) *Better than Life (Red Dwarf)*. London: Penguin.

New York Times (2016) 'A Surreal Life on the Precipice in Puerto Rico' (August 7).

NIV (2016) *New International Version Cultural Backgrounds Study Bible*. Grand Rapids, MI: Zondervan.

Nozick, R. (1974) *Anarchy, State and Utopia*. New York, NY: Basic Books.

Nussbaum, M. (1986) *The Fragility of Goodness*. Cambridge: Cambridge University Press.

(2000) *Women and Human Development*. Cambridge: Cambridge University Press.

(2003) 'Capabilities as fundamental entitlements: Sen and social justice'. *Feminist Economics* Vol. 9, No. 2–3, pp. 33–59.

Parfit, D. (1977) Class: 'The Self, the Future and the Rational Thing To Do'. Oxford University, Hillary Term.

(1983) *Reasons and Persons*. Oxford: Clarendon.

Plato *The Meno*. Available at http://classics.mit.edu/Plato/meno.html.

Rockström, J., Steffen, W., Noone, K., et al. (2009) 'Planetary Boundaries: Exploring the Safe Operating Space for Humanity'. *Ecology and Society* Vol. 14, No. 2, Art. 32. Available at http://www.ecologyandsociety.org/vol14/iss2/art32/.

Sacks, J. (2007) *The Home We Build Together: Recreating Society*. London: Continuum.

Sen, A. (1970) *Collective Choice and Social Welfare*. San Francisco, CA: Holden-Day.

(1992) *Inequality Reexamined*. Cambridge, MA: Harvard University Press.

(1999) *Development as Freedom*. Oxford: Oxford University Press.

(2004) *Rationality and Freedom*. Cambridge, MA: Belknap Press.

(2007) *Identity and Violence: The Illusion of Destiny*. London: Penguin.

Smart, J. J. C. and Williams, B. (1973) *Utilitarianism: For and Against* Cambridge: Cambridge University Press.

Stewart, F. (2005) 'Groups and Capabilities'. *Journal of Human Development* Vol. 6, No. 2, pp. 185–204.

Tasker, J. P. (2016) 'Trudeau cabinet approves Trans Mountain, Line 3 pipelines, rejects Northern Gateway'. *CBC news*. www.cbc.ca/amp/1.3872828 (29 November).

Thaler, R. H. (1980) 'Toward a Positive Theory of Consumer Choice'. *Journal of Economic Behavior and Organization* Vol. 1, pp. 39–60.

Thaler, R. H. and Sunstein, C. R. (2008) *Nudge: Improving Decisions about Health, Wealth and Happiness*. New Haven, CT: Yale University Press.

Welby, J. (2015) 'Building the common good'. In John Sentamu, ed. *On Rock or Sand? Firm Foundations for Britain's Future*. London: SPCK.

Wood, R. (2004) 'The Heresy of Solitary Faith'. *Christianity Today* (January), pp. 58–60.

4 | Measuring the Meta-Capability of Agency

A Theoretical Basis for Creating a Responsibility Indicator

MATHIAS NEBEL AND MA. TERESA
HERRERA RENDÓN NEBEL*

The importance of the agency aspect, in general, relates to the view of persons as responsible agents. Persons must enter the moral accounting by other not only as people whose well-being demands concern, but also as people whose responsible agency must be recognized.

(Sen, 1985a: 205).

Introduction

This chapter offers the theoretical basis to measure the meta-capability of agency. The focus on capabilities, as put forward by Sen to date, is built on a sharp distinction between agency-freedom and well-being freedom (Sen, 1985a: 185–87). Following the work of Bonvin and Farvaque (2004), Conill (2004), Cortina (2008) and Crocker (2009) on the normative importance of agency for well-being and development, we propose understanding agency as a meta-capability. Its specific capability space deals with the way in which each individual values and chooses one's own freedom. Like Ballet et al. (2007, 2008, 2014) we argue that agency capability is revealed in the way in which individuals act responsibly. In other words, the value they give to their freedom appears in the way in which they take on their responsibilities. Hence, we propose measuring the meta-capability of agency by means of the following three dimensions that make up

*We would like to thank Flavio Comim for his kind remarks that have helped to improve this chapter. We would also like to acknowledge the financial support received by the *Consejo de Ciencia y Tecnología Mexicano* (CONACYT), as well as the *Global South Scholar* programme of the *L'Institut de hautes études internationales et du développement* (IHEID). We would also like to thank the *Instituto Nacional de Estadística y Geografía de México* (INEGI) for its inestimable, constant support.

responsibility: (a) responsibility as referring to the relationship with oneself (in which I recognise myself to be subject to an obligation/promise); (b) responsibility as referring to the relationship with one's acts (in which we respond for them); (c) responsibility as referring to the relationship towards others (the other that calls me to responsibility). This last one is of special importance.

However, these three dimensions are not exclusively individual dimensions. They are constructed within social relations. More so, these dimensions of responsibility are socially constructed as minimum standard expectations of behaviour (the standard levels of responsibility required to function in a society). The law, for example, requires a certain level of responsibility from citizens with respect to their acts and with respect to others, whereas in the family people are tied together by strong expectation levels of responsibility towards the other. Thus, the meta-capability of agency results from the way in which an individual can express their responsibility in one of these social contexts.

Based on these theoretical developments, the second part of this chapter proposes a way of measuring the meta-capability of agency in terms of responsibility.[1] We conclude by presenting the various fields of application this indicator has, particularly at a level of public policies for development.

Importance of Responsibility for the Development of the Capability Approach

In 2005, in assessing the achievements and the future challenges of the capability approach, Robeyns (2005, 2009) highlighted the need to develop in the future the concept of *responsibility* to formalise the complex relationship that exists between *agency* and *capability*.[2]

---

[1] For this purpose, we had the invaluable support of the Instituto Nacional de Estadística y Geografía (INEGI) (Mexican National Institute of Statistics and Geography) to create an indicator to try to measure levels of agency in Mexico. In this chapter, you will find the questionnaire that was prepared for the INEGI and attached as a special module aimed at workers in the 2014 INEGI Household Questionnaire, as well as the hypotheses that underpin it.

[2] 'A capability theory of justice needs to specify where to draw the line between individual and collective responsibility, or how and by whom this decision should be made. There is a remarkable absence of any discussion about issues of responsibility in the capability literature, in sharp contrast to political

Her claim arises from the current lack of balance in the framework between *rights* and *obligations*; in other words between *freedom* on the one hand and *duties* on the other hand. While the former make up the central hub of Sen's contributions, obligations and duties regarding these rights and these freedoms are not developed. If well-being freedom is to be measured as a set of capabilities, then we should ask ourselves: what are the obligations that correspond to this well-being freedom? Which responsibilities does this set of capabilities imply in turn? Therefore, a reflection about responsibility – in other words, the way in which a person accepts and is committed to carrying out a purpose and/or a duty – seems essential for the coherence of the approach.

The Theory of Justice and the Notion of Responsibility

The recognition of the importance of the development of the notion of responsibility for the capability approach owes a great deal to the work by Bonvin and Farvaque (1998, 2004). These two authors, considering the debate surrounding Rawls' *Theory of Justice* (1971) as well as the mutations of the concept of 'welfare state' in the West, highlight the concept of responsibility as a key theoretical feature of the current development of social policies. Therefore, their work, on the one hand, deals with the main criticisms made of Rawls' Theory of Justice and, on the other hand, tries to develop what could be, within the capability approach, the role of responsibility.

After the publication of John Rawls' *Theory of Justice* (1971), numerous authors (Dworkin, 1981; Arneson, 1989; Cohen, 1989; Sen, 1992; Roemer, 1995) argued that the division of primary goods proposed by Rawls enables equality of opportunities to be reached. Several theoretical elements were proposed to highlight this failure. Dworkin (1981) claims that the distribution of primary goods extended to everyone does not take into account the *heterogeneity of the natural endowments* of each individual. Sen (1992) claims that equal opportunities cannot be achieved because the distribution of primary goods ignores the diversity of values given to the *set of*

philosophy and welfare economics, where this is one of the most important areas of debate ... Nevertheless, whether one wants to discuss it explicitly or not, any concrete capability policy proposal can be analyzed in terms of the division between personal and collective responsibility; but this terminology is largely absent from the capability literature' (Robeyns, 2009: 19).

capabilities by each individual. In addition, Roemer (1995) corrects Rawls by developing the role of personal *effort* and of the respective *merits* of each individual.

These authors challenge one of Rawls' central hypotheses: that the 'social distribution of responsibilities'[3] postulated by Rawls is *homogeneous.* The 'equality of opportunities' that the universal disposition of primary goods should generate supposes that each agent has the same responsibility. In other words, there is, in any given population: (a) a single and equal *ability for being responsible,* and (b) a uniform, equal *practice* of responsibility (Arneson, 1989). In other words, the ability to be free and responsible – as part of our human condition – makes up an anthropological presupposition of Rawls; a fact *pre-existing* his 'social division of responsibility'. In the same way as a common rationality exists behind the veil of ignorance, there is also an equality of responsibility; at no time can rationality or responsibility be considered as possible results of public policies (Bonvin & Farvaque, 2004: 18–19). Rationality as responsibility does not need to be distributed for Rawls because it already exists at the level of a *natural equality.*

However, historically and empirically, this is not the case.[4] The debate around the role and the objective of the Western welfare state stumbled on the existence of *obligations* that are correlative to the social rights that are granted. There are only rights if one first recognises duties. The diverse forms of rational dependency on benefits from the social welfare state (dependency trap) demonstrate that poverty cannot be simply considered as a shortcoming that a right to a social benefit could mechanically compensate (Arneson, 2011). The material compensation – often in a monetary form – for a real injustice suffered by an individual is not sufficient to offset their personal or structural origin (Stemplowska, 2009). The recognition of a right

---

[3] 'The account of primary goods includes what we may call a "social division of responsibility": society, citizens as a collective body, accepts responsibility for maintaining the equal basic liberties and fair equality of opportunity ... while citizens as individuals and association accept responsibility for revising and adjusting their ends and aspiration in view of the all-purpose means they can expect ... This division of responsibility relies on the capacity of persons to assume responsibility for their ends and to moderate the claims they make on their social institutions accordingly' (Rawls, 1993: 189).

[4] Rawls never proposed to carry out a historical or empirical analysis. Re-introducing history therefore moves the discussion away and beyond the Rawlsian argument.

to a material benefit does not enable the overall compromised social
equity to be restored. The benefit receiver's responsibility for their luck
intervenes crucially on the way in which they use the social benefit.
These were some of the features that authors such as Giddens (1998),
Bovens (1998), Lake (2001) and Hurley (2003) highlighted to propose
a reform of the paradigms of the welfare state. Their work addresses
the need to turn around the objective of social policies. They should no
longer be seen as benefits that make up for a past injustice, but as the
grounds for a future equality by means of incentives that come together
in the search for – but do not replace – each individual's responsibility.
Benefits should foster responsibility. Bonvin and Farvaque (2004) state
that, 'In such a framework, responsibility is not something given but
features as a goal of public action. ... In this view, the task of welfare
institutions is also to construct relevant information with the aim to
render people more responsible' (p. 19). These contributions to the
question of social welfare highlight the crucial importance of how
responsibility is socially constructed in a given society and individually enacted.

Moreover, Bonvin and Farvaque point out that the various criticisms
leveraged on the classical understanding of an equality of opportunities assume two highly different models of responsibility. They note:[5]

'Drawing on the various critics of mainstream equality of opportunity, two opposed approaches to responsibility may be identified: on
the one hand, responsibility is mainly conceived of as (i) a "luck vs.
choice" fixed starting point, (ii) a backward-looking conception, (iii) a
highly individualistic framework. ... On the other hand, responsibility
is envisaged as (i) an outcome of public policies rather than a starting
point, (ii) a forward looking conception, (iii) a combined institution-
al-individual framework'.[6]

---

[5] However, unlike Bonvin and Farvaque, we do not believe that there is a
   need to oppose these two approaches. Talking about approaches is, in any
   case, overstating them. These authors do not elucidate a clear concept of
   responsibility. It is more an incipient matter that progressively emerges
   separately from the main debate to look at equality of opportunities and
   social justice (Stemplowska, 2009). Their use of the concept is, however, fairly
   ingenious when compared with the many distinctions that ethics or law have
   with respect to forms and modalities of responsibility, or when compared to
   Hans Jonas' (1979) development of the notion of responsibility.
[6] Bonvin and Farvaque (2004), p. 21.

Sen's work exemplifies this ambiguous use of the concept of responsibility. Although the notion of responsibility undoubtedly plays a significant role in his approach to capability, this role is never formally developed. On the one hand, like Rawls, Sen sees freedom as a necessary, sufficient condition for responsibility to exist (Sen, 1992: 148–150, 1999: 283–285). For Sen, agency-freedom is anterior to well-being freedom; where agency exists there will also be responsibility (1985b: 197ss). He thus proposes responsibility as an ability that, like rationality, exists before the matters of well-being (1992: 148). However, on the other hand, when making the individual evaluative exercise of the functioning the central pillar of capabilities, Sen also grants each individual great responsibility with respect to the 'kind of lives they have reasons to value' (1992: 149). Sen argues that the transformation of primary goods is not homogenous in a given population, precisely because there are differences between what each individual considers to be the set of capabilities they value (1999: 190). Therefore, by not placing emphasis on the measuring of *achieved functioning* but on the measuring of a *capability space*, Sen turns the responsibility towards the future. A capability is the capacity to open up one's own welfare space in the midst of existing opportunities (1999: 30). In this latter point, we would also highlight Sen's originality with respect to a possible development of the implicit concept of responsibility. Following Berlin's distinction between positive and negative freedom (1969: 122–134), Sen recognises the social construction of any set of capabilities and, consequently, of responsibility (1999: 282ss, 2004: 381ss). However, Sen's commitment to ethical individualism on the one hand (Robeyns, 2005: 108), and on the other hand, his visceral opposition to communitarianism (Sen, 2007: 5–6), have left this aspect of his approach underdeveloped (Ballet et al., 2014: 9–16).

Therefore, it is no surprise that Robeyns (2005, 2009) identifies responsibility as a missing feature in the approach that would benefit from being theoretically developed. Moreover, if she identifies the relation between *agency and capability* as the matrix on which the effort will have to be made, it is precisely because this is the feature in which Sens's inheritance from Rawls is more marked. Questioning the existence of a uniform and equal level of agency previous to well-being freedom will be the key to developing a new, more coherent way of understanding the role of responsibility in the capability approach. This is our intention in the next section.

The Meta-Capability of Agency

The capability approach has developed into a rich framework with many authors contributing to a lively debate. Although the references to the works of Sen and Nussbaum continue to provide the basis for discussion, several more recent advances propose interpretations that are notably different from those of Sen or Nussbaum. One of these advances, of a Kantian nature, proposed by Conill (2004), Cortina (2007) and Crocker (2009), looks at the relationship between agency and capability. Our own contribution subscribes to this reinterpretation of the approach, but adds yet another feature, as we use Ricœur (1989) and Levinas (1974, 1996) as our main philosophical references, rather than Kant.

To be pedagogically relevant and to make the presentation as concise as possible, this part, as well as those following, are presented in thesis form:[7]

> Thesis 1. Evaluating and measuring well-being involves considering not just the non-exclusion between agency and capabilities, but their necessary reciprocity. The well-being of an individual or of a group requires, and is a function of, the degree in which it effectively possesses its 'quality of agency'. This reciprocity allows us to consider a non-absolute normative pre-eminence of agency over capability. This pre-eminence may be expressed by making the capability of agency the root or the source of the other capabilities.

Reciprocity between Agency and Capabilities

Sen distinguishes agency from capability based on the differences that exist between, on the one hand, general freedom (agency) and on the other hand, the specific field of the performance of freedom that constitutes the search for well-being (capability) (1985a: 185–187). The former considers the freedom that a person has to act for whatsoever purpose they choose to achieve.[8] The second contemplates a very

[7] Thesis form presents a succinct and synthetic position, which is then explained in the following paragraphs. It is an old form of presentation that has survived, especially in Germany.
[8] Agency 'is what a person is free to do and achieve in pursuit of whatever goals or values he or she regards as important' (Sen, 1999: 75). 'A person's agency

precise area of this agency freedom: that which refers to achieving well-being. Take note of the following two points:

(a) Sen never states that well-being freedom can be considered without the presumption of agency freedom (1985a: 186, 1992: 57). On the contrary, well-being freedom is but an integral part of agency freedom (1985a: 205). However, the *assessment* of well-being requires taking into consideration different informational spaces.[9] This is precisely the whole point of his Dewey Lectures (1985a). In the same manner that achievement information is to be complemented by opportunities and choice information; well-being freedom has to be complemented by information on agency freedom to get a clear picture of the quality of well-being achieved by a person. But these three informational spaces, while connected, are not necessary coherent.[10] A person can decide to put his well-being at risk to save the life of a child, prioritising agency freedom over well-being freedom. In this way, the individual conception of the 'good'[11] and

achievement refers to the realization of goals and values she has reasons to pursue, whether or not they are connected with her own well-being. ... Corresponding to the distinction between agency achievement and well-being achievement, there is a differentiation also between a person's 'agency freedom' and 'well-being freedom'. The former is one's freedom to bring about the achievements one values and which one attempts to produce, while the latter is one's freedom to achieve those things that are constitutive of one's well-being. (Sen, 1992: 56–57).

[9] 'Although the agency aspect and the well-being aspect both are important, they are important for quite different reasons. In one perspective, a person is seen as a doer and a judge, whereas in the other the same person is seen as a beneficiary whose interest and advantages have to be considered. There is no way of reducing this plural-information base into a monist one without losing something of importance. ... The well-being aspect may be particularly important in some specific contexts. ... On the other hand, in many issues of personal morality, the agency aspect and one's responsibility to others, may be central. The well-being aspect and the agency aspect both demand attention, but they do so in different ways and with varying relevance to different problems' (Sen, 1985a: 207–208).

[10] 'The ranking of alternative opportunities from the point of view of agency need not be the same as the ranking in terms of well-being, and thus the judgments of agency freedom and well-being freedom can move in contrary directions. So even though agency freedom is "broader" than well-being freedom, the former cannot subsume the latter' (Sen, 1985a: 207).

[11] 'It can be said that the well-being aspect of a person is important in assessing a person's advantage, whereas the agency aspect is important in assessing what a person can be in line with his or her conception of the good. The ability to do more good need not be to the person's advantage' (Sen, 1985a: 206).

'responsibility'[12] are mentioned by Sen as important agency features that enrich our understanding of well-being freedom (1985a). However, Sen takes a bold move and firmly states that, 'Insofar as each person's advantage commands attention and respect in moral accounting, the well-being aspect of the person has to be directly considered. This role cannot be taken over by agency information' (1985a: 207). For Sen, the agency aspects and well-being aspects of a person have different roles in moral accounting (1985a: 206). While the importance of agency-freedom is thus fully recognised by Sen, he takes the decision to put a moral *priority* on the well-being aspect of the person (over the agency aspect).[13]

(b) Second, Sen also states that agency freedom is hard to measure *for itself*. Its nature is that of an *open conditionality*: 'Whereas well-being freedom is freedom to achieve something in particular, viz. well-being, the idea of agency freedom is more general, since it is not tied to any one aim. Agency freedom is a freedom to achieve whatever the person, as a responsible agent, decides he or she should achieve'.[14] This means that agency freedom should not methodologically be examined in terms of any pre-specified objective (1985a: 204). But measurement difficulty can be solved, according to Sen. The plurality of conceptions of the good does not exclude the existence of 'open partial orderings'. These in turn allow for 'position differences' between persons without precluding the possibility of 'interpersonal comparisons' (1985a: 179–83). Sen is confident that 'Personal differences can be built parametrically into an evaluation function without losing objectivity' (1985a:196). But one important condition is posited by

---

[12] 'The importance of the agency aspect, in general, relates to the view of persons as responsible agents. Persons must enter the moral accounting by other not only as people whose well-being demands concern, but also as people whose responsible agency must be recognized' (Sen, 1985a: 205).

[13] The reasons for such priority are probably grounded in the moral pre-eminence of dignity and equality over other moral values, but this a guess.

[14] 'A person's "agency freedom" refers to what the person is free to do and achieve in pursuit of whatever goals or values he or she regards as important. A person's agency aspect cannot be understood without taking note of his or her aims, objectives, allegiances, obligations and – in a broad sense – the person's conception of the good. ... That *open conditionality* makes the nature of agency freedom quite different from that of well-being freedom, which concentrates on a particular type of objective and judges opportunities correspondingly' (Sen, 1985a: 203–4).

Sen: that of an 'invariability of authorship' formally expressed as responsibility when considering agency (1985a: 172–4, 183). This invariability, combined with the openness of partial ordering, are the axis allowing the construction of a partial ordering.

Nevertheless, Sen's distinction between agency and capability can, and must, be challenged (Nussbaum, 2000: 14; Alkire, 2005, 2008; Ballet, Dubois & Mahieu, 2007; Crocker & Robeyns, 2010). Why? In the first place, Sen's concern and argument, although legitimate, are artificial. It is an analytical distinction rather than an operational one. In fact, agency and capability cannot be distinguished in the real behaviour of a person. This can be seen in the numerous confusions that exist among researchers who 'apply' the approach and blithely measure autonomy or agency as a capability. Second, we must challenge Sen's distinction between agency and capability on the ground of the *innate freedom* and *responsibility* he posits (as the invariable axis allowing for agency measurement). In Sen's understanding our positive freedom is only constrained by our social context or body impairment (*negative freedom; adaptive preferences*). But he never seems to consider that the acquisition of agency freedom or responsibility is as much a *learning* process as it is a *choice*.[15]

We learn agency freedom.[16] On the one hand, over our childhood years, we must acquire the full mastery of our liberty and, on the other hand, the *will to be free* is also a process that many people reject, either in a flight to superficiality or by falling into various kinds of

[15] Sen has made significant contributions concerning the importance of processes to the act of choice, that is, 'how preferences may be sensitive to the choice process, including the identity of the chooser' (Sen, 1997: 745). However, it remains unclear to us how his argument about the importance of process to the act of choice really reaches the complexity of identity building. The dialectic between me and my-self (*idem* and *ipse* in Paul Ricoeur's work) would probably reverse the question and ask how the act of choice emerges in the building of an individual, thus leading the question toward 'education to freedom', which is precisely our point.

[16] The importance of education to the capability approach is one of the main contributions made by Martha Nussbaum. Here, the process through which we learn to be free is fully acknowledged and even set as one of the main objectives of public education (Nussbaum, 2006). However, it remains to be seen if institutional school education can really educate children to freedom. The will to educate to freedom can only too easily decay into subtle institutional forms of manipulation and indoctrination. School systems have mostly a bad record in the concept of educating to value.

dependences (in a way that is at least partially voluntary). Sen does not seem to consider that *we can willingly refuse to be free.*

If the learning of agency freedom is itself a process, then the priority set by Sen on the well-being aspect of a person over agency cannot be sustained any further. If we can show that *the quality of agency freedom* is a good that undergoes significant fluctuations in its acquisition and its distribution, then, without breaking Sen's methodological argument, agency itself must be considered a capability.

The Meta-Capability of Agency

In *Ethics of Global Development*, Crocker (2009) convincingly argues that there can be no separation between the quality of agency on the one hand, and the sets of particular capabilities on the other. On the contrary, he states that there is a *fundamental reciprocity* between effective possession of the quality of agency and achieving well-being (Crocker, 2009: 220). Indeed, the evaluative exercise that makes the set of achievable functions have a meaning requires the subject to be in full possession of his quality of agency. In other words, it requires the subject to be able, to have the *interior* capacity, to discern among the possible functioning options, those that are meaningful for the form of life he contemplates (Cortina, 2007: 226). Without this agency freedom, there would be no evaluative exercise by the subject and, consequently, no determination of a capability space relevant for the analysis. In this situation, it would be meaningless to differentiate between functioning and capabilities and the entire approach would lose much of its critical and analytical relevance.

What is the function of agency in well-being? Can one talk about a capability of agency? Crocker argues (i) that the quality of agency can be considered as a capability, and that (ii) a non-absolute normative pre-eminence of the quality of agency over other capabilities must be recognised (2009: 220–6).

In fact, agency is not a 'set amount' in us, but an ability that has been developed throughout our existence. Agency is the result of learning; it is the result of carrying out work on ourselves. The quality of agency is not a good that could be considered to have been acquired after a certain age, nor to have been simply declared as existing by a decree or a law, but it must be developed in each of us by means of a long process that leads the child through to adulthood. Even if every person had the same capacity of agency, we could not presuppose that each would enact it in the same way or control it in the same manner. We are born free, but we need to make this freedom ours.

Agency itself is the object of a fundamental choice: do I want to be a free agent? But this fundamental choice soon entails another decision about the concrete and specific means required to become a free agent. We have to choose the functionings that lead to the quality of agency. Yet precisely because agency may be valued differently by different people, we must acknowledge the existence of a specific capability: the capability of agency. Crocker (2009) writes, 'We might then call this ultimate freedom to exercise our agency – to be master of our own lives – the capability of capabilities, a meta-capability, or a super-capability. We might also say it is what makes us human' (2009: 223).

However, Conill (2004: 173–82), Cortina (2007: 224–7) and Crocker (2009: 221–4) do not stop here. They propose – in a Kantian interpretation of the approach– recognising a normative pre-eminence of agency over well-being. Although both must be considered intrinsic goods, agency has a pre-eminence over well-being: 'There is and should be a normative asymmetry between well-being and agency. Although both well-being ... and agency ... may be viewed as goods in themselves, agency is more important, for to choose well-being over agency (or vice versa) is itself an exercise of agency' (Crocker, 2009: 222). This *logical priority* becomes an *ethical pre-eminence*: agency – now defined as the free self-determination of a person– is not sought for any other purpose, but constitutes an end unto itself. However, this ethical pre-eminence of agency over well-being is not absolute. It must be upheld within a reciprocity with well-being. Therefore, agency presupposes that basic material needs, as well as ethical ones, are always covered in order to be functional. But once that important provision is made, says Crocker, a moral *and* practical priority of agency must be recognised over well-being (Crocker, 2009: 220ss). Accepting this point gives a considerable turn to the approach (Ballet et al., 2014: 26–9). It encourages new theoretical and practical research that could become crucial for the maturity of the proposition of a human, sustainable development.

The question that now arises is how to measure this meta-capability of agency. Below, we propose the notion of responsibility to give an account of the dynamic dimension of the quality of agency.

Responsibility as Proxy of the Capability of Agency

Thesis 2. Measuring the capability of agency consists of measuring the capacity a person has to exercise their own freedom. The notion of responsibility precisely captures the idea of people acting with freedom; in other words, it expresses the fact that someone is free in what they undertake. The notion of responsibility can be analysed along three different paths, each of which highlights an essential feature of the enactment of freedom: (a) responsibility as referring to the relationship with oneself (in the attestation); (b) responsibility as referring to the relationship with one's own acts (in which we respond for them); (c) responsibility as referring to the relationship towards others (the other that calls me to responsibility).

Responsibility versus Agency

Why favour the notion of responsibility to measure agency instead of, for example, the notion of autonomy? Why add yet another concept to an approach that is already marked by a complex vocabulary?

The capability of agency is described by Crocker as the capability to choose our own freedom. However, within the concept of freedom that Sen advocates, this is tautological and therefore illogical. In Sen's view: to choose my freedom, I must *already* be able to choose. As a result Sen rejects making agency a capability.

But it ceases being tautological if the concept of freedom is broadened to cover what must be freely accepted without having been chosen (Bovens, 1998: 27ss). In fact, there are many realities that we have not chosen but still consider as being ours (Nebel, 2014). This is the paradoxical case of death, which by being human only becomes ours if it is effectively accepted by the subject (*a* death as opposed to *my* death). This is also the case of our corporeal nature (*a* body must become *my* body), of our social condition or of the language and the culture in which we grow up (*my* people, *my* language, *my* culture). These are realities that we have not chosen but that we have *inherited* either as nature or as history. However, an inheritance can be accepted or can be declined. There is a choice. There is freedom.

The free acceptance of an inheritance is an act of freedom of a different nature than that of choosing items such as food, clothing or sport clubs. These inherited goods, even if they are turned down, leave an imprint or a mark on us. Therefore, one can reject the language, culture, society to which one belongs and even hate one's body and fight against one's death. But the language, the society, the body or the death will never stop being part of one's past or of one's life. However, the possibility of a rebellion or of rejection *shows that a significant part of freedom exists in the acceptance of these realities.* The adolescent who hates her body, for example, must learn to accept the way she is: to love in *this, her* body. The elderly person who rebels against his death must gradually make it theirs, otherwise the agony will be their total, definitive defeat. In any case, these processes of acceptance are neither instinctive nor homogenous in the population. They require a high level of freedom; they demand *free acceptance* and therefore *show marked differences* from one individual to another.

This is also the case with our freedom. Although we are born free, by nature this freedom must be accepted and this acceptance involves a commitment, in other words a responsibility to this 'being-free' that I accept to be. More so, this commitment is a process and a work on myself, as only by wanting to exercise my freedom do I learn to master my freedom.

Sen insists on the importance of choice as an act of freedom. What we wish to suggest here is that the act of freedom is definitively much broader than a simple choice. The act of freedom also includes appreciating, valuing, accepting what exists, creating meaning and duration, imagining possible futures, generating something unexpected, etc. It should be pointed out that with this widening of the approach, a turning point with the anthropological model mainly used by the capability approach is created (Ballet et al., 2014).

So, why talk about responsibility? Precisely because this notion describes the process of the accomplishment of freedom by a moral subject.[17] The concept of responsibility describes freedom as it is used by the subject as a subject; not as a right, not as an abstract ability, not as an external consequence to the subject, but as how the subject

---

[17] 'Here it is responsibility that provides the foundation for freedom; and since agency is a way of evaluating freedom, we can consider that agency is the use we make of our responsibility. Increasing the agency of individuals means allowing them to assume fully their responsibility, since increasing agency means extending the space of freedom and acknowledging that nothing external can constrain the freedom of self-constraint' (Ballet et al., 2014: 42).

acts with freedom. Responsibility expresses the subject's relations with their own freedom, with their acts and with others. The notion of responsibility therefore seems to be the most suitable to express this original capability which is the capability of agency; the capability of choosing our own freedom.[18]

Three Relations, Three Areas of Responsibility

We do not intend to systematically develop the concept of responsibility here, but to delimit three of its constitutive dimensions. Our aim is to structure a possible measurement of the capability of agency in terms of responsibility. These three dimensions refer to three relations: (a) Responsibility as referring to the *relationship with oneself*; (b) Responsibility as referring to the *relation with our own acts*; (c) Responsibility as referring to the *relationship with others*. Three types of responsibilities arise from these three relations: (a) A responsibility that constitutes the subject as the moral subject, or *anterior responsibility (ex-ante)*; (b) A responsibility that comes from the act towards the subject, or *posterior responsibility (ex-post)*; (c) A *responsibility from* and *for the other (ex-aliud)*. Hence mastering the capability of agency requires mastering these three aspects of responsibility.[19]

Now, because each is the object of an assessment and of a choice, these three aspects of responsibility make up a capability space. The assessment/choice of this capability space takes the form of the acceptance of an inheritance. It takes the form, in other words, of a *commitment to act as a free agent*. From the perspective developed here, such capability of agency forms a precondition to well-being freedom.[20]

---

[18] The importance of the concept of responsibility is verified by its simultaneous emergence in a whole host of authors as a required complement to the debate. See the first paragraph of this chapter.

[19] Our reflection refers mainly to two authors here: Hans Jonas (1979) and Paul Ricœur (1989). The fine organisation of the concept of responsibility to the approach of capability was developed by Mahieu (2008: 55–88) and Ballet et al. (2014: 24–42).

[20] The three levels of responsibility are not separate from each other, but have various forms of internal correlations. Although these three levels will very rarely be the same, one can however expect that they move symmetrically, in other words, as a whole. For the same reason, highly divergent levels of responsibility within a single individual must be considered as non-functional or pathological.

Anterior Responsibility

By anterior responsibility, we mean the subject's capacity to take on moral obligations or commitments. In other words, the capacity to commit oneself to do something in the future.[21] This responsibility is constituted as a counterpart to Kantian obligation. The order 'you must!' is addressed to an 'I'[22] that recognises itself as being able to take on this duty; a person, in other words, who responds to the obligation by saying 'yes, I will do it'. Kantian duty is built upon an anthropology of responsibility. Therefore, 'being responsible for ...' implies the subject's ability to 'make themselves responsible'. It is this capacity the subject has to take on for a duty that constitutes him as an ethical subject; without responsibility there is no moral subject. Thus, responsibility is not a posterior and *ad-extra* addendum to an already constituted subject, but a *sine-qua-non* feature of his autonomy. Agency – in terms of me being the author of my own determination – therefore requires the recognition of anterior responsibility. Furthermore, the subject, once he acts, acts morally because he has responsibility. This relationship to himself by means of anterior responsibility constitutes the first dimension of the capability of agency that we wish to measure.

This concept of responsibility emerges in Cortina (2007) and in the capability approach with Crocker (2009) as well as in Mahieu (2008) and Ballet et al. (2014). The former two, in a reflection marked by Kant, do not seem to measure the full impact anterior responsibility leverage on the capability approach. The latter two author groups do. They understand and assume that their interpretation of the capability approach *on this base* is markedly different to what Sen and Nussbaum have proposed to date. In fact, the notion of anterior responsibility means abandoning the idea of an ethical subject already constituted with whom the capability approach functions. There, the

---

[21] This paragraph owes a great deal Paul Ricœur's chapter 'Capabilities and Rights' published in Deneulin, Nebel and Sagovsky (2006). In this chapter, Ricœur proposes passing from the recognition of self to the maintenance of self by means of three capabilities that he identifies as: the *capability to speak, to act* and *to tell*. However, the contribution of this material is cryptic if it is not read in reference to its ethics (Ricœur, 1989).

[22] With Paul Ricœur, we do not see the subject as being transparent to himself in the perception he has of himself, but this perception passes through several mediations, among which the figure of the other is of immense importance. For Ricœur, the very constitution of one's own conscience includes the detour for the other.

ad-intra is a black box. It is constituted and given *a priori*. If the box is opened, if the *genesis* of this subject is questioned, the entire construction of this subject will potentially have to be integrated into the capability approach. Is this desirable? Is this necessary? The approach could dangerously lose its simplicity and applicability what we would add to it in complexity. The concept of anterior responsibility opens the Pandora's box that Sen, following Rawls, still refuses to open.

Like Ballet et al. (2014: 24–42, 57–60) we argue that this widening is essential. The genesis of the ability of responsibility allows the personal and social conditioners of the capability of agency to be revealed. To truly explain the individual variations of this capability in a population is only possible once we contemplate this genesis and its components. Without it, Sen's free agent becomes disembodied. Paradoxically, the capability approach investigates in detail the capabilities of the subject in his various contexts – family, social, educational, state, legal – but ignores how these same contexts have conditioned the *genesis of the agent*, i.e. the genesis of their capability of agency. The consequences of this short-sightedness of the approach are important. If a normative pre-eminence of the capability of agency over the other capabilities can be accepted, then the features necessary for its acquisition become crucial for the capability approach.[23]

Posterior Responsibility

Posterior responsibility considers the relation that exists between an act and a subject (Bovens, 1998: 29–31). It starts by determining what was done or what could be done, and only *then* looks for its cause. Posterior responsibility assigns an act to a person as its author. It is a reconstructed process. It moves *from* the action to look *for* a subject who can be assigned as its author. It identifies a person as having the responsibility for that particular act, investigating their degree of freedom and due prudence. In other words, it considers the relation of an

---

[23] Various current studies into the approach refer to this work that investigates the social and personal conditioners of agency (Alkire, 2005, 2008; Bruni, Comim and Pugno, 2008). Therefore, we believe that the technical development will have to be corrected by empirical studies that enable the crucial elements of the acquisition of this capability to be identified. Many assumptions, such as those of Ricœur, which identify attestation, language and acting as well as narration as crucial features of agency, must be verified empirically. This study postulates that one of the crucial contexts of the acquisition of the capability of agency is the work area.

act – both past as well as future – to a subject to determine the level of freedom with which it was/will be executed. The assignation of a responsibility is therefore not purely causal but involves measuring the degree of freedom, awareness and prudence with which it was executed (Ballet et al., 2014: 29–31, 35–9).

In its most common understanding, posterior responsibility has a strong legal–moral note. It habitually describes the process that an external court – a tribunal for example – undertakes during a trial to attribute and later assign the responsibility of some event to a subject in the most objective way possible. In these cases, a judge will investigate the events, looking for the fair weighting of the degree of freedom – planning, preparation, conscience, passion, violence, due prudence, etc. – with which an act was committed.[24]

The fair and objective reconstruction of the crime is important. It is a matter of investigating the level of personal responsibility as objectively and fairly as possible to then *impose it on the subject*. Posterior responsibility can be objectivised. It is not restricted to the inner, subjective recognition of a responsibility.[25] It can be leveraged upon an unwilling individual by a society (as upon a criminal, for example). In a positive way, posterior responsibility is socially constructed as a *required expectation* of behaviour. In other words, it is a minimal social norm that is required of everyone – a legal obligation – even if someone does not want to recognise themselves as being responsible/guilty.

---

[24] Posterior responsibility is usually linked to a moral notion of prudence by requiring a fine calculation of the possible consequences of an event. In a situation of knowledge and of finite projections (limited information), it is necessary to weigh up between various options and choose that which will achieve best results, that involves least uncertainty and that does not involve damages to third parties. This 'ethic of responsibility' was initially proposed by Max Weber (1919), but was broadly developed by Hans Jonas (1979). Sen, Nussbaum, Cortina and Crocker emphasise this aspect of a posterior responsibility.

[25] It is important to mention that for us, following Ricœur, anterior responsibility and posterior responsibility are united by constant reciprocity. The awareness of oneself, according to Ricœur, involves the mediation of the other. The human action is the target link, the real bridge between two consciences. In the same way, posterior responsibility certainly presupposes anterior responsibility, but the reciprocity is also certain, as the subject's capacity to recognise himself in his action involves posterior responsibility. Herein lies all the tension that Ricœur discusses in *Oneself as Another* [*Soi-même comme un autre*] that develops between the *idem* aspects and the *ipse* aspects in the subject's identity.

Living in society, the norm is that we have to assume the consequences of our actions (past as well as future).[26]

In short, posterior responsibility considers the relation of the real or hypothetical act to its author, investigating the level of freedom with which it was executed and establishes the obligations that this act involves for the subject.

Responsibility From and For the Other

The two first forms of responsibility we mentioned earlier are classical, although their presentation here is somewhat original. However, the same cannot be said of the third dimension of responsibility we propose below.

We refer to Lévinas (1974, 1982, 1989), who reflected on a responsibility which is based not on the self-awareness of the cogito but on the alterity of the face of the other that calls me to responsibility. According to the French philosopher, moral conscience does not arise from the Cartesian awareness of oneself. But it is the face of the other – in its absolute otherness, not reducible to my own subjectivity – that calls me to respond to a demand for justice that absolutely precedes me.[27] Here, then, responsibility is a *call from the other* with a *claim for justice* that always precedes me and that awakens in me, as a response to the call, my responsible being. To Levinas, I am born as an ethical subject based on this call.[28]

---

[26] It should be noted that this objectification of posterior responsibility in the legal system presupposes the existence of anterior responsibility.

[27] 'I speak of responsibility as the essential, primary and fundamental mode of subjectivity. For I describe subjectivity in ethical terms. Ethics, here, does not supplement a preceding existential base; the very node of the subjective is knotted in ethics understood as responsibility. I understand responsibility as responsibility for the Other, thus as responsibility for what is not my deed, or for what does not even matter to me; or which precisely does matter to me; is met by me as face' (Lévinas, 1982: 91–2).

[28] We do not intend to discuss Lévinas' position here, which is complex. We adhere to the interpretation of Lévinas' ethics proposed by Paul Ricœur in *Oneself as Another*. Ricœur incorporates the otherness of the face of the other in the social mediation by which the subject recognises itself as oneself. The otherness is here interiorised and returned to the internal forum of the subject (Ricœur, 1995). In other words, for Ricœur, this final dimension of responsibility is, along with the two others, one of the constitutive parts of the formation of the ethical subject. Anterior responsibility is not therefore closed on itself in a Kantian way, but is fundamentally open to the others, because

Lévinas takes a stance that radically rejects ethical individualism. His works develop an anthropology from the perspective of the otherness, therefore giving our social condition a crucial importance in the forming of the subject (completely different from the way proposed by communitarianism). While Kantian formalism affirms the relevance of others only by means of the universalisation of moral duty, Lévinas bases the universalisation of moral duty on the pre-existence of the face of the other that calls me to responsibility.[29]

What does this theoretical development imply for our purpose? It complements the two previous dimensions of responsibility with a third. Responsibility for the other is not to be considered as added separately and above the two previous ones. It is an integral part of the capability of agency.[30] Neither posterior responsibility nor anterior responsibility can be constituted without going through the mediation of the 'other than I' which – like culture, like history, like a far-off other or a fellow man– *precede me*. Responsibility from and for the other includes this anterior nature of the social relations in which the two other forms are progressively learned and perfected. The architectonic character of the responsibility from and for the other is fundamental.

its constitution necessarily goes through the mediation of the others (Ricœur, 1989: 167–98).

[29] From the capability approach point of view, this is seen as a possible bridge between individual capabilities and collective capabilities, as Ballet, Dubois and Mahieu defend in their 2007 article.

[30] The intimate bond that exists between anterior and posterior responsibility and responsibility for the other has been expressed, with some different nuances but using the same philosophical bases, by Ballet et al. (2014: 73–8). The key of this relation is the notion of identity, as conceived by Ricœur. Ballet et al. note: 'Let us recall the main points of the foregoing chapters. We first showed that a person is characterized by his or her responsibility. Next we tried to show that there is little point in separating the generic person from the particular person since these two concepts merge through the identity of the person. We went on to say that assuming his or her responsibility is for the person a way of personalizing the world, of forging an identity in the sense that accepting his or her responsibilities is how he or she becomes a person. Through action, the person forges him or herself and identity and because the person has chosen a given identity s/he acts in a particular manner. Action is not derived from identity in a causal manner; rather it is concomitant with it. Personal identity and practical identities are fused in a single person. Practical identities are the set of identities that constitute the social roles that we take on, and also the way we take them on board. We do have in fact multiple practical identities derived from the different social roles that we assume' (Ballet et al., 2014: 78).

In the same way, its lack can never be considered to be something trivial – the absence of a costly, superfluous accessory – but always as something serious. Its absence reveals some kind of fragility, instability or at least incoherence in the two previous modalities of responsibility.

This call to responsibility from the face of the other is character-ised by two fundamental requirements: the need for *justice* and the requirement of *solidarity*. Both arise as the horizon towards which this responsibility advances. Indifference towards the other will be, in a correlative way, the surest indicator for revealing the lack of this form of responsibility. From the perspective we adopt here, indifference to the other therefore reveals a *serious lack of responsibility, the absence of one of the dimensions that constitutes our capability of agency.* Therefore, this responsibility is measured by the response given to the call to responsibility, in other words, by the attention and the impor-tance that each individual gives to the call of justice that emerges from their surroundings.

Social Construction of Responsibility

Responsibility is never a pure individual capability or either a pure social construct (Bovens, 1998: 45–52). Consequently researchers do not measure a *pure* individual responsibility, or alternatively a *pure* social construct of responsibility (Ballet et al., 2014). They measure the *reality resulting from both*. They assess the level of responsibility that an individual agent is expected to perform *and* the strategies deployed by each individual in that social context. In other words, they measure the way in which the social structuring of responsibility constrains the individual actors to express their responsibility within these requisites.[31]

Indeed, our social environment is not a blank sheet of paper. The public square is overloaded with all kind and forms of normativity. The social space where we act is always structured.[32] Furthermore, this

---

[31] 'Responsibility refers us to two questions: what must I do as a person having a capacity for specific action, in a given context, with regard to what I consider to be good, fair or otherwise, as a function of the values I accept? Furthermore, how should I behave with regard to what other people expect of me in a given context, which also bears the imprint of values?' (Ballet et al., 2014: 74).

[32] The capability approach always took into account the importance of the social context in which individual freedom is expressed. The notion of 'negative freedom' refers to the social conditioners of well-being freedom, while 'adaptive preferences' say how individuals adapt their well-being expectations

structuring of the social space allows our actions to participate in larger social interactions. Participation in any kind of social activities requires one to abide to the social normativity imposed by this activity (Nebel, 2010). One classical example is that of language. To communicate with others, we need to use the social medium that constitutes a language. Only by expressing ourselves with the words of this language, only by conforming to the grammar that governs this language, may we communicate with others, make ourselves understood, involve them in the intelligibility of our action, be recognised in what we wish to undertake. In the same way as language conditions interpersonal communication, the social construction of responsibility also conditions the way in which an agent will value and express their responsibility.

One of the social spaces that most importantly conditions the levels of social responsibility is labour, more specifically how a firm organises and structures its labour force (Bovens, 1998: 3–8). Labour must be recognised as one of the social systems that most deeply conditions the levels of responsibility in a given population (due to the number of hours dedicated to professional activities, the formalised nature of the productive process and the intensity with which its normativity is imposed). Depending on the form that the rational organisation of the labour process takes, certain dimensions of responsibility are going to be favoured or hindered. For example, the workers' posterior responsibility can be valued, setting high expectation standards upon it, but at the same time dissuading any exertion of the responsibility for the other.

What is interesting to see here is how the rational organisation of the labour process usually sets expected standards of responsibility, demanding or limiting the expression of certain forms of responsibility. To measure responsibility is then to assess: (i) how the organisation of the labour process conditions the capacity of agency of the individuals, and (ii) how the individuals adapt their capability of agency to these standard expectations levels of responsibility. This is the hypothesis on which we will now construct our proposal for measuring the capability of agency in terms of levels of responsibility expressed in the rational organisation of the labour process.[33]

---

to express what the context permits (social interiorisation of the rationality of the structured field of the action).

[33] We are certainly aware that there are many types of production processes and that each one has diverse positions with different levels of expectation of responsibility (Bovens, 1998: 45ss). However, we reject the frequently assumed

The indicator of responsibility we propose shows, in a geolocalised[34] population, on the one hand, the levels of responsibility expressed by the population in their workplace and, on the other hand, the average levels of responsibility demanded by the structuring of the production processes in this region. Our aim is to create the required information to design public policies promoting the capability of agency.

Average Levels of Personal Responsibility: 'Natural' Responsibility; Real/Ideal Responsibility

To close this argument about the relevance of the concept responsibility, we have to address two further difficulties.

(a) There is a great temptation to consider that the responsibility expressed by the employees on their workplace should be compared to the responsibility of which they are 'naturally' capable 'at home' or 'in society'. The problem is that *no* social context will be neutral in terms of the social structuring of responsibility. There is no such thing as a 'pure' or 'natural' social context that corresponds to an individual's 'authentic' capability of responsibility. In other words, we lack a point of comparison. This does not mean that the person does not have, in a transversal way to all the social contexts, a level of responsibility that comes from the assessment and unique, highly personal integration of their capability of agency. As we said at the beginning of this section, the way in which the individual made the capability of agency *theirs* generates the diversity of agency levels that we observe. This

idea that the levels of responsibility within the rational organisation of the labour process are correlative to the hierarchical level occupied in it (Bovens, 1998: 89–92). By differentiating the three areas that make up responsibility, we believe that hierarchical levels lose their relevance to predict levels of responsibility. On the contrary, we could hypothesise that the relative impunity which the managerial posts of the production process usually enjoy (absence of sanctions) may in fact lead to decreasing levels of posterior responsibility; in the same way that these elevated hierarchical positions may be very ambiguous in terms of responsibility towards the other (which other? The shareholders/capital? The employees/labour?).

[34] Mexico has a very diverse and complex population still marked by the many pre-Colombian peoples that inhabited the country long before the Conquista. Strong cultural diversity exist between Mexican states, especially at the rural level. We geolocalised our data in order to see if responsibility indicator might be 'culturally shaped' in states like Oaxaca, Guerrero or Chiapas.

diversity does not disappear in the labour context. It is reflected in the dispersion of the various individual responses given to the social structuring of responsibility provided by the production process. The diversity of responses to this uniform context highlights the diversity of the personal levels of responsibility. Therefore, *it seems possible to read in the average of these individual responses an indicator of the real average level that the broad social context generates in such a population* (the sum of all the other social contexts). In this way, we might identify an average real level of responsibility of a population (at least concerning public matters). This approximation is nevertheless fragile and should not be used without due methodological prudence.

(b) A second significant theoretical difficulty will be to capture the difference that may exist between what the agent is and does and what they would like to be and do (Ego/Superego). Effectively, answers to the questionnaire will frequently find not what a worker is or does, but what they wish to be and do. In an area that so directly involves self-esteem, the importance of projection games between the ego and the superego is inevitable. Therefore, any attempt to measure responsibility levels must construct its questions in such a way as to detect these projections. Our questionnaire was designed to distinguish between the meta-discourse of the company as well as of the workers. We will call the first *ideal responsibility*, while the second will be termed *real responsibility*.

How to Measure Levels of Responsibility in the Labour Area

Hypotheses

In order to measure responsibility and bring about a specific questionnaire for the survey, we had to identify the main hypothesis we were working on. We thought that the previous theoretical discussion could be summarised in the following five propositions, which were used to build the survey:

• Measuring the capability of agency means measuring the ability the human being has to assess/choose their own freedom in a given social context.

- The notion of responsibility describes/expresses the free subject act-ing (in other words, when they value acting with freedom/choose to act freely).
- The notion of responsibility is constituted by three areas that high-light different features that make up the capability of agency: (a) A responsibility that constitutes the subject as a moral subject, or *ante-rior responsibility;* (b) A responsibility that flows from the action towards the subject, or *posterior responsibility;* (c) A *responsibility from* and *for the other.*
- The three areas of responsibility identified are socially structured by the national organisation of the labour process, under the form of standard expectations of responsibility levels.
- Individuals adapt and shape their levels of individual responsibil-ity to the standard expectations of the rational organisation of the labour process, either positively or negatively.

Assessment Chart

Based on these three dimensions of responsibility, we propose the fol-lowing assessment chart of the capability of agency.

The Scoring of the Questionnaire

The following questionnaire tries to capture the three levels of individ-ual, as well as structural, responsibility (rational organisation of the labour process). It was prepared for the INEGI Mexico and applied as an annex to a household questionnaire by the INEGI during the sum-mer of 2014 to a representative sample of more than 3,200 individuals in each of the states of Mexico. The answers to this questionnaire can therefore be read with numerous other pieces of information from the corresponding household questionnaire, as well as with other data-bases via this questionnaire.

The scoring of the questionnaire ranges from 1 to 0, in which 1 indicates maximum responsibility and 0 indicates an absence of it. It is important to note that the scoring is essentially qualitative. Only high levels of responsibility enable a person to be functional. Low levels are *pathological.* An example shows this clearly. A person who only recognises being responsible for what they really do from time to time (less than 50 per cent) is not functional in a company. In the same way,

	Seek to identify	Associated ethical features	Formal questions
Anterior responsibility	• Identifies the subject's capacity to take on the demands derived from their rational, free being.	• Rationality. • Duty (Kantian). • Attestation of oneself, in other words, recognition/maintenance of oneself. • Permanence of the subject.	• This dimension must overcome the existing distance between what the subjects are and what they wish to be. The formal questions will have to be adapted to the context so as to control these possible deformations in the questionnaires (ego/superego). • What is your confidence in your personal capabilities to achieve what you propose? • How do you take on the demands that arise in your social environment? • Can you identify with these demands of your social environment?
Posterior responsibility	• Identifies the causality of the agent in a series of acts (real or hypothetical), investigating the elements of their authorship (intentionality, knowledge, etc.).	• Assignation and recognition of oneself in one's acts. • Practical reason. • Possibility and limits of the projection of oneself. • Balance of risks/benefits (agent strategy). • Prudence.	• This dimension must be identified by means of one of the large areas of activity (in other words: work, home, school, etc.). • Do you recognise your mistakes? Do you master what you do? • Do you have the possibility of deciding on your action?
Responsibility from and for the other	• Identifies the subject's capacity to respond to the call to responsibility by the face of the other.	• Dignity. • Justice. • Solidarity.	• This dimension is the most elusive, it must be dealt with from the way in which the subject lives with respect to the other. • What kind of commitment do you have with those near you and those far from you? • Can you imagine yourself without the other? • What does their presence provide you with? • How do you question the misfortune of others?

someone who is not able to project themselves in the future and be faithful to what they are committed to more than 50 per cent of the time constitutes a problem for a company. Therefore, we propose the following scale (quantitative/qualitative) to read the results obtained:

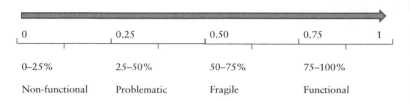

0	0.25	0.50	0.75	1
0–25%	25–50%	50–75%	75–100%	
Non-functional	Problematic	Fragile	Functional	

Research Hypothesis

The formulation of the questionnaire involves a certain number of hypotheses that the data collected will have to confirm or reject. We have divided these hypotheses into three main groups. The first covers the levels of individual responsibility of the workers. The second looks at the levels of responsibility implicit to the rational organisation of the labour process. The third deals with the hypotheses made on the different levels of individual responsibility and levels of labour requirements of responsibility.

Hypotheses Relating to Individual Levels of Responsibility

(a) There is no uniformity of the levels of responsibility in interpersonal comparisons. *We wish to verify that the Rawlsian presupposition of a uniform ability of responsibility within a population is not the case.*

(b) Each individual has levels of anterior, posterior and other responsibility that are different. *We wish to verify that the three levels of responsibility that we are researching can genuinely be different.*

(c) In each individual the three levels of responsibility fluctuate in a similar way. *We wish to verify that there are internal correlations between these three forms of responsibility; in other words, that a high level in one usually involves an equal or at least similar level[in another (fluctuation +/– 30 per cent).*

(d) There is a positive correlation between levels of poverty and levels of individual responsibility. *We wish to verify whether a deficit in the capability of agency, measured in terms of responsibility, is also linked to a certain level of poverty.*

(e) There is a positive correlation between levels of poverty and the levels of responsibility demanded by the production process. *We wish to verify whether low levels of responsibility demanded by the rational organisation of the labour process normally involve poverty.*

(f) There is a positive correlation between levels of regional success of the 'Opportunities' and 'Progress' programme and the overall level of responsibility of this region. *We wish to verify whether the transformation of the opportunities created by a development programme depend, in part, on the existing, average level of responsibility of a population.*

(g) There is a positive correlation between levels of education and levels of responsibility. *We wish to verify whether education has a determining influence on levels of individual responsibility.*

(h) There is a positive correlation between age and levels of responsibility. *We wish to verify whether life experience can be translated in terms of an increase of a person's overall level of responsibility.*

(i) There is a difference in overall responsibility depending on gender. *We wish to verify whether women have, in general, higher levels of responsibility than men, particularly at a level of responsibility for the other.*

Hypotheses Relating to Levels of Responsibility Promoted by the Rational Organisation of the Labour Process

(a) The levels of posterior responsibility demanded by the rational organisation of the labour process are equal or greater than 75 per cent; in other words, they require a functional posterior responsibility. *We wish to verify whether functional levels of posterior responsibility are essential to the rational organisation of the labour process. Lower levels would suggest a serious lack of efficiency of the rational organisation of the labour process, a very low productivity with high control costs.*

(b) The levels of anterior responsibility will be equal to or lower than 75 per cent; in other words, they get by without a functional anterior responsibility at an employee level. *We wish to verify whether Mexican industry sees creativity, initiative and risk-taking as being an important factor of the employees of the rational organisation of the labour process.*

(c) The levels of responsibility for the other will be, on average, low (lower than 50 per cent); the expression of this form of responsibility is done away with or impeded. *We wish to verify whether the dominant model of rational organisation of the labour process is a model of cooperation or of concurrence. Individuals are discouraged from any kind of cooperation that is not formally authorised; there is no community commitment for the good of the company and of the other employees. Individual employees are in constant internal concurrence with the others and may be quickly replaced.*

(d) There is a positive correlation between low levels of responsibility demanded by the rational organisation of the labour process and poverty. *We wish to verify whether low levels of responsibility demanded by the rational organisation of the labour process have a direct effect on low salaries (income) and poverty (measured in terms of human development).*

(e) There is a positive correlation between low levels of responsibility demanded by the forms of rational organisation of the labour process at a regional level and a low indicator of individual responsibility. *We wish to verify whether low levels of responsibility demanded by the process have a negative effect on the capability of agency of the employees and whether, inversely, they involve the introduction of companies that could prosper with these low levels of commitment among their employees. In other words, we wish to verify the creation of a vicious circle in which the lack of capability of agency feeds companies when their efficiency does not depend on functional levels of responsibility, which in turn, only propagate the lack of capability of agency. Drug trafficking, it should be noted, is going to create/impose total loyalty towards violence (total posterior and anterior responsibility).*

Hypotheses Relating to the Difference Between Levels of Individual Responsibility and Responsibility Promoted by the Rational Organisation of the Labour Process.

(a) There is no general correlation of the individual levels of responsibility and of responsibility demanded by the production processes. *We wish to verify whether, outside the rational organisation of the labour process, there are other factors that contribute to forming the capability of agency.*

(b) There is an adaptation of the levels of individual responsibility towards the required levels of responsibility demanded by the production processes inversely proportional to age and education. *We wish to verify whether, over time, experience as well as levels of education generate higher differences of capability of agency. Therefore, the most vulnerable people would be young people who would make their individual levels of responsibility correspond to the required levels of the production process.*

(c) There is a specific upward adaptation of the individual levels of posterior responsibility towards the levels required by the rational organisation of the labour process. *We wish to verify whether the rational organisation of the labour process generates a minimal social norm in a positive way for exercising posterior responsibility, greater than that which could exist at an individual level (cultural).*

Conclusion

In this chapter, we have proposed measuring the meta-capability of agency, in other words, measuring the ability that the human being has to exercise his own freedom. We have also upheld that the notion of responsibility describes the free subject acting (in other words, when they value acting with freedom/choose to act freely). At the same time, the notion of responsibility develops in three different parts, each of which highlights a feature that makes up the exercising of freedom: (a) responsibility as referring to the relationship with oneself (in the attestation); (b) responsibility as referring to the relationship with one's acts (in which we respond for them); (c) responsibility as referring to the relationship towards others (the other that calls me to responsibility).

Apart from these theoretical elements, we have proposed measuring levels of responsibility in the work area. Two features are at the centre of our questionnaire: (a) the individual levels of responsibility shown by employees at their workplace; (b) the standard levels of responsibility formally required by the rational organisation of the labour process. The result of these two variables gives us the real level of responsibility that the workers develop in the rational organisation of the labour process *and* the real level of responsibility that the rational organisation of the labour process requires of them.

The importance of the index we are trying to create is multiple-faceted. To conclude, we would like to underline what we hope this indicator will allow once it has been consolidated. However, first of all we would like to say that this index would be the first *National Indicator of Capability of Agency* that exists at an international level. As far as we are aware, no other state has developed a similar indicator to date. What is the point of such an index? Here is a non-exhaustive list:

(a) It enables an approximation of the average level of agency of a given population.

(b) It enables us to know what the average standard level of agency required for the labour context is in a given region.

(c) It enables the identification at a microeconomic level of industries or industry zones with high productive inefficiency.

(d) It enables the identification at a microeconomic level of industries or industry zones with high productive efficiency and a high degree of creativity.

(e) It enables the identification of areas of sub-development of the capability of agency within the population.

(f) It enables the identification of zones of economic activity that promote low levels of capability of agency.

(g) It enables the prediction, based on levels of capability of agency of the population, of what the level of transformation (of success) of a social or economic development programme could be.

(h) It enables the planning of unprecedented social and educational policies that could have the objective of remedying the lack of agency in a given population.

This list is obviously not complete, but states the enormous possibilities of this indicator. The confidence and invaluable support of the INEGI of this project pays witness to the creativity and originality that a country such as Mexico may have in the face of research which, in the field of human and economic development, has mainly taken place in the North.

References

Alkire, S. (2005). 'Subjective Quantitative Studies of Human Agency'. *Social Indicators Research* Vol. 74, No. 1, pp. 217–60.

(2008). 'Concepts and Measures of Agency'. In K. Basu and R. Kanbur, eds., *Arguments for a Better World: Essays in Honor of Amartya Sen.* Oxford: Oxford University Press, pp. 455–74.

Arneson, R. (1989). 'Equality and Equal Opportunity for Welfare'. *Philosophical Studies* Vol. 56, No. 1, pp. 77–93.

(2011). 'Rawls, Responsibility and Distributive Justice'. In M. Fleurbaey, M. Salles, and J. Weymark, eds., *Justice, Political Liberalism and Utilitarianism*. Cambridge: Cambridge University Press, pp. 80–107.

Ballet, J., Dubois, J. L., Mahieu, F. R. (2007). 'Responsibility for Each Other's Freedom: Agency as the Source of Collective Capability.' *Journal of Human Development* Vol. 8, No. 2, pp. 185–201.

Ballet, J., Bazin, D., Dubois, J. L., Mahieu, F. R. (2014). *Freedom, Responsibility and Economics of the Person*. London: Routledge.

Berlin, I. (1969). *Four Essays on Liberty*. Oxford: Oxford University Press.

Bonvin, M. and Farvaque, N. (2004). 'Social Opportunities and Individual Responsibility: The Capability Approach and the Third Way'. *Ethique Economique* Vol. 2, pp. 1–23.

Bovens, M. (1998). *The Quest for Responsibility, Accountability and Citizenship in Complex Organizations*. Cambridge: Cambridge University Press.

Bruni, L., Comim, F., Pugno, M. (2008). *Capabilities and Happiness*. Oxford: Oxford University Press.

Cohen, G. A. (1989). 'On the Currency of Egalitarian Justice'. *Ethics* Vol. 99 No. 4, pp. 906–44.

Conill Sancho, J. (2004). *Horizontes de economía ética: Aristóteles, Adam Smith, Amartya Sen*. Madrid: Tecnos.

Cortina, A. (2002). *Por una ética de consumo: La ciudadanía del consumidor en un mundo global*. Madrid: Taurus.

(2007). *Ética de la razón cordial : educar en la ciudadanía en el siglo XXI*. Oviedo: Nobel.

Crocker, D. (2009). *Ethics of Global Development: Agency, Capability and Deliberative Democracy*. Cambridge: Cambridge University Press.

Crocker, D. and Robeyns, I. (2010) 'Capability and Agency'. In C. W. Morris, ed., *Amartya Sen*. Cambridge: Cambridge University Press, pp. 60–90.

Deneulin, S., Nebel, M., Sagovsky, N. (eds.) (2006). *Transforming Unjust Structures: The Capability Approach*. Dordrecht: Springer.

Dworkin, R. (1981). 'What is Equality? Part II. Equality of Resources'. *Philosophy and Public Affairs* Vol. 10, No. 4, pp. 283–345.

Giddens, A. (1998). *The Third Way*. Bristol: Polity Press.

Hurley, S. L. (2008). *Justice, Luck and Knowledge*. Cambridge: Harvard University Press.

Jonas, H. (1979). *Das Prinzip Verantwortung*. Frankfurt am Main: Insel Verlag.

Lake, C. (2001). *Equality and Responsibility*. Oxford: Oxford University Press.

Lévinas, E. (1974). *Autrement qu'être ou au-delà de l'essence*. Nijhoff: Lattaye.

(1982). *Ethique et infini*. Paris: Fayard.

(1989). *Répondre d'autrui*. Neuchâtel: A la Baconnière.

Levinas, E. (1996). *Totalité et infini*. Paris: Gallimard.

Mahieu, F.R. (2008). *Responsabilité et crimes économiques*, Paris: L'Harmattan.

Mounnier, E. (1936). *Manifeste au service du personnalisme*. Paris: Montaigne-Esprit.

Nebel, M. and Herrera Rendon, T. (2006). 'A Hermeneutic of Amartya Sen's Concepts of Capability'. *International Journal of Social Economics* Vol. 33, No. 10, pp. 710–22.

Nebel, M. (2007). 'Fundamentos éticos de la capabilidad de afiliación'. *Estudios* Vol. 83, pp. 45–78.

(2010). 'Good Governance: the Practice of Social Power'. In S. Beretta and R. Zoboli, eds., *Global Governance in a Plural World*. Milan: Vita e Pensiero, pp. 23–61.

(2014). 'Identidad y Capabilidad'. In M. Nebel, P. Flores Crespo, and T. Herrera Rendon, eds., *Desarrollo como Libertad en América Latina. Fundamentos y Aplicaciones*. Mexico: Editorial Universidad Iberoamericana, pp. 143–161.

Nebel, M., Flores Crespo, P., Herrera Rendon, T. (2014). *Desarrollo como Libertad en América Latina. Fundamentos y Aplicaciones*. Mexico: Editorial Universidad Iberoamericana.

Nussbaum, M. (2006). 'Education and Democratic Citizenship: Capabilities and Quality Education'. *Journal of Human Development* Vol. 7, No. 3, pp. 385–95.

Prabhakar, R. (2002). 'Capability Responsibility, Human Capital and the Third Way'. *Political Quarterly* Vol. 73, No. 1, pp. 51–7.

Rawls, J. (1971). *A Theory of Justice*. Cambridge, MA: Harvard University Press.

(1993). *Political Liberalism*. New York, NY: Columbia University Press.

Ricœur, P. (1989). *Soi-même comme un autre*. Paris: Le Seuil.

(1995). 'Le concept de responsabilité. Essai d'analyse sémantique'. In P. Ricœur, ed., *Le Juste*. Paris: Le Seuil.

Robeyns, I. (2005). 'The Capability Approach: A Theoretical Survey'. *Journal of Human Development* Vol. 6, No. 1, pp. 93–114.

(2009). 'Capability and Theories of Justice'. In E. Chiappero Martinetti, ed., *Debating Global Society: Reach and Limits of the Capability Approach*. Milan: Feltrinelli, pp. 61–90.

Roemer, J. (1995). 'Equality and Responsibility'. *Boston Review* Vol. April/May (http://new.bostonreview.net/BR20.2/roemer.html; Accessed on 2 May 2016).

Scheffer, S. (2005). 'Choice, Circumstances and the Value of Equality'. *Politics, Philosophy and Economics* Vol. 4, No. 1, pp. 5–28.

Sen, A. K. (1985a). 'Well-being, Agency and Freedom: the Dewey Lectures 1984'. *Journal of Philosophy* Vol. 82, pp. 169–221.

(1985b). *Commodities and Capabilities*. Amsterdam: Elsevier.

(1992). *Inequality Reexamined*. Oxford: Oxford University Press.

(1997). 'Maximization and the Act of Choice'. *Econometrica* Vol. 65, pp. 745–79.

(1999). *Development as Freedom*. Oxford: Oxford University Press.

(2004). *Rationality and Freedom*. Cambridge, MA: Belknap-Harvard University Press.

(2007). *Identity and Violence*. London: Penguin.

Stemplowska, Z. (2009). 'Making Justice Sensitive to Responsibility'. *Political Studies* Vol. 57, No. 2 pp. 237–59.

5 | Equal Liberty, Reflective Equilibrium and Education

Defending Rawls from Sen's Criticisms

CAROLINE SOUZA AND GABRIEL GOLDMEIER

Introduction

In this chapter, social contract theory is defended as being the basis for considering the development of more just societies, in line with Western consensual values of equal civil and political liberties, equality of opportunity and promotion of social ties. Rawls' version of such a theory is supported but different contributions from capability approaches from Sen and Nussbaum are also considered. Thus, initially, classical social contract is proposed as a strong candidate to ground the understanding of principles that give basis to constitutional principles. Then, different critiques of this theory are connected with Rawls' defence of hypothetical contract: first, the defence of maximisation of utility and Rawls' response is presented, and then Rawls' incorporation of the communitarian claim towards a 'holistic' view of society is discussed. We next investigate Nussbaum's demands for expanding the scope of the contract and possible replies to this. Later, Sen's opposition to closeness and parochialism of contract theory and to Rawlsian transcendentalism are presented and addressed. However, although these criticisms are arguable, there are two improvements using the capabilities approach that must be considered. Through his appeal to social choice theory, Sen calls attention to the importance of improving the democratic process to sustain the liberal project. On the other hand, Mills' defence of non-idealised theories, which highlights the importance of expanding the observation of factual injustices in order to build a theory, is understood as a point of connection between Sen and Nussbaum's different understandings of the capabilities approach. This reflection orients the conclusion that states are only just insofar that their individuals share certain civic virtues.

Classic Social Contract as a Foundation for Constitutional Principles

The starting point of this reasoning is the idea, shared by contemporary Western individuals,[1] that civil and political liberties and equality of opportunities must be guaranteed by the state and communal ties amongst co-citizens must be encouraged. These ideas were historically developed[2] and align with 'very strong' principles, normally expressed in Western constitutions. It is very difficult for individuals (or their representatives) to change this situation, even if the desire for change is expressed by a majority group. Consequently, constitutional principles are not changed by ordinary democratic processes. Of course, throughout history, several constitutions have been rewritten or amended. Such processes, however, are exceptional and normally demand strong popular mobilisation. Unlike ordinary laws, constitutional principles are based on tradition – in the case of Western societies, they are based on traditions of communal ties, equal liberty and democracy – and, even if they are not exempt from current political debate (even if it is unusual, shared beliefs can change with time), they tend to be agreed upon by different political groups – which, mostly only interpret these principles differently.[3]

---

[1] The focus on these Western values does not mean that this chapter necessarily considers other societies' political developments wrong or unfair. The reason for such an appeal is that these foundational beliefs (in the case of Western countries) seem to be the best way to find theoretical reasons for political structures within them. In addition, it is important to highlight that we are not defending any type of policy that discourages many of non-Western cultural practices within Western borders. On the contrary, respecting different beliefs is part of this consensus.

[2] Siedentop, in *Inventing the Individual* (2014), presents a very interesting narrative related to this.

[3] Besides national ties, civil and political liberties are obviously guaranteed in all Western constitutions. Equality of opportunity, on the other hand, not always can be identified. In the US Constitution there is no mention to this idea. In the Brazilian Constitution, Article 211 'guarantees equalisation of educational opportunities'. Even if this idea is not found in particular constitutions, it is quite clear that the large majority of people from opposite political spectrums defend this idea in, it is not risky to say, all Western countries. The disagreement is not about the worth of equality of opportunities, but about what it means and how it should be implemented. In the US, it is in the basis of the 'American dream', the 'dream of a land in which life should be better and richer and fuller for everyone, with opportunity for each according to ability or achievement' (Adams, 1931: 214).

The existence of a consensus (paradigm) is as helpful in sciences as it is in politics, as it guarantees the stability needed to refine, respectively, 'truth' and 'justice'. Regarding reflections on 'truth' in natural sciences, Kuhn, in *The Structure of Scientific Revolutions* (1996[1962]), states that periods of normality, when a paradigm is widely accepted by a scientific community, are beneficial for the improvement of that area. Through the agreement of a main theory, scientists can join forces to refine the knowledge that comes from it. In Rawls' theory (1993, 1999a[1971], 2001), this stability comes from an 'overlapping consensus' of basic ideas, although he admits dissent from several important discussions, from abortion (1999b: 169) to redistribution of wealth (1993: 229–30). In this sense, constitutions – the symbol of overlapping consensus – give stability for the current political debate.

Even though Rawls defends the importance of constitutional agreements, it is wrong to imagine that he proposes the existence of a total consensus in public sphere. Actually, such a consensus is impossible and even unhealthy. Societies evolve from disagreement, which is standard norm in the political sphere. Rawls, mirroring a famous argument from Mill (2002[1859]), says:

[T]he ideal of public reason does not often lead to general agreements of views, nor should it. Citizens learn and profit from conflict and argument, and when their arguments follow public reason, they instruct and deepen society's public culture (1996[1993]: lvii).

However, it is necessary to better understand the meaning of ideas of communal spirit, equal liberty and democracy, which are the basis of Western constitutions. In this section, such a point is associated with a strong theoretical idea. In order to say that states are not founded on arbitrary principles (or based on the wishes of one dictator), political philosophers developed the idea that states are founded on the consensus of free people. This is known as social contract theory.

The three founding fathers of the social contract theory are Hobbes (1651), Locke (1690) and Rousseau (1762). Locke endorses a seminal idea proposed by Hobbes:

Men being ... by nature all free, equal, and independent, no one can be put out of this estate, and subjected to the political power of another, without his own consent. The only way whereby any one divests himself of his natural liberty, and puts on the bonds of civil society, is by agreeing with other men to join and unite into a community, for their comfortable, safe, and peaceable living one amongst another, in a secure enjoyment of their properties, and a greater security against any that are not of it. (2003[1690]: 141–2.)

However, despite this common idea, Locke's work differs significantly from Hobbes, as the latter starts with the premise that human beings are egoist, while the former considers that individuals are concerned about the good of the others (Nussbaum, 2006: 35). Rousseau (1762), suspicious of individuals' behaviour in society, suggests that a 'general will' should be developed in order to avoid egoism and allow people to cooperate in a way that benefits all, through defining common goals. For this reason, democracy and moral education play a central role in his project (1762). Thus, Rousseau's particular defence on how to educate and control people is considered 'non-liberal' and philosophers like Nussbaum say that he does 'not conceive of the social contract as a contract among independent individuals' in opposition to 'liberal theorists [like] Locke and Kant' (2006: 25).

In fact, Rawls and other contemporary sympathisers of social contract such as Nussbaum establish some limits to the liberal project. Equal liberty, communal spirit and democracy, central ideas in their view of social contract theory, are combined through cultivating civic virtues, that is, avoiding neutrality regarding moral education. In other words, for these social contract theorists, a just social organisation is the result of mutual agreement among all citizens, based on their freedoms of choice and their sense of belonging to a communal project. This reflection indicates that social contract is dependent on people's civic virtues.

Utilitarianism and Rawls' Hypothetical Contract

However, before exploring how social contract theory is dependent on civic virtues, it is interesting to analyse several criticisms of its classical format and some of Rawls' reinterpretations of social contract. It is possible to start such an analysis by understanding the distrust in the applicability of tacit contract and utilitarianism's offered solution to it. Of course, people are born in states already constituted and they do not have the option to disagree with it. 'In fact, all major social contract theorists – Hobbes, Locke and Rousseau – rely in different ways on arguments based on tacit consent. Here the central thought is that by quietly enjoying the protection of the state one is giving it one's tacit consent' (Wolff, 1996: 46). Hume (1748), however, claimed that this tacit consent with state's laws does not make sense, because common people do not have a real alternative of abandoning their original states if they disagree with them. In Hume's time, and even now, it remains difficult to move the individual away from their country of birth. Thus, in order to say that people agree with the idea of contract, additional reasoning is needed.

This lack of guarantee of people's tacit agreement on social contract gives way to a solution beyond tacit consent. Bentham (1780) introduced classical utilitarianism, a theory that dominated philosophical discussions for two centuries – at least in the field of economics, it still has many supporters – and relegated social contract theory to a secondary role. This new theory, in its classical format, presented two main characteristics. First, utilitarianism considers pleasure (well-being, happiness, etc.) and not liberty as the main good that humans strive to achieve. Because of this, people's consent on state's decisions is also considered less important. Thus, classic utilitarianism is focused on the maximisation of pleasure and not on consent regarding how the state should be organised. Rawls summarises classical utilitarianism by claiming that its 'main idea is that society is rightly ordered, and therefore just, when its major institutions are arranged so as to achieve the greatest net balance of satisfaction summed over all the individuals belonging to it' (1999a[1971]: 20). Thus, classical utilitarians do not demand that such social arrangement be promoted democratically, because it is most important for them to increase the average satisfaction of individuals.[4] In this sense, the problem of consent is solved and there is no need to create conditions for people to abandon their states, as the best situation for all would be guaranteed.

However, among political philosophers, this theory started losing sustainability as it allows obvious injustices and does not present any real concern with social stability. For classical utilitarianism, some people, at least theoretically, could be made slaves (or receive very low

---

[4] Classical utilitarianism is being discussed here rather than investigating more complex utilitarian proposals. Mill, for example, inserts demands on liberty and democracy in his theory and takes 'utility in a largest sense, grounded on the permanent interest of men as a progressive being' (2002[1859]). A reflection from Sandel (1998) aligns Mill's ideas with virtue ethics , but such analysis is outside of the scope of this chapter.

salaries, etc.) if doing so improves people's average well-being. This obviously promotes an unacceptable lack of consideration of individuals' dignity. Moreover, this practice would promote social instability, as oppressed people would develop an awareness of their lack of liberty and dignity and eventually not accept this situation. This society would not be cooperative. In this context, the classical utilitarianism solution was to restrict the utility principle by ad hoc intuitionistic constraints (Rawls, 1999a[1971]: xvi–xvii).

Avoiding these ad hoc solutions, in *A Theory of Justice* (1971), Rawls reasserts the central idea of equal liberty associated to social contract theory, but adds something new to the notion of people's free agreement. Instead of developing a reasoning based on the tacit agreement among real people, he defends a theory based on a *hypothetical contract*. His innovative proposal suggests that people should imagine themselves in a fictional *original position* of putting their own life plans into practice, though they are covered by a *veil of ignorance* which inhibits them from knowing their positions in society (1999a[1971]: 102–70). Thus, this idea takes into account two of the three main current Western civic values mentioned earlier which sustain all this reasoning: equal liberty, as all people are morally allowed to seek their own life plans; and spirit of community, because, by accepting institutions built through this veil mechanism, all people agree with not only defending their own privileges. These two values ground theories of justice, while democracy is the political procedure to guarantee the effectiveness of these values. By respecting people's right to follow their own life plans, their liberty and dignity are guaranteed and stability is reached.

Communitarianism and Rawls' Hypothetical Contract

However, there are other criticisms that are closely related to a problem identified by communitarians, who defend a 'holistic' view of societies, which considers social organisations as organic wholes, rather than an 'atomistic' understanding of societies, which sees them as a mere aggregate of individuals (atoms) (Sandel, 1982; Taylor, 1995). Communitarian thinkers such as MacIntyre (1981) and Sandel (1982) defend that the feeling of belonging to a community (eventually a nation), in just/virtuous societies, comes before the consent of individuals. In this sense, communitarians are not necessarily against the idea of a social contract, but they consider that people's attachments to their communities come prior to the idea of contract. This idea converges with the suggestion that communal ties are the basis of Western contemporary shared beliefs.

Pateman[5] sees the metaphor of the contract as useless to describe social relations based on justice, as she criticises the identification of social contract with something similar to the atomism mentioned above. Aligned with Hegel's (1820) description of civil society in opposition to the state, Pateman understands contracts as simulations of consents of self-interested people. Thus, '[c]ontract has a valuable commercial place, but ... it should be kept in that place ... and to insist that 'contract' is the metaphor for a free society is a very narrow view of humans and what they create' (Pateman & Mills, 2007: 15). For Pateman, the excessive individualism symbolised by the idea of contract is the main problem of this theory.

Contractualists like Hobbes surely sustain their theories in an atomistic view. Certain readers of Rawls identify the same characteristic in his project. The two main reasons for this understanding are: Rawls' definition of a just society as 'a cooperative venture for mutual advantage' (1971: 4); and the suggestion that, under the veil, individuals seek self-advantage (1971: 123). In this sense, Rawls would be departing from a similar premise used by Hobbes.

Nevertheless, this understanding is wrong. According to Nussbaum (2006: 64), the 'Veil of Ignorance is intended as an abstract model of benevolence. [Rawls] explicitly says that, by combining self-interest with ignorance, he hopes to get results that approximate to what we would get from benevolence with full information'. In order to avoid this confusion, in Rawls' *Political Liberalism* (1993), 'the locution 'a cooperative venture for mutual advantage' is replaced by 'society as a fair system of cooperation over time', and mutual advantage is not mentioned' (Nussbaum, 2006: 59)

Gauthier (1986), a neo-Hobbesian, denying this Rawlsian abstract appeal to benevolence, imagines that individuals would cooperate based only on their self-interest, because, in the end, the result of cooperation would be beneficial. Nevertheless, in a society where

---

[5] Pateman is not clearly identified with communitarianism. However, her point against classic social contract is based on a typical communitarian interpretation.

only self-interest is stimulated and civic values are not considered, some individuals or groups would probably be excluded. It is easy to imagine – and identify in our realities – obviously unjust societies in which rich people live in luxurious gated communities, while poor people live without any social benefit. Regarding this problem, Rawls proposes something different. His theory appeals to an intuition of the idea of justice – with historical roots – that respects people's life plans but limits their self-interest. This appeal makes Rawls' theory completely dependent on a certain sense of benevolence linked with a holistic/communitarian spirit.

Thus, Rawls' reinterpretation of the social contract embodies the communitarian claim to consider people's communal attachment before the idea of contract. It is this attachment that produces the feeling of benevolence towards co-citizens. Only if individuals somehow feel responsible for their co-citizens they will imagine society covered by the veil of ignorance. The idea of contract, however, serves to respect people's liberty to define their life plans. In this sense, it provides a reasonable answer to Pateman's accusation that the metaphor of contract is always associated with pure self-interest. For example, the appeal to the veil of ignorance in political reasoning allows arguments towards protecting 'poor' people from self-interested individuals who are only concerned with locking themselves into gated condominiums, ignoring the rest of the society.

Defining Social Contract Scope

Other problems related to the appeal to social contract theory are constantly presented by other authors. For example, Nussbaum (2006), although a sympathiser of social contract theory, addresses three different criticisms pertaining to the limits of social contract's scope. She understands that this theory is unable to provide a reasonable answer as how to fairly treat three specific groups: other species, people with disabilities, and foreigners. Nussbaum thinks that contract is useful for thinking about justice, but feelings of beneficence and benevolence towards a larger group must be considered.

In order to reply to Nussbaum's claim towards including other species, it is possible to argue that other species do not have the same moral status – based on current people's consensual beliefs – as humans. Because of this and because they do not have the same duties, they are not subjected to the same rights as humans. Of course, this fact does not mean that, for example, torturing an animal is acceptable. Regarding the second group, although Rawls' concerns are more focused on protecting those economically worse-off – through his principle of difference – he also indirectly proposes ways to protect people with disabilities. The veil of ignorance intends to model benevolence and helps to design institutions from the perspective of people who do not know if they are in a good or bad situation. Through this, Rawls stimulates people to imagine themselves in others' shoes in terms of 'class position or social status' but also 'natural assets and abilities, his intelligence and strength, and the like' (1999a[1971]: 125). (A different criticism against Rawls' disregard for inequalities suffered by women, black people and the lesbian, gay, bisexual, and transgender [LGBT] community is addressed later.) Finally, the exclusion of foreigners deserves more attention and this discussion is addressed in the next section.

Sen's Impartial Spectator versus Rawls' Contract Focused on the Nation

Sen, contrary to the previous criticisms, appeals to a bipartition in between two groups of Enlightenment thinkers to criticise the idea of contract. For him:

The [contractarian] approach has two distinct features. First, it concentrates its attention on what it identifies as perfect justice, rather than on relative comparisons of justice and injustice. ... Second, in searching for perfection, transcendental institutionalism concentrates primarily on getting the institutions right, and it is only indirectly concerned with the societies that would ultimately emerge ...

In contrast to the social contract approach, a number of other Enlightenment theorists took a variety of comparative approaches that were concerned primarily with removing identifiable injustices in the world – such as slavery, or bureaucracy-induced poverty, or cruel and counterproductive penal codes, or rampant exploitation of labor, or the subjugation of women (2009b: xv–xvi).

This distinction allows Sen to present two criticisms against contractualism: closeness to 'other people's *interests*'; and 'underscrutinised parochialism of values and presumptions in the local community' (2009b: xviii). In order to understand these criticisms, it is important to understand how Sen appeals to Smith's idea of impartiality (Smith, 2009). Impartiality, at least in Western cultures, is strongly associated with the Christian golden rule 'as ye would that men should do to you, do ye also to them likewise' (Luke 6:31[6])[7]. During the Enlightenment, Smith and Kant provided slightly different interpretations of this principle. Kant retained the idea of social contract, whilst Smith proposed the concept of the 'impartial spectator' to guarantee such impartiality.

Sen sees an advantage in Smith's proposal, as its impartiality is open, while social contract restricts this concept to a certain culture. This attitude would expand people's concerns towards foreigners and present a plurality of ideas that go further than parochial notions of justice. Through the impartial spectator device, we would 'view our sentiments from 'a certain distance from us' ... scrutinising not only the influence of vested interest, but also the impact of entrenched tradition and custom' (Sen, 2009a: 45). Appealing to this basic principle of justice, Sen intends to deal with issues not contemplated by social contract theory. In his words:

We can never survey our own sentiments and motives, we can never form any judgment concerning them, unless we remove ourselves, as it were, from our own natural station, and endeavour to view them as at a certain distance from us. But we can do this in no other way than by endeavouring to view them with the eyes of other people, or as other people are likely to view them. (2009a: 125)

However, Sen's discussion of what he calls the closed impartiality of Kantian/Rawlsian social contract, can be opposed by saying that some closeness is needed, because the heuristic device behind the reasoning about impartiality aims to simulate the establishment of constitutions that are *restricted to local nations*. In the end, decisions are taken within nation-states where people *pay taxes, vote and receive benefits*. As most of individuals' political actions happen within the

---

[6] King James' Bible version: www.kingjamesbibleonline.org/
[7] This claim does not mean that other cultures do not have different narratives to defend the same principle. For example, 'When Confucius was asked for a single word that summed up morality, he responded, "Is not reciprocity such a word? What you do not want done to yourself, do not do to others"' (Bloom, 2013: 212).

nation-state sphere, it makes sense that the theoretical reasoning regarding justice takes the nation as the main limit for reflections in this way. Challenging this view, cosmopolitans say that people's political actions should reach the whole of humankind. However, even if they have a moral point associated with a philosophical idealism, this goes against some world social structures based in nation-states built in the last few centuries.

Regarding this, Ben-Porath claims that 'nations are not a philosophical necessity, but a political reality that philosophers who focus on politics must contend with', because 'nation-state provides a unique set of opportunities [of belonging] that neither global nor subnational forms of membership currently provide' (2013: 81–2). Ben-Porath departs from a *factual observation* in order to derive *normative* political implications. The idea is that individuals must feel some commitment towards their national co-citizens, not because they have some natural duty associated with the same religion, ethnicity, etc., but because they are gregarious, and were accidentally born within the same political structure. She calls this accident a 'shared fate' and argues that 'by understanding citizenship as a matter of shared fate, we can achieve a rich view of commonality while simultaneously respecting the depth diversity in a pluralistic democracy' (2013: 84).

Nussbaum's criticism against the exclusion of foreigners in social contracts supports the view of those who consider her a defender of cosmopolitan citizenship (Callan, 2004: 77–80). However, Nussbaum does recognise the relevance of patriotism, which she defines as 'a strong emotion taking the nation as its object ... It is a form of love, and thus distinct from simple approval, or commitment, or embrace of principles ... This love involves the feeling that the nation is one's own' (2013: 208). As she understands it, the love from which patriotism derives is important because it inspires people to 'support the common good in ways that it involves sacrifice' (2013: 209). For Nussbaum, good patriotism is based on a kind of compassion that makes individuals 'stand for the well-being of all people' (2013: 210), within the nation's frontier or outside it. In this sense, Nussbaum acknowledges the major importance of patriotism for the health of nations and democracies and advocates that people should be educated so they may develop good patriotism. In this sense, patriotism, if properly cultivated, is the key to the development of communal ties which are important to improve the lives of people within the nations.

Of course, it also makes sense to think of global justice and moral duties towards foreigners, as world justice is far from being reached and it is not clear on which basis it has to be founded. Different ways to expand people's concerns towards foreigners have been proposed. Nussbaum (2013) writes about a cosmopolitan education. Sen appeals for the idea of the impartial spectator. The debate here, however, is focused on theoretical justifications for constitutional principles, and an idea of world constitution is far from being a reality. (Of course, reflections as proposed by Nussbaum and Sen can help the establishment of different types of treatises to improve justice around the world.)

Moreover, it is possible to reply to Sen's criticism against the closeness of social contract by noting that it does not necessarily generate parochialism. World-wide communication is a reality and the hypothetical contract does not demand that nations only follow their internal practices. For example, ideas outside Western cultures – for example, decreased mass consumption and increased connection with nature – can improve Western societies' principles of justice. In the information technology era, people from the most diverse parts of the world – including from non-Western cultures – are connected. Information spreads quickly and, now more than ever, it is possible for people from different cultures to share their own values and customs and to find ways to be close to each other. Modern world Western nations are not isolated from the rest of the world. Thus, the idea of a hypothetical contract does not exclude the possibility of viewing and considering distant points of view.

In addition to these responses to Sen's criticisms, it is also possible to address a criticism of how Sen uses the idea of impartial spectator. The impartial spectator's exercise requires individuals to engage in an impossible process of constant scrutiny of their moral judgments, because it entails people to continually judge their own moral decisions as if they were not part of their own community or nation, in other words, as if they were an outsider. On the other hand, a collective decision that inspires the model of hypothetical contract, which is also founded on an impartiality device – the veil of ignorance – seems to be a more effective approach. A hypothetical social contract model establishes basic parameters to guide individuals' public related decisions. Through simulating real-decision-making practices, such a device allows for people to understand their societies' foundations and their rights and duties towards their co-citizens.

'Transcendentalism': Sen versus Rawls

Sen also criticises what he calls 'transcendental theories of justice'. Sen understands that 'transcendental' theoretical projects pay little attention to people's real understandings of this issue (2009a: xi–xii). Sen then focuses his ideas on how to improve democratic processes and to address obvious injustices. Thus, he is concerned with presenting a set of basic rules (impartiality) and a methodology (social choice theory) behind the idea of equal liberty. In this way, it is correct to say that Sen does not develop a theory, unlike Rawls and Nussbaum, who propose, respectively, principles of justice and a list of ten central capabilities.[8]

However, it is possible to defend Rawls (and Nussbaum) by remembering that his project is sustained on the idea of reflective equilibrium. In his view, as some political issues are consensual in Western countries (such as the belief in civil and political liberty and equality of opportunities) but others are disputable (such as the limits for social and economic inequalities), a public debate to improve people's views about these issues is needed. If an effective back-and-forth process in which people's opinions and political theories are balanced is established, practices towards justice can be refined and social stability guaranteed.

This process defined by Rawls (1993, 2001) as general reflective equilibrium,[9] depends on the development of two different areas. On one hand, ordinary people must ultimately decide the destinies of their states. As democracy is a shared value in Western contemporary societies, it is important for the stability of these states that people participate in public decisions. Moreover, through democratic decisions

---

[8] Nussbaum is more aligned with Rawls. In her words, '[t]he primary task of my argument will be to move beyond the merely comparative use of capabilities to the construction of a normative political proposal that is a partial theory of justice' (2010: 6).

[9] This idea of general reflective equilibrium is an expansion of Rawls' proposed narrow and wide equilibriums (1971), which symbolise self-reflections that people do in private, first checking the coherence of their theoretical foundation and political beliefs (narrow equilibrium), later, comparing different theories (wide equilibrium). Rawls realised that his first reflective equilibriums did not favour a wide consensus, as societies are much more plural than what he had originally considered. Thus, because a comprehensive doctrine cannot be imposed and a consensus is a necessary condition for stability, he expanded his proposed dialogue between theory and practice. General reflective equilibrium, based on the dialogue between theories and real democratic sphere, is the way to take into account the consensual demand for democratic decisions.

based on correctly driven processes, fair decisions are taken, as Sen expects in his 'non-theoretical' proposal. On the other hand, political thinkers have an important role in designing theories in order to help the real political debate, offering ordinary people possible strategies to tackle political affairs. This is because, on average, people do not have the time to delve into questions regarding justice, because they are consumed by daily life activities. In this sense, the intellectual work of thinkers who dedicate their professional lives to these questions – in academia or not – is fundamental. Santos (2004: 31–6) and McCowan (2009: 89), for example, claim that academic institutions should help nations design their own national projects.

Taking this into account, Sen's criticism underestimates the role of transcendental theories, as theoretical principles are useful to help individuals in the political sphere make real decisions. It is important to note that agreeing with the importance of transcendental theories is not the same as agreeing with a specific transcendental proposal. In actual fact, a plurality of theories makes reflective equilibrium more powerful, because such plurality enriches the real political sphere with different theoretical ideas.

Improvement: Social Choice Theory

Rawls' responses to several criticisms of social contract theory do not mean that his ideas cannot present failures or limits. Although transcendentalism is useful/necessary to develop people's ideas of justice – making Sen's criticism exaggerated – it is important to defend Sen's idea that transcendental theories are not sufficient (2009a: 98–101). Thus, Sen's proposal to use social choice theory – the study of relation between 'the aggregation of interests, or judgments, or well-beings, into some aggregate notion of social welfare, social judgment or social choice' (Sen, 2008: 579) – is very welcomed, as it complements Rawls' project by developing the democratic dimension of general reflective equilibrium. Such a complement ameliorates Rawls' theory by *introducing reflections on how democratic decisions should happen*. Sen explains this theory as follows:

As an evaluative discipline, social choice theory is deeply concerned with the rational basis of social judgements and public decisions in choosing between social alternatives. The outcomes of the social choice procedure take the form of ranking different states of affair from a social point of view', in the light of the assessments of the people involved. This is very different from a search for the supreme alternative among all possible alternatives, with which theories of justice from Hobbes to Rawls and Nozick are concerned.

... A transcendental approach cannot, on its own, address questions about advancing justice and compare alternative proposals for having a more just society, short of the utopian proposal of taking an imagined jump to a perfectly just world. (Sen, 2009a: 96)

By appealing to social choice theory, Sen attempts to design a system of decisions in a context in which complete consensus is impossible. Thus, he helps to advance the practical (democratic) aspect of general reflective equilibrium. Regarding this, Sen's main concern is to develop ways to deal with challenges to democracy introduced Arrow's impossibility theorem (1963[1951]), a development of Condorcet' paradox of voting (1785):

[T]he demonstration of [Arrow's] impossibility has opened up investigations of the various limitations that constrain the format of traditional welfare economics (e.g., the avoidance of interpersonal comparisons of well-being). One result of this has been to draw welfare economics closer to moral philosophy. (Sen, 2002: 344)

In his own attempt to overcome Arrow's impossibility result, Sen (1969, 1970, 2002) pointed out some important problems with Arrow's formulation. Sen's main criticism relates to the unsuitability of Arrow's framework to deal with social and political matters that are not directly related to voting issues. He argues that there are many political and policymaking decisions that involve deeper judgments that go far beyond the mere ordering and aggregation of individual preferences and that include comprehensive moral judgments.

One of the main reasons presented by Sen to justify the inadequacy of Arrow's formulation to a wide range of policy-concerned problems is the possibility of voting rules based on majority decisions being incompatible with minimum requirements of individual liberty and, consequently, of minority rights – Sen's (1970) 'liberal paradox'. An example of this problem can be found in societies that prevent some minorities – such as the LGBT community – from having basic rights – for example, homosexual civil unions. Although it is possible that, in many cases, the majority of people in these societies would agree to

restricting the civil rights of these minorities, there is a broad superior consensual idea, at least in Western societies, that these people's
individual preferences, choices and freedom to lead the life they value
should be respected, regardless the opinion or preferences of others.

Thus, the main issue for Sen is how to aggregate individual choice
in such a way that generates a type of social choice concerned with
these broad superior notions of justice. In this sense, Sen (1970, 2002)
claims that *if* individuals only pay attention to their personal preferences when taking decisions on a political and policymaking level, it
can produce distorted results, especially those issues concerning important matters such as poverty and civil rights. Following only individual
preferences, such as in Arrow's original formulation, is not sufficient to
determine whether a given alternative is actually just in terms of distributive justice. By advocating for a broader informational space for
interpersonal comparisons of well-being, Sen favours moral judgments
that go beyond the recognition of one's own preferences, but which
entail the recognition of the conditions of the other. As Sen explains:

> To try to make social welfare judgments without using any interpersonal
> comparison of utilities, and without using any non-utility information, is
> not a fruitful enterprise. ... Once interpersonal comparisons are introduced,
> the impossibility problem, in the appropriately redefined framework, van-
> ishes. ... [S]uch comparisons are staple elements of systematic social welfare
> judgments. (2002: 273)

By appealing to individuals' concern with inequality to solve the
impossibility theorem, Sen introduces the need for founding individuals' choices on moral judgments and not only on their personal
preferences. Thus, although Sen does not establish a set of desirable
moral values, he affirms, in his attempt to understand to what extent
the majority rule could produce results that could harm individual
liberties, that '[t]he ultimate guarantee for individual liberty may rest
not on rules for social choice but on developing individual values that
respect each other's personal preferences' (1970: 155–6). There are
many different ways of developing these values. Sen's appeal to broadening individuals' knowledge about other people's life conditions is
one method. Nussbaum' and Rawls' proposals towards cultivation of
moral values are other options. From the field of deliberative democracy, different alternatives for developing values through the practice

of deliberation are suggested. Habermas' (1984, 1987) studies refer to this subject but are beyond the scope of the analysis presented in this chapter.

Improvement: Non-idealised Theories

Sen claims that people should observe real injustices to improve their participation in the democratic sphere, however, Mills, in order to deal with the other side of reflective equilibrium, proposes that thinkers also should observe real injustices to improve their theoretical reflections on this issue. Although a defender of hypothetical social contract, he criticises idealised elements of Rawls' proposal. As he says:

In modelling humans, human capacities, human interaction, human institutions, and human society on ideal-as-idealized-models, in never exploring how deeply different this is from ideal-as-descriptive-models, we are abstracting away from realities crucial to our comprehension of the actual workings of injustice in human interactions and social institutions, and thereby guaranteeing that the ideal-as-idealised-model will never be achieved. (2005: 170)

Mills is not against abstract theories *tout court*, but against '*deficient* abstractions of the ideal-as-idealised-model kind' (2005: 173), such as the Rawlsian one. Thus, he claims that past and present patriarchy and white supremacy (heteronormativity can also be included here) have to be seen by theories as central vectors of current injustices. Unlike Rawls, who does not mention historical gender, race and sexual orientation inequalities, Mills proposes to design a theory of justice 'starting from an already-existent non-ideal unjust society, to prescribe what ideally would be required from rectificatory justice. Nonetheless, such correction requires factual characterisation of past and present injustices, that is, a description' (Pateman & Mills, 2007: 232–3). In his view, the elimination of racism is under the current overlapping consensus (Pateman & Mills, 2007: 121). This appears to be true, as this prejudice, even if it is still being practiced, is not legally tolerated in any Western country.[10] Thus, because this problem,

---

[10] The concept of prejudice via sexism seems to be similar. Much more discussion regarding how homophobia is being treated by law in Western countries is needed. However, at least in the UK, the *Equality Act 2010* was implemented

consensually condemned, still exists (even if, most of times, through unconscious practices but also through shameful conscious behaviours), such a description of structural racism has to be considered in the hypothetical contract – the same can be said about structural sexism and homophobia.

Rawls' proposal is only focused on creating an ideal way to redistribute wealth and political power, and thus cannot 'capture the essentials of the situation of women and non-whites' (2005: 173), and additionally other minorities, such as the LGBT community. However, constant claims from women, black people and the LGBT community in the past half-century show that these prejudices are still felt and social tensions are far from being solved. Thus, in order to guarantee social cohesion, developing policies towards eliminating prejudices against women, non-whites, LGBT community, etc. is as important as increasing the material conditions of the poorer.

Mills, then, is not against ideal aims towards justice, but he 'suggest[s] that a non-ideal approach is also superior to an ideal approach in being better able to *realise* the ideals, by virtue of realistically recognising the obstacles to their acceptance and implementation' (2005: 181). In the same way, Nussbaum suggests that 'we must scrutinise Rawls's account of primary goods, with its commitment to measuring relative social positions (once the priority of liberty is fixed) with reference to wealth and income, rather than by some more heterogeneous and plural set of indices, such as capabilities' (2006: 64). Thus, Nussbaum's (2011: 33–4) list of ten central capabilities is an attempt to go further than the principles of justices presented by Rawls, and to be more realistic about social injustices. Sen famously avoids appealing to any type of theory but creates ways to remove identifiable injustices is in his agenda (2009: xv–xvi). Thus, because the importance of theories to help the development of justice is defended, Mills' 'ideal-as-descriptive-model' seems to be an interesting solution that reflects a meeting point between the understandings of the capabilities approach by both Nussbaum and Sen.

in order to protect people against discrimination in education, employment and provision of goods and services based on at least one of nine different characteristics (age, disability, gender reassignment, marriage and civil partnership, pregnancy and maternity, race, religion and belief, sex, and sexuality). This Act is directly associated with equality of opportunity, something under Western people consensus.

Some Conclusions and Indications of Further Analysis: Towards Identifying Civic Virtues

It is possible to further discussions of social contract by endorsing Nussbaum's positive view of a hypothetical social contract:

> The idea of basic political principles as the result of a social contract is one of the major contributions of liberal political philosophy in the Western tradition. In its various forms, the tradition makes two signal contributions. First, it demonstrates clearly and rigorously that human interests themselves – even if we begin with an artificially simplified conception of such interests – are well served by political society, a society in which all surrender power before law and duly constituted authority. Second, and even more significant, it shows us that if we divest human beings of the artificial advantages some of them hold in all actual societies – wealth, rank, social class, education, and so on – they will agree to a contract of a certain specific sort, which the theories then proceed to spell out. Given that the starting point is in that sense fair, the principles that result from the bargain will be fair. (2006: 10)

Following this idea, hypothetical contract intends to design the basic structures of a cohesive society based on liberal ideas. It aims to structure something that is under an overlapping consensus of not only rational, but reasonable, people. Hypothetical contract is associated with people's transcendental liberty, an ideal liberty that tries to simulate individual and collective choices imagining the design of a certain type of society that gives room for people to define their own destinies regardless of oppressions of class, gender, race, sexual orientation, etc. Moreover, the condition of possibility of these types of societies is the attachment of people to their nations. In this sense, constitutions are founded on these two ideas: transcendental liberties of all are respected and an idea of 'us' is promoted.

People's possession of certain public moral virtues is fundamental to this type of society. In this sense, it can be argued that it is desirable to balance people's tendencies to act towards their individual preferences with collective practices. Similarly, Sen, in order to solve Arrow's impossibility, claims that, in the democratic sphere, individuals have to take into account the circumstances of other individuals', not only their own. He then defends that spreading knowledge about other people's situation helps individuals to take democratic decisions with more concern about their co-citizens:

Arrow himself joined others in pursuing ways and means of broadening the informational basis of social choice. In fact, Condorcet too had already pointed in that direction in the 1780s in very general terms. There is a close motivational link here with Condorcet's passionate advocacy of public education and particularly women's education: Condorcet was one of the first to emphasise the special importance of the schooling of girls. There is also a close connection with Condorcet's deep interest in enriching societal statistics, and with his commitment to the necessity of continuing public discussion, since they all help to advance the use of more information in the procedures of public choice and in the exploration of social justice. (2009a: 96)

This discussion introduces reflections regarding the cultivation of civic virtues. Sen claims that more just decisions depend on broadening informational basis, spreading general knowledge, enriching societal statistics, etc. Such attitudes could favour individuals taking other people's interests into account when they participate in the democratic process. However, it is different from acting/voting towards favouring other people's interests. If individuals know about other people's situation, but only care about their own interests, such knowledge is useless.

Nevertheless, Rawls believes that most people in Western societies are somehow committed to their co-citizens' interests. Even so, this commitment exists in a quite abstract form. Thus, it is necessary to cultivate in people certain knowledge, skills and values in order to make sure they practice these civic virtues in real public sphere. Rawls, then, proposes:

[Political liberalism] will ask that children's education include such things as knowledge of their constitutional and civic rights. ... Moreover, their education should also prepare them to be fully cooperating members of society and enable them to be self-supporting; it should also encourage the political virtues so that they want to honor the fair terms of social cooperation in their relations with the rest of society. (1993: 199)

Rawls, thus, proposes introducing more content to civic education. Clarifying constitutional principles and encouraging political virtues linked with fair social cooperation is more than informing individuals about the situation of their co-citizens, as Sen suggests. However, both Sen and Rawls are quite minimalist in their ideas of the cultivation of moral virtues. Nussbaum, on the contrary, wrote at least three books – *Cultivating Humanity* (1997), *Not for profit* (2010) and

Political Emotions (2013) – focused on this theme. Through them, she presents her belief in:

> a type of liberalism that is not morally 'neutral', that has a certain definite moral content, prominently including equal respect for persons, a commitment to equal liberties of speech, association, and conscience, and a set of fundamental social and economic entitlements. (2013: 16)

Actually, this description is not far from the liberalism portrayed by Sen or Rawls. However, Nussbaum identifies the explicit need for the cultivation of a list of civic virtues to guarantee its success. Among the main virtues that Nussbaum considers essential are critical thinking, compassion and patriotism (non-nationalist).

Through this, Nussbaum also tries to find the right balance between the collective choice/communal life and people's individual freedom to orient the life they value. As presented above, Sen equally aims to establish this difficult balance through his contributions to the social choice theory. In the end, most of internal divergences related to the foundations of egalitarian liberalism – and, more specifically, between Sen and Nussbaum regarding the different foundations of their capabilities approach – rest on this balance. The great challenge is to find a way to endorse Western values guaranteeing the overlapping consensus and, at the same time, to respect people's opinions in a democratic sphere. It is this attitude that guarantees the stability and the refinements of justice aimed at by Rawls.

References

Adams, James Truslow. *The Epic of America*. New York, NY: Simons Publications, 1931.

Arrow, Kenneth. *Social Choice and Individual Values*, 2nd edn. New Haven, CT and London: Yale University Press, 1963[1951].

Ben-Porath, Sigal. Education for a shared fate citizenship. In D. Allen and R. Reich, eds. *Education, Justice and Democracy*. Chicago, IL: University of Chicago Press, 2013.

Bentham, Jeremy. *An Introduction to the Principles of Morals and Legislation*. Oxford: Claredon Press, 1907[1780].

Bloom, Paul. *Just Babies*. New York, NY: Broadway Books, 2013.

Callan, Eamonn. Citizenship and education. *Annual Review of Political Science*, 2004, 7: 71–90.

Condorcet, Marquis de. *Essay on the Application of Analysis to the Probability of Majority Decisions.* 1785.

Gauthier, David. *Morals by Agreement.* Oxford: Oxford University Press, 1986.

Habermas, Jurgen. *The Theory of Communicative Action I: Reason and the Rationalization of Society.* Boston, MA: Beacon Press, 1984.

The Theory of Communicative Action II: Lifeworld and System. Boston, MA: Beacon Press, 1987.

Hegel, Georg. *Philosophy of Right.* Kitchener: Batoche Books, 2001[1820].

Hobbes, Thomas. *Leviathan.* London: Andrew Crooke, 1651.

Hume, David. Of the Social Contract. In *Essays and Treatises on Several Subjects.* London, 1777[1748].

Kuhn, Thomas. *The Structure of Scientific Revolutions.* Chicago, IL: University of Chicago Press, 1996[1962].

Locke, John. *Two Treatises of Government.* New Haven, CT: Yale University Press, 2003[1690].

MacIntyre, Alasdair. *After Virtue.* Notre Dame, IN: University of Notre Dame, 1981.

McCowan, Tristan. *Rethinking Citizen Education.* London: Continuum, 2009.

Mill, John Stuart. *On Liberty.* London: Dover Publications, 2002[1859].

Mills, Charles. 'Ideal Theory' as Ideology. *Hypatia* vol. 20, no. 3, pp. 165–84, 2005.

Nussbaum, Martha. *Cultivating Humanity.* Cambridge, MA: Harvard University Press, 1997.

Frontiers of Justice. Cambridge: Harvard University Press, 2006.

Not for Profit. Princeton, NJ: Princeton University Press, 2010.

Creating Capabilities. Cambridge: Harvard University Press, 2011.

Political Emotions. Cambridge: Harvard University Press, 2013.

Pateman Carole, Mills Charles. *Contract and Domination.* Malden, MA: Polity Press, 2007.

Rawls, J. *Political Liberalism.* New York, NY: Columbia University Press, 1996[1993].

Rawls, John. *A Theory of Justice – Revised Edition.* Cambridge: Harvard University Press, 1999a[1971].

Rawls, J. *The Law of People with The Idea of Public Reason Revisited.* Cambridge: Harvard University Press, 1999b.

Rawls, John. *Justice as Fairness: A Restatement.* Cambridge: Belknap Press, 2001.

Rawls, J. *Justice: What's the Right Thing To Do?* New York, NY: Farrar, Straus and Giroux, 2009.

Rousseau, J. -J. *Do Contrato Social.* Sao Paulo: Abril Cultural, 1978[1762].

Emílio ou da educação. Sao Paulo: Martins Fontes, 1995.

Sandel, Michael. *Liberalism and the Limits of Justice*, 2nd edn., Cambridge: Cambridge University Press, 1998[1982].

Santos, Boaventura de Sousa. *A Universidade no Séc. XXI: Para uma Reforma Democrática e Emancipatória da Universidade*. Sao Paulo: Cortez Editora, 2004.

Sen, Amartya. Quasi-transitivity, rational choice and collective decisions. *The Review of Economic Studies*, Vol. 36, No. 3 (Jul., 1969), 381–93.

The impossibility of a paretian liberal. *Journal of Political Economy*, Vol. 78, No. 1 (1970), 152–7.

Rationality and Freedom, Cambridge, MA: Harvard University Press, 2002.

Social choice. In S. Durlauf and L. Blume, eds, *The New Palgrave Dictionary of Economics*, Vol. 7, 2nd edn. New York, NY: Palgrave MacMillan, 2008.

The Idea of Justice. Cambridge: Harvard University Press, 2009a.

Introduction. In R. P. Hanley, ed. *Adam Smith: The Theory of Moral Sentiments*. New York, NY: Penguin books, pp. 11–22, 2009b.

Siedentop, Larry. *Inventing the Individual*. Cambridge: Harvard University Press, 2014.

Smith, Adam. *The Theory of Moral Sentiments*. New York: Penguin books, 2009[1759].

Taylor, Charles. Cross-Purposes: The Liberal-Communitarian Debate. In Charles Taylor, ed. *Philosophical Argument*. Cambridge: Harvard University Press, 1995.

Wolff, Jonathan. *An Introduction to Political Philosophy*. Oxford: Oxford University Press, 1996.

6 | On Epistemic Diversity, Ontologies and Assumptions in Capability Approaches

JOSH PLATZKY MILLER

Introduction

Philosophy should engage with the world as it is and as it could be. Political philosophy, in particular, should engage with the complexities and possibilities of existent politics, and not simply with ideal-types from a particular ideological disposition. Unfortunately, in this sense, political philosophy has tended to operate idealistically, within a set of assumptions that are generally ahistorical (or, rather, falsely universalise specific historical moments of Western Europe) and are attached to a single epistemology; that is, Western or Eurocentric liberal political thought (Geuss, 2008: 8).

Capability approaches are ostensibly more connected to the reality of people's lives, intending to recognise contextual variation between people's circumstances, and with particular (but not exclusive) attention intended towards those who are most capability-deprived: those cast as the world's poor and disenfranchised (Stewart & Deneulin, 2002: 62). However, many of those working with the concept of capabilities carry a number of problematic assumptions. These take certain features of social reality as a given, to the exclusion of others, and limit the possibilities for seeing the world differently, or for creating new configurations. Such assumptions can inhibit those trying to operationalise capabilities from achieving their objectives, mask possible worthy objectives, such as by imposing artificial limits on what can be counted as a 'capability',[1] or even produce and reproduce relations of domination, exploitation, or injustice.

This chapter deals with two significant features at the core of most capability approaches. The first aspect is the attention paid to the capabilities of individuals, and the assumptions about personhood

---

[1] That is, an artificial delimiting of the 'informational basis' of concern (Sen, 2000: 56).

built therein; second, the overemphasis on the nation-state and the relatively simplistic, Eurocentric analysis thereof. In both of these cases, at least two things are assumed: first, which entities are most important in capability discussions, and second, how they are important.

The purpose of these comments is not to provide a new capability theory based on alternative assumptions; rather, it is to point to some of the weaknesses embedded in the assumptions that are generally carried in work on capabilities, and to point to potential ways to avoid these pitfalls.

Ontology and 'What Counts'

The Individual

Within capability approaches, individuals[2] constitute the focal point of analysis: individuals' capability sets are to be expanded and realised, and individuals suffer from capability deprivation. Nussbaum (2011), for example, claims that capability perspectives ask 'what is each person able to do and to be?' when approaching questions of justice and decency (p. 18). Sen (2000) writes about how individuals 'can effectively shape their own destiny', and adds that they can also 'help each other' (p. 11). In a brief discussion of personhood, Sen (2000) presents a view of personhood in which individuals are 'entities that experience and have well-being' and that have an 'agency role' in acting and taking responsibility for one's actions (p. 190).

It is true that capability approaches are not necessarily 'methodologically individualist'[3] in a strict sense; and that they can, in fact, take into account social relations in various ways, and recognise individuals' associations with multiple social groups (Sen, 2009: 244–7).[4] Robeyns (2005) similarly claims that CAs do not rely on 'ontological individualism'[5] because they recognise 'the social and environmental

---

[2] Generally, but not necessarily, understood as individual humans. See Nussbaum (2007).

[3] Understood by Robeyns (2005) as 'the view that everything can be explained by reference to individuals and their properties only' (p. 108).

[4] In its strongest form, Sen (2009) specifically recognises that 'individual human beings ... are quintessentially social creatures' (p. 247).

[5] The claim that 'only individuals and their properties exist, and that all social entities and properties can be identified by reducing them to individuals and their properties' (Robeyns, 2005: 108).

factors that influence the conversions of commodities into functionings', and because the conversion of capabilities into functionings requires individuals' choices, which are influenced by social factors (p. 108).[6] Robeyns maintains, however, that CAs can, and should, be ethically individualistic (2005: 109).[7]

However, there are two points to be made here: first, not all of those who make use of capability approaches would always be quite so nuanced (or even see the point in 'fussing' about the semantics of individualism), and may simply be concerned with individuals without these qualifiers. Second, while sensitive to some social interaction, these influential approaches nevertheless tend to adopt particular forms of individualism embedded in their operative assumptions, which take the individual to have primary ontological, not only ethical, significance.[8]

Views of personhood that begin with the individual, and thereafter 'bring in' social influence, have dominated (European) liberal philosophy for centuries, but are by no means the only option. Menkiti (1984), for example, provides an introduction to various views that have been significant in a variety of African philosophies (perhaps most famously those characterised as Ubuntu). One general summary of these views is expressed in the phrase 'I am because we are'; in other words, there is an ontological and epistemic priority given to the community, rather than to the individual (Menkiti, 1984: 171). Kaphagawani (2004) notes that on this conception, what constitutes personhood is (amongst other aspects) a foundational interrelation between people and a person's individuation from a (pre-existing) community (p. 337). Such conceptions thus go beyond the idea of a person that 'brings in social influences' (Sen, 2009: 244), because the concept of a person (chronologically, ontologically and ethically) would be incoherent without their constitutive relations to others and to the communities which mould them.[9]

---

[6] Although there is contention as to the extent to which this is true, even within mainstream development thought, e.g. Stewart and Deneulin (2002).

[7] That is, 'when evaluating different states of social affairs, we are only interested in the (direct and indirect) effects of those states on individuals' (Robeyns, 2005: 107).

[8] Even though, as Douglas and Ney (1998) argue, the proposals for capability expansion rely thoroughly on other people and institutions (p. 62), and that the individual is only 'nominally to the fore' (p. 72).

[9] This is one of various points of difference notable in alternative conceptions of personhood, Cf. Comaroff and Comaroff (2011).

This is not the space to assess and compare the positions, but rather to note that there are conceptions of intersubjective personhood which hold social or community elements to be significantly stronger than is granted in most liberal philosophy.[10] Perhaps more importantly, these are conceptions that may be held by the very people that would be targeted by those trying to operationalise the capability approach, particularly through development projects aimed at those individuals deemed to be the 'most capability deprived'. It is not essential here to determine fully the truth of one or another theory. Rather, it is important to recognise that practical interventions, on the basis of fundamentally individualistic assumptions, can at the very least be in tension with the lives and activities of those who experience the world from different perspectives. Worse, these assumptions can serve to justify or reproduce the injustices of historical domination, particularly colonial imposition of values, and forced integration into oppressive economic, epistemic, and political systems (Escobar, 2015).

The Nation-State

If individuals are the targets of interventions in most capability approaches, then nation-states are regularly taken to be the actors which are to expand the capability sets, or are seen as the obstacles that impose 'unfreedoms'. The focus here is frequently on making these approaches 'operationalisable' through 'policy recommendations' for changing nation-states, thereby derivatively affecting individuals' capabilities and functionings.[11] One of the primary ways to 'operationalise' capabilities is through the Human Development Index (HDI), which focuses on an admittedly-narrow selection of capabilities, and creates comparisons between and rankings of nation-states on this basis (Klugman et al., 2011). Notwithstanding various direct critiques of the HDI, the focus here is on an assumption that is frequently taken for granted in capabilities, and is carried through into the HDI: that the world is fairly straightforwardly divisible into territorially-bounded nation-states, and that people more-or-less neatly fit into these entities.[12]

---

[10] See Warner, and Nebel and Herrera-Nebel (Chapters 3 and 4 in this book), as well as Calestani (2009) and Escobar (2015).

[11] E.g. Nussbaum (2011: 19).

[12] Not all literature relating to capabilities subscribes to this; see, e.g. Sen (2009: 129, 143).

There is a host of well-known issues with the nation-state, not least the fact that it is a theoretical construct emerging from a particular social milieu in (Western) Europe that has been assumed of, and imposed on, the rest of the world. There is a sizeable literature explaining how, for example, the colonial state was constructed and imposed for the purposes of extraction of resources and domination of people into actual slavery or de facto forced labour, and that the post-colonial state is frequently an overdeveloped 'security' and policing apparatus for the perpetuation of exploitative labour practices.[13] Issues such as these account for some of the theoretical and practical issues inherent in contemporary efforts to develop capabilities and remove unfreedoms. However, capability discussions infrequently account for these kinds of historical injustices. One risk in taking the nation-state as a basic unit of analysis is thus to minimise the extent to which peoples' lives, opportunities, and self-conceptions are shaped by the ongoing legacies of these oppressive histories.

It is not only in the 'postcolonies' that the background assumption of the nation-state can be problematic. In regions considered 'highly developed' (in terms of HDI), such assumptions can affect struggles against injustice, the removal of unfreedoms, and the expansion and realisation of capabilities. In the HDI for 2015, Norway, Australia, and Switzerland were ranked as the top three most-developed countries in the world (UNDP, 2015: 208).[14] One initial concern is that such a ranking leads one to applaud Norway and Switzerland for their success in providing a high quality of life for their citizens, while masking the ways in which racism, xenophobia, and immigration policies affect the capabilities of those who are not deemed 'Norwegian' or 'Swiss'.[15] The HDI could, however, conceivably be adapted to recognise discriminatory practices internal to the country. A deeper problem is that those who are not already living within what is considered Norwegian or Swiss territory are artificially precluded, particularly

---

[13] See Fanon (1961) and Mamdani (1996).

[14] In the inequality-adjusted rankings, they are all in the top four (UNDP, 2015: 216). However, even inequality-adjusted measures retain the foundational assumption of national borders, with measurements being between countries or between people within a given country. Similarly, disaggregated or regional-level data still relies on data collected at a national level (Fukuda-Parr, 2003).

[15] See Freeman (1995: 884), Grosfoguel et al. (2015), Gullestad (2002), and Skenderovic (2007).

through immigration regimes, from capability-related opportunities.[16] The reliance on the conceptual category of the nation-state as a pre-supposition can hide how this political entity is constructed on the basis of exclusionary and discriminatory practices.

The role of the Australian state is particularly telling. Recently, the hierarchies of how lives are valued, and whose capabilities matter, have become obvious in the country's brutal immigration policy that utilises 'non-national' space to 'hold' human beings who attempt to travel to the country's territory.[17] Leaked files from an Australian detainment camp located on the island country of Nauru indicate widespread abuse of people who have been detained on the basis of Australian immigration policy (Farrell et al., 2016). Australian state officials have attempted to absolve themselves of responsibility, claiming that Nauru is 'not part of Australia' (Peralta, 2016). Furthermore, many of those implicated in maintaining these anti-human conditions are not directly agents of the Australian state as such, but subcontracted private security firms such as G4S, known for its denial of capabilities to people across the world (Siegfried, 2014).

The HDI might well measure Australia as having done well at providing for (particularly white) citizens and their capabilities. This apparent achievement, however, masks various oppressive practices and daily injustices from interpersonal relationships through to state policy, both historically and currently. It is the same state (and at times, has even been the same department) that formally presides over both the continuing legacy of historical injustices against Australia's Aboriginal populations, and the abovementioned discriminatory and harmful immigration policies.[18] This case further makes apparent the problem of 'extra-territorial non-jurisdictions', used by powerful (so-called 'developed') states, armed forces, and corporations to undermine human freedoms and capabilities.[19]

Capability approaches could still be useful for those looking for theoretical frameworks to support people at risk in their own contexts or who try to create their lives in new contexts according to what they have 'reason to value' (Sen, 2000: 10). Tools like the HDI can

[16] Aspects of this can be cast as 'exclusionary neglect' and 'inclusionary incoherence' (Sen, 2009: 138–9).
[17] See Delaney (2016), Hyndman & Mountz (2008) and Mares (2001).
[18] See National Aboriginal Freedom Movement (2015).
[19] Guantánamo Bay is another obvious example.

be employed by those looking for practical guidelines on how to use capability frameworks for the expansion of people's real freedoms and their capability sets. However, these are significantly affected by the actual complexities of inter- and intra-state politics, not just states' ostensible obligations, or provision of resources or rights. The extent of this is not ordinarily captured either by most capabilities approaches or, subsequently, by tools like the HDI.

Those wishing to use these frameworks and tools must therefore incorporate sensitivity to historical legacies, particularly the ways in which historical injustices manifest today. Additionally, rather than taking borders as delineations from which to theorise or research, they should acknowledge that artificial disparities in capabilities can be created because of those borders. This is salient for understanding the complexities of multi-layered phenomena such as migration, particularly when people – who might already be relatively marginalised or vulnerable – face imposed vulnerabilities and capability deprivations due to border regimes.[20] Moreover, this is important with regard to those countries that are regarded as the 'best' in terms of their level of human development and the capabilities of their citizens. This is because precisely these countries are involved in active capability deprivation and maltreatment (increasingly through unaccountable private actors only indirectly mandated by the state) of people who, by an accident of their birth, are considered to be outside the responsibility of a given nation-state and 'don't count' for their statistics.

Alternative Theories and Approaches

Assemblage Theory

The focus on individuals and states can hide multiple other levels at which thinking about capabilities might be relevant: not simply how a community might constrain an individual's capabilities (through taboos, for instance), but how it might constitute a person's capability set by creating the conditions of possibility for individuals to have certain capabilities in the first place (Comim, 2008: 635). Extending this analysis, it becomes possible to see how a community itself may have

---

[20] See Mbembe (2000) and Mignolo (2000).

capabilities that are normatively relevant. One possible ontological approach that can help in reconceptualising these issues is Assemblage Theory and its characterisations by DeLanda (2006, 2017).

Assemblage Theory takes neither the individual nor the group (nation, country, class, etc.) to be ontologically or epistemically privileged. Rather, assemblages are created through the interrelations between their parts, which have properties that are 'irreducible' to the properties of their parts (DeLanda, 2011), and which can be best understood by tracing that assemblage's historical roots (DeLanda, 2006: 29). Crucially, assemblages have the capacity to act and influence the world in ways that can change even their constituent components (DeLanda, 2006: 2). This theory is not micro-, macro-, or meso-reductionist; instead, it accounts for 'intermediate levels to show the many different levels at which explanations can be framed' (DeLanda, 2009).

At the risk of over-simplification, one can consider the international system as an assemblage of international organisations, states, international law, and so on; states as assemblages of communities, cities, regulatory frameworks and institutions, and the like; communities are assemblages that include individual people; individual people are assemblages of organs, desires, memories, and more. None of these exist in isolation to the other, and there is no 'final layer of ultimate reality to which larger assemblages can be reduced' (Harman, 2008: 371).

There are multiple implications of this framework for capability approaches. Significantly, Assemblage Theory helps to avoid some conceptual traps in assumptions made about individuals and nation-states. It also creates the theoretical space to focus on substantial issues that might otherwise be obscured, or difficult to understand, in most capability discourse, such as the experiences of people 'in limbo' in Australian privatised offshore immigration detention centres, or Kurdish experiences in territories (nominally) controlled by regional nation-states.[21]

Communities Approach

This approach is conducive for multiple levels of analysis, particularly one often omitted from capability discussions: that of a sub-national

---

[21] For more on what can be construed as Kurdish collective attempts to expand and realise their capability sets, with a particular focus on gender and without a state, see Knapp et al. (2016). More generally, Comim (2008) argues that capabilities could conceivably be just such a 'multi-level concept' (pp. 637, 645).

group, especially a community or a social movement. Sen recognises that one could speak of group-level capabilities (2009: 244).[22] However, his primary concern here is with the way in which groups 'think': that, because of a commitment to seeing individuals as the primary actors, it is unclear how groups are more than mere aggregations of individuals, in which it is those (or other) individuals' attitudes, beliefs, and values that are – derivatively – held by the group (p. 246).

A community seen through the perspective of Assemblage Theory is a social product of the people that constitute it, but is also relatively-autonomous, constituting those same people (and, in turn, constitutes and is constituted by larger-scale assemblages, which might be referred to as a 'society' or a 'nation').[23] One example of a community-level capability that could be normatively relevant is that of food sovereignty, understood (in rights-speak) as 'the right of peoples to healthy and culturally appropriate food produced through ecologically sound and sustainable methods, and their right to define their own food and agriculture systems' (La Via Campesina, 2007). This can be conceived as a collective right that entails the capabilities, not of any given individual, but of communities to produce or access food on their own terms. In this case, such capabilities focus on how communities are able to produce food in ways that they, as a group, have 'reason to value', and to sustain themselves and their practices. The functionings associated with these capabilities are, in practice, often actions taken in opposition to the entities usually tasked with implementing (or imposing) 'development' projects, including the state, the private sector, and aid interventions that create new forms of colonial exploitation (La Via Campesina, 2007).

These are collective capabilities,[24] irreducible to a purely individual analysis. A given farmer alone may not be able to produce, in the appropriate way, the entire set of foods that would meet the conditions of food sovereignty. Furthermore, the value of a food or agriculture system is not held exclusively in the minds of individuals within a community: it is a part of the geography of the area in which a community lives, it is in group rituals, habits, customs, histories, stories, taboos,

---

[22] Although other writers, such as Robeyns (2000: 18), dispute this.

[23] In contrast to Sen's warning (2009: 246–7), components of one assemblage can easily be components of other assemblages, for instance with people having multiple group affinities at once (DeLanda, 2006: 18).

[24] Or, in Comim's (2008) phrasing, 'social capabilities' (p. 644).

festivals and so on. Understood in this way, no single individual could value the system as a whole because its value is constituted by the group as a historical assemblage, and by the interrelations between people and the world around them throughout time. Indeed, insofar as individuals may come to value or hold beliefs about their food system, these attitudes may well be derived from what might be considered the social or community attitude,[25] rather than holding the individual to be the ultimate point of analysis as Sen does (2009: 246).[26]

Insofar as the communities in question are also mobilised politically for the defence of their ways of life, they can be additionally considered as a social movement. This therefore provides one example of how social movements, generally analysable as assemblages on their own terms,[27] are able to create their own internal capabilities: they are able to both extend and realise the capability sets of their communities to food sovereignty. Indeed, social movements in general can create internal learnings that are significant within the movement, but which also speak to the general concerns of many capability theorists, such as in terms of having voice in a political community (McGregor, 2014: 219–20).[28]

Those using capability approaches tend to rely on the assumed building blocks of an individual and the state. This is reductive. Even if making these assumptions opens some possible lines of analysis, they foreclose numerous significant possibilities – often ones that are most relevant for those who would be the target of development interventions, such as the peasant movements and communities associated with La Via Campesina.

---

[25] Or perhaps more accurately, their form/stream of life (Sen, 2009: 119–21).

[26] Concerns over community-based sectarianism or exclusionary practice, summarised in writings such as Comim (2008: 636–7), are beyond the scope of this chapter. Suffice to say that issues at this level of practicality are insufficiently good reasons for not theorising in ways that properly account for social groupings (Comim, 2008: 642). For instance, it may be possible for *communities* – and their constituent individuals – to collectively reason and organise themselves, in ways that overlap or correspond with normative elements of capability approaches. Take, for example, the participatory processes and practices of Democratic Confederalism in Rojava (Knapp et al., 2016).

[27] See McFarlane (2009) and McGregor (2014).

[28] Amongst other avenues, pursuing this line of thought also opens up space for thinking about the relationships between cities and capabilities. See Amin (2008), Dovey (2011) and McFarlane (2011).

Conclusion

Capability approaches have tended to reproduce a 'coloniality of knowledge' (Grosfoguel, 2013: 87). The various ways in which this manifests includes the recognition of particular actors, and how they are to act or be treated – explored here through conceptualisations of the individual and the state.[29] A number of pathways avoid these pitfalls, tending to lead away from the traditional theorising in capabilities frameworks (and in academic political philosophy, ethics, and economics more generally). Nevertheless, they are worth exploring if theorising of capabilities is to retain a sense of action-focused, historically-located realism that pays attention to who is theorising and acting, and about or for whom (Geuss, 2008).

Can capability approaches be reconstructed and made more useful for, in Biko's (1978) words, a 'quest for true humanity', with all of its social complexity? Perhaps, although it is also possible that these changes may not be viable within existing capabilities frameworks. Nevertheless, there are a host of intimate and systemic ways in which injustices mark our social lives and our world – constituting us and creating our capabilities, as much as limiting them. If capability approaches cannot engage with the range of challenges, then this should be recognised for what it is: not necessarily a set of approaches or theoretical tools to be entirely abandoned, but put in its place and used with care, and with the recognition of the power and limitations that such knowledge can have.

References

Amin, A. (2008). Collective culture and urban public space. *City*, 12 (1), 5–24.

Biko, S. (1978). *I Write What I Like*. Johannesburg: Heinemann Publishers.

Calestani, M. (2009). An anthropology of 'the hood life' in the Bolivian Plateau. *Social Indicators Research*, 90 (1), 141–53.

Comaroff, J. and Comaroff, J. L. (2011). On Personhood: A Perspective from Africa. In *Theory from the South: Or, How Euro-America Is Evolving Toward Africa* (pp. 45–56). Boulder, CO: Paradigm Publishers.

---

[29] Other issues could include, for instance, what capabilities are acknowledged or omitted from most analyses.

Comim, F. (2008). Social capital and the capability approach. In D. Castiglione, J. W. van Deth, & G. Wolleb (eds.), *The Handbook of Social Capital* (pp. 624–51). Oxford: Oxford University Press.

DeLanda, M. (2006). *A New Philosophy of Society: Assemblage Theory and Social Complexity*. London: Continuum.

(2009). *The Geography of Assemblage Theory*. Available at: www.you tube.com/watch?v=9kAwq7TACyk&list=PL121B56E661F64649

(2011). *Assemblage Theory, Society, and Deleuze*. Available at: www .youtube.com/watch?v=J-I5e7ixw78

(2017). *Assemblage Theory*. Edinburgh: Edinburgh University Press.

Delaney, B. (2016, April 30). *Eva Orner on Chasing Asylum: 'Every Whistleblower that I Interviewed Wept'*. Retrieved 1 July, 2016 from www.theguardian.com/australia-news/2016/apr/30/eva-orner-on-chasing-asylum-every-whistleblower-that-i-interviewed-wept

Douglas, M. and Ney, S. (1998). *Missing Persons: A Critique of the Social Sciences*. Berkeley, CA: University of California Press.

Dovey, K. (2011). Uprooting critical urbanism. *City*, 15 (3–4), 347–54.

Escobar, A. (2015). Degrowth, postdevelopment, and transitions: a preliminary conversation. *Sustainability Science*, 10 (3), 451–62.

Fanon, F. (1961). *The Wretched of the Earth* (1963 edn.). (C. Farrington, Trans.) New York, NY: Grove Press.

Farrell, P., Evershed, N. and Davidson, H. (2016, August 10). The Nauru files: cache of 2,000 leaked reports reveal scale of abuse of children in Australian offshore detention. *The Guardian*.

Freeman, G. P. (1995). Modes of immigration politics in liberal democratic states. *The International Migration Review*, 29 (4), 881–902.

Fukuda-Parr, S. (2003). The human development paradigm: Operationalizing Sen's ideas on capabilities. *Feminist Economics*, 9 (2–3), 301–17.

Geuss, R. (2008). *Philosophy and Real Politics*. Princeton, NJ: Princeton University Press.

Grosfoguel, R. (2013). The structure of knowledge in westernized universities: epistemic racism/sexism and the four genocides/epistemicides of the long 16th century. *Human Architecture: Journal of the Sociology of Self-Knowledge*, 11 (1), Article 8, 73–90.

Grosfoguel, R., Oso, L. and Christou, A. (2015). 'Racism', intersectionality and migration studies: framing some theoretical reflections. *Identities: Global Studies in Culture and Power*, 22 (6), 635–52.

Gullestad, M. (2002). Invisible fences: egalitarianism, nationalism and racism. *Journal of the Royal Anthropological Institute*, 8 (1), 45–63.

Harman, G. (2008). DeLanda's ontology: assemblage and realism. *Continental Philosophy Review*, 41 (3), 367–83.

Hyndman, J. and Mountz, A. (2008). Another brick in the wall? Neo-refoulement and the externalization of asylum by Australia and Europe. *Government and Opposition*, 43 (2), 249–69.

Kaphagawani, D. N. (2004). African conceptions of a person: a critical survey. In K. Wiredu (Ed.), *A Companion to African Philosophy* (pp. 332–42). Oxford: Blackwell.

Klugman, J., Rodríguez, F. and Choi, H.-J. (2011). The HDI 2010: new controversies, old critiques. *The Journal lf Economic Inequality*, 9 (2), 249–88.

Knapp, M., Flach, A. and Ayboğa, E. (2016). *Revolution in Rojava: Democratic Autonomy and Women's Liberation in Syrian Kurdistan.* (J. Biehl, Trans.). London: Pluto Press.

La Via Campesina. (2007). *Declaration of Nyéléni.* Nyéléni Village, Sélingué, Mali: Forum for Food Sovereignty.

Mamdani, M. (1996). *Citizen and Subject: Contemporary Africa and the Legacy of Late Colonialism.* Kampala: Fountain Publishers.

Mares, P. (2001). *Borderline: Australia's Treatment of Refugees and Asylum Seekers.* Sydney: University of New South Wales Press.

Mbembe, A. (2000). At the edge of the world: boundaries, territoriality, and sovereignty in Africa. *Public Culture*, 12 (1), 259–84.

McFarlane, C. (2009). Translocal assemblages: space, power and social movements. *Geoforum*, 40 (4), 561–7.

(2011). Assemblage and critical urbanism. *City*, 15 (2), 204–24.

McGregor, C. (2014). From social movement learning to sociomaterial movement learning? Addressing the possibilities and limits of new materialism. *Studies in the Education of Adults*, 46 (2), 211–27.

Menkiti, I. A. (1984). Person and community in African traditional thought. In R. A. Wright (Ed.), *African Philosophy: An Introduction* (pp. 171–81). Lanham, MD: University Press of America.

Mignolo, W. D. (2000). *Local Histories/Global Designs: Coloniality, Subaltern Knowledges, and Border Thinking.* Princeton, NJ: Princeton University Press.

National Aboriginal Freedom Movement. (2015). *Aboriginal Sovereign Manifesto of Demands.* Canberra: Aboriginal Embassy.

Nussbaum, M. C. (2007). *Frontiers of Justice: Disability, Nationality, Species Membership.* Harvard, MA: Harvard University Press.

Nussbaum, M. (2011). *Creating Capabilities: The Human Development Approach.* Cambridge, MA: Harvard University Press.

Peralta, E. (2016, August 11). Australia's Immigration Minister Plays Down Claims Of Abuse On Refugee Island. NPR.

Robeyns, I. (2000). *An Unworkable Idea or a Promising Alternative? Sen's Capability Approach Re-examined*. Leuven: University of Leuven, Center for Economic Studies Discussions Paper Series (DPS).

(2005). The Capability Approach: a theoretical survey. *Journal of Human Development*, 6 (1), 93–114.

Sen, A. K. (2000). *Development as Freedom*. New York, NY: Alfred A. Knopf.

(2009). *The Idea of Justice*. London: Allen Lane.

Siegfried, K. (2014, March 12). *Private Security Firms Prosper as more Migrants Detained*. Available at: www.irinnews.org/analysis/2014/03/12/private-security-firms-prosper-more-migrants-detained

Skenderovic, D. (2007). Immigration and the radical right in Switzerland: ideology, discourse and opportunities. *Patterns of Prejudice*, 41 (2), 155–76.

Stewart, F., and Deneulin, S. (2002). Amartya Sen's contribution to development thinking. *Studies in Comparative International Development*, 37 (2), 61–70.

UNDP. (2015). *Human Development Report 2015: Work for Human Development*. New York, NY: United Nations Development Programme.

7 Collective Agency Capability

How Capabilities Can Emerge in a Social Moment

RAZIA SHARIFF

Introduction

Sen's instrumental freedoms are seen as foundational in the capability approach in understanding the ways in which functioning and capabilities can be developed. This chapter builds on these instrumental freedoms using critical theoretical insights and research undertaken using the case history of Shahbag, a social moment when collective agency capabilities emerged in Bangladesh in 2013. The research was based on case histories from coding and analysis of thick descriptive interviews held with 59 people involved in different aspects of the Shahbag Moment along with triangulated data from real time coverage in media and social media. By interrogate Sen's instrumental freedoms using critical theoretical insights and informed by the analysis of the case histories, this chapter develops a stronger understanding of how collective agency capabilities emerge through economic emancipation, political empowerment, social network capital, transparent communication, security and trust.

Collective Agency Capabilities

For the purposes of this paper we start with a brief overview of relevent aspects of the capability approach. The capability approach 'concentrates on our capability to achieve valuable functionings that make up our lives, and more generally, our freedom to promote objectives we have reason to value' (Sen, 1992: xi). Capabilities are the chosen functionings (beings and doings) that a person can achieve, where the person has the 'agency' or freedom to choose from possible options. Freedom not only has instrumental value but is intrinsically important for a good social structure (Sen, 1992: 41). Sen believes that the 'freedom of agency ... is qualified and constrained by the social, political and economic opportunities that are available to us' (Sen, 1999: xi–xii).

He argues that there are principally five types of instrumental freedoms: political freedom to scrutinize and criticize authority; economic facilities, the opportunities to have and use economic resources/entitlements; social opportunities, to live in society where others enjoy goods; transparency guarantees, to be able to trust others and know that information is clear and honest; and protective securities, to prevent deprivation (Sen, 1999: 38–40). He argues that 'there is a strong rationale for recognising the positive role of free and sustainable agency' (Sen, 1999: 11). For Sen, freedom is the process that allows the agency of actions and decisions, given the opportunities available, based on personal and social circumstances. There are thus 'conversion factors' in the personal, social and environmental domains that can influence agency, the achievement of being and doing, and the capability sets that are negotiated (Morris, 2010: 68). Thus 'individual freedom is, quintessentially a social product and there is a two way relationship between the (i) social arrangement to expand individual freedoms and (ii) the use of individual freedoms to improve the respective lives but also to make social arrangements more appropriate and effective' (Sen, 1999: 31). Agency freedom is one's freedom to bring about achievements one values and which one attempts to produce either through one's own efforts 'instrumental agency success' or that are aimed to be 'realised' even if not directly through one's efforts (Sen, 1992: 57). However this can be hampered by adaptive preferences where 'lifelong habituations to adverse environments induces people to accept current negative situations with cheerful endurance' (Sen, 1984: 309). Therefore where wellbeing and quality of life is subjective, there can be a misrepresentation of an individual's objective reality and circumstances.

More recently Sen has argued that we need to focus on comprehensive outcomes, by analysing the actions, the agencies involved, and the processes used to understand aspects of freedom (Sen, 2009: 215). Agency then is the individual's right to judge which opportunities to use as we value them, but Sen notes that we need to consider the social influences both in terms of what we value and what influences operate on what we value in what we choose, think and do (pp. 244). Morris, (2010:72) writes, 'Sen, we shall argue, draws on his ideal of agency to argue that each group should itself select, weigh, trade off, and sequence capabilities as well as prioritise them in relation to other normative considerations such as agency, efficiency and stability'.

However critical theorists such as Foucault would assert that individuals may be conditioned by networks of power as to what they value and prioritise and are only truly free when they resist with a permanent critic and push the boundaries of what is possible. This is touched upon in earlier case work by Sen and Dreze in India, when they highlighted the distinction between 'reasoned agency' acting for a goal or purpose, and 'critical agency' scrutinising and deliberating about reasons and values (Sen and Dreze, 2002: 19). They argued 'what is needed is not merely freedom and power to act, but also freedom and power to question and reassess the prevailing norms and values (Sen and Dreze, 2002: 258). Hence agency relates to personal and collective process freedoms, the process through which goals are attained (Comim et al., 2011: 4) and is critical in connecting capabilities and functionings (Sen, 1999: 19). Therefore in our understanding of agency we need to analyse actions and their agencies and the processes used beyond the power to act through resisting prevailing norms and values.

Pelenc et al. (2013) argues that these socially dependent capabilities of the individual does not allow us to understand the wide range of mechanisms for social change (citing Evans (2002), Zimmer and Freise (2008)). He further concurs with others that they fail to explore the interactions between capabilities and social structures (Ibrahim, 2006) and do not make it possible to address capabilities that can only be achieved through group action (Panet and Duray-Soundron, 2008). There also seems to be limited consideration of the consequences that interdependence may have on capability (Dubois and Ballet, 2007: 194). In addition, there is limited understanding of how the agency capability depends on the context, and personal situation within which they find themselves as capabilities are situated and contingent (O'Neill, 2001: 197).

As suggested more recently by Pelenc et al. (2015), 'there have been few empirical studies on how collective agency and capabilities are generated by a group of individuals (see Ibrahim, 2006) ... (*but*) collective action can help establish social and environmental conversion factors and instrumental freedom ...' (Pelenc et al., 2015: 226). Pelenc cites Ballet et al. (2007) to argue that collective capabilities allow states of being through collective actions that would not be possible if individuals acted alone. Pelenc has suggested that collective agency formation leads to collective capability emergence, which is built on in this chapter. Although the findings from the research concur with the main arguments presented by Pelenc regarding collective agency and capabilities, it is evident that there are a multiplicity of factors that impact on the conditions that enable collective agency and capability to develop. It has been argued that individual freedoms are dependent on collective capabilities, and that 'for the less privileged attaining development as freedom requires collective action. Organized collectivities ... are fundamental to 'peoples' capabilities' to choose the lives they have reason to value' (Evans, 2002: 57). We now build on this understanding of collective agency capability with critical theoretical insights.

Critical Theoretical Insights

Critical theorists provide a broader ontology of social change than that provided by the capability approach and thus explore the process of transition and change. In the project of pursuing a just, free and fair society, we build on post-structuralists' understandings to differentiate three types of political philosophy (May, 1994) as particular approaches to social transformation. The first (formal) approach assumes that the individual is a rational self-interested being, where the state institutions must intervene in order to ensure justice and equality (liberalism); the second (strategic) suggests that the state systems and structures in place alienate people from who they are and what they create, and that they must come together to struggle and campaign for social justice against the system (Marxism); the third (tactical) sees power as operating in a different way, such that without realising it people reproduce social systems, and that all individuals and institutions participate in perpetuating current conditions of injustice but have the potential to resist (critical theorists). The Theory of Justice by Rawls and later critiqued by Sen (2009) would be found in the first two traditions with Rawls social contract and just institutions, and Sen's realist social choice theory approach. The critical theoretical stance in the third approach goes beyond normative assumptions of current conditions of society, and the traditional notion of individuated efforts for social change, offering post-structuralist insights into changing the fundamental dynamics of contemporary society. This 'tactical' political philosophy and approach to social transformation and understanding of power is built on through this research.

The domination of capitalism is seen as a key barrier to just social change by critical theorists. Weber suggested that modern capitalism subverted the dream of a normative organic community (Surin, 1990: 42) and Hegel went further suggesting that the total sublimation of civil society into the state had been brought to completion by capitalism this century (Hegel, 1981). Negri elaborates further '... that in the present global capitalist conjuncture the state and civil society have in fact been meta-morphosised into moments of a new complex ... the abolition of any final distinction between the state and civil society has been brought about by integrated world capitalism which has very considerable implications for the traditional Marxist politics of civil society'(Surin, 1990: 43). So civil society, the traditional space for potential social transformation, is no longer seen as independent and free of state and market interference. Even so, the economic and political base are not the only determinants of freedom and social change.

Foucault's conviction is that 'both classical political science and Marxist social theory failed in the project of adequately understanding the predominant mechanisms of social integration in developed societies because both are bound to the theoretical prejudice of a concept of power situated at pre modern forms of power' (Honneth, 1997: 154). Foucault questions the Marxist analysis of power being deduced from the economy and believes in concentrating on the techniques of power, in a certain context to understand its mechanisms of governmentality (Foucault, 2004: 13, 30). Sen does not address the problem that Foucault has raised, as we cannot take for granted that existing forms of capitalism and democracy will deliver the freedoms he advocates. Given that capitalist modes of wealth distribution are unequal, we need to explore alternative mechanisms for resource distribution based on need, not markets, and power for economic instrumental freedoms to exist, and alternative forms of deliberative democracy that engage society.

Gramsci's work offers a rediscovery of the economic, political and social sphere not only seeing it as the production of goods, but also of social relations (Mouffe, 1979: 123). By taking this line of argument further one could argue that economic determination in social relations, i.e. not only the need to have money and resources to live but also your position and role in society, impacts on Sen's instrumental freedom of social opportunities, to live in society where others enjoy goods, and thus has significant implications on capability and potential agency. Your economic position in society affects your social relations and networks, and therefore the capabilities and functioning, and the freedom of agency you can exercise.

Gramsci (2007) also offers insights into our understanding of the political sphere with his conception of hegemony. His ideas, contemporary theorists argue, were teleologically driven, based on mechanical determinism through political class and ideological struggle in the civil society sphere. Hegemony was created through a 'war of position' (consensus) rather than a 'war of manoeuvre' (conflict), but only if civil society was developed and strong enough. Hegemony, he argued, operates principally in civil society in the decisive nucleus of economic activity when there is an organic crisis. It has been further argued that '[a]n historic political bloc has to be dismantled and a new one constructed so as to permit the transformation of the relations of production (Mouffe, 1979: 67). Hegemony therefore is a dynamic process of being and becoming, and can be achieved either via: limited hegemony/passive revolution, where the bourgeoisie neutralise other social forces; or expansive hegemony/active revolution, where the interests of the subaltern are adopted in full (Jones, 2009). Hegemony is established through the organisation of consent by maintaining systems of alliances through political and ideological struggle of social relations and organisations that embody them in civil society (Simon, 1982). Active revolution needs 'organic leadership' (intellectual and moral), which Gramsci sees limited to its existence within the political party. Intellectuals must be organic to those they educate and persuade in order to have hegemony. The organic intellectual functioning as a deputy/agent to organise hegemony in civil society, needing to have an emotional bond with the people in order to be a 'permanent persuader', organiser, constructor and active participant in practical life (Gramsci, 2007: 10). Here then for Sen's instrumental freedoms political opportunities are possible through empowerment, but only through a space generated in civil society of organic leadership and expansive hegemony or active revolution.

For Foucault there are three forms of struggle: against domination; against forms of exploitation; and against subjectivity and submission (Dreyfus and Rabinow, 1983: 212). Rather than agency, Foucault argues that it is resistance that can effect change. Furthermore that resistance to existing social development can come only from within society and from those places that have not been fully co-opted (Couzens Hoy, 1986: 14). Thus through the decentering of agency and political empowerment, where the subject's construction of subjectivities in relation to existing regimes and networks of power is collectively transformed, new patterns of behaviour in relation to other networks and structures can transform society. This view of the political sphere fits into and expands Sen's instrumental freedom of political capability to scrutinise and criticise authority, i.e. where the empowered agent can collectively resist and transform the conditionality of power networks.

Sen's instrumental freedoms in relation to society, trust and security are expanded further through this case history research, although critical theorists do comment on aspects of the social political in relation to network capital, and the ability to use social networks for political purposes. Thus resistance, rather than capability and agency (as argued by Sen) is the very essence of freedom. Individual resistance on its own is insufficient for social change. Any meaningful struggle must transcend sectorial identities and articulate a 'collective will' or resistance, a 'populism' constructed through political action of particular demands, which create a populist demand for the very social entities to be emancipated (Laclau, 2007). A process of 'crystallisation' must occur around a demand and the plurality of links becomes singular through its 'condensation' around a popular identity (Laclau, 2007: 93–4). Thus there is in any society a reservoir of raw anti-status-quo feeling which crystallises in some symbol quite independent of the forms of their political articulation and it is their presence we intuitively perceive when we call a discourse or a mobilisation 'populistic' (Laclau, 2007: 123). Political empowerment is thus a movement from bio power to bio politics where 'civil society is an expression of their collective freedom ... as a counterbalance to the state' (Davidson, 2008: 9). Here then collective social will is used to develop pressure for political change on a given issue at a given moment in time. Social networks are fundamental for collective will to develop, as argued by Bourdieu (1977).

For Bourdieu, the 'habitus', a set of dispositions that engender agents to act and react in different ways, shapes agency, but it is the hegemonic elites who shape the 'habitus' (Cleaver, 2007). Bourdieu argued that 'the habitus engenders all the thoughts, all the perceptions, and all the actions' (Bourdieu, 1977: 95), 'as a system of lasting transposable dispositions which integrate past experiences as a matrix of perceptions, appreciations and actions' (Bourdieu, 1977: 83). Within these systems there are 'fields' networks of positions defined by a particular distribution of knowledge that endows the field with a specific practical logic; the field is not a static structure but 'spaces of struggle' reconstructed by agents within the habitus (Chouliaraki and Fairclough, 1999). Significantly, knowledge of this habitus and field means the ability to transpose and extend it, thus agency is the actor's capacity to reinterpret and mobilise an array of resources in terms of the systems and cultural schema to new contexts by competent members of society, so the capacity of agency is a given (Sewell, 1992: 18–20). Furthermore, the occupancy of different social positions in different fields gives people the knowledge of different schemas to access different amounts of resources in the system and different possibilities for transformative action, as structure empowers agents differently (Sewell, 1992: 21). So although the structures and schema of society exist and control behaviours and actions, through knowledge and understanding of these schema and structures by individuals in different parts of the system there is the potential to mobilise resources to resist. This understanding of the social has significant implications for Sen's instrumental freedoms, as social networks and capital, where people from different social positions come together to form a collective that can effect change.

From a literature review, we anticipated the existence of social transformative networks with social capital within the existing habitus that could, through collective agency, bring together people from different networks and fields. We suggested that political opportunities would exist in the structures, that there would be political empowerment through people's collective action to effect change in structure through their collective agency. It was also identified that a non-capitalist allocation and use of resource mobilisation could lead to economic emancipation with resources allocated based upon need not wants, a form of 'crowd sourcing' through collective agency. However, security and transparency were freedoms that were not adequately addressed by the literature.

The Shahbag moment in Bangladesh in 2013 offers a unique example of how collective agency capability emerged, and this is now detailed below.

The Shahbag Moment in 2013

In order to understand the reason and significance of the Shahbag Moment, we need to recap on the significance of the re-establishment of the International Crimes Tribunal (ICT) trials, the Bangladesh liberation war from Pakistan in 1971, and the people's demands for secularism, democracy, nationalism and socialism. The creation of Pakistan was based on the two-nation theory or religious partition of East and West Pakistan. Separated by 1500 km of Indian land. Pakistan was seen as 'a unique experiment in state making' as it was built on religious nationalism, with two geographically separate wings (Van Schendel, 2009: 107). Even though in reality 'compared with the other nations of South Asia, the dominance of a relatively well-defined Bengali ethnic and linguistic group provides the country with a strong level of social cohesion' (Lewis, 2011: 27), Bengal was not given the option at the time of partition to be an independent state. In 1970, the first Pakistani election was held based on adult franchise where the Awami League (AL), who campaigned on a Regional Autonomous Plan (based on the Lahore Resolution of 1940 which allowed for the confederation of two separate states) and the ideals of secularism, democracy, socialism and nationalism won an absolute majority. In 1971, after power transition negotiations failed there was a military crackdown by the Pakistan army in Dhaka, East Pakistan to try and squash the move for autonomy. During the 'war' that ensued, Bengali people resisted, the Pakistani army started killing and torturing all known supporters of autonomy with the help of local pro-Pakistani Muslim collaborators.

In 1971, Bangladesh was born after a 9 month war, some refer to it as a 'genocide' by the Pakistani army and 'razakaars' collaborators predominantly from the Muslim Jammat Islam Party (JI), as at least 300,000 to a million people were killed, half a million raped and tortured, with 40 million people being displaced or becoming refugees in neighbouring India. The first constitution of Bangladesh was based on the AL's ideological pledge to secularism, not in the sense of the absence of religion, but the neutrality of religion, so that nobody would be allowed to use religion as a political weapon (Lewis, 2011: 29). In 1972, a Bangladesh Collaborators (Special Tribunal) Order was passed and in 1973 the International Crimes Tribunal Act was created to establish a special court for crimes against humanity by Bengali collaborators during the 1971 genocide. The Special Tribunal had 2,484 cases and sentenced 752 people with a further 11,000 in jail awaiting a sentence. There was a military coup in 1975 where the leader of the AL, Sheikh Mujibur Rahman, and his family were killed, apart from two daughters who were abroad at the time. Subsequently, an Ordinance was passed to repeal the 1972 Order and 1973 Act to give amnesty to the collaborators and all the prisoners were released. In 1978, the Bangladesh Nationalist Party (BNP) revoked the ban on JI as a political party in Bangladesh, and in 1988 Ershad (JP) Islam was declared the state religion. 'Three competing visions of the nation, Bengali, Bangladeshi and Muslim and two models of Government, autocracy and democracy, have towered over political life in Bangladesh since the 1970s' (Van Schendel, 2009: 215).

However, during this time ongoing activities tried to maintain the history of the liberation war, against military regimes that attempted to destroy all evidence and to rewrite history. Thus 'until the restoration of democracy in 1991, after a long mass opposition, movement was eventually translated into a peaceful "peoples power" removal of Ershad' (Lewis, 2011: 75) – however, these activities remained underground. In 1992, the Nirmul Committee (NC) was established to resist the killers and collaborators of the Bangladesh Liberation War with the support of 101 high profile cultural, academic and political personalities. They established a mock trial, 'Gonoadalot' or People's Court to try key collaborators including the head of JI. Bangladesh Nationalist Party were in power and charged the members of the NC with treason, stating that their activities were unlawful. 'The NC survives and has become an important rallying point for secular and anti-fundamentalist forces in Bangladesh' (Van Schendel, 2009: 217). The AL won the subsequent elections, and focused on ensuring that the true history of the liberation war was known and trying the killers of Sheikh Mujibur Rahman and his family. In the elections in 2001, when the BNP came back into power again, this time with an alliance with JI, key collaborators were given Ministerial positions. The pro liberation party, the AL, won the election in 2008 with a pledged to re-establish the Special Court to try the collaborators. They started legal proceedings and the Ordinance of 1975 was found invalid, with the International Crimes Tribunal Act of 1975 being upheld and given constitutional protection. In 2010, after numerous delays, the special court was re-established as part of the ICT.

Internationally there was much resistance to the establishment of the ICT nearly four decades after the crimes had been committed, by the government, without external international judges and because Bangladesh allows capital punishment. The first verdict for the first case was guilty with a sentence of the death penalty, but the defendant managed to leave the country before being convicted. The verdict of the second case was announced on the 5th February 2013, where the defendant was found guilty and given a sentence of life imprisonment. He left the court room showing a 'v' sign of victory. This was the trigger for the emergence of the Shahbag Moment.

At its peak the Shahbag Moment that erupted in February 2013 and gathered along the main Shahbag interchange in Dhaka, Bangladesh's capital, had over 150,000 participants. It also spread with 471 platforms established across the country and in 26 different capitals abroad through the Bengali diaspora. The Shahbag Moment emerged after the verdict announcement on the 5th February from young people and bloggers taking the initiative to make a stand on the issue of justice, rather than against the ICT or government. Unlike usual 'human chains', marches and demonstrations that fizzle out, ordinary people and senior personalities showed support and solidarity to the cause for justice in huge numbers. Rather than sporadic, traditional and usual practices of rally speeches, marches, human chains, strikes, protests and demonstrations by different groups, they initiated the use of cultural non-violent sit-in protests with never-ending circles of protestors. By using TV, newspapers and social media to spread the message and ensuring that the movement remained apolitical and by denying leading politicians the platform to address the gathering, they gained the trust of ordinary people. Another unique feature was that women and children were actively participating in the movement as they felt it was a safe space, because the authorities were providing logistical support and protection to the movement. Business and ordinary people were providing support to the protesters and the movement spread across the country and through the diaspora abroad. The government responded and the process was initiated to address the demands of the movement by introducing the Amendment Bill in Parliament. Propaganda against the movement by the BNP and JI suggested that the Government was behind the movement and were controlling it, as on the 15th February the movement announced that it would stop the 24 hours sit-in as the Bill was going before Parliament. Unfortunately a blogger was killed that evening; this changed the mood of the movement and shifted the emphasis of the demands to targeting JI. The propaganda also changed to emphasis the atheist, anti-Islamic nature of the movement, especially when the Amendment Bill was passed on the 17th February and included the right to try organisations like JI. The government did not want Islamic sentiments to be hurt, and the demands of Shahbag groups started to split and shift from the demand for justice which had united and attracted the support of ordinary people, to being anti-JI. Some bloggers took the freedom of expression too far against the religious sentiments of the majority and people demonstrated their unease, after the swell of sympathy for the killing, by gradually disengaging from Shahbag. The morals of the Shahbag protesters were brought into question by the counterpropaganda, as non-believers, women and men were together all night, and some bloggers were writing anti-Islamic blogs. By the end of February, JI and other Muslim groups instigated violence against the Shahbag movement, burning the national flag and the physical space of Shahbag returned to normal.

Shahbag was not about leadership but the strength of the people, and the commitment of young people for the cause, offering a platform, a safe public space for people to express their true feelings, which created a paradigm shift in a 'moment', capturing the heart and soul of the ordinary people for justice. Media coverage and social media amplified the Shahbag message for justice and the original initiators of the movement could only manage the ongoing flow of people who were self motivated by their consciences to participate and support the movement. The core initiators were 'unknown faces', and groups shifted their positions to align with the spirit of the cause for justice first. It was a messy decision making process, but the never-ending circles of groups of people participating gave the movement strength and participated in activities that they believed would contribute to the cause, no one could control the movement, it was self evolving, they could only guide the flow. The government was seen as being responsible for protecting the public and responding to the demands given the number of people who supported it. There was no risk for participating in the movement as it was a non-violent cultural protest, so women and children joined in as a learning empowering experience, adding to the credibility of the movement's cause. Some people went to see the entertainment, to feel the energy and participate, or to 'be seen' at Shahbag, to demonstrate support for the popular cause, but the atmosphere and dynamics of the movement, although about hanging the war criminals, was positive, engaging, festive and safe. The Shahbag moment was a unique paradigm shifting event in Bangladesh's history. It is remembered as an event led by the new generation who were not even born during the liberation war, but who, using social media, ignited a passion amongst ordinary Bengali people to secure justice for the victims of the liberation war.

Recent publications including the *Rutledge Handbook of Bangladesh* (2016) have acknowledged the significance of Shahbag but have framed it within a nationalism verses Islamisation context.

Shahbag movement opened the floodgates and revealed once again, what the nation as a whole had repressed for four decades. While the Shahbag movement created a space for people whose voices had been shut out, its secular orientation also provoked radical Islamists who turned to violence to express their opposition. Shahbag exposed the dilemma of seeking justice for war crimes decades after the war ended, in a context where retributive justice became the primary demand because of decades of repressed trauma and denied justice (Riaz and Rahman, 2016: 52–3).

However, as argued earlier, it was primarily the identity with injustice that led to Shahbag, when the focus turned to Bengali verses Muslim identity; after the initial demands had been met, collective agency capability was lost. Bengali culture and secular nationalism was used as a repertoire during Shahbag, but it was not the core reason for participation – the main reason was a search for justice. The Islamic backlash was due to the fact that senior Muslim political leaders were on trial. They were on trial not because they were Muslim or senior political leaders, but because they had committed crimes against humanity while collaborating with the Pakistani army to try and stop the independence of Bangladesh. Shahbag therefore should not be framed in the first instance as an example of Bengali secular nationalism but as an example of the freedom of individuals to collectively demand the need for justice even after 40 years. Another consideration suggested was that in Bangladesh, as there were no existing predominant cultural discourses or hegemony the discursive opportunity structures were fluid (Sajjad and Hardig, 2016), the public discourse on Shahbag changed from Bengali secularism and justice to being spoiled, nonbelievers and atheists. The shift in the discourse moved from the demand pivoted around justice and promoting a progressive secular Bengali identity to banning JI, and accusations of insulting the Muslim Bangladeshi identity. It has been argued that there has been an ongoing contested issue regarding national identities in Bangladesh since 1971 between a secular Bengali identity and Muslim Bangladeshi identity

(Hossain, 2015). However, Shahbag demonstrated shifting identities and networks which mobilised ordinary people, including Muslims, to support the cause for justice in the ICT trials.

Developing a Process Framework for Instrumental Freedoms

The process framework outlined in Figure 7.1 is based on Sen's instrumental freedoms and assumes the interactions these have with each other, structures and practice in the emergence of collective agency capabilities. The figure shows five key points to reflect the five instrumental freedoms, and how they change for collective agency capabilities to emerge. The different instrumental freedoms have been developed based on theoretical insights of the changes needed to

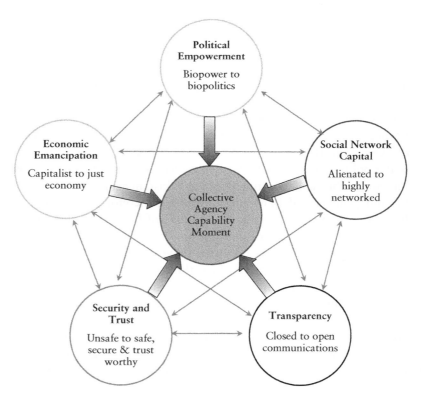

Figure 7.1 Instrumental freedom changes needed for collective agency capability to emerge

shift from a normal state to one with collective agency capability. For example, Sen's instrumental freedom of political freedom has been developed as political empowerment, based on theoretical insights from Gramsci and Foucault, with bio power leading to biopolitics, i.e. from individual empowerment to the empowerment of the collective and all those involved as displayed during Shahbag. Each of the instrumental freedoms are developed in more detail along with their interrelation based on the findings from the Shahbag moment. These elaborations should aid a more dynamic representation of the levels of being, doing and impact within the framework of instrumental freedoms. The three levels of being, doing and impact emerged through the coding of the Shahbag interviews as a way of understanding the patterns, conditions and processes before, during and after Shahbag, where structure and practice was normalised, where collective agency and resistance emerged and were responded to in structure and practice, and the impact collective agency capability had. The descriptions represent the interactive and constructionist nature of the formation of collective agency capabilities.

The capability approach and Sen's freedoms offers a normative position to evaluate social arrangements and the extent to which they support people's freedom and agency to promote their capabilities and achieve the functionings they value (Alkire, 2005: 3). This individualistic approach in capabilities, however, misses the role that structures or living together play in facilitation the exercise of agency (Deneulin, Nebel and Sagovsky, 2006: x) Although Sen's focus in relation to instrumental freedoms relate to capabilities and functionings at a given moment in time, this framework attempts to show the dynamic and interactionist construction of capabilities and functionings during the emergence of collective agency capability in a given moment in time. In Figure 7.1, each instrumental freedom contributes to collective agency capability in different ways, for each freedom a shift must occur to allow collective agency capability to emerge: political empowerment needs to occur with a shift from biopower to biopolitics; economic emancipation occurs through a shift from capitalism to a just economy; social network capital develops from having an alienated society to one that is highly networked with organic solidarity; for security there is a shift from an unsafe suspicious environment to one of feeling safe and secure and trusting others; and for transparency the shift is from a closed, uninformed public to one where communications are open and transparent and easy to access. Similarly, at the core of this figure is the dynamics that structures must shift from being rigid to responsive, and practice must shift from being normalised to resisting. The process of change from level one being, to level two doing and level three impact for each instrumental freedom, is now outlined in more detail.

Social Network Capital

This freedom relates to the type of society and networks that exist, whether networks are alienated with mechanical solidarity, or highly networked with organic solidarity. It also involves whether there is social, symbolic and cultural capital (Bourdieu, 1973) and how strongly there is bridging capital or interconnections between different networks. This was a crucial aspect of generating collective agency and capability, as without some form of social network capital between different spheres in society, the critical mass needed for collective agency capability to emerge and have an impact would have been greatly reduced (Crossley, 2002; Sewell, 1992). In the first level of being, then, there was sufficient existing network capital to establish a public space or field to raise the issue, and enough latent network capital for others from different spheres to be made aware of it and inform others. In the second level, the network capital was strong enough and the issue significant enough to warrant the reactivation of latent networks, bringing together a wide range of people to mobilise resources, participate and influence structures and practices for change. In the case of Shahbag the legacy of the liberation war and people's historical connection to it cut across active networks to mobilise a diverse range of people together from all walks of life for a common cause (Hardt and Negri, 2009; Laclau, 2007). In the third level, once the initial demands had been met, network identities shifted and changed, other identities become a priority and latent networks that had come to the fore had dissipated. New networks and connections were formed and latent networks strengthened from the interactions generated during the process of the collective agency capability. A multitude was formed, but not sustained, for the political project, a populous or collective will led to the creation of practice and structural shifts in the pursuit of justice. Singularities from a diverse range of fields in the habitus with different networks, schemas and resources mobilised collectively to resist the norm and effect change.

Economic Emancipation

This freedom relates to the economic infrastructure's ability to respond based on need and a just economy (Sheehan, 2003) rather than being motivated by a capitalism monopoly, where profit and market mechanisms control the economy. In the case of Shahbag, this was demonstrated through the act of individuals and businesses donating their resources and time to engage in the movement, and the crowd sourcing and resource mobilisation to support the movement. In the first level the economic priorities were not monopolised by monetary profit (i.e. capitalistic); individuals felt that the opportunity cost of engaging in nonprofit making initiatives for Shahbag was less than if they did not engage, i.e. that they were able to engage in the movement without it being to the detriment of their long term economic wellbeing. In Shahbag, people from all walks of life, rich and poor felt the need to prioritise participating and supporting the movement in whatever way they could. In the second level when the movement became established, the economic infrastructure, private business and government agencies responded and supported the movement logistically to make the movement sustainable based on the needs of the movement, rather than a profit motive. Shahbag also flourished through crowd sourcing and resource mobilisation, but this would have been time limited without infrastructure support. Hence, during Shahbag, while most gave in kind resources because they supported the cause, some individuals and businesses also saw involvement as a marketing and sponsorship opportunity, a kind of symbolic capital to be associated with and supporting something that was gaining such wide positive media coverage and public attention. However, in level three when the initial demands had been met, and the discourse and narrative became more negative because of counter propaganda, the opportunity cost balance changed. The momentum in resource mobilisation and crowd sourcing was weakened and logistics and other forms of economic support were withdrawn, thereby weakening Shahbag's collective agency capability. For a moment, for the cause of justice, those who participated in Shahbag were economically emancipated, they valued the need to support Shahbag and a just economy based on the movement's collective needs above their individual capitalist economic wants.

Political Empowerment

Here we refer to political structures and parties as well as individual's political agency of biopower (Foucault, in Burchell et al., 1991; Hardt and Negri, 2001), and how they conform or resist power dynamics in their habitus. Structurally, political powers may be weak or strong, hollow or engaging in a given context, but it is the way that they respond to the movement, positively or negatively that is a determining factor for collective agency capability to occur. In the case of Shahbag, the justice system and political powers were seen with suspicion of compromising the judgement, but when the people of Shahbag resisted, they supported, facilitated and responded positively to the demands. In the first level, political structures and parties offered potential opportunities for change, they created the opportunity by establishing the ICT but were perceived as having negated the possibility for justice. Although a window of opportunity had been opened through the trial, it was seen as being closed because although the defendant was found guilty, he was not given the maximum penalty, a death sentence. This stimulated a response of biopower from a collective of individuals to seize the opportunity, and assert the right to re-open the door of possibility. For collective agency capability to be established a sufficient critical mass needs to be formed for the political project to deliver change, which is what made Shahbag so significant. In level two political structures and parties reacted positively (AL), negatively (JI) and tried to ignore the critical mass (BNP), but because Shahbag continued and grew all parties had to respond. The biopower of the individuals resisting the status quo and normalisation turned into biopolitics of the collective critical mass ensuring the movements voice was heard. As the critical mass at Shahbag was nonviolent and cultural it gained much more positive coverage. Shahbag engaged women and children and individuals from across different networks and fields and so had a much higher potential to succeed and not to be ignored and suppressed by political structures and parties. For Shahbag the non-violent, cultural protest against injustice, the unifying identity of Bengali identity, engaged women and children and young people born after the liberation war demonstrated political empowerment. This was the hallmark of its success in securing collective agency capability, and being supported by political structures and parties. Political structures were able to generate a context where the flourishing of collective agency capabilities were protected, but it was the collective of free singularities, individuals who collectively came together with agency and capability that created the changes in structure and practice. The process of engaging in the movement was described by most interviewees as inspiring, rejuvenating and empowering, and as the demands were for justice, a higher cause, it was much more acceptable to the general public. Ongoing dialogue and negotiations online and in the public domain lead to solutions being found that amicably fulfill the demands of the protestors. In level three, once demands had been met, the initial ethos and priorities of the movement changed. The momentum of the movement was seized for other causes of concerns which did not resonate with the critical mass. As a consequence, collective agency capability was weakened, biopolitics fragmented and become divided, and individuals used their biopower and agency to disengage. From a critical theoretical lens, the political project for which the critical mass had been crystallised was achieved and, like a swarm, the singularities dissipated.

Security and Trust

This is where collective agency capabilities mean a shift from an unsafe suspicious environment to one which is safe, enabling, secure and trustworthy where people respect each other. It is worthwhile noting that all those interviewed regarding Shahbag referred to the unique environment where everyone respected and supported each other, where there were no incidents, and where women and children felt safe – a situation that was unique for a public open space in Bangladesh. Young people put their traditional politics aside to support each other and focus on the main demands. The Shahbag was nonviolent and cultural, a celebratory atmosphere where people could participate, share and learn. Social movement theorists have highlighted the role that culture can play in framing and offering a repertoire of protest activities that give meaning and resonate with the wider public and engage them in actions (Goodwin and Jasper, 2004; Johnstone, 2009). In addition, the police offered three rings of security to ensure the movement was not attacked by JI and their allies. Some argue that they had a public duty to do so, others that this was a way to engineer and control the movement. This aspect of the movement was key in engaging a wide range of audiences, especially women and children, which legitimised the space and the demand. In level one the environment of ongoing intimidation and violence by JI and their allies did not offer security, safety and trust; the environment was one of daily threats and fear. On level two, the new field created by the collective in Shahbag generated an implicit understanding between all those involved of respect, nonviolence and trust, building cultural capital. On level three, once the main demands had been achieved the necessity of unity and a common identity was reduced, counterpropaganda and the withdrawal of logistical security and support made the space less secure, and people disengaged.

Transparency

This relates primarily to communications, media and social media and whether access to knowledge and information is open or closed and how trustworthy the source is. If information is contradictory and confusing people are less likely to engage on mass. However, as in the case of Shahbag, if the issue is a fundamental injustice and the demands are honest and from the heart, it is more likely to resonate with a diverse range of people. Social media played a key role in ensuring that there was a reliable source of information that was open and transparent. Although on level one structural communications were closed, e.g. the judgement regarding the verdict at the ICT, the channels for public debate were open and free, so that the issue was widely disseminated and discussed. On level two, the necessity of communication to a wide audience was fundamental to ensuring a critical mass of engagement and mobilisation of resources, ensuring that the message and frame was positive and reflective of the movement's demands. There were ongoing online 'propaganda wars' but the individual was able to choose and select their information source and make an informed decision whether to engage or not. On level three, media interests began to wane and distorted interpretations were developed to create 'new news', but communication channels remained open and transparent on social media. There was a backlash against opinions being too open and free, which instigated counterpropaganda, as was the case at Shahbag, and the narrative regarding secular, atheist and blasphemous blogging.

This chapter has attempted to bring together and develop an understanding of Sen's instrumental freedoms through a critical theoretical lens, and the insights of the Shahbag moment. It has developed a process framework in structure and practice across the three levels of being, doing and impact. It has argued that by using critical theoretical insights to interrogate Sen's instrumental freedoms, we can develop a process framework that demonstrates how instrumental freedoms support the emergence of collective agency capability using a case history of the Shahbag moment.

References

Alkire, S. (2005) Why the capability approach? *Journal of Human Development*, 6(1), 115–33.

Ballet, J., Dubois, J. and Mahieu, F. (2007) Responsibility of each others freedom: agency as a source of collective capability. *Journal of Human Development Capabilities*, 8(2), 185–201.

Biggeri, M., Ballet, J. and Comim, F. (2011) *Children and the Capability Approach*. Palgrave: Macmillen.

Bourdieu, P. (1973) *Cultural Reproduction and Social Reproduction*. London: Travistock.

(1977) *Outline of a Theory of Practice*. Cambridge: Cambridge University Press.

Bourdieu, P. and Wacquant, L. (1992) *An Invitation to Reflexive Sociology*. Chicago, IL: University of Chicago Press and Polity.

Burchell, G., Gordon, C. and Miller, P. (1991) *The Foucault Effect: Studies in Governmentality*. Chicago, IL: University of Chicago Press.

Chouliaraki, L. and Fairclough, N. (1999) *Discourse in Late Modernity: Rethinking Critical Discourse Analysis*. Edinburgh: Edinburgh University Press.

Cleaver, F. (2007) Understanding agency in collective action. *Journal of Human Development and Capability*, 8(2), 223–44.

Couzens Hoy, D. (1986) *Micheal Foucault: A Critical Reader*. London: Blackwell.

Crossley, N. (2002) *Making Sense of Social Movements*. Buckingham: Open University Press.

Davidson, A. (2008) The uses and abuses of Gramsci. *Thesis Eleven*. 91, 1, 68–94.

Deneulin, S., Nebel, M. and Sagovsky, N. (Eds.) (2006) *Transforming Unjust Structures: The Capability Approach*. London: Springer.

Dreyfus, H. and Rabinow, P. (Eds.) (1983) *Michael Foucault: Beyond Stucturalism and Hermeneutics*. Chicago, IL: University of Chicago Press.

Dubois, J. and Ballet, J. (2007). Responsibility for each others' freedom: agency as the source of collective capability. *Journal for Human Development and Capability*, 8(2), 185–201.

Evans, P. (2002) Collective capabilities, culture and Amartya Sen's development as freedom. *Studies in Comparative International Development*, 37(2), 54–60.

Foucault, M. (2004) *Lecture: Society must be Defended*. Translated by D. Macey. London: Penguin Books.

Goodwin, J. and Jasper, J. (Eds.) (2004) *Rethinking Social Movements: Structure, Meaning and Emotion*. London: Rowman and Littlefield Publishers.

Gramsci, A. (2007 [1971]). *Selections from the Prison Notebook*. Q. Hoare and G. Smith (Eds. and Trans). London: Lawrence and Wishart.

Hardt, M. and Negri, A. (2001) *Empire*. Massachusetts: Harvard University Press.

(2009) *Commonwealth*. Belknap Press: Harvard University Press.

Hegel, G. (1981) *The Berlin Phenomenology*. London: Reidel Publishing Company.

Honneth, A. (1997) *The Critique of Power: Reflective Strategies in a Critical Social Theory*. London: MIT Press.

Hossain, A. (2015) Contested national identity and political crisis in Bangladesh: historical analysis of the dynamics of Bangladesh society and politics. *Asian Journal of Political Science*, 23(3), 366–9.

Ibrahim, S. (2006) From individual to collective capabilities: the capability approach as a conceptual framework for self help. *Journal for Human Development and Capability*, 7(3), 398–416.

Johnstone, H. (2009) *Culture, Social Movement and Protest*. Burlington: Ashgate Publishing Ltd.

Jones, S. (2009) *Antonio Gramsci*. London: Routledge.

Laclau, E. (2007) *Emancipations*. London: Verso.

Lewis, D. (2011) *Bangladesh Politics, Economy and Civil Society*. Cambridge: Cambridge University Press

Marx, K. (1853) On the Jewish Question, in Tucker, R. (Eds.) (1978) *The Marx Engels Reader*. New York: Norton and Company, 26–46

May, T. (1994) *The Political Philosophy of Post Structural Anarchism*. Pennsylvania, PA: Penn State University Press.

Morris, C. (2010) *Amartya Sen*. New York: Cambridge University Press.

Mouffe, C. (Ed.) (1992) *Dimensions of Radical Democracy: Pluralism, Citizenship, Community*. London: Verso.

(2009) *The Democratic Paradox*. London: Verso.

Negri (2005) *The Politics of Subversion: a Manifesto for the 21st Century*. Polity Press

O'Neill, O. (2001) Agents of Justice. *Metaphilosophy*. 32, 12, 180–95.

Panet, S. and Duray-Soundron, C. (2008) Introduction General. In Dubois, J., Brouillet, A., Bakhshi and Duray-soudron, C. (Eds.) *Repenser l'action collective: une approche par les capability*. Paris: L'Harmattan.

Pelenc, J., Lompo, M., Ballet, J., Dubois, J. (2013) Sustainable human development and the capability approach: integrating environmental responsibility and collective agency. *Journal of Human Development and Capability*, 14(1), 77–94.

Rabinow, P (Ed.) (1991) *The Foucault Reader: An Introduction to Foucault's Thought*. London: Penguin Social Sciences.

Rawls, J. (2009) *The Theory of Justice*, Revised Edition. Harvard: Harvard University Press.

Riaz, A. and Rahman, M. (Eds.) (2016) *Routledge Handbook of Contemporary Bangladesh*. Oxford: Routledge.

Sajjad, T. and Hardig, A. (2016) Too many enemies: mobilization, marginalisation and political violence. *Terrorism and Political Violence*, 29, 6, 1106–1125.

Sen, A. (1992) *Inequalities Re-examined*. New York, NY: Clarendon Press.
(1999) *Development as Freedom*. Oxford: Oxford University Press.
(2009) *The Idea of Justice*. London: Penguin Books.

Sen, A. and Dreze, J. (2002). *India: Development and Participation*. Oxford: Oxford University Press.

Sewell, W. (1992) The Theory of structure: duality, agency and transformation. *American journal of Sociology*. 91, 1, 1–29.

Sheehan, S. (2003) *Anarchism*. London: Reaktian Books.

Simon, R. (1982) *Gramsci's political thought: An Introduction*. London: Lawrence and Wishart Ltd.

Surin, K. (1990) Marxists and the withering away of the state. *Social Texts*. 27, 35–54

Van Schendel, W. (2009) *A History of Bangladesh*. Cambridge: Cambridge University Press.

Zimmer, A. and Freise, M. (2008) Bringing society back in: Civil society, social capital and third sector. *Civil Society and Governance in Europe*. 19–42

The Operationalisation Frontier

8 | Sen's Capability Approach, Social Choice Theory and the Use of Rankings

FLAVIO COMIM

Introduction

The concept of 'ranking' plays an important role in Amartya Sen's capability approach and in his conceptualization of Justice. It derives from Arrow's (1951) formulation of social choice and Sen's early attempts at broadening the informational basis of social choice through the use of ranges of weights for generating partial orderings (Sen, 1970a, 2002). Within this context, the use of rankings can be adapted to a wide range of conceptual distinctions important to Sen's capability approach, such as those of sympathy and commitment (1977) and agency and well-being freedom and achievement (2005).

Moreover, rankings and weights are key ingredients in Sen's conceptualization of the links between reflected social valuation, public reasoning and collective choice given that, according to him, any serious social judgment should accommodate non-commensurabilities and pluralities of values (in individual and collective choices). These values do not need to be restricted to what Sen called 'culmination outcomes' but can be part of 'comprehensive outcomes' (Sen, 2002 [1997]), including not simply characteristics of the processes of choice but also key features of decision-making such as obligations and responsibilities.

An investigation of Sen's distinct concepts of rankings is necessary to human development for at least three reasons. First, it can show how people's goals can go well-beyond personal self-interest (Sen, 1985a), a hypothesis widely shared by Nussbaum (2013). Second, it can illustrate the key relevance of social choice theory in the formulation of Sen's capability approach (an aspect insufficiently discussed in the capability literature, see Qizilbash, 2007). Finally, it can give more concreteness to Sen's argument for public reasoning and the importance of a broad notion of rationality in the capability approach (Scanlon, 1998).

The aim of this chapter is to explore the links between Sen's capability approach and its Social Choice foundations, investigating the role of rankings in their characterization. It examines operational ways to work with multidimensionality and noncommensurability where competing indicators can give rise to different rankings of alternatives based on different criteria or informational spaces. For instance, subjective indicators of satisfaction with public services can give rise to rankings that can disagree with objective rankings based on basic capabilities (Drèze and Sen, 2013). This chapter also examines concepts such as 'intersections', 'internal consistency', 'range of weights', 'partial rankings', 'goals' and 'reflected evaluation' among other concepts involved in use of rankings. It does not try to offer a blueprint for how to deal with distributive conflicts and aggregative considerations, but rather examines how to use consequence-sensitive reasoning (Sen, 1979) in a variety of contexts.

With these objectives, the chapter is divided into three parts. The first part examines the social choice foundations of the capability approach, contextualizing the role of 'rankings' in valuation processes. The second part discusses the operational use of rankings and their characteristics, showing how they can be used for individual and social welfare evaluations. Finally, the third part explores some implications for conceptualizing the use of the capability approach within a human development perspective.

Social Choice and the Capability Approach

What is the approach that Amartya Sen uses in his empirical works? From *Poverty and Famines* (1981a) to *An Uncertain Glory* (2013) (with Jean Drèze),[1] it is difficult to find explicit references to a single approach when Sen examines issues such as poverty, health, education and inequality. Indeed, one could *prima-facie* say that Sen has tried many different evaluative approaches throughout his career. In the field of social welfare, it seems that its first attempt was using 'the meta-ranking approach' (1974, 1979), followed by 'the named goods approach' (1979), 'the capability approach' (1979), 'the vector view' (1980/1), 'the capabilities right system' (1982), 'the positional

---

[1] In *An Uncertain Glory* the authors refer often to 'human capabilities' but not to the capability approach as an evaluative framework.

approach' (1983) and 'the intersection approach' (1986). All these approaches had some points in common, namely, they were all part of Sen's defence of pluralism in normative evaluations and they were all constituents of his overarching approach based on Social Choice Theory (SCT) whose roots can be found in his path-breaking *Collective Choice and Social Welfare* (1970). In fact, this sequence of apparently different approaches only reveals that Sen was just trying to brand a single approach based on his SCT, as discussed below.

When it comes to the 'capability approach' (CA) the most certain thing is that it refers to the choice of informational spaces in assessing social possibilities. On the one hand, this is coherent with Sen's defence of pluralism. For him, life is diverse and heterogeneous and for this reason normative judgments made by different people under different circumstances are bound to be complex giving rise to different methods to examine them. On the other hand, the fact that Sen does not appeal systematically to the CA as a way of examining social welfare judgments suggests that the CA is only part of a broader framework of analysis that can be found elsewhere.

Indeed, in several opportunities[2] Sen (e.g. 2002, 2009) has manifestly expressed that his overarching framework for normative evaluations is Social Choice Theory. The CA is indeed strategically key for Sen's SCT in broadening the informational basis used in social evaluations,[3] but it does not seem to provide the same range of tools and analytical structure that comes with SCT. It is indeed remarkable how the links between the CA and SCT have not been further explored by the CA secondary literature.[4]

---

[2] Sen (2002) refers to the revised version of his Nobel Prize paper, 'The Possibility of Social Choice' (1998).

[3] In *Development as Freedom* (1999), Chapter 3, Sen refers to 'capability information' and 'capability perspective' (see e.g. p. 81) applying it through the use of (i) the direct approach, (ii) the supplementary approach, (iii) the indirect approach, suggesting that capabilities are key ingredients but not the main framework of analysis.

[4] Sen (2009: 94–5) explains that, 'Because the apparent remoteness of formal social choice theory from matters of immediate interest, many commentators have tended to see its applicability as being extremely limited. The uncompromising mathematical nature of formal social choice theory has also contributed to this sense of remoteness of the discipline of social choice from applicable practical reason'. He strongly criticizes this interpretation saying (p. 95) 'I would argue that not only is this conclusion wrong, almost the exact opposite may be true', in particular, as 'an evaluative discipline'.

In one of the very few notable exceptions in this literature, Qizilbash (2007) examines the links between the CA and SCT trying to explore their differences and complementarities. He does not seem to disagree with the above remark that the relevance of the CA is mostly for providing broader informational spaces for evaluation (what he calls a 'thin view'). However, he tends to see SCT as a field of application of the CA[5] based on public reasoning (what he calls a 'thick view'). This in itself is not a problem, but it raises the question of why does everyone continue to call the CA 'an approach', if its field of application is given by a different approach? Indeed, essential items for any evaluative approach, such as selection of weights, seem to be within Sen's thick view, as argued by Qizilbash (2007: 176). As much as his interpretation provides an articulated and consistent view of Sen's CA and SCT it leads to an *overlap of approaches* when, for instance, he concludes that 'Sen's thick view [he referred to it earlier as an approach] thus provides a framework [an approach?] for applying the capability approach ...' (2007: 185). One could try to scrutinize the conceptual differences between 'view', 'perspective', 'approach' and 'framework' but they are bound to have little practical relevance.

Sen (2009: 232) clarifies that the CA 'does not, on its own, propose any specific formula about how that information [on capabilities] may be used' and in addition (pp. 232–33) that 'it does not lay down any blueprint for how to deal with conflicts between, say, aggregative and distributive considerations'. It is clear that given Sen's pluralism, he wishes to avoid imposing specific recommendations about how societies should establish their priorities and define their social policies. But at the same time, it seems that the core of an evaluative exercise is not addressed by the CA, what raises again the same question about to what extent shall we call it 'an approach?' We should not confuse this argument with a claim for predefining weights in valuation exercises (because this would be tantamount to eliminating the role of individual and public scrutiny). As he summarizes (2009: 296–97),

---

[5] Qizilbash (2007: 170) argues that 'Sen also suggests that some relevant issues about the application of the capability approach, particularly issues relating to weights and the selection of valuable capabilities or functionings, are social choice problems'. He reiterates this point when discussing the use of aggregative indexes and arguing that (p. 176) 'Nothing in Sen's thin view commits one to following any of these routes, since the thin view *only* advocates the importance of the spaces of capability and functioning' (my italics).

'Capability is, in fact, no more than a perspective in terms of which the advantages and disadvantages of a person can be reasonably assessed'.

Within the context of SCT, the broadening of informational spaces (for instance, by using capability spaces) is important as a possible way for circumventing Arrow's (1951) impossibility theorem. The problem goes back to Lionel Robbins' (1938) critique of interpersonal comparisons of utility and how Pareto optimality has been used to bridge this gap within contemporary welfare economics. As Sen (1996: 55) has put it, 'the most likely route of escaping the Arrow dilemma in making social welfare judgments lies not in any marginal modification of one of the Arrow axioms, but in the general direction of enriching the informational input into the analysis'. In particular, by using 'capabilities' that are objective (in contrast to subjective utilities) Sen can assemble different types of interpersonally comparable information.[6] However, his argument is not about capabilities *per se* but about pluralism given that the mechanical use of a single formula, even if based on capabilities, would be similarly inadequate. As he argued, the informational base of capabilities can illuminate individuals' real opportunities 'But that does not, in any way, 'close' the issue of informational bases of social choice' (1996: 61). First, because capability rankings would be incomplete and partial just as any other ranking; second, because other considerations (for instance about processes[7]) can also be relevant and finally because the existence of conflicting demands cannot all be resolved by capability spaces.

But what could be said of SCT? Most importantly, what are the main features of Sen's SCT that would be relevant for examining human development issues? To what extent can SCT's analytical structure provide an approach to the use of capability spaces in social evaluations? Answering these questions would put in evidence the use of

---

[6] The question is not overcome by using of cardinality. In his classic *Collective Choice and Social Welfare* (1970a) Sen demonstrates that even following the cardinal route would not completely solve the problem of interpersonal comparability within Arrow's framework.

[7] In 'Elements of a Theory of Human Rights' Sen (2004: 336) argues that 'Although the idea of capability has considerable merit in the assessment of the opportunity aspect of freedom, it cannot possibly deal adequately with the process aspect of freedom, since capabilities are characteristics of individual advantages, and they fall short of telling us enough about the fairness or equity of the processes involved, or about the freedom of citizens to invoke and utilize procedures that are equitable'.

different forms of rankings in Sen's work. Thus, the main characteristics of Sen's SCT for systematic social welfare judgments are[8]:

1. Pluralism: as the recurrent example of 'the three children and a flute' illustrates[9], it is possible to find evaluations that have to face competing reasons that are equally impartial, non-arbitrary and valid. In this sense, pluralism can be seen as an argument for evaluations based on informationally-rich accounts of state of affairs and as a clear critique of welfarism (that reduces or eliminates diverging principles and conflicts into a common amorphous denominator). Behind Sen's pluralism there is the idea, following Adam Smith, that people can have a variety of motivations (or moral sentiments). In terms of Sen's own contribution to SCT, an important milestone was his work on 'the impossibility of a Paretian liberal', not simply because it was the first formal formulation of individual rights in welfare economics but because it introduced, with its pluralism, non-consequential features into welfare evaluations (Suzumura, 2011).

2. Comparative analysis: as the example of one trying to choose between 'a Picasso and a Dali'[10] illustrates, one does not need to use an ideal reference in order to choose between alternatives that one faces. Indeed, assessments can be made within the limits of the possibilities of what is available and what it is possible to compare, rather than between 'optimal'[11] options. In his early SCT work, Sen (1970a, item 7.4) investigates the range of possibilities for comparing options (following Arrow's 1951 approach of *ordering* a sequence of pairwise alternatives) and introduces the concept of 'partial comparability'. Thus, between the world of non-comparability,

---

[8] Sen presents 'social choice as a framework for reasoning' in Chapter 4 of *The Idea of Justice*. He characterizes social choice by calling attention to seven elements. In his (2012) paper on 'The reach of social choice theory' he expanded to eight elements. Here, I chose to focus on the most distinguished of these elements, avoiding some possible subtleties and overlaps in Sen's classifications. For instance, his particular focus on comparative analysis seems conducive to partial solutions and his discussion of reasoned scrutiny appears to demand explicitness and public reasoning.

[9] This example has more recently appeared in several parts of *The Idea of Justice* (2009) (see, for instance, pages 12–15, 201 and 396–7).

[10] See *The Idea of Justice* (2009: 16–17).

[11] Sen (2002: 160) argues that there can be cases where one *best* alternative (optimization) is not necessary for maximization (choosing an alternative that is not worse than others).

where interpersonal comparisons are ruled out, and the world of full-comparability, where utilities are all commensurable, choosing what can be compared can be of direct relevance to the problem that has to be faced.[12] Although 'comparability' and 'partiality' are different concepts, they appear together when working with 'incomplete rankings'. They are compatible with the concept of 'maximization' that does not need full comparability given that it only requires that we do not choose an alternative that is worse than another (Sen, 2000: 486). Two options in an incomplete ranking, but that are better than all alternatives, can each be chosen following maximization.[13]

3. Reasoned scrutiny: as the example of someone who believes that 'the moon and the sun have the same size'[14] shows, people's views depend on their positionality that should be open to revision at both an individual and at a social level. Going beyond one's parochialism and revising one's evaluations is essential for being objective in one's views. Quite often individual and public scrutiny are part of similar processes, because the best way of achieving impartiality is to open one's views to informed debates and interactive discussions to see whether arguments can survive. Indeed, individual reflected evaluation is not enough. It needs to be open to public reasoning, as a way of testing the reach, reliability and robustness of evaluations. More concretely, Sen argues for 'open impartiality' as the most important strategy for achieving positional objectivity (Sen, 1993). Reasoned scrutiny comes with a strong argument against mechanical judgments; a constant critique that characterizes most of Sen's contributions to SCT and shapes his related criticisms of Welfarism and of Rawls's *Theory of Justice*.

Together, pluralism, comparative analysis and reasoned scrutiny provide the bones of Sen's social choice approach whose analytical structure, following in the footsteps of Arrow's SCT, can often be seen in Sen's work in the use of rankings in valuation processes. In fact,

---

[12] Comparability can thus be seen as question of degree. More importantly, as argued by Sen (1970a: 102) is that 'Complete comparability is not merely a doubtful assumption, it is also quite unnecessary'.

[13] As Sen has argued (2000: 487), 'This is the way maximality is defined in the mathematical literature, both in pure set theory, and in axiomatic economic analysis'.

[14] See *The Idea of Justice* (2009: 156).

much more than the use of capability informational spaces, the use of rankings can be understood as 'an approach' in Sen's analysis because it provides a methodological framework for helping with valuation exercises. As Sen argues (2009: 95), 'The outcomes of the social choice procedure take the form of ranking different states of affairs from a "social point of view", in the light of the assessments of the people involved'.

To sum up, as much as the role of the capability 'approach' seems indispensable for Sen's broadening of informational spaces in social welfare evaluations, it has a limited role and much more needs to be said about how SCT provides an overarching framework for social evaluations. Moreover, the use and interpretation of rankings needs to be further investigated.

Rankings and Their Characteristics

We often talk loosely about 'public policy' or 'societies' preferences' without due concern to the fact that what we call 'social preferences' very much depends on how individuals in a particular place collectively form their judgments and establish their joint priorities. Following this simple idea, introduced by Bergson, that social welfare can be represented by a function based on individual welfares, Arrow (1951) represents choice mechanisms by ordering relations or rankings.[15] An important distinction in this framework is between ordering tastes (about individuals' own utility) and values (about individuals' standards of equity or 'socializing desires'). Sen (1970a: 2) emphasizes that the concept of *orderings* is 'the basic constituent of collective choice' and explains that different orderings can be characterized depending on how they satisfy properties between binary relations, such as transitivity or completeness.[16] Whereas much of the SCT depends on the existence of complete orderings, Sen (1970a: 99) introduces the notion of 'partial ordering' (taking into account the fact that orderings do not have to be complete and not all elements are fully comparable, but there is some comparability/intersection between them) to show how

---

[15] In Arrow's and Sen's formulations, orderings are established based on binary relations where x R y means 'x is at least as good as y'.

[16] For instance, a 'quasi-ordering' is a ranking that satisfies reflexivity and transitivity, whereas an 'ordering' satisfies in addition the property of completeness. A 'partial ordering' satisfies reflexivity, transitivity and anti-symmetry.

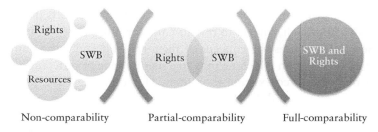

Non-comparability   Partial-comparability   Full-comparability

Figure 8.1 From non-comparability to full-comparability

it is possible to find out intermediate cases between non-comparability and full-comparability, as illustrated by Figure 8.1.

Sen (1974) further develops his early arguments about broader evaluation structures by introducing the notion of 'ordering the orderings' or 'ranking of rankings' or 'meta-ranking' as a framework for defining how people can morally deliberate among different sets of preferences. Starting from a pluralist perspective, he acknowledges that people can have legitimate non-commensurable moralities that might not be mechanically reducible to welfarist metrics. Thus, he introduces the analytical structure given by the notion of meta-rankings where people could exercise their morality by choosing one preference pattern over another. Sen (1982 [1977]: 99) argues that focusing on a single preference ordering is too simple and that 'The *purely* economic man is indeed close to being a social moron'.[17] A more elaborate analytical structure for orderings is therefore needed.

Imagine a ranking *A* that reflects your selfish personal welfare, a ranking *B* that represents an enlightened personal welfare (of reasonable people à la Rawls) and a ranking *C* that represents altruist welfare. The role of a meta-ranking is to allow a moral articulation between these different moral systems, for a given context, searching for 'the most moral' system in question, provided that it proves at all possible, or alternatively, finding a different ranking, say, *M*, that helps ordering each ranking vis-à-vis each other. Just as Sen (1970a) has argued, the resulting meta-ranking can be incomplete, reflecting a partial ordering. Thus, a meta-ranking is a broader structure not only in informational

[17] Sen (1982 [1977]: 89) argues that 'choice may reflect a compromise among a variety of considerations of which personal welfare may be just one' (e.g. commitment).

terms (allowing pluralism) but also in examining trade-offs in a comparative approach, subject to revision and scrutiny.

Sen (1981b) uses the concept of meta-ranking under the name of 'the vector view' in which he puts together a range of different (utility and non-utility) co-existing moralities. However, the basic principle of non-commensurability between different types of information and the need for reasoned scrutiny (and weights) remains the same as in the original formulation. Some additional element might be relevant for cutting across different types of information depending on the particular motivation involved. In fact, Sen (1981b: 207) suggests that 'the question of weighting of different types of pleasures or desires [should be] left open as an additional moral exercise'. Because life is complex and heterogeneous, and individuals' reasons and motivations are often divergent, pluralism is the most sensible principle to adopt. Non-commensurability is pervasive and a comparative analysis generating partial rankings might produce 'partial but useful' guidance.

In very basic terms, rankings can be different[18] not simply in terms of their specific ordering of options (for instance, a ranking that following a single criterion that considers options 'a' better than 'b' and 'b' better than 'c' is different from another that considers 'c' better than 'b' and 'b' better than 'a') but in terms of how they assemble different criteria, each producing its corresponding ordering. As much as the range of different criteria can be quite large, it is common to see criteria formulated around four kinds of informational spaces, namely:

1. Resources: monetary or non-monetary
2. Subjective well-being: pleasures, desires, desire fulfillment or choice
3. Rights: abstract or concrete; general rights or human rights
4. Capabilities: basic or non-basic

Whereas much of the capability literature, as we can see for instance in Comim et al. (2008), follows a narrow reading of the approach, exclusively focusing on capabilities as informational spaces for welfare evaluations, it remains a challenge to work with broader informational spaces in a more inclusive and encompassing ways.

---

[18] Strictly speaking, as mentioned before, rankings can be different according to the properties (or axioms) that they satisfy, such as reflexivity, completeness, transitivity, asymmetry, among others (see Sen, 1970a: 9 for a good introduction).

Within this context, following Sen's SCT, the main alternatives for working with rankings, that can operate within a variety of informational spaces, are:

1. Complete rankings: for any pair of alternatives, we can always say whether one is better than the other or if they are indifferent. Many well-known rankings, such as the Human Development Index (HDI) or the Happiness Score (HS) are presented as complete rankings. However, in a SCT comparative analysis, rankings do not have to be complete. Quite the opposite, as Sen (1985b: 20–1) mentions, 'The tyranny of "required completeness" has had a disastrous effect on many other problems in economic measurement, offering us a false choice between silence and babbling'.

2. Partial rankings: even when total comparability is not secured, it is possible to find grounds for some comparability between options. Formally speaking, Sen (1982 [1970b]: 209) notes that 'Partial comparability is the generic term to be used for every case of interpersonal comparability lying in between unit comparability and non-comparability', thus defining comparability as question of degree.[19] When it comes to partial orderings, incompleteness can be justified both on fundamental and pragmatic reasons (Sen, 1992). It is important to note that a partial ranking reflects a minimum standard, a lower limit, of what can be asserted without contradicting any of the other rankings.[20]

3. Intersection of shared rankings: the advantage of searching for a 'shared' partial ranking through the intersection of the set of chosen measures is that it can represent greater clarity and internal consistency than the ones achieved with partial rankings due to incompleteness. Sen (1997 [1973]: 72–3) explores the concept of 'intersection quasi-orderings', arguing that 'Such an intersection quasi-orderings has the advantage of avoiding exclusive reliance

---

[19] In the context of *The Idea of Justice*, Sen argues that (2009: 398) 'The basic issue here, which is simple enough when shorn of the analytical formalities, is the need to recognize that a complete theory of justice may well yield an incomplete ranking of alternative courses of decision, and that an agreed partial ranking will speak unambiguously in some cases and hold its silence in others'.

[20] Sen (1985b: 25) argues that 'Where the person would decide to draw the line is ultimately a matter of what view he or she would take of the nature and basis of the valuational exercise and the status of other views expressed in p* [the remaining set of partial or complete orderings]'.

on any particular measure and on the complete ordering generated by it which reflects its arbitrary features', alerting tough that the resulting ordering can be severely incomplete. An intersection of shared rankings does not eliminate the possibility of position-relative rankings within the context of 'situated evaluation' (Sen, 2000) but it is helpful in operationalizing the role of public reasoning in the definition of common standards of social well-being.

4. Lexicographic rankings: they are organized around hierarchical criteria in such a way that the first criterion of the ranking should be satisfied before we move on to the second and the second before we move to the third, and so on. This kind of ranking became well known after Rawls (1971) used it in his *A Theory of Justice*. In fact, he argued that (p. 43) 'I shall, in fact, propose an ordering of this kind by ranking the principle of equal liberty prior to the principle regulating economic and social inequalities'. Rawls gave total priority to liberty (the first principle) but other criteria, based for instance, on rights, could be used to put together a lexicographic ranking. In the case of a social ordering, this can be more complicated because the rights that individuals have might not be translated into the right of determining the relative ranking of an alternative within a social ranking (Nozick, 1974: 165). Lexicographic rankings do not prevent *per se* selection and discrimination among alternatives, but can often be used as a mechanical procedure.

5. Meta-rankings: these have the effect of broadening the valuational framework by adding an extra layer of deliberation in the choice of the organizing criterion. Reasoned scrutiny and public reasoning (in the context of open impartiality) are key ingredients in overcoming positionality and local parochialism in defining the 'most moral' ranking. It is true, as Sen remarks that (1996: 60), 'Our standards are not always uniform, ambiguities do exist, and there is often much scope for argument about what the standards should be'. For this reason we should not expect meta-rankings to provide complete rankings. Meta-rankings are not only about pluralism, non-commensurability, tolerance to divergences but mostly about a moral articulation based on flexible judgments about what is valuable and for what reasons. Meta-rankings take for granted the existence of irreconcilable divergences and do not see them as a negative state of affairs; instead, their incomplete and partial nature can be seen as a testimony to democracy and public reasoning.

The above categories of rankings should be understood in the context of the SCT core principles, namely, pluralism, comparative analysis and reflective scrutiny what means that we should not see them as 'rules of thumb' or 'mechanical procedures' to work with orderings. As Sen (1996: 61, footnote 23) warns us, 'The programme of relying entirely on *one* overall index that covers different considerations would be defective not only in the case of exclusive reliance on capability considerations, but also in proposals to have some other similarly aggregative index'. However, it might be worth considering that the concept of rankings and more broadly the notion of meta-rankings within SCT can provide an 'approach' for handling the evaluation of individual and social welfare. A meta-ranking could assist (in the sense of offering options for working with rankings and for their interpretation) in the selection of one ordering over another or a combination of them. By doing so, people can (individually and socially) exercise their powers of discretion, normally denied in complete utilitarian or rights-based rankings. Because people are diverse and have different motives and reasons behind their evaluations, it could be said that 'the meta-ranking approach may be seen as an attempt to exploit the psychology of mixed reasons' (Van der Veen, 1981: 355) in line with pluralism and examined scrutiny. Issues of altruism, cooperation, reasonableness, among others are of particular interest for the use of meta-rankings.

Implications for Human Development

The main consequence of considering the SCT as the overarching approach behind Sen's Social Welfare Analysis is that the capability 'approach' has a much more limited role than 'an approach'. This means more concretely that it should be used within Sen's informational pluralism. In addition, this implies a wider interpretation of the CA as a taxonomy of different informational spaces without a particular obsession with the use of capabilities for evaluating individuals' advantages or states of affairs. Going back to the main informational spaces discussed above, it is likely that different spaces will come with different criteria and that among them there will be a certain hierarchy established by different cultures and societies. Whatever the criteria that might come with them based on lexicographical orderings, sufficient thresholds or even a mechanical combination of certain key values, it is important to note that we have moved to a different question, namely, how to combine different informational spaces (with their respective criteria) in order to evaluate certain individual or social states of affairs?

One could try to establish (first-order) partial rankings between primary goods, capabilities, rights, human rights, subjective well-being and resources and use a matrix to ask questions when these do not match. For instance, when increasing resources are not translated into adequate capabilities (or functionings) one would be entitled to further investigate the conversion factors behind these processes. Similarly, when high subjective well-being is not supported by basic capabilities one should examine conditions that could lead to the adaptive preferences problem. An increase of resources when not translated into higher subjective well-being could be considered a problem of a hedonic treadmill. One would expect a close matching between human rights and basic capabilities, but when this is not the case one should examine the public reason basis for establishing these capabilities. The important point here is that by following the SCT as an approach would allow a more fruitful strategy in using capabilities as a limited strategy for operationalizing informational pluralism rather than demanding it to do all the job of a comprehensive approach (which it is unable to deliver anyway).

In other words, pluralism[21] allows us to consider all these informational spaces without pushing for an *a priori* superiority of any of them. But these spaces cannot be considered at face value without being scrutinized, as noted. For instance, the argument that 'resources are imperfect indicators of human well-being'[22] (that has become a 'human development mantra') signals the importance of evaluating how resources are used. Similarly, subjective well-being or happiness can provide an evidential role[23] in welfare evaluations (Sen, 2008) and should not be rejected because of its shortcomings. Rights and liberties should not be put 'on an absolute pedestal', as argued by Sen (2009: 59) because they should be seen alongside other concerns.[24]

---

[21] Pluralism seems to expand even further Arrow's condition of 'unrestricted domain' of social choice. For a good explanation see Craven (1992).

[22] See for instance Sen (1999: 80) that contributed to the popularization of this argument, together with UNDP's *Human Development Reports*.

[23] Happiness can be relevant as a criterion in assessing individual well-being and social achievement for other reasons. They are explored for instance in Sen (2008: 26–7).

[24] Sen criticizes Rawls's prioritization of liberty, arguing that 'It is indeed possible to accept that liberty must have some kind of priority, but total

A comparative analysis will prevent procedures that mechanically prioritize one criterion over others (without scope for deliberation) because this would turn reasoning into non-consequential forms. Instead, Sen (2000: 480) argues for 'broad consequential evaluation', emphasizing the importance of a more explicit and integrated framework of judgmental evaluation.

Rankings based on consequential evaluation should not be limited to 'culmination outcomes' (focusing only on final results) but should pay attention to 'comprehensive outcomes' (including the choice process,[25] in particular 'chooser dependence'), as explained by Sen (2002 [1997]). Other valuational issues are also relevant, such as the role of responsibility, obligations (perfect, imperfect) and duties, all of them related to the concept of individual agency. Sen (1985a) distinguishes between 'well-being freedom' and 'agency freedom'. In his words (1985a: 203) 'A person's 'agency freedom' refers to what the person is free to do and achieve in pursuit of whatever goals or values he or she regards as important. A person's agency aspect cannot be understood without taking note of his or her aims, objectives, allegiances, obligations, and – in a broad sense – the person's conception of the good'. The agency aspect seems to offer decisiveness (decision power throughout the set of alternatives) over other rankings in the context of a meta-ranking.[26] Agency can generate rankings that are different from those based on well-being orderings (Sen, 2009: 287).

Nevertheless, it should be noted that as important as informational pluralism is, it does not offer on its own analytical tools for actually passing judgment on individual and social states of affairs. For this it is

---

unrestrained priority is almost certainly an overkill' (2009: 65). However, Sen's criticism is very general because it applies both to 'rights-independent evaluations' (Utilitarists) and to 'rights-inclusive non-consequential procedures' (Libertarians) (2000: 493).

[25] The classical example is about the difference between 'winning an election' (culmination outcome) and 'fairly winning an election' (comprehensive outcome).

[26] Traditional concern with welfare has a much more limited scope within this framework. As argued by Sen (1985a: 206) 'the important thing to recognize is that the well-being aspect and the agency aspect of persons have dissimilar roles in moral accounting. They invite attention in *disparate* ways. At the risk of over simplification it can be said that the well-being aspect of a person is important in assessing a person's *advantage*, whereas the agency aspect is important in assessing what a person can do in line with his or her conception of *the good*'.

essential to follow a comparative analysis where a more extensive use of partial rankings and other forms of rankings can give the necessary flexibility for adapting different methods to distinct contexts. A single example should suffice to illustrate its consequences: let us take the case of the HDI.

The HDI has been constructed without the observance of several criteria put forward by Sen in his SCT: it does not follow pluralism in representing diverse informational spaces relevant for human development, it does not follow partial or intersection rankings but rather it forces complete rankings defined over continuous variables (even considering that with the introduction of geometric means in 2010 the degree of commensurability among different variables has been reduced) and it does not offer a participatory process for the definition of the index, opting instead for mechanical processes of aggregation of culmination indicators (ignoring 'comprehensive outcomes' in the characterization of countries' development). There are several problems that arise from the non-observance of these criteria, many of which have already been observed by UNDP (2010). But one of these problems that has been ignored is that the development picture that emerges should be much more fragmented in different groups (rather than the usual classification between very-high, high, medium and low human development categories). Initial simulations carried out using PyHasse software suggest that at least nine categories of development should be considered when a comparative analysis is taken more seriously into account.

When discussing the role of intersection quasi-orderings, Sen (1997 [1973]: 73) uses a Hesse diagram with a simple ordering with five countries and two noncomparabilities, arguing that (p. 72) 'Such an intersection quasi-ordering has the advantage of avoiding exclusive reliance on any particular measure and on the complete ordering generated by it which reflects its arbitrary features'. Here, the degree of incompleteness is just a measure of the conflict between different measures. The fact is that the level of complexity in using intersection of quasi-ordering for a larger number of countries and measures derived from different informational spaces can be quite high.

Finally, it should be acknowledged that 'reasoned scrutiny' is not an easy category to be employed. It is much easier to criticize mechanical algorithms for normative exercises rather than to implement schemes that promote people's participation and voice. Having said that, it seems that the structure provided by meta-rankings allows the choice of a distinct separate ranking among those rankings in question or the choice or introduction of a different ranking or concern in ordering all rankings altogether. Rather than being a mechanical procedure, like pre-established (explicit or implicit) weights, the meta-ranking structure proposes to add further reflections about the whole exercise of ranking. For instance, a meta-ranking could take into account the percentage of average public spending in health and education to weight the other rankings or consider an intersection of shared-rankings with human rights rankings or environmental rankings. The fundamental point about the links between reasoned scrutiny and meta-rankings is that somehow they should reflect the complexities of different moral compasses that can be used to represent individuals' public or individual priorities.

Conclusions

The main objective of this chapter was to call attention to the importance of SCT as the overarching framework behind Sen's CA. This should not be a new point, given the number of times that Sen himself has introduced SCT as his main framework of analysis. But it is remarkable how the capability literature has ignored the links between SCT and the CA. The discussion started questioning the role of the capability approach as an approach, highlighting instead the relevance of SCT as a broader approach for human development. In particular, it focused on its main characteristics, namely, pluralism, comparativeness and reasoned scrutiny as the key assets for working empirically with human development variables.

It also explored some alternatives for working with rankings, exploring the differences between complete rankings, partial rankings, intersection of rankings and finally meta-rankings. The use of rankings is at the heart of SCT as an approach not because of pluralism (a characteristic better left to the CA) but because of the comparative nature of social choice exercises. The characteristics of these comparisons are at the heart of Sen's main contributions to the discipline of social choice. It links well especially in regards to meta-rankings with its corresponding need for reasoned scrutiny.

From a very simple structure based on a plurality of informational spaces it is possible to build a matrix to verify what types of stories they are telling about individuals and states of affairs. The use of a wide range of rankings can unveil the different degrees of incompleteness of these stories and as such it can provide an analytical structure for thinking about human development on the lines suggested by Sen's SCT. These are some provisional conclusions, unspecific to the use of HDI rankings, but that could be the foundation for further work on using SCT as an approach for human development.

References

Arrow, K. (2012 [1951]) *Social Choice and Individual Values*, 3rd edn. New Haven, CT: Yale University Press.

Comim, F., Qizilbash, M. and Alkire, S. (2008) *The Capability Approach: Concepts, Measures and Applications*. Cambridge: Cambridge University Press.

Craven, J. (1992) *Social Choice: A Framework for Collective Decisions and Individual Judgments*. Cambridge: Cambridge University Press.

Dreze, J. and Sen, A. (2013) *An Uncertain Glory: India and Its Contradictions*. Princeton, NJ: Princeton University Press.

Nozick, R. (1974) *Anarchy, State, and Utopia*. Oxford: Blackwell, pp. 26–35, 150–66.

Nussbaum, M. (2013) *Political Emotions: Why Love Matters for Justice*. Cambridge: The Belknap Press.

Qizilbash, M. (2007) Social choice and individual capabilities. *Politics, Philosophy and Economics*, 6 (2), 169–92.

Rawls, J. (1971) *A Theory of Justice*. Oxford: Oxford University Press.

Robbins, L. (1938) Interpersonal comparisons of utility: A comment. *The Economic Journal*, 48 (192), 635–41.

Scanlon, T. (1998) *What We Owe to Each Other*. Cambridge: Harvard University Press.

Sen, A. (1970a) *Collective Choice and Social Welfare*. San Francisco, CA: Holden-Day.

(1970b) Interpersonal aggregation and partial comparability. In Sen, A. (ed.) *Choice, Welfare and Measurement*. Cambridge: Harvard University Press, pp. 203–21.

(1974) Choice, orderings and morality. In Korner, S. (ed.) *Practical Reason*. Oxford: Oxford University Press, pp. 54–67.

(1979) The welfare basis of real income comparisons: A survey. *Journal of Economic Literature*, 17 (1), 1–45.

(1981a) *Poverty and Famines: An Essay on Entitlement and Deprivation*. Oxford: Oxford University Press.

(1981b) Plural utility. *Proceedings of the Aristotelian Society*, LXXXI, 193–215.

(1982 [1977]) Rational fools: a critique of the behavioural foundations of economic theory. In Sen, A. (ed.) *Choice, Welfare and Measurement.* Cambridge: Harvard University Press, pp. 84–106.

(1985a) Well-being, agency and freedom. *Journal of Philosophy*, 82 (4), 169–221.

(1985b) *Commodities and Capabilities.* Oxford: Oxford University Press.

(1992) *Inequality Re-examined.* Oxford: Oxford University Press.

(1993) Positional objectivity. *Philosophy and Public Affairs*, 22 (2), 126–45.

(1996) On the foundations of welfare economics: utility, capability and practical reason. In Farina, F., Hahn, F. and Vannucci, S. (eds.) *Ethics, Rationality and Economic Behaviour.* Oxford: Clarendon Press, pp. 50–65.

(1997 [1973]) *On Economic Inequality.* Expanded edition. Oxford: Clarendon Press.

(1999) *Development as Freedom.* Oxford: Oxford University Press.

(2000) Consequential evaluation and practical reason. *The Journal of Philosophy*, XCVIII (9), 477–502.

(2002) The possibility of social choice. In Sen, A. (ed.) *Rationality and Freedom.* Cambridge: Belnak Press, pp. 65–118.

(2002 [1997]) Maximisation and the act of choice. In Sen, A. (ed.) *Rationality and Freedom.* Cambridge: Belnak Press, pp. 158–205.

(2004) Elements of a theory of human rights. *Philosophy and Public Affairs*, 32 (4), 315–56.

(2008) The economics of happiness and capability. In Bruni, L., Comim, F. and Pugno, M. (eds.) *Capabilities and Happiness.* Oxford: Oxford University Press, pp. 16–27.

(2009) *The Idea of Justice.* Cambridge: Harvard University Press.

(2012) The reach of social choice theory. *Social Choice and Welfare*, 39, 259–72.

Suzumura, K. (2011) Welfarism, individual rights, and procedural fairness. In Arrow K. J., Sen, A., and Suzumura, K. (eds.) *Handbook of Social Choice and Welfare*, Volume II. Oxford: North Holland/Elsevier, pp. 606–85.

UNDP (2010) *Human Development Report.* New York: United Nations Development Programme.

Van der Veen, R. (1981) Meta-rankings and collective optimality. *Social Science Information*, 20, 345–74.

9 | Selecting Capabilities for Development

An Evaluation of Proposed Methods

MORTEN F. BYSKOV

Introduction

Several methods for the selection of capabilities and functionings have been proposed within the capability literature. Which method should we prefer when selecting capabilities and functionings that are normatively relevant for development? In this chapter, fifteen proposed methods, categorized as *ad hoc*, foundational, procedural, and mixed (or multi-stage) methods, are identified and discussed.[1] *Ad hoc* methods base their selection of capabilities on pragmatic considerations, foundational methods on some ultimate normative value or principle, procedural methods on more open-ended, democratic information, while mixed (or multi-stage) methods employ two or more foundational and procedural methods in conjunction.

It is argued that selecting capabilities and functionings relevant for human development requires a mixed (or multi-stage) method. *Ad hoc* methods are dismissed because of their lack of methodological and normative justification, foundational methods due to a lack of democratic legitimacy and contextual sensitivity, while procedural methods are found vulnerable to implicit biases and adaptive preferences. Mixed (or multi-stage) methods, however, can provide both methodological and normative justifications as well as provide democratic legitimacy and contextual sensitivity.

The chapter adds to the capability literature in two ways. First, it provides an up-to-date systematic and comprehensive discussion of the many distinct methods for the selection of capabilities and functionings found within the capability literature.[2] Second, it identifies

---

[1] An overview of the general and specific methods, identified within the capability literature, and their main proponents can be found in Table 9.1.
[2] It should be noted, though, that Alkire (2002) undertook a similar endeavor in regards to the different list of capabilities and functionings in the capability

key advantages of, and concerns with, the different methods. The chapter thus answers an important question: by which method should we select normatively relevant capabilities and functionings for development purposes?

The chapter is structured as follows: Before the identified methods are discussed, the first section introduces and discusses a persistent disagreement between capability scholars interested in the selection of relevant capabilities, namely whether it is a philosophical or a democratic task. It is argued that the binary distinction between the democratic and philosophical positions is too simple to capture the diversity of methods by which capability scholars have attempted to sketch a list of relevant capabilities. The next four sections introduce, analyze, and discuss the four general methodological categories – *ad hoc*, foundational, procedural, and mixed (or multi-stage) methods – as well as their more specific methods in turn. From this discussion, it is concluded that the multi-stage method, which I label *synthesizing methods*, is best suited to the task selecting normatively relevant capabilities and functionings because it can integrate theoretical and empirical, technical and procedural insights alike.

Philosophical, Democratic, and Practical Concerns in Selecting Capabilities

The capability literature has traditionally presented the issue of selecting relevant or valuable capabilities as a disagreement between those who hold that it is a public task and those who argue that some essential capabilities can and should be selected by normative philosophers. While the former, procedural or democratic position has commonly been associated with Sen, the latter, philosophical position is often attributed to Nussbaum and her followers (Byskov, 2016: 3).

Although it is true that the methods for the selection of relevant capabilities can be more or less democratic and more or less philosophical, this binary distinction between the democratic and philosophical positions is too simple to capture the diversity of methods by which capability scholars have attempted to sketch a list of relevant capabilities. Ballon (2013: 7), for example, identifies three general methods

---

literature. Alkire, however, did not engage in the critical analysis and discussion of *how* these lists were brought about – a gap that this chapter will fill.

used in the empirical capability literature: normative views, quantitative methods, and especially designed surveys. *Normative views* base their selection of capabilities either *ad hoc* on the values of the researcher or on moral theory (e.g. a theory of justice). *Quantitative methods* extract relevant capabilities from statistical data, either by summarizing the information in the original dataset or by confirming them through further quantitative analysis. Finally, *especially designed surveys* gather information about relevant and valuable capabilities through qualitative studies, often with a specific purpose. Other methods recognized in the literature include democratic deliberation and participatory exercises (Burchardt and Vizard, 2011: 95).

Whereas Ballon (2013) merely surveys and categorizes some of the empirical capability literature, this chapter goes beyond Ballon's categories to analyze and discuss the *justification* of the proposed methods for the selection of capabilities. Before the various methods are discussed, three preliminary remarks should be made. First, it is important to note that the chapter will not provide a comprehensive survey of the empirical capability literature. In that respect the reader is referred to Ballon (2013) and Robeyns (2006) as good starting points. Rather, the following sections will be an amalgamation of the literature, examples of the various methods through references to empirical studies and practical uses, where appropriate, will of course be provided.

Second, not all of the identified methods are explicitly concerned with development and some are only secondarily concerned with the selection of capabilities. This, however, does not exclude the possibility that they may actually be appropriate for the selection of capabilities relevant for development purposes and thus warrant further scrutiny in this regard. While most of the identified methods are found to be question-begging when applied to selecting capabilities for development purposes, *it is by no means* intended to deny their applicability in other regards nor that they may play a valuable part of a method for the selection of relevant capabilities for development or otherwise. In fact, the aim is to show that all of these methods may provide us with crucial insights for the selection of relevant capabilities for human development, although neither method is in itself *sufficient* for this purpose (see also Alkire (2008) for a similar conclusion).

Third, a list of capabilities can have different purposes. For example, a list of basic capabilities may be used to specify a capability theory of justice while the relative welfare of a society may be indicated by a list of functionings that its citizens have. A list of capabilities and functionings relevant for human development may have two main purposes. First, it can be used to *evaluate* existing human development policies and, second, to *develop* new ones. In the first case, the existing states of affairs and human development practices are interpreted and judged through the lens of a list of capabilities; in the latter case, the list of capabilities provides the normative requirement, which should be implemented in practice.

Without further ado, let me proceed to the analysis, categorization, and evaluation of the methods proposed within the capability literature. An overview of the methods can be found in Table 9.1. The fifteen identified methods are divided into four general methodological categories: *ad hoc*, foundational, procedural, and mixed (or multi-stage) methods.[3] We can characterize the four methodological categories in the following way:

- *Ad hoc* methods are characterized by their lack of methodological justification. These methods do not adhere to any normative theories, but rather base their selection of capabilities on *ad hoc* considerations, such as the purpose of the study, the researcher's own values, or practical and pragmatic concerns. For example, a welfare economist may simply take an existing dataset, and base their selection on whatever functionings are included in that dataset. The selection is then fully determined by the choice of the dataset and the available functionings in the dataset.
- Foundational methods hold that a list of capabilities and functionings can be derived (solely) from some ultimate normative value or principle, such as human agency, human dignity, or human rights, which grounds the selection. As such, foundational lists tend to claim to be universally applicable, although the items on the lists may be further specified to suit local circumstances.
- Procedural methods derive a list of capabilities from an open-ended empirical or deliberative procedure. As such, these methods base the selection on people's (reasoned) subjective preferences. A list of capabilities is thus contingent on the social, cultural, and political

---

[3] It should be noted that each of these terms might carry different connotations depending upon one's discipline. I shall here use the terms in the philosophical tradition and otherwise explain exactly how they are to be understood.

Table 9.1 *Overview of methods for the selection of capabilities and functionings proposed within the human development and capability literature*

General methodology	Description	Specific methods		Selected authors
Ad hoc methods	Selection based on *ad hoc* considerations **Characteristics:** Provisional; contextual; pragmatic or intuitive justification	Purpose of study		Human Development Index (UNDP, 2015), Sen (1985a, b), Slottje (1991), Klasen (2000)
		Researcher's own values/normative views		
		Pragmatic concerns and practical issues		
Foundational methods	Normatively relevant capabilities and functionings are derived from normative values and principles **Characteristics:** Absolute; universal; theoretical justification	Deductive reasoning	Internalist essentialism	Early Nussbaum (1990; 1992), Qizilbash (1998)
			Dialectically necessary judgments	Claassen and Düwell (2013)
		Overlapping consensus		Later Nussbaum (2011b)
		Human rights theory		Vizard (2006, 2007, 2010), Fukuda-Parr (2011), Osmani (2005), Sengupta (2002)
		Technical knowledge		
		Others		

Method	Characteristics	Approach	References
Procedural methods	Normatively relevant capabilities and functionings are contingent on the social, cultural, and political context **Characteristics:** Democratic; open-ended; contextual; empirical or discursive justification	Deliberative democracy	Anderson (1999, 2003), Crocker (2005, 2008), Drydyk (2005), Sen (1999a, b, 2001, 2002), Sen and Scanlon (2004), Drèze and Sen (2002)
		Qualitative analysis — Narrative approaches	Hodgett and Deneulin (2009), Biggeri et al. (2006), Phelps (2006), Clark (2002, 2005)
		Participatory approaches	Biggeri et al. (2006), Clark (2009), Frediani (2007), Doyal and Gough (1991)
		Quantitative analysis — Data-driven selection	Schokkaert and Oortgem (1990), Lelli (2001)
		Confirmatory methods	Kuklys (2005), Krishnakumar (2007), Comim (2008)
Mixed (or multi-stage) methods	Integrates two or more technocratic and procedural methods **Characteristics:** Holistic; dialectical; conflicting; both theoretical and empirical/discursive justification	Comparative methods	Brock (2009), Burchardt and Vizard (2011), Vizard (2010), Holland (2014a,b)
		Synthesizing methods	Alkire (2002), Claassen (2011), Khader (2011)

context and is justified based on empirical findings and/or the political and deliberative discourse.

- Mixed (or multi-stage) methods combine one or more foundational method(s) with one or more procedural method(s). As such, mixed methods aim to integrate different sources of knowledge (e.g. normative theory, human rights theory, qualitative and quantitative analyses, democratic deliberations) to provide a dialectical and holistic approach.

In the following sections, I analyze and discuss each general methodological category, and their more specific methods, in turn. It is shown that the first three methodologies – i.e. *ad hoc*, foundational, and procedural methods – all have serious shortcomings when applied to the context of selecting capabilities and functionings for human development purposes.[4]

Ad hoc *Methods*

The first set of methods for the selection of capabilities distinguishes itself by its lack of methodological justification. That is, these methods base the selection of capabilities and functionings on *ad hoc* or pragmatic considerations, such as personal values, intuitions, or availability of data, and hence lack both robust normative and methodological justifications. As these methods and their subsequent lists of capabilities lack normative and methodological justification, I shall not regard them as sufficiently justified to warrant further discussion other than to mention them in the name of completeness. We can distinguish three such methods. The first set of methods base their selection of capabilities on the particular purpose of the study. The second uses the researcher's own values as the basis for the selection (Ballon, 2013: 7, 9–10) while the third set selects capabilities out of pragmatic concerns, e.g. a lack of reliable or available data on some capabilities (Hodgett and Deneulin, 2009: 66).

First, the capability approach can be applied to many specific purposes and the relevant capabilities may vary between these different purposes. For example, we may want to investigate a rural community's

---

[4] Each specific method may be more suitable for other tasks, such as the development of a capability theory of justice, particular empirical studies, or the conceptualization of a specific domain, such as education or health care.

access to clean drinking water. For such an investigation it stands to reason that some capabilities are more relevant than others. While access to clean water reservoirs, wells, and means of transportation are crucial capabilities in this context, other capabilities, such as having the freedom to be a mother or to be sheltered, are less important, although crucial in other respects. Restricting the selection of relevant capabilities in this way is entirely *ad hoc* and specific to the purpose. In doing so, the researcher fails to consider whether the capabilities in question are at all relevant to the specific community or whether they are normatively important (although, of course, the researcher may have a good intuition in both regards).

Second, Ballon (2013: 9) identifies a set of empirical studies in which the list of capabilities is based on the interests and/or values of the researcher. Again, the selection of capabilities here is made *ad hoc* because the researcher does not base it on any evidence of its normative importance for people's well-being and development (although, of course, the researcher may very well be correct in his/her assumption). The Human Development Index (HDI) selection of capabilities (i.e. basic education, longevity, and income) may be seen as an example of such *ad hoc* selection process. Although the value of these three indicators has been defended in the Human Development Reports, the decision to restrict the number of capabilities was predominantly on a political basis as it fostered clarity and brevity. Accordingly, the HDI has often been accused of providing an incomplete and superficial picture of human well-being and development.

Third, Hodgett and Deneulin (2009: 66) note that many researchers do not base their selection of capabilities on normative or practical reason, but rather on "pragmatic concerns of data availability." Because some capabilities are notoriously difficult to measure, they are often not considered by researchers. There are three reasons underlying researchers' omission of certain capabilities. First, there may be no data available on that particular capability and it may be difficult to obtain any due to it being difficult to measure for one reason or another (e.g. it could be a culturally sensitive subject). For example, data on domestic violence is not readily available and victims of domestic violence are often averse to discuss the subject. Thus, researchers may make the pragmatic decision to include other dimensions of gender equity while excluding domestic violence. Second, the available data may not be reliable or reflect reality. For example, the survey may not investigate all sources of information, while subjects may misrepresent or report false data. Whilst omitting such incomplete or unreliable data might be valid, this decision is nonetheless based on pragmatic considerations. Finally, the researchers themselves may be vulnerable to cognitive biases that lead them to ignore certain otherwise relevant dimensions.

Thus, in sum, there may be a variety of pragmatic or practical reasons why capability scholars – especially empirical researchers – may choose to include or omit certain capabilities. These reasons, nevertheless, remain entirely *ad hoc*, as they are not based on considerations of the normative relevance or value of these capabilities. *Ad hoc* methods for the selection of relevant capabilities are inadequate and inappropriate exactly because they fail to consider the relevance and justification of its capabilities and functionings. A selection of capabilities for development purposes must be minimally justifiable, both as a matter of normative theory (Nussbaum, 2003: 47; Claassen, 2011: 496) or democratic legitimacy (Robeyns, 2005: 199; Jaggar, 2006; Claassen, 2011: 491; Byskov, 2016: 5). The following two sections thus discuss two general methodologies, which aim to provide either a theoretical grounding or a procedural justification of a list of capabilities and functionings.

Foundational Methods

Methods belonging to the second category arrive at a list of capabilities and functionings through theoretical reasoning (as opposed to deriving it from empirical studies). As such, they all rely on generalized hypotheses about what is necessary for decent human life or a just state of affairs. We can identify three sets of foundational methods: deductive reasoning, overlapping consensus, and technical knowledge. In this section each is discussed in turn.

The most prominent type of foundational method is *deductive reasoning*. Deductive reasoning is the idea that one starts out with a normative theory, which includes some ultimate and fundamental value(s) or principle(s), such as human dignity or agency, and then work backwards to identify the capabilities and functionings that are necessary for people to have in order to satisfy this normative theory. In other words, from what is morally desirable we can deduce a list of relevant capabilities. Especially the early Nussbaum (1990, 1992) uses a version of deductive reasoning, which she labels "internalist essentialism."

Nussbaum's *internalist essentialism* identifies human characteristics by asking us whether or not we agree with certain common sense judgments about human life. For example, does human life involve social relationships? Someone denying this common sense judgment faces a trilemma (Nussbaum, 1995: 108–9). If she cannot convince everyone else of her conviction, she must either sever ties with her friends and family and go live by herself, or she must contradict her own conviction that human life does not include social relationships. Nussbaum claims that it is implausible that people would be convinced that human life does not involve social relations and since the second option comes at such a high cost it is doubtful whether anyone would choose it. If these assumptions hold, Nussbaum argues, we should include the capability for social relations, such as holding friendships and participating in a community, on a list of essential characteristics of human life.[5]

Claassen and Düwell (2013) have criticized Nussbaum's method of internal essentialism. While sympathetic to Nussbaum's project of identifying essential capabilities through a process of deductive reasoning, Claassen and Düwell (2013) argue that insofar as the critic of Nussbaum's list is sufficiently willing to deny some of the items on the list, he is perfectly able to do so. For example, though Nussbaum include the capability for humor on her list, while omitting the capability for aggression, it is perfectly conceivable that someone may live an aggressive life without humor and that "we have no reason to think that the costs of that person doing so are unbearably high" (Claassen and Düwell, 2013: 500).

As an alternative to Nussbaum's method, Claassen and Düwell (2013) suggest that there are certain capabilities that any agent must necessarily accept insofar as she is an agent; something that would be self-contradictory to deny because the denial itself necessitates having this capability. Claassen and Düwell (2013: 501) find this argument in Gewirth's (1978, 1996) concept of *dialectically necessary judgments*. Dialectically necessary judgments are the things we cannot deny on pain of self-contradiction (Claassen and Düwell, 2013: 504–5). The method of dialectically necessary judgments starts out from the claim that in order to make *any* moral judgments, it is dialectically necessary for

---

[5] It should be noted, however, that Nussbaum (2000: 83) acknowledges that her list of capabilities does not include all characteristics that we recognize as human (such as the propensity for violence and cruelty), but only those capabilities that can be morally defended.

us to value having the capability for agency because agency is a necessary condition for making moral judgments in the first place (Claassen
and Düwell, 2013: 504). From the claim that we recognize ourselves as
agents, Gewirth argues that it is dialectically necessary for us to value
the means for that enable us to exercise our agency, namely freedom
and well-being, broadly defined. (Claassen and Düwell, 2013: 505).
Accordingly, a list of capabilities and functionings should include the
freedoms and the well-being necessary to exercise our agency.

However, there are many issues that are relevant for development,
which do not concern the necessary means for agency and many questions can be answered both affirmatively and negatively without violat-
ing one's agency. Consider, for example, the issue of teen pregnancies,
which is a big problem in low- and middle-income countries, according to WHO (2015). Should the capabilities for sexual education and
contraception be a matter of development out of dialectical necessity?
It is difficult to see how denying oneself the right to these capabilities
is self-contradictory to the exercise of one's agency or that the generic
features of one's agency – well-being and freedom – are thereby denied.
It is perfectly consistent for someone to deny these capabilities without
consequently having her agency, well-being, or freedom threatened.
That is, the capabilities for sexual education and contraception are
arguably not linked to one's capacity for making moral judgments and,
hence, denying them would not (necessarily) amount to denying one's
agency or the necessary means to exercise this agency.

Of course, it would be an entirely other matter if these rights were
denied *by someone else* and whatever we think about development, it
should not clash with the rights of all agents to well-being and freedom. But because the method of dialectical necessary judgments starts
from what *oneself* as an agent, defined as the capacity to make moral
judgments, can or cannot deny as a matter of self-contradiction, it
remains indeterminate in cases where one does not deny one's agency
or generic features thereof, namely well-being and freedom. While
the example does not entail that the method of dialectically necessary
judgments must remain entirely silent on these issues, it does imply
that the method cannot by itself fulfill the role of selecting relevant
capabilities for human development purposes.

Departing from her internalist essentialism, Nussbaum (2011b)
has more recently justified her list of capabilities, following Rawls,
by relying on an *overlapping consensus*. The method of overlapping

consensus proceeds by identifying the capabilities and functionings, which different ethical systems can agree to. As an example, religious freedom can be subject to an overlapping consensus among different religious ethical systems insofar as they all want the freedom to practice their religious beliefs, although they disagree on many other issues.

Barclay (2003), Ferracioli and Terlazzo (2014) and Robeyns (2016), however, have argued that several of the items on Nussbaum's list cannot be subject to an overlapping consensus. For example, as Robeyns (2016: 14–15) argues, it is difficult to envision how pro-choice and pro-life activists could ever come to an overlapping consensus on the issue of having the capability to abortion, which is contained under the capability of bodily integrity on Nussbaum's list (Dixon et al., 2011). Nussbaum's list of capabilities, Robeyns concludes, is not only controversial with regards to some of the items on the list, it will also be quite limited in terms of which capabilities we can actually reach an overlapping consensus on.

Nussbaum could respond, though, that the objection is based on the empirical fact that different agents disagree on one particular item on her list, *not* on whether, given adequate normative arguments and reasons, a group of reasonable deliberators would be able to arrive at an overlapping consensus on *some* list of central capabilities, possibly including the right to abortion. In other words, this response goes, Nussbaum's defense of abortion as a central capability is based on normative arguments and reasons that sufficiently reasonable agents can *hypothetically* agree to – come to an overlapping consensus on – and thus not on any assumption about what capabilities and functionings that are, empirically speaking, subjects of consensus.

In response, Robeyns (2016: 14) argues that even if we take the overlapping consensus to be between reasonable agents, the persistent disagreements within the philosophical literature on many issues of ethics in general and social justice in particular, including the right to abortion, support the conclusion that a list of central capabilities, arrived at through an overlapping consensus, would indeed be quite minimal at best or impossible at worst. It is often possible to invoke sound normative arguments and reasons in support of antagonistic positions.[6]

---

[6] See also Alkire (2002: 36–43) for three additional issues that make Nussbaum's overlapping consensus method unsuitable for development purposes.

The last foundational method derives a list of capabilities and functionings from *technical knowledge*. Within the capability literature technical knowledge has especially been obtained from *human rights theory*. Here, a list of capabilities may be found in academic works as well as in international conventions and declarations on human rights (Vizard, 2007: 234–5).[7] Human rights are entitlements a person has by virtue of being human and which other people and institutions in turn have an obligation to provide them with (Fukuda-Parr, 2011: 75; Sengupta, 2002: 843). Thus, in combining the capability approach with human rights theory, the proponents of a human rights-based capability framework hold that – similar to Claassen and Düwell (2013) and Nussbaum (2011a,b) – we can identify some basic capabilities, which a person is entitled to in virtue of being human/a human agent and which must accordingly be fulfilled.

Can a human rights-based capability framework form the basis for the selection of capabilities relevant for development purposes? Human rights theory may certainly supplement the capability approach in many ways. As (Vizard, 2007: 227) argues, the capability approach is underspecified and incomplete and a human rights theory may help provide a) "a theoretical basis for making judgments about the relative values of different capabilities" and b) "adequate grounds for explaining how the elements of a subset of basic and central (or highly valuable) capabilities might be specified and justified." Moreover, whereas the question of obligation is largely ignored within the capability approach, human rights theory may provide an account of legal accountability (Fukuda-Parr, 2011: 77–8; Vizard, 2007: 248; Sengupta, 2002: 843, 873).

Yet, as Fukuda-Parr (2011: 75) notes, human rights are usually not directly concerned with development issues. The main issue is that human rights are concerned with the basic capabilities we are entitled to as a matter of justice (Sengupta, 2002: 845), whereas human development arguably concerns more than only justice. Vizard (2007: 245) admits these limitations: even if human rights can be extended to concern development issues, "[l]ists of basic capabilities derived from lists of internationally recognized … should be viewed as *minimal* lists generated by just one of the various background or supplementary theories and methods."

---

[7] As Vizard (2007: 237) argues, such lists are not fixed or set in stone, but are under continuous revision.

A more general issue with the foundational methods, including those building on technical knowledge, is that they are decidedly top-down: a list of normatively relevant capabilities and functionings is essentially decided at a theoretical level and then applied in practice. This top-down approach has been met with two objections, which we can refer to, respectively, as *the objection from democratic legitimacy* and *the objection from epistemology* (Claassen, 2011: 491–4; Byskov, 2016: 5–6). The objection from democratic legitimacy holds that a technocratic list is illegitimate because it bypasses those who are meant to benefit from it (Claassen, 2011: 491; Jaggar, 2006; Byskov, 2016: 5; Robeyns, 2005: 199). That is, "[i]f the people to whom the list will apply reasonably feel that it is imposed on them, then the list will lack the necessary legitimacy" (Robeyns, 2005: 199) because "such lists should be the outcome of a democratic process, or a process of public reasoning" (Claassen, 2011: 491). The objection from epistemology, on the other hand, holds that there are epistemological limits to what the theorist or development expert can know about, which capabilities matter to citizens (Claassen, 2011: 504; Byskov, 2016: 6). If this is so, then a list of capabilities will be incomplete in terms of substance. For a list of capabilities to adequately address concerns for democratic legitimacy and epistemic correctness it must be arrived at through a process in which local stakeholders have had the authority and opportunity to influence the outcome.

Proponents of the foundational methods could argue that the two issues of epistemology and democratic legitimacy can be avoided if we acknowledge that the normative theories, by which foundational methods derive a list of capabilities, implicitly rely on a discourse ethics. Discourse ethics is the idea that the normative validity of an argument – such as a proposed list of capabilities – can be derived from a reconstructive analysis of what counts as a normatively valid argument in everyday moral discourse. If foundational methods rely on a development ethics, this response goes, they can avoid the two objections – from democratic legitimacy and epistemology, respectively – because they actually derive their normative validity from a reconstructive analysis of deliberative practices and social norms.

Yet, this response seems to be inadequate as a defense of foundational methods – defined as the proposition that a list of capabilities and functionings can be justified with reference to some ultimate normative principle or value – because they then also (implicitly) rely on

procedural methods, such as empirical investigations, anthropological analyses, historical investigations, or democratic deliberations. If
it is the case that foundational methods, either implicitly or explicitly
make use of such procedural methodology, we may want to categorize
them as mixed (or multi-stage) methods, that integrate foundational
and procedural methods.

This is not to say, however, that foundational methods cannot bring
anything valuable to the discussion on development. Foundational
methods can add a critical perspective based on normative values and
principles to a discussion, which is vulnerable to moral relativism insofar as they also aim to include local perspectives and values. Thus, in
sum, while foundational methods may be relevant for the identification of normatively relevant capabilities and functionings for human
development, they are in themselves inadequate at fulfilling this task.

Moreover, we still need to investigate whether a foundational
method is needed at all in this regard or whether a procedural method
can provide such critical insight without grounding the selection of
capabilities and functionings in an ultimate normative value or principle. Accordingly, the following section discusses the category of
procedural methods.

Procedural Methods

There are a number of approaches, which base a selection of capabilities more or less squarely on people's corrected or reasoned, yet
subjective, beliefs, values, or preferences. Rather than making theoretical strides to identify capabilities based on an ultimate normative
value or principle, the proponents of these methods base a selection
of capabilities on investigations into the capabilities people value and/
or need. In this sense, they rely on bottom-up (rather than top-down
or theoretical) *procedural methods* to the selection of capabilities and
functionings. At least three procedural methods can be identified.
Quantitative analyses base their lists of capabilities on statistical data,
qualitative analyses on in-depth inquiries into the reasons and preferences of selected groups of agents, and *deliberative democracy* selects
capabilities based on the reasoned and expressed preferences of deliberators in democratic process.

Before we proceed to analyze and evaluate the three procedural
methods, I need to address the concern that selecting capabilities and

functionings through a pure procedural method is a non-starter. Even procedural methods, this objection states, rely on the normative view that a list of capabilities and functionings can only be justified with reference to people's actual values and preferences. If this is true, the objection concludes, it makes a purely procedural method impossible from the outset.

However, we need to distinguish between the justification of the method and the process of selecting capabilities and functionings. Although the procedural methods may need to rely on normative theories – such as discourse ethics or deliberative democratic theory – when justifying why we should prefer a procedural method, it does not necessarily follow that a list of capabilities and functionings can be derived from adherence to such a foundational theory. In other words, what distinguishes procedural from foundational methods is the fact that procedural methods do not derive relevant capabilities and functionings from some ultimate normative value or principle (although such values and principles may play a role in justifying the choice of method) but from an open-ended inquiry into people's actual values.

The first set of procedural methods that we can identify is quantitative analyses. Quantitative analyses uses statistical analysis of how people value certain capabilities, providing insights about which capabilities people find most relevant (Vizard, 2010: 1). Ballon (2013: 7, 10–12) argues that we can use statistical data to identify relevant and valuable capabilities in two ways. The first method deduces relevant capabilities and functionings from the values expressed by the surveyed subjects. She calls this *data-driven selection*. Data-driven capability selection merely summarizes the statistical data rather than questioning it. The second method, to the contrary, seeks to confirm the assumptions and hypotheses of economic models against the datasets. Ballon labels these approaches *confirmatory statistical methods*. Confirmatory statistical methods specify hypotheses about human well-being and development and compare these to the statistical data in order to confirm, corroborate, or disprove them.

One major weakness of quantitative analysis, however, is that it does not capture information and data, which cannot be quantified or aggregated (Hodgett and Deneulin, 2009: 66–7). Moreover, statistical data is not always available or reliable and is thus not considered. Hodgett and Deneulin (2009: 66) give the example of domestic violence. Although the risk of domestic violence can be considered an important aspect of gender equity, there is often no reliable data available and it is difficult to quantify the experience of domestic violence. Ignoring certain capabilities for pragmatic reasons leaves the outcome of the qualitative analysis incomplete and somewhat random and thus unsuitable for the task of selecting capabilities for human development purposes.

As a consequence, Hodgett and Deneulin (2009: 68) argue that it would be prudent to supplement or replace quantitative analysis with *qualitative analyses*. Qualitative analyses base a list of capabilities on inquiries into the values and preferences of individuals and groups. We can identify two uses of qualitative research within the capability literature: narratives and participatory programs. *Narrative approaches* to the selection of relevant capabilities allow people to make sense of their own experiences and express their needs and values in life stories. Listening to these stories, researchers look for common themes and recurring issues (Hodgett and Deneulin, 2009: 74). Whereas statistics aggregate people across race, religion, nationality, ethnicity, and age, narratives place people and their experiences in an environmental, personal, and social context (Hodgett and Deneulin, 2009: 70).

Since people's lives and experiences cannot be separated from their environmental and sociocultural setting (Hodgett and Deneulin, 2009: 67) it is important to note that there is a risk that their narratives may not reflect real desires, but rather the social norms and cultural values (Biggeri et al., 2006: 68) or the power relations in the group where the selection is made. Thus, Biggeri et al. (2006: 68) argue that the process should be "conductive to the reflective reasoning around individual preferences" in order to (ideally) "detach them from the constraints of the adaption to personal experiences." Consequentially, Biggeri et al. (2006) supplement the narrative approach with a *participatory approach*, which aims at facilitating the critical reflection and discussion among a group of individuals, either with different or similar backgrounds. The participatory method is partly an open approach allowing the participants to exchange ideas and experiences; partly a critical exercise in which participants reflect on and discuss these ideas and experiences (Chambers, 1997: 102).

Generally, the qualitative methods have a number of limitations (Hodgett and Deneulin, 2009: 77). First, they are limited in terms of scope (Cooke and Kothari, 2001; Frediani, 2007: 9). Due to practical constraints it is often only possible to conduct a small sample of interviews or consultations and thus not necessarily represent the whole population who will be affected by the implementation of a list of capabilities. Secondly, even if the collection of data were balanced and representative, the researchers may still manipulate the result according to their aims (e.g. by only including the positive or negative responses). Thirdly, people's narratives are influenced by the institutional setting. Not only may the method used to conduct the interviews or consultations influence how people express themselves, people's experiences and languages are also affected by their social and cultural background. It is not always easy to disentangle people's real experiences from these backdrops.

Moreover, a special issue relating to the qualitative methods concerns the *subjectivity* of the people's experiences and the vulnerability to implicit biases and adaptive preferences. Implicit bias is an unconscious attitude someone may have towards other people, groups, or things. Someone may, for example, have a negative view of government intervention and thus oppose tax raises even though he might in the end benefit from such a tax policy. Adaptation of preferences occurs when someone lowers or raises her expectations due to the circumstances she is in. Someone may, for example, find her perspectives so hopeless that she gives up on her dreams, while someone who had something good happen to him may accordingly expect more good things to happen.

It should be noted, though, that some capability scholars have argued that, while some people may suffer from implicit biases and adaptive preferences, people are *in general* aware of their own values and the extent to which they are satisfied (Barr and Clark, 2009; Clark, 2009) or that evidence of adaptive preferences is inconclusive (Clark and Qizilbash, 2008: 536). However, this is not a common view among capability scholars (and moral psychologists). For example, Khader (2009, 2013) identifies several cases where individuals adapt their preferences despite not suffering from any of the traditional ways of thinking about adaptive preferences, such as lack of adequate information, agency, autonomy, or self-interest, while Conradie and Robeyns (2013) and Ibrahim (2011) document that although people's aspirations are less vulnerable to adaptation than the critics may think, they are nevertheless negatively affected by conditions of poverty and oppression.

If this were true, democratic bottom-up approaches to the selection of capabilities may risk conflicting with normative standards and principles (Burchardt and Vizard, 2011: 99–100). As Nussbaum (2003: 47) argues, "[s]ome human matters are too important to be left to whim and caprice, or even to the dictates of cultural tradition. To say that education for women, or adequate health care, is not justified just in case some nation believes that it is not justified seems like a capitulation to subjective preferences."

What proponents of procedural methods argue is that creating favorable conditions for preference formation, such as better access to information, more critical reflection, and increased interaction and deliberation, can reduce the risk of preference adaptation. However, all of these measures are *complimentary* to the qualitative method and rely on a normative conception of what non-adaptive preferences look like. What is more, it seems that in arguing for the creation of such favorable conditions we are already making a judgment about what capabilities and functionings are normatively important, namely those that allow people to form non-adaptive preferences. To wit, qualitative methods cannot constitute a "pure" procedural approach to selecting capabilities and functionings because it must incorporate some foundational insights in order to avoid the charge of being vulnerable to adaptive preferences and implicit biases.

Can we establish a purely procedural approach to selecting capabilities and functionings? Sen in particular (see Sen, 1999a, b, 2001, 2002, Sen and Scanlon, 2004; Drèze and Sen, 2002) has been a strong proponent of the view that a third procedural method, namely deliberative democracy, can help overcome the issues relating to implicit biases and adaptive preferences.[8] Deliberative democracy, as Anderson (2003: 250) puts it, "is the institutional embodiment of practical reason for a collective agency composed of equal citizens." Through deliberation, people are, on the one hand, able to express their values and preferences, while, on the other hand, this process forces them to confront the values of themselves and others with good arguments thus fostering their reasoned revision.

Sen (1999a: chapter 6; 2001: 10–11)[9] argues that deliberative democracy is important for three reasons. First of all, democratic participation is *intrinsically* important because it is a capability in and of itself.

---

[8] Crocker (2008, 2005), Drydyk (2005), and Anderson (1999, 2003) have been at the forefront of conceptualizing a capability theory of deliberative democracy.

[9] See also Crocker (2008, chapter 9) for an in-depth discussion of the importance of democracy, especially in relation to the way it enhances people's agency.

Providing access to deliberative democratic procedures thus serves directly as an expansion of people's capability sets. Second, deliberative democracy is *instrumentally* important because it enhances the opportunity for people's opinions to be heard and democratic rights may help to hold policy-makers accountable insofar as they have to face people's criticisms and seek their support. Third, and most importantly, deliberative democracy serves a *constructive* role. The constructive role of deliberation is directly aimed at addressing the charge of implicit bias and adaptive preferences. The formation of *reasoned* values and preferences, Sen (1999a: 153; see also Anderson, 2003: 249) argues, crucially depends on public discussion: as people engage in public deliberations they are forced to confront the biases and adaptive preferences of themselves and others and revise them in light of better evidence. It seems, then, that a deliberative democratic method can avoid relying on a foundational method because the critical reflection on people's values and preferences is built into the method itself. Even if these critical insights came from normative theory, they would only constitute a contribution to the deliberative exercise.

The deliberative method faces three major issues, however. First, the circumstances surrounding democratic deliberations are often non-ideal at best and at worst severely dysfunctional. Consider, for example, that development is often needed in societies with high socioeconomic inequality, low educational levels, and poor access to democratic institutions (such as a free press). Individually, these circumstances may hamper democratic ambitions, but put together they make the prospect of a proper public deliberation extremely weak. Socioeconomic differences have been shown to be reproduced in democratic participation giving more representation (and, presumably, political power) to the better-off (Huber et al., 1997) while a lack of free press restricts citizens' access to information. Furthermore, as Smith (2014) argues, people are generally bad at deliberating because they suffer from a variety of biases in the process of making decisions. Even well-educated deliberators, Smith argues, fail to be self-critical and give due consideration to the arguments of others. In other words, if these objections hold, the assumptions underlying the constructive role of deliberation are undermined, casting serious doubts on the deliberative democratic method of selecting capabilities.

Second, even if the qualitative and deliberative approaches could solve the issue of biases and adaptive preferences, the deliberative method's requirement of reasoned scrutiny runs contrary to the method's ambition of representing the plural values of deliberators (Argenton and Rossi, 2013). For deliberation to lead to the positive construction of shared values and goals, on Sen's deliberative account agents must be "reason giving and autonomous" individuals who are "sufficiently neutral toward competing conceptions of the good" (Argenton and Rossi, 2013: 137). Yet, this is quite substantively a liberal understanding of what it means to be a deliberative agent; one in which the deliberators are expected to deliberate in a particular way, namely through reasoned introspection and exchange of reasoned arguments. This is in conflict with Sen's commitment to pluralism, according to Argenton and Rossi, because it only accommodates pluralism in its reasonable forms. By requiring deliberators to scrutinize their own beliefs and values and provide generally acceptable reasons for them, the deliberative method is "an essentially homogenous moralized consensus, based on the unwarranted silencing of some of the most challenging expressions of pluralism" (Argenton and Rossi, 2013: 137).[10]

Third, in order to avoid these two objections above, as Claassen (2011) and Walzer (1981) point out, deliberative democratic methods must themselves rely on a substantive democratic theory that delineates what a just democratic procedure looks like. For deliberative democracy to constitute a reliable method, we already assume that stakeholders have a range of capabilities and functionings, such as access to robust democratic institutions and information as well as the capacity for critical reflection and deliberation, which in turn requires adequate cognitive skills and access to education (Bohman, 1997: 325–6).

Thus, it seems that even on the level of selecting capabilities and functionings, the deliberative method cannot escape the predicament that was outlined at the beginning of this section. Recall, it was here argued that even though procedural methods may adhere to a foundational theory (e.g. deliberative democratic theory) at the level of justifying the method, it does not necessarily follow that we are thereby committed to a list of capabilities and functionings. However, if the practical implementation of a deliberative method indeed requires the

[10] Consider, for example, as Argenton and Rossi (2013: 137) do, a religious person who believes that questioning her own beliefs would condemn her to Dante's Seventh Circle of Hell reserved for blasphemers.

capabilities and functionings as highlighted by Bohman, it *does* follow that we are committed to a substantive list of capabilities and functionings, namely those that are necessary for a functioning democratic deliberation. Even though the list of capabilities and functionings that follows may be quite minimal and imperfect (Byskov, 2016: 11) – i.e. restricted to democratic capabilities and not comprehensive of what is normatively relevant for development – the deliberative democratic method as a purely procedural method is illusive because it does to some extent rely on a foundational method.

In sum, although the procedural methods can address two of the concerns that we identified with the foundational methods – namely, lack of democratic legitimacy and contextual sensitivity – selecting capabilities procedurally, either through empirical research or public deliberation, requires that we move beyond a purely procedural method to include insights from a foundational method about what constitutes a just or reliable democratic deliberation. In the final section, two methods, which combine two or more foundational and procedural methods, are explored.

Mixed (or Multi-Stage) Methods

I have in the previous sections identified three general categories of methods for the selection of capabilities and functionings – *ad hoc*, foundational, and procedural methods – and argued that neither is suitable, on its own, to fulfill the task of selecting capabilities relevant for development purposes: *ad hoc* methods lack any robust justification of the particular items, "purely" foundational methods lack democratic and epistemological legitimacy, while "purely" procedural methods are vulnerable to subjectivism.

The silver lining, however, is that both the foundational and procedural methods may satisfy *different aspects* of a list of capabilities. On the one hand, democratic and participative exercises are important because they capture the *process* aspect of a selection of capabilities (Sen, 1997; Robeyns, 2003: 69). In short, it makes a difference in terms of legitimacy whether a list of capabilities is derived from normative theory or has been through a democratic process, even if the lists are identical (Robeyns, 2005; Jaggar, 2006). Moreover, local stakeholders may provide information about the local socioeconomic conditions and social norms that development experts and policy-makers have little access to (Byskov, 2017). On the other hand, though, democratic bottom-up approaches may reproduce unjust sociocultural norms and local power relations (Nussbaum, 2003: 47; Claassen, 2011: 496). Setting out normative standards and principles is thus an important aspect of a justifiable list of capabilities that can only be fulfilled by a theoretical exercise (Claassen, 2011: 498–9; Byskov, 2016: 4–5).

Some capability scholars have attempted to capture this duality of aspects by adopting or proposing *mixed (or multi-stage) methods* for the selection of capabilities and functionings. Mixed or multi-stage methods combine two or more foundational and procedural methods in order to create an integrated approach to the selection of capabilities and functioning. Robeyns (2003: 71), for example, argues that a list of capabilities "should be drawn up in at least two stages. The first stage can involve drawing up a kind of 'ideal' list, unconstrained by limitations of data or measurement design, or of socio-economic or political feasibility. The second stage would be drawing up a more pragmatic list which takes such constraints into account."

By integrating procedural and foundational aspects, in this way, the ambition is to capture what Sen (1997) has labeled the *comprehensive outcome* of selecting capabilities. As Sen argues, we should distinguish between the culmination outcome and the comprehensive outcome of a list of capabilities. While the culmination outcome only takes into consideration whether the final list of capabilities can be justified – i.e. none of the items on the list violate principles of justice – the comprehensive outcome also considers the justifiability of the procedure by which the list was brought about. Mixed (or multi-stage) methods aim to justify both the procedure as well as the particular list of capabilities.

Robeyns herself does not specify her mixed (or multi-stage) method further nor take a stance on the normative relationship between the two or more stages. Within the capability literature we can identify two specific kinds of mixed (or multi-stage) methods. *Comparative methods* start out by identifying an abstract and idealized list of capabilities in theory, which is then specified through an empirical or deliberative exercise. It is important to note that in cases of conflict, top-down comparative methods hold that the list derived from theory has overriding status. (As such, the empirical/deliberative exercise is merely for comparative purposes making the method decidedly top-down.) *Synthesizing methods*, to the contrary, embraces the potential conflict between lists derived from, respectively, theory and empirical/deliberative exercises by facilitating a dialectical "conversation" between the two stages. This conversation can have two purposes: on the one hand, the empirical/deliberative exercise can inform the (normative) theory while, on the other hand, the (normative) theory can provide a critical view on the empirically or deliberatively developed list. In the following I discuss both methods in turn and argue that the task of selecting capabilities for human development purposes is best managed by adopting a synthesizing method.

Brock (2009), Burchardt and Vizard (2011), and Holland (2014b) adopt a "two-stage" method, which informs and specifies an abstract normative theory through empirical or deliberative means. While Holland (2014b: 188–192) follows Nussbaum in specifying ten central capabilities and showing how they are affected by local environmental conditions, Burchardt and Vizard (2011: 92) combine "'bottom-up' deliberative/participative strategies on the one hand, and internationally recognized human rights standards on the other." Brock (2009: 5) similarly argues that real discussions on public policy "can usefully inform" her cosmopolitan account of global justice.

The first stage of the selection process aims at identifying overlapping and shared ideal principles – for example, in the international human rights treaties and conventions (Burchardt and Vizard, 2011: 100–2), in a hypothetical overlapping consensus (Holland, 2014b: 188–92), or in a cosmopolitan account of global justice based on an original position approach (Brock, 2009) – which can provide a normative basis for the list of capabilities. The second stage plays either or both of two primary roles within top-down comparative methods. On the one hand, it may adapt or refine the abstract list to local socioeconomic and environmental circumstances, taking such constraints into concern (Burchardt and Vizard, 2011: 102–3; Robeyns, 2003: 70–1). Brock (2009: part II), for example, investigates five discussions within public policy, which she uses to inform and refine her theory of global justice (Brock, 2009: part III). As such it satisfies the epistemological objection that theorists may not know what matters to the local stakeholders.

On the other hand, the second stage may also satisfy the issue of democratic legitimacy by including "a process of deliberation and debate, giving the general public and those at risk of discrimination and disadvantage a defining role in identifying and justifying the selection of central and basic capabilities" (Burchardt and Vizard, 2011: 102). The main problem with such two-stage methods as the ones adopted by Brock (2009), Burchardt and Vizard (2011), and Holland (2014b) is that the two stages may arrive at conflicting lists of capabilities. That is, there may be cases where the second empirical/deliberative stage identifies capabilities, which do not only supplement the normative theory's list of capabilities, but are actually incompatible with it. How should such conflicts be resolved? Brock (2009: 73–4), Burchardt and Vizard (2011: 104) and Holland (2014b: 137–8) all stress the priority of the list of capabilities derived from normative theory over the list of capabilities derived from an empirical or deliberative exercise. In this sense, the method ultimately becomes top-down, imposing the normative theory on the people to whom it applies, while the empirical/deliberative exercise merely poses as a comparison and confirmation of the normative list.

If this is true, then the top-down comparative method cannot meet standards of democratic legitimacy: while it is true that granting overriding priority to the list derived from normative theory ensures that the list of capabilities arrived at in the second stage does not violate basic normative principles – including a list of basic capabilities – in practice it has the consequence that a list of capabilities only has validity *insofar as it aligns with* the normative theory and its (substantive) list of capabilities. In other words, the empirical/deliberative process cannot in itself (or only secondarily – if at all) justify a certain selection of capabilities. But this ability is arguably the hallmark of a comprehensive outcome. A selection of capabilities gains democratic legitimacy exactly because it is not imposed on the people to whom it applies. This should lead us to reject the top-down comparative method as suitable for the selection of capabilities and functionings for development purposes.

How can we retain democratic legitimacy while minimizing the risk that the final list of capabilities violates basic normative principles (assuming that there will always be some tension between the two)? A second set of mixed methods may promise to rectify this democratic shortcoming. *Synthesizing methods* to the selection of capabilities accord equal priority to the two (or more) stages and engage them in an ongoing dialectical dialog with the aim of enhancing and improving both the normative theory and the democratic decision-making process. Rather than being antagonistic, then, the two (or more) stages are seen as different contributions that provide critical insights to the process of making a selection of capabilities that is, on the one hand, normatively justifiable and, on the other hand, democratically and contextually sensitive. In the remainder of this section, I discuss three such synthesizing methods to the selection of capabilities.

Alkire (2002), Claassen (2011) and Khader (2011) all adopt (or propose to adopt) a three-stage method, which engages in a dialectical or dialogical exercise between theoretical reflection, empirical investigation, and public deliberation. The three stages are, respectively, (i) from practice to theory, (ii) from (refined) theory to practice, and (iii) a synthesis. The dialectical dialog is present at all stages of Alkire, Claassen, and Khader's methods. On the first stage, Alkire, Claassen and Khader start out by identifying a normative theory, which can and should be supplemented or refined through a participatory (Alkire, 2002: 43–7), empirical (Claassen, 2011: 504–5) or deliberative (Khader, 2011: 20–1) exercise. The reasons they provide for this are different, however.

Alkire (2002: 43–4), for example, identifies a preliminary list of basic capabilities, which she then uses to facilitate a process of practical reasoning with her participants in order to further specify the list of capabilities to local values and circumstances. To Claassen (2011: 504), the empirical investigation is meant to address the objection from epistemology: the theorist cannot by herself know what is relevant to those who are affected by a list of capabilities and she must therefore "learn from public debates about capabilities [or] even conduct social scientific research to find out which capabilities people value most" and with suitable modification allow the results of this practical investigation to influence and enhance her ideal list of capabilities. As Claassen (2011: 505) further writes, "[t]he philosopher's individual epistemological limits are compensated for by drawing upon the knowledge of (many) others." Khader (2011: 21), on her part, aims to address the objection from democratic legitimacy, arguing that "we want people to be judged by a conception of flourishing that is widely perceived as legitimate."

In the second stage, this refined normative theory is then used as a starting point for a process of practical reasoning (Alkire, 2002: 46) or offered for public deliberation and endorsement (Claassen, 2011: 501) or as an input in a participatory dialog with local stakeholders (Khader, 2011: 22). Thus, where the first stage worked from practice to theory, the second stage of their methods move from (refined) theory back to practice. Again, the reasons Alkire, Claassen, and Khader give for this move are different. The primary reason for offering the refined normative theory for public deliberation and endorsement is primarily a matter of democratic legitimacy, according to Claassen (2011: 500–2). Claassen (2011: 501) admits that if a list were to be applied directly and solely based on authority of the theorist, it would indeed lack democratic legitimacy. Yet, as Claassen (2011: 501) further argues, the theorist should not demand compliance with her list independently of public deliberation but rather offer it "as an input into a democratic process run by others."

To Khader, meanwhile, the second stage of her method has epistemological motivation. Whereas the first stage of her method intends to specify a normative theory – in particular, a cross-cultural conception of human flourishing based on a deliberative exercise – in the second stage this refined normative theory (i.e. of human flourishing) can help identify an unjust state of affairs (in Khader, 2011: 22) case, whether someone is suffering from adaptive preferences). Similarly, Alkire intends the second stage to have epistemic consequences for her participants: by engaging them and challenging their beliefs and values, Alkire (2002: 46) aims to make her participants reflect on, reason about, and refine the list of capabilities and functionings they find valuable and the reasons why they do so based on their own personal, historical, and socioeconomic context.

The third stage of Alkire, Claassen, and Khader's methods serves as a synthesis where normative and descriptive content form a critical input that aims to enable local stakeholders – participants in development projects (Alkire); deliberators (Claassen); individuals suffering from adaptive preferences (Khader) – to make informed decisions about which capabilities are normatively relevant, for themselves or in general. As Claassen (2011: 505) argues, "the fact that a group of people empirically holds the belief that realizing capability x is a moral demand does not mean that these beliefs are morally correct."

Hence, Alkire (2002: 46), Claassen (2011: 505), and Khader (2011: 22) argue, we need to engage in a critical dialogue with stakeholders. Through this critical dialog, the democratic and epistemological concerns come together. On the one hand, whereas Burchardt and Vizard (2011) and Holland's (2014b) mixed approaches endorses paternalistic intervention when encountered with a potential source of reproduction of an unjust state of affairs, Alkire, Claassen, and Khader's methods hold that the decision ultimately lies with the public themselves.[11] On the other hand, whereas Burchardt and Vizard (2011) and Holland's (2014b) approaches only sought to confirm the normative theory through an empirical exercise, Alkire, Claassen, and Khader hold that it is the normative theory that must inform the individual or public deliberation process.

It might be argued, though, that the synthesizing method does not avoid the problem of indeterminacy that the comparative method resolves by giving overriding normative status to normative theory. That is, because the synthesizing method gives equal status or priority to the foundationally and procedurally established lists of capabilities, it cannot resolve disputes that arise between these lists. We can respond to this criticism in two ways. First, disagreements are an inherent part of political discourse. Within political discourse we often have to make compromises that result in non-ideal solutions. That does not mean that these solutions are unjust. Nor does it, secondly, mean that we should discontinue process of deliberation of coming to a mutual understanding. What we disagree on now may be resolved in the future. Thus, what the synthesizing method proposes is an ongoing process that may provide a non-ideal list of capabilities and functionings, which is under continued scrutiny and revision as we repeat the stages of dialectic deliberation described above.

In sum, a synthesizing method as a method for the selection of capabilities has the most potential, I contend, as a method for selecting capabilities for development purposes. This is because it manages to address several of the concerns that we have raised against other methods, most importantly normative justifiability, democratic legitimacy, and contextual sensitivity.

Concluding Remarks

This chapter identifies, analyzes, and discusses four general categories of methods for the selection of normatively relevant capabilities and functionings, comprising fifteen more specific methods. *Ad hoc methods* base a list of capabilities on the values of the researcher or

---

[11] See, however, Claassen (2014) who does allow for some paternalist interventions to ensure basic agential functionings.

practical concerns, *foundational methods* derive a list from technical knowledge and reasoning, *procedural methods* identify capabilities through either empirical studies or a deliberative process, while *mixed (or multi-stage) methods* integrate two or more foundational and procedural methods.

It has been argued that the three former methodologies – *ad hoc*, technocratic, and procedural methods – have serious shortcomings when applied to the task of selecting capabilities for development purposes. Generally, these shortcomings are either a lack of contextual sensitivity, normative justification, or democratic legitimacy. However, adopting a mixed (or multi-stage) method can ameliorate these shortcomings.

In particular, we would do best to adopt the method labeled *synthesizing methods*. Synthesizing methods aim to engage critically with local stakeholders in a three-stage procedure. While the purpose of the first stage is to enrich the normative and descriptive theory through empirical and deliberative exercises, the second stage offers this refined theory as an input to a democratic procedure with the aim of enhancing the informational bases of the participants. Lastly, in the third stage, local stakeholders engage in a critical deliberation with the ideal outcome of an informed and widely endorsed list of capabilities and functionings. Synthesizing methods can satisfy our concerns of contextual sensitivity, normative justification and democratic legitimacy.

References

Alkire, S. (2002) *Valuing Freedoms: Sen's Capability Approach and Poverty Reduction*. Oxford: Oxford University Press.

(2008) "Choosing Dimensions: The Capability Approach and Multidimensional Poverty." MPRA Working Papers No. 8862.

Anderson, E. (1999) "What is the point of equality?" *Ethics*, 109 (2): 287–337.

(2003) "Sen, ethics, and democracy." *Feminist Economics*, 9 (2–3): 239–61.

Argenton, C. and Rossi E. (2013) "Pluralism, preferences, and deliberation: A critique of Sen's constructive argument for democracy." *Journal of Social Philosophy*, 44 (2): 129–45.

Ballon, P. (2013) "The selection of functionings and capabilities: A survey of empirical studies." *Partnership for Economic Policy (PEP)*.

Barclay, L. (2003) "What kind of liberal is Martha Nussbaum?" *SATS – Nordic Journal of Philosophy*, 4 (2): 5–24.

Barr, A. and Clark, D. (2009) "Do the poor adapt to low income, minimal education and ill-health?" *Journal of African Economies*, 19 (3): 257–93.

Biggeri, M., Libanora, R., Mariani, S. and Menchini, L. (2006) "Children conceptualizing their capabilities: results of a survey conducted during the first Children's World Congress on Child Labour." *Journal of Human Development*, 7 (1): 59–83.

Bohman, J. (1997) "Deliberative democracy and effective social freedom: capabilities, resources, and opportunities." In James Bohman and William Rehg (Eds.) *Deliberative Democracy. Essays on Reason and Politics*. Cambridge, MA: The MIT Press, pp. 321–48.

Brock, G. (2009) *Global Justice: A Cosmopolitan Account*. Oxford: Oxford University Press.

Burchardt, T. and Vizard, P. (2011) "'Operationalising' the capability approach as a basis for equality and human rights monitoring in 21st century Britain." In D. Elson, Sakiko Fukuda-Parr, and Polly Vizard (Eds.) *Human Rights and the Capabilities Approach: An Interdisciplinary Dialogue*. London, UK: Routledge.

Byskov, M. F. (2016) "Democracy, philosophy, and the selection of capabilities." *Journal of Human Development and Capabilities*, 18 (1): 1–16.

(2017) "Third wave development expertise." *Oxford Development Studies*, 45 (3): 352–65.

Chambers, R. (1997) *Whose Reality Counts?: Putting the First Last*. London: Intermediate Technology.

Claassen, R. (2011) "Making capability lists: Philosophy versus democracy." *Political Studies*, 59 (3): 491–508.

(2014) "Capability paternalism." *Economics & Philosophy*, 30 (1): 57–73.

Claassen, R. and Düwell, M. (2013) "The foundations of capability theory: comparing Nussbaum and Gewirth." *Ethical Theory and Moral Practice*, 16 (3): 493–510.

Clark, D. A. (2002) *Visions of Development: A Study of Human Values*. Cheltenham: Edward Elgar Publishing. Available at: http://books .google.com/books?hl=en&lr=&id=vutLazwFZiUC&oi=fnd& pg=PR6&dq=%22capability+approach%22&ots=C0r31hbzf4& sig=h9r6cTmuDXJ2J79phqre4VXBpRk.

(2005) "Sen's capability approach and the many spaces of human wellbeing." *The Journal of Development Studies*, 41 (8): 1339–68.

(2009) "Adaptation, poverty and well-being: Some issues and observations with special reference to the capability approach and development studies." *Journal of Human Development and Capabilities*, 10 (1): 21–42.

Clark, D. A. and Qizilbash, M. (2008) "Core poverty, vagueness and adaptation: A new methodology and some results for South Africa." *The Journal of Development Studies*, 44 (4): 519–44.

Comim, F. (2008) "Measuring capabilities." In Flavio Comim, Mozaffar Qizilbash, and Sabina Alkire (Eds.) *The Capability Approach: Concepts, Measures and Application.* Cambridge: Cambridge University Press, pp. 157–200.

Conradie, I. and Robeyns, I. (2013) "Aspirations and human development interventions." *Journal of Human Development and Capabilities,* 14 (4): 559–80.

Cooke, B. and Kothari, U. (2001) *Participation: The New Tyranny?* London and New York, NY: Zed Books.

Crocker, D. (2005) Sen and deliberative democracy. In Alexander Kaufman (Ed.) *Capabilities Equality: Basic Issues and Problems.* New York, NY and London: Routledge, p. 155.

(2008) *Ethics of Global Development: Agency, Capability, and Deliberative Democracy.* Cambridge: Cambridge University Press.

Dixon, R., Nussbaum M., Baines, B., Barak-Erez D. and Kahana, T. (2011) "Abortion, dignity and a capabilities approach." Public Law and Legal Theory Working Papers No. 345, pp. 1–19. Available at: http://chicagounbound.uchicago.edu/cgi/viewcontent.cgi?article=1009& context=public_law_and_legal_theory

Doyal, L. and Gough, I. (1991) *A Theory of Human Needs.* New York, NY: Palgrave Macmillan.

Drèze, J. and Sen, A. (2002) "Democratic practice and social inequality in India." *Journal of Asian and African Studies,* 37 (2): 6–37.

Drydyk, J. (2005) "When is development more democratic?" *Journal of Human Development,* 6 (2): 247–67.

Ferracioli, L. and Terlazzo R. (2014) "Educating for autonomy: Liberalism and autonomy in the capabilities approach." *Ethical Theory and Moral Practice,* 17 (3): 443–55.

Frediani, A. A. (2007) "A participatory approach to choosing dimensions." *Maitreyee, E-Bulletin of the Human Development and Capability Association,* 7: 7–10.

Fukuda-Parr, S. (2011) "The metrics of human rights: Complementarities of the human development and capabilities approach." *Journal of Human Development and Capabilities,* 12 (1): 73–89.

Gewirth, A. (1978) *Reason and Morality.* Chicago, IL: The University of Chicago Press.

(1996) *The Community of Rights.* Chicago, IL: The University of Chicago Press.

Hodgett, S. and Deneulin, S. (2009). "On the use of narratives for assessing development policy." *Public Administration,* 87 (1): 65–79.

Holland, B. (2014a) "15 Nussbaum, Rawls, and the ecological limits of justice: Using capability ceilings to resolve capability conflicts." In Flavio

Comim and Martha Nussbaum (Eds.) *Capabilities, Gender, Equality: Towards Fundamental Entitlements*. Cambridge: Cambridge University Press, pp. 382–413.

(2014b) *Allocating the Earth: A Distributional Framework for Protecting Capabilities in Environmental Law and Policy*. Oxford: Oxford University Press.

Huber, E., Rueschemeyer, D. and Stephens, J. D. (1997) "The paradoxes of contemporary democracy: formal, participatory, and social dimensions." *Comparative Politics*, 29 (3): 323–42.

Ibrahim, S. (2011) "Poverty, aspirations and well-being: Afraid to aspire and unable to reach a better life – voices from Egypt." SSRN Scholarly Paper ID 1747798. Rochester, NY: Social Science Research Network.

Jaggar, A. M. (2006) "Reasoning about well-being: Nussbaum's methods of justifying the capabilities." *Journal of Political Philosophy*, 14 (3): 301–22.

Khader, S. J. (2009) "Adaptive preferences and procedural autonomy." *Journal of Human Development and Capabilities*, 10 (2): 169–87.

(2011) *Adaptive Preferences and Women's Empowerment*. New York, NY: Oxford University Press.

(2013) "Identifying adaptive preferences in practice: Lessons from postcolonial feminisms." *Journal of Global Ethics*, 9 (3): 311–27. doi:10.1080/17449626.2013.818379.

Klasen, S. (2000) "Measuring poverty and deprivation in South Africa." *Review of Income and Wealth*, 46 (1): 33–58.

Krishnakumar, J. (2007) "Going beyond functionings to capabilities: An econometric model to explain and estimate capabilities." *Journal of Human Development*, 8 (1): 39–63.

Kuklys, W. (2005) *Amartya Sen's Capability Approach: Theoretical Insights and Empirical Applications*. Berlin: Springer.

Lelli, S. (2001). "Factor analysis vs. fuzzy sets theory: Assessing the influence of different techniques on Sen's functioning approach." *KU Leuven Center for Economic Studies Discussion Paper Series* 01 (21): 1–35.

Nussbaum, M. (1990). "Aristotelian social democracy." In R. Bruce Douglas, Gerald M. Mara, and Henry S. Richardson (Eds.) *Liberalism and the Good*. New York, NY: Routledge, pp. 203–52.

(1992) "Human functioning and social justice in defense of Aristotelian essentialism." *Political Theory*, 20 (2): 202–46.

(1995) "Aristotle on human nature and the foundation of ethics." In J. E. J. Altham and Ross Harrison (Eds.) *World, Mind and Ethics: Essays on the Ethical Philosophy of Bernard Williams*. Cambridge: Cambridge University Press, pp. 86–131.

(2000) *Women and Human Development. The Capabilities Approach*. Cambridge: Cambridge University Press.

(2003) "Capabilities as fundamental entitlements: Sen and social justice." *Feminist Economics*, 9 (2–3): 33–59.

(2011a) "Capabilities, entitlements, rights: Supplementation and critique." *Journal of Human Development and Capabilities*, 12 (1): 23–37.

(2011b) *Creating Capabilities. The Human Development Approach.* Cambridge, MA: Belknap Press of Harvard University Press.

Osmani, S. R. (2005) "Poverty and human rights: Building on the capability approach." *Journal of Human Development*, 6 (2): 205–19.

Phelps, T. G. (2006) "Narrative capability: Telling stories in the search for justice." In Severine Deneulin, Mathias Nebel, and Nicholas Sagovsky (Eds.) *Transforming Unjust Structures. The Capability Approach.* Dordrecht: Springer, pp. 105–20.

Qizilbash, M. (1998) "Poverty, Concept and Measurement." 12. Research Report Series. Islamabad: Sustainable Development Policy Institute.

Robeyns, I. (2003) "Sen's capability approach and gender inequality: Selecting relevant capabilities." *Feminist Economics*, 9 (2–3): 61–92.

(2005) "The capability approach: A theoretical survey." *Journal of Human Development*, 6 (1): 93–117.

(2006) "The capability approach in practice." *Journal of Political Philosophy*, 14 (3): 351–76.

(2016). "Capabilitarianism." *Journal of Human Development and Capabilities*, 17 (3): 397–414.

Schokkaert, E. and vanOotegem, L. (1990). "Sen's concept of the living standard applied to the Belgian unemployed." *Recherches Économiques de Louvain / Louvain Economic Review*, 56 (3/4): 429–50.

Sen, A. 1985a. *Commodities and Capabilities.* Oxford: Oxford University Press.

1985b. "Well-being, Agency and Freedom: The Dewey Lectures 1984." *Journal of Philosophy* 82 (4): 169–221.

(1997) "Maximization and the act of choice." *Econometrica*, 65 (4): 745–79. doi:10.2307/2171939.

(1999a) "Democracy as a universal value." *Journal of Democracy*, 10 (3): 3–17.

(1999b) *Development as Freedom.* New York, NY: Knopf.

(2001) "Democracy and Social Justice." In Farrukh Iqbal and Jong-Il You (Eds.) *Democracy, Market Economics, and Development. An Asian Perspective.*Washington, DC: World Bank, 7–24.

(2002) *Rationality and Freedom.* Cambridge, MA: Harvard University Press.

Sen, A. and Scanlon, T. (2004) "What's the point of democracy?" *American Academy of Arts and Sciences Bulletin*, 57 (3): 9–11.

Sengupta, A. (2002) "On the theory and practice of the right to development." *Human Rights Quarterly*, 24 (4): 837–89.

Slottje, D. J. (1991) "Measuring the quality of life across countries." *The Review of Economics and Statistics*, 73 (4): 684–93.

Smith, A. F. (2014) "Political deliberation and the challenge of bounded rationality." *Politics, Philosophy & Economics*, 13 (3): 269–91.

UNDP (2015). *Human Development Report 2015*. New York, NY: United Nations Development Programme.

Vizard, P. (2006). *Poverty and Human Rights: Sen's Capability Perspective Explored*. Oxford: Oxford University Press.

(2007) "Specifying and justifying a basic capability set: should the international human rights framework be given a more direct role?" *Oxford Development Studies*, 35 (3): 225–50.

(2010) "Developing and agreeing a capability list in the British context: what can be learnt from social survey data on 'rights'?" *CASE Working Papers* 142. Available at: http://eprints.lse.ac.uk/43866/

Walzer, M. (1981) "Philosophy and democracy." *Political Theory*, 9 (3): 379–99.

World Health Organization. (2015). Adolescent Pregnancy. Geneva: WHO. Available at: http://who.int/maternal_child_adolescent/topics/maternal/adolescent_pregnancy/en/

10 From Resources to Functioning
Rethinking and Measuring Conversion Rates

ENRICA CHIAPPERO, PAOLA SALARDI
AND FRANCESCO SCERVINI

Introduction

What is usually considered one of the most relevant, distinctive features of the capability approach is the attention paid to human diversity as a core element in determining individual well-being. Indeed, the individual ability to transform resources into achievements differs across people, shaped by internal (personal) characteristics, such as gender, age, ethnicity, health conditions or mental status, and by external features related to the physical and social environments in which people live. In the capability literature, internal and external characteristics are usually referred to as 'conversion factors' and the underlying process of converting resources into well-being is defined as a 'conversion process'. The rationale of this approach is that two individuals with the same amount of resources may not achieve the same functionings or, conversely, two individuals may require a different set of resources to achieve the same functionings.

This conversion process can be understood as a (functioning) production function, in which individual achievements are the final outcome generated by a production function whose inputs are the resources available to the individual and whose shape/characteristics are determined or affected by the conversion factors. Consistently, two individuals with the same inputs/resources may end up with different outputs/achievements due to the different production functions/conversion factors. The idea of conceiving the individual well-being process as a production function dates back to Gary Becker's contribution on the household production literature and it has also been mentioned in the capability literature, in particular, by Kuklys (2005), Muellbauer (1987) and Sen (1985).

Although there is a wide consensus in the capability literature on this general theoretical structure, it is not fully clear how the conversion process works. In particular, it is unclear how the conversion factors combine and interact with each other, and the joint effect of resources and conversion factors in the production of achievements – what we will define as 'conversion rates'. It is not a single factor that determines individual advantage or disadvantage, but rather the combination and interrelation between personal characteristics and a plurality of contextual factors that affect individuals' positions and may determine individual differences in terms of functionings or capabilities. For instance, being a woman, or disabled, or belonging to a minority ethnic group does not automatically mean that one is disadvantaged, even if there may be a higher concentration of disadvantaged people in these groups. Rather, it is the interaction between these personal characteristics and other external factors – including family socioeconomic background, geographical location, cultural norms and institutional factors – that will contribute to exacerbating or reducing inequalities.

We think that a more precise definition of 'conversion rate', both theoretical and empirical, can be helpful for several reasons: (i) it could serve as a possible 'benchmark' to the literature, as there is still no general consensus on a clear definition of conversion rate, at least empirically; (ii) it could then avoid the confusion between conversion factors, factor scores and conversion rates that sometimes emerges in the literature, especially empirical; (iii) it could help to identify the best way to estimate conversion rates. Above and beyond these, the ultimate goal of a more precise and clear definition and estimation of conversion rates is to provide policy makers with a reliable instrument to design and implement public policies targeted at individuals who are less able to convert resources into functionings.

Literature Review

Empirical work on conversion rates is rather limited, but it is possible to distinguish three main strands of literature on this topic. The first strand includes papers primarily aimed at estimating the capability or functioning generating functions (Addabbo et al., 2004; Anand and Van Hees, 2006; Burchardt and Le Grand, 2002; Krishnakumar, 2007; Krishnakumar and Ballon, 2008). Most of the papers estimating capabilities assume that they are unobservable entities that can only be proxied through a set of indicators. They consistently make use of a class of latent variable models that include factor analysis, structural equation models (SEM) and multiple indicators and multiple causes models (MIMIC), which allow for investigating the causal effect of economic resources and conversion factors on capabilities. Among these, Burchardt and Le Grand (2002) estimate the share of voluntary and involuntary unemployment in UK controlling for a set of 'opportunities', which are individual characteristics affecting the decision about participating in the labour market. The marginal effect of the latter on the former can be interpreted as (a sort of) conversion rate. Addabbo et al. (2004) use a very complex model based on fuzzy sets and SEM–MIMIC models to estimate capabilities in the framework of child well-being, by first identifying the most important conversion factors and then estimating their role in the production of capabilities. Anand and van Hees (2006) built a survey designed to measure capabilities using a targeted set of questions. Analysis of the correlation between a list of covariates and capabilities can approximate the concept of conversion rates. Krishnakumar (2007) identifies some external factors that may shape the conversion process in the generation of capabilities and estimates their effects as a sort of by-product of her SEM-MIMIC model. Krishnakumar and Ballon (2008) refine the empirical analysis in Krishnakumar (2007) employing micro-data from Bolivia and estimate the effect of 14 different 'exogenous causes' affecting capabilities.

A second way of accounting for different abilities in the conversion process comes from the equivalence scales literature applied to the capability approach (Lelli, 2005; Zaidi and Burchardt, 2005). Welfare comparisons between heterogeneous entities, typically between households, require consideration of the fact that households differ not only in terms of size and composition, but also across other sociodemographic characteristics. These characteristics can affect both their capacity to generate income as well as their needs and, hence, their ability to achieve a given level of well-being. Zaidi and Burchardt (2005) apply the equivalence scales methodology for calculating the extra-costs of living associated with disability, using a range of standard of living indicators, income and disability. They show that disability generates substantial additional costs. Lelli (2005) estimates an equivalence scale for the functioning 'being well sheltered', controlling for the effect of a given set of characteristics (household size and compositions, age, gender, occupation, education, marital status among others). She finds that differences in shelter functioning achievement seem to be only partially explained by income differences.

These two strands of literature present a concerted attempt to operationalize the capability approach, investigating the linkages between resources and achievements, controlling for a variety of characteristics. However, in most of these papers the role of conversion factors is only explicative or derivative. In none of these cases there is an estimation of the *rate of* conversion produced. Instead, conversion factors remain incorporated into the explicit or implicit underlying assumptions that connect resources and achievements.

By contrast, the third strand of literature is characterized by a direct and explicit account of the conversion process. A first attempt can be found in the seminal work of Kuklys (2005), which aims to estimate conversion rates both *per se* and as part of the functioning generating function.[1] Kuklys' (2005) book offers a foundational guide to the econometric operationalisation of the capability approach. Among several interesting insights, it includes a clear distinction between conversion factors (the set of characteristics affecting the production of a given functioning), factor scores (the average effect of conversion factors on functionings, independent of the resources available), and conversion rates (Kuklys, 2005: 5). The latter are understood as how the 'productivity' of resources changes according to different conversion factors, or, in other words, how individuals with different characteristics are differently able to convert resources into functionings. However, this clear theoretical definition is not fully and clearly mirrored in the empirical strategy that follows.

Following from this starting point, few papers have attempted specifically to estimate conversion rates: Chiappero-Martinetti and Salardi (2008) and Salardi (2008) adopt a similar empirical strategy in two different frameworks: after an exploratory regression model with discrete outcomes, in which functionings depend on income and a set of conversion factors, conversion rates are estimated by taking the difference between factor scores (as defined in Kuklys, 2005) for different subsamples of the population. A series of papers by Binder and Broekel (2011, 2012a, b), closely related to one another, approach the same problem using an alternative two-stage procedure. First, they attempt to identify, non-parametrically, a functioning production efficiency frontier and the individual distance from the frontier. Second,

[1] In the same work, she also estimated a 'psychometric equivalence scale' for disabled individuals in UK (Kuklys, 2005).

using a simple parametric linear regression model, they seek to establish the determinants of individual efficiency. More recently, Hick (2016) tries to disentangle the effects of different conversion factors in the generation of income on the one hand, and of material deprivation on the other hand, using an OLS regression model.

The common feature of all of the papers is that they estimate a correlation or causal effect of individual, social, or environmental characteristics on individuals' functionings or capabilities. More or less explicitly, and with differences of definitions and operationalisation, all of the authors seek to investigate how individuals with different characteristics are differently able to convert resources into functionings. However, in our view these papers have generally continued to mix the concepts of conversion rates and factor scores, as defined by Kuklys (2005). In her work, factor scores are the direct effect of resources and conversion factors on functionings, controlling for a set of characteristics, while conversion rates represent the effect of different characteristics on the conversion process of resources into functionings. In the next section we describe in detail our proposal and compare it with the methodologies most commonly applied by other papers.

Our Proposal

This section is devoted to offering an intuitive introduction to our definition of conversion rates and then to suggesting how they can be estimated. Consistent with the theory of the functioning production function, following Kuklys (2005) and Sen (1985) we can represent the process as follows:

$$\mathbf{b}_i = f_i(c(\mathbf{x}_i)|\mathbf{z}_i)$$

where $\mathbf{b}$ is the vector of functionings of individual i, $\mathbf{x}$ is the set of resources she owns, $c(\cdot)$ and $f(\cdot)$ are conversion functions generating commodities from resources and functionings from commodities, respectively. The vector $\mathbf{z}$ represents all of the conversion factors, which affect the process of conversion from resources to functionings.

We make use of an example in order to clarify the exposition. Consider the functioning 'being in a good state of health'. The production of such a functioning involves a virtually unlimited number of aspects and characteristics, including, among others, income and availability of healthcare facilities, age and gender, occupational status and exposure to unsafe working conditions, pollution, etc.

Definitions

The first issue is then to classify all of these items into three broad categories: resources, commodities and conversion factors. In our view, and having in mind a functioning production function, *resources* should have three characteristics: first, they can be used to get the commodities; second, they can be targeted by public policies; and, as a consequence, third, they can be at least partially or indirectly redistributed across individuals. The previous literature has focused on monetary resources, mainly income or wealth. However, we argue that the list of resources should be extended and include, for instance, public provision and availability of public goods or goods provided by the public sector. In our example, income and wealth can obviously contribute to producing a good state of health: they can be used to access high quality medical care, screenings and health insurance if needed, and also to buy healthy food, to have a healthy life-style and so on. However, education is also important for getting the 'right' commodities: a wealthy individual is not necessarily aware of which medical screenings she needs, healthy habits, nutritional properties of different foods and so on. Moreover, low-educated individuals may underestimate the effects of unhealthy behaviours, such as smoking, drinking or using narcotics, they may be unable to fully understand therapeutic indications, and so on. Indeed, a medical study by Wolf et al. (2005), for instance, found a strong positive correlation between literacy and health, even after controlling for sociodemographic characteristics. Finally, public goods and services should also be included among resources. Indeed, they can be used to get commodities and functionings as effectively as private resources, either as substitutes or complements, or independently of private resources. In the production of good health, for instance, some systems provide universal public healthcare, others mostly private healthcare, others consist of a mixed system. In this framework there is little sense in considering private income the only resource available to produce and achieve health functioning.

The list of *commodities* includes all those goods and services directly related to the functionings, and are therefore very specific: for instance, in the production of 'a good state of health' it includes drugs and medicines, examinations, and medical care when needed, as well as gym memberships, low-fat, low-carb or any kind of food specific to individuals' dietary requirements, and so on.

Conversion factors are all those characteristics (traditionally divided into three categories: individual, social, and environmental) that may or may not directly affect the production of the relevant functionings, but which potentially affect the process of conversion from resources to functionings, either because resources are used differently by individuals with different characteristics or because commodities have different effects on different individuals (Sen, 1999). Following the previous example of the functioning 'being in a good state of health', the list of conversion factors is virtually endless. Individual conversion factors include personal intrinsic characteristics that, in principle, cannot be modified, such as gender, age or ethnicity, as well as IQ, metabolic rate, temperament, other genetic characteristics and features. Social factors may refer to the narrow household context, including marital status, household size and composition, health status, occupational status and job characteristics of other family members, or to the broader social context, including interpersonal relationships, groups of peers and friends and their habits and lifestyle, and any other social factor. Finally, environmental factors include all those conversion factors broadly related to environment and its quality, such as air, water, soil and noise pollution, local and regional climate and so on.[2] However, this distinction among conversion factors is empirically convenient but theoretically arbitrary, as it is possible to adopt different classifications, depending on the nature of the functioning investigated and of the factors considered. In particular, one possible criterion to classify conversion factors should be policy relevance: indeed, they should be analysed and classified in order to suggest sensible policies to improve the condition of some categories of individuals.

Within this framework, *conversion rates* capture how, and to what degree, conversion factors affect the conversion process of resources into functionings. An example can help to illustrate this concept: two individuals with the same resources may nonetheless obtain very different health outcomes because of the air pollution in the place they

[2] Sen (1999) classifies the various types of contingencies that can affect the conversion of income in functionings into four main categories: personal heterogeneities, diversities in the physical environment, variation in social climate, and differences in relational perspectives.

live, of different genetic proneness to some illnesses, of their age, or of any other element that may affect the way resources are translated into good health. Indeed, given the same amount of private income and wealth, education and public resources, an individual living in a rural area may find it more difficult to access medical care than one living in a city; an individual living close to heavy industries may not be able to find clean air and water; an individual with a high responsibility, stressful job may have worse health status than a pensioner, and so on.

Conversion rates should not be confused with factor scores, which capture the average effects of factors on functionings (e.g. how healthy on average are individuals at different ages or living in differently polluted areas, independent of their resources), and the average effect of resources (e.g. how healthy on average are individuals with different income or education, independent of the conversion factors).

Finally, there might be, in principle, a residual category of characteristics that may have a direct impact on the production of functionings, while leaving the conversion process of resources into functionings unaffected. However, outside very specific cases the distinction between conversion factors and these *other characteristics* must be empirically estimated rather than theoretically defined: whenever (i) the conversion rates of a factor are estimated to be the same for all the resources, independently of conversion factors, and (ii) the factor has a significant impact on the functioning, then the factor cannot be classified as a 'conversion factor', but rather as a factor that only affects the functioning, but not the conversion process. Back to our example, it is difficult to imagine *ex-ante* some individual, social or environmental characteristic that directly affects individual health status without affecting the conversion process of income, wealth or education into health status. However, after the estimation of the functioning generating function, it could be possible to find some characteristics with this feature. We classify these possible characteristics as 'other factors'.

Estimation Procedure

Having defined all of the relevant variables, we review the estimation procedures adopted by the previous literature and then introduce a new methodology. We can begin with the work by Kuklys (2005): chapter 3 develops a model to estimate functionings, while chapter 5 is devoted to the estimation of an equivalence scale for disabled individuals. Although applied to different purposes, the estimation procedures are similar and consist of finding the average effects of income (the only resource considered in both cases) and other sociodemographic indicators (conversion factors) on the functioning of interest (health and housing in chapter 3, income satisfaction in chapter 5). Indeed, Kuklys (2005) was looking for factor scores, rather than conversion rates. The estimation procedure followed by Lelli (2005) is very similar although it is more focused on finding the factor scores for disabled individuals in order to generate a specific equivalence scale. Zaidi and Burchardt (2005) follow the same general strategy with an important improvement: they estimate factor scores for different household compositions. They get closer to our definition of conversion rate, as they estimate the different effect of the conversion factor 'household composition/occupational status' (divided in six categories: single, couple with one disabled and couple with two disabled, both for pensioners and non-pensioners) on the functioning 'any savings'. Chiappero-Martinetti and Salardi (2008) adopt an analogous procedure in order to estimate the conversion rates for three different functionings in Italy: they estimate factor scores for several subgroups, according to age and gender. Similarly, Salardi (2008) computed different factor scores for health status in Brazil according to gender and ethnicity. Finally, Hick (2016) looks back to Kuklys (2005) and Zaidi and Burchardt (2005) in order to find the factor scores (in his paper defined as 'conversion factors', different from the definitions put forward by Kuklys, (2005), and in this chapter) for the functioning 'material deprivation'. The three papers by Binder and Broekel (2011, 2012a, b) take a very different approach and introduce the concept of 'conversion efficiency', theoretically analogous to conversion rates, but empirically similar to an efficiency frontier. Indeed, they exploit non-parametric techniques to estimate conversion efficiency using a two-stage procedure: first, they estimate individual efficiency in the production of functionings based only on available resources; second, they explain individual efficiency with individual conversion factors (age, job status, marital status, disability and living in London) through standard OLS regressions by gender.

In our view, however, none of these methodologies precisely fits the theoretical definition of a conversion rate. Instead, they estimate factor scores either for the whole sample, or – at best – for different subcategories of individuals separately. What we propose here, in order to be as consistent as possible with the theoretical definitions in Kuklys (2005) and in the previous section, is to *estimate conversion rates as the coefficients on the interacted terms between one resource and one or more conversion factors in a single equation regression model*. This proposal has several advantages with respect to the models used by the works reviewed previously. With respect to the non-linear models and efficient frontier models by Binder and Broekel (2011, 2012a, b), it is simpler and more parsimonious, because it involves a single equation procedure, and it clearly distinguishes among functionings and conversion factors, unlike their non-parametric first stage. With respect to other models it is more precise, as it estimates the differential effect of the resources for each possible category of conversion factors. Indeed, by adding an interacted term in a single equation model, it is possible to estimate and compute not only the conversion rates, but also the factor scores and possibly interesting differences between them. Another important feature is that it relies on simple econometric models based on commonly used and agreed hypotheses, making the results immediately clear to a large audience.

This methodology is a step forward compared to Chiappero-Martinetti and Salardi (2008), Salardi (2008) and Zaidi and Burchardt (2005) whose methodology is the most similar to what we propose here. Indeed, they estimate average factor scores for different categories of individuals by running separate regressions on different subsamples. By contrast, we see four advantages in adopting the methodology suggested here. First, it exploits the entire sample, increasing the efficiency of the estimate, rather than splitting the sample into several sub-samples. Second, it allows for an immediate comparison of the conversion rates for different categories, by running equality of coefficients tests, in order to assess whether conversion rates are different from zero and different across categories. Third, it allows for investigating multiple interactions without the loss of efficiency due to low sample sizes. Fourth, it does not compare the average effects of different subsamples of individuals, but the additional effects of some conversion factor on the same sample, making the comparison more consistent and immediate.

Finally, consistent with our concept of conversion rates, this methodology allows for computing the interacted effects between resources. It seems likely that the effectiveness of a resource in the production of functionings depends not only on conversion factors, but also on other resources. This issue has never been raised in the literature because 'resources' has often been used to represent a single variable, i.e. income. However, in light of our broader definition of resources it may be interesting to investigate the possible complementarity or substitutability of resources in order to implement effective policies.

Required Data and Empirical Issues

What are the most suitable data in order to estimate conversion rates? The answer is that it depends on the nature of the functionings being investigated, and on the estimation method. However, there are some common issues in the estimation of conversion rates that require specific characteristics of the dataset.

Endogeneity is the most frequent empirical issue faced in the estimation of conversion rates, as it is in any impact evaluation exercise. As it is well-known (see for instance Angrist and Pischke, 2009, or Wooldridge, 2010), it arises from two possible characteristics of the data: (i) there is a problem of reverse causality whenever the dependent variable – i.e. the functioning in this case – may affect one of the regressors, such as the resources or the conversion factors. In our example, the problem arises if the functioning 'being in a good state of health' affects the resources (e.g. this is the case if health affects individual income, particularly in case of long-term illnesses), the conversion factors (e.g. health may affect occupational status, area of residence, household size and composition, and so on, but not exogenous characteristics such as age, gender, parental background and others), or both; (ii) there is an omitted variable issue if there is one (or more) unobservable variables that jointly determine at least one of the regressors and the dependent variable. We may think of some unobservable variable, for instance individual genes, which affect both the functioning 'being in a good state of health' and some of the conversion factors (IQ, metabolism, chronic diseases), or even the resources (education might be affected by some genetic characteristics). The traditional solutions to these issues consist either in finding some instrumental variable (i.e. variables that are correlated with the endogenous regressors but not the dependent variable) or relying on a 'fixed effects' model (i.e. ruling out all of the time-invariant individual characteristics by taking deviations from the mean). For the former, it is usually difficult to find a valid instrument, but this depends crucially on the features of the dataset and on the nature of the functionings under investigation; for the latter, it requires a sufficiently long panel data structure, something that is very difficult to find at the individual level for sufficiently large samples. Other traditional ways out from the endogeneity issue, such as regression discontinuity design, counterfactuals and randomized experiments, or quasi-experiments seem more suitable to determine causalities rather than conversion rates, and anyway require a panel dataset. However, although such a strategy has never been applied in the literature on functionings and conversion rates, it is theoretically possible to design an experiment, or to exploit a discontinuity, such that a conversion factor is exogenously changed and thus estimate its effects on the role of resources in the production of functionings. Again, the most suitable methodology depends crucially on the nature of the functionings and on the structure of the dataset.

Another frequent limitation that researchers face in this field is data availability: it is very difficult to find surveys that include sufficient information about the determinants of a given functioning. Indeed, in principle one should be able to retrieve information on all of the relevant resources, on all of the conversion factors, and of course on the functioning itself. Ideally, as noted above, these data would have a longitudinal component, in order to observe the same individuals/households over time, and thus rule out a possible source of endogeneity. Finally, it could be of some interest also to compare the results across countries, in order to link conversion rates to institutional characteristics, by exploiting consistent cross-country surveys. Of course, the severity of issues of data availability depends on the nature of the functioning, but this is one of the main reasons why the literature has focused on a relatively small number of resources and conversion factors. Moreover, among the works reviewed in this paper, only Lelli (2005) includes any kind of cross-country comparison, using barely comparable data for Italy and Belgium. All the other works focus only on a single country, with most of them exploiting the richness of data of the British Household Panel Survey.

Conclusions

This chapter begins from a concern that the literature on the capability approach has failed to offer a consistent definition of conversion rates, generating some confusion in the empirical estimation of how conversion factors influence the role of resources in the production of functionings. Authors have applied quite different econometric procedures in order to estimate conversion rates, either explicitly or implicitly, and factor scores. In the light of this heterogeneity, this chapter is a first attempt to rationalize, from a theoretical point of view, a clearer definition of conversion rates, and the characteristics of key related variables.

Empirically, we propose an econometric strategy to estimate conversion rates that is consistent with the theoretical definitions in Kuklys (2005), which are developed in this chapter. In our view, this empirical approach has several advantages: it rigorously fits the theoretical definition; it is sufficiently simple, so that results can be easily read and interpreted and rely on standard, well-known econometric approaches; and it is parsimonious, so that it is possible to implement it with the surveys commonly used by the literature. Finally, we review some frequent issues encountered in this type of estimation, related to the existence of endogeneity and to the quality of data available.

We are conscious that a commonly agreed definition requires a wide discussion within the scientific community and that, even starting from the same theoretical concept, several possible estimation methods can be employed in order to quantify conversion rates. At least for now a 'best practice' does not exist. However, we hope that this contribution can be both a useful reference for future research in this field and a clear starting point to animate the debate of these issues.

References

Addabbo, T., Di Tommaso, M. L. and Facchinetti, G. (2004) *To what extent fuzzy set theory and structural equation modelling can measure functionings? An application to child well being*, CHILD Working Paper 30/2004, Centre for Household, Income, Labour and Demographic economics.

Anand, P. and van Hees, M. (2006) Capabilities and achievements: An empirical study. *The Journal of Socio-Economics*, 35(2), 268–84.

Angrist, J. D. and Pischke, J.-S. (2009) *Mostly Harmless Econometrics: An Empiricist's Companion*. Princeton, NJ: Princeton University Press.

Binder, M. and Broekel, T. (2011) Applying a robust non-parametric efficiency analysis to measure conversion efficiency in Great Britain. *Journal of Human Development and Capabilities*, 12(2), 257–81.

(2012a) The neglected dimension of well-being: Analyzing the development of 'conversion efficiency' in Great Britain. *The Journal of Socio-Economics*, 41(1), 37–47

(2012b) Happiness no matter the cost? An examination on how efficiently individuals reach their happiness levels. *Journal of Happiness Studies*, 13(4), 621–45.

Burchardt, T. and Le Grand, J. (2002) Constraint and Opportunity: Identifying Voluntary Non-employment, CASE Paper, 55, Centre for Analysis of Social Exclusion, London, UK.

Chiappero-Martinetti, E. and Salardi, P. (2008) Well-Being Process and Conversion Factors: An Estimation, HDCP-IRC Working Paper Series 3/2008.

Hick, R. (2016) Between income and material deprivation in the UK: In search of conversion factors. *Journal of Human Development and Capabilities*, 17(1) 34–54.

Krishnakumar, J. (2007) Going beyond functionings to capabilities: An econometric model to explain and estimate capabilities. *Journal of Human Development*, 8(1), 39–63.

Krishnakumar, J. and Ballon, P. (2008) Estimating basic capabilities: A structural equation model applied to Bolivia. *World Development*, 36(6), 992–1010.

Kuklys, W. (2005) *Amartya Sen's Capability Approach: Theoretical Insights and Empirical Applications*. Berlin: Springer.

Lelli, S. (2005) Using functionings to estimate equivalence scales. *Review of Income and Wealth*, 51(2), 255–84.

Muellbauer, J. (1987) Professor Sen on the Standard of Living. In Sen A. K. (Ed.), *The Standard of Living*. Cambridge: Cambridge University Press.

Salardi, P. (2008) The Estimation of the Health Functioning Production Function for Brazil In Essay on Poverty, Inequality and Well-being, PhD Thesis, Catholic University of Milan, 115–67.

Sen, A. K. (1985) *Commodities and Capabilities*. Amsterdam: North Holland.

(1999) *Development as Freedom*. New York, NY: Alfred A. Knopf.

Wolf, M. S., Gazmararian, J. A. and Baker, D. W. (2005) Health literacy and functional health status among older adults. *Archives of Internal Medicine*, 165(17), 1946–52.

Wooldridge, J. M. (2010) *Econometric Analysis of Cross Section and Panel Data*. Cambridge, MA: MIT Press.

Zaidi, A. and Burchardt, T. (2005) Comparing incomes when needs differ: Equalization for the extra costs of disability in the UK. *Review of Income and Wealth*, 51(1), 89–114.

11 Demystifying the Use of Simultaneous Equation Models for Operationalising the Capability Approach

JAYA KRISHNAKUMAR AND
RICARDO NOGALES

Introduction

Understanding what constitutes human wellbeing as well as how to measure it have been constant challenges for economic theory and policymaking. Most of the studies that address this challenge in mainstream economics operate within the framework of utility maximisation behaviour, thus associating wellbeing with a subjective perception of satisfaction. Other conceptual developments, however, have taken a strong stand against utility as the *only* adequate evaluative space of human wellbeing, one of the most prominent and influential among them being the Capability Approach (CA), whose key author is Nobel Laureate Amartya Sen (Sen, 1980, 1985, 1992, 2009). This approach has been a main inspiration for many modern conceptions of human wellbeing such as the human development concept put forward by UNDP (1990), or the Going Beyond GDP of the European Commission[1] or even the Better Life Index of the OECD.[2] At the same time, its intentional silence on setting practical guidelines for concrete policy action for the improvement of human wellbeing has also been pointed out by many authors, such as Comim (2001), Robeyns (2006), Gasper (2007), Comim, Qizilbash and Alkire (2008) and Chiappero-Martinetti and Roche (2009).

It is undeniable that the richness of the CA is quite difficult to translate into practical terms for at least two reasons. The first is the diversity and complexity of informational spaces that it brings into focus for a proper evaluative judgment about wellbeing and the second is

---

[1] See http://ec.europa.eu/environment/beyond_gdp/download/bgdp-summary-notes.pdf
[2] See www.oecdbetterlifeindex.org

the fact that some underlying fundamental concepts are often hard to directly observe. First, the CA has a *pluralistic* and *multidimensional* view of wellbeing that calls for a simultaneous account of the multiple informational spaces highlighted in this approach as well as the relationships among these spaces. The capability set, defined as the set of *potential* lifestyle outcomes from which a person has the freedom to choose, is given normative priority as the evaluative space *par excellence* for assessing individual *advantage* (Gasper, 2007; Schokkaert, 2009). However, capabilities are hard to observe as they regroup materialised lifestyle outcomes and non-materialised ones.

The second practical difficulty of the CA concerns obtaining information on potential lifestyle outcomes. There are essentially two ways of going about it. The first way is to get direct information through new questionnaires on people's choices and lifestyle outcomes (e.g. Anand et al., 2005, 2009; Anand & van Hees, 2006). The second way relies on secondary data sets which contain information on various aspects of people's lives including their achievements and circumstances. The first method requires careful framing of the questions for respondents to understand the distinction between capabilities (*potential* outcomes) and functionings (*actual* outcomes). Further it also requires the use of appropriate analytical tools to account for the *subjective* nature of the capability responses while making interpersonal comparisons. On the other hand, secondary data sets are generally large nationally representative samples that contain information on most of the informational spaces considered in the CA – resources, individual characteristics, family and social circumstances, institutional and political factors – except possibly for capabilities, which can then be inferred using *all* the other information sets by means of appropriate statistical and econometric techniques (e.g. Di Tommaso, 2007; Krishnakumar, 2007; Krishnakumar & Ballón, 2008).

Both methodologies have their own strengths and limitations. This chapter focuses on the suitability of the second method for three reasons. First, secondary data at the individual level coming from household surveys is widely available in most countries, as opposed to primary data specifically collected to capture people's choices and capabilities in different domains of individual wellbeing.[3] Second, lack

---

[3] Notable exceptions are Argentina and the UK (see Open University's Capability Measurement Project: www.open.ac.uk/ikd/research/human-capabilities/capabilities-measurement-project).

of resources for regularly conducting such specific surveys at a national level implies that they are not likely to be implemented in most countries for years to come. Finally, secondary data are generally collected by national statistical offices after a serious discussion among competent government officials and experts, and hence enjoy wide acceptance amongst policymakers. Thus, it is indeed useful to exploit the information contained in secondary data sets within a suitable econometric framework to acquire a sound empirical knowledge on the key informational spaces of the CA as well as the relationships among them.

Before getting to the heart of the matter, we would like to clarify that this chapter is mainly concerned with wellbeing freedom in terms of the *opportunity* aspect. The *process* aspect is only present, if at all, in the relations between external (e.g. political and institutional) factors and individual capabilities. In addition, we do not at all address agency freedom in this chapter. On the other hand, we look at the operationalisation of the CA, not only in terms of obtaining information on various potential lifestyle outcomes but also in terms of providing a theoretical structure which can incorporate the main features of the approach, its informational spaces and more importantly the causal and associational links among the different information sets, thereby leading to an operational model which can be confronted with real life observations to arrive at useful policy recommendations.

In what follows we elaborate on the idea that a Simultaneous Equation Model (SEM) has all the required characteristics for taking the richness of the CA to the complex reality of the world in an effective manner. We emphasise that it is not merely concerned with people's capabilities but also with all other relevant informational spaces that interact with and influence capabilities as well as wellbeing. Thus a SEM goes beyond a simple operationalisation of the concept of capability and includes the various pathways through which these capabilities influence one another and are influenced in turn, by particular external circumstances. The use of this type of models to successfully implement the CA in different contexts is steadily increasing over the recent years within a vein of social scientists, especially economists (see e.g. Anand et al., 2010; Addabbo et al., 2014; Krishnakumar & Nogales, 2016a; Tellez et al., 2016; Wendelspiess, 2017 and Zhou et al., 2016).

The chapter is organised as follows. The following section briefly recalls the main some key features of the CA that we are concerned with in this chapter, namely the aspects of wellbeing freedom and achievements, at the individual level. The next section discusses the different steps involved in matching the various elements of a theory with corresponding elements of reality through appropriate modelling, performing a reality check with the resulting model and using the empirically validated model for suggesting 'good' actions for changing the current situation into a more desirable one according to the theory. The suitability of a SEM with latent variables for modelling the CA and confronting it with real life data is substantiated in the fourth section. The fifth section briefly presents two empirical illustrations and then the last section concludes the topic.

The Capability Approach in Brief

This section briefly recalls the main features of the capability approach as far as wellbeing freedom is concerned. According to the CA, human development is the expansion of people's freedom to lead the life they have reason to value (Sen, 1999), which goes far beyond their perception of satisfaction. Whether or not an individual is capable of freely choosing the states of *beings* and *doings* in life that she values, is cornerstone to understanding her wellbeing. Indeed, Sen has strongly commented on the theoretical limitations of utility as the informational basis for wellbeing assessment. In fact, Sen argues that freedom to achieve valued lifestyle outcomes is both the end and the means to development. We now briefly recall the essential aspects of the CA, in particular its pluralistic view of wellbeing and the relationships between different informational spaces.

In this approach, a person's wellbeing is described in terms of what she manages to do or be in life. These *beings* and *doings*, which we will denote as b_i, are called *functionings* and are the result of an individually-varying transformation of a bundle of resources or commodities that are at the person's disposal, which is denoted as $[x_j]$. Individual heterogeneity plays a key role in this theory thereby affirming that different people may achieve different functionings given the same resources. This idea has been formalised by Sen (1985, 1987) as follows:

$$b_i = f_i(c(x_j)) \tag{11.1}$$

where $c(x_j)$ represents the *characteristics* of the resources that the individual can make use of and *convert* into actual functionings. This conversion is personal and affected by factors that change from one individual to another, which is what the individually-varying function $f_i(\cdot)$ represents. These conversion factors may be taken in a large sense to include personal, environmental, social or even political features. In a theoretical formulation one can either postulate that b_i depends on x_i as well as the conversion factors say z_i either additively or multiplicatively, i.e. either the level of b_i is different for two individuals with different z_i even if they have the same resources x_i, or that the effect of x_i on b_i can depend on the individual characteristics z_i in addition to the latter having its own effect. Thus f_i can be:

$$b_i = f_i(c(x_i), a(z_i))$$

or

$$b_i = f_i(c(x_i), a(z_i), c(x_i) \times a(z_i)) \tag{11.2}$$

The *value* of a certain vector of achieved functionings b_i is also personal and hence denoted by an individually-varying *valuation function*, say $v_i(\cdot)$.

$$v_i = v_i(b_i) = v_i(f_i(c(x_i))) \tag{11.3}$$

Following Sen (1985), the value of b_i for individual i represents the *goodness* of the life described by the functioning vector b_i and Sen is very clear that it does not represent the utility or happiness derived from it. However, Sen allows for the theoretical possibility of utility or happiness being one particular valuation criterion among many possible valuation criteria $v_i(\cdot)$, although he strongly disputes it. The happiness corresponding to b_i is therefore denoted by a separate function $h_i(\cdot)$, and it does not represent a valuation function.

Finally, one of the central concepts of the approach, namely the *capability set*, is defined as the set of potential states of *beings* and *doings* that an individual *can* achieve given the resources and conversion factors. This is described as her *advantage*. Thus the advantage is the *set of potential valued states of life from which an individual is able to choose*. Formally, a person's capability set, denoted as Q_i, is the set of all potential functionings b_i that an individual *is able to* achieve by choosing (a) one particular conversion function, f_i, from an individual-specific set of possible functions F_i and (b) one specific set of resources or commodities, x_i, from an individual-specific set of possibilities X_i, called entitlements:

$$Q_i = [b_i \mid b_i = f_i(c(x_i), a(z_i)), \; f_i \in F_i, \; x_i \in X_i] \tag{11.4}$$

At any point, the actual achieved functionings vector of an individual say y_i is the result of a particular choice from this capability set, which may either be purely individual or combined with some family or cultural constraints. Denoting these external factors that enter the choice process as m_i, we can write:

$$y_{i,k} = \phi_k(Q_{i,k}, m_i) \quad \text{for all } k = 1 \dots K \tag{11.5}$$

To sum up, the CA involves different informational spaces: resources (x_i), individually-varying personal and surrounding factors (z_i), capability set (Q_i) or potential functionings (set of all b_i), and achieved functionings (y_i) as well as value (v_i) and happiness (h_i). It advocates for the capability set as the preferred informational space to assess wellbeing freedom, over the actual achievements or the resources that generate the capability set. Thus it defines development as an expansion of the freedom to choose multidimensional valued functionings.

Our brief description of the CA highlights its pluralistic view of human life. Even if it gives normative priority to the capability set, it does not fail to recognise that achieved functionings and resources, taken in a large sense to include personal resources as well as social and institutional infra-structural support, are necessary informational spaces to understand wellbeing.

Why Model the Capability Approach?

The CA is an *approach* to wellbeing and not a fully specified theory per se (Robeyns, 2006). Sen himself states the following when referring to the implication of the CA for a theory of justice:

the capability perspective does point to the central relevance of the inequality of capabilities in the assessment of social disparities, but it does not, on its own, propose any specific formula for public decisions (Sen, 2009: 232).

Thus the practical usability of the CA depends on the effective translation of its conceptual framework into a *theoretical structure,* which can be taken to the ground reality for a practical evaluation of any state of affairs in terms of the different elements that it contains, in particular wellbeing and freedom to achieve. This implies a suitable structuring of the multiple concepts and ideas that the CA contains into different information sets and relationships (Comim, 2001).

Any theory is ultimately an *attempt* at understanding real life phenomena in a logical and structured manner. In the context of development and wellbeing, it is to be conceived as a framework on the basis of which one can draw meaningful and useful conclusions about ways to improve people's wellbeing as well as their freedom to achieve. Thus by operationalisation of a theory or a theoretical approach, we mean a confrontation (*matching*) with reality in order to verify its applicability and usefulness in a practical setting.

Applied econometric modelling provides a valid methodology for verifying the ability of a certain theoretical framework to match real facts. Evidence-based analysis is a widely used and scientifically valid evaluation method for assessment of theoretical statements and policy actions, and rigorous econometric modelling plays a major role in this decision-making process. In our view, this same methodology can be and should be employed to take the CA to practical situations and evaluate different states of affairs in terms of the theoretical concepts that it stands for, such as wellbeing, advantage, agency, and so on, using empirical data. Only by matching a theoretical formulation with empirical data can one make informed decisions on wellbeing assessment and policy impact.

Thus operationalisation, in the sense of going from theory to practice for a proper assessment of its empirical relevance as well as its use for a better understanding of the complex reality and policy implications, involves the following four steps.

Step 1: Theoretical structure building. Starting from the conceptual formulation of the approach, this step focuses on building a theoretical structure that enables an empirically relevant representation of the different informational sets involved and the relations among them, in such a way that the resulting structure can be mapped on to reality. Often, this can be depicted by a diagram containing different variable sets and the theoretical paths among them. It goes without saying that the particular variables entering the different informational sets may and will differ from one context (society) to another, and possibly from one period to another for the same society.

Step 2: Modelling. This step is concerned with the translation of the proposed theoretical framework into a model given by a set of equations describing the theoretical relations among the above variable sets, that can be quantified (estimated) using appropriate empirical data while respecting technical rigour.

Step 3: Empirical analysis. This step focuses on the estimation of the model using empirical data and analysis of the results for a better understanding of the empirical content of different informational sets and the relations that operate among them in reality. It is in this step that one critically examines the validity of the theoretical framework as well as the statistical assumptions made for estimation purposes.

Step 4: Practical use. Having validated the empirical model in the previous step, this step relates to the effective use of the empirical model for evaluating and predicting the impact of policy actions, based on a practical understanding of how the objects of key interest actually evolve and influence each other.

The above applied econometric approach provides a valid way to acquire a solid understanding of the real world and hence can be suitably employed for a practical implementation of the CA in varied contexts and situations. Even if we argue that it constitutes a valid methodology in any field, we do not claim that this is the *only* way to address the operationalisation of the CA. In fact it can be gainfully complemented with other procedures for enhancing our knowledge of the real world. Further, it is also possible to combine or integrate the capability approach with other theories for a useful application of the CA to answer important practical questions on human wellbeing and policy making (Robeyns, 2006). We will come back to this last point in our section on empirical illustrations.

Simultaneous Equation Models

Earlier in this chapter we highlighted some essential aspects of the CA to bring out its pluralistic view of wellbeing, its human life-centred conception of development and its context-dependence. The previous section discussed a valid way of taking any theory (or theoretical approach) to reality for gaining empirical knowledge and guiding policy actions. In this section, we aim to establish the suitability of the SEM as an appropriate modelling tool for implementing the different features of the CA and confronting it with real life data along the lines suggested in the previous section.

Let us first consider the key notion in this approach that distinguishes it from other wellbeing approaches namely the capability set. As explained earlier, the concept of *potential* functionings makes it hard to directly observe the capability set of an individual due to its counterfactual nature.[4] Sen himself states:

> In fact, the capability set is not directly observable and has to be constructed on the basis of presumptions (just as the 'budget set' is also constructed on the basis of data regarding income, prices and presumed possibilities of exchange). (Sen, 1992: 52)

People have generally resorted to one of two different strategies for coping with this issue – either by using direct questionnaires asking people what they could be and do, or by inferring the wellbeing freedom of individuals using multiple informational sets – resources, conversion factors, achieved functionings and so on (like using income, prices and presumed possibilities of exchange to construct the budget set in the above citation of Sen). As the SEM modelling framework allows for the possibility of including observable and unobservable concepts in the theoretical structure, both ways can be adequately modelled by a SEM, although it is particularly suited for the second situation. Hence in what follows we focus on the adequacy of a SEM in the absence of direct information on capabilities, which is largely the case (and will probably remain so) for most countries of the world.

In a nutshell, we assume that the capability set, or let us say 'the freedom to choose' is a latent (unobserved) variable, and the (observed) achieved functionings are partial manifestations of it. This idea is exactly the same as that commonly adopted in fields like psychology in which, for example, it is assumed that the *personality* of an individual is not something that can be directly observed and measured but is revealed through many observed 'behaviours' or 'behavioural characteristics'; similarly, the *ability* of a person is not directly measurable but through a set of indicators of performance in various tests. Thus one can also assume that the freedom to choose valued functionings is a latent variable (or could be many latent variables if we examine this

---

[4] The capability set incorporates both materialised and non-materialised functionings that are available to a person. As we can only observe materialised functionings, a large portion of the capability set is in fact a set of *potential* functionings, which have not been chosen by the person. Thus measurement of capability sets requires a *counterfactual* viewpoint to include potential functionings.

freedom in many dimensions of wellbeing), and can be inferred from various informational sets, in particular: (a) the achieved functionings which are partial manifestations of capabilities, (b) the resources, and surrounding factors such as economic, social, political and institutional systems that influence the capability set (wellbeing freedom), (c) the individual characteristics that play a role in the conversion of resources into potential functionings and (d) family, societal or cultural preferences or constraints that interfere in the choice of particular functionings from the capability set. In fact, this is very much in line with Sen's argument that: 'the assessment of capabilities has to proceed on the basis of observing a person's actual functionings, to be supplemented by other information' (Sen, 1999: 131).

Any model contains endogenous and exogenous variables; the former being the variables determined by the model and the latter being variables determined outside of the system of equations. Let us consider an analysis of K dimensions of wellbeing and denote the advantage (freedom to choose or capability set) in each one of them as $Q_{i,k}$ for $k = 1 \ldots K$, where index i denotes the individual. These Q_i are part of the endogenous variables of our model. We allow for interdependencies among the different freedoms: advantages in one dimension (say the capability to be healthy) may influence advantages in other dimensions (say the capability to be educated).

Recall that capabilities are obtained by the conversion of resources or commodities (in a large sense including economic, social and political circumstances), denoted as x_i, into potential functionings b_i, with individual, social and environmental conversion factors z_i that affect the process of 'production' of advantages. Thus among the exogenous variables, we may include policy variables, environmental circumstances, and a variety of individual or household characteristics. Thus, respecting the CA formulation that Q_i is the set of all possible b_i's, we have:

$$Q_{i,k} = g_k(Q_{i,j \,|\, j \neq k}, x_i, z_i) \quad \text{for } k = 1 \ldots K \tag{11.6}$$

where $g_k(\cdot)$ represents the mathematical function that yields people's advantage or capability set in the k-*th* dimension for a given x_i, z_i. From a technical point of view, this function may be linear or nonlinear, can include interactions among the different exogenous factors, as well as allow for context-dependent variables and heterogeneous parameters.

Furthermore, the SEM framework also allows for some resources to be endogenous, by considering that they may be affected by some advantages. This is a useful way to avoid possible technical misfits and the so-called endogeneity bias in parameter estimates. Formally, suppose that the *l-th* element of vector x_i could be possibly endogenous, i.e. may itself be influenced by capabilities as well as influencing them, this may be taken into account by an additional equation:

$$x_{i,l} = \varphi_l \left(Q_{i,k|k=1\ldots K}, x_{i,o|o \neq l}, w_i \right) \text{ for some } l \tag{11.7}$$

where $\phi_l(\cdot)$ represents the mathematical function that explains the l-th resource and may contain other exogenous determinants w_i.

Equations (11.6) and (11.7) are called structural equations in a SEM terminology and they represent a mathematical translation of the theoretical relations that materialise the principles put forward by the CA. It is important to note that these equations aim to provide *explanations* for the multiple advantages considered in the analysis, and need to satisfy certain theoretically justified exclusion conditions for identification purposes.

However, as we have stated before, advantages or capability sets depict potential functionings regrouping both materialised functionings and non-materialised ones. Not all advantages get translated into actual achieved functionings. As mentioned earlier, either the individual chooses which ones to achieve or she may be constrained to select some options due to family or cultural factors. Thus the achieved functionings y_i are 'choices' (including constrained ones) from the capability set given the individual factors m_i:

$$y_{i,k} = \phi_k(Q_{i,k}, m_i) \quad \text{for all } k = 1 \ldots K \tag{11.8}$$

where $\phi(\cdot)$ are functions representing the individual act of 'choice' among the potential states of life. These individual factors therefore account for different choices made by different individuals having the same capability set or advantage. These relations are called *measurement equations* in a SEM terminology; from a technical point of view, these equations can take a linear or non-linear form,[5] thus accounting

---

[5] One may often have to resort to the nonlinear form as many functionings are measured as discrete variables, either in a binary form (e.g. literate or not) or in an ordered categorical form (e.g. having attained primary, secondary or tertiary level of education). Examples of functionings in other dimensions can be 'enjoying access to social security in a job' (work dimension) or 'not suffering

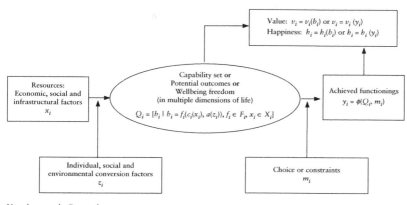

Note that x_i, z_i, b_i, Q_i, y_i and m_i are vectors
It is possible that for some elements of x_i, say $x_{i,t}$, we have the reverse relation: $x_i = \varphi_l \left(Q_{i,k|k=1 \ldots K}, x_{i,olo\neq l}, w_i \right)$

Figure 11.1 The capability approach in a diagrammatic form

for continuous (quantitative) or discrete (qualitative) indicators as well as subjective or objective information on achieved states of life.

In Figure 11.1 we present the theoretical structure of the CA in the form of a diagram as far as wellbeing freedom is concerned, with the key information sets represented by multidimensional variables as well as the relations among them given by the equations of the model. Before taking this model to real life data, stochastic elements are introduced in all the equations to account for unknown shocks and appropriate assumptions are made on them.

Thus we see that an econometric model in general and a SEM in particular is highly suitable to reproduce the richness of CA's theoretical structure with considerable technical flexibility, and offers an apt and useful way of taking the theory to real-life data in the quest for an empirically valid explanation of how advantage and wellbeing relate to resources, 'conversion factors', as well as individual, family, societal and cultural characteristics. Furthermore, even if it is not its main purpose, a SEM can also yield scores or estimates of individual advantages in all the considered dimensions of wellbeing. These estimates may be interpreted as indices of *individual freedom to achieve* and allow for

from a certain disease' (health dimension). The measurement equations will be nonlinear for all these indicators.

comparisons over time or between different groups of people for a deeper investigation of specific disadvantages and possible remedies.

Two Illustrations

In this section, we wish to illustrate the above arguments with the help of two empirical studies that we have conducted and that are the object of two separate academic contributions. Here we summarise the studies from the point of view of how the CA has been operationalised in both contexts by means of a SEM with latent variables. These studies also demonstrate the usefulness of integrating other theoretical approaches with the CA in the search of effective practical policy guidelines for the improvement of human well-being.

First illustration: A CA-based practical framework for policy guidance against unfair social disparities

This study develops an econometric model for assessing the social justice aspect of public policies that aim at improving individual wellbeing, adopting a multidimensional definition of the latter inspired from the CA. We use Bolivian nation-wide representative micro-level data for our empirical analysis. In what follows we focus us on how the four-step procedure is implemented in the study to highlight the suitability of the SEM framework to take into account the relevant informational sets for conducting the analysis, as well as drawing useful conclusions on policy effects. The reader is referred to Krishnakumar and Nogales (2015, 2016a) for detailed explanations.

Step 1: Theoretical structure building. Our study builds upon an influential approach in the social justice domain developed by Roemer (1998), namely the Equality of Opportunity approach. This approach states that in an ideal state of equality of opportunities, characteristics or situations beyond the control of an individual, called *circumstances* (denoted as C_i in our model) should not matter in the determination of any individual well-being outcome. Instead, differences in outcomes should only be the reflection of either differences in willingly and freely taken actions called *efforts* (denoted as E_i) arising from differences in tastes and natural individual heterogeneity, or random factors such as luck. As the efforts themselves can be affected by circumstances, perfect equality of opportunity requires the absence of these indirect effects of circumstances as well. We incorporate this link between efforts and circumstances in our model.

We defend the idea that the Equality of Opportunity approach can be fruitfully extended by bringing in some key ideas from the CA in order to provide a rich and powerful framework to understand wellbeing generation and its connection with public actions. In particular, (i) we make the case for an extension of the Equality of Opportunity framework to a multidimensional setting in which several dimensions of wellbeing and their interrelations are taken into account and (ii) we advocate the explicit consideration of efforts as key drivers of wellbeing instead of treating them as unobservable confounders merged with modelling errors. Here, let us also note that a parallel can be drawn between Roemer's circumstances and Sen's conversion factors as they both relate to personal factors that influence wellbeing opportunities.

In Roemer's framework, public policies (denoted as *pol*) play the role of instruments for *levelling the playing field*. Should they contribute to the attenuation of the direct influence of circumstances on a lifestyle outcome and/or their indirect influence through efforts, one can say that they promote equality of opportunity for wellbeing.

Thus, we extend Roemer's approach to a broader and different evaluative space to argue that equality of wellbeing opportunity (EOp) occurs when *circumstances* (C_i) do not play any role in the determination of *multiple* wellbeing advantages or freedoms to achieve, rather than a single lifestyle outcome. We state that an equality of *advantages* is the appropriate way of going about achieving EOp rather than an equalisation of *actual* outcomes as the latter involves an element of 'choice', which should be preserved. These ideas are inspired by Sen's intervention at the Tanner Lecture on Human Values delivered in 1979, where he put forth what he called *basic capability equality* as a partial guide to moral goodness that is associated with the notion of equality and justice. He argued for this notion of equality of basic capabilities as a moral guide that has important advantages over other notions such as equality of resources or equality of perceptions of satisfaction. Although Sen does not explicitly and deliberately state equality of capabilities as a desired goal, we take this position in this paper and implement it in an empirical study.

Finally, a word of caution. We are not denying the relevance of equality of outcomes from a redistributive angle especially due to the role played by luck (see Atkinson, 2015 for further explanation). However, we argue that the legitimate objective of equality of opportunity should be concerned with opportunities for wellbeing taken in the multidimensional sense as advocated by the CA.

Step 2: Modelling. As explained in our description of the CA, freedom to achieve or potential wellbeing is determined by resources (including economic, social and institutional factors) and conversion factors, among which we distinguish between circumstances that are beyond an individual's control such as gender, age, ethnicity, parental characteristics, as well as efforts and other controls. As the aim of the study is to investigate the role played by policy variables in reducing inequality of opportunity through their effect on the impact of some of the circumstance variables, we also include policy variables in the structural equations. Thus our 'capability' or wellbeing freedom equation is refined to bring out the classification of the resources and conversion factors into circumstances C_i, efforts E_i, policy effects pol, and the remaining variables r_i:

$$Q_i = g_{Q_i}(Q_i, C_i, E_i, pol, r_i) \tag{11.9}$$

To this we add another equation that allows for the possibility that efforts may themselves be influenced by the circumstances of the individual and some other individual determinants s_i:

$$E_i = \varphi_{E_i}(Q_i, C_i, E_i, pol, s_i) \tag{11.10}$$

Perfect equality of opportunity for advantage occurs if $\dfrac{\partial Q_i}{\partial C_i} = 0$, which has to be calculated using both sets of vector equations. If this derivative is not zero (i.e. no perfect EOp), then we say that a policy configuration *promotes* equality of opportunity if it goes in the right direction of *reducing* the magnitude of the impact of circumstances.

Now we specify a linear system of equations for Equations (11.9) and (11.10) considering advantages and efforts as latent endogenous variables (denoted as θ_i) and including two types of exogenous variables: (a) policy variables and policy-sensitive circumstances (x_i) and (b) other exogenous variables that are needed for identification purposes (k_i) that combine r_i and s_i. Thus the structural part is written as:

$$A\theta_i - Tx_i - Bk_i - \varepsilon_i = 0 \tag{11.11}$$

where A, T and B are coefficient matrices that are configured according to appropriate inclusion and exclusion restrictions for identification purposes, and ε_i is a vector of error terms representing unknown factors. To account for the 'levelling the playing field' role of public policies, the impact of circumstances T is postulated to be affected by policy variables:

$$T = \psi_T(pol) = \Gamma + \Pi \cdot pol \qquad (11.12)$$

Because our empirical data set does not contain observations on potential outcomes and efforts, the model considers efforts and capability sets as latent variables and includes the corresponding measurement equations involving multiple effort indicators and achieved functionings.

Step 3: Empirical analysis. Estimating this model with Bolivian data yields quite a rich set of results. Here we highlight two particularly important findings. We find that being indigenous severely hinders the advantage for material living conditions and the exercise of efforts, which is an unfair cause of inequality of opportunities for this wellbeing dimension. This result is in line with the vast literature on persistent and severe disadvantages of ethnic minorities in terms of access to (quality) education and real chances for positions in the competitive job market (see e.g. Nuñez & Villegas, 2016). We calculate that the fact of being indigenous is associated with a 181 per cent reduction of the advantage for material living conditions, compared to non-indigenous people. However, public social service expenditure does contribute to reducing this unfair disadvantage.

On the other hand, expenditure on infrastructure exacerbates the negative effect of being indigenous on material wellbeing advantage implying that the indigenous population benefits less from such expenditures than the others. Although somewhat striking, this result is in line with similar findings for other countries such as Pakistan and India (Keefer & Khemani, 2005), South Africa (Mershon, 2015) and other developing economies such as China, Russia and Indonesia (Gomez, 2015). One possible explanation for this fact can be found in imperfect political decisions that force flows of public expenditures towards powerful minorities, and another one in the considerable geographical difficulties to access the poorest and most vulnerable part of the population.

Step 4: Practical use. Our framework allows us to carry out simulation exercises to examine counterfactual scenarios by simulating the effect of changes in policy variables under the clause of 'all other things being equal'.[6] As an example, simulating a reduction of 50 per cent

---

[6] As the estimation of our SEM yields numerical mathematical functions that can be used to calculate values of the dependent variables (advantages in this case) for any combination of values of the explanatory variables (including policy

in social expenditures at the municipal level and re-assessing the effect of being indigenous, we find that the magnitude of the negative effect increases around 38 per cent in the simulated scenario, thus confirming that these expenditures are indeed helping to reduce the unfair disadvantage of the indigenous people.

Furthermore, our empirical model also allows us to calculate the (optimal) level of expenditure required to completely eliminate unfair disparities due to being indigenous, all other things being equal. Our computations show that social service expenditure should rise, on average, by around 303 per cent per person each year! Thus the current expenditure level is quite far from the optimal level.

Second illustration: A CA-based practical framework for understanding work-related wellbeing

In this study, we focus on a dimension of human development that, in our view, remains understudied in the CA-related literature, namely work-related wellbeing, or work *advantage*. Once again, we use Bolivian data for empirical support, which comes from the World Bank's Survey Towards Employability and Productivity (STEP) program. More details about this study can be found in Krishnakumar and Nogales (2016b).

Step 1: Theoretical structure building. Ever since classical theories proposed by Mincer (1974) and Becker (1994), educational achievements have been directly associated with job market outcomes, and the vast majority of the related literature focuses on earnings. Drawing inspiration from the CA, which advocates for a pluralistic definition of wellbeing, this study takes a stand that work-related wellbeing, which we term *work advantage*, cannot be described by one single indicator and several work-related aspects need to be considered in order to obtain a full picture of the goodness of a job. This view also coincides with that of the International Labour Organization (ILO), which has been promoting the multidimensional concept of decent work with its four pillars of full and productive employment, social protection, rights at work and social dialogue (see e.g. Ghai, 2003). This goes to show how important elements of the CA are compatible with theoretical frameworks of mainstream economics which are often inspired by utilitarianism.

configurations), the simulation exercises consist in the computation of individual advantages for different policy configurations under different circumstances.

This study examines the relationship between educational investments and this broader notion of work wellbeing by investigating how the different type of skills produced by education influence work-related aspects. An adequate framework for relating educational investments to skills is given by Heckman's theory on the technology of skill formation (see Heckman & Mosso, 2014). Our study proposes to blend the capability vision with this theory by looking at how education enhances work wellbeing through the development of multiple skills.

Briefly speaking, skills are divided into two broad types: (i) cognitive skills, referring to a person's acquired knowledge or intelligence ($Q_{C, i}$) and (ii) non-cognitive skills ($Q_{NC, i}$), referring to personality traits or socio-emotional abilities. Let us regroup both types of skills in vector $\theta_i \equiv [Q_{C, i}, Q_{NC, i}]$. According to Heckman's theory, skill acquisition is a dynamic process that starts in the early stages of life. In this process skills are interdependent in the sense that skill-stocks at a certain period in lifetime lay the foundation for the formation of skill-stocks in the next period, i.e. *skills beget skills*. Literature (see e.g. Heckman & Kautz, 2012) highlights two main determinant factors in this dynamic skill formation process: investments in skill formation (I_i), such as education, and parents' skills (θ_i^P), which are taken to be constant over time in this setting.

Finally, turning to work-related wellbeing, we propose to consider multiple aspects going beyond earnings or salaries, even if they are not perfectly observable, to include information about many other dimensions of work advantage including employment opportunities, work conditions and social protection. Then, we relate these dimensions to cognitive and non-cognitive skills, other conversion factors, resource variables and controls.

Step 2: Modelling. Adopting a time index t and considering T development stages in skill formation, the skill formation process can be represented as:

$$\theta_{i, t} = g_\theta(\theta_{i, t-1}, I_{i, t}, \theta_i^P) \text{ for } t = 1 \dots T \quad (11.13)$$

Work advantage is observed in period $T + 1$, i.e. after the skill formation process is finished. Let us denote it as vector $Q_{i, T+1}$. Following the theoretical reasoning of the CA, we formulate work advantage to be a function of the individual's resources $x_{i, T+1}$, and conversion factors which include cognitive and non-cognitive skills possessed at the end of the 'education' period, i.e. $\theta_{i, T}$. To these variables, we add parental skills as is often done in the literature due to the existence of inter-generational transmission of skills (see e.g. Dohmen et al., 2012 and Burke et al., 2013) and as also suggested in Heckman's technology of skill formation theory. This results in a modified version of Heckman's model with work advantage as the dependent variable and supplementary context-relevant variables on the right hand side of the equation[7]:

$$Q_{i,T+1} = g_Q(\theta_{i,T}, \theta_i^P, x_{i,T+1}) \tag{11.14}$$

Substituting successively for $\theta_{i,T}$ and its lags from Equation (11.13), work advantage is obtained as:

$$Q_{i,T+1} = g_Q(I_{i,1}, \dots, I_{i,T}, \theta_i^P, x_{i,T+1}) \tag{11.15}$$

Once again, the model allows for the possibility of endogeneity of some of the explanatory variables, in particular educational investments, as noted in the literature (see e.g. Heckman & Cunha, 2007). In such a case, the equation needs to be analysed together with an investment function:

$$I_{i,t} = \varphi_I(\theta_{i,t}, \theta_i^P, \lambda_{i,t}) \quad \text{for } t = 1 \dots T \tag{11.16}$$

where vector $\lambda_{i,t}$ depicts other possible determinants of the investment decision.

As work advantage and skills are not directly measured, we consider them as latent endogenous variables that we will denote as a vector η_i. Both are captured using multiple achievement indicators. Finally, we reformulate the model in such a way to cover both the cases of exogenous and endogenous educational investments within the same specification. We divide the explanatory variables into two groups: investment-related variables (W_i) and all other variables that are always strictly exogenous (X_i). Adopting a linear form, our structural relations can be written as:

$$A\eta_i - \Gamma W_i - BX_i - u_i = 0$$

---

[7] In the model proposed by Heckman, the dependent variable is usually taken to be one observable aspect of people's life such as earnings, drug use or violent behavior and only skills, i.e. the right hand side variables, are treated as latent. However, we propose that skills as well as work advantage should be considered as unobservable with appropriate multiple indicators for both. Furthermore, skills are elements of paramount importance, but they are not originally interpreted as *means* or *resources* in the sense of the CA, as we propose in this study.

where A, Γ and B are coefficient matrices that include appropriate inclusion and exclusion restrictions and matrix W_i depicts either direct measurements of investments or their estimates yielded by the first of a standard IV-2SLS for correcting endogeneity bias.

Step 3: Empirical analysis. Based on the information available in our data set, we use various reading, writing, comprehension and numeracy scores as indicators of cognitive skills, and the Big Five personality traits as well as three additional socio-emotional characteristics as indicators of non-cognitive skills (see e.g. Heckman & Kautz, 2012; Jia et al., 2013). Our indicators of work advantage can be regrouped under three dimensions – employment opportunities, decent work time and safe work environment.

Among our most salient results, we find that both cognitive skills and non-cognitive skills have positive effects on all dimensions of work advantage, with the effect of the former greater than that of the latter. For instance, we show that the median individual in the *highest quintile* of distribution of cognitive skills has an advantage of employment opportunities that is 0.42 standard deviations greater than the *average*; the median individuals in all other quintiles of these skills are at a disadvantage with respect to the average. We find a very similar qualitative relation between this dimension of work advantage and non-cognitive skills; the corresponding figure for comparing the median individual in the fifth quintile with the person of reference (average) is 0.39. This shows the extent to which this dimension of work advantage is heavily concentrated within a skilled elite in the country.

Furthermore, we also note that disadvantage in terms of decent working time mainly affects people in the lowest quintile of the cognitive skills distribution, but the magnitude of this effect is found to be lower compared to the figures presented above. The median individual in this quintile has an advantage that is 0.16 standard deviations lower than that of the average individual in this dimension. Similarly, the lowest quintile of the non-cognitive skills distribution concentrates individuals that are at a disadvantage in terms of a safe work environment, as measured by the physical strain that it implies for the worker.

Step 4: Practical use. Our empirical results confirm that investments for skill acquisition such as years of schooling and timely school start have significant direct influences on both cognitive and non-cognitive skills and through them, on work advantage. For instance, we show that individuals with a relative advantage in cognitive skills have had at least 12.5 years of education (completed secondary education plus short pre-college courses). Similarly, *advantaged* individuals in terms of non-cognitive skills are concentrated among people who have at least completed primary education (8 years of schooling). As non-cognitive skills may be considered more malleable than cognitive skills through the life cycle,[8] this calls for a special attention to be given to the organ-isation of curricula at different levels of education so that more years of education effectively translate into better non-cognitive skills. This is particularly important in the Bolivian case, as public and private schools and universities in the country are constantly revising a com-petency-based teaching and learning process (Pichardo et al., 2008).

Concluding Remarks

The CA provides a broad and rich framework for analysing wellbeing and agency freedom using multiple information spaces and the relations among them. However, this same richness poses formidable challenges for its operationalisation because of its underlying complexity. A selec-tion of researchers across different disciplines has attempted to rise up to this challenge, proposing different mechanisms of taking the theory to real-life data. In this chapter, we have attempted to show that the different informational spaces and their links can be adequately por-trayed in a theoretical set-up that can be translated into a Simultaneous Equation Model (SEM) with latent variables. A SEM has quite a few advantages that makes it highly suitable to address many crucial ana-lytical issues such as possible non-observability of certain concepts, multiple indicators to represent a single concept, interdependencies among different variable sets, possible feedback effects, policy impacts and individual heterogeneity. It can therefore be effectively applied to widely available micro-level data in most countries.

We do not claim that this is the only way of operationalising the CA. In particular, we stress that whenever direct primary data on capabili-ties are available, they do provide valuable information about people's advantage, which can also be analysed through the lens of a SEM or other equally valid technical tools. However, given the current scarcity of this type of primary data in many countries, we defend the usefulness

---

[8] It is sometimes argued that cognitive skills may relate more closely to raw intel-ligence and hence may be largely inherited (see e.g. Heckman & Kautz, 2012).

of a SEM to make inference on *freedom to choose* using data on all the factors that could possibly influence potential outcomes. By representing as closely as possible the key features of the theoretical framework of the CA and matching them with the practical information available, a SEM is able to operationalise the approach for a better understanding of the mechanisms at play in the real world.

It is also important to mention that even if a SEM allows for as much complexity as needed, certain functional and distributional assumptions are typically introduced in order to estimate the equations of the model; this is common practice in any scientific attempt to describe reality through a theoretical model. However, what is really important is that these theoretical simplifications are tested and validated in a rigorous manner. In that sense, we wish to emphasise that the results of a SEM need to be interpreted in combination with the theoretical simplifications just as in any other scientific modelling exercise. Similarly, the results are only as valid as the data and lack of good data availability can sometimes limit any empirical exercise to a simplified setting. However, this does not imply that one cannot use the empirical model, as the results still do convey useful information for practical decision-making as long as the diagnostic tests do not reject the assumptions. As no model can perfectly reproduce all the complexities of real life, reality being more complex than the model is not an excuse for not studying reality through a model. It is the nature of any theory (not just an econometric model) to depict the world in terms of different 'agents' acting according to different decision rules, and processes leading to certain results, i.e. appropriate theorisation must come first. A SEM or any other econometric model must be understood simply as a translation of a theoretical framework into a suitable form so that it can be confronted with real world data.

Finally, qualitative surveys concerning a small set of individuals also offer particularly rich insights about various aspects of their wellbeing and their inter-relations. However, this approach may lack external validity given that the particular context of this group of individuals is difficult to reproduce elsewhere. We believe that, in the quest of understanding wellbeing and its determinants, a mix of quantitative and qualitative approaches has a great potential to offer useful information for public decision-making and grasping important details of people's livelihoods. It may shed useful light on people's actions and reactions to their reality and thus provide more information on agency freedom and agency wellbeing, which we have not touched upon in this chapter. We leave the operationalisation of the agency aspect of the capability approach for future research.

References

Addabbo T., Di Tommaso M. L., Maccagnan A. (2014) Gender differences in Italian children's capabilities. *Feminist Economics*, 20(2): 90–121.

Anand P., van Hees M. (2006) Capabilities and achievements: An empirical study. *The Journal of Socio-Economics*, 35: 268–84.

Anand P., Hunter G., Smith R. (2005) Capabilities and wellbeing: Evidence based on the Sen-Nussbaum approach to welfare. *Social Indicators Research*, 74(1): 9–55.

Anand P., Hunter G., Carter I., Dowding K., Guala F., van Hees M. (2009) The development of capability indicators. *Journal of Human Development*, 10(1); 125–52.

Anand P., Krishnakumar J., Tran B. (2010) Measuring welfare: Latent variable models for happiness and capabilities in presence of unobservable heterogeneity. *Journal of Public Economics*, 95(3–4): 205–15.

Atkinson A. B. (2015) *Inequality – What Can Be Done?* Harvard: Harvard University Press.

Becker G. S. (1994) Human Capital Revisited. In *Human Capital: A Theoretical and Empirical Analysis with Special Reference to Education*. Chicago, IL: The University of Chicago Press.

Burke T. J., Woszidlo A., Segrin C. (2013) The intergenerational transmission of social skills and psychosocial problems among parents and their young adult children. *Journal of Family Communication*, 13(2): 77–91.

Chiappero-Martinetti E., Roche J. M. (2009) Operationalisation of the Capability Approach, from theory to practice: A review of techniques and empirical applications. In E. Chiappero-Martinetti (Ed.) *Debating Global Society: Reach and Limits of the Capability Approach*. Milan: Fundazione Giangiacomo Feltrinelli.

Comim F. (2001) Operationalising Sen's Capability Approach. Conference: Justice and Poverty, Examining Sen's Capability Approach (Cambridge, 5–7 June 2001).

Comim F., Qizilbash M., Alkire S. (Eds.)(2008) *The Capability Approach: Concepts, Measures and Applications*. Cambridge: Cambridge University Press.

Di Tommaso M. L. (2007) Children's capabilities: A structural equation model for India. *The Journal of Socio-Economics*, 36: 436–50.

Dohmen T., Falk A., Huffman D., Sunde U. (2012) The intergenerational transmission of risk and trust attitudes. *The Review of Economic Studies*, 79(2): 645–77.

Gasper D. (2007) What is the capability approach? Its core, rationale, partners and dangers. *The Journal of Socio-Economics*, 36(3): 335–59.

Ghai D. (2003) Decent work: Concepts and indicators. *International Labour Review*, 142(2): 113–45.

Gomez E. (2015) Health expending and inequality in the emerging economies. Report supported by the EU and Oxfam.

Heckman J., Cunha F. (2007) The technology of skill formation. *American Economic Review*, 97(2): 31–47.

Heckman J., Kautz T. (2012) Hard evidence on soft skills. *Labour Economics*, 19(4): 451–64.

Heckman J., Mosso S. (2014) The economics of human development and social mobility. *Annual Review of Economic, Annual Review* 6(1): 689–733.

Jia H., Jia R., Karau S. (2013) Cyberloafing and personality: The impact of the Big Five traits and workplace situational factors. *Journal of Leadership & Organizational Studies*, 20(3): 358–65.

Keefer P., Khemani S. (2005) Democracy, public expenditures and the poor: Understanding political incentives for providing public services. *The World Bank Research Observer*, 20(1): 1–27.

Krishnakumar J. (2007) Going beyond functionings to capabilities: An econometric model to explain and estimate capabilities. *Journal of Human Development*, 8(1): 29–63.

Krishnakumar J., Ballón P. (2008) Estimating basic capabilities: A structural equation model applied to Bolivia. *World Development*, 36(6): 992–1010.

Krishnakumar J., Nogales R. (2015) Public policies for wellbeing with justice: A theoretical discussion based on capabilities and opportunities. *International Journal of Wellbeing*, 5(3): 44–62.

(2016a) Do public policies promote equality of opportunity for wellbeing? An econometric analysis using Bolivian data. *Working Paper Series 16-06-2*. Geneva: Institute of Economics and Econometrics, University of Geneva.

(2016b) Skills as mediators between education and work advantage. *Working Paper*. Geneva: Institute of Economics and Econometrics, University of Geneva.

Mershon C. (2015) The political determinants of public goods provision in South Africa. Working Paper. University of Virginia

Mincer J. (1974) *Schooling, Experience and Earnings*. New York: Columbia University Press

Nuñez H., Villegas H. (2016) Dicriminación étnica en Bolivia: Analizando diferencias regionales y por nivel de calificación. *Revista de Economía*, 32(2): 201–18.

Pichardo M. C., Garcia T., Justicia F., Llanos C. (2008) Efectos de un programa de intervención para la mejora de la competencia social en niños de educación primaria en Bolivia. *International Journal of Psychology and Psychological Therapy*, 8(3): 441–52.

Robeyns I. (2006) The capability approach in practice. *Journal of Political Philosophy* 14(3): 351–76.

Roemer J. (1998) *Equality of Opportunity*. Cambridge MA: Harvard University Press.

Schokkaert E. (2009) The capabilities approach. In P. Anand, P. Pattanaik and C. Puppe (Eds.) *The Handbook or Rational and Social Choice*. Oxford: Oxford University Press.

Sen A. K. (1980) Equality of what? In *The Tanner Lecture on Human Values, I.* Cambridge: Cambridge University Press, 197–220.

(1985) *Commodities and Capabilities*. Amsterdam: North Holland.

(1987) *The Standard of Living*. Cambridge: Cambridge University Press.

(1992) *Inequality Reexamined*. Oxford: Oxford University Press.

(1999) *Development as Freedom*. Oxford: Oxford University Press.

(2009) *The Idea of Justice*. Cambridge, MA: Harvard University Press.

Tellez J. M., Krishnakumar J., Bungener M., Le Galès C. (2016) Capability deprivation of people with Alzheimer's disease: An empirical analysis using a national survey. *Social Science & Medicine*, 151: 56–68.

UNDP (1990) *Human Development Report*. Oxford: Oxford University Press.

Wendelspiess F. (2017) On the role of agent-based modelling in the theory of development economics. *Review of Development Economics* 21(3), 713–30.

Zhou L., Lin H., Lin Y. (2016) Education, intelligence and wellbeing: Evidence from a semi-parametric latent variable transformation model for multiple outcomes of mixed types. *Social Indicators Research*, 125(3): 1011–33.

PART III

The Application Frontier

12 | Human Development in India
Comparing Sen and his Competitors

DES GASPER

Introduction: 'India Shining'?

A valuable set of papers some years back entitled *Illfare in India – Essays on India's Social Sector* (Harriss-White and Subramaniam, 1999) reflected on India's disappointing progress, in some cases even non-progress, on many 'social' fronts in the fifty years after the independence year of 1947. India, home of civilizations for 5,000 years, home too to ample wealth and talent, housed the greatest concentration of human misery, suffering and wasted potential in the world. Economic growth had shifted from a long-term trend under British rule before 1947 of around 1.5 per cent per annum, little more than the rate of population growth, up to a 3.5 per cent per annum trend, and population growth had revealingly considerably accelerated to an average close to 2 per cent per annum for 1951–1981. Real economic growth further accelerated to 5 per cent per annum in the 1980s and 6 per cent in the 1990s. However, compared to many other countries in Asia and elsewhere, India made weak progress to change illfare into welfare. Its figures for human development compared unfavourably in several respects even with those of much of Sub-Saharan Africa (Drèze and Sen, 1995, 2002). Despite the idea of India (Khilnani, 1997) that had been gradually consolidated since the nineteenth-century, a shared national project of citizenship and provision of its requisites had remained weak after 1947, due to a fragmented hierarchical society and social consciousness. The Dalit leader B. B. Ambedkar had broadly predicted this failure. Tabling the new Constitution in Parliament in 1949, he warned that an India that remained caste-ridden could not form a nation. In such a society, investing in mass education for example has implied empowerment of the rural poor, women and Dalits, and received no priority from the powers-that-be.

In a review article on *Illfare in India* I argued that the abstracted, aggregated, impersonal frameworks from economics that had predominated in much official policy and planning, and even in many of the book's chapters, had helped to veil such issues. They led at most to regrets over a weak state rather than to understanding of a strong and cruel one (Gasper, 2001). Frameworks from economics had contributed to India's poor human development performance, through the disciplinary exclusion of analyses of class, caste and the state, and the lack of attention to issues as fundamental to poverty as age, disability or mental illness, amongst others, and to the intersections of multiple dimensions of disadvantage. Conventional economics had provided little counterweight to the perceptual, ethical and political 'disability' of Indian elites and Indian state institutions in regard to basic need.

As perhaps partial acknowledgement of this weakness, the editors of *Illfare in India* chose to conclude the volume with a chapter from an already published book: the final chapter of Amartya Sen and Jean Drèze's 1995 study of India's economic development and its failings in human development. That book and its 2002 and 2013 successors have thrown a powerful light on the omissions and distortions of Indian development, drawing on Sen's theorizing on capability gaps and entitlement failures.

Since the mid-1990s, India's economic transformation has accelerated. The associated pride has found expression in slogans like 'India Shining', the premature 2004 election banner of the BJP, the broadly right-wing Hindu nationalist party. For many in both the private and public sectors the epitome and talisman of success has been the rate of GNP growth, symbol of national self-respect; considered so important that every type of egg may be broken in order to make a bigger national GNP omelette. Forced displacement from places of residence has occurred on a huge scale, frequently with little or no compensation (see e.g. Perspectives, 2008); and the nominal growth of gross national product is accompanied by vast disinvestment environmentally and sometimes even possible decline of net national wealth (Dasgupta, 2001).

This chapter looks at work of a cross-section of Indian leaders of ideas on public affairs in the early twenty-first-century, to give a comparison with Sen's thinking on Indian development. It takes four such pictures, after reviewing *Illfare in India* to give a baseline from 1999. Second comes Sen's most recent volume on India, *An Uncertain Glory*, written with Drèze[1]; third, a business inspired vision, that of

---

[1] I understand Sen's books with Drèze to derive from intense collaboration based on Sen's theories – capability theory, entitlements analysis and his ideas about

management-strategy guru C. K. Prahalad; fourth, a technology-plus-management perspective, from IT entrepreneur and state-reformer Nandan Nilekani; and fifth, the technology-centred nationalist-inspired vision of former President Abdul Kalam. Nilekani represented one strand in the Congress Party, the dominant power-vehicle from 1947 through to 2014. We look too at ideas of the dominant post-Congress politician, BJP Prime Minister Narendra Modi, to see how he draws from the various strands, and to help in considering the degree of potential political force of Sen's vision.

The unit for comparison is, except for Mr. Modi's speeches, a full book subjected to close reading to assess the quantity and quality of attention given to issues of 'human development' and 'social sectors'. The chapter analyses how and how far these writers consider those issues, within their overall imaginaries of India's past, present and future – the sets of vocabularies, concepts, characters (including the identified groupings and nations), assumptions, topics, ideals, and comparators that they engage with or employ, the scenes they paint and the horizons both retrospective and prospective that they proffer. Through this comparison it identifies also the topics, concepts, characters and values that they may exclude or marginalize. This leads to an elucidation of the 'narratives', the story-lines of past, present and prospective national trajectory that they variously tell, woven around these frames and constructed with these vocabularies.

The approach is influenced by the work of Benedict Anderson (1991) and Sunil Khilnani (1997), amongst others, and by the concerns of Nehru, Ambedkar and their contemporaries two to three generations before, arguing about what sort of 'India' they sought to construct and the requisites of doing so. Sen has reviewed and contributed to such discussions (2005). 'Members' of India's (and almost any other) national 'community' know hardly any of its other members personally. Every country is a creation of the human mind: in the specification of its spatial borders and historical borders (for when did it begin? – typically it is posited to have existed before it acquired its present legal status) and in specification of what supposedly unites it other than its spatial borders, and what rationalizes the borders and

democracy, justice and public reason; while in the books discussing India, Drèze does the larger part of consequent empirical work. This understanding reflects the books' prefaces, other reports on their construction, and their close compatibility with Sen's earlier and ongoing work.

proposed historical characterization. In the modern world what also often purportedly unites a country is a vision of its future, as a way of building shared commitment across highly diverse present-day groups.

Anderson reflected on the images of their (asserted) country created by national dreamers, often expatriates: first, of an ideal supposedly existent in the past; second, of the present reality; and third, of an ideal future; for example in the musings of Gandhi in South Africa or of the elite Muslim men in Cambridge University a generation later who conceived 'Pakistan'. The emergence of the notion and state of India have been much analysed along these lines, often with reference to the language of unity-in-diversity favoured by, for example, Nehru. Sen (2006) has advanced a related but different framework, for reasoned individuality and a person's recognition of his/her plural affiliations. Contemporary Europe illustrates the difficulties of creating a shared 'imagined community' on a sub-continental scale. Yet India has made progress in doing so, including over the years since 1947 and not only when it was united by imperial colonizers and struggles against them.

This chapter explores some of the imaginaries currently employed, to consider in perspective what vision of Indian development Sen offers. We will see that, compared to the other authors, Sen highlights the poorest groups, caste, gender, sanitation, and relevant comparison cases in Asia, notably Bangladesh; that he perhaps misses opportunities to distinguish his work from the others by strongly probing the power systems that underlie the Indian polity, as well as issues like children and migration; and that he says little on what seem to be other authors' most prominent and glamorous selling-points: high technology, contemporary capitalist business models, and lyrical nationalism.

Illfare in India, 1947–1999: Waiting for Human Development

India's figures for human development compare dramatically unfavourably in many respects with those of not only East and Southeast Asia but also much of Sub-Saharan Africa, as underlined by Drèze and Sen in work beginning in the 1980s and repeated each decade since then. Barbara Harriss-White and S. Subramaniam's 1999 collection *Illfare in India – Essays on India's Social Sector* documented much of this disappointing record. It provided an audit of achievements, failures, and policies, written five decades on from 1947, at a time when 'Inequality in India [had begun] on a path of confident expansion' (Subramaniam and

Harriss-White, 1999: 39) and a new BJP-led national government had just taken power. It aimed 'to counter the increasing prevalence of complacency and alienation, and to challenge readers to engagement' (p. 17). Audits, especially if uncomfortable, may fall on deaf ears though, unless a language is found that has the force of new revelation or reaches new and more motivated audiences. Reiteration of the same sorts of findings to the same sorts of audiences in the same sort of language might not be effective. I suggest that the book's own languages, way of seeing, and resulting vision remained overall unsatisfactorily perched on the edge of conventional economics approaches (Gasper, 2001). However its turn to Sen and Drèze for its closing chapter indicated a search for something more, and recognition of how conventional development economics downplayed the multidimensional nature of poverty.

An Audit of India's 'Social Sector', 'Special' Needs and Special Cases

The term 'welfare' can mean how well people live, or what is done by others to help the needy. The book shared this dual focus: it considered how people suffer, and 'the social sector'; given its methods it was stronger on the latter. 'Sectors' are parts of an economy. Economic statisticians and macro-economists record (some of the) resources expended in what they see as the various sectors. Compared to the other sectors though, the 'social sector' spans much of the life of every single person. It is only a 'sector' to economists. Harriss-White's survey paper on the 'social sector' defined it as 'comprising poverty reduction interventions, health, education, nutrition, social assistance and social welfare' (1999a: 304). Crucially, she explained 'the poor record of anti-poverty policy ... in reaching the weakest members of Indian society', for these 'have a high incidence of individuals with special needs through advanced age, disability and chronic sickness (including mental illness), destitution, abandonment and widowhood. Conventional anti-poverty measures are inappropriate for such circumstances' (1999a: 314). Nagaraj's essay on employment and employment promotion programmes documented the diversity, sporadicity and diffuseness of employment in India, and drew an implication that policy should be responsive to local variation and complexity and hence be specified locally. Yet even this fine study discussed employment without reference to the disabled, to human variation.

Harriss-White's essay on disability, 'On To a Loser', noted that few of the mentally retarded in India, and relatively few even of the dumb, survived to adulthood (pp. 138–9). The Indian state was 'currently unwilling, rather than unable' (pp. 152–3) to support their families to fulfil their basic needs. It also barely regulated the work of the private for-profit and non-profit sectors. Astonishingly, economic cost–benefit analysis, a method established for choosing between types of commercial and quasi-commercial project, apparently dominated in allocation of resources for disabled people. The method excludes benefits not expressible in money and typically neglects the needs of people without purchasing power. Recent work influenced by capability theory underlines the need for a more person-focused lens. Trani et al. (2015: 1) report that: 'Public stigma and multidimensional poverty linked to SMI [Severe Mental Illness] are pervasive and intertwined. Particularly for low caste and women, it is a strong predictor of poverty. Exclusion from employment linked to negative attitudes and lack of income are the highest contributors to multidimensional poverty'.

Conventional Economics as Disabled and Disabling in Studying Poverty

All the twelve long papers in *Illfare in India* were by economists, with two exceptions (Athreya and Radhakrishnan). For documenting and auditing ill-fare the methods of conventional economics are essential but insufficient. The book, not untypically, contained no case of a specific ill-faring person, not one piece of testimony or 'voice of the poor', not one life history, and little of the languages of feelings and of care. Studies that identify particular real people in their complexity, in their social and historical contexts – such as those by Das (1996) and Breman and Das (1999) – are indispensable complements to economists' abstractions (Gasper, 2000). Economists have tended to see development as a technical exercise, whether of appropriate state investments, or 'getting prices right', or finding the right levers of 'human resource development', not also centrally as a human struggle against far more than economic constraints and as a political struggle for human rights. In India, a technocratic approach has had special attraction, as a way of supposedly bypassing the political blocks, a way of effecting social change through a type of technical fix rather than by political struggle and moral change.

Other chapters in the book reflected the abstracted generalized depersonalized gaze of even well-intentioned conventional economists. It contained almost no discussion of culture and relatively little of race, gender and women's movements, and little on political strategies for change. Two chapters devoted themselves to adjusting human development indexes for the Indian states, according to how, respectively, poverty and basic education are distributed between two groups, first the Scheduled Castes and Tribes and second the rest of the population. The adjusted indexes led to minor changes in the ranking of states, no more. Non-aggregated figures, comparing Scheduled Castes/Tribes with other groups, per state and across states, are far more helpful than adjusted re-aggregated poverty indices. They would show how tens, in fact hundreds, of millions of Indians have been excluded from basic services. Analyses of more sharply defined disadvantaged groups (for example, Dalit women, the blind, the crippled, disabled women) would also be more helpful.

Explaining the Record

Robert Cassen's essay linked India's typically low incremental output/capital ratios to its relatively poorly educated workforce (Cassen, 1999). Manabi Majumdar discussed the miserable performance in basic education to 1997 and probed too the sources and excuses for policy failure. Wretchedly funded schools for the poor offer limited prospects for the pupils. Neglect of basic education for huge numbers of people has then been rationalized by the tax-averse and by some in the State, as justified by the poor's alleged lack of desire for schooling and by their prior need to supplement family incomes through child labour. These rationalizations re-create the causes: the uneducated remain desperately poor and hindered in both perceiving and grasping the benefits of schooling.

Contributors bemoaned weakness of the state rather than exposing its strength and cruelty. Official speeches and the hopes of planners can be mistaken for 'Indian politics'; but, as at the world scale, the exclusion of the poor has been often intentional not only accidental. As shown by the superior achievements in many comparable countries, shortage of resources in India has not been the reason for inaction. If taxes were collected without evasion there would be ample resources (Subramaniam and Harriss-White, 1999: 37–8).

Athreya's essay on adult literacy and programmes noted how 'failure to implement the constitutional promise for free and comprehensive elementary education' (1999: 228) had left vast tasks for adult literacy programmes, yet they had received even lower priority, less than one per cent of the education budget. A successful large-scale adult literacy programme in Maharashtra in the early 1960s was ignored nationally. Only with the Janata administration of 1977–9 did national leaders show urgent interest in educating the 'broad masses', but the ambitious 1978 plan was downgraded step-by-step by successive governments. What remained was in the usual top-down, sectorally restricted, sickly format with centrally set targets all too readily 'achieved' by false reporting. A breakthrough occurred at the end of the 1980s. A team of motivated and politically backed top administrators and activists led by Anil Bordia (the Education Secretary) launched campaigns of mass mobilization to achieve functional literacy, a method used abroad already for decades. Athreya noted the key roles of participation in the successes of this movement, and its decline as it was extended into less welcoming areas of the country and recaptured by an authoritarian and sectoralist bureaucracy. In large parts of the country 'empowerment of non-literates through the mass campaigns implied ... empowerment of the rural poor, the women and the Dalits' (p. 255) and threatened many powers-that-be. Such programmes were reined back. Nagaraj's essay similarly documented the need to design employment programmes as part of social transformation and breaking-up of semi-feudal relations; instead employment programmes operated with centrally set targets for centrally defined measures which promoted marginal types of work in sectors with little demand or demand growth. Social transformation and local autonomy were feared and resisted.

Despite such evidence, *Illfare in India* connected little to analyses of political forces for and against reduction of illfare, and of 'the unarticulated reluctance of the [Indian] state to be a vehicle of empowerment of the suppressed sections of society' (Introduction: p. 31). Radhakrishnan (1999)'s paper on the politics of caste reservations over several decades was the exception. Mass franchise politics had typically reinforced caste society; and elites from 'Other Backward Castes' had been the main beneficiary of reservations policies due to their balancing electoral position and their ability to sufficiently control and deliver vote-banks. Elsewhere in the book, caste figured very little, except as a statistical category for the economists.

What Next?

Recommendations included 'according a high priority to health education programmes as a strategy for promoting good health' (Muraleedharan, p. 123) because 'many of the health problems of the poor can be solved to a large extent through health education' (p. 128). Yet they were not. The same could be said for measures of public sanitation. Many medical professionals had evolved into profit maximizers, and 'as a result we are facing certain basic issues, primarily ethical in nature, that restrict access to appropriate care' (p. 130). Some other essays concluded similarly, but ethics and what can influence them were not taken up elsewhere in the book. It hardly used the language of human rights, or any other explicit moral framework for critique such as basic capabilities.

Unusually, the concluding contribution to *Illfare in India*, a set of original papers, was a version of a chapter published four years earlier. Drèze and Sen's *India – Economic Development and Social Opportunity* (1995) was turned to for potential illumination and inspiration. We consider now the successor volume *An Uncertain Glory* (2013), the latest in the series where Drèze and Sen have analysed India's economic and human development; to see in which ways the book transcends *Illfare in India* and in which not.

Drèze and Sen: India's Uncertain Glory

Amartya Sen's theorizing combines an elegant universality with a strong humanistic focus. Its hallmark has been to focus economic analysis on the lives of individual ordinary people and the plurality of interwoven factors that affect and constrain them. His lexicon of 'human development' places the economy as subsidiary to people, rather than leaving persons and society as a lesser box within an economic accounting. His capability approach can be used to focus and synthesize an audit of illfare and contribute to a motor for change: a moral compass for concern and prioritization. His entitlements approach helps then in design of programmes for public action conceived in terms far broader than only State expenditure. The theories are well known, much discussed, and well in evidence in his books on India.[2] They will not be

---

[2] Human development theory is discussed more explicitly in the 1995 and 2002 books but not repeated in the 2013 book. This book aims (like Prahalad, Nilekani and Abdul Kalam) to reach a general audience and so has no wish

the centrepiece here. Instead we consider how they are used to characterize and address the specifics of Indian realities, and what might be their limits. The theories' humane motivation is reflected in Sen's continuing active commitment to the less advantaged in India: he retains citizenship, spends much of each year there, and works intensively on its issues of human development, especially in partnership with Drèze.

The 1995 book had proposed that the then-recent 73rd and 74th constitutional amendments to revive *panchayati raj* institutions provided opportunities to build local political communities that represent all India's population, if supplemented 'with an expansion of public initiatives and social movements aimed at more widespread literacy, a stronger political organisation of disadvantaged groups and a more vigorous challenge to social inequalities' (Drèze and Sen, in Harriss-White and Subramaniam, 1999: 392). But by 2013 they noted that India could look back on over thirty years of rapid economic growth and miserable advances in human development (Drèze and Sen, 2013: ix). To bring this home, *An Uncertain Glory* uses extensive comparison not only with China or Brazil but with Bangladesh, India's neighbour: a much poorer country and with considerably lower economic growth than India in the past generation, that had much worse human development indicators than India in the 1970s but that a generation later had far outstripped it. This theme figures strongly in the Preface, the international comparisons chapter, and the health chapter. A similar comparison exists with some parts of sub-Saharan Africa. The book documents the sorry story of human development in India, sector by sector, for example in regard to nutrition, child mortality and environmental damage. In parallel it traces the priority tacitly given in each sector to supporting more affluent groups, through policies that are too often misleadingly designated 'populist'.

Drèze and Sen rely on data from the World Bank's *World Development Indicators* and on careful 'case-by-case assessment' (p. 28). Their degree of specific knowledge of other countries far outstretches that in the other books we will examine; for example in noting that Sri Lanka, far better educated than India, has no private schooling system along Indian lines (p. 58). The chapter on education explodes once more the

to foreground theory. Capability theory is part of Sen's human development framework, as are entitlements analysis and his ideas on justice; it is not the whole (Gasper, 2007, 2008), even though some supporters like to call the full package 'the capability approach'.

myth that poor people are not interested in sending their children to school, when some actual schooling is supplied (p. 110); and documents and analyses in painful detail the continuing disaster of much of the government school system in India – and the new disasters in much of the private school system, where absence of serious competition, plus parental gullibility, often allow large-scale profit-making for little educational benefit.

The chapter on health, equally meticulous, judicious and depressing, explores India's prominence at the bottom of numerous performance tables, related to the decline of the public system in most of India – despite lessons from around the world, including the USA, and the domestic achievements in some states, notably Tamil Nadu – and to the vested interests and biases of private health industry providers, insurance companies and richer users who are not willing to use or contribute to a shared public facility. The book's curiosity on the specifics of ordinary people's lives extends to the delicate topic of sanitation, which is discussed extensively. 'In India, a full 50 percent of households had to practice open defecation in 2011', six or seven times the proportion in Bangladesh; and 'women … are often constrained to rise before dawn and have no convenient way of relieving themselves after that' (p. 63).

The chapter on poverty and social protection shows how miserly and incomplete have been the identification of households and persons in poverty in India, and how grudging and counterproductive the deliberately exclusive forms of selection, targeting and 'user fees' for basic health and education. Self-identification as poor is shown to be a more appropriate mechanism, as seen for example in the rural employment 'guarantee' scheme. Drèze and Sen's thoughtful documented assessments of that programme and of 'new style' public food distribution are not conducted in terms of party political labels. Nor do they engage with the religious undertones in current actions and inaction: of stigmatizing the supposedly undeserving poor, ignoring the unworthy, cursing evil-doers.

In comparison to the books which we look at next, *An Uncertain Glory* is harder to summarize. It centres on careful examination of data and steering between myths at either extreme; for 'the resolution of particular policy issues demands a specific, case-by-case assessment of arguments in favour and against', with reference to the 'effects on people's lives' (p. 28). It contains few memorable anecdotes or interviews with leaders and celebrities. There are no shining heroes and simple villains. Democracy remains its very reluctant hero. 'It is deeply disappointing that more use has not been made of the opportunities offered by a political democracy and a free society to solve the problems that so many Indians continue to face' (p. 16). Indeed the book admits that 'we know very little about which institutions matter' for development (p. 36), and in reality this point applies also with regard to Western forms of political democracy. The full chapter on corruption devotes special attention to institutions for transparency, in addition to seeking to influence behavioural norms and reduce societal tolerance for corruption.

In these chapters the agents are not strongly highlighted. We read a thoughtful diagnosis of mistakes, oversights, blind spots; but less about the agents who commit them, and their passions and perceptions, likes and dislikes (in contrast to Mander, 2015, for example). Chapter 8 addresses India's specific inheritance, caste: disgust-based extreme social hierarchy. It probes outcomes much more than roots. When measured in terms of income per capita rather than personal expenditure per capita, inequality in India is at South African levels, far higher than traditionally estimated; and is much higher yet when the absence of public services is included (p. 280). Subsidies to petroleum and fertilizer greatly exceed all government health expenditure; the exemption of crude oil and mineral oils from customs duties loses revenue that could pay for the national food security proposals twice over; and so on, and on (pp. 270–72). Upper castes totally dominate the upper ranks in business, government and media.

Chapter 9 squarely faces the charge that the scale, persistence and even intensification of 'inequalities in India, which were discussed in earlier chapters, provides strongly incriminating evidence against taking Indian democracy to be adequately successful in consequential terms' (p. 244); and concludes that the system has mostly failed to fulfil the duties outlined in the Directive Principles of the Constitution. The chapter recounts the embarrassing character and indolence of so many of India's democratically elected legislators. At this point Sen seeks to distinguish ballot-box democracy from his Millian ideal of 'government by discussion' and Rawlsian notion of 'the exercise of public reason' (pp. 257–9). But public discussion in India, as he and Drèze show, are completely dominated by affluent groups and their concerns. Indian media provide little or no coverage of the lives of half the country (except in constant attacks on pro-poor programmes, p. 284), and are not even conscious of the bias: 'the relatively privileged seem to have created a social [and mental] universe of their own' (p. 268). 'The possibility of space missions seems to capture the imagination of the privileged far more than flush toilets' (p. 281). In these respects, India is a microcosm of the world. The chapter ends without a proposed solution, although it draws encouragement from the Right to Information Act. It leads instead into a final chapter: 'The Need for Impatience'. This summarizes again the wretched performance by international standards and the failures to understand the real content of the growth-models in Asia and elsewhere since the 1940s. It offers no vision of an exciting national project that would transform India from quasi-apartheid.

Do Drèze and Sen contain proportionately too much depressing audit and too much sober faith in democratic deliberation to be able to underpin an inspiring political programme? (Gasper, 2009). Do they offer a set of mobilizing 'myths' about an imaginable desirable attainable future, anger-inducing enemies (injustice, corruption and lack of dignity are instead presented coolly as problems to be analysed and counteracted), and inspirational 'heroes' to be loyal to, other than the now relatively tame and tarnished ideals of democracy and rational deliberation? We find such rousing features in the work of Abdul Kalam and Nandan Nilekani, and in popular versions of the business evangelism articulated by Sen's doppelganger, Professor C. K. Prahalad.

Whose Fortunes Lie at the Bottom of C. K. Prahalad's Pyramid?

Sen and Drèze's work gained influence in some corners of the Indian state during the recent phase of the Congress Party's long rule, in 2004–14. Yet by the time of the start of a second major phase of BJP rule in national government in 2014, combined now with greater BJP predominance at regional level, we can see major shifts compared to the mental and political worlds of the 1990s. Most notable is the rise of private-sector dominated discourse, power and prestige. Big business expressions of self-pity can still be found but have been superseded by a more confident, pro-active and even sometimes socially constructive stance. In the emergence of such discourse perhaps the most influential single thinker, in his writings and through the advisory roles he took up, was the late C. K. Prahalad (1941–2010) of the University of Michigan, the man who persuaded many top leaders of big Indian corporations to recognise that they operate in a society not only an economy (Paramanand, 2014: 72).

Prahalad was one of the top corporate strategy academics worldwide in the 1990s and 2000s, co-creator of 'core competences' thinking. He offered intellectual perspectives to articulate how Indian business mind-sets were changing and to influence them himself. At organizational level he had proposed the need to be aware of, and if necessary reform, an organization's 'dominant logic'– its set of mental maps that derive from its past experience but may be outdated and dysfunctional for the future (Paramanand, 2014). He had encouraged corporations to think big, bold and afresh: 'if your aspirations are not greater than your resources, you're not an entrepreneur'.[3] Resources are secondary; they can usually be mobilized for good ideas, from investors, partners, consumers or suppliers. So businesses should think in terms of opportunities rather than constraints; for example, opportunities linked to the presence in many Indian slums of multiple-income non-tax-paying households. They should not copy current 'best practices' but instead seek 'next practices', innovations that transform price-performance ratios. Businesses and nations in the global South can even become world leaders, because they can leapfrog the established competitors who are stuck in the physical, social and mental infrastructures of previous technological eras. The scale of Prahalad's personal impact on many large companies in India, through consultancies, exhortations and informal advice as well as his writings, meant that his strategy of changing mental maps has in effect been applied at national scale in India across much of the corporate sector, facilitated by his standing internationally.[4] Later we will see how Nandan Nilekani has consciously essayed such a management re-think for India as a whole, not least for the Indian state.[5]

---

[3] From an interview in *Strategy and Business*, 9 August 2010: www.strategy-business.com/article/00043?pg=all.

[4] For example, Prahalad influenced Unilever globally – stimulating the Unilever Sustainable Living Plan and their Standards of Corporate Behaviour – long before he published *The Fortune at the Bottom of the Pyramid*.

[5] However, Nilekani never mentions Prahalad.

As expressed in the foreword to his famous *The Fortune at the Bottom of the Pyramid* best-seller, Prahalad became preoccupied from Christmas 1995 onwards with how business could help the poor. 'Why is it that with all our technology, managerial know-how, and investment capacity, we are unable to make even a minor contribution to the problem of pervasive global poverty and disenfranchisement?' (Prahalad, 2005: xi). Even before his slogan of 'The Fortune at the Bottom of the Pyramid' (BoP), he became the most influential proponent of the idea that business can 'do well by doing good'. While open to many criticisms, the BoP idea has great flexibility, being applicable to any market sector and open to combination with Prahalad's further notion of the 'co-creation of value' through cooperative interaction between a business, its customers and suppliers. Ideas, requests, innovations, feedback can come from all sides. The slogan evolved from 'Fortune at the Bottom ...' to 'Fortune with the Base of the Pyramid'. It provides an ennobling sheen for even investments for middle-income groups very remote from the real bottom.[6] An India-specific sister label, 'Indovation' (Birtchnell, 2013), emerged specifically for low-cost innovations for low-income consumers.

Besides acquiring saintly status in Indian big business circles, Prahalad's ideas rose in both major political parties. Rahul Gandhi's adviser Sachin Rao was a student and disciple of Prahalad from a period at the University of Michigan (Rao, 2005).[7] A piece entitled 'Major Indian political parties quote Social Entrepreneurial thinkers' notes these remarks by Uma Hemachandran:

... with the unexpected upset [loss] of the BJP in the [2004] elections, in part due to inadequate attention to those struggling at the bottom, the party is now taking a page, quite literally, out of CK Prahalad's 'Bottom of the

[6] An article in *The Hindu*, 4 July 2010: 'Call for fulfilling C. K. Prahalad's unfinished agenda', cited various business leaders: 'Godrej & Boyce Manufacturing Limited Chairman and Managing Director Jamshyd N. Godrej [said] Tata's Ginger Hotels, and Godrej's Chotukool, a refrigerator for rural households, were born out of Prahalad's ideas ... Hindustan Unilever former Vice-Chairman D. Sundaram said that Professor Prahalad was the driving force behind Pureit, a solution to provide safe drinking water at low price and Shakti, a project empowering rural women by distributing FMCG [Fast Moving Consumer Goods] through them'.

[7] Rao and others undertook an e-choupal type case-study for Prahalad, which is in the BOP book's CD-Rom, and at: 'Indiagriline – EID Parry' at www.bus .umich.edu/FacultyResearch/ResearchCenters/EIDParry.pdf.

Pyramid'. She references a speech by BJP's LK Advani, in June 2008 where he says, '*In this context, I must say that I am highly impressed by C.K. Prahalad's theory about 'The Fortune at the Bottom of the Pyramid'. I agree with his approach to poverty alleviation, which states that 'if we stop seeing the poor as victims or as a burden and start recognizing them as resilient and creative entrepreneurs and value-conscious consumers, a whole new world of opportunities will open up'.*[8]

Much of the business talk and business journalism stands in contrast to the realities described by long-term in-depth social research on an India marked by increasing differentiation and dramatically divergent fortunes. Mazumdar and Agnihotri (2014)'s huge multi-year study of women's work-related migration in the whole of India reveals some of the major blind spots. It undertook surveys in numerous parts of the country, both in places of origin and destination, complemented by other discussions. Women's work-related migration has grown enormously but has been conventionally mis-conceptualized and greatly under-recorded, including in major government statistical publications. The criterion of change of usual place of residence leaves out the huge numbers of short-term migrants, which have soared since the 1990s and include now a high proportion of women, as a result of the agrarian crisis in much of the country and the marked decline in secure employment of women in most sectors in the era of market-led growth. 'Armies of women [are] migrating in search of [seasonal] work', reported one observer they cite – as one can see on the sides of national highways. But, due to a view that 'real' migration means permanent transfer from rural to urban areas, short-term migrants only entered official figures as recently as 2007–2008. Even then, those whose migratory cycles exceed six months remain excluded; and the employment-related component in movements that are also for marriage is overlooked. Much social science continues to relatively neglect migration (Jan Breman's work in India has been a major exception); and it is hardly mentioned in *An Uncertain Glory*.

Mazumdar and Agnihotri investigate a range of modes of migration, including: circulatory; short-term seasonal; irregular short-term; medium-term; daily or weekly long-distance commuters, including urban to

[8] Posted on July 11, 2008 on 'The Social Ecosystem' http://blog.ambientengines .com/2008/07/11/major-indian-political-parties-quote-social-entrepreneurial-thinkers/

rural; and migration for unpaid family care. Their study demonstrates the concentration of migrant women workers from the scheduled castes and tribes in the most marginal, poorly-remunerated, and physically arduous employment, especially in short-term and circulatory migration and work in agriculture and brickmaking. The relatively fast-growing and higher-status urban service occupations are largely the preserve of urban upper-caste women. The rural economy increasingly marginalizes poorer groups, who have the least access to the relatively few relevant formal sector jobs generated in the urban economy.

Sunil Tankha observes (personal communication) from his research on institutional preparedness for climate change adaptation that government staff at local levels in India consider that most agriculturalists have no future, and hence that adaptation can only be through out-migration to towns and cities. An unprecedented scale of population transfer may lie ahead. In parallel, given the limits on urban job creation, there may be further massive growth of the types of labour arrangement described by Mazumdar and Agnihotri, reminiscent of the systems in apartheid South Africa. Circulatory workers, displacees, bonded labour and the like are topics far in the background for Prahalad. Let us look for them in the emblematic book of Nandan Nilekani and in the vision of former President Abdul Kalam. We consider which topics are on the menu and how they are served up.

Nilekani: Imagining India – as America

The Infosys IT entrepreneur and multi-millionaire Nandan Nilekani (1955–) has emerged as a leading national reformer, including as head of the Unique Identification Authority from 2009 to 2014. He was a Congress parliamentary candidate in 2014. Infosys has led in the huge growth of India's software sector, including in support of the offshore Business Process Outsourcing (BPO) that has mobilized bright low-cost Anglophone staff. His 500-page *Imagining India – Ideas for the New Century* presents a wide-ranging analysis and vision for the country (Nilekani, 2009). It extends a bullish Western-oriented technology-based perspective to India as a whole, approached as a further business-process re-engineering challenge albeit on a mega-scale. *Imagining India* synthesizes notions of transformation through technology, business management and markets. It represents in some ways a reverse image of *An Uncertain Glory*.

Main Themes

'I have attempted to analyse India through the evolution of its ideas ... [because] every country is governed through some overarching themes and ideas', writes Nilekani (p. 8). In contrast to Drèze and Sen, *Imagining India*'s first chapter presents a crude but memorable storyline of India's past, present and future. First came the Nehruvian creation of modern India, 1947–64, dominated by 'the state'. This Nehruvian India, not a much older India, is highlighted as the enemy: 'the state' is stagnant, stifling and deeply risk-averse. Second came the semi-transition effected by economic liberalization in 1991. Here the story is more nuanced than those told by many external commentators, for example as (typically) in *The Economist* newspaper or by Dutch observer Roel van der Veen, for Nilekani recognizes that each stage has laid a basis for the next.[9] Third, a rosy future of take-off into economic and social freedom lies ahead, that can be realized by adopting Nilekani's ideas. The chapters that follow in his Part I on India Re-Imagined concern the ingredients of that rosy future: the 'demographic dividend', the private sector, the English language, IT, the rise of Indian multinational companies and global economic opportunities, and the emergence of a widely-felt sense of national identity. Together these ingredients allow an inspiring envisioned trajectory for India as a world leader in C21: it has the IT skills, the knowledge of

---

[9] Roel van der Veen, author of *What Went Wrong with Africa*, an Africa specialist in the Netherlands Ministry of Foreign Affairs, undertook a sabbatical in 2005–6 to write on the triumphs of economic liberalization in India: 'India's Road to Development'. He presented a pro-market view-from-outside, with no intra-national differentiation despite the different trajectories of Punjab, Kerala or Bihar. In his story a large proportion of India's budget had been spent on social services that could not be economically sustained. Allegedly India had changed more since 1991 than in centuries previously – even though in reality after being stagnant or falling under colonial rule life expectancy had risen markedly during 1947–91, while economic growth moved from the colonial 1.5% p.a. to an average around 4% p.a. In contrast, Nilekani's view-from-inside notes the upward shift in economic growth from the early 1980s (pp. 73–7, 475), from a 3.5% p.a. trend to a 6% trend – based partly on starting to reap fruits from earlier investments such as in the Indian Institutes of Technology where he himself studied. Van der Veen's narrative highlights only the liberalization of 1991, seen as similar to the fall of the Berlin Wall. Only after 1991 does social mobility allegedly begin. This simplistic analysis appears at length in van der Veen (2010) and reflects standard views in Dutch business circles and the associated political parties.

English, a window-of-opportunity phase when the country has a high proportion of working-age population as its baby boom is followed by secular birth-rate decline, the high savings, low-cost professionals and business culture for it to become a leader in an era of computerized transparent accountable efficient business and public administration, including for running elections and taxation. IT can bring efficiency, effectiveness and equity, sustaining a social order that gives everyone access to everything, including through nationwide economical access to credit. E-governance will remove venal 'gate-keepers' and transform public services.

Characters (and Absences)

Nilekani gives a business-sector representation of Indian history. The bad guys are: first, British colonialism and the 'legacies of the East India Company' (p. 67), with little reference to any pre-British legacies and none to Indian society as the product of many successive conquests; second, the British legacy of an Indian English-speaking elite that patronizes post-colonial 'masses' (p. 12); and, foremost, the swollen inert state, supported by the backward political Left. 'The state' is allegedly a leftist incubus, yet is one that for example 'failed to implement [mass education]' (p. 15). Marching with the state is a parasitic class of state employees with defined-benefit pensions, subsidized by taxation that could have served the poor (p. 415), and of unaccountable academics working in feeble underfunded universities (at least before the 2007– 12 National Plan). A total of four million employees in central government in a country of over one billion people is presented as absurdly large. The iconic villain is Mrs Gandhi (baldly labelled 'Indira'), who imposed market restrictions and nationalizations and is presented as doling out subsidies rather than investing in long-term development. 'The state' that she and her father created is described as very strong when it came to frustrating capitalists but as weak when it came to supporting the poor – due to its wrong ideas. Nilekani does not disaggregate 'the state' much; 'the state has failed to implement mass education', but in fact that is primarily a subnational-level responsibility.

The good guys are the suffering, but innovative, Indian business sector. For Nilekani, software engineer turned computer empire manager, America is the tacit model. Japan, the richest Asian country and the

first to economically transform, is not even mentioned – unlike for
Drèze and Sen who stress its nineteenth-century drive towards mass
education – let alone for example Sri Lanka, Thailand or Indonesia, all
of which are within Drèze and Sen's field of reference. In Indian terms
this is a Bangalore book, with greater plausibility for India's more
progressive South.[10] It talks of Bombay, not Mumbai, the name introduced in 1995. It does not talk of Calcutta/Kolkata, under any name.
Europe is not the model; it is condemned as having an unaffordable
welfare state. Nor is Latin America favoured: supposedly large parts
of it have 'turned to socialism ... and [it] is mired in stagnant growth'
(sic; p. 56); Brazil allegedly had a socialist government (p. 289), rather
than a mildly social democratic one. The book makes many international comparisons though, to spur pride and performance. The choice
is between being 'a country that greatly disappoints when compared
to our potential or one that beats all expectations' (p. 362) – the voice
of an ambitious professional seeking pride when encountering others
in global meeting places. Notably absent from the comparisons, again
unlike in Drèze and Sen's work, is Bangladesh, ignored despite its
greatly superior record in 'the social sector'. Perhaps South India feels
no need to look in that direction.

Within Nilekani's 'cast of characters', Muslims receive very little
attention, despite forming a high proportion of the poorest in India
and often suffering particular forms of exclusion (e.g. many are Dalit
Muslims); likewise for the disabled and the displaced, notwithstanding
his enthusiasm for roads construction. Indians are conceived in this
book as individual consumers, clients and (potential) 'human capital'
(e.g. p. 402). Using such a conception India becomes seen as one, an
entity that is being unified by markets, by technology and by English.
Amongst the forces defending and advancing the use of English are
Dalits, he underlines. Caste does feature in his discussions, as a barrier that is manipulated by politicians and that must be surpassed by
shifting to the perspective in terms of individual citizens and consumers. Caste is seen as evolving not frozen. But while M. N. Srinivas's
prediction is repeated, that the market economy will dissolve caste,
Nilekani admits that so far India has continued to be organized more

[10] Nilekani at one point talks of 'India's English-speaking areas – the southern
and western states' (p. 467).

in terms of castes than of society-wide classes and the corresponding issues such as social security (p. 288).

He does not disaggregate far in class terms. A claim is cited that a $2.5 [sic] rise in urban consumption spending increases rural household incomes by almost one dollar (p. 231) – but whose are those rural incomes? Which groups do they belong to? Nilekani does not see the implications of his own anecdote of people in drought-prone areas who have sold their ration cards in order to buy food (p. 255); he sees it as an argument against ration cards ('dole outs') rather than as an indicator of some groups' desperation and not only of other groups' corruption.

Farmers figure in the narrative, slightly, as mired in 'age-old, outdated agricultural practices' (p. 441) and dupes of a subsidy system that leads to exhaustion of their groundwater and poisoning of their soil (p. 435). They supposedly suffer under the 'tragedy of the commons' (p. 442), and yet they live in 'communities' (p. 443) that could jointly manage common resources if rights were formalized. Nilekani agrees with Drèze and Sen on the need to strengthen local governance in order to respond to local conditions and defend local interests and environment.

The chapter on social insecurities identifies another major character, 'the family': people's refuge from the rugged public arena and overwhelmingly 'the primary caretaker' (p. 405). As family systems change dramatically, including through large-scale migration and urbanization, how can supplementary or replacement national systems be built, he asks.

Topics (and Absences)

Part II of *Imagining India* is on the key challenges to be solved in fulfilling the vast opportunity and happy vision identified in Part I, and on steps taken in the previous decade or more. It has chapters on primary schooling, nationally integrated markets, urban governance and its absence, and physical infrastructure and its decades-long neglect. All these chosen topics reflect the needs and perspective of business.

Schooling for the 'masses' receives a full chapter, on its desperate condition in upper-caste dominated settings and on attempts from the 1980s onwards to remedy this. Nilekani does recognize here that the Constitution granted education to state governments not central control, but the ambiguity of the term 'state' assists his storyline. In the 1970s, Mrs Gandhi moved education to the concurrent list, and a decade later Rajiv Gandhi started using that power. The 93rd Amendment made basic education for children a fundamental right from 2001, and in the same year the Supreme Court made midday meals for children in school obligatory. The challenge remained to turn public schooling into meaningful education, in the face of unconcerned state-level governments. Private schooling has mushroomed, drawing children away from public schooling that is often mediocre or worse.

Part III is about systemic reform: reforming the state and basic state–citizen relations, that remained stagnant while business has boomed; transcending caste, not institutionalizing it via augmented reservations; reforming labour markets, to reduce the privileges of formal sector employees and so allow labour-intensive expansion not via rights-less casual workers as at present; and reforming universities. The picture of politics remains one of saying that leaders lack 'vision' (p. 313). His observation that 'the reforms that attract such [intense] knee-jerk opposition are the very ones that [would] bring the poor significant economic freedoms and power, the kind that would allow them to choose better schools, access welfare more effectively' (p. 312) is treated as a paradox rather than as revealing the nature of existing class-rule by elites and the organized middle classes.

Part IV explores in detail upcoming challenges in health (notably, ageing), social provision (pensions and social security), environment and energy supply, for each of which attention must be given now not only later. The health chapter, for example, talks of what has probably been the least active ministry of health in the world (p. 384), preoccupied mainly with birth control and that presided by 2000 over 'a system in ruins' (p. 393). Nilekani accepts that private sector entry can never suffice in health, for 'health is too much of a public good ... [for] creating awareness, controlling epidemics and ensuring basic nutrition and vaccination for even the poorest citizens – the government has to play a role, as market solutions for these services are neither effective nor universal' (p. 386). The National Rural Health Mission launched in 2005 has taken some major steps; but public-funded health education remains very weak, and the health implications of other policies (like overuse of subsidised pesticides, and blocking foreign investment in the retail sector to build cold storage chains) are not considered, he says.

Despite long chapters on both health and pensions, Nilekani barely mentions sanitation.[11] The scope of his agenda matches urban elite concerns and American think-tank debates, about the affordability of different types of social security scheme and how to meet growing energy demands. Environmental protection rightly has a chapter, but sanitation does not. Disability too does not feature.

In all his areas, ICT, in which India has real comparative advantage, is presented as having transformative power, including for state–citizen–business relations; for example through 'IT-enabled [electricity] grid intelligence' (p. 470). ICT can allow a real Right-to-Information, beyond just the legal right instituted in 2005. It can bring affordable medical care to remote locations. Maps and land records can be digitized and harmonized. A unified 'national smart ID' would transform India by confirming each citizen's status, assets, rights, responsibilities and credit-status, bypassing venal middlemen and gate-keepers, and making entitlements transferable nationwide. IT must become 'the centrepiece of our development and reform strategy' (p. 383).

In contrast to the papers in *Illfare* and to Abdul Kalam or Sen, Nilekani makes no open call for ethics, despite his concerns with accountability and public goods. There is no expectation of any change of character. Instead technology will make the difference. While Kalam calls for inspiration of children, instilling commitment to the nation, Nilekani does not discuss children other than as the potential beneficiaries of schooling.

Methods and Sources

Nilekani reviews literature casually, citing sources that support a view he advocates. He collects innovative policy ideas and examples, anecdotes and 'business myths', for example about misspending in rural programmes, how old villagers informally monitor road works (pp. 146–7), the miraculous impacts of road-building, and how dissatisfied villagers send their children to online education provided via IT kiosks.[12] Most

[11] On p. 176 Nilekani claims that an Indian has now invented the dry toilet, something already invented in Southern Africa in the 1970s and disseminated widely since then, for example as the Blair VIP latrine.
[12] P. 255 brandishes an unqualified claim that 'a million rupees spent on roads can reduce poverty seven times more effectively than the same spends on anti-poverty programmes'.

of the ideas and some of the anecdotes are from interviews with a
stream of celebrity intellectuals, many of them American or America-
based. Nilekani draws authority from his access to and intimacy with
them, citing them by first name ('Montek' Singh Ahluwalia, 'Martin'
Feldstein, 'Tom' Friedman, 'Daniel' Yergin, and so on) or as 'Dr. [X]'
and 'Professor [Y]', plus 'Sir Nicholas Stern' and 'My friend and the
former President of Mexico Ernesto Zedillo' (p. 304). Each of the
stream of celebrity informants 'tells me' and 'points out' (never 'told
me' or 'pointed out'), in the hot-off-the-press insider-knowledge style
of a business-magazine article. The style has strengths too. The variety
of sources allows a panoramic richness of insights that is greater than
in for example the economist-dominated *Illfare in India* or even in
An Uncertain Glory.[13] Drèze and Sen use a great range of sources but
do not capture attention in the same way with diverse examples and
anecdote. Authority is invoked too from Nilekani's role in the rise of
Infosys, which has brought him assets declared in the 2014 election as
7,700 crore rupees (over a billion euros).[14]

Overall Message and Vision

Nilekani's is an American-style vision, perhaps derived from a certain
image of the USA. 'Tom' Friedman's *The World is Flat* is an implicit
model in style and content, the 2005 global best-seller which appeared
soon before Nilekani decided to write his book.[15] Stories from Horatio
Alger's nineteenth-century American novels, of hard-working young
fellows rising from rags to riches, are cited at the beginning and end of
Nilekani's chapter on reforming labour markets, as the relevant ideal
for India. India must have systems of social support but not 'populist' 'social crutches' that cripple people's own saving and self-reliance
(p. 413), discourage work and will arguably not be sustainable when its

---

[13] For example, an observation on how the rise of affordable synthetic clothing in
the 1980s sharply reduced visual differentiation between castes (p. 166).

[14] Nilekani found it 'disconcerting' that '[Prime Minister] Manmohan Singh
has offered [only] careful, qualified praise for reforms and at one point even
expressed concern over the "vulgar display of wealth" in post-reform India'
(p. 296).

[15] *The World is Flat* opens with Friedman's visit to Infosys, led by Nilekani, in
Bangalore. It describes BPO operations at length, and how teams of world-
class Indian professionals work flat-out to produce escapist computer games
for the US market.

demographics and economy both age. Negative income tax can be used to help those who cannot make their own savings contributions, he argues.[16]

The declared programme is to move away from a hierarchical world of elites who patronize 'undifferentiated "masses"' through across-the-board hand-outs of subsidies that benefit indiscriminately and bring distortions and corruption; to instead support citizens who have differentiated needs and opportunities, by measures of generalized empowerment, direct cash benefits and increased net incomes (pp. 309, 485); and to establish a 'balance' between state, market and civil society. 'Human capital' is used as a term of praise (e.g. p. 402), that will come to replace the old idea of needy masses. The heroes are business and technology, that via freeing and extension of markets (e.g. into carbon pricing and trading) can save 'the people' from 'the state'. Subsidies, such as on petrol, electricity and water, overwhelmingly benefit the better-off and must be scrapped. Markets will absorb any amount of labour displaced by increases in farm-size, he believes (p. 306), claiming remarkably that urban labour markets have absorbed all entrants (p. 482) and that India is close to full employment. It is an extraordinary business vision. Technology not ethics is the deus ex machina.

In Mission Mode: Abdul Kalam

A. P. J. Abdul Kalam (1931–2015), the rocket and space flight scientist, published *Ignited Minds* just before he was chosen in 2002 under the BJP-led government to become India's eleventh President (Abdul Kalam, 2002). The book consists of public lectures, but offers an interesting comparison to the massive enterprises of Prahalad, Nilekani and Drèze–Sen. Kalam presented a nationalist rather than a capitalist vision, including elements shared by many in the BJP. Whereas Nilekani and Prahalad write primarily about systems driven by self-interest, and Sen/Drèze write for enlightened humanists, for Kalam, 'The motive force has to be love for the country' (p. 183), 'pride in being a member of a great civilization' (p. 186), and a primary identity as

---

[16] Nilekani herewith responds to the classic argument for elements also of state provision since 'Neither the market nor NGOs allow universal claims based upon social welfare rights' (Harriss-White, 1999b: 137).

'a proud citizen of India' (p. 189), in whose mind is 'embed[ded] the thought "Nation is bigger than the Individual"' (p. 195).

Kalam shared with many visions of market- and managerial-magic the enthusiasm for technological innovation, and added a style of boyish dreams. He espoused rerouting India's waters to supply its dry west, and creating IT-serviced villages so that India will not become a land of cities. He presented a combination of national mythology ('Ancient India was an advanced knowledge society', p. 119), spiritualism and techno-vision, in which economic, military and technical strength is the road to gaining international respect (p. 78). 'The only way to show the strength of the country is the might to defend it. Strength respects strength and not weakness. Strength means military might and economic prosperity' (pp. 111–12). Military spending is defended in terms also of tech spin-offs that will help health care (p. 16) and for building national confidence (p. 23). He dreamed of large-scale arms exports (p. 183). Sen's criticism of the Indian nuclear tests in 1998 was rejected – 'Dr. Sen looked at India from a Western perspective' (p. 110). Netaji-like, the foreign countries he chose as models of admirable national pride are Japan and Germany (p. 113).

In terms of cast of characters, while Nilekani seldom discusses Muslims, Kalam, an ecumenical practising Muslim and from an older generation, referred continually to all religious groups. Like Mahatma Gandhi, Nehru and Congress he was a product of an era in which undivided India was almost 30 per cent Muslim; Muslims were central in conceptualizations of India's character and composition. In a post-Partition India where Muslims are only 10–15 per cent of the population, the Jan Sangh/BJP arose and (originally) declared Muslims alien or marginal to India's nature; India became partly defined in contradistinction to Pakistan. *Ignited Minds* mentions Pakistan once, as a far less mature and admirable nation (p. 109); India must ensure that others no longer view the two as similar. Bangladesh is mentioned once too (p. 105), but not as a comparator, merely as a speck to be brushed away, without comment, when Indians remove the Bangladeshi flag from some islands in the Bay of Bengal.

Indians should 'operate in mission mode, with a vision' (p. xv) to make India 'a developed nation by the year 2020' (p. ix), he urged, extending the themes of his earlier book *India 2020* (Abdul Kalam and Rajan 1998). 'Mission' here combines missionary national commitment, exemplified by Aravind Eye Hospital (one of Prahalad's case studies too), and the goal-focused urgent teamwork of the space flight and the military strike. When writing *Ignited Minds* Kalam had just stepped down as Chief Scientific Advisor to the Prime Minister, after concluding that he wished to devote himself to inspiration of children and 'to help discover the nature of India's true self in [and by] its children' (p. 10). After writing *India 2020* he had felt that 'our problem is that we may present this before the government, but how do we create people with values to carry out such a big vision? What we need is a cadre of value-based citizens' (p. 74). To the earlier book's five priority areas (identified from India's possession of 'core competences' therein) – agriculture and food processing; energy; education and healthcare; IT; and 'the strategic sector', a priority label that he reserved for weapons, nuclear energy and space – he added spiritual revival, to be promoted through compulsory teaching in schools. India shares a common spirituality, he argued, that when mobilized can unite it and make it stronger than any other nation.

While children appeared in Nilekani only as subjects of schooling and as future 'human capital', they appear in Kalam as torchbearers of the bright future of the nation. Neither examines the sorry state overall of child welfare in India (see e.g. Chanda, 2014). Kalam's plan for transforming India is to provide children with appropriate role models, to fan and guide their idealism, not only support their skills acquisition and individual advancement. 'Education and the teacher–student relationship have to be seen not in business terms but with the nation's growth in mind. A proper education would help nurture a sense of dignity and self-respect among our youth' (p. 26). In contrast to Nilekani's Horatio Alger figures, the role models proffered include many famous Indian physicists. Kalam drew particular pride from India's development of advanced weapon systems and highlights his 'dream of marketing an advanced weapon system [internationally] ahead of the so-called developed countries' (p. 66). This is part of how 'India would become the jagadguru (world leader)' (p. 76).

The combination of these elements – nationalism, historical pride, technological bravura, warm expressed concern for children and youth, ecumenical spirituality – helped to give Kalam a mass appeal, not least among many young people. Numerous titles by him can be found in the average bookshop around India. Like Prahalad and Nilekani he articulated big aspirations and horizons for individual and national greatness. Whereas the core character in Sen is the reasoning, dialogical, concerned citizen, for Kalam, Prahalad and Nilekani it is the thrusting innovative individual operating in a committed corporate or national team. Kalam differs from Prahalad and Nilekani in his stress on altruistic, ethical, patriotic motivations.

Let us review. Prahalad and Nilekani offer the dynamism and drama of markets and high-tech; Kalam adds the romance and passion of openly espoused nationalism. Drèze and Sen offer an analysis richer than the others in most dimensions, for example including serious attention to a range of comparable countries and to gender inequalities (Chapter 8). They probe more deeply than through the standard abstractions of economics that remained strong in *Illfare in India*. But, despite a deep commitment to democracy, their work lacks the flair of a political programme. Their studies lack heroes and villains, or the authorial aura of IT billionaireship, rocket science or US business school smarts. The current-day BJP attempts to draw in all those themes, mixing nationalism, religion, markets and high-tech, plus some of the concerns of Drèze and Sen, such as the challenge of sanitation.

The BJP's Opportunity: Sanitation and the Clean India campaign

In India ... distance from your own shit is the virtual marker of class distinction.

(Appadurai, 2004: 80)

There has been much discussion of the worldview of India's Prime Minister since 2014, Narendra Modi (1950–), and his record in practice as Chief Minister of Gujarat (2001–2014). Nair (2013) gives a content analysis of 68 of Modi's speeches to 2013, translated into English on his website, plus a commentary on his accompanying body language and facial expressions. She identified a dichotomous vocabulary. Table 12.1 italicizes the words that are heavily used.

Emergent from the word counts analysed was a strong pattern of contrasts in Modi's speeches ... one in every pair of vocabulary items outperforms its counterpart by an extremely significant statistical margin: for example, global versus local; industry/business versus labour; power (not the hydroelectric sort, which we factored out) versus money; youth versus age; poor versus rich; and technology versus the social sciences ... the sharp verbal

Table 12.1 *Word choices in Narendra Modi's speeches*

Word	Number of uses of the word	Number of uses of the contrasted word	Contrasted word
Hindu	0	534	*Development*
Technology	127	0	Humanities
		0	Social sciences
Rich	15	211	*Poor*
Business	109	19	Labour
Strength/strengths	128	2	Weaknesses
Vivekananda	70	8	Nehru
		6	Ambedkar

Source: Nair, 2013

divergences found in Modi's speech could indicate a personality unwilling or unable to engage in nuanced dialogue and debate, with a limited and unipolar view of the world. (Nair, 2013)

One sees a storyline in which technology and business, India's perceived strengths, bring development and uplift its poor, in the spirit of Vivekananda (1863–1902), apostle of a revived Hinduism that would drive India's revival. But, as with Prahalad, 'the poor' here excludes the bottom quintile or more. Mr. Modi's 'Vibrant Gujarat' ranked rather low amongst Indian states regarding indicators 'on human development, poverty relief, nutrition and education. Gujarat ranks 13th in India in poverty and 21st in education. Nearly 45 per cent of children under five are underweight and 23 per cent are undernourished, putting the state in the "alarming" category on the India State Hunger Index'.[17] In the associated disputation, Jaffrelot (2013) argued that economic growth and development in Gujarat have been strongly concentrated in urban areas and already better-off groups, while the lives of Dalits and Adivasi in rural areas have deteriorated; Arvind Panagariya, later Modi's appointee as head of Niti Aayog, the successor to the Planning Commission, told an opposing story of respectable human development gains (Panagariya, 2013).

[17] Source: http://en.wikipedia.org/wiki/Narendra_Modi; accessed 10 April 2015.

Whatever the details in Gujarat, the BJP has come to profile itself as a national party, not exclusively as a party of a hurt and defensive Hindu identity. It is now an anti-Congress party which characterizes Congress not primarily as the party of Hindu-Muslim-everyone unity but as the party of corruption, statism and inertia. Like any power-seeking large party, the BJP is a coalition; originating as the Bharatiya Jan Sangh, an RSS offshoot, it later absorbed elements of the former Swatantra and Janata parties.[18] It has lately sought to enrich the mix by donning a quasi-Gandhian mantle of social service in the cause of cleanliness. The discrepancy between its projection of 'India Shining' and some continuing realities had become too great, not least when many foreign-based Indians and their offspring were reluctant to revisit the motherland.

'Your children talk about going to India, but they turn their nose up at us because they think it's dirty', Modi told an audience at Fiji National University on November 19. 'I'm going to make such a country your children will want to come and see. They will never again turn their nose up at India'.[19]

Undoubtedly influential also were reports from international agencies that Indians not only predominantly defecate outdoors, which has

[18] The RSS is a Hindu nationalist movement and social service organization founded in 1925. It created the Bharatiya Jan Sangh political party (BJS) in 1951, which was replaced by the BJP in 1980. One strand within the BJS was the 'Integral Humanism' concept articulated by party ideologue Deendayal Upadhyaya (1916–68). His Wikipedia entry indicates: 'Integral Humanism was adopted by the BJS as its official doctrine and subsequently passed on to the BJP'. The article cites BJP (ex-Janata) intellectual Subramanian Swamy, in his book *Hindus Under Siege*: 'IHT [Integral Humanism Theory] recognized that in a democratic market economy an individual has technical freedom of choice but the system without safeguards fails to accommodate the varying capabilities and endowments of a human being. Since the concept of survival of the fittest prevails in such a system, therefore some individuals achieve great personal advancement while others get trampled on or disabled in the ensuing rat race. We need to build a safety net into our policy for the underprivileged or disabled while simultaneously rewarding the meritorious or gifted. Otherwise, the politically empowered poor in a democracy who are in a majority will clash with the economically empowered rich who are the minority, thereby causing instability and upheaval in a market system'. Swamy's *India and China, A Comparative Perspective* articulated IHT's ideal of 'harmonizing material progress with spiritual advancement'. Upadhyaya's purist followers considered that the BJP-led government of 1998–2004 paid only lip service to his teachings.

[19] https://shethepeople.tv/news/come-visit-our-safe-clean-india/ (January 27, 2015).

major implications for health in a densely populated country, but that
most of the world's open defecation occurs in India.

The World Health Organization and United Nations Children's Fund
(UNICEF) estimate that there are more than 620 million people practising
open defecation in the country; over 50 per cent of the population. With
[perhaps] 638 million people defecating in the open and 44 per cent [of]
mothers disposing their children's faeces in the open, there is a very high
risk of microbial contamination (bacteria, viruses, amoeba) of water which
causes diarrhoea in children. Children weakened by frequent diarrhoea epi-
sodes are more vulnerable to malnutrition and opportunistic infections such
as pneumonia. About 48 per cent of children are suffering from some degree
of malnutrition. (*The Hindu*, 21 November 2013)

While the 2011 reported figures were an advance on 2001 when
63.6 per cent lacked a toilet, India's standing had declined relatively:
'While more than half of India's people go to the toilet outdoors, in
Bangladesh and Brazil only 7 per cent do. That figure is 4 per cent in
China, UNICEF data shows'.[20]
Besides elite humiliation in international league tables and in relation
to hesitant foreign visitors, hopefully playing a role too is an awareness
of the dangers and humiliations directly involved for those obliged to
engage in 'open defecation'. Arjun Appadurai invites us to face, with
special reference to India's growing cities, 'the politics of shit':

Human waste management, as it is euphemistically described in policy
circles, is perhaps the key arena where every problem of the urban poor
arrives at a single point of extrusion, so to speak. Given the abysmal housing, often with almost no privacy, that most urban slum dwellers enjoy,
shitting in public is a serious humiliation for adults ... Living in an ecology
of fecal odors, piles and channels, where cooking water, washing water and
shit-bearing water are not carefully insulated from one another, adds high
risks of disease and mortality to the social humiliation of shitting in public
view. (Appadurai 2004: 78–9).

Nilekani's book barely mentions sanitation, let alone discussing it in
detail like Drèze and Sen did. Nor did Prahalad, unsurprisingly for he was
concerned with advising potential profit-makers. Unsurprising too was

[20] http://veritas-lux.blogspot.nl/2013/11/indians-and-their-shit-looking-at.html
(accessed March 2015).

the silence of Abdul Kalam, whose eyes were raised to the heavens. But Nilekani proffered an overall vision for managing India, and sanitation fell outside that field of vision. In contrast, on this front the new Prime Minister Modi – an RSS product since youth, assigned by the movement at age 35 to serve in the BJP – took the verbal offensive. His 2014 Independence Day speech promised toilets for girls and boys in all schools. On 2 October 2014, he launched Swachh Bharat Abhiyan (Clean India Mission); he 'nominated nine famous personalities for the campaign, and they took up the challenge and nominated nine more people and so on'.[21]

Swachh Bharat Abhiyan is a revamping of a longstanding programme, running since at least 1986 under various names. The declared date for nationwide open-defecation-free status was advanced from 2022 to 2019, the 150th anniversary of Gandhi's birth. However, in contrast to the massive advances in neighbouring Bangladesh and even Nepal, India's programmes have remained marred and dominated by state indifference, corruption, and bogus reporting to fulfil artificial targets (see e.g. Om, 2014). Of the hundred million or so toilets supposedly built through government-support in India from 1999 to 2012, variously 40 to 60 million were identified as 'missing' – collapsed, abandoned or never existent.[22]

Ashish Chaturvedi notes how the $20 billion National Urban Renewal Mission (NURM), launched in 2008 with a large solid waste management component, had made little progress. 'It was assumed that the private sector would be successful where the government has failed ... In most cities, although the informal sector provides key services for waste management it is not a part of the "formal" waste management narrative'.[23] Mander (2014) goes deeper, adding dimensions noted by Appadurai:

... Little in the current discussions about cleanliness reflect ... the acknowledgment that India's dirt derives mostly from its huge historical inequality,

---

[21] See Wikipedia entry on Swachh Bharat Abhiyan.

[22] 'Of the 97.3 million toilets that it claims to have built, the [Drinking Water and Sanitation] ministry's 2012 survey suggests that at least 27.64 million toilets are unaccounted for, and an additional 14.15 million are defunct'. (A 2 October 2014 report in *India Today*), see: http://indiatoday.intoday.in/story/clean-india-modi-govt-toilets-missing-defunct-india/1/393894.html.

[23] www.communityledtotalsanitation.org/blog/modis-clean-india-campaign-dont-waste-opportunity?utm_source=newsletter&utm_medium=email&utm_campaign=Community-Led%20Total%20Sanitation%20newsletter. 9 October 2014.

and from [public investment] neglect of India's people of disadvantage ... India's millennia-old caste system is founded on great social anxieties about pollution, and little is considered as ritually polluting as human excreta. Those at the lowest depths of the caste hierarchy – and even among these mostly girls and women – are assigned the most socially humiliating duty of cleaning excreta. The two laws that outlaw manual scavenging have still not ended this practice ... Public investments in modern sanitation technologies are not made by the railways and municipalities simply because impoverished low-caste people are available to do this work.

... Toilets for schools are mandated by the Right to Education Act 2009 but the State simply has not raised significantly its investments in school education to fulfil this ... Census 2011 data [indicate] that 63% households in recognised notified slums have either open or no drainage for waste water and 34% slum households have no latrine in the premises ... The figures are significantly higher for non-recognised slums, and absolute for the homeless ... [None] of these problems can be solved by pious pledges [under the Clean India Mission] by middle-class people to keep their surroundings clean.

How does the upper-caste-dominated BJP position itself in this terrain? Tariq Thachil's prizewinning Cornell PhD on *Why The Poor Vote For Hindu Nationalism In India* (Thachil, 2009; later appearing as Thachil, 2014) observed that: 'the strategies available to other political parties, such as enacting pro-poor policies or promoting lower caste leaders, were untenable options for the BJP. Such approaches involved unacceptable compromises to the interests of the party's upper caste constituencies' (2009: 242–3). He argued that: 'neither conventional clientelist techniques used by elite parties, nor strategies of ideological polarization favoured by religious parties, explain the BJP's pattern of success with poor Hindus [including Dalits and Adivasi tribals]. Instead the party has relied on the efforts of its 'social service' organizational affiliates in the broader Hindu nationalist movement [notably the RSS]' (2009: ii). In the 2008 Chhattisgarh state elections, for example, the BJP is widely seen as having retained power by 'stealing' the Congress-style policy of broad-coverage public distribution of rice (Drèze and Sen, 2013: 2007). However, as seen by failures that year elsewhere, 'the [BJP's] service approach seems unlikely to even initially succeed where it faces effective governance [by a competitor party] and a politically active subaltern citizenry' (Thachil, 2009: 259).

P. K. Vijayan (2012) suggested that such analyses miss something else that is fundamental: 'Hindu nationalism or Hindutva ... [rests also] on the Brahmanical masculine hegemony that it is founded on, incites and strives continually to intensify ... [T]here is a larger and more pervasive discursive field from which Hindutva draws sustenance, [that should be theorized] in gendered structural terms' (p. 217). Prime Minister Narendra Modi may represent a potent combination of 'the service approach' and a particular image of muscular masculinity.

Concluding Reflections: Does a Capability Approach Inspire?

Not only have Indian elites overall given continuing low priority to promoting fulfilment of many basic needs for half the population, compared to elites in East Asia and other comparable cases; many of the elites have mentally seceded from national obligations, joining instead the global market extolled by Thomas Friedman and others (Gasper, 2005). Others remain explicitly committed to the national project but have adopted a belief that economic growth is the only path to good, sometimes displaying a worship of money that we may need ideas from Simmel (2011 [1907]) to try to grasp. Various factors might over time contribute to counter-currents, such as the needs for international competitiveness and respectability, and increasing political mobilization of lower castes.

This chapter has explored some of the imaginaries currently employed – the scenes they paint, their casts of characters and how these are grouped and labelled and characterized, the challenges and opportunities they highlight and those they ignore, the world outside India which they present or imply or seek to emulate, and the horizons both retrospective and prospective that they proffer. In particular one can consider how and how far they consider issues of 'human development', within their overall imaginaries of India's past, present and future. Table 12.2 summarizes the comparisons.

The two final columns of the table present the central foci: the analysis by Amartya Sen and Jean Drèze, for contrast with the pictures from some comparable competitors; and the pattern of attention of the currently dominant leader, Narendra Modi, compared with all the authors. Modi draws mainly on the visions of Sen's

Table 12.2 Sen and Drèze in comparison to five other analyses of India. Patterns of attention and lack of attention to topics in human development

	Illfare in India, 1947–99	C. K. Prahalad, Fortune at the BOP	Nandan Nilekani, Imagining India	A. P. J. Abdul Kalam, Igniting Minds	Drèze and Sen An Uncertain Glory	Prime Minister Modi's BJP
Rationale for inclusion	Provides a baseline for viewing more recent work	Management orientation; strong links to big business	Management and high tech; link to Congress Party	High-tech plus nationalism	Humanism, democracy and participation	Which of the preceding elements does it reflect?
Sanitation	No	No	No	No	Yes	Yes
The poorest	Yes	Concerns 3rd and 4th quintiles but not 5th	No	No	YES	Talks of the poor not of the rich
Ageing	(Yes)		Yes	No	No	
Disability	Yes	(Yes)	No	No	(Yes)	
Migration	No	No	As a solution	No	No	No
Displacement	No	No	No, but much about roads	No	(Yes)	
Caste	(A little)	No	Yes, plus 'communities'	No	Yes	No
Muslims	No	No	No	Yes	Yes	No (nor Hindu)
Power System	(Little)	No	YES, as Leftist incubus	No	(Little)	
The state	(A little)	State as incompetent but reformable	State as obstacle; reformable	(No)	State as reformable	State as reformable
Business	No	YES	YES	(No)	(No)	YES
Intersectionality, real cases	(Little)	Some	Some; via anecdotes	Some	(Multi-dimensional poverty)	

(cont.)

Table 12.2 (cont.)

	Illfare in India, 1947–99	C. K. Prahalad, Fortune at the BOP	Nandan Nilekani, Imagining India	A. P. J. Abdul Kalam, Igniting Minds	Drèze and Sen An Uncertain Glory	Prime Minister Modi's BJP
Children	(As pupils)		As pupils	As minds, creators, value-holders	As pupils, with details on ill-/welfare	Yes, as great
Pre-British	No	No	No	Yes, as great	No	(Yes)
British colonial	No	No	Yes, as problem	(No)	Yes	
Nehru(s)	(A little)	No	Yes, as a major problem	(No)	(No)	Attention instead to Vivekananda
(American-style) globalization	(Little)	Yes	Yes, as the answer. Asset of English.	(Yes)	Yes	Yes
China	(No)	(Yes)	(Little)	No	Yes	
Bangladesh	No	No	No	No	Yes	No
ICT	(No)	Yes	YES	Yes	No	Yes
Ethics	(Needed)	(implicit)	No	YES	Yes	Yes, service
The Nation	(Little)	(implicit)	Yes	YES	Yes	YES
Gender	(Little)	(A little)	(Little)	No	Yes	(?)

Blank spaces: the issue is not relevant or not answerable in yes/no terms, or the answer is not known to the author

Brackets: a modest degree of attention

Capital letters: strong emphasis

competitors – managerialism, high-tech, outspoken nationalism – but also astutely sometimes from the social service concerns of Sen and Drèze, including in respect of sanitation. Drèze and Sen operate at the reasoned level of universalistic humanists, not the excited – and exciting – visions of dreaming engineers, nationalist leaders and chauvinistic crowds. It is not clear that the vision they present has enough political connection to the dreams and aspirations, motivations and consolations, hopes and hates of enough of India's elites, old and new, or its busy middle strata, or its impoverished masses. The foci on unmet basic needs of the bottom two quintiles in India (over 500 million people), including the embarrassing theme of sanitation, and the psychic and political obstacles related to caste may strike fewer chords with a majority of either the electorate or the current and aspirant elites than do the visions of their competitors: military muscle, arms exports, e-commerce, e-governance, space stations, making fortunes through 'next practices', capturing global markets for IT-based services, and/or American-style faith in the private sector rather than the hard labour of reforming state schools. The eminently reasonable and highly relevant comparisons with Bangladesh may have zero impact within India, like comparisons earlier with Sri Lanka or also nowadays with Nepal. These countries may not exist in Indian mental maps.

Looking back at Harriss-White and Subramaniam's overview of *Illfare in India*, when reviewing it 15 years ago I drew the hypothesis that the frameworks from economics that had predominated in much official policy and planning had helped to veil and thereby exacerbate India's poor human development performance – through the lack of attention to basic issues like age, disability and mental illness, and of class, caste and the state. The work of Sen and Drèze has helped to counter these biases. However, we need to add more to the discussion, including with reference to themes of identity, disgust and humiliation, and hope. For Indian democracy, even more than democracy elsewhere, seems to work differently from the models of democratic reasoning that Sen has expounded. As he himself notes, India's extreme inequality, including in education and health, undermines the content within its democratic forms.

As suggested by the comparisons with other authors, Sen and Drèze's work contains gaps. It consists perhaps too exclusively of policy audit and reliance on sober democratic deliberation, lacking the ingredients to underpin an inspiring action programme. Policy audit alone is not sufficient to capture attention, trigger outrage and drive action. Its appeal to a general ideal of freedom could be weak in offering an inspirational identity and horizon of hope, let alone a mobilizing narrative storyline, including 'myths' of past, present and future trajectory, accessible and appealing simplifications, and motivator feelings of disgust and of enemies to overcome.

The chapter recurrently considered, as one vital touchstone, the degrees of attention given to basic sanitation, traditionally the blindest of blind spots in Indian development. It concluded with the attention to this area officially advocated by new Prime Minister Narendra Modi, and the BJP strategy of attracting support through attention to some forms of 'social' provision, a way of 'stealing the clothes' of their somnolent opponents. Sanitation deserves special attention, given its significance not only for health but for recognition, status and respect, fundamental elements in the project of building a solidary, cooperative, effective, self-respecting national community (cf. Gasper and Comim, 2018). One can think back also though to the post-Emergency period in the late 1970s, when as we saw the Janata coalition came the closest in India's first 50 years to taking serious action on basic education, but crumbled in face of its internal contradictions and the domestic resistance. We will see what happens in the coming years to the BJP in its updated attire and what influence human development theory can bring to bear.

References

Abdul Kalam, A. P. J. (2002) *Ignited Minds: Unleashing the Power within India*. New Delhi: Viking.

Abdul Kalam, A. P. J. and Rajan, Y. S. (1998) *India 2020: A Vision for the New Millennium*. New Delhi: Viking.

Anderson, B. (1991) *Imagined Communities: Reflections on the Origin and Spread of Nationalism*. Revised and extended edition. London: Verso.

Appadurai, A. (2004) The capacity to aspire: Culture and the terms of recognition. In *Culture and Public Action*, Vijayendra Rao and Michael Walton (Eds.). Stanford, CA: Stanford University Press, 59–84.

Athreya, V. (1999) Adult literacy in India since Independence. In Harriss-White, B. and S. Subramaniam, 227–64.

Birtchnell, T. (2013) *Indovation: Innovation and a Global Knowledge Economy in India*. Basingstoke: Palgrave Macmillan.

Breman, J. and Das, A. (1999) *Down and Out: Labouring under Global Capitalism*. Delhi: Oxford University Press.

Cassen, R. (1999) Population and development revisited. In Harriss-White, B. and S. Subramaniam, 47–72.

Chanda, P. K. (2014) Troubling paradox: Child poverty and child wellbeing in India. MA thesis. The Hague: International Institute of Social Studies.

Das, A. (1996) *Changel*. Delhi: Penguin.

Dasgupta, P. (2001) *Human Well-Being and the Natural Environment*. Oxford: Oxford University Press.

Drèze, J. and Sen, A. (1995) *India – Economic Development and Social Opportunity*. New Delhi: Oxford University Press.

(2002) *India: Development and Participation*. Delhi: Oxford University Press.

(2013) *An Uncertain Glory – India and Its Contradictions*. London: Penguin.

Friedman, T. (2005) *The World Is Flat – A Brief History of the 21st Century*. New York: Farrar, Straus & Giroux.

Gasper, D. (2000) Anecdotes, situations, histories: Reflections on the use of cases in thinking about ethics and development practice. *Development and Change*, 31(5), 1055–83.

(2001) Waiting for human development: A review essay on Illfare in India. *Review of Development and Change*, VI(2), 295–304.

(2005) Beyond the inter-national relations framework: An essay in descriptive global ethics. *Journal of Global Ethics*, 1(1), 5–23.

(2007) What is the capability approach? Its core, rationale, partners and dangers. *Journal of Socio-Economics*, 36(3), 335–59.

(2008) From 'Hume's Law' to policy analysis for human development: Sen after Dewey, Myrdal, Streeten, Stretton and Haq. *Review of Political Economy*, 20(2), 233–56.

(2009) From valued freedoms, to polities and markets: The capability approach in policy practice. *Revue Tiers Monde*, no. 198 (April–June), pp. 285–302.

Gasper, D. and Comim F. (2018) Public goods and public spirit. In *Agency, Democracy and Participation in Global Development*, L. Keleher and S. Kosko (Eds.); Cambridge: Cambridge University Press.

Harriss-White, B. and Subramaniam S. (Eds.) (1999) *Illfare in India – Essays on India's Social Sector in Honour of S. Guhan*. New Delhi: Sage Publications.

Harriss-White, B. (1999a) State, market, collective and household action in India's Social Sector. In Harriss-White, B. and S. Subramaniam (Eds.), 303–28.

(1999b) On to a loser: Disability in India. In Harriss-White, B. and S. Subramaniam (Eds.), 135–59.

Jaffrelot, C. (2013) Gujarat elections: The sub-text of Modi's 'hat trick' – High tech populism and the 'neo-middle class'. *Studies in Indian Politics*, 1(1), 79–95.

Khilnani, S. (1997) *The Idea of India*. London: Hamish Hamilton.

Majumdar, M. (1999) Exclusion in education: Indian states in comparative perspective. In Harriss-White, B. and S. Subramaniam (Eds.), 265–99.

Mander, H. (2014) Need to clean our biases first, then our streets. *Hindustan Times*, 22 October. Available at: www.hindustantimes.com/columns/need-to-clean-our-biases-first-then-our-streets/story-ANaXDka4dS2N-q8Puox2sYM.html

(2015) *Looking Away: Inequality, Prejudice and Indifference in New India*. Delhi: Speaking Tiger.

Mazumdar, I. and Agnihotri, I. (2014) Traversing Myriad Trails: Tracking Gender and Labour Migration across India. In *Migration, Gender and Social Justice*, T-D. Truong et al. (Eds.). Heidelberg: Springer. 123–52.

Muraleedharan, V. (1999) Technology and costs of medical care. In Harriss-White, B. and S. Subramaniam (Eds.), 113–34.

Nagaraj, K., (1999) Labour market characteristics and employment generation programmes in India. In Harriss-White, B. and S. Subramaniam (Eds.), 73–109.

Nair, R. B. (2013) Manwatching Mister Modi. *Outlook*, 24 June. Available at: www.outlookindia.com/article/Manwatching-Mister-Modi/286143

Nilekani, N. (2009) *Imagining India – Ideas for the New Century*. New Delhi: Penguin India.

Om, H. (2014) *Making Sense on Sanitation: The Case of Uttar Pradesh and Bangladesh*. Saarbrucken: GlobeEdit. Earlier as MA thesis, The Hague: International Institute of Social Studies.

Panagariya, A. (2013) Narendra Modi's real report card. *Business Standard*, 28 October.

Paramanand, B. (2014) *CK Prahalad – The Mind of the Futurist*, Chennai: Westland Ltd.

Perspectives (2008) *Abandoned: Development and Displacement*. 2nd edition. Delhi: Perspectives Team, Hindu College, Delhi University.

Prahalad, C. K. (2005) *The Fortune at the Bottom of the Pyramid*. Upper Saddle River, NJ: Wharton School Publishing.

Radhakrishnan, P. (1999) Caste, politics and the reservation issue. In Harriss-White, B. and S. Subramaniam (Eds.), 163–95.

Rao, S. (2005) Reflections on the MAP and working with Dr. C. K. Prahalad. *Journal of Management Inquiry,* 14(2), 178–80.

Sen, A. (2005) *The Argumentative Indian*. London: Allen Lane.

(2006) *Identity and Violence*. London: Allen Lane.

Simmel, G. (2011 [1907]) *The Philosophy of Money*. London: Routledge.

Subramaniam, S. and Harriss-White, B. (1999) Introduction. In *Illfare in India*, Harriss-White, B. and S. Subramaniam (Eds.), 17–43. New Delhi: Sage Publications.

Thachil, T. (2009) *The Saffron Wave Meets The Silent Revolution: Why The Poor Vote For Hindu Nationalism In India*. Ithaca, NY: Department of Government, Cornell University.

(2014) *Elite Parties, Poor Voters: How Social Services Win Votes in India*. New York: Cambridge University Press.

Trani, J.-F. Bakhshi, P. and Kuhlberg, J. et al. (2015) Mental illness, poverty and stigma in India: A case control study. *British Medical Journal Open*, 2015;5:e006355. doi: 10.1136/bmjopen-2014-006355

Van der Veen, R. (2010) *Waarom Azië rijk en machtig wordt*. [Why Asia is Becoming Rich and Powerful]. Amsterdam: LM Publishers.

Vijayan, P. K. (2012) Making the Pitrubhumi: Masculine hegemony and the formation of the Hindu nation. PhD thesis, The Hague: International Institute of Social Studies.

13 Sustainable Human Development Measurement Issues

A New Proposal

MARIO BIGGERI AND VINCENZO MAURO

Introduction

Measuring multidimensional development of countries is a core issue in current international debate on sustainable Human Development (HD) and to target and monitor the Sustainable Development Goals (SDGs) and the 2030 agenda.[1] Sustainable HD can be defined as a process of promotion and expansion of valuable opportunities/capabilities[2] (Sen, 1999; Anand and Sen, 2000; Biggeri and Ferrannini, 2014) and it is considered a policy objective for the United Nations Development Programme (UNDP) and other development agencies in addition to some countries.

In order to synthesize multidimensional HD outcomes, different approaches have been proposed in the empirical literature (Anand and Sen, 1997; Bourguignon and Chakravarty, 2003; Ranis et al. 2006; Alkire and Foster, 2011; Klugman et al., 2011). The Human Development Index (HDI) is the pivotal indicator of sustainable HD paradigm and it is still recognized as holding a relevant role in political terms in the development arena[3] versus the GDP primacy (Klugman et al., 2011: 7–8).

Despite the large amounts of available literature that discusses HDI, there are some relevant issues that deserve attention both from a theoretical and empirical perspective. First, the construction of the HDI was

---

[1] 17 SDGs are general for any country and during the process a set of indicators and targets have been identified and set-up (see JHDCA, 2015 special issue).

[2] The HD definition draws on elements from basic needs and from the capability approach (CA), and it puts people at the centre of its concerns according to the pillars indicated by Mahbub ul Haq: equity, efficiency, empowerment and sustainability (UNDP, 1996; Comim et al. 2008; Deneulin, 2009).

[3] HDI is intended as a broader approach looking at the conditions of all people in the society i.e. 'conglomerative perspective' vs 'deprivation perspective' that is concentrating specifically on the living conditions of the poor (Anand and Sen, 1997: 1). These perspectives complement each other in the HDI.

driven to a great extent by the cross-country data available in 1990, as well as the need to generate a simple compelling policy message. As underlined by many researchers, it does not include all capabilities that might be of interest (Fukuda-Parr, 2000). Furthermore, issues regarding substitutions between dimensions were raised by several authors since the HDI's inception (e.g. Desai, 1991), who pointed out that the level of priority to be given to a dimension was invariant to the level of attainments.

The HDI released in 2013 substitutes the arithmetic mean of the three components with a geometric mean (UNDP, 2013). This new approach adds relevant properties[4] such as the 'penalisation' of countries' heterogeneous outcomes (also referred to as 'prioritization') (Klugman et al., 2011). Despite this substantial improvement, this method could still present some problems especially if the number of dimensions increases (Ranis and Stewart, 2010). For example, as acknowledged by the authors, if some of the components are zero (or close to zero), the geometric mean conduces to some well-known problems of calculations and interpretability (Klugman et al., 2011: 24).

The aim of this chapter is to introduce the Multidimensional Human Development Index (MHDI). It is a method that allows researchers and practitioners to expand the classical HDI dimensions penalizing heterogeneity by applying the Multidimensional Synthesis of Indicators (MSI) approach introduced by Mauro et al. (2016).

The MSI is a class of functions that allows a general statistical procedure to aggregate different dimensions of HD into a unidimensional index. The level of priority given to a dimension is connected to the overall level of attainments. It has some significant advantages in relation to what has been put forward by the Human Development Research Office (HDRO) because it overcomes the technical problems encountered by the new HDI while partially addressing the so-called 'inescapable arbitrariness' in the choice of the degree of the mean – an issue discussed by Anand and Sen (1997) – as well as allowing further exploration of the link between human freedom and HD.

The procedure of aggregation of different dimensions entails many different phases. Despite their relevance, this chapter is not going to focus on some key issues such as the process of selection of dimensions,

---

[4] For instance, eliminating the practice of capping variables that surpass the upper bounds (Klugman et al., 2011: 16)

their transformation, the implicit weighting issue, the harmonization of indicators and the inequality issue.[5] In this chapter we focus only on the aggregation function, presenting an empirical example with six dimensions.

The chapter is structured into five parts. In the second section, we further introduce the sustainable HD theoretical perspective. In the third section, we present the MHDI. In the fourth section we provide an example with real data at the country level, while in the conclusion the main findings are reviewed.

The Sustainable Human Development Perspective and Its Measurement at Country Level

The interpretative framework proposed in the HDR is built on the idea of sustainable HD as a process to expand valuable capabilities at the country level, considering the outcomes of each country as a proxy for dwellers' 'opportunities' and more precisely 'opportunity freedom'. Indeed, HD is a process to expand the basic capabilities – abilities and opportunities – of people to lead the kind of life they have reason to value. We are interested in the different opportunities that a human may face in different countries or more in general in a territorial context.[6]

The opportunities of a country are shaped by the levels and interactions (as well as synergies) between different development outcomes. Therefore each dimension can be interpreted both as a goal and as an instrument (Mehrotra and Jolly, 1997; Sen, 1999; Anand and Sen, 2000; Ranis et al., 2000a, b, 2006; Biggeri and Ferrannini, 2014).[7] For instance, the capability to be educated has an intrinsic value but also a relevant instrumental value that enhances other capabilities, and vice versa (Mehrotra and Biggeri, 2007; Mehrotra and Delamonica, 2007).[8]

---

[5] See for instance Foster and Lopez Calva (2010) and Alkire and Foster (2010).

[6] The HD progress (i.e. human flourishing) springs throughout virtuous synergies among positive HD outcomes. These synergies can be found at different levels: at the individual and household level (micro), at the local system of development level (meso), at the country level (macro) and at the international level.

[7] The capabilities/opportunities we have are dependent upon the access to instrumental capabilities and income. The three HDI components (health, education and income) can also be interpreted as instrumental to our well-being and capabilities: the opportunities a country can offer.

[8] This recalls Sen's broader distinction between (1) the primary end and (2) the principal means of development. When development is seen as a process of

Going back to the notion of capabilities as being *corealisable*, one should try to restrict the substitutability as between the basic variables. This would make the deprivations multiplicative, each feeding off the others. Such a weighting would heighten the plight of the very poor and make the gradient of HD steep (Desai, 1991: 536).

In order to produce some empirical evidence, we present a list of six dimensions to operationalize the MHDI. As already mentioned in the introduction, we are not going to focus on the process of selection of dimensions.[9] This issue deserves more attention: as stated by Klugman et al. (2011), the measurement difficulties for some immaterial dimensions coupled with political controversies makes the incorporation of new dimensions into the HDI in itself very difficult. Last but not least, Sen (1999, 2002) and many CA scholars insist on public reasoning and scrutiny as ways of selecting dimensions.

The six dimensions chosen for the operationalization of the MHDI are: health, education, command over resources, environment, labour opportunities, political and civil freedom. This choice adds three extra dimensions to the standard three dimensions included in the HDI.[10]

The purpose of including 'command over resources' is that there are many important capabilities which are critically dependent on one's economic circumstances (instrumental), 'resource availability' is only

expanding the real freedom that people enjoy, 'The intrinsic importance of human freedom as the preeminent objective of development has to be distinguished from the instrumental effectiveness of freedom of different kinds to promote human freedom'(Sen, 1999: 37), 'the instrumental freedoms link with each other and with the ends of enhancement of human freedom in general' (Sen, 1999: 10).

[9] Different methods can be used separately or combined can be used to choose domains/dimensions (Alkire, 2007, 2008; Biggeri and Mehrotra, 2010) and also specific procedures to conceptualize capability dimensions (see for instance Robeyns, 2003, and Biggeri et al., 2006 or Biggeri and Libanora, 2010).

[10] For instance, Ranis et al. present a 'pragmatic' list for evaluating HD based on the analysis of the literature review that takes into account also the economic development aspects or better 'command over resources' (Ranis et al., 2006). In Ranis et al. the dimensions selected the following dimensions: (1) The HDI itself. This broadly covers bodily well-being, material well-being and mental development. Of course, it itself is a multidimensional indicator. We include it as a single indicator because it is the generally accepted measure of achievement on HD. (2) Mental well-being. (3) Empowerment. (4) Political freedom. (5) Social relations. (6) Community well-being. (7) Inequalities. (8) Work conditions. (9) Leisure conditions. (10) Political security. (11) Economic security. (12) Environmental conditions (2006: 328–9).

318 *The Application Frontier*

an instrument for other ends – indeed, income is just one way of seeing this command' (Anand and Sen, 2000: 84).[11] However, it is also clear that, after a certain level, extra income does not determine an increase of HD if there are not policies towards HD, especially at an aggregate level.[12]

Moreover, it is important to point out that although Sen has argued that for evaluative purposes, the appropriate space' is that of substantive freedoms and capabilities (1999), we can only observe achievements rather than the full range of achievable functionings (i.e. capability set). Conceptually, 'there is no difference as far as the space is concerned between focusing on functionings or on capabilities. A functioning combination is a point in such a space, whereas capability is a set of such points' (Sen, 1992: 50). Indeed, 'The actual set of achievements on any variable, of course, indicates that it is a one of the set of possible choices, but the range of choices presumably goes much beyond actual performance, as options not chosen are not included' (Ranis et al., 2006: 324). Hence, from the point of view of our analysis we can compare the individual achieved functionings to the 'best' and the 'worst' achieved functioning (realized). In other words, the sustainable HD outcomes in terms of achieved functionings can give an idea of the potential functionings for the individual unit in a given context (country) (Brandolini and D'Alessio, 1998).

Multidimensional Human Development Index

In order to properly monitor well-being over time and for all subgroups of a population of interest, a synthesis aggregating different indicators must be a function that satisfies some desirable properties. First, any change in the situation of any country considered in the analysis must

<hr>

[11] Furthermore, GDP per capita signals deprivation of economic provisions including public basic social services and private opportunities as pointed out by Anand and Sen (1997, p. 8). Moreover, the ability to command resources with which a person can lead a positively freer life in a number of fields gives us an indirect account of many significant aspects of HD (Anand and Sen, 2000: 99).

[12] Mahbub ul Haq identified four essential pillars/principles in the HD process: equity, efficiency, participation/empowerment and sustainability (UNDP, 1996; Alkire and Denaulin, 2009; UNDP, 2013). Therefore, the resource availability needs to take into account not only the income level but also social and environmental sustainability by future generations (UNDP, 1996).

be captured by the index. This condition, that we refer to as 'strict monotonicity', guarantees that any improvement (worsening) in any indicator observed for any country results in an increase (decrease) of the synthetic score. Second, the function must be continuous. Small changes in the data must result in small changes in the index.

Moreover, a good synthesis should take into account the heterogeneity between accomplishments. Countries with significant differences between their achievements should have an overall score penalized by this heterogeneity. This property is closely linked to the degree of substitutability among indicators, that cannot be generally assumed as perfect (unless the heterogeneity is zero).

The last property introduced is the manageability of the elasticity of substitution rate between sub-indexes, a property entailed in many synthetic indicators based on higher-order means (Biggeri and Mauro, 2010; Klugman et al., 2011; UNDP, 2013). This property is implicitly taken into account by the MHDI. A common issue with synthetic indicators is that the elasticity of substitution between basic indicators is strictly dependent on the choice of a parameter (usually the order of the mean). Anand and Sen (1997) underline how there is no flexibility in the rate of substitutability between indicators once this parameter is set. They refer to this problem as 'inescapable arbitrariness in the choice of the parameter' (1997: 16).

The idea advanced by the MSI (Mauro et al., 2016) is that a full flexibility in the degree of substitutability can be retained by directly linking it to a function of the general level of well-being for each unit. A lower degree of substitutability assigns implicitly a higher relative weight to the lowest score achievements, especially for poor countries.

More formally, let X be the nxk data matrix with generic entry x_{ij} the j-th achievement for unit i. Then

$$\text{MSI}_i = 1 - \left[\frac{1}{k} \sum_{j=1}^{k} (1 - x_{ij})^{g(x_i)} \right]^{\frac{1}{g(x_i)}}$$

where k is the total number of dimensions and $g(x_i)$ is a generic real-valued function of the i-th row of matrix X, with $g(\cdot) \geq 1.g(\cdot) > 1$

The function $g(\cdot)$ allows a high degree of flexibility in the index. As a result, theoretical considerations regarding the structure of substitutability rates between achievements can be taken into account.

If the function is constant $g(\cdot) = \alpha$, with $\alpha > 2$, then the synthesis becomes a higher-degree average (with a lower degree of substitutability; see an example of where $\alpha > 2$ in Anand and Sen, 1997). As α increases, the iso-capabilities curves mapping the levels of individual outcomes consistent with a given level of well-being tend to a Leontief functional form where there is no substitutability between achievements (Klugman et al., 2011).

Although these scenarios represent important cases presented in literature, the value added by our proposed approach is that the degree of substitutability can be directly linked to the general level of well-being of each unit[13] through a non-constant function $g(\cdot)$. Given the instrumental value of most dimensions, this means that a sharp deprivation in a specific dimension might not only cause an overall deprivation (intrinsic value) but also negatively affects other dimensions as well. Put simply, this synthesis penalizes heterogeneity. This consideration mirrors Sen's notion of 'development as freedom' (Sen, 1999). Further information (or assumptions) on the structure of substitutability rates relating to the population can lead to more detailed and complex reiterations of the functional form[14] of the function $g(\cdot)$.

The MHDI is a particular case of MSI where the units are the countries, the dimensions of analysis are the usual three of the HDI plus other new dimensions, and the function chosen is $g(\cdot) = \mu^{-1}$, where μ is the arithmetic mean[15] of x_i. This is a simple and intuitive way to allow a flexible penalization of heterogeneity in achievements: countries with higher outcomes are less penalized, while poorest countries are more heavily penalized, as heterogeneity (or lack thereof) is interpreted as lack of effective freedom or opportunities (Ranis and Stewart, 2010). In other words, the degree of substitutability is a function of the

---

[13] Bourguignon and Chakravarty (2003), for instance, propose individual poverty.

[14] The choice of μ for measuring the level of individual well-being used to characterize the heterogeneity structure is not purely arbitrary. A sensitivity analysis using different measures (e.g. an iterative method leading to a sufficient degree of convergence after 3–4 iterations) showed no significant differences in the final measurements, so that a simple function as the arithmetic mean seems the most natural choice in absence of additional information on the structure of substitutability rates.

[15] The MSI requires $g(\cdot) \geq 1$, so that all the dimensions must be bounded between 0 and 1.

overall achievement of the country estimated through an arithmetic mean of the indicators.[16]

There is no upper limit to the flexibility of function $g(\cdot)$. In fact, such flexibility is in line with Sen where opportunities or capabilities are intended as freedoms of a country and can be easily linked to their flourishing (Brandolini and D'Alessio, 1998; Ranis and Stewart, 2010). Therefore, as stated in the previous section, outcomes reached on different dimensions in a country are a proxy of the opportunity open to a person in a certain context.[17] Moreover, the smaller the level of general development, the higher the need for synergy between dimensions.

Results of the Empirical Analysis

In this section we present the results of an illustrative analysis on the MHDI. Six dimensions were examined. Health, education and command over resource are the components of HDI and the variables chosen are therefore 'life expectancy', 'education', 'GDP' index (for these variables the source is the Human Development Report and an online database showing trends from UNDP).

The new three dimensions that are presented are environment, labour opportunities, and political and civil freedom. Data are obtained from The World Bank's World Development Indicators (WDI).

The dimension of environment is represented by carbon dioxide (CO_2) emissions.[18] These emissions are those stemming from the burning of fossil fuels and the manufacture of cement. They include carbon dioxide produced during consumption of solid, liquid, and gas fuels and gas flaring. The data source is the Carbon Dioxide Information Analysis Centre, Environmental Sciences Division, Oak Ridge National Laboratory, Tennessee, USA.

The dimension of labour opportunity is captured by unemployment rates. This variable refers to the share of the labour force that is without work but available for and seeking employment. Definitions of labour

[16] The function is not defined for $\mu = 0$, therefore we exclude the particular case where all variables are 0.

[17] We are not going to consider the inequality issue here as stated in the introduction.

[18] The variable 'CO_2 emissions' has been previously transformed using a logarithmic scale.

force and unemployment differ by country. The data source in this case is from the International Labour Organization: Key Indicators of the Labour Market database. The political dimension is measured through the Freedom index. This index is calculated combining political rights and civil liberties ratings, indicating the general state of freedom in a country or territory. The data on political rights and civil liberties categories are taken from the Freedom House and they contain numerical ratings between 0 and 12 for each country or territory.[19] Data are obtained from a survey measuring freedom (the opportunity to act spontaneously in a variety of fields outside the control of the government and other centres of potential domination) according to two broad categories: political rights and civil liberties. Political rights enable people to participate freely in the political process, including the right to vote freely for distinct alternatives in legitimate elections, compete for public office, join political parties and organizations, and elect representatives who have a decisive impact on public policies and are accountable to the electorate. Civil liberties allow for the freedoms of expression and belief, associational and organizational rights, rule of law, and personal autonomy without interference from the state.

All the six variables were measured in 2005 for sixteen countries. In this explorative analysis the selection of the countries is not so relevant so the selection is based on data availability and different locations and levels of well-being (Bangladesh, Brazil, Botswana, Chile, China, Costa Rica, France, India, Italy, Japan, Norway, Russian Federation, South Africa, United Arab Emirates, USA and Zambia).

The original data are first redirected towards a common positive direction, and then normalized using a function of the range.[20] In Table 13.1 the MHDI normalized components HDI and new dimensions are reported for 2005.

In Table 13.2 a comparison is provided an example with the results of two common indexes and the MSI calculated on a matrix of data on the sixteen countries, in 2005. In the table we see the standard deviation of the normalized values (as a measure of variability within units), the arithmetic mean, the geometric mean and the MHDI.

---

[19] The minimum value was set at −1 because the value 0 (e.g. that for China) cannot be considered the worst possible situation.

[20] The minimum (maximum) used for this transformation was set at approximately 10 per cent less (more) than the observed minimum (maximum).

Table 13.1 *HDI components and new dimensions and proxy variable normalized for selected countries, year 2005*

	Min	Max	Range	Mean	St. Dev.
GDP	0.41	1.00	0.60	0.78	0.20
Education	0.52	0.99	0.47	0.85	0.14
Life expectancy	0.30	0.96	0.66	0.75	0.21
Une2005	0.10	0.91	0.81	0.74	0.24
Freedom	0.15	0.92	0.76	0.70	0.27
CO_2 (log)	0.09	0.95	0.86	0.54	0.25

Source: Our elaboration on WDI (World Bank, 2010) and HDI Trends (UNDP, 2010)

Table 13.2 *A comparison between arithmetic mean, geometric mean and MHDI*

Country	St. Dev.	Arithmetic	Geometric	MHDI	Differ. Geom.	Differ. MHDI
Bangladesh	0.218	0.650	0.621	0.618	−4.6%	−4.9%
Botswana	0.281	0.594	0.490	0.544	−17.6%	−8.5%
Brazil	0.057	0.793	0.791	0.791	−0.2%	−0.2%
Chile	0.130	0.818	0.808	0.811	−1.2%	−0.9%
China	0.271	0.644	0.563	0.601	−12.5%	−6.7%
Costa Rica	0.074	0.833	0.831	0.831	−0.3%	−0.3%
France	0.193	0.835	0.812	0.819	−2.8%	−1.9%
India	0.124	0.693	0.684	0.683	−1.3%	−1.4%
Italy	0.206	0.828	0.799	0.811	−3.4%	−2.1%
Japan	0.225	0.828	0.791	0.808	−4.5%	−2.4%
Norway	0.250	0.838	0.790	0.813	−5.9%	−2.9%
Russia	0.261	0.643	0.589	0.600	−8.3%	−6.6%
South Africa	0.258	0.587	0.532	0.541	−9.3%	−7.8%
UAE	0.389	0.653	0.489	0.564	−25.1%	−13.6%
USA	0.300	0.807	0.720	0.771	−10.8%	−4.4%
Zambia	0.229	0.580	0.543	0.542	−6.4%	−6.6%

Source: Our elaboration on WDI (World Bank, 2010) and HDI Trends (UNDP, 2010)

The last two columns report the decrease of both the geometric mean and the MHDI compared to the arithmetic mean.

The arithmetic mean implies perfect substitutability between dimensions, and therefore does not penalize heterogeneity, while the other two indexes produce lower scores (the magnitude of the decrease with respect to the arithmetic mean is reported in the last two columns). Both geometric mean and the MHDI are sensitive to the level of well-being, with poorest units more penalized than others. These indexes produce similar results in cases of low heterogeneity (Brazil, Chile, Costa Rica), while appear significantly different for countries with a high variability in the achievements (United Arab Emirates, USA, China, South Africa). As the achievements are homogeneous, the hypothesis of perfect substitutability is acceptable, and both the geometric mean and the MHDI produce results that are similar to the arithmetic mean.

As the standard deviation of the achievements increases, the assumption of perfect substitutability appears less reliable. The countries with higher variability (UAE, USA, Botswana, China, Russia, South Africa, Norway) have their results penalized by both the geometric mean and the MHDI. The difference between the geometric mean and the MHDI is that the penalization of the former is a function of the heterogeneity of the achievements (i.e. of the variance of the different indicators chosen), while for the latter, it is also a function of the level of well-being of the country. Norway, for example, that presents a medium-high degree of variability, it is significantly penalized by the geometric mean (−5.7 per cent), while the penalization induced by the MHDI is less than half (−2.9 per cent). This is due to the high level of overall well-being in Norway, captured by the MHDI, according to the assumption that the lower the level of development, the greater the need for synergy between dimensions.

The penalization induced by the geometric mean appears excessively sensitive. For example UAE has −25.1 per cent in presence of dimensions that are extremely deprived (this is due to the functional form of the index that is too sensitive to values close to 0). The MHDI, still penalizing this extreme situation of poverty and heterogeneity (−13.6 per cent) appears more robust to these 'small' values in the achievements. The results are relevant also in terms of changes in ranking despite the limited number of countries analysed. For instance, Norway ranks first according to the arithmetic mean, while it is dramatically penalized by the geometric mean, under which it ranks seventh. The

MHDI does not penalize Norway so strongly. This is due to the high level of overall well-being in Norway, captured by the MHDI, according to the assumption that the lower the level of development, the greater the need for synergy between dimensions.

Although the MHDI helps overcoming the 'inescapable arbitrariness' issues mentioned by Anand and Sen (1997), it still maintains some elements of subjectivity in the choice of the functional form of $g(\cdot)$ or its parameters. We do not claim to have solved this arbitrariness issue, but rather to have proposed an index that allows a more flexible approach towards the management of the relationships between the dimensions of interest. In our opinion, the tools provided by the *MSI* can be important for a better understanding of the crucial dynamics of the synthesis. Even if a certain degree of arbitrariness in some choices is still inescapable, having a deep understanding and a flexible approach can significantly increase the awareness and consciousness of these choices.

Conclusion

According to Sen, '"Human development" accounting involves a systematic examination of a wealth of information about how human beings in each society live. It brings an inescapably pluralist conception of progress to the exercise of development evaluation' (Sen, 2000: 18). However, most development indexes, including the HDI, have still not been able to offer enough flexibility in handling heterogeneity problems arising from multidimensionality. The MHDI maintains, as dimensions increase, the balance between intuitive appeal and explanatory power. In particular, we focused on the synergies between HD outcomes. We introduced the MHDI applying the MSI approach. The MHDI index allows us to assign higher scores to countries with homogeneous levels of the outcomes (i.e. more synergic) and with a higher level of well-being. Our assumption is that the lower the level of development, the greater the need for synergy between dimensions.

It is important to notice that, if sufficient data are available, the analysis can be conducted at different level of aggregation (e.g. local areas). An extension of the work includes the possibility of considering different synergies at different level of growth of a country. Moreover, the MHDI potentially allows the identification and the analysis of HD patterns in terms of outcomes' performance from a cross and time perspective and from a social and economic distinction.

Acknowledgements

The authors acknowledge the financial support from the EuropeAid project 'Umanamente' in the initial part of the research project. The authors are grateful for the comments and help of Marco Bellandi, Marco Bellucci, Giovanni Canitano, Annalisa Caloffi, Enrica Chiappero Martinetti, Flavio Comim, Jaya Krisnakumar, Andrea Ferrannini, Richard Jolly, Federico Perali, Gustav Ranis, Filomena Maggino, Giovanni M. Marchetti, Marco Sanfilippo and Enrico Testi. This chapter also benefited from comments received from participants at the following events: the conference on 'Twenty Years of Human Development: The Past and the Future of the Human Development Index', St Edmund's College, University of Cambridge, UK, 28–29 January 2010; the PRIN project events between 2011 and 2013 financed by MIUR; the workshop on 'Capabitaly' in Rome 7 April 2014; the conference of AIQUAV in Florence, December 2015; the Cambridge Capability Conference, at the Centre of Development Studies, University of Cambridge, 13–14 June 2016, and the HDCA conference in Tokyo at the Hitotsubashi University, August 2016. The authors have also benefited from continuous interactions with academics participating in the Italian colloquia on the capability approach.

References

Alkire, S. (2007) 'The missing dimensions of poverty data: Introduction to the special issue'. *Oxford Development Studies*, 35 (4), 347–59.

(2008) 'Choosing dimensions: The capability approach and multidimensional poverty'. In N. Kakwani and J. Silber (Eds.) *The Many Dimensions of Poverty*. Basingstoke: Palgrave Macmillan.

Alkire, S. and Foster, J. E. (2010) Designing the inequality-adjusted human development index (IHDI). Human Development Research Paper 2010/28.

(2011) 'Counting and multidimensional poverty measurement'. *Journal of Public Economics*, 95 (7), 476–87.

Anand, S. and Sen, A. K. (1997) 'Concepts of Human Development and Poverty: A Multidimensional Perspective'. Human Development Papers 1997. New York: UNDP.

Anand, S. and Sen, A. (2000) 'The income component of the human development index'. *Journal of Human Development*, 1 (1), 83–106.

Biggeri M., Ferrannini A. (2014) 'Opportunity Gap Analysis: Procedures and Methods for Applying the Capability Approach in Development

Initiatives', *Journal of Human Development and Capabilities*, 15 (1), 60–78.

Biggeri, M., Libanora R. (2010), 'From Valuing to Evaluating: Tools and Procedures to Operationalize the Capability Approach' in M. Biggeri, J. Ballet, F. Comim (Eds.), *Children and the capability approach*, Palgrave Macmillan.

Biggeri M., Mauro V. (2010), Comparing Human Development Patterns across Countries: Is it Possible to Reconcile Multidimensional Measures and Intuitive Appeal? Working paper, n° 15/2010, Dipartimento di Scienze Economiche, Università di Firenze.

Biggeri, M., Libanora, R., Mariani, S. and Menchini, L. (2006) 'Children conceptualizing their capabilities: Results of the survey during the first Children's World Congress on Child Labour'. *Journal of Human Development*, 7 (1), 59–83.

Brandolini, A., and D'Alessio, G. (1998) 'Measuring well-being in the functioning space'. In E. Chiappero Martinetti (Ed.) *Debating Global Society: Reach and Limits of the Capability Approach*. Milan: Fondazione Giangiacomo Feltrinelli, pp. 91–156.

Bourguignon, F., Chakravarty, S. R. (2003), 'The measurement of multidimensional poverty', *The Journal of Economic Inequality*, 1 (1), 25–49.

Comim, F., Alkire, S. and Qizilbash, M. (2008) *The Capability Approach: Concepts, Measures and Applications*. Cambridge: Cambridge University Press.

Desai, M. J. (1991) 'Human development: Concepts and measurement'. *European Economic Review*, 35 (2/3), 350–7.

Fukuda-Parr, S. (2000) 'Rescuing the human development concept from the HDI: Reflections on a new agenda'. In A. K. S. Kumar and S. Fukuda-Parr (Eds.) *Readings in Human Development*. New Delhi: Oxford University Press.

Klugman, J., Rodríguez, F., Choi, H. J. (2011), 'The HDI 2010: new controversies, old critiques', *The Journal of Economic Inequality*, 9 (2), 249–88.

Mauro, V., Biggeri, M., Maggino, F. (2016), 'Measuring and Monitoring Poverty and Well-Being: A New Approach for the Synthesis of Multidimensionality'. *Social Indicators Research*, pp. 1–15.

Mehrotra, S. and Biggeri, M. (2007) *Asian Informal Workers: Global Risk Local Protection*. London: Routledge.

Mehrotra, S. and Jolly R. (Eds.) (1997) *Development with a Human Face: Experiences in Social Achievement and Economic Growth*. Oxford: Clarendon Press.

Mehrotra, S. and Delamonica, E. (2007) *Eliminating Human Poverty: Macro-economic Policies for Equitable Growth*. London: Zed Press.

Ranis, G. and Stewart, F. (2010) Success and Failure in Human Development, 1970–2007. Human Development Research Paper 10. New York: UNDP–HDRO.

Ranis, G., Stewart, F. and Ramirez, A. (2000a) 'Strategies for success in human development'. *Journal of Human Development*, 1 (1), 49–69.

(2000b) 'Economic growth and human development'. *World Development*, 25 (2), 197–209.

Ranis, G., Stewart, F. and Samman, E. (2006) 'Human development: Beyond the Human Development Index'. *Journal of Human Development*, 7, 323–58.

Ranis, G., Stewart, F. and Samman (2007) 'Country patterns of behaviour on broader dimensions of human development'. In J. Antonio Ocampo, K. S. Jomo and K. Sarbuland (Eds.) *Policy Matters, Economic and Social Policies to Sustain Equitable Development*. London: Zed Books.

Robeyns, I. (2003) 'Sen's capability approach and gender inequality: Selecting relevant capabilities'. *Feminist Economics*, 9 (2–3), 61–92.

Sen, A. K. (1999) *Development as Freedom*. Oxford: Oxford University Press.

Sen, A. K. (2000) 'A decade of human development'. *Journal of Human Development*, 1 (1), 17–23.

UNDP (1996) Human Development Report. New York: Oxford University Press.

(2013), Human Development Report. New York: Oxford University Press.

14 | Inequality and Capabilities
A Multidimensional Empirical Exploration in Chile

MACARENA ORCHARD[*] AND MARTINA YOPO[*]

Introduction

In the past decades, research and debates on inequality have shifted from an economic approach focused exclusively on income distribution to a multidimensional approach that addresses the heterogeneous and complex nature of inequality. In this context, the capability approach has made a significant contribution to the conceptual reflections and empirical measurements of multidimensional inequality by creating tools that enable determining and observing the different aspects that condition the individual capability to achieve valuable functionings to experience wellbeing and live a worthy life. Drawing on the use of capabilities to assess the multidimensional nature of inequality, this chapter aims to provide empirical evidence of inequality in Chile by showing the asymmetrical distribution of capabilities within the Chilean population and identifying their distribution among social groups. By conducting statistical analyses with data from the Human Development Survey 2011 in Chile (Programa de las Naciones Unidas para el Desarrollo [PNUD], 2012), that contains a multidimensional and context-specific operationalisation of capabilities for the Chilean society, this chapter contributes to advance the study of multidimensional inequality through the capability approach. First, we discuss the emergence and development of a multidimensional perspective on inequality in recent years, and its conceptual and empirical advancement from the capability approach. Second, the chapter describes the construction of a list of significant capabilities for Chilean society and

[*] Former researcher of the Human Development Programme, United Nations Development Programme (UNDP) in Chile. The authors would like to thank the research team of the Human Development Programme for supporting this article by facilitating the dataset and the capabilities indicators which are used in it. The intellectual property of these indicators is of the research team (PNUD, 2012).

its empirical operationalisation for the Human Development Survey 2011 (PNUD, 2012). Third, we suggest a method to analyse the distribution of these capabilities and present and discuss the results of their general and specific distribution in the Chilean population, and their association with social groups determined by socioeconomic status, gender, and age. Finally, the chapter presents some reflections on the capability of capabilities to empirically observe the multidimensional nature of inequality in Chile, and the particularities of the distribution of capabilities within Chilean society.

The Multidimensional Approach to Inequality

In the past decades, there has been a significant shift in the debate on inequality. A multidimensional approach to the theoretical understanding and empirical measurement of inequality has emerged as an alternative to overcome its prevalent narrow understanding based on the asymmetrical distribution of income calculated through measures such as the Gini coefficient (Heshmati, 2004; Crow et al., 2009; Decancq, 2011). This multidimensional approach is based on a broader and more profound understanding of inequality that goes beyond income distribution and addresses the diversity of aspects that condition the capacity of individuals to live a worthy and satisfactory life. Among many others, Kreckel (1976), Sen (1992), and Therborn (2013) have emphasised that inequality refers to an asymmetrical distribution of life chances that affects the capability of human beings to freely pursue life objectives and choose a life of dignity and wellbeing. This multidimensional approach to inequality has gained importance not only in academic research and debates, but also in the policy design and implementation of international organisations and national governments. In this context, for example, both the (United Nations Development Programme [UNDP], 2013) and the Equality and Human Rights Commission in England, Scotland and Wales (Alkire et al., 2009) have incorporated a conceptual and empirical approach to inequality that goes beyond differences in income distribution.

Within a multidimensional approach, there are different perspectives to define and operationalise inequality. Although the aim of this chapter is not to provide a comprehensive categorisation of theoretical and empirical approaches to multidimensional inequality, we illustrate some of the main perspectives that are currently used in social research to address inequality beyond the distribution of income. We have identified at least three perspectives. First, there are perspectives that focus on a particular set of variables that affect individual wellbeing and that are used as a basis to establish comparisons between individuals in a population. Following the Human Development Index (HDI), some studies like Decancq (2011) and Binelli et al. (2015), base a multidimensional assessment of inequality on the combination of empirical indicators related to an individual's income, health and education, while others like McKay (2002) and Heshmati (2004) consider a broader range of indicators including happiness, welfare and security among others. Second, there are perspectives that focus on the broader theoretical dimensions that define inequality and group different empirical variables according to those dimensions. Kreckel (1976), Langer and Brown (2007) and Therborn (2013) among others, define dimensions such as 'material inequality', including variables like income, wealth and control over the means of production, 'existential inequality', including variables like personhood, autonomy, dignity, freedom, respect and self-development, and 'cultural inequalities', including variables like religion, language, ethnocultural practices and their recognition. Third, there are perspectives that focus on how a variable or a set of variables are distributed between different social groups characterised by particular identities or common features like gender, class, age, race, among others. For example, in mapping global inequalities, Crow et al. (2009) focus on health, materiality, gender, migration and culture as significant axes of inequality. Despite their differences, these perspectives tend to agree that the conceptually differentiated dimensions and variables of inequality are empirically interwoven, interdependent and intertwined, and at the same time irreducible to each other due to their particular content and dynamics (Kreckel, 1976; McKay, 2002; Therborn, 2013; Binelli et al., 2015). We argue that although these perspectives make a significant contribution to assess the multidimensional nature of inequality, they fail to take into account the subjective standpoint in determining the aspects that are relevant for an equal, just and worthy life. As we will discuss in the following section, this is something that has received greater consideration in the capability approach, and thus it constitutes a valuable contribution to complement the aforementioned perspectives.

Inequality and the Capability Approach

Perhaps the most significant contribution to the conceptual and empirical assessment of the multidimensional nature of inequality has been developed within the capability approach. The foundations of the relationship between capabilities and a multidimensional approach to inequality can be found in the work of Sen (1992, 2000). Sen's approach to inequality differs significantly from the utilitarianism implicit in neoclassical economic theory (Walsh, 1995/1996), and is based on a critique of the limited and neglecting character of conceptions based exclusively on income distribution. As he argues, 'the extent of real inequality of opportunities that people face cannot be readily deduced from the magnitude of inequality of *incomes,* since what we can or cannot do, can or cannot achieve, do not depend just on our incomes but also on the variety of physical and social characteristics that affect our lives and make us what we are' (Sen, 1992: 28). Thus, Sen suggests that the informational focus of inequality should be based on the distribution of capabilities as the freedoms that people enjoy to do things they have reason to value (Sen, 2009). This means that inequality understood in terms of capabilities differs significantly from the standard focus on welfare economics, because instead of concentrating on income, wealth, and utilities, it emphasises that wellbeing depends on the capability to achieve valuable functionings (Walsh, 1995/1996). From this perspective, inequality is understood as the difference in capabilities that people have to develop the life they aspire to and it exists within a plurality of spaces and a diversity of individuals. To transit from an income perspective to a capability perspective in the assessment of social disparities allows both overcoming the narrow domain of income distribution and provides a comprehensive framework to address the conceptual and empirical aspects of multidimensional inequality through the lens of what people value to achieve wellbeing and live a worthy life. That this subjective standpoint matters for the assessment of inequality is one of the fundamental pillars of Sen's (2000) capability approach.

In discussing multidimensional inequality, Aristei and Bracalente (2011) argue that the capability approach has been the foundation of a growing consensus in recent years in favour of assessing inequality beyond monetary income. Drawing on Sen's work, a significant body of literature has used the capability approach to conceptualise or measure the multidimensional nature of inequality (Robeyns, 2003; Burchardt and Vizard, 2009, 2011; Crow et al., 2009; Burchardt and Vizard 2011; Wang, 2011; Binelli et al., 2015). In this body of work, a wide and diverse range of capabilities including physical health, mental wellbeing, identity, bodily integrity and safety, social relations, respect, political empowerment, education and knowledge, paid work, leisure activities, among many others, have been defined as an effective conceptual and methodological tool in the empirical assessment of inequality. This increasing relevance of the intersection between capabilities and inequality was also observed in the Cambridge Capability Conference (2016) organised by the Centre of Development Studies of the University of Cambridge; this theme was echoed among other participants, for example in the presentation 'Inequality and the Capability Approach' by Tania Burchardt and Rod Hick, and in the poster 'Children's Capabilities and Education Inequality – how types of schooling play a role in Pakistan' by Amna Ansari.

This chapter draws on this significant body of work and aims to advance it by providing empirical evidence of the multidimensional nature of inequality in Chilean society through an analysis of the asymmetrical distribution of capabilities within the Chilean population and identifying their distribution among social groups. We choose the capability approach for two main reasons. On the one hand, because the capability approach focuses on the diverse range of aspects that affect the human capacity to achieve wellbeing, it is multidimensional and provides a comprehensive framework to address the different opportunities and constraints to achieve valuable functionings to live a worthy life from the standpoint of the individuals that experience them. On the other hand, because the capability approach allows overcoming a theoretical a priori definition of the central dimensions of inequality by stressing that the definition of dimensions that should be considered to assess inequality should be guided by public reasoning (Sen, 2009). We consider that this opens the possibility to develop a context-specific approach to the analysis of multidimensional inequality, as it invites a reflection on the distribution of functionings that people have reason to value in Chilean society. Certainly, there have been authors within the capabilities approach, such as Nussbaum (2003) who have argued that a universal 'list' of capabilities should be established, something that Sen (2009) himself has criticised. But even Nussbaum (2003) has acknowledged that it is important to account for pluralism and have sensitivity to cultural differences in defining the capabilities that are relevant to achieve wellbeing. For that reason she argues that the list of central capabilities should always be subjected to supplementation or deletion according to any society's account of its most fundamental entitlements, and to specification and deliberation by citizens and their legal frameworks. Stressing this point is crucial, as the risk of universalism tends to be quite high in the literature on multidimensional inequality that is not inspired by the capability approach.

Data, Method and Analysis

To empirically observe the multidimensional nature of inequality in Chilean society, this chapter draws on the operationalisation of capabilities developed in the Human Development Report (PNUD, 2012) in Chile. Inspired by the aforementioned philosophical debate on the selection of capabilities (Nussbaum, 2003; Sen, 2009), and attempting to avoid both the limits of universalism and particularism as well as the problem of adaptive preferences (Teschl and Comim, 2005), the list of capabilities was produced though a small-scale deliberative process. This procedure was guided by a normative principle named 'culturally-sensitive universalism' (PNUD, 2012: 126). This principle acknowledges the importance of both universal standards and local public reasoning and deliberation in defining a specific 'list' of capabilities to assess the wellbeing of the Chilean population. With this framework in mind, the research team carried out a series of workshops where people from different genders, socioeconomic status, and age were invited to discuss the 'things' that were more important in their lives. The participants were offered a preliminary list of elements that was created by the research team inspired by different lists such as that from Nussbaum (2003) and The Universal Declaration of Human Rights, among others. The systematisation of lists carried out by Alkire (2008) was particularly fruitful for this exercise. This list was intentionally defined as openly as possible, and participants were invited to add or delete elements from it. They were also exposed to the possibility to assess their preferences by means of deliberation, as they were required to reach consensus as a group. Afterwards, the outcomes of these workshops were analysed and an exploratory list of 11 capabilities (see Table 14.1) that are central for the wellbeing of

Table 14.1 *List of 11 capabilities*

(1) Enjoying good health
(2) Having physical and material basic needs covered
(3) Knowing oneself and having an inner life
(4) Feeling secure and free from threats (in terms of illness, crime and others)
(5) Participating and having an influence in society
(6) Experiencing pleasure and emotions
(7) Maintaining significant ties with other people
(8) Being recognised and respected in one's dignity and rights
(9) Knowing and understanding the world in which one lives
(10) Enjoying and feeling part of nature
(11) Having and developing one's own life plan

Chileans was suggested.[1] This list is significantly multidimensional as it includes vital, existential, relational and political elements.

These capabilities were then empirically operationalised and included in a questionnaire applied to a probabilistic sample of Chileans[2] (n = 2,535). Each capability was operationalised in terms of its 'effective functioning' and its 'subjective evaluation', in an attempt to distinguish between the actual possession of the functioning and the subjective assessment that each person makes of it. For instance, the capability of being healthy was measured in terms of its functioning as the possession of any limiting physical illness in the last 12 months, whereas in terms of its subjective evaluation it was measured through a scale in which respondents were asked to evaluate their own health in general terms. In turn, the capability of being recognised and respected in one's dignity and rights, was measured in terms of its functioning as the frequency by which respondents had experienced disrespect or mistreatment in the last 12 months, whereas in terms of its subjective evaluation was measured through a scale in which respondents were

---

[1] The details of this exercise can be found in PNUD (2012: 344).

[2] The Human Development Survey (PNUD, 2012) was applied to a probabilistic sample of the Chilean population over the age of 18. A stratified three stage cluster sampling approach was performed, with a sampling error of 1.9 per cent. The sample was stratified according to variables such as region and zone (urban-rural), and it was weighted according to region, zone, gender and age in order to correct any deviation of population's parametric data.

asked to evaluate to which extent they feel their rights and dignity are respected in Chilean Society.[3] This procedure created 22 indexes standardised from 0 to 1; 11 indexes of each capability's effective functioning and 11 indexes of each capability's subjective evaluation. We want to stress that this operationalisation can certainly be improved. To some extent, these indicators are closer to actual beings and doings than to the freedom to develop them. Also, the objective element is quite difficult to measure for certain capabilities. Nevertheless, they offer an opportunity to understand the distribution of functionings that we know are valued by Chileans. That it is why we consider them useful as proxies of capabilities in Chilean Society.

An interesting outcome of the analysis of these 22 indexes, which was already highlighted by PNUD (2012), is that all of them are unequally distributed in Chilean society. In fact, when analysed separately, all of them present differences that are statistically significant according to gender, socioeconomic status and age (PNUD, 2012: 161–5). At the same time, all are significantly associated with the subjective wellbeing of Chileans, which is operationalised through measurements such us the life satisfaction and the Cantril scale.[4]

In light of this rich material, in this chapter we would like to advance the empirical observation of the multidimensional nature of inequality in Chilean society by proposing an additional approach to the analysis of the distribution of these capabilities in the population. As it has been noted in the literature (e.g. Aristei and Bracalente, 2011), the empirical observation of multidimensional inequality involves several complexities. One of them is associated to the definition of whether the different dimensions of inequality should be analysed separately

---

[3] The list of variables included in each index can be found in PNUD (2012: 357–8). For extension constraints, we decided not to include the whole list of variables here. The report can be downloaded from: http://desarrollohumano.cl/idh/informes/2012-bienestar-subjetivo-el-desafio-de-repensar-el-desarrollo/.

[4] The life satisfaction scale consists of the question: 'all things considered, how satisfied are you with your life as a whole these days?', and it has been used, for instance, in several waves of the World Value Survey. The Cantril scale corresponds to an adapted version of the original Cantril Self-Anchoring Striving Scale developed by Cantril (1965) and consists of the question: 'please imagine a ladder with steps numbered from 1 to 10, the top of the ladder represents the best possible life for you and the bottom of the ladder represents the worst possible life for you. On which step of the ladder would you say you personally feel you stand at this time?' This scale has been used, for instance, in the Gallup's World Poll. For a discussion on these scales see Bjørnskov (2010).

or in an aggregated form. Another one is related to the definition of empirical thresholds that enable us to claim that a person (or country) possess an adequate level of any of the relevant dimensions involved in the analysis. Having these challenges in mind, we designed a procedure to analyse the distribution of these 11 capabilities in the Chilean population. This procedure is inspired by Sen's assertion that, beyond the distribution of individual capabilities, the capability's approach is 'ultimately concerned with the ability to achieve *combinations* of valued functionings' (Sen, 2009: 233).

First, we transformed these 22 indexes into 11 indexes that summarised the information on each capability.[5] Although the 'objective functioning' and the 'subjective evaluation' of each capability do not always present the same distribution in the population – an outcome which is interesting in itself – we suggest that we can still work with the two dimensions of each capability together. In fact, we can theoretically consider each dimension as a subdimension of each capability. Thus, we created 11 indexes by simply adding and weighting both dimensions in order to represent the 50 per cent of each individual's capability. As a result, 50 per cent of each index is compounded by the answers that respondents gave to questions that measured their level of capabilities in an objective manner, and the remaining 50 per cent is compounded by the answer that respondents gave to questions which measured their subjective evaluation of their level of capability. This exercise produced 11 indexes of capabilities, standardised from 0 to 1, whose means and standard deviations in the population can be found in Table 14.2. Also, we present the distribution of these indexes according to sex, socioeconomic status and age. Note that almost all these indexes show statistically significant differences in the population by gender, socioeconomic status and age. By comparing the means of these capabilities on each subgroup of the population (in particular, the magnitude of both the t and the f statistics), it is possible to observe that there are some capabilities that present higher differences in the population, according to sex, socioeconomic status and age, than others. For instance, the difference in the capability of 'knowing' is particularly high among men and women, whereas the difference in the capability of 'having a life plan' is particularly relevant in the

---

[5] We developed all analyses using SPSS v. 22.

Table 14.2 Means of the 11 capabilities indexes in the population and their distribution according to sex, age and socioeconomic status

Population	Health	Basic needs	Self-knowing	Human security	Participation	Pleasure	Ties	Respect	Knowing	Nature	Life plan
Mean	0.70	0.62	0.68	0.55	0.47	0.6	0.65	0.64	0.55	0.37	0.65
Std. deviation	0.26	0.17	0.19	0.15	0.18	0.20	0.17	0.18	0.21	0.26	0.27
Sex											
Male	0.71	0.64	0.68	0.57	0.48	0.62	0.65	0.64	0.58	0.39	0.67
Female	0.69	0.61	0.68	0.52	0.46	0.58	0.65	0.64	0.52	0.35	0.62
T test	2.07[*]	3.82[***]	−0.36	7.44[***]	2.99[**]	5.34[***]	1.33	0.77	8.09[***]	4.54[***]	4.3[***]
Socioeconomic status[a,b]											
ABC1	0.8	0.87	0.74	0.64	0.54	0.71	0.75	0.69	0.74	0.49	0.77
C2	0.74	0.73	0.73	0.6	0.52	0.64	0.71	0.65	0.68	0.4	0.74
C3	0.73	0.64	0.69	0.56	0.47	0.6	0.67	0.63	0.57	0.38	0.68
D	0.67	0.56	0.65	0.52	0.44	0.57	0.61	0.62	0.49	0.35	0.6
E	0.64	0.51	0.65	0.48	0.44	0.58	0.58	0.64	0.43	0.31	0.54
F statistic	22.46[***]	317.97[***]	19.72[***]	67.79[***]	24.93[***]	22.33[***]	64.20[***]	6.11	176.68[***]	19.27[***]	53.74[***]

Age

18–24	0.79	0.65	0.7	0.57	0.41	0.66	0.7	0.63	0.57	0.45	0.73
25–34	0.77	0.65	0.68	0.58	0.41	0.63	0.7	0.64	0.59	0.39	0.71
35–44	0.74	0.62	0.68	0.56	0.48	0.58	0.65	0.63	0.56	0.36	0.65
45–54	0.67	0.62	0.67	0.55	0.50	0.57	0.64	0.62	0.56	0.34	0.63
55 years +	0.63	0.6	0.67	0.51	0.49	0.59	0.61	0.66	0.5	0.34	0.59
F statistic	36.09***	8.57***	3.13	18.54***	29.50***	12.62***	26.84***	6.81***	16.79***	13.82***	23.56***

*$p < 0.05$; **$p < 0.01$; ***$p < 0.001$

[a] We are using here one of the most used socioeconomic classification systems in Chile, which is based on two criteria: educational attainment and occupational activity of the head of household. If any of that information is missing, the classification operates according to the possession of a set of goods. ABC1 represents the upper class, C2 the upper-middle class, C3 the middle class, D the lower-middle class, and E the lower class.

[b] This classification includes the level of education of the head of household, which should be taken into account when analysing the association with the capability of 'understanding'.

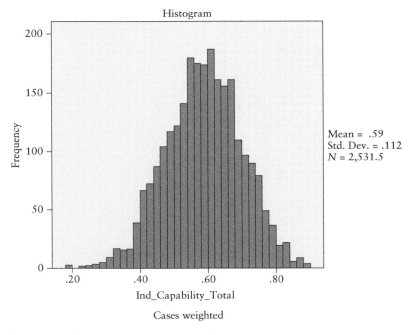

Figure 14.1 Histogram of the General Capabilities Index

case of socioeconomic status. Finally, the difference in the capability of 'being healthy' is very high according to age.

The previous analysis is very useful to understand the relevance of performing a separate analysis of each capability. As noted, it shows that some capabilities present higher differences in the population according to sex, socioeconomic status and age than others. However, the aggregate analysis of these 11 capabilities is also telling. To show this, we created a single general index by calculating the mean of the 11 capabilities together. This index also runs from 0 to 1 and it has a distribution closer to normal (see Figure 14.1). We name it the 'General Capabilities Index'. Akin to the individual indexes, the General Capabilities Index shows statistically significant differences in the population by sex, socioeconomic status and age (see Table 14.3), which confirms that women, the elderly and people from more disadvantaged socioeconomic backgrounds exhibit a significantly lower level of capabilities in Chile. This index constitutes a key tool to

Table 14.3 Means of the General Capabilities Index by gender, age and socioeconomic status

| | Sex | | Age | | | | | | Socioeconomic Status | | | | |
	Male	Female	18–24	25–34	35–44	45–54	55 years +	ABC1	C2	C3	D	E
Mean	0.60	0.57	0.62	0.61	0.59	0.58	0.56	0.70	0.65	0.60	0.55	0.53
Test	t = 6.74***		F = 24.14***					F = 173.55***				

*p < 0.05; **p < 0.01; ***p < 0.001

approach the study of multidimensional inequality in Chilean society. Although it tends to reduce complexity, it enables us to convey in one single figure the average possession of several functionings which are valued by the Chilean population. Thus, the study of its distribution is a key tool to measure the level of multidimensional inequality in Chile.

To analyse how unequal is the distribution of the General Capability Index, we decided to construct a 'capabilities quintile ratio', following the same rationale behind the 'income quintile ratio' used by UNDP to measure income inequality[6] (see Table 14.4). This measure compares the ratio of the average level of capabilities of the 20 per cent of the population who possess the highest level of capabilities according to the General Capabilities Index, to the average level of capabilities of the 20 per cent of the population who possess the lowest level of capabilities based on the same index. Even though this is a simple measure, we believe that it is easy and intuitive enough to contribute to the understanding of the magnitude of multidimensional inequality in Chile. The results show that people pertaining to the highest capabilities quintile (quintile 5) poses almost two times more capabilities than people pertaining to the lowest capabilities quintile (quintile 1). The ratio is especially high for the capabilities of 'enjoying nature', 'knowing' and 'life project', and is lower for capabilities such us 'respect' and 'self-knowing'. This outcome is relevant as it stresses the fact that there are capabilities that are more unequally distributed than others, enabling us to highlight the importance of understanding the multidimensional nature of inequality beyond income distribution. Chile has one of the most unequal income distributions in the world. According to the UNDP, Chile had an income quintile ratio of 13.5 in 2013, and the World Bank estimated a Gini Index for Chile of 50.5 for the same period.[7] In terms of the capabilities indexes, this inequality is partly captured by the distribution of the capability of 'having basic needs covered', which includes a measure of income in its operationalisation. Although the analysis of this capability cannot replace the analysis of income distribution, it is interesting to observe how in terms of our

---

[6] This measure defines inequality as the ratio of the average income of the richest 20 per cent of the population to the average income of the poorest 20 per cent of the population. More information can be found at: http://hdr.undp.org/es/content/income-quintile-ratio.
[7] This information can be found at: http://data.worldbank.org/indicator/SI.POV.GINI?locations=CL.

Table 14.4 *Capabilities quintile ratio of the General Capabilities Index and the 11 capabilities indexes*

	General Capabilities Index	Health	Basic needs	Self-knowing	Human security	Participation	Pleasure	Ties	Respect	Knowing	Nature	Life plan
Means Quintile 1*	0.43	0.52	0.47	0.53	0.44	0.36	0.43	0.49	0.54	0.35	0.18	0.39
Means Quintile 5*	0.74	0.86	0.78	0.80	0.66	0.59	0.76	0.80	0.73	0.74	0.59	0.86
Ratio	1.73	1.65	1.66	1.51	1.51	1.65	1.75	1.63	1.34	2.08	3.19	2.21

*The quintiles have been defined according to the distribution of the General Capabilities Index

indexes the capability of having basic needs covered does not exhibit the highest level of inequality. This result suggests that there are some capabilities which might be even more asymmetrically distributed than income.

Finally, we would like to reflect on how multidimensional inequality operates in people's lives. This involves replying questions such as: How do these capabilities relate to each other? Does having a low level of capabilities in one particular dimension always imply having a low level of capabilities in the other dimensions? We approached these questions by means of a cluster analysis. Even though this is an exploratory statistical technique, we argue that it is appropriate for our purposes for two reasons. First, it allows understanding the most typical combinations of levels of capabilities in the Chilean population, and therefore, to have a sense of whether these capabilities are organised as 'constellations'. Second, by studying the association of these clusters with different measures of wellbeing, this method allows the different 'thresholds' of capabilities to emerge empirically. This method has been previously used to explore other subjective constructs in Chilean society (Güell et al., 2015) and has proven to be fruitful in this context. We carried out a cluster analysis based on the K-means method. This method creates clusters of cases by maximising the differences among cases according to a set of grouping variables. We instructed the programme to look for optimum structures of 2, 3, 4, 5 and 6 clusters. As standard in this procedure, we use the Euclidean distance as a measurement of distance and the 11 indexes of capabilities, standardised from 0 to 1, as grouping variables. Once we obtained the clusters, we analysed which of these structures created the clearest and more balanced differences among the 11 capabilities. We also analysed the level of association of these different structures with two variables that can be considered proxies of wellbeing, such as the life satisfaction scale and the Cantril scale (both operationalised from 1 to 10). We decided to select the structure of clusters that presented both the more significant association with wellbeing and the most balanced distribution of capabilities. This structure would reflect the structure of the inequality of capabilities in Chile, by showing which 'constellations of levels of capabilities' were associated with higher or lower levels of wellbeing. To determine this we carried out one-way ANOVA analyses for all the structures of clusters in the 2 wellbeing scales and the 11 capabilities. To select the best structure of clusters, the F-statistic was used as

Table 14.5 *F statistics of Capabilities' Indexes and wellbeing measurements in the different clusters structures*

	F statistic[*]				
	Structure of 2 clusters	Structure of 3 clusters	Structure of 4 clusters	Structure of 5 clusters	Structure of 6 clusters
Health	235.0	4,597.5	406.2	1,701.6	1,859.4
Basic needs	902.0	418.0	340.6	234.5	239.6
Self-knowing	426.5	188.6	163.9	113.8	115.9
Human security	447.1	223.3	175.4	126.8	108.9
Participation	286.5	139.8	113.0	105.9	77.9
Pleasure and emotions	558.7	290.5	299.2	246.0	166.8
Ties with others	817.7	347.1	327.6	275.7	222.5
Respect	90.5	46.8	50.2	42.4	27.7
Knowing	1,272.7	509.0	468.0	309.6	283.6
Nature	537.0	265.3	570.4	668.3	656.9
Life plan	1,930.1	708.0	1237.9	608.9	663.5
Life satisfaction scale	301.8	143.1	119.6	89.2	76.7
Cantril scale	374.2	169.2	135.3	95.8	95.4

[*]All the tests are statistically significant ($p < 000.1$)

a reference. According to these analyses, we selected the structure of 4 clusters, which presents the most clear and balanced distribution of capabilities and that exhibits one of the higher association with the wellbeing of the population (see Table 14.5). This means that the procedure detected 4 groups of cases in the population that have similar levels and combinations of levels of capabilities, which also exhibits the most different levels of capabilities and wellbeing.

As we can observe in the Table 14.6, this structure reflects almost an ordered grouping of the 11 capabilities. However, there are some interesting particularities for each group that enable us to understand that having a certain level of one capability does not always involve having the same level in another. The subjects pertaining to the first cluster

Table 14.6 *Means of Capabilities' Indexes and wellbeing in the structure of four clusters*

	Cluster 1: High capabilities	Cluster 2: Middle high capabilities	Cluster 3: Middle low capabilities	Cluster 4: Low capabilities	General population
Health	0.82	0.68	0.81	0.38	0.70
Basic needs	0.74	0.63	0.55	0.48	0.62
Self-knowing	0.77	0.69	0.63	0.55	0.68
Human security	0.63	0.54	0.51	0.45	0.55
Participation	0.55	0.47	0.41	0.39	0.47
Pleasure and emotions	0.74	0.57	0.60	0.42	0.60
Ties with others	0.77	0.65	0.60	0.50	0.65
Respect	0.69	0.63	0.63	0.56	0.64
Knowing	0.70	0.59	0.43	0.37	0.55
Nature	0.61	0.25	0.38	0.18	0.37
Life plan	0.83	0.79	0.38	0.40	0.65
Life satisfaction	8.18	7.43	6.83	5.94	7.27
Cantril scale	7.89	7.10	6.46	5.67	6.95

(28.6 per cent of the population), have a higher level of capabilities than the average population on each of the measured capabilities and they also present the higher levels of wellbeing. The individuals that comprise the second cluster (32.8 per cent of the population) have a middle high level of capabilities, closer to the population average mean on each capability, with the exception of the capability of 'having a life plan', in which they present a higher level than the average population. They also present a higher level of wellbeing than the general population. The third cluster (22.6 per cent of the population) presents a middle low level of capabilities. The individuals of this group tend to be below the average population on all capabilities, with the exception of the capability of 'being healthy', in which they present a very high level, and the capability of 'enjoying nature' in which they are slightly above the general population. Also, among the four clusters, they present the lowest level of the capability of 'having a life plan'. Their level of wellbeing is also below the general population. Finally, the individuals of the fourth cluster (15.9 per cent of the population) present low levels of capabilities on all measured capabilities, being under the average population mean on each capability. They have particularly low levels of the capability of 'being healthy' and 'having the basic needs covered', and they present very low levels of wellbeing.

It should be noted that these clusters are also significantly associated with gender, socioeconomic status and age. This reflects again the intersectional character of multidimensional inequality in Chile. For instance, the percentage of women and men on each group differ greatly in the 'high capabilities' and the 'middle low capabilities' cluster (see Table 14.7). There is also a significant association with socioeconomic status, in which the 'high capabilities' cluster has the highest proportion of upper class individuals, whereas the 'low capabilities' cluster has the highest percentage of lower class individuals. It can also be observed that the younger groups of the population have a major presence in the 'higher capabilities' cluster than the older groups, and, in turn, the older groups have a greater presence in the 'low capabilities' cluster.

Conclusion

This chapter has suggested that the capability approach has enormous theoretical and empirical potential to improve our understanding of the multidimensional nature of inequality. Drawing on data from the Human Development Survey (PNUD, 2012), this chapter analysed the distribution of 11 context-specific capabilities for the Chilean population by performing a separate analysis of each one of these capabilities, an aggregated analysis of these capabilities by creating a General Index of Capabilities for Chile, and by analysing the magnitude of the unequal distribution of these 11 capabilities and how they operate in different constellations in the population through a cluster analysis. The results indicate that capabilities are unequally distributed in Chilean society and that this inequality is significantly structured by sex, age and socioeconomic status. This substantive empirical evidence contributes to highlight the great capability of capabilities to assess the multidimensional nature of inequality.

Several lessons can be learned from these results to further advance research on multidimensional inequality through the capability

Table 14.7 *Distribution of the clusters according to sex, age and socioeconomic status*

	Socioeconomic Status					
Clusters	ABC1	C3	C3	D	E	Total
High capabilities	71.1%	45.9%	32.3%	17.7%	9.8%	28.6%
Middle capabilities	22.1%	38.3%	36.8%	31.4%	29.3%	32.8%
Middle low capabilities	6.4%	10.9%	19.6%	28.0%	33.9%	22.6%
Low capabilities	0.5%	5.0%	11.4%	22.9%	27.0%	15.9%
Total	100.0%	100.0%	100.0%	100.0%	100.0%	100.0%
Chi squared test	Chi = 477.40***					

*$p < 0.05$; **$p < 0.01$; ***$p < 0.001$

	Sex		Age					Total
	Male	Female	18–24	25–34	35–44	45–54	55 years +	
High capabilities	33.8%	23.5%	45.2%	38.5%	26.7%	25.9%	20.4%	28.6%
Middle capabilities	33.0%	32.6%	29.2%	32.1%	34.9%	33.8%	32.9%	32.8%
Middle low capabilities	19.1%	26.0%	18.8%	17.9%	25.7%	22.5%	24.4%	22.6%
Low capabilities	14.0%	17.9%	6.8%	11.5%	12.7%	17.7%	22.4%	16.0%
Total	100.0%	100.0%	100.0%	100.0%	100.0%	100.0%	100.0%	100.0%
Chi squared test	Chi = 43.11***		Chi = 126.285***					

*$p < 0.05$; **$p < 0.01$; ***$p < 0.001$

approach. Firstly, that addressing the complex character of multidimensional inequality requires both single and aggregate analysis of capabilities in order to highlight the particular and interrelated character of the substantive freedoms that individuals have to achieve wellbeing. Second, that developing accurate empirical measurements of multidimensional inequality in particular social environments requires generating context-specific lists of capabilities that merge both a priori conceptual frameworks and emergent empirical elements. Finally, intersectionality is essential to account for the multidimensional nature of inequality, because the particular social features of an individual determine significantly freedoms and constraints on their capability to live a worthy life.

References

Alikire, S. (2008) Choosing dimensions: The capability approach and multidimensional poverty. Munich Personal RePEc Archive, Paper 8.862.

Alkire, S., Bastagli, F., Burchardt, T., et al. (2009) Developing the Equality Measurement Framework: Selecting the indicators. Research Report 31. Equality and Human Rights Commission, 1–525.

Ansari, A. (2016) Children's capabilities and education inequality: How types of schooling play a role in Pakistan. Cambridge Capability Conference, Centre of Development Studies, University of Cambridge. Cambridge, 13–14 June 2016.

Aristei, D. and Bracalente, B. (2011) Measuring multidimensional inequality and wellbeing: Methods and empirical applications to Italian regions. *Statistica LXXI*, (2), 239–66.

Binelli, C., Loveless, M. and Whitefield, S. (2015) What is social inequality and why does it matter? Evidence from Central and Eastern Europe. *World Development*, 70, 239–48.

Bjørnskov, C. (2010) How comparable are the Gallup World Poll Life Satisfaction Data?, *Journal of Happiness Studies*, 11 (1), 41–60.

Burchardt, T. and Vizard, P. (2009) Developing and equality measurement framework: A list of substantive freedoms for adults and children. Research Report 18. Equality and Human Right Commission, pp. 1–67.

(2011) 'Operationalizing' the capability approach as a basis for equality and human rights monitoring in twenty-first-century Britain. *Journal of Human Development and Capabilities*, 12 (1), 91–119.

Burchardt, T. and Hick, R. (2016) Inequality and the capability approach. Cambridge Capability Conference, Centre of Development Studies, University of Cambridge. Cambridge, 13–14 June, 2016.

Cantril, H. (1965) The Pattern of Human Concerns. New Brunswick, NJ: Rutgers University Press.

Crow, B., Zlatunich, N. and Fulfrost, B. (2009) Mapping global inequalities: Beyond income inequality to multi-dimensional inequalities. *Journal of International Development*, 21, 1051–65.

Decancq, K. (2011) Measuring global well-being inequality: A dimension-by-dimension or multidimensional approach? *Reflets et Perspectives de la Vie Economique*, 11 (4), 179–96.

Güell, P., Orchard, M., Yopo, M. and Jiménez-Molina, A. (2015) Time perspectives and subjective wellbeing in Chile. *Social Indicators Research*, 123 (1), 127–41.

Heshmati, A. (2004) Inequalities and their measurement. Discussion Paper No. 1219. The Institute for the Study of Labour, 1–17.

Kreckel, R. (1976) Dimensions of social inequality: Conceptual analysis and theory of society. *Sociologische Gids*, 23 (6), 338–62.

Langer, A. and Brown, G. K. (2007) Cultural status inequalities: An important dimension of group mobilization. Working Paper No. 41. Centre for Research on Inequality, Human Security and Ethnicity, University of Oxford, 1–15.

McKay, A. (2002) Defining and measuring inequality. Inequality Briefing Paper No 1. Overseas Development Institute, 1–6.

Nussbaum, M. (2003) Capabilities as fundamental entitlements: Sen and social justice. *Feminist Economics*, 9 (2), 33–59.

Programa de las Naciones Unidas para el Desarrollo (2012) Desarrollo Humano en Chile. *Bienestar Subjetivo: El Desafío de Repensar el Desarrollo*. Santiago: PNUD.

Robeyns, I. (2003) Sen's Capability Approach and Gender Inequality: Selecting Relevant Capabilities. *Feminist Economics*, 9 (2–3), 61–92.

Sen, A. (1992) *Inequality Re-examined*. New York: Oxford University Press.
   (2000) *Development as Freedom*. New York: Alfred A. Knopf.
   (2009) *The Idea of Justice*. Cambridge, MA: The Belknap Press of Harvard University Press.

Teschl, M. and Comim, F. (2005) Adaptive preferences and capabilities: Some preliminary conceptual explorations. *Review of Social Economy*, Vol. LXIII, No. 2, 229–48.

Therborn, G. (2013) *The Killing Fields of Inequality*. Cambridge and Malden: Polity.

United Nations Development Programme (2013) *Humanity Divided: Confronting Inequality in Developing Countries*. New York: UNDP.

Walsh, V. (1995/1996) Amartya Sen on inequality, capabilities and needs. *Science & Society*, 59 (4), 556–69.

Wang, L. (2011) Social exclusion and inequality in higher education in China: A capability perspective. *International Journal of Educational Development*, 31, 277–86.

15 | Living Wages in International Supply Chains and the Capability Approach

Towards a Conceptual Framework

STEPHANIE SCHRAGE AND KRISTIN HUBER

Introduction

Over the past decade, globalisation has led to an increased fragmentation of production of goods and services into different stages and activities along international supply chains. One industry that has in particular experienced the expansion of an international division of labour is the garment industry. Western corporations have, over the past decades, increasingly outsourced and offshored labour-intensive manufacturing stages in the garment production, which has induced the rapid evolvement of international supply chains in the garment industry. The international garment industry has recently attracted considerable attention by the media, civil society and the general public with regard to its abysmal working conditions. The collapse of the factory building of Rana Plaza in Bangladesh in 2013 has gruesomely illustrated the precarious safety situation in garment factories producing items for international markets. Besides safety issues, the wage levels of workers in the garment industry are also criticised by civil society organisations such as the Clean Clothes Campaign (CCC), Oxfam or the Worker Rights Consortium (WRC) (Musiolek, 2011: 6; Oxfam, 2014; WRC, 2013). Wages in the garment sector are often too low to safeguard the well-being of workers and their families. In Cambodia, for example, labour rights organisations have reported that malnutrition is a severe problem and that the wages of garment workers have in the past only sufficed for the consumption of half the recommended daily calorie intake (CCC, 2013: 11; ILRF, 2016). Legal minimum wages are often too low to guarantee a good life for workers in international supply chains. According to the CCC, the minimum wage in Bangladesh in 2014 was more than five times lower than the wage required to secure an adequate living standard (CCC, 2014).

Yet, the right to a living wage is recognised as a human right. Article 23 (3) of the Universal Declaration of Human Rights (1948) stipulates a worker's 'right to a just and favourable remuneration ensuring for himself and his family an existence worthy of human dignity'. Because current legal minimum wages often are not sufficient to guarantee this right in many garment producing countries, in the recent past, labour rights activists and other civil society organisations have started calling on multinational enterprises (MNEs) to voluntarily raise wages in their supply chains to a living wage level. For the garment industry, as a pioneer industry in many developing countries and already in the focus of labour rights organisations, these calls have been especially loud.

Despite being considered a human right, the definition of what a living wage exactly means is still highly contested (Anker, 2011). Usually, the living wage is defined as the wage that safeguards a worker and his family's 'basic needs' (Shelburne, 1999). It is supposed to not only ensure their existence, but also their means of development. Unlike a minimum wage, it is not set by political actors, but from a minimum level of well-being (Carr et al., 2015; Krugman, 1997). However, what exactly should be included within this minimum level of well-being remains unclear, so that little progress has been made so far in terms of wage raises (Anker, 2011). Over the past few years, a variety of different propositions on how to calculate and implement living wages for international supply chains have been put forward by various different actors, including non-governmental organisations (NGOs), academics and multistakeholder initiatives (MSIs) (see e.g. ACT, 2015; Anker, 2006; FWF, 2011; Miller, 2013; Musiolek, 2011). As a consequence, the international garment industry has seen the emergence of multiple and overlapping standards with considerable variation. In this chapter, we use the term 'living wage approaches' as an umbrella term to refer to this variety of initiatives. The different approaches to paying a living wage lead to vastly different results in terms of how high such a wage should be and how a raise in wages can be achieved. While approaches such as Action Collaboration Transformation (ACT) or the Wage Ladder do not foresee a prior calculation of living wages, but rather focus on the steps to wage raising implementation (ACT, 2015; FWF, 2011), other approaches, like the Asia Floor Wage (AFW) (Musiolek, 2011) or the Anker methodology (Anker, 2006), focus on different formulas to deliver exact living wage figures.

In this chapter, we argue that the question of 'what are the basic needs of a person?' cannot be answered independently of the normative concept of a good life. The capability approach (CA), as developed by Sen (2000) and with its further development by Nussbaum (2000, 2007, 2011), provides a normative view of what a good life entails. The CA proposes a shift in the evaluation of living standards focusing on an individual's actual opportunities and real freedoms rather than on their means of living, such as income (Sen, 2011). According to the CA, cultural, economic and political capabilities must exist in order for an individual to lead a good life (Sen, 2000). Sen (2011: 231–2) circumscribes the CA by outlining that it focuses 'on the freedom that a person actually has to do this or be that – things that he or she may value doing or being'. Thus, while poverty can be assessed monetarily, monetary measures of poverty are imperfect in the sense as they give little information about the well-being of persons, i.e. about the freedom that individuals have available and that they can use to fulfil their role in society (Sen, 2000; 2011). Following the logic of the CA, in this chapter, we propose that a living wage approach cannot be evaluated merely in monetary terms, but that it needs to recognise the capabilities a worker and his or her family have available at a certain wage level. Within the academic debate on living wages, few authors have already pointed to the value of the CA for understanding living wages (e.g. Aiken & Haldane, 2004; Austin, 2014: 162; Brenner, 2002: 6–7; Carr et al., 2015, 2016; Carrasco-Songer, 2011; Liebig et al., 2004: 27–29; Stabile, 2008: 94). Existing research so far, however, has primarily focused on establishing a general link between the CA and living wages, e.g. by using the CA as a justification for why a living wage should be paid (e.g. Aiken & Haldane, 2004; Austin, 2014: 162; Stabile, 2008: 94), but has so far not addressed how the CA can be used to evaluate existing living wage approaches. While Carr et al. (2015) and Carr et al. (2016), in their recent empirical studies, provide a list of capabilities that can be enabled through the payment of a living wage, their research focuses on a developed country (New Zealand), and neither establishes how the CA can be used to assess and improve the design of approaches for calculating and implementing living wages.

This chapter aims to address this research deficit by developing a conceptual framework for the analysis and assessment of different approaches to setting and implementing a living wage in international supply chains, such as the international garment industry, informed by the CA. Since the establishment of a living wage within international garment supply chains can be perceived as a challenge of transnational governance (Doh, 2005; Rasche, 2012; Scherer & Palazzo, 2008), and given that MNEs are called upon to voluntarily raise the wages paid to workers to compensate for the insufficient legal requirements of developing countries' governments, we draw on the literature on international accountability standards (IAS) for corporations in developing our framework. IAS are 'voluntary predefined rules, procedures and methods to systematically assess, measure, audit and/or communicate the social and environmental behaviour and/or performance of firms' (Gilbert et al., 2011: 23–4). IAS have emerged to fill governance voids that exist along international supply chains and to assist MNEs in fulfilling their increasingly political role in society (Korten, 2015; Rasche, 2009: 193–4). In the case of living wages, IAS as voluntary standards for MNEs can be argued to be of particular importance because governmental hard law, i.e. legal minimum wage regulation, is often insufficient to safeguard the well-being of workers in international supply chains. In this chapter, we argue that by integrating the CA with research on IAS, we can develop a conceptual framework that allows for mapping and evaluating currently existing living wage approaches and identifying their respective strengths and weaknesses for improving the living conditions of workers in international supply chains.

With this chapter, we contribute to three streams of literature. First, we contribute to the scholarly discourse on the role of labour and wages in the context of the CA (Bartelheimer et al., 2012; Bonvin, 2012; Leßmann, 2012, 2014) by linking the CA with the current debate on living wages. Second, we contribute to the literature on IAS (Behnam & MacLean, 2011; Gilbert & Rasche, 2008; Gilbert et al., 2011) by adapting it to the context of living wage approaches. Third, we complement the living wage debate (Anker & Anker, 2013; Carr et al., 2016; Parker et al., 2016) by developing a framework to compare and analyse living wage approaches for international supply chains, informed by the CA.

This chapter proceeds as follows: First, we give an overview of the history and development of the living wage debate and introduce living wage approaches from theory and practice. Second, we elaborate on the role of work and remuneration within the CA and deliver a justification for the payment of a living wage from a CA perspective.

Third, we address the underlying systemic reasons as to why wages in the international garment industry are so low. Fourth, we introduce IAS and a model to compare and analyse IAS, defining living wage approaches as a type of IAS. Fifth, we develop a framework based on the literature on IAS and the CA to compare and analyse living wage approaches. We then apply the newly developed framework to the approach for determining a living wage as proposed by the Asia Floor Wage Alliance. We conclude by outlining avenues for future research.

The Living Wage Debate

A living wage is generally defined as a wage that provides a basic income covering not only the subsistence of workers and their families, but also their participation in society and protection against an unforeseen future (Parker et al., 2016: 1). The living wage concept has a longstanding tradition in both theory and practice. It can be traced back to Plato and Aristotle in ancient Greece (Anker, 2011; Stabile, 2008) and to the Middle Ages when, influenced by moral and religious teachings, early attempts were made to define an acceptable wage rate that should provide for more than just biological existence (Ryan, 1906; Shelburne, 1999: 6). Adam Smith, who is generally considered as the founder of modern economics, in the Wealth of Nations (1776: 479) established the need for paying a living wage to workers by writing about necessaries beyond physical existence that should be provided to everyone:

By necessaries I understand, not only the commodities which are indispensably necessary for the support of life, but whatever the custom of the country renders it indecent for creditable people, even of the lowest order, to be without ... Under necessaries therefore, I comprehend, not only those things which nature, but those things which the established rules of decency have rendered necessary to the lowest rank of people.

In 1919, the Constitution of the International Labour Organization (ILO) first recognised the right for workers to a living wage (Anker, 2011: 1), highlighting 'the provision of an adequate living wage' as a condition for social justice (ILO, 2010: 5). In 1948, the living wage became part of the Universal Declaration of Human Rights (UN, 1948) and of the American Declaration on the Rights and Duties of

Man (Inter-American Commission on Human Rights, 1948). In 1961, the right for workers to receive a living wage was recognised by the European Social Charter (Council of Europe, 1961) and in 1966 by the United Nations (UN) International Covenant on Economic and Social Cultural Rights (UN, 1966). In 2014, the United Nations Development Programme (UNDP) first called for living wages to become a declared aim of business initiatives for the reduction of global poverty (UNDP, 2014).

So far, academic discussions of living wages have mainly focused on historical accounts of the living wage concept (Shelburne, 1999; Stabile, 2008) or on the moral justification of living wages (Cawthorne & Kitching, 2010; Krugman, 1997; Liebig et al., 2004). Over the past few years, living wages have also been discussed in the business ethics community in the context of the debate on the moral admissibility of 'sweatshops' (e.g. Arnold & Bowie, 2003, 2007; Coakley & Kates, 2013; Kates, 2015; Maitland, 1997; Miller, 2003; Preiss, 2014; Radin & Calkins, 2006; Snyder, 2009, 2010; Sollars & Englander, 2007; Zwolinski, 2007). Additional to the debate over whether and on what grounds the payment of a living wage is morally required, there is an ongoing controversy over what elements a living wage should cover and which methodology is best suited for calculating living wages (Anker, 2006, 2011; Brenner, 2002; King, 2016; Miller, 2013). In terms of living wage calculations, two approaches in particular have received considerable attention over the past years: the Anker methodology (Anker, 2006; Anker & Anker, 2013) and the approach provided by the Asia Floor Wage Alliance (Musiolek, 2011). Richard Anker, on the one hand, has calculated living wages for the certification organisations of the International Social and Environmental Accreditation and Labelling (ISEAL) Alliance and the ILO (Anker & Anker, 2013; Manquila Solidarity Network, 2014: 6). For ISEAL, Anker, together with his wife, developed an elaborate methodology to calculate the costs of living of a worker in three categories: food, housing and other essential needs (Anker & Anker, 2013) (see Figure 15.1).

The Asia Floor Wage Alliance, on the other hand, is an initiative of more than 60 trade unions and NGOs, initially founded in India (Musiolek, 2011: 9; Scheper & Menge, 2013: 51). Its goal is to establish a regional minimum living wage for the most important garment producing countries in Asia (Musiolek, 2011: 8). The AFW is calculated by means of a simple formula based on the food costs of a household,

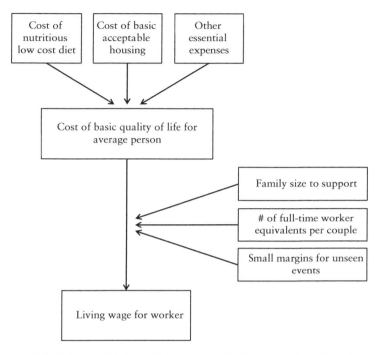

Figure 15.1 Anker and Anker's living wage calculation methodology for ISEAL
Source: Anker & Anker, 2013

assuming 50 per cent of the household income for non-food spending that is supposed to cover housing, clothing, health care, education, transport and savings. Converted into Purchasing Power Parity Dollars ($PPP), a fictional currency of the World Bank, the average living wage of all surveyed countries is calculated and converted back into local currencies, constituting the AFW (AFW, 2016; Scheper & Menge, 2013: 51–4). In addition, the Asia Floor Wage Alliance aims at fostering workers' education and, in the long term, wants to establish supply chain-wide wage negotiations (Manquila Solidarity Network, 2014: 3–4). Currently, the Asia Floor Wage Alliance has provided estimations for living wages for Bangladesh, China, India, Indonesia, Cambodia, Malaysia and Sri Lanka (Musiolek, 2011: 8). As the AFW represents a much-discussed living wage approach, which has specifically been designed for the garment industry, in this chapter, we will focus on this particular initiative.

One critique that has been raised against any living wage approach is that they seldomly address how, beyond calculation, living wages can be implemented in practice. Anker (2006: 336) states that steps to implementing higher wages are especially important in developing countries, which are the focus of this chapter, because in developing countries the gap between actually paid wages and living wages currently is generally larger than in developed countries. Against this background, in practice, a variety of further approaches have been brought forward in the past few years, focusing more on practical implementation of living wages. Examples include the Wage Ladder (FWF, 2011), a pragmatic step-by-step approach to living wages on a factory level brought forward by an alliance of MSIs that encourages implementers to simply collect all available living wage calculations, map them on a ladder and work their way upwards, and the ACT initiative (Action, Collaboration, Transformation) (ACT, 2015), which is an alliance of clothing brands and retailers (e.g. H&M, Inditex, Tesco and Primark), garment producers and the international trade union IndustriALL that aims to achieve raises in wage levels through the establishment of collective bargaining procedures in textile sourcing countries.

However, the debate over which living wage approach is best suited to address the issue at hand and what a living wage should cover is still ongoing. In our view, the question of how high a living wage should be cannot be answered independently of a concept of the good life. Instead of merely focusing on material resources necessary for subsistence, such as the cost of basic housing, the capability approach directs attention to the real freedoms people may enjoy at a given wage level. We therefore argue for the need to bring the CA into the current discussion on living wage approaches. Accordingly, we suggest that living wage approaches should be judged by the changes they provide for workers in terms of capabilities, choices, and freedoms. Rather than guaranteeing the provision of certain costs (see, for example, Anker or AFW), a living wage should be geared towards guaranteeing basic capabilities. While some authors have already pointed to the value of the CA for understanding and justifying living wages (e.g. Aiken & Haldane, 2004; Austin, 2014: 162; Carr et al., 2015, 2016; Stabile, 2008: 94), so far, no framework exists allowing for a detailed assessment of current living wages approaches analysing whether and how far capabilities are taken into account.

We therefore develop a conceptual framework involving the CA and including criteria of both calculation and practical implementation as parameters to evaluate living wage approaches. The framework helps to discover the strengths and weaknesses of existing living wage approaches concerning the provision of decent living conditions for workers in terms of capabilities. Before establishing the dimensions relevant for such a framework, we first address the components of the CA and the role of work and remuneration within the CA.

The Capability Approach, Work and Remuneration

The CA distinguishes between capabilities and achieved functionings. According to the CA, capabilities and achieved functionings represent the value-objects when it comes to evaluating the well-being of individuals (Sen, 1995). Achieved functionings cover all realised beings and doings of an individual, e.g. being educated or uneducated, ill or healthy, working or unemployed. Capabilities are potential functionings. They determine the realm of opportunities of an individual and are central to the CA as they allow for an evaluation of people's freedoms (Sen, 2000: 74–6). Capabilities do not have to be realised, but are of latent nature. This leads to a central concept in the CA – the concept of choice. Quality of life, in the CA, is determined not by achieved functionings, but by capabilities – individuals living in freedom can choose according to their own idea of a good life which of their capabilities they want to transform into achieved functionings. According to Sen, only individuals themselves can define which capabilities are necessary for them to lead a good life (2000: 74–81, 87). Within the category of capabilities, Sen also refers to the term of 'basic capabilities', which are still to be determined by the individuals themselves, but can be generalised to some extent as they refer to the ability of satisfaction of 'elementary and crucially important functions', such as hunger or thirst (Sen, 1995: 45). According to Sen (1985: 217), basic capabilities 'yield straightforward notions of rights' (see Nussbaum, 2000, 2011 for further extensions on the notion of basic capabilities).

Alongside capabilities and achieved functionings, the CA specifies a number of further concepts. Monetary and non-monetary resources represent means, which allow people to acquire goods or services that in turn represent instruments to achieve well-being or an expansion of freedom (Robeyns, 2005: 98–9). Yet, how far means can be transformed into capabilities is affected by conversion factors. Conversion factors can be either personal, e.g. health, gender, education, age, or social, e.g. norms, legal systems, traditions; or finally environmental, e.g. weather, infrastructure or climate. Moreover, the concept of agency plays and important role in the CA. Agency refers to 'what the person is free to do and achieve in pursuit of whatever goals or values he or she regards as important' (Sen, 1985: 203). Sen added the concept of agency to the CA in order to account for the fact that people do not only act in order to expand their own well-being, but also on behalf of others (Sen, 2000: 18–19; 1985: 206–7) or in accordance with their broader aims, allegiances or conception of the good (Sen, 1985: 203). The choice of which capabilities to transform into achieved functionings is not only determined by the individual's particular well-being freedom, but mostly by their more general agency freedom (Sen, 1985: 203) (for further extension on the notion of agency see the chapter by Nebel & Herrera-Nebel's elsewhere in this book).

Sen, in his conceptualisation of the CA, considers many more aspects such as the role of democracy (Sen, 2000: 146–59), rights (Sen, 2000: 148–9), or subjective information and views in achieving and securing capabilities (see the chapter by Comim elsewhere in this book on different informational spaces of the CA). For the purpose of this chapter, in the following, however, we focus on the roles of work and remuneration within the CA, as these are constitutive aspects to the debate on living wages.

The CA recognises work as a major component of a good life. In the multidimensional view of life of the CA, work is not only seen as a burden resulting in necessary income, but also as a part of people's identity and the reason for the acceptance and appreciation they receive from society (Sen, 2000: 94–6). With freedom as the highest goal within the CA, the ideal employment of an individual and its type and duration can be self-chosen in order to maximise the individual's capabilities (Bonvin, 2012: 17; Leßmann, 2014: 48).

Within the CA, work is mainly viewed as one of the many functionings an individual can achieve – the functioning to be 'working'. Whether or not an individual has the capability to work is dependent on conversion factors, such as facilities for child care, education, infrastructure for transport, conditions of the labour market, etc. (Bonvin,

2012: 14; Leßmann, 2014: 50). Despite being such an important component of a good life and having great influence on a person's identity, so far, there has been little research on work within the CA (Leßmann, 2014: 50). This is especially interesting as work plays a significant role within the model of the CA: the capability to work results in remuneration, which can buy new goods and services and can influence not only an individual's monetary resources, but also non-monetary resources, such as education or health, hence clearly exerting a substantial influence on an individual's overall capability set. The capability to work can also directly influence conversion factors. Personal conversion factors can be influenced by work through, for example, providing an individual with new knowledge and experience, resulting directly in development. Social conversion factors can be influenced, for example, through the appreciation an employed person experiences from his or her surroundings, or by a working woman encouraging other women to work as well. Environmental conversion factors can be influenced, for example, by the product of work, such as newly built streets, changing the infrastructure of a country (see Figure 15.2).

Sen is aware that capabilities can influence one another. He defines capabilities as freedoms that are linked to each other and can result in one another. While some freedoms are instrumental to gaining others, other freedoms are constitutive and directly contribute to development (Sen, 2000: 36–40). The capability to work, on the one hand, is an instrumental freedom, resulting in remuneration, new resources, new goods and services and thus in new capabilities. On the other hand, work is a constitutive freedom, providing the worker not only with money, but also with a meaningful job, a purpose, appreciation, knowledge and experience, positively influencing conversion factors and directly leading to development. Sen himself distinguishes between three aspects of work: the income aspect (work delivers an income to a working individual), the production aspect (work results in products) and the aspect of appreciation (work provides an individual with the appreciation of doing something meaningful) (Sen, 1975: 5). This interplay of work as an instrumental and a constitutive freedom, resulting in remuneration and development, leads to a cycle influencing an individual's set of capabilities. Figure 15.2 illustrates this cycle between work, remuneration and capabilities.

Applied to the idea of a living wage for international supply chains, we cannot assume that the work itself, e.g. in garment factories,

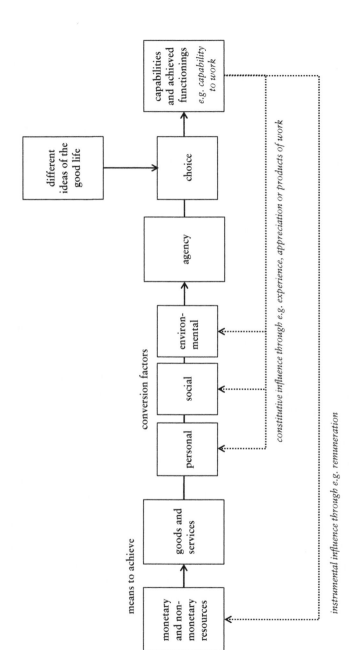

Figure 15.2 The role of work and remuneration in the model of the capability approach
Source: Authors, modified from Robeyns, 2003, 2005

significantly expands capabilities. Most of the time the job of a garment worker is not freely chosen, but merely the best option amongst many poor options (Miller, 2003: 97), and the work is little qualified and repetitive, the capability to work as a constitutive freedom might not play such an important role in our case. The instrumental freedom to work resulting in remuneration, however, helps explain why the payment of a living wage is important from the perspective of the CA. The interrelation of the capability to work and the remuneration entailed by it, which influences available resources, goods, and services, results in a cycle which determines an individual's overall capability set. Whether this is a positive capability expanding cycle, or a negative capability decreasing cycle, is determined by the payment of a living wage. Tisdell and Sen (2004: 147), for example, have shown that if income levels drop below a critical threshold, this can lead to an erosion of individuals' capabilities. The living wage can thus be seen as the threshold from which remuneration resulting from work expands the capability set instead of decreasing it (Carr et al., 2016) – i.e. from which the wage gives an individual more freedom than work takes from it.

A living wage approach, instead of considering that work results in sufficient monetary resources for an employee's subsistence, needs to consider how the wage affects workers' capabilities, by addressing in how far it influences non-monetary resources, available goods and services and conversion factors. A living wage should guarantee workers basic capabilities, which can be determined contextually. The CA views monetary measurements of poverty as insufficient and poverty as entailing more than just lack of money (Sen, 2000: 87–92). When comparing living wage approaches, the value-object should hence be capabilities and not resources. In order to be a measure against poverty, a living wage approach should therefore provide both a meaningful calculation of how high a living wage has to be under consideration of the workers' basic capabilities, as well as means of implementation helping workers to develop these capabilities.

At first sight, the concept of a living wage and the CA might seem contradictory: while the CA is a pluralistic concept, paying close attention to the individual's unique views and needs, the concept of a living wage is an aggregative one. Despite the subjectivity of the question of the good life, it will be unfeasible to calculate a living wage on an individual level, such that local aggregation will always be necessary in order to calculate and implement a living wage. Sen recognises the possibility for achieving (at least partial) social consensus on capabilities (2000: 78–9, 110, 158, 249, 253–4). While he is against any form of mechanical judgment of an individual's well-being, such as the gross domestic product (GDP), in *Collective Choice and Social Welfare* (1970: 99), Sen establishes that welfare levels of individuals are partially comparable such that it can be assumed that a more equal distribution of income will lead to a higher collective welfare. He later, however, argues that a process of public reasoning and discussion is necessary for selecting relevant capabilities that are to be promoted on a societal basis (Sen, 2011: 241–3). For living wage approaches, it is important to recognise both the possibility of partial comparability of capabilities and the emphasis Sen puts on public reasoning. In the context of a living wage, the aggregation of capabilities should hence be the outcome of a collective and public discussion and reasoning process of workers, who through this process get a chance to voice their individual preferences regarding which capabilities they deem relevant. As outlined above, from a CA perspective, the payment of a living wage is a necessary condition for individuals to develop their capabilities. In the next section, using the example of the international garment industry, we discuss why raising wages in international supply chains to a living wage level currently is so difficult.

Wages in the International Garment Industry

The reasons why wages in the international garment production in many developing countries are too low to safeguard the well-being of workers and their families are manifold and deeply rooted within the structure of the industry, which is characterised by the interdependency of three different levels (ETI, 2015: 9, 2016: 31). These levels relate to the garment factories, the local labour markets, and the transnational level of organisation of production of garments in international supply chains.

Some of the reasons for the low levels of wages lie within the characteristics of the *garment factories* themselves. The international garment industry is a pioneer industry in many developing countries. It takes neither specialised knowledge nor advanced technology or infrastructure to set up a garment factory, which leads to much of today's garment production being undertaken in the poorest of developing countries, and due to low barriers to entry and exit also enables the industry to move to new countries very quickly and flexibly once wage levels start rising (Labowitz & Baumann-Pauly, 2014: 6–13). Furthermore, in comparison to other industries, garment factories remain at a low level of efficiency, which reduces the factories' margins, leaving little surplus to be passed on to the workers (Musiolek, 2011: 6). Given this lack of efficiency, wages are more flexible than other production costs, so that under the pressure of price competition they are the first to fall despite increasing costs of living (ETI, 2015). In addition, payment systems within factories are non-transparent and often discriminating, neither fostering workers' personal development nor their productivity (ETI, 2015: 38).

On a *labour market* level, low wages in garment production are mainly driven by the weak bargaining position of garment workers. Garment workers are mostly young and uneducated women, who are often also migrants and have little knowledge of their own rights. The wage question is thus also closely related to the issue of gender discrimination. Moreover, garment workers are rarely unionised (Musiolek, 2011: 6–7). Joining a union often means jeopardising one's job (Bhattacharjee et al., 2009: 76). Any workers who still take the risk to join, however, do not significantly improve their bargaining power. Union strikes and protests in countries like Cambodia, Myanmar or Bangladesh are often oppressed by governments (Manquila Solidarity Network, 2014: 2); in China and Vietnam unions are completely government owned and controlled (Bhattacharjee et al., 2009: 76), and most unions in garment producing countries are not internationally organised, which makes it difficult for them to negotiate on equal terms with the MNEs at the other end of the supply chain (Bhattacharjee et al., 2009: 72). Moreover, under the pressure of competition between garment-producing countries and in order to facilitate growth, legal minimum wages are often set far below a living wage level by garment producing countries' governments (Oxfam, 2014: 5). This practice of continuously underbidding one another in terms of wages and labour standards is termed the 'race to the bottom' (Lee, 1997: 181–3). In addition, production is often unofficially subcontracted to workshops that fly under the radar of the control of MNEs or governmental agencies (ETI, 2015: 32; Musiolek, 2011: 7).

On the level of *international garment supply chains*, various factors result in low wages. The business models of Western brands are built around low-cost production, leading to an instant competitive disadvantage for the brand that starts increasing wages in their supply chain (Oxfam, 2014: 6). Even if MNEs want to make an effort to achieve increased wages in the garment production, this is quite difficult for them due to the characteristics of the supply chain. International garment supply chains are complex, non-transparent and influenced by various different actors. They connect factories and suppliers with importers and import agencies, with retailers and brands, and with consumers. This minimises the share of the purchasing price that ends up in a factory worker's pocket and makes it difficult to transfer money from one end of the supply chain to another. Even though global garment supply chains are characterised as mostly buyer-driven, their complexity reduces the buyer's influence on factories as many buyers do not even know where exactly their products are manufactured (Bhattacharjee et al., 2009: 75; Labowitz & Baumann-Pauly, 2014: 6; Musiolek, 2011: 10). This lacking influence of buyers is aggravated by two further issues: the purchasing practice of many Western brands and retailers is to buy low order volumes on short notice with many different suppliers in order to minimise the risk of supply shortfalls and meet the demand for 'fast fashion'. This practice also minimises the buyer's influence on a factory's management and wage policies (FWF, 2014: 5). Another issue is the practice of subcontracting. Contracted factories often pass on orders to other factories to ensure delivery beyond their own capacity. Subcontracting often happens without notifying buyers and also to unregistered production facilities (Labowitz & Baumann-Pauly, 2014: 6). The combination of these factors has led to a situation where unduly low wages have become rooted in the structure of the industry (summarised in Figure 15.3).

Even if MNEs, decide to act against low wages, their efforts are often fruitless, as the complexity of supply chains and the practice of subcontracting make it difficult for them to raise production wages on their own. In order to be able to address the systemic dimension of too low wages in the international garment industry, a uniform and joint approach – i.e. a standard – is needed including all relevant stakeholders, i.e. brands, retailers, agencies, importers, suppliers, factories, governments of buying and supplying countries, trade unions, consumers and NGOs. A uniform approach could foster transparency in the supply chain and fairness of profit allocation. It would enable different brands and retailers to collaborate and thus combine their influence

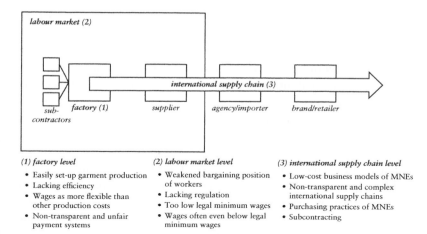

Figure 15.3 The systemic dimension of too low wages in the international garment industry – challenges on three levels

on factory management. Moreover, it would remove wages from the competition around the lowest production costs and enable MNEs to raise wages in their supply chain without competitive disadvantage. Furthermore, a uniform approach to living wages that ensures consistency of application within and between countries might also be able to put an end to the 'race to the bottom' and the threat of MNEs moving from one country to another with lower wage levels.

The challenges to guarantee a living wage are manifold and, among other reasons, induced by unduly low legal minimum wages and the suppression of unions – of which the sources are to be found with governments in either case. Against this background, MNEs as powerful actors in international supply chains must raise wages independently of legislation on the basis of voluntary standards, so-called international accountability standards (IAS).

International Accountability Standards

NGOs and MSIs have made various propositions on how to take action concerning the wage situation of workers in international supply chains and have called on MNEs to voluntarily commit to raising wages. This led to a proliferation of different living wage approaches that are currently being discussed with regard to their suitability as a standard for the international garment industry. Over the past few years, these approaches or standards of voluntary commitment in research have been summarised under the name of 'international accountability standards', which we shall briefly introduce.

IAS include all 'voluntary predefined rules, procedures and methods to systematically assess, measure, audit and/or communicate the social and environmental behaviour and/or performance of firms' (Gilbert et al., 2011: 23–4). Examples of well-known IAS are the certification standard Social Accountability 8000 (SA 8000), the principle-based standard of the UN Global Compact, or the reporting standard of the Global Reporting Initiative (GRI). Despite large differences between these standards with regards to their contents, they all fall under the term of IAS as they have a common goal: to support corporations in dealing with the needs and requirements of their stakeholders and justifying their actions and providing organisational accountability (McIntosh, 2003; Paine et al., 2005; Rasche, 2009: 192). According to Rasche and Esser (2006: 252), organisational accountability is 'the readiness or preparedness of an organisation to give an explanation and a justification to relevant stakeholders for its judgments, intentions, acts, and omissions'. Accountability means being able to deliver transparency to stakeholders and bear the consequences for mistakes (Crane & Matten, 2007; Gilbert et al., 2011: 23–4). Against the background of missing international regulation, voluntary accountability of MNEs has become more and more important (Gilbert et al., 2011: 23; Korten, 2015; Rasche, 2009: 193–4).

Over the past few decades, the number of voluntary standards for corporations has grown significantly, leading to a vast landscape of overlapping standards (Leipziger, 2010; Rasche, 2009: 193). In order to classify IAS and make them comparable, Rasche (2009) developed a conceptual framework. He suggests that accountability standards can be compared and analysed based on 'the content of their underlying norms, the implementation processes they suggest, and their context of application' (Rasche, 2009: 192). Living wage approaches, such as the Anker methodology, the AFW, the Wage Ladder or ACT, can be understood as particular forms of IAS. They are voluntary and predefined and come with rules, procedures and methods for organisations, especially MNEs, to systematically assess, measure, audit and communicate their performance with regard to the payment of decent wages in their supply chain. Moreover, living wage approaches deliver voluntary and private solutions, in a context where governmental hard law, i.e. legal minimum wages, is often insufficient to safeguard the well-being of workers. We therefore draw on the model developed by Rasche (2009).

Based on the threefold distinction between *content, process* and *context*, Rasche (2009) suggests that specific characteristics and strengths and weaknesses of IAS can be identified. For each of these three dimensions, Rasche (2009: 195–6) suggests guiding questions and example issues to focus on. The guiding question of the first pillar (*content*) of Rasche's model is 'What content-related rules does the standard propose?' Rasche suggests evaluating standards with respect to their specificity and legitimacy. Regarding specificity, rules should be formulated in a precise and specific way in order to leave as little room for interpretation as possible and enable all kinds of parties to implement a standard (Rasche, 2009: 196). With a view to legitimacy, Rasche states that the legitimacy of a standard's rules is strongly related to the legitimacy of the organisation behind a standard (Kostova & Zaheer, 1999; Rasche, 2009: 197–8). Organisational legitimacy mainly results from the inclusive dialogue with all relevant parties. Regarding IAS, this means that a standard ideally is developed in an inclusive multistakeholder dialogue, in which affected parties can voice their interests (Rasche, 2009: 197–8). Multistakeholder initiatives (MSIs), which bring companies, organisations of civil society, and sometimes other parties, such as governments, academics or unions into dialogue (Utting, 2002), in this context represent promising mechanism of private regulation.

The second pillar (*process*) comes with the guiding question 'What implementation processes does the standard propose?' It addresses the implementability and accountability of IAS. In order to ensure that its rules are implementable, a standard must provide specific and easy-to-understand implementation processes that match the available resources of implementers (Rasche, 2009: 197–8). In terms of accountability, Rasche states that a standard ideally should establish complaint mechanisms for issues of non-compliance, evaluation mechanisms for monitoring results, transparency-enhancing mechanisms towards stakeholders, or participation mechanisms to include the most important stakeholders (Blagescu & Lloyd, 2006; Rasche, 2009: 198–9).

The guiding question of the third pillar (*context*) is 'In which context can the standard be applied?' Rasche (2009: 199) suggests addressing the scope an IAS claims to be valid for, i.e. local vs international, and in which countries the standard is actually used, as many IAS claim to apply internationally, as well as taking into consideration the industry focus of a standard, i.e. whether it is specific to a particular industry or can be applied across multiple industries. Figure 15.4 summarizes Rasche's model.

With its focus on content, process and context, Rasche's framework allows for a broad analysis and comparison of IAS. Yet, in order to identify which living wage approach should be favoured over another, we argue that his framework needs to be further specified in terms of the CA because, as outlined above, the question of what wage is required to allow for a decent living cannot be answered independently of a conception of a good life. Accordingly, in the next section, we propose to extend Rasche's framework with the CA such that it accounts for the fact that living wage approaches should be geared to guaranteeing basic capabilities to workers.

Living Wage Approaches and Capabilities: Towards a Conceptual Framework

In this section, we outline how the three dimensions of *content, process* and *context* of Rasche's framework can be detailed to account for capabilities in the context of living wages in international supply chains.

		Content	Process	Context
Guiding Question		What content-related rules does the standard propose?	What implementation processes does the standard propose?	In which context can the standard be applied?
Exemplary Issues to Compare and Analyze Standards		*Specificity of Norms* Are the rules proposed by the standard specific enough to foster implementation?	*Implementability* Are the required implementation processes specifically laid out?	*Geographic Scope* In which countries/regions is the standard primarily used?
		Legitimacy of Norms Was the standard developed in a multi-stakeholder way?	*Accountability* Does the standard require the creation of accountability processes?	*Industry Focus* In which industry (or industries) can the standard be used?

Figure 15.4 A model to compare and analyse accountability standards
Source: Rasche, 2009

The first pillar (content) deals with the rules a standard sets for implementers. Here, Rasche sets a focus on the specificity and legitimacy of rules (Rasche, 2009: 196–7). Regarding specificity, in terms of living wage approaches, this mainly concerns the calculation of a living wage – how high is the wage that implementers have to pay their workers? According to what formula should it be calculated? As Anker (2011: 12) states, in order to raise wages to a living wage level, it is necessary to advance the debate on how high exactly a living wage should be and reach an agreement on a specific wage. In terms of living wage approaches as voluntary standards for MNEs, this is especially crucial in order to give implementers a target, encourage progress towards this target and make progress measurable.

Apart from being specific, there are further requirements to the calculation formula of a living wage that can be drawn from the CA. When distinguishing between means and capabilities it becomes clear that while means, such as resources and available goods and services, are only instrumental to well-being and freedom, capabilities are the value object informing about an individual's well-being. For living wage approaches, this means that surveys on household spending prior to a living wage calculation should focus on capabilities rather than means. It needs to be established whether or not an approach proposes a wage that guarantees basic capabilities for workers and their families. As we saw in Figure 15.1, many living wage approaches such as Anker or the AFW so far mainly calculate a living wage based on prior and externally set levels of resources, instead of taking basic capabilities into account. On top of that, surveys of workers regarding household spending need to focus not only on how high their spending on certain functionings are, but also on what basic capabilities they view as necessary part of a good life. Thus, surveys on household spending prior to the living wage calculation should address which capabilities workers consider as crucial for a good life. Subsequently, costs for these capabilities can be surveyed. A living wage is a wage that allows workers to lead the life that they have reasons to consider worth living and that secures basic capabilities.

In order for workers to find agreement on these basic capabilities, from a CA perspective, public reasoning processes are necessary. The main reason for the lacking agreement on a calculation formula for a living wage is the subjectivity of the question of a persons' essential needs (Anker, 2011: 11–12). While moral pluralism is what makes calculating a living wage so complicated, this pluralism is particularly valued by the CA. According to Sen, only individuals can decide what they need in order to lead a good life (Sen, 2000). However, as stated earlier, Sen argues that individual welfare is partially comparable, such that it can be assumed that a more equal distribution of welfare will lead to a higher collective welfare (Sen, 1970: 99). Regarding the calculation of a living wage, this implies that it should be based on an aggregation of preferences, which is the outcome of a public reasoning process that engages workers, taking into account as many individual choices as possible. After asking workers 'Which basic capabilities do you view as a crucial part of a good life?' workers should reason with one another finding agreement on the capabilities to be considered in their living wage calculation.

With a view to the legitimacy of rules, Rasche states that they should be developed in a multistakeholder process (Rasche, 2009: 197–8). As wage issues are rooted systemically at various levels within the garment industry and other industries, and are influenced by a variety of different participants, it is important that a living wage approach is uniformly adopted and standardised, involving all relevant stakeholders. In order to induce all stakeholders to participate in a standard, rules of this standard must be jointly developed. Sen (2011: 22–3, 215–17) equally highlights the significance of processes in realising capabilities. Referring to a 'comprehensive outcome', he notes that not only does the actual outcome matter but also the process through which it emerges. From a CA perspective, it is especially important that workers participate in the development of a standard. The participation of either workers themselves or of union delegates representing them is both means and end itself from a CA perspective. It represents a means, as workers' acceptance of a standard is crucial and as they have knowledge of their own wage situation that cannot be replaced; and it is an end, as having a voice in matters concerning one's life can be perceived as an important capability in itself.

The second pillar (process) deals with the implementation processes and accountability processes that a standard suggests. Regarding the implementation processes of a standard, Rasche suggests that these should be specifically laid out (Rasche, 2009: 197–8). In terms of living wage approaches, it is important that implementation processes go beyond the calculation of a living wage and that they contribute to furthering the capabilities of workers (Anker, 2011: 336; Ryan, 1906: 18).

According to Sen (2000: 87–92), poverty entails more than just lack of money. In order to be a measure against poverty, a living wage approach has to provide not only monetary figure, but also means of implementating to help workers in their development of capabilities and change their conversion factors in order for them to be truly lifted out of poverty. For instance, each living wage approach should foster education, efficiency and productivity of workers, and also their unionisation and bargaining power. In order to liberate the labour markets in developing countries, so that basic economic principles can take effect and wages reach equilibrium, it is important for living wage approaches to empower workers and to support collective bargaining. Despite the individualistic grounding of the CA, Sen recognises the capabilities of group formation (Drèze & Sen, 2002: 29) and collective political will formation (2000, 2011) as important freedoms. Sen views social arrangements as valuable, if they expand individual liberty (2000: 31). In the context of living wages, the capabilities of group forming and collective political will formation and the social arrangement of unions are particularly important for workers to negotiate on equal terms with the other powerful actors involved in the system and thus to expand their freedom. As Bonvin (2012: 17) notes, 'process freedom in the capability perspective implies an adequate combination between collective rationality (organised along processes of democratic deliberation and bargaining) and individual rationalities'.

In terms of accountability processes, Rasche (2009: 198–9) suggests that a standard should entail at least one of the following: complaint mechanisms, evaluation mechanisms, transparency-enhancing mechanisms, or participation mechanisms. While all of these are important for the context of living wage approaches, transparency-enhancing mechanisms and participation mechanisms especially play a role in solving the lack of transparency of international garment supply chains that are influenced by various different actors. Sen (2000: 10, 40) also highlights 'transparency guarantees' as important instrumental freedoms. Such guarantees 'have a clear instrumental role in preventing corruption, financial irresponsibility and underhand dealings' (Sen, 2000: 40). Thus, the extent to which a particular approach fosters transparency and accountability has important implications for the advancement of the capabilities of a worker.

The third pillar of the framework (context) deals with the geographic scope and industry focus of an approach (Rasche, 2009: 199).

In terms of living wages, it is important to highlight the country/region- and industry-specific challenges to raising wages. As described above, in the international garment industry, there are various industry-specific challenges that add up to the systemic dimension of low wages in the industry, which are probably different in other industries. A living wage approach should consider these industry-specific factors. The same is valid for country- and region-specific challenges leading to poverty wages within a certain area. Societal and legal differences between countries and varying worker preferences will lead not only to different calculations of living wages, but also to different implementation measures being necessary. While many IAS claim to be valid internationally (Rasche, 2009: 199), this is not necessarily true for living wage approaches. Figure 15.5 summarises the framework to compare and analyse living wage approaches.

Applying this extended framework to living wage approaches thus allows for identifying strengths and weaknesses of different approaches in promoting freedoms and functions that workers have reasons to value. In order to illustrate the practical relevance of the developed

	Content	**Process**	**Context**
Guiding Question	What content-related rules does the approach propose?	What implementation processes does the approach propose?	In which context approach be can the applied?
Exemplary Issues to Compare and Analyse Living Wage Approaches	*Specificity of Rules and Calculation based on Capabilities* Are the rules proposed by the approach specific enough to foster implementation? Does the approach include a specific calculation formula or wage? Does the proposed wage guarantee basic capabilities for workers? Was capability aggregation outcome of public reasoning? *Legitimacy of Rules* Was the approach developed in a multi-stakeholder way? Were workers included in the development of the approach?	*Implementability* Are the required implementation processes specifically laid out? Do the implementation processes further workers' capabilities? *Accountability* Does the approach require the creation of accountability processes, e.g. complaint mechanisms, evaluation mechanisms, transparency enhancing mechanisms, participation mechanisms?	*Geographic Scope* Are region/country specific characteristics considered in the approach? *Industry Focus* Are industry specific characteristics considered in the approach?

Figure 15.5 A framework to compare and analyse living wage approaches
Source: Authors, modified from Rasche (2009)

framework, in the following section, we use the framework to assess the earlier introduced living wage approach, the Asia Floor Wage.

Example: The Case of the Asia Floor Wage

When applying our proposed framework to the AFW, strength and weaknesses of this particular living wage approach in terms of the CA become apparent. Regarding the first pillar (content), the AFW proposes rules that are specific and straightforward. Implementers are asked to pay a given wage – the calculated AFW – to workers in their supply chains (Musiolek, 2011). The AFW provides not only a formula, but also the calculated wage as a clear target for MNEs. While the calculation of the AFW is easy to understand and transparent, it is based on pre-defined food basket research and it remains unclear whether or not the proposed wage guarantees basic capabilities of workers. For example, it does not include surveys asking workers for basic capabilities that they perceive as necessary to lead a good life. Suggesting that workers spend their non-food budget on housing, clothing, health care, education, transport and savings (AFW, 2016), the AFW rather focuses its calculation on means than on capabilities. There are no public reasoning processes behind the calculation of the AFW. Moreover, the Asia Floor Wage Alliance as the organisation behind the AFW is not a complete MSI, as it does not include companies. Also, it leaves out important parties such as governments. Nonetheless, the strength of the AFW is that it is an approach created in a developing country by concerned parties. Workers played an important role in the development of the AFW (Musiolek, 2011: 9; Scheper & Menge, 2013: 51), which is positive from a CA perspective.

Regarding the second pillar of the framework (process) it becomes clear where the AFW has the most potential for improvement. While the Asia Floor Wage Alliance also runs programmes for workers' education and aims at supply chain-wide negotiations (Manquila Solidarity Network, 2014: 3–4), it does not specify how implementers are supposed to reach the target of the AFW. Therefore, implementation processes do not really go beyond calculation, leaving implementing MNEs alone with the question of how to raise wages at the other end of the supply chain and how to enable workers in terms of their capabilities in order to really lift them out of poverty. Also, the AFW does not include any accountability processes.

The third pillar (context) concerns the geographical scope and the industry focus of an approach. The AFW focuses on Asia; calculations exist for seven garment-producing Asian countries. In an adapted version, it is also applicable to garment producing countries in Eastern Europe (Manquila Solidarity Network, 2014: 5). By calculating an average from various local living wage estimates, the AFW succeeds in making countries' living wages comparable. However, it does not take into account that capabilities and conversion factors, and therefore living wages, vary between countries, regions and individuals. From a CA perspective, locally adapted living wage formulas are to be favoured over averages as capabilities are essentially context-dependent. Moreover, the formula the AFW applies, suggesting 50 per cent of the household income to be spent on nutrition, is often criticised as not generalisable (see e.g. Anker, 2011: 38; Scheper & Menge, 2013: 51–4). In terms of its industry focus, the AFW was especially developed for the garment sector and so far has only been used within this industry. Aiming at excluding wages from the competition around the lowest production costs by making country wages comparable, the AFW already meets some of the garment industry specific characteristics described above. In order to really address the systemic dimension of low wages in the international garment industry, however, a much larger focus on implementation processes for wage increases would have to exist, addressing the roles of all parties involved.

The application of the developed framework thus highlights various areas for improvement for the AFW from a CA perspective. The calculation of the AFW instead of focusing on means for living should take into account capabilities that workers view as a crucial part of a good life. Moreover, the approach should focus more closely on implementation and accountability processes in order to give guidance to implementing MNEs, enable workers' capabilities and meet the systemic dimension of low wages in the garment industry.

Conclusion

Wages in the international garment industry currently are often too low to safeguard the well-being of workers and their families. Against this background, in the recent past, a number of suggestions for the calculation of a living wage have been made by various groups, leading to an ongoing debate on what basic needs a living wage should cover. In this chapter, we have argued that the question of how to set a living wage is strongly related to the question of a good life. In order to take into account this normative component, we drew on Sen's CA. Moreover, we have proposed that living wage approaches can be understood as a particular form of international accountability standards as they target MNEs to voluntarily raise wages according to a predefined standard. In order to assess strengths and weaknesses of currently existing living wage approaches, we therefore integrated research on IAS with the CA in a conceptual framework. Our framework informs the debate on living wages in four ways. First, living wage calculations should focus on capabilities rather than on means and living wages should guarantee basic capabilities to workers. Second, the capabilities relevant to a calculation for a living wage should take contextual factors into account and ideally result from a transparent process of public reasoning. Third, beyond calculations, living wage approaches should include capability enhancing implementation processes. Finally, locally adapted living wages should be favoured over international approaches, in order to account for context specific capabilities and conversion factors.

It is however important to note that the living wage is not an indicator to measure an individual's well-being, but an instrument to further well-being and a condition for development. The living wage is not the target wage at which ultimate welfare of an individual is reached; it rather represents a threshold, i.e. a wage floor, from which development should start. Beyond receiving the payment of a living wage, many more aspects will play a role for an individual's well-being as it is conceptualised by the CA.

The application of the developed framework to the AFW has uncovered a number of shortcomings of this particular approach from a CA perspective. Among other things, the AFW can be criticised for not focusing its calculation on capabilities but on means, and for omitting implementation processes, which would enable workers to increase their capabilities in order to really lift them out of poverty.

Further research is needed to address how different actors can foster the implementation of living wages in international supply chains (Parker et al., 2016: 5). Moreover, further research will be needed to address how the capabilities relevant for a living wage calculation can be identified. Sophisticated survey methods will be necessary in order to move living wage calculation beyond a level of costs towards the assessment of capability levels. Findings by Anand et al. (2005) and Anand et al. (2009) on the measurement of capabilities might be of some assistance. Additionally, empirical studies will be necessary in order to connect capabilities to different wage levels. Future empirical research could cover topics such as how much freedom workers enjoy at certain wage levels.

References

ACT. (2015) Action collaboration transformation: Factsheet. Available at: www.hiil.org/data/sitemanagement/media/ACT%20Factsheet.pdf, accessed 13 May 2016.

AFW. (2016) Five steps. Available at: http://asia.floorwage.org/5-steps, 19 Feb 2016.

Aiken, W. and Haldane, J. (2004) *Philosophy and Its Public Role: Essays in Ethics, Politics, Society and Culture*. Exeter: Imprint Academic.

Anand, P., Hunter, G. and Smith, R. (2005) Capabilities and wellbeing: Evidence based on the Sen-Nussbaum approach to welfare. *Social Indicators Research*, 74(1): 9–55.

Anand, P., Santos, C. and Smith, R. (2009) The measurement of capabilities. In K. Basu and R. Kanbur (Eds.), *Arguments for A Better World. Vol. 1: Ethics, Welfare and Measurement*. Oxford: Oxford University Press, 283–310.

Anker, R. (2006) Living wages around the world: A new methodology and internationally comparable estimates. *International Labour Review*, 145(4): 309–38.

  (2011) Estimating a living wage: A methodological review. Available at: http://is.muni.cz/repo/1131138/anker_2011_ilo.pdf, 25 Jul 2015.

Anker, R. and Anker, M. (2013) A shared approach to estimating living wages: Short description of the agreed methodology. Available at: www. isealalliance.org/sites/default/files/Descripton%20of%20Living%20 Wage%20Methodology%2020131124.pdf, 21 Feb 2016.

Arnold, D. G. and Bowie, N. E. (2003) Sweatshops and the respect for persons. *Business Ethics Quarterly*, 13(2): 221–42.

  (2007) Respect for workers in global supply chains: Advancing the debate over sweatshops. *Business Ethics Quarterly*, 17(1): 135–45.

Austin, M. J. (2014) *Social Justice and Social Work: Rediscovering a Core Value of the Profession*. Thousand Oaks, CA: Sage Publications.

Bartelheimer, P., Leßmann, O. and Matiaske, W. (2012) Editorial: The capability approach: A new perspective for labor market and welfare policies? *Management Revue*, 23(2): 91–7.

Behnam, M. and MacLean, T. L. (2011) Where is the accountability in International Accountability Standards? *Business Ethics Quarterly*, 21(1): 45–72.

Bhattacharjee, A., Gupta, S. and Luce, S. (2009) Raising the floor: The movement for a living wage in Asia. *New Labor Forum*, 18(3): 72–81.

Blagescu, M. and Lloyd, R. (2006) Global accountability report: Holding power to account. Available at: www.worldvision.or.kr/business/pdf-down/2006_GAR.pdf, 29 Jan 2016.

Bonvin, J.-M. (2012) Individual working lives and collective action. An introduction to capability for work and capability for voice. *Transfer: European Review of Labour and Research*, 18(1): 9–18.

Brenner, M. (2002) Defining and measuring a global living wage: Theoretical and conceptual issues. Available at: www.peri.umass.edu/fileadmin/pdf/gls_conf/glw_brenner.pdf, 10 Jul 2015.

Carr, S. C., Parker, J., Arrowsmith, J. and Watters, P. A. (2015) The living wage: Theoretical integration and an applied research agenda. *International Labour Review* 155(1): 1–24.

Carr, S. C., Parker, J., Arrowsmith, J., Watters, P. and Jones, H. (2016) Can a 'living wage' springboard human capability? An exploratory study from New Zealand. *Labour & Industry*, 26(1): 24–39.

Carrasco-Songer, M. (2011) Effects of the living wage on low-wage workers' wellbeing: An examination of Asheville, NC. Available at: http://inside.warren-wilson.edu/~socanth/Directed_Research_2011/MariaCarrasco-Songer.doc, 27 Jul 2015.

Cawthorne, P. and Kitching, G. (2010) Moral dilemmas and factual claims: Some comments on Paul Krugman's defense of cheap labor. *Review of Social Economy*, 59(4): 455–66.

CCC. (2013) Shop 'til they drop: Fainting and malnutrition in garment workers in Cambodia. Available at: www.cleanclothes.org/resources/national-cccs/shop-til-they-drop/view, 13 May 2016.

(2014) Im Stich gelassen. Available at: http://lohnzumleben.de/im_stich_gelassen/, 13 May 2016.

Coakley, M. and Kates, M. (2013) The ethical and economic case for sweatshop regulation. *Journal of Business Ethics*, 117(3): 553–8.

Council of Europe. (1961) European social charter. Available at: http://polis.osce.org/library/f/2667/466/CoE-ITA-RPT-2667-EN-466.pdf, 18 May 2016.

Crane, A. and Matten, D. (2007) *Business Ethics: Managing Corporate Citizenship and Sustainability in the Age of Globalization*, 2nd edn. Oxford: Oxford University Press.

Doh, J. P. (2005) Offshore outsourcing: Implications for international business and strategic management theory and practice. *Journal of Management Studies*, 42(3): 695–704.

Drèze, J. and Sen, A. K. (2002) *India: Development and Participation*, 2nd edn. Oxford: Oxford University Press.

ETI. (2015) Living wages in global supply chains: A new agenda for business. Available at: www.ethicaltrade.org/resources/living-wages-in-global-supply-chains, 2015, 16 Jan 2015.

—— (2016) Base code guidance: Living wages. Available at: http://s3-eu-west-1.amazonaws.com/www.ethicaltrade.org.files/shared_resources/eti_living_wage_guidance.pdf?0bxlCUtP7Kr661Kz78pgvsH4Qk-p7r6rJ, 29 May 2016.

FWF. (2011) Wage ladder background study. Available at: www.fairwear.org/ul/cms/fck-uploaded/documents/fwfpublications_reports/wageladderbackgroundstudy.pdf, 30 Jul 2015.

—— (2014) Living wage engineering: A study by Fair Wear Foundation – With initial observations about the links between outdoor industry brand practices, wages, pricing, and the cost to consumers. Available at: www.fairwear.org/ul/cms/fck-uploaded/documents/fwfpublications_reports/LivingWageEngineering20141.pdf, 2014, 17 Jan 2016.

Gilbert, D. U. and Rasche, A. (2008) Opportunities and problems of standardized ethics initiatives: A stakeholder theory perspective. *Journal of Business Ethics*, 82(3): 755–73.

Gilbert, D. U., Rasche, A. and Waddock, S. (2011). Accountability in a global economy: The emergence of international accountability standards. *Business Ethics Quarterly*, 21(1): 23–44.

ILO. (2010) Constitution of the International Labour Organisation. Available at: www.ilo.org/public/english/bureau/leg/download/constitution.pdf, 24 Jul 2015.

ILRF. (2016) Living wage. Available at: www.laborrights.org/issues/living-wage, 13 May 2016.

Inter-American Commission on Human Rights. (1948) American Declaration of the Rights and Duties of Men. Available at: www.cidh.oas.org/Basicos/English/Basic2.American%20Declaration.htm, 18 May 2016.

Kates, M. (2015) The ethics of sweatshops and the limits of choice. *Business Ethics Quarterly*, 25(2): 191–212.

King, P. (2016) Setting the New Zealand living wage: Complexities and practicalities. *Labour & Industry*, 26(1): 8–23.

Korten, D. C. (2015) *When Corporations Rule the World*, 3rd edn. Oakland, CA: Berrett-Koehler Publishers.

Kostova, T. and Zaheer, S. (1999) Organizational legitimacy under conditions of complexity: The case of the multinational enterprise. *Academy of Management Review*, 24(1): 64–81.

Krugman, P. (1997) In praise of cheap labor: Bad jobs at bad wages are better than no jobs at all. Available at: www.slate.com/articles/business/the_dismal_science/1997/03/in_praise_of_cheap_labor.html, 17 May 2016.

Labowitz, S. and Baumann-Pauly, D. (2014) Business as usual is not an option: supply chains and sourcing after Rana Plaza. Available at: www.stern.nyu.edu/sites/default/files/assets/documents/con_047408. pdf, 16 Jan 2015.

Lee, E. (1997) Globalization and labour standards: A review of issues. *International Labour Review*, 136(2): 173–89.

Leipziger, D. (2010) *The Corporate Responsibility Code Book*, 2nd edn. Sheffield: Greenleaf Publishing.

Leßmann, O. (2012) Applying the capability approach empirically: An overview with special attention to labor. *Management revue*, 23(2): 98–118.

—— (2014) Arbeit und ein gutes Leben: Erfassung von Verwirklichungschancen im Capability-Approach. In Friedrich-Ebert-Stiftung (Ed.), *Was macht ein gutes Leben aus? Der Capability Approach im Fortschrittsforum.* Bonn: Fortschrittsforum, 47–57.

Liebig, K., Schmidt, P. and Stamm, A. (2004) Living Wages: Ermittlung und Einführung existenzsichernder Löhne. Available at: www.coc-rundertisch.de/inhalte/publikationen_rt/Living_Wages.pdf, 03 Jul 2015.

Maitland, I. (1997) Sweatshops and bribery: The great non-debate over international sweatshops. *British Academy of Management Annual Conference Proceedings*, 8–10 Sep. London, 240–67.

Manquila Solidarity Network. (2014) Global survey of living wage initiatives. Available at: http://en.maquilasolidarity.org/sites/maquilasolidarity.org/files/Global_review-living-wage-initiatives-MSN-Sep2014_0. pdf, 24 Sep 2015.

McIntosh, M. (2003) *Living Corporate Citizenship: Strategic Routes to Socially Responsible Business.* London, New York: Prentice Hall Financial Times.

Miller, D. (2013) *Towards Sustainable Labour Costing in UK Fashion Retail.* Manchester: University of Manchester.

Miller, J. (2003) Why economists are wrong about sweatshops and the antisweatshop movement. *Challenge: The Magazine of Economic Affairs*, 46(1): 93–122.

Musiolek, B. (2011) The Asia Floor Wage Campaign: Decent income for garment workers in Asia. Available at: www.eu-china.net/upload/pdf/materialien/2011_Musiolek-Asia_Floor_Wage.pdf, 30 Jun 2015.

Nussbaum, M. C. (2000) *Women and Human Development: The Capabilities Approach.* Cambridge: Cambridge University Press.

—— (2007) *Frontiers of Justice: Disability, Nationality, Species Membership.* Cambridge, MA: Belknap Press of Harvard University Press.

—— (2011) *Creating Capabilities: The Human Development Approach.* Cambridge, MA: Belknap Press of Harvard University Press.

Oxfam. (2014) Steps towards a living wage in global supply chains. Available at: www.oxfam.org/sites/www.oxfam.org/files/file_attachments/ib-steps-towards-living-wage-global-supply-chains-101214-en.pdf, 27 Jul 2014.

Paine, L. S., Deshpandé, R., Margolis, J. D. and Bettcher, K. E. (2005) Up to code: Does your company's code meet world-class standards? *Harvard Business Review*, 82(12): 122–33.

Parker, J., Arrowsmith, J., Fells, R. and Prowse, P. (2016) The living wage: Concepts, contexts and future concerns. *Labour & Industry*, 26(1): 1–7.

Preiss, J. (2014) Global labor justice and the limits of economic analysis. *Business Ethics Quarterly*, 24(1): 55–83.

Radin, T. J. and Calkins, M. (2006) The struggle against sweatshops: Moving toward responsible global business. *Journal of Business Ethics*, 66: 261–72.

Rasche, A. (2009) Toward a model to compare and analyze accountability standards: The case of the UN global compact. *Corporate Social Responsibility and Environmental Management*, 16(4): 192–205.

(2012) Global policies and local practice: Loose and tight couplings in multi-stakeholder initiatives. *Business Ethics Quarterly*, 22(4): 679–708.

Rasche, A. and Esser, D. E. (2006) From stakeholder management to stakeholder accountability. *Journal of Business Ethics*, 65(3): 251–67.

Robeyns, I. (2003) The capability approach: An interdisciplinary introduction. Available at: http://citeseerx.ist.psu.edu/viewdoc/download?-doi=10.1.1.196.1479&rep=rep1&type=pdf, 31 Jan 2016.

(2005) The capability approach: A theoretical survey. *Journal of Human Development*, 6(1): 93–117.

Ryan, J. A. (1906) *A Living Wage: Its Ethical and Economic Aspects*. New York: Macmillan Co.

Scheper, C. and Menge, J. (2013) *Menschenwürdige Löhne in der globalisierten Wirtschaft: Positionen, Durchsetzungshürden und Lösungsansätze*. Duisburg: Institut für Entwicklung und Frieden.

Scherer, A. G. and Palazzo, G. (2008) Globalization and corporate social responsibility. In A. Crane, A. McWilliams, D. Matten, J. Moon and D. S. Siegel (Eds.), *The Oxford Handbook of Corporate Social Responsibility*. Oxford: Oxford University Press, 413–31.

Sen, A. (1975) *Employment, Technology and Development: A Study Prepared for the International Labour Office within the Framework of the World Employment Programme*. Oxford: Clarendon Press.

Sen, A. K. (1970) *Collective Choice and Social Welfare*. San Francisco, CA: Holden-Day.

Sen, A. K. (1985) Well-being, agency and freedom: The Dewey lectures 1984. *Journal of Philosophy*, 82, 4, 169–221.

Sen, A. K. (1995) *Inequality Re-examined*, 3rd edn. New York: Russell Sage Foundation.

(2000) *Development as Freedom*. New York: Alfred A. Knopf.

(2011) *The Idea of Justice*. Cambridge, MA: Belknap Press of Harvard University Press.

Shelburne, R. C. (1999) The history and theory of the living wage concept. Available at: http://works.bepress.com/cgi/viewcontent.cgi?article=1039&context=robert_shelburne, 27 Aug 2015.

Smith, A. (1776) *An Inquiry into the Nature and Causes of the Wealth of Nations:* Oxford: Clarendon Press.

Snyder, J. (2009) Efficiency, equity and price gouging: A response to Zwolinski. *Business Ethics Quarterly*, 19(2): 303–6.

(2010) Exploitation and sweatshop labor: Perspectives and issues. *Business Ethics Quarterly*, 20(2): 187–213.

Sollars, G. G. and Englander, F. (2007) Sweatshops: Kant and consequences. *Business Ethics Quarterly*, 17(1): 115–33.

Stabile, D. (2008) *The Living Wage: Lessons from the History of Economic Thought*. Cheltenham, Northampton: Edward Elgar.

Tisdell, C. A. and Sen, R. K. (Eds.) (2004) *Economic Globalisation: Social Conflicts, Labour and Environmental Issues*. Cheltenham: Elgar.

UN. (1948) Universal Declaration of Human Rights. Available at: www.un.org/en/universal-declaration-human-rights/, 17 May 2016.

(1966) International Covenant on Economic, Social and Cultural Rights. Available at: www.ohchr.org/EN/ProfessionalInterest/Pages/CESCR.aspx, 18 May 2016.

UNDP. (2014) Barriers and opportunities at the base of the pyramid. Available at: www.undp.org/content/dam/undp/library/corporate/Partnerships/Private%20Sector/undp-psd-iicpsd-barriers_and_opportunities_BOP_full%20report_updated_2014.pdf, 26 Jul 2015.

Utting, P. (2002) Regulating business via multi-stakeholder initiatives: A preliminary assessment. In R. O. Jenkins, P. Utting and R. Alva Pino (Eds.), *Voluntary Approaches to Corporate Responsibility. Readings and a Resource Guide*. Geneva: NGLS; UNRISD, 61–130.

WRC. (2013) Stealing from the poor: Wage theft in the Haitian apparel industry. Available at: www.workersrights.org/freports/WRC%20Haiti%20Minimum%20Wage%20Report%2010%2015%2013.pdf, 13 May 2016.

Zwolinski, M. (2007) Sweatshops, choice, and exploitation. *Business Ethics Quarterly*, 17(4): 689–727.

16 | *For a Happy Human Development*

TADASHI HIRAI

Introduction

Human development (HD), influenced by the capability approach, has gained widespread acceptance over the past two decades thanks to the annual publication of the UNDP's *Human Development Report*. It has put forward a vision of development as an expansion of substantive freedoms rather than simply the pursuit of economic growth. According to HD, people's views and evaluations are crucial for public reasoning and for promoting bottom-up development strategies (Sen, 1999; Nussbaum, 2000). Despite its conceptual emphasis on what 'people value and have reason to value', it might well be open to the problem of malleability of subjective assessment, and hence tends to prefer assessing well-being objectively in practice. To make development work, economic growth is not enough, but the betterment of objective well-being (achievable by the multidimensional Human Development Index) is not completely adequate either. With subjective evaluations being indispensable in individual valuation, a key challenge is to reflect individual valuation systematically without being vulnerable to subjective whim.

In this context, it is important to remember that both the founders of the capability approach recognise the role of subjective well-being in evaluative exercise. Whilst Sen argues that happiness plays an evidential role in checking whether people succeed or fail to get what they have reason to value (Sen, 2008), Nussbaum argues that (subjective) emotions play a motivational role in searching for human flourishing, or 'real' happiness (Nussbaum, 2008). Extending their argument, this chapter will explore a systematic usage of happiness and subjective information to reflect individual valuation on states of affairs. The malleability of happiness would be overcome if its background is considered by assessing the satisfaction of human needs, an objective requirement to be human, as Nussbaum (2001) insists on the necessity of adjusting false desires to natural ones in pursuit of human flourishing or eudaimonia. This way of assessing happiness has a potential to make effective use of subjective information within the HD framework without fear of deformed valuations.

To this end, two versions of the capability approach will be first featured to clarify the different interpretation of happiness between Sen and Nussbaum. Following that, a conceptual examination will be made regarding eudaimonia as defined by the literature. It will lead not only to the necessity of differentiating it from cognition that is based on simple value judgments but also to the relevance of its distinction to two versions of the capability approach. The remaining sections will introduce two measures that can be used for eudaimonia and then select one for its application to Nussbaum's version. Ultimately, this chapter maintains that Nussbaum's version can correspond to eudaimonia whilst Sen's version has a stronger claim than cognition but a weaker claim than eudaimonia, and that at least Nussbaum's version has a possibility of being operationalised by the self-determination theory (SDT) which offers the measures most faithful to the original concept of eudaimonia.

Happiness in the Capability Approach: Nussbaum vs Sen

While sharing the significance of capabilities for the evaluation of our well-being and for the perspective of justice, the capability approach has two versions: One is the comparative by Sen and the other is the constitutional by Nussbaum.[1] Whereas Sen's version is more permissive by stressing the importance of individual valuations that are scrutinised by public discussion and so leaving individuals to decide what to value to constitute one's advantage, Nussbaum's is more assertive by requiring basic social justice for its assessment prior to individual valuation. Although Sen does not accept all individual values by emphasising the significance of public reasoning and thus does not suggest any particular value or sets of values between individuals and the public, it could be possible to see that he places individual values

---

[1] In Nussbaum's words, 'Sen typically focuses on the comparative use of capabilities. ... My version of the approach uses the idea of capabilities as the core of an account of minimal social justice and constitutional law' (Nussbaum 2011: 70–1).

prior to public reasoning while Nussbaum demands universal values prior to individual ones.

Indeed, the distinction has been argued in a series of Nussbaum's work from the Aristotelian perspective. In particular, the following statement clearly expresses her view vis-à-vis Sen's:

> [i]t seems to me ... that Sen needs to be more radical than he has been so far in his criticism of utilitarian accounts of well-being, by introducing an objective normative account of human functioning and by describing a procedure of objective evaluation by which functionings can be assessed for their contribution to the good human life. I think that Aristotle will provide substantial assistance in this task. For Aristotle's ethical thought contains an account of human functionings ... that is non-eternal, but still objective – and objective in a way that still leaves room for a certain sort of sensitivity to cultural relativity. (Nussbaum, 1988: 176)

Along these lines, Nussbaum proposes a list of basic capabilities (central capabilities in her words) arguing that '[a]t a bare minimum, an ample threshold level of ten Central Capabilities is required' (Nussbaum, 2011: 32) for human flourishing. It is deliberately narrow and partial so as to be confined to a core group of entitlements that can become the object of an overlapping consensus (Nussbaum, 2008). In other words, it clarifies a central group of very fundamental entitlements without which minimal justice has not been done (Nussbaum, 2006, 2008). In this respect, her list follows the basic needs literature (Gasper, 1996, 2004) and thus leaves room to tackle the problem of adaptive preferences (Teschl & Comim, 2005). By manifesting universal values, the list promotes the construction of political principles according to virtues, as Franklin acknowledges the role of society in a prescriptive manner following Aristotle: 'the *polis* provides a set of rules that guide appropriate action for those who have not yet developed virtuous ways. For those without the benefit of self-discipline and "right desire" the *polis* structures social behaviour' (Franklin, 2010: 150) Once the threshold level of fundamental entitlements is satisfied, plural structure of societies is accepted: '[i]t seems likely, at any rate, that moving all citizens above a basic threshold of capability should be taken as a central social goal. When citizens are across the threshold, societies are to a great extent free to choose the other goals they wish to pursue' (Nussbaum, 1999: 43). This plural structure is called 'multiple realisability' (Nussbaum, 2000).

Nussbaum's argument follows very closely to Aristotle's doctrine. As an Aristotelian philosopher, she proposes the concept and the list of capabilities based on two stages originally set up by Aristotle – namely the fulfilment of universal values and the achievement of unique potentials, which consist of the two requirements for eudaimonia. In her words: 'In the Aristotelian approach, it is obviously of the first importance to distinguish two stages of the inquiry: the initial demarcation of the sphere of choice, of the "grounding experiences" that fix the reference of the virtue term; and the ensuing more concrete inquiry into what the appropriate choice, in that sphere, *is*' (Nussbaum, 1993: 249–50, italics in original).

Less specific is Sen's notion of capabilities. Unlike Nussbaum, he neither requires capabilities to be virtuous nor creates a list or threshold of core capabilities, and rather values a process of public discussion in determining valuable capabilities and their thresholds. Although stressing the significance of the concept of injustice rather than transcendental justice (Sen, 2009) which sounds similar to Nussbaum's argument of the requirement of a bare minimum for social justice, he refrains from *a priori* specifying a basic universal norm to detect injustice. Given this, he leaves more room for the identification of capabilities, and thus his requirement of capabilities seems weaker than Nussbaum's.

This point leads to the different role that Sen and Nussbaum attach to happiness information: while Sen sees happiness as evidential, Nussbaum sees it as motivational. To the extent that Sen does not specify an objective normative account, the resulting happiness would be more malleable depending on the circumstances to which one belongs, and thus he sees it simply as evidential. In contrast, happiness by Nussbaum is filtered by the list to be satisfied for human flourishing and thus could be more reliable without much vulnerability to the problem of deformed valuations, which ends up acknowledging the role of happiness as motivational.

Happiness in Positive Psychology: Eudaimonia vs Cognition

This section will clarify the distinction between cognition and eudaimonia. In the preceding research, it seems that eudaimonia has been used frequently in the field of psychology and positive psychology in particular, even though it does not follow the original concept by

Aristotle and rather corresponds to cognition. As will be seen, this distinction is all the more significant for the capability approach, given that it is concerned with two versions of the approach (i.e. those from Sen and Nussbaum).

In the psychological literature, approaches to happiness have been categorised into hedonism and eudaimonism. Initially, the latter was reinterpreted as *personal expressiveness* (Waterman, 1990). However, it seems that personal expressiveness differs from the original concept of eudaimonia, in that this concept has been transformed, in the course of operationalisation, into a type of happiness based on a cognitive judgment that is too open without a moral anchor. Thus it is imperative to acknowledge an essential feature of eudaimonia that is missing from Waterman's reinterpretation.

Waterman recognises that daimon, or true self, consists of two potentialities: potentialities that are shared by all humans by virtue of our common specieshood; and unique potentials, which distinguish each individual from all others. For the purpose of operationalisation, however, Waterman (1990: 55) raises four significant departures from the original concept of eudaimonia, so that it can be measured from the psychological perspective as follows:

(a) Considering eudaimonia to have a subjective component embodying the experiences that flow from efforts to live in truth to one's daimon by striving to develop one's skills and talents for purposes deemed worth having in life.

(b) Considering eudaimonia as a subjective condition to be experienced as a function of discrete aspects of one's life, rather than one's life as a whole.

(c) Broadening the range of the constituents of eudaimonia beyond contemplation and moral virtue as discussed by Aristotle, to include efforts directed at the development of one's talents and the furthering of one's purposes, as these are consistent with the daimon.

(d) Viewing eudaimonia as available to children and adolescents, rather than restricting its possibility to adults as was done by Aristotle.

The first point (a) 'eudaimonia as a subjective condition' is justifiable to the extent that pleasure is regarded as a byproduct of eudaimonic living by Aristotle. That is, a positive feeling follows when individuals promote their potentials and/or their purposes in living. In this regard it (subjective well-being in their term) can be seen as an indicator of eudaimonia (Ryan et al., 2008) as will be examined later. The second point (b) 'eudaimonia as a function of aspects of one's life' makes sense as well. It parallels with the claim of the capability approach in which our quality of life is assessed in a multi-dimensional way (e.g. Nussbaum, 2000; Alkire, 2002) unlike utility in utilitarianism or GDP in the economic growth model. The fourth point (d) 'eudaimonia as available to children and adolescents' is also acceptable. Waterman broadens the target of eudaimonia other than adults for they can act in ways that further their potentialities and thus lead the type of life worth living for their ages. Consequently, it is not necessary to wait until adulthood to measure eudaimonia.[2]

Unlike the three points so far, the third point (c) 'broadening the range of the constituents of eudaimonia' seems to ruin the original concept of eudaimonia in exchange of its measurement. Rephrasing the article, eudaimonia is achievable as long as efforts are directed towards the development of one's talents and the promotion of one's purposes regardless of contemplation and moral virtue. Indeed, he later states that '[e]xperiences of personal expressiveness (eudaimonia) are a *sign* of the success the individual is having in furthering his or her talents and/or purposes in living' (Waterman, 1990: 60, brackets and italics in original). Here the necessity of common value, an indispensable feature of eudaimonia, seems missing. In this view, one could achieve eudaimonia as long as one *believes* in some efforts to promote one's talents and purpose in living, even if such beliefs are moulded in controlled or unjustified circumstances. This line of argument is thus similar to the views of many cognitive theorists (e.g. Bandura, 1977, 1989; Scheier & Carver, 1985; Carver & Scheier, 1990; Seligman, 1991). Their common argument is that psychological health would follow if one feels that adequate progress is being made toward one's goals regardless of what these goals are.

Against their claims, Kasser and Ryan (1993, 1996) advocate that the cognitive theory does not prevent harmful consequences, to the extent that it simply requires one to be optimistic or confident regarding one's attainment. For example, they argue against cognitive

---

[2] It is relevant to the necessity of cultivating competence or 'internal capabilities' towards eudaimonia, as argued by Nussbaum throughout her work.

efficacy views, in that financial success they believe as a factor to foster happiness does not function to produce happiness even when one succeeds. The Easterlin's Paradox in the materialistic society is a major example of cognitive misjudgment. What matters here is the content of the goal, which the cognitive theory misses.[3] The content of the goal leads to a proper adjustment in cognitive judgments and is supported by the satisfaction of *basic human needs*. In this regard, value ought to be distinguished from need, to the extent that value is simply a belief pertaining to desirable end states or modes of conduct (Schwartz & Bilsky, 1987, 1990; Schwartz, 1992). Likewise, quoting Fromm (1981), Ryan and Deci (2001) advocate that it is necessary to distinguish between the desire that is only subjectively felt leading to momentary pleasure and the objective need that is rooted in produces eudaimonia. Indeed, desire is regarded as a part of value in their work by stating: '[e]udaimonic theories maintain that not all *desires* – not all outcomes that a person might *value* – would yield well-being when achieved' (Ryan & Deci 2001: 145, italics added).[4] The bottom line is that our values are not set automatically towards eudaimonia, and to that extent cognitive judgments require to be adjusted by the satisfaction of basic human needs, which in turn allows us to cultivate a common value for human flourishing.

Against this view, the eudaimonic criteria based on needs is criticised by Diener et al. (1998) because the definition of well-being is often defined by experts who specify the needs criteria. Instead, they justify their research of subjective well-being that allows individuals to tell experts what makes their life good. In an extreme case it would be then logical for the cognitive theory and subjective well-being to repudiate even basic education just to avoid being paternalistic. But this seems hard to justify in reality. It is least likely that those who lack a proper background (needs) lead to a proper cognitive judgment (eudaimonia). In other words, only those who have such base

---

[3] In this regard, Deci and Ryan (2000) lament that the concept of *needs* has been repudiated and replaced by the concept of *goals* as the dominant motivational concept after the dramatic shift toward the cognitive theory beginning around the 1960s, and as a result goal-related efficacy has been stressed regardless of the content of the goal.

[4] In this regard it makes sense that Sen uses the expression 'one has reason to value' rather than simply 'one values'; by the filter of 'reasoning' wrong desires can be avoided. However, unlike Nussbaum he does not require the satisfaction of basic human needs for reasoning and valuation, as will be examined shortly.

can have a proper value which leads to a right cognitive judgement and adjustment for a good life. In this regard Rawls claims the necessity of primary goods in order to make our life plan rational by stating that 'primary goods should turn out to be those things which are generally necessary for carrying out such plans successfully whatever the particular nature of the plan and of its final ends' (Rawls, 1971: 411). Note here that primary goods include not only material goods but also 'primary social goods' such as liberties, opportunities and self-respect which can be regarded as human needs. Then it can be rephrased that without those needs (primary goods) people cannot construct a proper life worth of value (a rational plan). Indeed, as noted by Ryan et al. (2008) Aristotle's model of eudaimonia included a list of specific virtues and excellences that constitute a good life among which are courage, generosity, wisdom and being fair and just in relation to others, all of which can be regarded as the needs to be truly human.

Moreover, the necessity of basic human needs ('organismic needs' in their words) is further strengthened in the concept of personality integration (Sheldon & Kasser, 1995). Personality integration is conceptualised in terms of both coherence which involves how goals connect with each other and congruence which involves how goals connect with organismic needs. Out of two components of personal integration, congruence is regarded as more beneficial than coherence, on the ground that coherence between goals provides weaker predictors of the well-being outcomes than does congruence between goals and organismic needs. This argument seems parallel with the concept of daimon by Aristotle which composes both potentialities shared by all humans and unique potentials distinguishing each individual from all others. It can be rephrased that organismic needs or potentialities shared by all are prior to personal goals or individuals' unique potentials for eudaimonia.[5]

Overall, the cognitive theory does not usually consider the content of the goal and the reason underneath it, as long as the goal is based on an individual value. In its turn, eudaimonia requires the fulfilment of potentialities shared by all humans or human needs in addition to the fulfilment of unique potentials each person holds. Moreover, the former element (fulfilment of human needs) is even more beneficial than the latter (fulfilment of individual unique potentials) for our well-being

---

[5] In this regard, the level of personal expressiveness by Waterman would turn out to be higher with congruence than coherence.

according to the concept of personality integration. Now going back to Waterman, his concept of eudaimonia reflects the fulfilment of surface-level potentiality according to one's own belief only, while putting the requirement of human needs aside in exchange for the operationalisation. It means that his concept not only misses a part of eudaimonia but also the more important part of it, which ends up being reduced to a type of happiness based on cognitive judgments. To sum up, human needs should be fulfilled to transform their cognitive judgments into a flourishing life, which differentiates eudaimonia from cognition. In other words, distinguishing needs from mere desires or unscrutinised values and goals can help focus efforts to defining the ends a person has reason to value, so essential to the capability approach (to Nussbaum's version more precisely) from a constitutional perspective. One step further, applying the difference to the argument in the previous section, Sen's version would be in a middle ground between cognition and eudaimonia; it is stricter than the former by calling public scrutiny in society, and weaker than the latter by not demanding universal values. In contrast, Nussbaum's version is compatible with eudaimonia by requiring the fulfilment of universal values in addition to the achievement of unique potentials. In this context, Bruni and Porta (2005) praise Nussbaum's capabilities approach for its objective operationalisation of a good human life in constitutional and political spheres.

Eudaimonic Measures

It has been found on the conceptual level that eudaimonia differs from cognition in terms of its additional requirement of basic human needs as a common value. In this regard, the former is narrower/stricter than the latter. Based on this clarification, many measures involving value judgments fall into: (1) concerning life satisfaction (e.g. General Social Surveys (Layard, 2005; Frey, 2008); satisfaction with life scale (Diener et al., 1985); domain satisfaction approach (Van Praag & Ferrer-i-Carbonell, 2004); life cycle happiness (Easterlin, 2008)) or (2) reflecting control to/efficacy of one's own life (e.g. mastery scale (Pearlin & Schooler, 1978); self-efficacy scales (Bandura, 2006); efficacy scale (Sherer et al., 1982)). Overall, all the measures enumerated here can be categorised as cognitive but not eudaimonic, given that they allow individuals to make their own individual judgments (which aim at the fulfilment of respective unique potentials) without any requirement of human needs. Consequently, they are not able to avoid value misjudgments, to the extent that individual values and goals can be formed by distorted reasoning either in a controlled or unjustified environment. In contrast, the psychological well-being and the self-determination theory remain to be possible eudaimonic metrics. Indeed both measures specify some dimensions as requisite for human flourishing.

Psychological Well-Being

The psychological well-being (PWB) by Ryff and others originates from a critical standpoint of two preceding literatures: psychological well-being and personal growth models, and extends them in pursuit of eudaimonia. On the one hand, the existing literature of psychological well-being since Bradburn (1969) was criticised by Ryff (1989b), because it does not define the essential features of positive psychological functioning. Indeed, its indicators (i.e. positive affect, negative affect and life satisfaction) were, she argues, developed not to represent psychological well-being in itself but rather to verify how certain macro-level social change affects people's sense of psychological well-being. Facing the lack of theoretical rationale, therefore, she argues for the necessity of adjusting it to reflect the important aspects of positive psychological functioning.

On the other hand, acknowledging that the existing literatures of personal growth models (e.g. self-actualisation (Maslow, 1968), fully functioning person (Rogers, 1961), individuation (Jung, 1933), maturity (Allport, 1961)) theoretically consider growth as innately and biologically motivated and thus propose that it would occur naturally as long as conditions were right and impediments were removed. Ryff (1985) nonetheless points out that they miss the consideration of process, namely how growth is to be achieved in an empirical sense. In particular, she criticises their ignorance of historical and cultural variation and their neglect of life cycle, both of which lead to implicit value judgments. In terms of sociocultural influences on personal characteristics, for example, Ryff (1987) compares American and Japanese culture and finds that American values lead to the promotion of personal characteristics such as independence, autonomy, achievement, individualism and competitiveness, whereas Japanese values lead to personal characteristics such as interdependence, self-discipline, politeness and group identity. To make it generalised, Ryff and Singer (1998) advocate that one's purposes, obligations and reasons for living vary dramatically by the social structure and its hierarchical system. PWB is thus aware of sociocultural variations in conceptions of growth to make the scope of inquiry more relative and more dynamic, unlike the existing personal growth models which are essentially based on Western and middle-class values (Ryff, 1985, 1989b). Further to sociocultural influences, Ryff (1989a) argues for the significance of reflecting people's own definitions of positive functioning at their respective life stages for successful aging, so that they can be constantly revised, refined and elaborated. PWB hence takes seriously both the theoretical investigation of well-being and empirical inquiry on the assessment of the fit with the values of those to whom they are applied (Ryff, 1989c).

To make PWB both theoretically sound and empirically applicable, six dimensions are selected based on the personal growth models. The choice was made because many supporters of the models have written about similar features of positive psychological functioning which can be integrated into a more parsimonious summary (Ryff, 1989a, b). The dimensions are: self-acceptance, positive relations with others, autonomy, environmental mastery, purpose in life and personal growth. Each dimension represents different aspects of positive functioning (Ryff, 1989b). This multidimensional approach is prescriptive by specifying the important elements of positive psychological functioning in advance and thus meant to be distinct from subjective well-being (Ryff & Keyes, 1995). Comparing these newly constructed measures with the six dimensions, she reveals that the existing indices of psychological well-being (e.g. positive affect, negative affect, life satisfaction) fail to reflect aspects of positive functioning illustrated in the theoretical literature. It means that they are guided by narrow conceptions of positive functioning, not only in that the emphasis is given to short-term affective well-being at the expense of more enduring life challenges, but also in that life satisfaction, despite its more enduring and long-term quality, does not reflect some essential aspects of well-being (e.g. autonomy, personal growth, positive relations with others).

In short, the significance of PWB vis-à-vis the existing literature is two-fold: to overcome the limited theoretical ground in psychological well-being and the limited empirical ground in personal growth models. Ultimately, PWB aims to pursue the realisation of one's true potential and purposeful living, following Aristotle's eudaimonia (Ryff, 1989b, 1995; Ryff & Singer, 1998).

Self-Determination Theory

As with PWB, the self determination theory (SDT) explicitly expresses the overlap with the concept of eudaimonia. Indeed, it intends to reflect eudaimonia which is regarded as 'a central definitional aspect of well-being' (Ryan & Deci, 2001: 146). The uniqueness of SDT is to investigate both the *content* of goals and the *regulatory processes* through which the goals are pursued (Deci & Ryan, 2000).

In order to examine the content of goals, SDT examines values associated with goals in relation to well-being outcomes and categorises them into intrinsic and extrinsic. It finds that intrinsic goals (e.g. self-acceptance, affiliation, community feeling) are the goals that foster growth towards a thriving way and thus typically promote well-being, whereas extrinsic goals (e.g. financial success, fame, image) are the goals that foster excessive ego involvement and social comparison and thus typically undermine well-being (Kasser & Ryan, 1993, 1996; Deci & Ryan, 2000; Sheldon et al., 2010). Moreover, extrinsic values are found inconsistent with intrinsic values while each type of values consistent within themselves (Kasser & Ryan, 1996; Grouzet et al., 2005). Although some extrinsic goals are surely important to a certain degree, when they become stronger than intrinsic goals, well-being is worsened (Vansteenkiste et al., 2008). This pattern has been found in people of a wide range of ages (Sheldon & Kasser, 2001; Vansteenkiste et al., 2004) as well as in cultures regarded as both collectivist and individualist (Ryan et al., 1999; Schmuck et al., 2000; Grouzet et al., 2005). Going beyond goal importance per se, SDT thus stresses the content of goals and further identifies the three basic psychological needs – autonomy, competence and relatedness – as determinant for well-being or eudaimonia (Deci & Ryan, 2000; Ryan & Deci, 2000, 2001).

The requirement of the basic psychological needs makes SDT universal. While acknowledging the fact that sociocultural circumstances in which one is embedded have an immense influence on one's values (Kasser et al., 1995), SDT maintains that the relation between the three basic psychological needs and well-being be invariant regardless of these differences (Ryan & Deci, 2000) and thus be used as an anchor to investigate their relation to the varied values (Deci & Ryan, 2000). To put it another way, these underlying needs are universally relevant, although being expressed differently across societies and cultures that hold different values. In this respect, Chirkov et al. (2003) argues that differences in the extent to which people readily assimilate different cultural forms are a function of how those specific cultural orientations and practices meet or do not meet the basic psychological needs.[6] By specifying these needs as universal to all humans, therefore, SDT has clear normative criteria, unlike other relative theories that regard the contents of any cultural goals as equally good (Deci & Ryan, 2000).

In addition to the content of goals – intrinsic or extrinsic – SDT also considers regulatory processes of goals, namely whether goals are to be regulated by autonomous motivations or controlled motivations (Deci & Ryan, 2000; Ryan & Deci, 2000). Autonomous motivations let people freely engage in activities that they find enjoyable or of personal value and thus persist without reinforcement from operationally separable consequences, whereas controlled motivations involve people engaging in activities because they feel pressured or compelled to do so (Vansteenkiste et al., 2008). Here again the difference in regulatory processes depends on conditions with or without the support for the basic psychological needs: autonomous motivations are supported by social contexts that promote the needs (Brown & Ryan, 2004). Among the three basic psychological needs, autonomy is regarded as the most important, in that perceived autonomy is required for motivations to be intrinsic, while perceived competence is necessary for any type of motivations. This point reassures that SDT does not see control or efficacy alone (e.g. mastery scale, self-efficacy scales, efficacy scale) as sufficient to explain high volitional activities based on intrinsic motivations.[7] Relatedness is also important but only to the extent that

---

[6] A series of works by Schwartz (Schwartz & Bilsky, 1987, 1990; Schwartz, 1992, 1994) demonstrate the existence of 10 universal human values, create a circumplex to propose the structural relations among them and propose that the cultural difference is caused by the relative importance among them across cultures. Based on this framework, comparative argument on intrinsic-extrinsic difference across countries is made by Kasser and Ryan (1993, 1996) and then extended by Grouzet et al. (2005).

[7] In this regard, the concept 'personal strivings' by Emmons (1989) is investigated in Sheldon and Kasser (1995): personal strivings that help bring about extrinsic possible futures are associated with distracting daily activities (e.g. smoking, watching television), while personal striving linked to intrinsic possible futures are associated with meaningful daily activities (e.g. helping friends, thinking about one's future). It indicates that not all personal strivings defined by Emmons lead to well-being enhancement.

intrinsic motivations are more likely to flourish in a secure relational condition. With both the content and the regulatory processes of goals, SDT has much in common with the capability approach, which addresses freedom in terms of opportunities and processes (Sen, 1999) on the one hand, and requires the satisfaction of central capabilities in pursuit of eudaimonia (Nussbaum, 2011) on the other.

Further to the dichotomy between intrinsic and extrinsic motivations, SDT examines the degree of 'internalisation of extrinsic motivation' (i.e. external, introjected, identified and integrated) in order to reflect the reality that people often need to follow extrinsic motivations to live as social agents, and reveals that the degree to which people can incorporate cultural values into the self depends on the degree to which the needs satisfaction is supported (Deci & Ryan, 2000; Ryan & Deci, 2000). In other words, social contexts supportive of the basic psychological needs not only enhance intrinsic motivations but also facilitate the internalisation of extrinsic motivations in case of necessity, and consequently promote intrinsic goals; social contexts thwarting the basic psychological needs strengthen more controlled regulations and consequently promote stronger extrinsic goals.

Overall, SDT advocates that both content and process affect well-being outcomes through the satisfaction or thwarting of the basic psychological needs (Deci & Ryan, 2000). Intrinsic goals such as community contribution facilitate the satisfaction of the needs and tend to be more autonomous, whereas extrinsic goals such as financial success facilitate the thwarting of the needs and tend to be more control-oriented or ego-involving (Kasser & Ryan, 1993, 1996; Deci & Ryan, 2000; Ryan et al., 2008). It is also confirmed that there is a synergistic effect when intrinsic goals are pursued in an autonomy-supportive context (Vansteenkiste et al., 2004) and further that intrinsic goals have additional impact on well-being over and above autonomous motivation because the content of goals has a direct impact on well-being even after controlling for the motives (processes) people have for pursuing them (Vansteenkiste et al., 2004, 2008). The suitability of SDT for a eudaimonic assessment is indeed clearly explained in Ryan et al. (2008). More importantly, SDT has a potential for operationalising the capability approach not only due to its focus on the content and process of goals but also due to its open-end feature, as will be considered in the next section.

Eudaimonic Measure for the Capability Approach

In the previous section, the main features of PWB and SDT have been reviewed respectively in order to examine whether they can be used as eudaimonic metrics. The next step is to identify which is more relevant to the capability approach. The topics covered here are: basic human needs, autonomy and hedonics.[8]

Basic Human Needs

First, as argued at the conceptual level, the satisfaction of basic human needs is an important requisite for eudaimonia together with cognitive judgments, and thus is better to be reflected in eudaimonic measures. It particularly corresponds to the well-being assessment proposed by Nussbaum as discussed earlier. In this regard, both PWB and SDT determine what contents (that reflect needs) constitute eudaimonia. PWB consists of six contents: self-acceptance, positive relations with others, autonomy, environmental mastery, purpose in life and personal growth, whilst SDT consists of three contents: autonomy, competence and relatedness. Comparing the contents of each measure, it seems that personal growth and environmental mastery correspond to competence; positive relations with others to relatedness; autonomy to autonomy; and self-acceptance and purpose in life to all the three contents of SDT. It is therefore fair to suggest that both measures demand similar dimensions of basic human needs for eudaimonia, despite the different number and label. Indeed, Ryan and Deci (2001) clearly states that SDT largely agrees with PWB concerning the content of eudaimonia (with the exception of their differing definitions of autonomy, as discussed below).

Related to the requirement of the basic human needs, SDT, unlike PWB, distinguishes intrinsic values from extrinsic values and

---

[8] Alkire (2008) covers both PWB and SDT among others as possible agency measures for the capability approach and further advocates that SDT is more promising than PWB due to its multidimensional analysis, its carefully distinguished concept of autonomy and its consideration of multiple practices. In contrast, anchoring the pursuit of eudaimonia, this chapter selects PWB and SDT because of the requirement of *basic human needs* and further proposes that SDT seems more promising not only because of the rich concept of *autonomy* but also the inclusion of *hedonic type of happiness*.

demonstrates the link between the value types to the existing social system. Extending the study on universal content and structure of human values by Schwartz (1992) and the study on value types behind goals by Grouzet et al. (2005), Kasser et al. (2007) finds the inconsistency between American corporate capitalism and eudaimonia, because the extrinsic values typically associated with capitalism (e.g. self-interest, competition, financial success) are empirically negatively correlated with the intrinsic values associated with eudaimonia (e.g. caring about the broader world, having closer relationships with others, feeling worthy and free).[9] This finding is particularly suggestive of the challenges in the current materialism-stricken world. Ryan et al. (2008) further argue that modern capitalistic societies have a much closer fit with hedonic conceptions of well-being, although materialism has a limitation even in the sphere of hedonics let alone eudaimonia.

Of course it is often difficult to divide values between intrinsic and extrinsic. Further to this point, the pursuit of extrinsic values could be justified. For example, the pursuit of culturally valued extrinsic goals can increase self-esteem and buffer anxiety (Greenberg et al., 1992); extrinsic values may help people attain higher incomes which in turn enhance subjective well-being (Diener & Oishi, 2000); the acquisition of materialistic resources and other signs of status can confer distinct reproductive advantages (Geary, 1998; Gangestad, 2000). Similarly, Grouzet et al. (2005) points out that financial success has a less extrinsic character in the poorer cultures than in the wealthier cultures, to the extent that financial success in the former is probably more likely to concern basic survival for loved ones than in the latter where financial success is often a means to acquire status, image and popularity. Nonetheless, the distinction in values is important. To support this, Grouzet et al. (2005) finds that the intrinsic and extrinsic clusters are strongly consistent within themselves and strongly opposed to each other across samples from diverse nations. It implies that, rather than focusing on intrinsic values while excluding extrinsic values, prioritising the former *relatively* to the latter is more realistic and important for eudaimonic living. Indeed, this line of argument parallels with the capability approach, which emphasises the distinctive feature of

---

[9] Note here that Kasser et al. (2007) specifies American corporate capitalism among other forms of capitalism. It implies that the capitalistic system works not necessarily as extrinsic.

ends-values (e.g. freedoms) and means-values (e.g. economic growth) and prioritises the pursuit of the former with the latter not unimportant in the field of development.

Autonomy

The indispensable feature of autonomy has been repeatedly highlighted in the capability approach. And yet, given its abstract nature, it is important to examine the conception of autonomy in each measure and to investigate their compatibility with the capability approach.

In PWB, the concept of autonomy is similar to the notions of *control*, unlike in the capability approach where capabilities do not always demand control (Sen, 1999). It is greatly affected by individualistic view deriving from a series of the personal growth models as follows: a resistance to enculturation to become self-actualiser (Maslow, 1968); a deliverance from convention to avoid following the collective feats, beliefs and laws of the masses (Jung, 1933); an emphasis on an internal locus of evaluation based on personal standards rather than looking to others for approval (Rogers, 1961); and a sense of freedom from the norms in the process of turning inward in the later years (Erikson, 1959; Neugarten, 1968). Therefore, autonomy is seen in PWB as the notions of control and independence (Ryff, 1989a, b) which is not feasible within collectivism (Ryff, 1985). In this regard, she distinguishes her concept of autonomy from Waterman's concept of individualism which is compatible with social values by promoting cooperative interdependence.[10] It reinforces the difference between PWB and the capability approach in the concept of autonomy, to the extent that the capability approach rather appreciates effective freedom which does not necessarily require one's direct control and independence.

In SDT, on the other hand, autonomy is defined as *volitional* regardless of control and independence, as referring 'not to being independent, detached, or selfish but rather to the feeling of volition that can accompany any act, whether dependent or independent, collectivist or individualist' (Ryan & Deci, 2000: 74). It contrasts with not dependence but with heteronomy 'in which one's actions are experienced as

---

[10] More precisely, the concept of autonomy in PWB would be revised by the influence of empirical studies on psychological well-being, the other backbone of PWB. Nonetheless, the feasibility is uncertain.

controlled by forces that are phenomenally alien to the self or that compel one to behave in specific ways regardless of one's values or interests' (Chirkov et al., 2003: 98). In this regard, a person pursuing a reward 'agentically' is not thought of as autonomous (Vansteenkiste et al., 2008). Instead, autonomy in SDT involves fully endorsing the actions in which one is engaged and/or the values expressed by them, thus following one's integrated sense of self (Deci & Ryan, 2000; Chirkov et al., 2003), and further corresponds to one's reflective capacity (Ryan et al., 2008) which is required for eudaimonia. This point is particularly relevant to SDT's claim on the necessity of considering the degree of internalisation of extrinsic motivations in addition to intrinsic motivations.

Overall, PWB views independence/individualism in autonomy, which is less compatible with dependence/collectivism. It is not true of SDT, in which having a supportive relation with parents allows their adolescents to depend on them and this in turn facilitates autonomy rather than diminishes it (Vansteenkiste et al., 2008). This definition makes autonomy more universal across cultures. In this respect, Alkire (2008) notes its similarity with Sen's concept of agency in terms of universal applicability. SDT indeed acknowledges that the forms that autonomy takes can differ according to what is culturally meaningful. For example, Deci and Ryan (2000) argues that Americans tend to feel autonomous when making their own decisions whereas East Asians may feel more autonomous when endorsing and enacting values of those with whom they identify. Similarly, an empirical study by Chirkov et al. (2003) verifies autonomy to be associated with the enhancement of well-being in both Western and Eastern cultures regardless of the forms taken. In this respect, Vansteenkiste et al. (2008) advocates that a person can fully internalise a collectivist value to be autonomous as well as can fully internalise an individualist value to be autonomous. Indeed, the concepts of 'conformity', 'constraint' and 'demand' often categorised into collectivism are compatible with autonomy if one fully internalises external guidelines, although they are not if one obeys someone out of fear of punishment and thus externally controlled (Chirkov et al., 2003; Ryan et al., 2008). Therefore, autonomy does not necessarily imply independence from others; one can be autonomously dependent as well as autonomously independent (Chirkov et al., 2003; Vansteenkiste et al., 2008). This concept of autonomy enables SDT to apply to any cultures and societies while respecting diversities and multiple realisability, which the capability approach advocates. One step further, categorising norms supporting equality as horizontal vis-à-vis hierarchal social relations as vertical, Chirkov et al. (2003) finds that horizontal practices are more highly internalised than vertical practices regardless of the individualistic or collectivist contexts. This implies that autonomy is more relevant to horizontal practices vis-à-vis vertical practices than to individualism vis-à-vis collectivism. All these arguments put forward by SDT would be appreciated by the capability approach, in that SDT succeeds in reflecting such a rich concept of autonomy in a number of empirical studies whereas the capability approach still struggles with its operationalisation.

Hedonics

The final issue to be investigated for the comparison between PWB and SDT is regarding how to deal with hedonics. It has been argued so far that both measures reflect eudaimonic type of happiness rather than hedonic type. However, it is another issue whether the latter is also taken into account or out of concern.

On the one hand, SDT acknowledges two main routes to hedonics and their impacts: some result from selfishness, materialism, objectified sexuality and ecological destructiveness and end up jeopardising well-being in a long run; and others accompany eudaimonic way of living and lead to enduring hedonism (Ryan et al., 2008). Indeed, this unique feature of hedonics is empirically confirmed in SDT in the context of the intrinsic-extrinsic distinction, by demonstrating that pleasure falls midway between the two values whereas the others can be divided into either value (Grouzet et al., 2005; Ryan et al., 2008).[11] More importantly, following Aristotle's claim that pleasure is a byproduct of eudaimonia, SDT considers hedonic type of happiness as one of outcomes associated with eudaimonia, while stressing its contents and processes. Consequently, it regards the basic psychological needs and the regulatory processes as the mediating roles or

---

[11] Elsewhere, Schwartz (1992, 1994) also acknowledges a duality of meaning in hedonism, by finding that hedonism falls between two dimensions: 'self-enhancement' which is closely related to extrinsic values (e.g. image, popularity) and 'openness to change' which is closely related to intrinsic values (e.g. competence, purpose in life).

indicators of eudaimonia rather than eudaimonia in itself (Ryan et al., 2008), which enables it to leave room for hedonic type to be considered as a part of eudaimonia, indeed as one of its common outcomes. This interpretation of hedonics fits well with the capability approach, in which hedonic type of happiness is regarded as intrinsic in itself and thus an important part of living conditions – 'an important human functioning' (Sen, 2008: 26) and 'an intrinsically valuable source of richness and goodness in human life' (Nussbaum, 1990: 84) – while eudaimonic type of happiness is regarded as evidential or motivational respectively. In contrast, PWB regards six selected dimensions as eudaimonia in itself rather than its indicators (Ryan & Deci, 2001) and does not include any dimension reflective of hedonics in them. This means that PWB neither covers hedonic type of happiness nor leaves room for it to be an indicator, which indicates that hedonics is not taken into account as a part of eudaimonia in PWB.

So far, PWB and SDT have been investigated with a focus on three issues: basic human needs, autonomy and hedonics. The requirement of basic human needs is proposed by both measures despite the difference in number and labelling. Even though PWB demands more contents for needs than SDT, it has been found that all correspond to the basic psychological needs in SDT with reservation of the conceptual difference of autonomy (which comes next). Therefore, both PWB and SDT could be a candidate in this regard for the application to Nussbaum's version in pursuit of eudaimonia. However, it is not true of the remaining two issues. Whereas SDT leaves room for hedonics to be a part of eudaimonia, PWB does not. Given that hedonic type of happiness is regarded as an important functioning and capability and thus as a crucial feature of our lives, SDT is more relevant to the capability approach. When it comes to the concept of autonomy, PWB regards it as control and independence which is not necessarily required for autonomy defined in the capability approach. In contrast, the SDT regards autonomy as equivalent to volition regardless of locus of control, much in the same way that the capability approach regards it as effective freedom rather than one's direct control. Moreover, its systematic consideration of regulatory processes in autonomy (i.e. not only intrinsic motivations but also the degree of internalising external motivations) would be appreciated by the capability approach and useful for its operationalisation. While the similarity between SDT's concept of autonomy and Sen's concept of agency was argued by

Alkire (2008), this remark seems all the more true of Nussbaum's view to the extent that SDT's autonomy cannot be addressed fully without the demand of basic human needs from the Aristotelian perspective.

All in all, reflecting a subjective side of well-being, PWB does not fit with neither versions of the capability approach in terms of both the concept of autonomy and the treatment of hedonics despite the requirement of basic human needs. In contrast, SDT fits well with both Sen's and Nussbaum's versions in terms of the concept of autonomy and the inclusion of hedonics and further with Nussbaum's version for the requirement of basic human needs. Moreover, both SDT and Nussbaum leave the possibility of other human needs to be considered in the future (Ryan et al., 2008; Nussbaum, 2000), by following Aristotle's concept of virtues: 'we must ... not look for precision in all things alike, but in each class of things such precision as accords with the subject-matter, and so much as is appropriate to the inquiry' (Aristotle, 1098a6-9). Thus they have chosen specific basic human needs and central capabilities, which are nonetheless open-end and revisable.

Conclusion

In this chapter, it has been argued that eudaimonia should not be seen as equivalent to cognition. Whereas the latter requires individual value judgments only, the former requires universal values prior to individual value judgments. In other words, whilst the latter demands the fulfilment of potentials each person holds regardless of the satisfaction of basic human needs, the former demands the satisfaction of them for a good human life prior to the fulfilment of individual unique potentials. This distinction seems particularly relevant to two versions of the capability approach: while Nussbaum's constitutional version presupposes universal values to be human/humane prior to individual values and is thus compatible with eudaimonic approach, Sen's comparative version stresses individual values prior to common values led by public scrutiny and seems thus compatible with cognitive approach but not fully so to the extent that it necessitates public scrutiny which is not required in the cognitive approach. This distinction is consistent to their interpretation of happiness: while Nussbaum regards it as motivational by advocating the requirement of basic human needs, Sen, without their requirement, regards it simply as evidential to be a part of informational space for evaluative exercise. At least Nussbaum's version has potential to overcome the problem of deformed valuations, by putting individual valuations right in the process of creating central capabilities, namely satisfying basic human needs.

Eudaimonic approach and its measures could avoid one's reasons to be biased as much as possible by requiring basic human needs and thus keep value misjudgments at a minimum, whilst cognitive approach and its measures allow one to make value judgments regardless of one's reasons to be biased or not. SDT, identified as the most appropriate basis for eudaimonic metrics above, is promising to provide a way to operationalise Nussbaum's version by reflecting individuals' voices for evaluative exercise in a more systematic manner without being much bothered by the problem of deformed valuations.[12] In contrast, various cognitive metrics can be used to support Sen's version by providing more evidence even though it might be vulnerable to subjective whim. In either way, subjective information is a substantial part of the capability approach. Above all, Nussbaum's version, suitable for global advocacy, can be operationalised with the help of SDT in pursuit of a happy human development where objective well-being is to be harmonised with subjective well-being.

References

Alkire, S. (2002) *Valuing Freedoms: Sen's Capability Approach and Poverty Reduction.* Oxford: Oxford University Press.

(2008) 'Subjective measures of agency'. In L. Bruni, F. Comim and M. Pugno (Eds.) *Capabilities and Happiness.* Oxford: Oxford University Press, 254–85.

Allport, G. W. (1961) *Pattern and Growth in Personality.* New York: Holt, Rinehart, & Winston.

Aristotle (2009) *The Nicomachean Ethics.* Translated by D. Ross. Oxford: Oxford University Press.

Bandura, A. (1977) 'Self-efficacy: Toward a unifying theory of behavioral change'. *Psychological Review,* 84: 191–215.

---

[12] A possible connection between SDT and the capability approach has been argued by both the specialists in SDT (Vansteenkiste et al., 2008) and the specialist in the capability approach (Alkire, 2008) in a seminal book, *Capabilities & Happiness* (Bruni et al., 2008). However, they focus on the relevance of SDT to Sen's version. Nonetheless, as thus far described, SDT is compatible with Nussbaum's view rather than Sen's.

(1989) 'Human agency in social cognitive theory'. *American Psychologist*, 44 (9): 1175–84.

(2006) 'Guide for constructing self-efficacy scales'. In F. Pajares and T. Urdan (Eds.) *Self-Efficacy Beliefs of Adolescents*. Greenwich, CT: Information Age Publishing, 307–37.

Bradburn, N. M. (1969) *The Structure of Psychological Well-Being*. Chicago, IL: Aldine.

Brown, K. W. and Ryan, R. M. (2004) 'Fostering healthy self-regulation from within and without: A self-determination theory perspective'. In P. A. Linley and S. Joseph (Eds.) *Positive Psychology in Practice*. Hoboken, NJ: John Wiley and Sons, Inc., 105–24.

Bruni, L., Comim, F. and Pugno, M. (2008) *Capabilities and Happiness*. Oxford: Oxford University Press.

Bruni, L. and Porta, P. L. (2005) Introduction. In L. Bruni and P. L. Porta (Eds.) *Economics and Happiness: Framing the Analysis*. Oxford: Oxford University Press, 1–28.

Carver, C. and Scheier, M. (1990) 'Origins and function of positive and negative affect: A control-process view'. *Psychological Review*, 97: 19–35.

Chirkov, V., Ryan, R. M., Kim, Y. and Kaplan, U. (2003) 'Differentiating autonomy from individualism and independence: A self-determination theory perspective on internalization of cultural orientations and well-being'. *Journal of Personality and Social Psychology*, 84 (1): 97–110.

Deci, E. L. and Ryan, R. M. (2000) 'The "what" and "why" of goal pursuits: Human needs and the self-determination of behavior'. *Psychological Inquiry*, 11 (4): 227–68.

Diener, E., Emmons, R. A., Larsen, R. J. and Griffin, S. (1985) 'The satisfaction with life scale'. *Journal of Personality Assessment*, 49 (1): 71–5.

Diener, E., Sapyta, J. J. and Suh, E. (1998) 'Subjective well-being is essential to well-being'. *Psychological Inquiry*, 9: 33–7.

Diener, E. and Oishi, S. (2000) 'Money and happiness: Income and subjective well-being across nations'. In E. Diener and E. M. Suh (Eds.) *Culture and Subjective Well-Being*. Cambridge, MA: MIT Press, 185–218.

Easterlin, R. A. (2008) 'Life cycle happiness and its sources: Why psychology and economics need each other'. In L. Bruni, F. Comim and M. Pugno (Eds.) *Capabilities and Happiness*. Oxford: Oxford University Press, 28–59.

Emmons, R. A. (1989) 'The personal strivings approach to personality'. In L. A. Pervin (Ed.) *Goal Concepts in Personality and Social Psychology*. Hillsdale, NJ: Erlbaum, 87–126.

Erikson, E. (1959) 'Identity and the life cycle'. *Psychological Issues*, 1: 18–164.

Franklin, S. S. (2010) *The Psychology of Happiness: A Good Human Life.* Cambridge: Cambridge University Press.

Frey, B. S. (2008) *Happiness: A Revolution in Economics.* Cambridge, MA; London: MIT Press.

Fromm, E. (1981) 'Primary and secondary process in waking and in altered states of consciousness'. *Academic Psychology Bulletin*, 3: 29–45.

Gangestad, S. W. (2000) 'Human sexual selection, good genes, and special design'. In D. LeCroy and P. Moller (Eds.) *Evolutionary Perspectives on Human Reproductive Behavior.* New York: New York Academy of Sciences, 50–61.

Gasper, D. (1996) 'Needs and basic needs'. In G. Kohler (Ed.) *Questioning Development: Essays on the Theory, Policies and Practice of Development Interventions.* Marburg: Metropolis Verlag, 71–101.

(2004) *The Ethics of Development: From Economism to Human Development.* Edinburgh: Edinburgh University Press.

Geary, D. C. (1998) *Male, Female: The Evolution of Human Sex Differences.* Washington, DC: American Psychological Association.

Greenberg, J., Solomon, S., Pyszczynski, T. et al. (1992) 'Why do people need self-esteem? Converging evidence that self-esteem serves an anxiety-buffering function'. *Journal of Personality and Social Psychology*, 63 (6): 913–22.

Grouzet, F. M. E., Kasser, T., Ahuvia, A. et al. (2005) 'The structure of goal contents across 15 cultures'. *Journal of Personality and Social Psychology*, 89 (5): 800–16.

Jung, C. G. (1933) *Modern Man in Search of a Soul.* New York: Harcourt Brace.

Kasser, T. and Ryan, R. M. (1993) 'A dark side of the American dream: Correlates of financial success as a central life aspiration'. *Journal of Personality and Social Psychology*, 65 (2): 410–22.

(1996) 'Further examining the American dream: Differential correlates of intrinsic and extrinsic goals'. *Personality and Social Psychology Bulletin*, 22 (3): 280–7.

Kasser, T., Ryan, R. M., Zax, M. and Sameroff, A. J. (1995) 'The relations of maternal and social environments to late adolescents' materialistic and prosocial values'. *Developmental Psychology*, 31 (6): 907–14.

Kasser, T., Cohn, S., Kanner, A. D. and Ryan, R. M. (2007) 'Some costs of American corporate capitalism: A psychological exploration of value and goal conflicts'. *Psychological Inquiry*, 18 (1): 1–22.

Layard, R. (2005) 'Rethinking public economics: The implications of rivalry and habit'. In L. Bruni and P. L. Porta (Eds.) *Economics and Happiness: Framing the Analysis.* Oxford: Oxford University Press, 147–69.

Maslow, A. H. (1968) *Toward a Psychology of Being*. New York: Van Nostrand Reinhold.

Neugarten, B. L. (1968) 'The awareness of middle age'. In B. L. Neugarten (Ed.) *Middle Age and Aging*. Chicago: University of Chicago Press, 93–8.

Nussbaum, M. C. (1988) 'Nature, Function, and Capability: Aristotle on Political Distribution'. *Oxford Studies in Ancient Philosophy 1988*, supplementary volume, 145–84.

(1990) *Love's Knowledge: Essays on Philosophy and Literature*. Oxford: Oxford University Press.

(1993) 'Non-relative virtues: An Aristotelian approach'. In M. C. Nussbaum and A. Sen (Eds.) *The Quality of Life*. Oxford: Oxford University Press, 242–69.

(1999) *Sex and Social Justice*. New York; Oxford: Oxford University Press.

(2000) *Women and Human Development*. Cambridge: Cambridge University Press.

(2001) *Upheavals of Thoughts: The Intelligence of Emotions*. Cambridge: Cambridge University Press.

(2006) *Frontiers of Justice: Disability, Nationality, Species Membership*. Cambridge, MA; London: The Belknap Press of Harvard University Press.

(2008) 'Who is the happy warrior? Philosophy poses questions to psychology'. *The Journal of Legal Studies*, 37 (S2): S81–S113.

(2011) *Creating Capabilities: The Human Development Approach*. Cambridge, MA; London: The Belknap Press of Harvard University Press.

Pearlin, L. I. and Schooler, C. (1978) 'The structure of coping'. *Journal of Health and Social Behavior*, 19 (1): 2–21.

Rawls, J. (1971) *A Theory of Justice*. Cambridge, MA; London: The Belknap Press of Harvard University Press.

Rogers, C. R. (1961) *On Becoming a Person: A Therapist's View of Psychotherapy*. Boston, MA: Houghton Mifflin.

Ryan, R. M. and Deci, E. L. (2000) 'Self-determination theory and the facilitation of intrinsic motivation, social development, and well-being'. *American Psychologist*, 55 (1): 68–78.

(2001) 'On happiness and human potentials: A review of research on hedonic and eudaimonic well-being'. *Annual Review of Psychology*, 52: 141–66.

Ryan, R. M., Chirkov, V. I., Little, T. D., Sheldon, K. M., Timoshina, E. and Deci, E. L. (1999) 'The American dream in Russia: Extrinsic aspirations and well-being in two cultures'. *Personality and Social Psychological Bulletin*, 25: 1509–24.

Ryan, R. M., Huta, V. and Deci, E. L. (2008) 'Living well: A self-determination theory perspective on eudaimonia'. *Journal of Happiness Studies*, 9: 139–70.

Ryff, C. D. (1985) 'Adult personality development and the motivation for personal growth'. In D. Kleiber and M. Maehr (Eds.) *Advances in Motivation and Achievement*: Vol. 4. Motivation and Adulthood. Greenwich, CT: JAI Press, 55–92.

(1987) 'The place of personality and social structure research in social psychology'. *Journal of Personality and Social Psychology*, 53 (6): 1192–202.

(1989a) 'Beyond Ponce de Leon and life satisfaction: New directions in quest of successful aging'. *International Journal of Behavioral Development*, 12: 35–55.

(1989b) 'Happiness is everything, or is it? Explorations on the meaning of psychological well-being'. *Journal of Personality and Social Psychology*, 57 (6): 1069–81.

(1989c) 'In the eye of the beholder: Views of psychological well-being among middle and old-aged adults'. *Psychology and Aging*, 4: 195–210.

(1995) 'Psychological well-being in adult life'. *Current Directions in Psychological Science*, 4 (4): 99–104.

Ryff, C. D. and Keyes, C. L. M. (1995) 'The structure of psychological well-being revisited'. *Journal of Personality and Social Psychology*, 69: 719–27.

Ryff, C. D. and Singer, B. (1998) 'The contours of positive human health'. *Psychological Inquiry*, 9 (1): 1–28.

Scheier, M. and Carver, C. (1985) 'Optimism, coping and health: Assessment and implications of generalized outcome expectancies'. *Health Psychology*, 4: 219–47.

Schmuck, P., Kasser, T. and Ryan, R. M. (2000) 'Intrinsic and extrinsic goals: Their structure and relationship to well-being in Germany and US college students'. *Social Indicators Research*, 50: 225–41.

Schwartz, S. H. (1992) 'Universals in the content and structure of values: theoretical advances and empirical tests in 20 countries. *Social Psychology*, 25: 1–65.

(1994) 'Are there universal aspects in the structure and contents of human values?' *Journal of Social Issues*, 50 (4): 19–45.

Schwartz, S. H. and Bilsky, W. (1987) 'Toward a universal psychological structure of human values'. *Journal of Personality and Social Psychology*, 53 (3): 550–62.

(1990) 'Toward a theory of the universal content and structure of values: Extensions and cross-cultural replications'. *Journal of Personality and Social Psychology*, 58 (5): 878–91.

Seligman, M. E. P. (1991) *Learned Optimism*. New York: Alfred A. Knopf.

Sen, A. (1999) *Development as Freedom*. Oxford: Oxford University Press.

(2008) 'The economics of happiness and capability'. In L. Bruni, F. Comim and M. Pugno (Eds.) *Capabilities and Happiness*. Oxford: Oxford University Press, 16–27.

(2009) *The Idea of Justice*. London: Penguin.

Sheldon, K. M. and Kasser, T. (1995) 'Coherence and congruence: Two aspects of personality integration'. *Journal of Personality and Social Psychology*, 68 (3): 531–43.

(2001) 'Getting older, getting better? Personal strivings and psychological maturity across the life span'. *Developmental Psychology*, 37 (4): 491–501.

Sheldon, K. M., Gunz, A., Nichols, C. P. and Ferguson, Y. (2010) Extrinsic value orientation and affective forecasting: Overestimating the rewards, underestimating the costs. *Journal of Personality*, 78 (1): 149–78.

Sherer, M. J., Maddux, E., Mercandante, B., Prentice-Dunn, S., Jacobs, B. and Rogers, R. W. (1982) 'The self-efficacy scale: Construction and validation'. *Psychological Reports*, 51: 663–71.

Teschl, M. and Comim, F. (2005) 'Adaptive preferences and capabilities: Some preliminary conceptual explorations'. *Review of Social Economy*, LXIII (2): 229–47.

Van Praag, B. M. S. and Ferrer-i-Carbonell, A. (2004) *Happiness Quantified: A Satisfaction Calculus Approach*. Oxford: Oxford University Press.

Vansteenkiste, M., Simins, J., Lens, W., Sheldon, K. M. and Deci, E. L. (2004) 'Motivating learning, performance, and persistence: The synergistic effects of intrinsic goal contents and autonomy-supportive contexts'. *Journal of Personality and Social Psychology*, 87 (2): 246–60.

Vansteenkiste, M., Ryan, R. M. and Deci, E. L. (2008) 'Self-determination theory and the explanatory role of psychological needs in human well-Being'. In L. Bruni, F. Comim and M. Pugno (Eds.) *Capabilities and Happiness*. Oxford: Oxford University Press, 187–223.

Waterman, A. S. (1990) 'Personal expressiveness: Philosophical and psychological foundations'. *The Journal of Mind and Behavior*, 11 (1): 47–74.

17 Capability of Capabilities and Aspirations of the Middle Classes in India

MEERA TIWARI

Introduction

There is a rich array of literature that investigates the numerous characteristics, complexities and the role of middle classes as actors in society. This research ranges from material that notes middle classes as agents of change and progress, drivers of economic development to being catalysts for political change (Adelman and Morris, 1967; Landes, 1998; Moore, 1998; Easterly, 2001; Loayza et al., 2012; Alesina et al., 2012). One of the earliest references to the term 'middle classes' is found in the writings of Aristotle where he suggests that the best political communities are those that are formed by the middle classes. Further, states with larger middle classes are more likely to be better governed (306 BC, as noted in Decornez, 1998). Moore (1993) in his seminal work – *Social Origins of Dictatorship and Democracy* – referred to the middle classes as the bourgeoisie. He felt that this class drove the political processes towards democracy, asserting that societies with a powerful landowning cohort turn into dictatorships, while those with a strong bourgeoisie become democratic.

In recent years, as a number of developing countries march into the club of middle-income countries, the emergence of an amorphous category that sits between the very poor and the very rich appears to be rekindling the debate on the role of the middle classes in the progress of the society. Within the Indian context, while the country continues to be home to the largest number of $1.90 (in $2011, Purchasing Power Parity (PPP)) a day poor, highest number of undernourished children in the world with dismal child and maternal mortality figures, it is also home to the world's fourth largest number of billionaires (Forbes, 2016a). Further, while it was projected to overtake the UK economy by 2020, India surpassed the UK economy for the first time in more than 100 years in the latter part of 2016 (Forbes, 2016b). The ascendance of a class in between these two distinct categories is the subject of inquiry of this chapter. The study uses the capability approach (CA) to understand the functionings, capabilities and aspirations of the Indian middle classes that have resulted in their categorisation as the consuming class and the 'climbers' (Natarajan, 1999). The chapter then draws on Bourdieu's concepts of *habitus* and *doxa* to further the understanding of the social and cultural context and the norms that enable the opportunity to have the spectrum of life opportunities, i.e. *the capability of capabilities* that shape the aspirations of this class. Thus enriching the Capability Approach literature on capabilities and aspirations.

The purpose of this research is to assess how the aspirations, mobility and values of this expanding class, wielding significant influence in policy making, fit within the larger development agenda. With increasing emphasis on the inequality of opportunities in the current development discourse, understandings of the drivers of opportunities and aspirations of certain cohorts and how these impact on the opportunity structure of the disadvantaged cohorts, is critical in addressing the inequality concerns. The chapter explores whether this consuming and 'climbing' class facilitates, displays apathy or impedes addressing the inequalities to expand opportunities for the poor. The inquiry is timely, located within the recent literature, which suggests the relatively privileged classes continue to command disproportionate access and influence over public goods, media and social policy. Further, this asymmetric opportunity structure comprises mostly the demands that benefit the affluent with feeble gains for the deprived classes (Dreze and Sen, 2013: 266–73). The chapter will be both conceptual and empirical drawing on the current literatures and secondary data as well on small qualitative surveys undertaken in Mumbai.

The chapter is organised into five sections. Following the introduction the discussion in the second section explores the literature on the understandings of aspiration and applies the CA lens to further unpack the concept. The next section provides an overview of the middle classes locating the emergence of this class within an Indian context. The discussions then examine the aspirations and values that lend this class its distinct features identified in the first half of the section. Bourdieu's concepts of habitus and doxa are then deployed to further the understanding of how the aspirations and values of the middle classes are shaped. Then we investigate how aspirations of the middle classes fit in with the wider development discourse in India with high levels of inequality in some of the key domains of the sustainable development goals. This is followed by the conclusions of the chapter.

Understanding Aspirations through the Capability Approach

The word 'aspiration' originates from the Latin word *aspiratio* meaning breathing, although its usage to describe 'steadfast longing for a higher goal'; 'earnest desire for something above one' or 'a strong desire for realisation' can be tracked back to the sixteenth century. These definitions imply connotations of something beyond the fulfilment of basic needs of life as also noted by Conradie (2013). She refers to the term 'aspiration' as evoking notions of an individual's dreams, alluding to their ambitions, ideals and drive to achieve goals that would bring satisfaction beyond the essentials and routines of survival. Appadurai's (2004) contribution to highlighting the process of how aspirations are formed is significant in drawing attention to the norms, values, culture and contexts that foster and shape these wants and the drive to achieve. Here, the concept of adaptive preferences (Sen, 2002; Clark, 2002) plays an important role. Adaptive preference explains how people's ability to make judgments about what they want and desire, their ambitions and happiness can be misleading if their information and opportunity contexts are feeble, constrained or absent. In an earlier study, Ray (2003) explored the relationships between aspirations, poverty and economic change, further grounding the concept in the social context of the individual or the group. He refers to an individual's 'similar' or 'attainable' zone – the individual's window from which he/she draws aspirations. This attainable zone comprises the lives, attainments and success stories of individuals in a person's social sphere of familiarity. This can be illustrated by considering that it may be easier for a teenage in India to draw aspiration from Mahatma Gandhi than Abraham Lincoln. Further, within this 'attainable' zone, a poor person who has succeeded in breaking out of the poverty traps in a village to become a medical professional or qualified for entrance into engineering has a bigger influence on the aspirations of the village teenagers than Mahatma Gandhi. Ray also draws attention to the information flows that can affect how an individual's aspirations are crafted in a similar way to how the notion of adaptive preferences shape the aspirations.

Aspirations can be individual, i.e. of one person and or collective, i.e. of a community, albeit within the adaptive preference caveat mentioned previously, in addition to the problems linked to the dominant group bias in influencing the group goals (Copestake and Camfield, 2010). The article by Copestake and Camfield (2010) used field data from Peru, Thailand and Bangladesh, and further builds on Appadurai's (2004) and Ray's (2003) arguments on the material and non-material components of aspiration to formulate a multidimensional concept of aspirations. The discussions and the conceptual and methodological framework deployed in the article further open the inquiry into distinctions between happiness and aspiration. Copestake and Camfield interchangeably use the terms 'happiness' and 'aspirations'. Fifteen 'highest rated aspirations' are represented in a table entitled 'Highest rated items that are necessary to be happy in each country' (p. 622). Aspiration is considered a drive to achieve a goal that would bring satisfaction or happiness beyond the essentials and routines of survival. Hence food, livelihood, water, sanitation, children's education, housing and health could be considered as essentials or the basic needs of all humans in the present age. Within the normative context of CA, however, there may be perceptual blurring sometimes between what is considered the essentials of life and what falls within the remit of 'aspirational' goals. To illustrate this further, consider a teenager who may derive happiness by having the opportunity to go to a school. His aspiration may be to become a teacher, engineer, a medical professional or set up his own business. The understandings of aspiration in this chapter hence draw on the eudaimonic notions – 'human flourishings' – that resonate with the self-actualisation goals of Maslow's hierarchy of needs (1943, 1954). The perceptual blurring noted above builds on the arguments that Sen (2008) makes regarding happiness itself being an important human functioning. Furthermore, achievement of other things one values and has reason to value – the functioning – influences our happiness. Therefore, happiness is derived through the achievement of functionings for essentials of life as well as the aspirational goals.

The literature on aspirations spans the disciplines of anthropology, sociology, psychology, economics and more recently its emergence has been observed in development studies. The research in the development studies arena is mostly located in the newer understandings of noneconomic dimensions of poverty. It draws attention to low aspirations or aspirational deficit as one of the conditions of being in poverty.

Building on this feature, some literature proposes expansion of aspirations of the poor to be part of the poverty mitigation strategies as noted by Conradie and Robeyns (2013). In particular the authors refer to works of Ray (2003), Appadurai (2004), Bernard et al. (2008) and Ibrahim (2011).

Ray (2003), exploring the relationship between aspirations and poverty defines aspirations as the 'social grounding of individual desires' (p. 1) and articulates that it is the condition of poverty that 'stifles dreams or at least the process of attaining dreams' (p. 1). He suggests therefore that poverty and failure of aspirations are linked in a mutually reinforcing cycle. The paper further develops the concept of an aspiration gap that could be explored to address individual behaviour and effort. Appadurai's (2004) conceptualisation of the 'capacity to aspire' is largely recognised as spurring the debate and several studies on locating aspirations within culture and social contexts. He alludes to a feeble or absent capacity to aspire amongst the poor as one of the key impediments to overcoming their poverty. Hence, as part of a poverty mitigation strategy he suggests a better understanding of the cultural assumption and enabling the poor to aspire for a better life. This, according to Appadurai (2004) would lead to the poor accessing more opportunities by articulating their functionings, expanding their capabilities and exercising freedoms (pp. 66–70). Building on Ray's (2003) concepts of *aspiration window* and *aspiration gap* and Appadurai's (2004) *capacity to aspire*, Bernard et al. (2008), using notions of fatalism within the context of the poor in Ethiopia, argue for a third key concept that they call the *aspiration failure*. They describe fatalism as the 'lack of proactive and systematic effort to better one's own life and the implied acceptance of their circumstances' (p. 2). The paper puts forward an aspiration failure framework within which a feeble capacity to aspire can lead to a poor or no effort/investment towards better wellbeing, manifesting itself as fatalism or aspiration failure. Ibrahim (2011), using a case study from Egypt, advances the aspirational failure concept in terms of capability deficit and dynamics of aspirational failure that happens through a downward spiral and intergenerational transmission. As with the others, she too suggests aspiration-enabling policies to help the poor overcome their poverty and improve their wellbeing.

In summary then, it can be said that aspirations are ideals and a drive to achieve goals that would bring satisfaction beyond the essentials and routines of survival. Aspirations can be individual or collectively grounded in the social and cultural norms and context. Aspirations have the capability for unlocking potential that can enable enhancement of wellbeing and access to better opportunities in life. These are generic features of aspirations that have been explored within the context of the poor in the literature reviewed so far. This chapter examines how the aspiration window, the aspiration gap and the capacity to aspire of the middle classes in India are shaped and how these fit within the wider development discourse.

The Middle Classes

The origins of the middle classes in the modern Western discourse can be traced to Marxist literature (Marx and Engels, 2004). In the class analysis that formed the basis of the Communist Manifesto, Marx deployed a binary conceptualisation of society in terms of the bourgeoisie – owners of the means of productions and the employers of wage labour, and the proletariat – the labourer class and the workforce of the bourgeois masters. The existence of yet another group in between the bourgeoisie and the proletariat or the rich and the poor is absent in the Marxian class analysis. This is also noted in Jaffrelot and van der Veer (2008: 11), who draw attention to the missing middle class analysis in the Marxist critique of capitalism. In the Weberian reading of the class structure, the 'petty bourgeoise' and the 'intelligentsia' are certainly the mainstays of the middle classes. The plural here seems more relevant than the singular given the dual nature of the intermediary stratum as noted by Jaffrelot and van der Veer (2008: 12). This group commands more secure resources than the poor but not the levels of surplus enjoyed by the rich, considers itself quite distinct from the rich or the poor and belonging to the 'middle class'. A notoriously elusive social category, the middle class is a phenomenon of the capitalist era. The phrase was used for the first time in Britain by the end of the eighteenth century, to designate those who have some education, who have some property and some character to preserve (Wahrman, 1995: 443). More recently, Piketty in his seminal work *Capital in the Twenty-First Century*, points out that within the persistent concentration of wealth at the upper decile in Europe (60 per cent) and the USA (70 per cent), emergence of a patrimonial (propertied) middle class should not be underestimated (Piketty, 2014: 260–2). While significant in numbers accounting for

40 per cent of the population, its ownership is between one-quarter and one-third of the national wealth. The significance of this class, Piketty suggests, is transforming the social landscape, the political structures and the terms of conflict in the society.

As societies became more modernised, the social structure became more complicated (Jaffrelot and van der Veer, 2008: 12). Kharas and Gertz (2010) further draw attention to the rise of a significant middle class in the 'low and lower-middle income' countries amidst the multipolar world of the twenty-first century. While this new middle class (NMC) is less wealthy than the European middle class, it does wield considerable consuming power and potential as noted in Knorringa and Guarin (2015). With the emergence of the service sector (tertiary sector) and the subsequent development of this group, there was even more stratification and differentiation. The classification was primarily based on socio-economic criteria such as occupation and the standard of living. Guarin and Knorringa (2014) contest that the homogeneity of the middle classes arose through assumptions of common ways of socio-political participation, life styles and material acquisitions. However, Jaffrelot and van der Veer's (2008) focus on patterns of consumption emerging as the dominant focal point to which the middle classes in the Global South appear to be converging, continues to hold ground, albeit with further challenges from authors such as Upadhya (2008).

There is extensive of literature investigating the numerous characteristics, complexities and the role of middle classes as actors in the society. These topics range from middle classes as agents of change and progress, drivers of economic development, to being catalysts for political change. The earliest references to 'middle classes' are found in the writings of Aristotle. It highlights the positive contribution a dominant middle class can make in a society. This theme is further explored by Moore (1993). He attributes a strong middle class for driving the political processes towards democracy while societies with a powerful land-owning class turn into dictatorships.

Easterly (2001), using a theoretical construct of the middle class consensus which he defines as a national situation with low levels of class and ethnic differences, takes the somewhat inconclusive explanations of cross-country development variations provided by endogenous factors such as saving rates and national policies further to search for other causes. Two key streams of literature – the first located in the debates on economic factors of resource endowment, inequality and growth and the second in the discourse on the heterogeneity of social classes and growth – inform Easterly's national consensus hypothesis for understanding the middle classes. Using a comprehensive range of variables/proxies for growth, middle classes and ethnic polarisation in regression models, Easterly concludes that higher the class homogeneity in societies, i.e. a dominant middle class, the better the human capital and institutional capital accumulation. This in turn leads to higher levels of income and growth. The institutional capital here refers to national policies, functioning institutions, political stability and urbanisation. While the paper urges caution and rejects extreme measures such as ethnic cleansing towards becoming homogenous societies, the inter-changeability of the word *diversity* with polarisation, societal divisions and heterogeneity with negative connotations is problematic. Such usage leads to a narrow and restrictive understanding of diversity excluding any positive contribution diverse societies make to growth and wellbeing. Further, the paper does not engage with the process of creating middle classes that is increasingly linked to asymmetries in access to resources and opportunities, use of public goods and spaces (Fernandes, 2004; Upadhya, 2008). Hence the national consensus lens offers at best partial insight and skewed arguments into the contributions of the middle classes.

Issues of how the aspirations of the middle classes might impact on the increasing inequalities expressed through constraint opportunities for the low income or the poor cohorts preventing them from any form of social mobility have not been examined. This domain is emerging as one of the key issues in the worsening inequalities debate both within the developed countries (Stiglitz, 2012; Dorling, 2014) and the developing country contexts captured in the sustainable development goals.

The Indian Context

Before delving into the aspirations of the middle classes in India, an understanding of the emergence and evolution of this class in India is necessary. Through initial academic treatment of the subject, Mishra (1961) contemplated that the Indian middle-class had emerged due to British social policy, the introduction of new economic system, industry and with the growth of new professions in the eighteenth century. He argues that the Indian middle classes were created by the British to carry out the lower level administration of the empire. In order to reduce the cost of being trained personnel from UK to carry out the mundane tasks of running the everyday businesses of the empire, Macaulay created the infamous system of education in 1835 where he had envisaged the creation of a class that would be Indian in its origins but British in its mannerisms and personality (Acharya, 1988). The middle classes in India have been growing in size over the last century, more particularly after its independence from the colonial rule. However, the Indian middle class story witnessed a qualitative shift during the early 1990s with the introduction of economic reforms and an increasing integration of the Indian economy into the global markets. These reforms lead to substantial expansion of opportunities and remunerations in the business service and the IT sector.

While there is inevitable tension between the value systems associated with class, which is based on hierarchical, collective values, the caste background of the middle classes made them more cohesive in terms of shared values (Jaffrelot and van der Veer, 2008: 17). Fernandes and Heller (2006) argue that the new middle class is a tangible and significant phenomenon, but one whose boundaries are constantly being defined and tested. They note that the past two decades have witnessed a significant reconfiguration of class forces marked in particular by the ascendance of a new middle class that is conventionally portrayed as the natural carrier of India's intensified embrace of economic liberalisation. Public commentators, media images, and academic analyses have depicted this class as a consumer-based group benefiting from economic reforms. They contend that the contours of the NMC can be grasped only as a class-in-practice, that is, as a class defined by its politics and the everyday practices through which it reproduces its privileged position. This conceptualisation provided by Fernandes and Heller moves away from a static opposition between structural and political/cultural/ideological processes. Sociocultural inequalities and identities (such as those based on caste and language) are seen as an integral part of the process of middle class formation. The result, they argue, is that patterns of middle class illiberalism that is strongly shaped by such inequalities and exclusions. Harriss's (2005) work with the politics of the poor and the activism of the middle classes in Chennai lends credence to this argument. In his working paper he notes that while 'Civil society' is the arena for middle class activism and assertion; to a significant extent the middle classes engage in such activism whilst the urban poor engage in politics (Harriss, 2005: 32).

The 1998 National Council for Applied Economic Research (NCAER) report on Indian market demographics classified the consumer groups into three categories: the very rich, the consuming class and the climbers (Natarajan, 1999). However, the size of this group is not more than 200 million which means that at one-fifth of the population, this group remains a minority. Despite this the group remains the point of reference for the officials and the policy makers (Jaffrelot and van der Veer, 2008: 19). This is also because whilst this class accounts for a small proportion of the total population in India, in absolute numbers the Indian middle classes exceeds the total population of many countries of the developed West. They provide for a viable market-base and cultural universe for global capital to operate and flourish in India (Jodhka and Prakash, 2011: 43). The declining interest in parliamentary elections among the urban upper caste middle class of India can primarily be explained by its growing rejection of the existing form of democracy and the rise of the new plebeian brand of politics. At the same time, the upper middle class benefits more than any other group from economic liberalisation. Jaffrelot argues that the middle class is so powerful that it does not need to vote at all (Jaffrelot, 2008: 50–2).

Upadhya (2008) looks at the middle class as an ideological construct that has become a primary category of social identity for a significant section of the Indian population. She constructs this in a continuum from the Nehruvian period to the present. The explosion in consumption, especially of consumer and luxury goods, has been a very visible phenomenon in urban India over the past two decades. This is attributed to rising incomes of some sections of the middle classes, the growth of local business opportunities and the consequent emergence of new entrepreneurial groups together with easier availability of such commodities. Yet this linkage between middle class identity and consumption is not straightforward or transparent. It can neither be simply assumed that the new consumer class had a homogenising effect on the middle classes, nor that it has been uncritically absorbed without resistance or alteration. Moreover, the middle classes are highly diverse in terms of cultural and social backgrounds, and with enormous variation in attitudes towards, and practices of, consumption across different sections, linked at least in part of 'traditional' identities of caste, region and community.

Emerging residential patterns in cities such as Mumbai, Delhi and Bangalore, with large upwardly mobile class populations, reflect and reinforce the process of social fragmentation and dis-embedding. Most software engineers and other young professionals prefer to buy flats in large, upscale, self-contained apartment complexes that have been built around the city specifically to cater this class. They find living in such enclaves convenient because services such as security, maintenance, recreation and domestic help are provided or readily available. Within these gated communities, an army of maids, cooks, drivers and nannies look after family needs and domestic work, freeing professional couples from chores and childcare so that they can concentrate on their careers. In addition, the standard layout of flats in these complexes produces a new small model of middle class living different from that of the older generation middle and lower middle classes. These modern apartment complexes, and the lifestyles they promote, help to create a hegemonic and homogenised 'new middle class' (NMC) cultural style, while fragmenting older kinship or caste based neighbourhoods (Upadhya, 2008: 67–8).

In contrast to the understandings of the Indian NMC within a socio-cultural framework as noted above, there is also emerging literature exploring the NMC through a GDP growth and drivers of economic growth dominant framework. India's NCAER has been leading the research into income based definitions and boundaries of middle classes. Two categories are identified: 'seekers', with annual household income between Rs 200,000–Rs 500,000 and 'strivers' with annual household income between Rs 500,000– Rs 1,000,000 at 2001–2 prices. This equates to approximately $8–$20 per capita per day (2005 PPP) for seekers and $20–$40 per capita per day for strivers. Based on this categorisation the NCAER survey estimations put 153 million people in the NMC in 2009–10, accounting for 12.8 per cent of all households. At the global level, while there is no agreement on any definition for an income-based class, numerous researchers and institutions including the World Bank (2012), Birdsall (2010), Kharas (2010) and Meyer and Birdsall (2012) use a $10 per capita (2005 PPP) as the threshold for the global middle class. With $10 as the minimum and $50 as the upper ceiling and deploying India's National Sample Survey (NSS), Meyer and Birdsall (2012) provide a lower estimate of around 70 million people in the NMC cohort. An important point to note here is the rate of expansion of this class as per the NCAER's estimates of 2001–2 of 5.7–12.8 per cent in 2009–10, very much reflecting the rise in the NMC following the robust GDP growth trend in the country during this period. In another study, Sridharan (2010), locates the shift to higher incomes and the growing affluence of the urban income-based categories to the deregulation of the economy in the 1990s. Nayyar (2012) draws attention to the service sector as spear heading the GDP growth in the Indian economy during this period and one that is expected to continue resulting in 58 per cent of employment in the tertiary sector by 2009–10. Maitra (2011) further builds on economic-growth-enhancing notions of the middle class through durable goods ownership identification and recommends a policy focus. These studies indicate further expansions in the NMC in line with the strong growth projections for India.

Briefly then, the NMC in India can be understood as an expanding cohort that can be identified with higher incomes, a lifestyle that is supported by these income levels, norms of livelihood and financial security, education and access to resources and networks.

The Middle Class Aspirations

Appadurai's (2004) and Ray's (2003, 2006) attention to the social and cultural context and the norms that shape individual and collective aspirations of the poor can also be explained in terms of Bourdieu's concepts of *habitus* and *doxa*. Bourdieu, using his research in the French education system, defines *habitus* as a 'matrix of perceptions, appreciations and actions' Bourdieu and Nice (1977: 83) which are learnt at school and in the home. Further, these structures can both allow and restrict practices and goals giving rise to what he defines as *doxa* – a universe of the 'undiscussed' and self-evident Bourdieu and Nice (1977: 166). The larger social context within which the NMC are located can be conceptualised as its doxa. This would comprise the social structures such as professional and family networks, resource availability through access to credit and family finance, mobility, access to high standard of education and health services and strong information flows. These predictable structures facilitate a functioning agency and well-informed judgments about their ambitions and wellbeing based on current knowledge. These are the *opportunity structures* referred to in Alsop et al. (2006) within the context of agency and levels of empowerment attainments. Alsop et al. (2006) argue that agency can be restrictive within a weak opportunity structure, albeit with reference to the poor. The importance of institutional and opportunity structures as prerequisites for a functioning agency and its meaningful execution is further reinforced by Ibrahim and Alkire (2007) and Narayan (2005).

While high deprivation cohorts are the foci of much of the literature regarding empowerment and poverty reduction, the crucial requirement of an opportunity structure is relevant in the achievement of goals in non-poor domains too. The social context of the NMC, i.e. their doxa shapes, powers a strong and predictable opportunity structure.

Hence, adaptive preference is easily overcome where it might be present. The attainable zones are dynamic and provide plentiful pathways to achievements in life. The self-evident norms of education, livelihood securities and wellbeing focus on propelling the individual into an upward spiral of wealth and stability. Figure 17.1 illustrates changes in the capability set of the urban NMC through improvements in education, employment and income levels since 1993–4. There is a distinct trend showing steep increases in the educational levels from 12 per cent graduates to 21 per cent in 2004–5, GDP contribution by the service sector from 44 per cent to 62 per cent in 2004–5 and enhancements in the income categories. The trend also indicates a declining 'deprived income' cohort with an emerging bulge comprising the 'aspiring' and the 'seekers'. The changing boundaries reflect the amorphous feature of the NMC. The aspirations of the NMC are realised through capability enhancements in higher education, better livelihoods and incomes.

The following paragraphs explain the interplay between the NMC habitus, doxa and the aspiration spiral. The habitus of the NMC comprises the family traditions, social, cultural and religious practices and values. As within the normative framework of the CA, these would be family specific within the larger societal universe of this middle class household: the doxa. Figure 17.2 presents a conceptual model of the dynamics between the NMC doxa, habitus and aspirations.

Within the NMC doxa – the larger universe of self-evident norms of higher education, livelihood securities, wellbeing, resource structures and networks, the individual's habitus – the specific traditions and values drive the aspirations. The collective habitus of the NMC influences and creates the doxa. Driven by one's aspirations, the NMC individual strives to achieve his/her goals by expanding their capabilities/opportunities in life through the available and existing structures and networks.

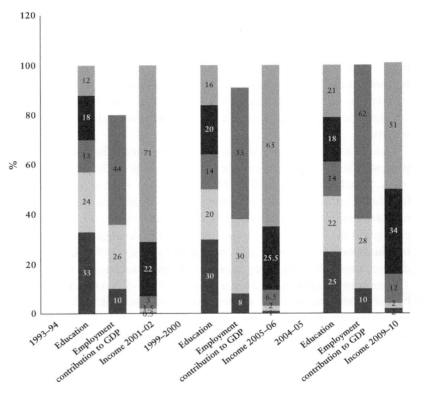

Figure 17.1 NMC capability expansion
Education: Illiterate, Literate primary, Middle school, Secondary, Graduate
and above
Employment: Primary, secondary, tertiary (services)
Income (INR): Rich >1,000,000; Strivers 500,000–1,000,000; Seekers
200,000–500,000; Aspiring 90,000–200,000; Deprived <90,000
Source: Sridharan (2010)

A functioning and enabling opportunity structure is made possible
both by external agencies – the state and the private sector (relational
agency) as well as by the NMC doxa that espouses the demand for
such structures. This idea resonates with Nussbaum's conceptions
of combined capabilities (Lessmann, 2007, Nussbaum, 2011: 22–3).
Nussbaum defines combined capabilities as 'internal capabilities plus
the social/political/economic conditions in which functioning can
actually be chosen' (p. 22). Further, she notes the blurred boundary

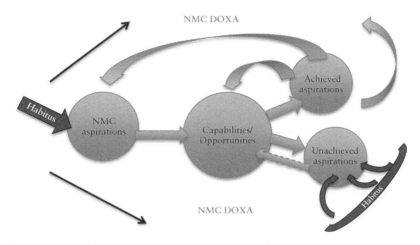

NMC DOXA

NMC DOXA

Figure 17.2 NMC Doxa, habitus and the upward aspiration spiral

between internal and combined capabilities, drawing attention to the external opportunity structure that is necessary for the internal capability to function. Her arguments illustrate the intricately woven landscape of the external opportunity structure essential for creating opportunities and its access by the citizens. A similar point is made by Fernandes and Heller (2006) by drawing attention to the processes adopted by the NMC to access local and state bureaucracy for seeking preferential entitlements in both public and private spaces. Such pathways though lie outside the democratic processes, lack transparency and favour the resolution of NMC issues over the concerns confronting the poor.

The achieved aspirations further engender new aspirations for some individuals in line with Maslow's hierarchy of needs. Additionally, the achieved aspirations also strengthen the opportunity structure by providing pathways to achievement and becoming part of Ray's (2003) attainable zone. This in turn would support aspirations of other NMC individuals as discussed in section previously. The aspirational spiral thus lifts the individual into higher levels of achievements, strengthens the opportunity structure and encourages the same individual to aspire for other higher goals, leading to another step on the social mobility ladder. Those who have unachieved aspirations in most cases have access to social capital and networks comprising family, friends and contacts as well as to a resource structure. Guided by one's habitus,

Table 17.1 NMC *aspiration–agency–capability mapping*

Doxa: macro environment	Habitus: micro environment	Aspiration	Agency needed	Capability and freedoms needed
Networks, social capital, resource access, information availability and access	Values and tradition: seek higher education, find a secure job, strive to improve material wellbeing and ownership of assets, invest in next generation	Professional career	Individual, relational	Education and access to institutions, mobility
		Wellbeing of family	Individual, relational	Healthcare systems, resource networks
		Own a house	Individual	Financial means and access, information
		Children's higher education, career, family	Individual	Means, information, resource networks,
		Own a car	Individual	Resources, access and information
		Travel for leisure	Individual	Means and information
		Be part of a group, participate in activism	Individual and collective	Access to information, group acceptance

the individual is nudged back into the opportunity structure and given a second chance to enhance his/her capability and achieve the aspiration. The habitus thus creates a safety floor below which the individual is prevented from falling.

Table 17.1 outlines the agency, capability and freedoms required to achieve aspirations of the NMC located within their habitus and doxa. The aspiration genre noted in the table is derived from data on ownership of cars and other assets, small surveys conducted in Mumbai,

Patna and Delhi and existing data from NCAER. These indicate dominance of individual agency, followed by relational agency[1] and a feeble presence of collective agency. The NMC life goals.

Attaining higher education, a secured professional career, home ownership and wellbeing of the family are located within the doxa and the habitus of the NMC. This perhaps could be the key difference between the aspirations of the poor and the NMC. The poor do not have the opportunity structure, the networks or the safety that the NMC habitus and doxa create and reinforce. The habitus and the doxa of the NMC create a capability of capabilities terrain: the opportunity to create more opportunities and access these choices that propel them to achieve their life goals.

The Current Development Discourse and the Middle Class Aspirations

Since the beginning of this century with the launch of the millennium development goals (MDGs) in 2000, and the somewhat more elaborate sustainable development goals (SDGs) in 2015, much of the global development discourse has been shaped by the global goals. While UNDP's recognition of the need for urgent attention to sustainable development by formally taking up the recommendation of the Rio+20 Conference in 2012 to produce a set of SDGs is encouraging, the road ahead to achieving these calls for much caution. The proposed SDGs aim to build on the MDGs and converge with the post 2015 development agenda (UN, 2014). By bringing the sustainable development debate to forefront (instead of being tucked away as targets), and as the anchor for the post-2015 agenda, there is clear indication of global commitment to climate change and to address the increasing inequalities. This is reflected in adopting several key dimensions of inequality in addition to health, gender and education being proposed as goals: water and sanitation (Goal 6); energy (Goal 7); inclusive growth and employment for all (Goal 8); reduce inequality within and between countries (Goal 9); make cites and human settlements inclusive and

---

[1] Relational agency refers to the social and institutional context that shapes the opportunities and resources that can be accessed by individuals. For a detailed discussion and its implementation, see Cleaver (2007), Ibrahim and Alkire (2007) and Tiwari (2014).

resilient (Goal 11); sustainable consumption and production (Goal 12); peace and inclusive institutions and justice for all (Goal 16).

Conceptually, how can these be achieved or what are the ingredients necessary to facilitate the achievement of these goals within the framework of CA? Table 17.2 indicates the mapping in terms of unachieved functioning, capabilities/instrumental freedoms and agency required to facilitate the attainment of the three selected SDGs as an example. Let us start with SDG 6: Ensure availability and sustainable management of water and sanitation for all. The starting point is the progress made in the MDGs which was noteworthy with drinking water target met in 2010 albeit with over 650 million people still using unimproved drinking water sources. While progress was made in sanitation provision with 2.1 billion gaining access to improved sanitation since 1990, the target has been missed. The cohorts with unachieved functionings of this SDG are the poorest communities in South Asia and Sub Saharan Africa. Examination of how progress has been possible in this domain (WSP, 2012) reveals collective action through community participation and partnership with state and/or the NGOs to create access, ownership and address information gaps (the instrumental freedoms). These in turn inform and change adaptive preferences and bring about behavioural changes where needed. The constitutive freedoms are the outcomes (the targets) that would be achieved through the required agency and instrumental freedoms of those with the unachieved functioning of the water and sanitation SDG. An examination of the mapping matrix in Table 17.2 also shows dominance of the following two factors. First, the groups with unachieved functionings are more likely to be the poorest, although in some SDGs such as Goal 8 (inclusive growth and employment), Goal 13 (climate change and its impacts) and Goal 16 (peaceful and inclusive societies and accountable and inclusive institutions) , the NMC and the very rich are also affected albeit to a much lesser severity. Second, collective and relational agencies are needed in all of the SDGs noted. As mentioned in the table, individual agency is the starting point: the individual must have a functioning for which she/he would like to act and do something to achieve. In the resource constraint communities whose habitus and doxa are underpinned by a much insecure and vulnerable context, the achievement of functionings is more likely through collective agency galvanising collective means and strengths than through an individual effort. The role of relational agency is also critical in

Table 17.2 *Selected SDGs, agency, instrumental and constitutive freedoms*

SDG	Unachieved functionings	Capability needed: Instrumental freedom	Type of agency needed	Outcome for SHD by 2030: Constitutive freedom
Goal 6: Water and Sanitation	Water scarcity affecting 40 per cent global population is projected to rise > 650 million people use unimproved drinking water Around 1 billion people practice open defecation (OD). 2.4 billion people use poor sanitation facilities	Opportunity to address: water scarcity and inequalities in access Opportunity to access clean drinking water Adequate sanitation provision, access to information on adverse impact of OD on health	Collective and relational: those that do not have access cannot achieve through *individual agency, albeit that is the starting point*	*Sustainable management of water and sanitation for all* • Equitable, safe, affordable water • End OD, access to sanitation and hygiene for all • Reduce pollution, eliminate dumping, halve untreated water • Increase water efficiency • Water management, trans boundary co-operation • Protect and restore water ecosystems • Capacity building to support developing countries • Strengthen local community participation
Goal 7: Energy	1.3 billion people with no access to electricity, 2.6 billion people without clean cooking facilities: 84 per cent of these are in rural areas	Access to affordable and sustainable energy sources	Collective and relational to avail the services, individual as above	*Access to affordable, sustainable energy for all* • Increase share of renewable energy • Double rate of energy efficiency • Global co-operation for clean energy research • Infrastructure and technology for sustainable energy services in developing countries
Goal 8: Inclusive growth and employment for all	Global unemployment rate for youth is three times > adult Employment opportunities in developing and developed countries have diminished	Participative freedoms, education opportunities to enable participation in the growth process	Individual, relational and collective, seen in the Living Wage campaign	*Inclusive, productive, decent work for all* • LDCs to have 7 per cent + growth • Diversification, innovation, high-value added and focus on labour intensive sect • Decent job creation, growth of micro environment • Strengthen domestic institutional capacity • Eradicate: forced and child labour, slavery, trafficking, child soldiers • Protect labour rights

Source: Author's research, data from UNDP (2015)

terms of opportunity provision through public goods via the state and/ or common goods via the NGOs. Third sector organisations such as BRAC and Grameen Bank in Bangladesh are attributed with having a significant role in the overall noteworthy progress made in the country particularly with reference to the education, health and incomes of women (Dreze and Sen, 2013: 58–64).

In the selected SDGs in Table 17.2 the NMC have insignificant presence, although as noted earlier the sustainability issues in the medium to long term in particular will impact everyone, irrespective of the resource networks that appear to mitigate the severity for the rich and middle classes in the short term. Further, the rise of NMC and the aspirations driving them up the mobility ladder appear to be more individual and family-centric where a strong individual agency is the driving force. Relational agency has a role but the resource networks enable aspirational achievement even within a weak institutional infrastructure. Notions of mechanisms that bypass the routine and the electoral processes to enable the privileges and the achievements of the NMC are also discussed in Fernanades and Heller (2006) and Baud (2015).

Conclusions

Conceptual mappings that we saw in Tables 17.1 and 17.2 suggest that the Indian NMC aspirational spiral is underpinned by the NMC habitus and doxa, which enable command over a resource and opportunity structure. The NMC habitus and doxa also create a safety floor and an upward aspirational spiral that nudges unachieved aspirations into other opportunities and reinforce achieved aspirations into professional mobility. The aspirations are driven by an individual agency, which is critical in their achievement. These are no doubt the positive features of the NMC habitus and doxa that can largely be attributed to the rise and recognition of this group as a separate class. The rapid emergence of this group, however, poses some challenges.

The mobility of this class is grounded in values and norms of a modern world that not only distances them from the majority population on low-income insecure jobs but also undermines the existence of the latter. Inequalities in consumption of public services, infrastructure and physical space together with the state's agenda for making Indian cities 'world class' has squeezed and pushed the already marginalised communities in the cities, as also noted by Dupont and Ramanathan (2008) and Upadhya (2008).

The three SDGs selected as examples in Table 17.2 indicate essential requirements of strong collective and relational agencies to facilitate their achievement. In the current context therefore the NMC aspirations appear incompatible in supporting the selected SDGs. One could argue that given their small numbers within the Indian context, this incompatibility can be ignored to allow and encourage their upward mobility. However the disproportionate command and consumption especially within urban contexts poses challenges for the wider development agenda.

Such characteristics of the NMC in India differentiate them from the earlier conceptualisations in the literature that attribute the middle classes with being change agents for the larger society and driving the democratic processes. Within a similar context, Dreze and Sen (2013: 266–73) draw attention to the influence domains of the privileged classes. These enable the middle classes to have an asymmetric reach to all public goods, biased allocation to public revenue and disproportionate voice in the media. Dreze and Sen call it 'a failure of public reasoning' when the privileged are allowed to have far more attention in public spheres while the deprivations of the majority remain largely invisible in any meaningful way.

The NMC engagement with the state often circumvents the democratic processes while their lifestyles often disenfranchise the urban poor from their entitlements. The change is definitely 'negative' albeit worthy of applaud at the personal progress and rapid mobility. After all, the purpose of development is to enhance and facilitate the well-being of people. Here, tensions can be understood within the notions of *means* and *ends* within the capability approach. While the 'ends' of achieving the NMC aspirations are located very much within the development discourse, some of the 'means' by which the NMC are achieving these are problematic. The process often restricts the aspirations and freedoms of the marginalised communities. A considered engagement with the habitus and doxa of the NMC can perhaps influence wider collective goals and collective agency together with a more inclusive approach to other habitants of the city. Bringing their experiences and life skills into the attainable zone of marginalised communities together with helping to forge pathways to achieve aspirations, the NMC could create the *capability of capabilities* for the poor, as they have created for themselves and become drivers of positive change.

References

Acharya, P. (1988) 'Is Macaulay still our guru?' *Economic and Political Weekly*, 23(22), 1124–30.

Adelman, I. and Morris, C. T. (1967) *Society, Politics, and Economic Development: A Quantitative Approach*. Baltimore: Johns Hopkins Press.

Alesina, A., Cozzi, G. and Mantovan, N. (2012) 'The evolution of ideology, fairness and redistribution'. *Economic Journal*, 122(565), 1244–61.

Alsop, R., Bertelsen, M. and Holland, J. (2006) *Empowerment in Practice From Analysis to Implementation*. Washington D.C.: World Bank Institute.

Appadurai, A. (2004) 'The capacity to aspire: culture and the terms of recognition', in V. Rao and M. Walton (Eds.) *Culture and Public Action*. Washington, DC: The World Bank, pp. 59–84.

Baud, I. (2015) 'The emerging middle classes in India: Mobilizing for inclusive development?', *European Journal of Development Research* 27(2), 230–37.

Birdsall, N. (2010) The (indispensable) middle class in developing countries. In: R. Kanbur and M. Spence (Eds.) *Equity and Growth in a Globalizing World*. Washibgton, DC: *World Bank on behalf of the Commission on Growth and Development*, 157–87.

Bernard, T., Taffesse, A. S. and Dercon, S. (2008) 'Aspirations-and-WellBeing-Outcomes-in-Ethiopia': towards an empirical exploration'. Available at: http://www.dfid.gov.uk/r4d/PDF/Outputs/IIG/E13-Aspirations-and-WellBeing-Outcomes-in-Ethiopia.pdf (accessed March 2016).

Bourdieu, P. and Nice, R. (1977) *Outline of a Theory of Practice*. Cambridge: Cambridge University Press.

Clark, D. A. (2002) *Visions of Development: A Study of Human Values* (London: Edward Elgar).

Cleaver, F. (2007) 'Understanding agency in collective action', *Journal of Human Development*, 8(2), 222–44.

Conradie, I. (2013) 'Can deliberate efforts to realise aspirations increase capabilities? A South African case study'. *Oxford Development Studies*, 41(2), 189–219.

Conradie, I. and Robeyns, I. (2013) 'Aspirations and human development interventions'. *Journal of Human Development and Capabilities*, 14(4), 559–80.

Copestake, J. and Camfield, L. (2010) 'Measuring multidimensional aspiration gaps: a means to understanding cultural aspects of poverty'. *Development Policy Review*, 28(5), 617–33.

Decornez, S.S. (1998) 'An empirical analysis of the American middle class (1968–1992)', Ph.D. Dissertation, Vanderbilt University, Nashville, USA, August. Sage.

Dorling, D. (2014) *Inequality and the 1%*. London: Verso Books.

Dreze, J. and Sen, A. (2013) *An Uncertain Glory: India and Its Contradictions*. New Delhi: Allen Lane, 266–73.

Dupont, V. and Ramanathan, U. (2008) 'The courts and the squatter settlements in Delhi – Or the intervention of the judiciary in urban governance'. In I. Baud and J. De Wit (Eds.) *New Forms of Urban Governance of the in India*. New Delhi, India, Sage Publications, 312–343.

Easterly, W. (2001) 'The middle class consensus and economic development'. *Journal of Economic Growth*, 6, 317–35.

Fernandes, L. (2004) 'The politics of forgetting: Class politics, state power and the restructuring of space in India'. *Urban Studies*, 41(12), 2415–30.

Fernandes, L. and Heller, P. (2006) 'Hegemonic aspirations'. *Critical Asian Studies*, 38(4), 495–522.

Forbes, (2016a) Forbes Rich List 2016. Available at: www.ibtimes.co.uk/forbes-rich-list-2016-which-countries-have-most-billionaires-1547107.

(2016b) India's economy surpasses that of Great Britain. Available at: www.forbes.com/sites/realspin/2016/12/16/indias-economy-surpasses-that-of-great-britain/-62068c8b39eb.

Guarin, A. and Knorringa, P. (2014) 'New middle-class consumers in rising powers: Responsible consumption and private standards'. *Oxford Development Studies*, 42(20), 151–71.

Harriss, J. (2005) Middle class activism and poor people's politics: An exploration of civil society in Chennai. Working Paper. London School of Economics.

Ibrahim, S. (2011) *Poverty, Aspirations and Wellbeing: Afraid to Aspire and Unable to Reach a Better Life – Voices from Egypt*. X: Brooks World Poverty Institute.

Ibrahim, S. and Alkire, S. (2007) 'Agency and empowerment: A proposal for internationally comparable indicators'. *Oxford Development Studies*, 35(4), 379–403.

Jaffrelot, C. (2008) 'Why should we vote?: The Indian middle class and the functioning of the world's largest democracy'. In C. Jaffrelot and P. van der Veer (Eds.) *Patterns of Middle Class Consumption in India and China*. New Delhi: Sage, 35–54.

Jaffrelot, C., and van der Veer, P. (2008) 'Introduction'. In C. Jaffrelot and P. van der Veer (Eds.) *Patterns of Middle Class Consumption in India and China* New Delhi: Sage, 11–34.

Jodhka, S. S. and Prakash, A. (2011) The Indian middle class emerging cultures of politics and economics (No. 12). The Konrad-Adenauer-Stiftung. Available at: www.kas.de/wf/doc/kas_29624-544-30.pdf?111205131841

Kharas, H. (2010) The emerging middle class in developing countries. Working Paper 285. Paris: OECD.

Kharas, H. and Gertz, G. (2010) 'The new global middle class: A cross-over from West to East'. In C. Li (Ed.) *China's Emerging Middle Class: Beyond Economic Transformation*. Washington, DC: Brookings Institution Press, 32–54.

Knorringa, P. and Guarin, A. (2015) 'Inequality, sustainability and middle classes in a polycentric world'. *European Journal of Development Research*, 27, 202–4.

Landes, D. (1998) *The Wealth and Poverty of Nations*. New York: Norton.

Lessmann, O. (2007) *Effective Freedom and Combined Capabilities: Two Different Conceptions of Capability*. Available at: www.ortrud-lessmann.de/resources/Lessmann2007.pdf

Loayza, N., Rigolini, J. and Llorente, G. (2012) 'Do Middle Classes Bring Institutional Reforms?' Policy Research Working Paper No. 6015. World Bank, Washington, DC. © World Bank. https://openknowledge.worldbank.org/handle/10986/19866

Maitra, S. (2011) Who are the Indian middle class? A mixture model of class membership based on durables ownership. Available at: http://dept.econ.yorku.ca/~smaitra/SMaitra_middle_class_mixture_May2011.pdf

Marx, K. and Engels, F. (2004) *The Communist Manifesto*. London: Penguin.

Maslow, A. H. (1943) 'A theory of human motivation', *Psychological Review*, 50(4), 370–396.

(1954) *Motivation and Personality*. New York: Harper and Row.

Meyer, C. and Birdsall, N. (2012) New estimates of India's middle class: Technical note. Washington, DC: Centre for Global Development.

Mishra, B. B. (1961) *Indian Middle Classes – Their Growth in Modern Times*. London: Oxford University Press.

Moore, B. (1993) *Social Origins of Dictatorship and Democracy: Lord and Peasant in the Making of the Modern World*. X: Beacon Press.

Moore, M. (1998) 'Death without taxes: Democracy, state capacity and aid dependence in the fourth world'. In M. Robinson and G. White (Eds.) *The Democratic Development State: Political and Institutional Design*. Oxford: Oxford University Press, 84–121.

Narayan, D. (2005) *Measuring empowerment: Cross-disciplinary perspectives*. Washington, DC: World Bank.

Natarajan, I. (1999) *India Market Demographic Report, 1998*. New Delhi: NCAER.

Nayyar, G. (2012) 'The quality of employment in India's services sector: Exploring the heterogeneity'. *Applied Economics*, 44(36), 4701–19.

Nussbaum, M. C. (2011) *Creating Capabilities: The Human Development Approach*. Cambridge, MA: Harvard University Press.

Piketty, T. (2014) *Capital in the Twenty-First Century*. Cambridge, MA: The Belknap Press of Harvard University Press.

Ray, D. (2003) *Aspirations, Poverty and Economic Change*. Mimeo. Available at: www.citeseerx.ist.psu.edu/viewdoc/summary?doi=10.1.1.67.1319.

(2006) 'Aspirations, poverty and economic change'. In A. V. Banerjee, R. Bénabou and D. Mookherjee (Eds.) *Understanding Poverty*. Oxford: Oxford University Press, 409–43.

Sen, A. (2002) 'Health: Perception versus observation'. *British Medical Journal*, 324, 860–1.

(2008) 'The economics of happiness and capability'. In L. Bruni, F. Comim and M. Pugno (Eds.) *Capabilities and Happiness*. New York: Oxford University Press, 16–27.

Stiglitz, J. E. (2012) *The Price of Inequality*. London: Allen Lane.

Sridharan, E. (2010) 'The growth and sectoral composition of India's middle class: Its impact on the politics of economic liberalisation'. *India Review*, 3(4), 405–28.

Tiwari, M. (2014) 'CA, livelihoods and social inclusion: Agents of change in rural India'. In M. Tiwari and S. Ibrahim (Eds.) *Capability Approach: From Theory to Practice*. X: Palgrave, 29–51.

UN (2014) Prototype Sustainable Development Report, United Nations Department of Economic and Social Affairs, New York, https://sustainabledevelopment.un.org/content/documents/1454Prototype%20Global%20SD%20Report2.pdf

UNDP (2015) Sustainable Development Goals, 17 Goals to Transform Our World. Available at: https://www.un.org/sustainabledevelopment/sustainable-development-goals/

Upadhya, C. (2008) 'Rewriting the code: Software professionals and the reconstitution of Indian middle class identity'. In C. Jaffrelot and P. van der Veer (Eds.) *Patterns of Middle Class Consumption in India and China*. New Delhi: Sage, 55–87.

Wahrman, D. (1995) *Imagining the Middle Class: The Political Representation of Class in Britain, c1780–1840*. Cambridge: Cambridge University Press.

World Bank (2012) Economic mobility and the rise of the Latin American middle class. Available at: www.openknowledge.worldbank.org/bitstream/handle/10986/11858/9780821396346.pdf

WSP (2012) *Scaling Up Rural Sanitation, Water and Sanitation Program*. World Bank. Available at: www.wsp.org/sites/wsp.org/files/publications/WSP-What-does-it-take-to-scale-up-rural-sanitation.pdf

18 The Value of Individual and Community Social Resources

PAUL ANAND AND IRIS MANTOVANI

Introduction

It is increasingly recognised that social, as well as financial resources, play a crucial role in contributing to quality of life. The long-standing interests in the concept by the World Bank help to highlight the practical importance for global economic development (Grootaert and Bastelarer, 2001) and there have been a number of influential studies exploring impacts of social capital in business knowledge transfer (Inkpen and Tsang, 2005), health (Kim et al., 2011), economic growth (Beugelsdijk and Schaik, 2005), adaptation to environmental change (Adger, 2010), successful fisheries (Gutiérrez et al., 2011) and happiness (Rodríguez-Pose and Berlepsch, 2014), to name but a few. The term social capital is widely used and although there is some debate about its exact appropriateness, environments of high social quality have been shown to be conducive to economic activity and good quality of life in a wide range of societies (Woolcock and Narayan, 2000; Karayiannis and Hatzis, 2012). Research on capabilities has latched onto the problems with the term 'social capital' but risks missing out on the importance of social resources both at an individual level as well as the community level (as highlighted by Heckman and Corbin (2016), for example). This chapter helps to address the gap by highlighting the potential value both of individual social skills and community social resources.[1]

---

[1] For one thing, social capital seems to follow a different dynamic to financial or physical capital in that its use may increase rather than deplete its value. However, the conversion factors of the capability approach, which measures the ability to transform resources into doings and beings that reasonable persons value, clearly do in part depend on a person's internal and external social resources. In this chapter I shall focus particularly on the internal social resources of the individual, such as their networks as well as the external social resources (for example, trust) that are available for use by virtue of the communities they inhabit. My motivation is essentially thematic and pragmatic – if we accept the need for an approach to development that emphasises the human rather than just the financial factors, then it is sensible to

Research on the benefits of social resources has contributed to and been part of the idea that countries should not merely seek to maximise growth (measured financially) but rather pursue forms of progress that are socially inclusive and wellbeing oriented. In turn, these ideas leave open the possibility that some forms of growth could erode or 'crowd out' social goals and resources (Frey, 1994). We know a lot about the meanings and consequences of social resources although it would seem that there are few published attempts at valuation, with the arguable exception of studies that model the contribution of social capital to economic growth. That said, in recent years growing interest in happiness (often more strictly life-satisfaction based) methods of valuation have led to the production of valuations of significant social events (from being a victim of crime to the loss of a family member) which have the capacity to feed into policy analysis. There are strong parallels here with the interest in methods of environmental valuation, for policy-makers to know how much priority should be given to any particular environmental externality not reflected in markets transactions, some kind of evaluation is essential. Similarly, economists are becoming interested in the social aspects of wellbeing, which are not normally reflected in a country's national accounts; there is need not for measures of such resources but for assessments of their value. The capability approach draws motivation in part from well-understood and accepted critiques of reliance on market valuations alone, but one can argue, as we do here, that it should not throw the proverbial baby of information and analysis out with the bathwater of imperfect measures. It has advocated consultation and reasoning as contributions to the understanding of value and these are indeed valuable contributions but there is often a need to quantify, both to aid priority setting and communication between different groups and the approach has not said much about its own approach to valuation. However, the approach is based on some relations between resources and experiential wellbeing and so we shall use these relations to justify the use of a life-satisfaction valuation method on the understanding that one is extracting informational value from experience not using observed behaviour as a gold standard metric of value and entitlement. We use therefore a quantitative approach but interpret the results

take social resources into account. Our working hypothesis is that development policies that fail to do so run the risk of being inefficient and possibly worse.

as indicators rather than measures. Much has been said in recent times about the measurement of material poverty but here we want to make a slightly different point, namely, that social resources might also play a role not only in characterising deprivation but also in helping people and policy makers find pathways away from it.

We believe this is the first set of research to provide an economic valuation of social resources and also to make a distinction in doing so between individual and community social capital.[2] Potentially, therefore, the estimates could contribute to understanding methods for valuing social capital as well as its value in this current setting. Beyond these economics and policy concern, social resources contribute to other aspects of life quality of life, ranging from health and safety to autonomy and social inclusion that are not always closely correlated with national income based measures of progress (Sen, 1999; Diener and Biswas-Diener, 2011; Huppert and So, 2013). For all these reasons it is useful to know how much value people derive from the social resources to which they have access. Estimates, which are contextualised in comparison with others, indicate that social resources are indeed of positive, significant value and that it merits priority in policy making. This approach also raises theoretical conceptual and methodological questions about how 'capability' research can or should engage with the literature on social resources and this is addressed more fully in our concluding discussion. For the moment, however, one shall simply assume intuitively that the 'human' approach to development to which the capabilities approach has given rise is open to the idea that not only outcomes but also inputs should have a distinct human or social aspect. But how might this be done?

If we go back to the only formal version of the approach developed by Sen (1985) we might note the importance of three equations. First,

---

[2] The relations underlying the life satisfaction method used are those found in Sen's (1985) original formal version of the approach (see also Bruni et al (2008) on the complementarities between the capability and happiness perspectives. Capabilities researchers are concerned, rightly, about the limits for claims that actual preferences have, given their adaptive nature, and so we should be mind of a potential asymmetry here. The costs of bads may be undervalued and the pursuit of goods can be self-defeating, but neither concern seems to bear directly on what we might think if we find that rather than being invisible, social resources actually seem to have a significant positive value on average. See also Powdthavee for a related economic evaluation of friendship as well as Knack and Keefer (1997) who look at the contribution of social resources to economic growth.

valued activities and states depend on resources and abilities to covert the latter into the former. Second, experienced happiness depends on valued activities and states. Third, the set of all activities and states possible given a person's resources and abilities can be defined as a measure of their advantage. This provides a relatively general grammar for the analysis of wellbeing that could be meaningfully applied across a wide stretch of human anthropology and history. In this chapter, we draw on the equations in a way that is novel and perhaps even controversial but that hopefully provides capabilities researchers a coherent way of incorporating social resources into their analysis and thinking. In the first instance, we take the view that resources are social as well as financial and that means that the social quality of the environment in which one lives is potentially a factor that could impact development (whether human or economic). Typically, despite resources being a general concept, capabilities research tends to operationalise the concept financially: We argue in this chapter for the value of also including non-financial resources. Second, it can be noted that whilst the 'problem of adaptive preferences' is correctly used to avoid taking indifference to undesirable states or acts at face value, this has also led to a throwing out of the baby with the bathwater problem as experienced utility judgments often do have some informational value about the judgments about goods and bads that people make. There is no single ideal gold standard method for finding out what people have reason to value, for example, and so in trying to understand valuations, we cannot avoid triangulating the results of different methods being mindful of their relative strengths and weaknesses. In this case, one can conclude that the rankings derived from the life satisfaction method do have informational value about the significance of social resources.

The remainder of this chapter is structured as follows. The second section provides a discussion of the concept of social resources drawing particularly on the existing social capital literature and motivates the method of valuation used in the paper described in third section. The following two sections introduce the data and some descriptive results concerning the variation of social capital across socioeconomic and demographic groups. The sixth section presents and discusses the estimation of the marginal utility of income and social capital, together with estimates for the value of social capital whilst the chapter concludes with a discussion of how social resources are important both theoretically within the capability and for the practice of human development that it seeks to support.

Social Capital and Valuation Methods

The literature has tended to use the term 'social capital' to refer to kinds of social resources we consider valuable and for present purposes we follow this practice. Various definitions exist but the concept of a social resource created through formal and informal relationships between people within a community is widely accepted. As such, social capital refers to the environment that people live in, and comprises the collective resources to which individuals, families, neighbourhoods and communities have access (see for instance, Harper, 2001).[3] The idea that involvement and participation in groups can have positive consequences for individuals and societies alike is not new, as Portes (1998) notes, and can be dated back at least to work by the sociologist Durkheim (1897/1951) whose influential work on the subject saw group life as an 'antidote to anomie and self-destruction'.[4]

Even if it is a valuable resource, social capital is also a non-market service and its value is not measured routinely and reflected in national GDP figures as is the case with physical and human capital.[5] A major challenge for policy is, therefore, is one of valuation. Traditionally, three main methods have been used to ascertain the value of non-market goods from people's preferences and market behaviours: (1) revealed preference, (2) hedonic price and (3) stated preference (or

---

[3] A definition particularly oriented to growth and development issues can be found in World Bank (Dasgupta and Serageldin, 1999) which argues that it 'refers to the institutions, relationships, and norms that shape the quality and quantity of a society's social interactions. Increasing evidence show that social cohesion is critical for societies to prosper economically and for development to be sustainable. Social capital is not just the sum of the institutions [that] underpin a society – it is the glue that holds them together'.

[4] See Portes (1998: 2).

[5] Historically, the measurement of the stock of social capital has been conducted through a count of the involvement in formal organisations and clubs, e.g. bowling clubs, rotary charters, and teacher-parent organisations (Putnam, 1995). Research has distinguished between 'bonding', 'bridging' and 'linking' social capital, which serve the purpose of 'getting by' in life on a daily basis, 'getting ahead' in society, and 'garnering resources or power', respectively. Subsequently, empirical measures have reflected a distinction between social resources that are particular to individuals, and those available to all (effectively, public goods), and this is a distinction which our data allows us to make in our analysis. There has been a major debate about whether social capital is in decline – see for example Sarracino (2010) – and this work, whilst not directly contributing to that debate does help to indicate the materiality of such changes, if they are real and widespread.

contingent valuation) methods. With revealed preference techniques, estimates of value are uncovered using evidence of how people behave in the face of real choices in complementary or substitutive markets. Rao et al. (2003), for example, use a revealed preference approach to estimate the cost of safe sex as the price penalty that prostitutes incur for using condoms with their clients. This method relies on there being a natural experiment that identifies a counterfactual group of people not exposed to the same treatment – and such a group may not always exist. By contrast, Gibbons and Machin (2008) use a hedonic regression analysis to estimate the value of public services and school quality. This method relies on there being a marketable good, such as housing, whose price changes systematically with the quality of the non-marketed good – in this case, both public services and school quality taken together. As long as house prices are in equilibrium, houses only differ to the extent that they are located in areas with differing exposures to the good, house prices will reflect the good's value – but of course these can be strong assumptions to make in practice. Finally, a third method often used in valuation studies and not based on market observations asks respondents directly about the value they place on the good. Using this so-called 'stated preference' approach, Atkinson, Healey and Mourato (2005) have estimated that different types of crime can cost each victim up to £36,000 in the UK. Where there are no market data, the approach can be difficult to avoid but it has been noted that it is susceptible to strategic responses if people think that their answer may affect public provision but have little impact on their own financial contributions.

This chapter offers a fourth, alternative method for valuing social capital. The essence of our approach is to develop data on social resources and to calculate valuations based on impacts, equivalent to income changes, from life satisfaction equations.[6] This approach does not require any assumptions about market equilibria, the existence of choices, or the consistency of choice with life satisfaction. Respondents are simply asked to provide a subjective measure of life satisfaction which is then modelled using potential determinants and controls. There is no requirement, furthermore, for respondents to have perfect

---

[6] Such methods are now entering into economic policy analysis also – see for example Fujiwara, Oroyemi and McKinnon (2013).

information about the non-market good or service being valued nor is there any need for them to reveal or state a preference. Thus preference anomalies are not involved and value estimates are constructed on the basis of how the non-market good in question actually affects a person's experienced life satisfaction.

A central assumption of the approach, however, is that self-reported life satisfaction is a good indicator of overall utility. Whilst all self-reported measures are subject to various biases of one sort or another, there is a large research literature from psychology and health that shows such measures can be reliable and valid.[7] There is also mounting evidence that the relation between life satisfaction and several important sociodemographic and economic factors is stable across different studies (Frey and Stutzer, 2002), that major events in a lifetime – such as divorce, job loss or bereavement – often have permanent effects on one's life satisfaction (Lucas et al., 2003) and that the importance of different domains of life – for example health, intimacy and material well-being – is also relatively stable (Cummins, 1996). Similarly Anand et al. (2009) find that a wide range of quite different capability dimensions show up in life satisfaction equations – there are many different kinds of things that make a life go well and these show up in data because we do not adapt instantly – or even nearly completely in the case of status changes. That said, it is also now accepted widely that different measures of experience track slightly different aspects of life quality and for this reason we shall also report analyses using a weighted index of four such measures. Overall then, the primary aim is to show how estimates of social resources can be derived using this method.

An Experience-Based Method for Valuing Social Resources

As our approach assumes that self-reported life satisfaction is a good proxy for value (utility) and estimates a utility function U, that depends positively on household income, y, and on social capital SC, it is reasonable to use a standard compensating variation measure of value. This is just the amount of money or value required to compensate a person for some event (traditionally a price change) that gives rise to a gain or loss in utility. In the present case, the compensating variation

[7] See Clark, Frijters and Shields (2006).

for social capital, CV, can be obtained by identifying the utility gain derived from a unit increase in social capital.[8] More explicitly and formally, a life satisfaction equation can be written thus:

$$U^0(y^0, SC^0) = U^1(y^0 + CV, SC^1) \tag{18.1}$$

In this case, the superscript 0 and 1 denote utility before and after some change in social capital. Using a linear life satisfaction equation, the expected utility given any particular value of social capital can be written as:

$$E(U_i|SC_i, y_i, X_i) = \beta_0 + \beta_y y_i + \beta_{sc} SC_i + \gamma' X_i + \varepsilon_i, \tag{18.2}$$

where X represents all additional covariates. CV then becomes a solution to the equation,

$$E(U_i|SC_i^0, y_i^0, X_i) = E(U_i|SC_i^0 + 1, y_i^0 + CV, X_i), \tag{18.3}$$

which in turn implies that

$$CV = \frac{\beta_{SC}}{\beta_y} \tag{18.4}$$

In economic applications of the life satisfaction approach, income usually enters in logarithmic form to account for the diminishing marginal utility of income.[9] Under this specification, CV is the solution to the equation,

$$E(U_i|SC_i^0, \ln(y_i^0), X_i) = E(U_i|SC_i^0 + 1, \ln(y_i^0 + CV), X_i) \tag{18.5}$$

---

[8] Although not previously used to estimate the value of social capital, as far as we aware, this approach has been applied to the valuation of domestic violence (Santos, 2013); volunteering (Fujiwara, Oroyemi and McKinnon, 2013); the inflation/unemployment trade-off (Di Tella, MacCulloch and Oswald, 2001); droughts (Carroll, Frijters and Shields, 2009) and floods (Luechinger and Raschky, 2009); informal care (Van den Berg and Ferrer-i-Carbonell, 2007); bereavement (Oswald and Powdthavee, 2008; Deaton, Fortson and Tortora, 2009); urban renewal (Dolan and Metcalfe, 2008), air quality (Van Praag and Baarsma, 2001; Luechinger, 2009; Levinson, 2012); terrorism (Frey, Luechinger and Stutzer, 2004); and commuting time (Stutzer and Frey, 2004). There is a much larger literature now on satisfaction with particular aspects of life – see for instance literature on personal finance (Brown, Taylor and Price, 2005); aesthetics (Baddeley, 2007); work (Poggi, 2010); development (Graham, 2005) as well reviews by Clark et al. (2008); Dolan et al. (2008) and Dolan and Galizzi (2015).

[9] Fujiwara and Campbell (2011).

which implies that

$$CV = \exp\left(-\frac{\beta_{SC}}{\beta_y} + \ln \bar{y}\right) - \bar{y} \tag{18.6}$$

where $\bar{y}i$ is average household equivalised income.[10] In our results (the results of our empirical estimation presented in this chapter), valuations are reported based on both linear and logarithmic formulations as described. Some significant variations arise as a result although they are not sufficient to make dramatic changes to the ranking of changes in social capital compared with other factors.

Data and Empirical Methods

The data used in this study derive from a unique dataset discussed in more detail in Anand, Roope and Gray (2014). The original survey instrument was designed to generate data on various aspects of life quality and the final survey was delivered in the UK and US in 2012 by YOUGOV, an opinion polling and market research organisation.[11] In both countries, the respective panels of respondents were drawn equally from several geographic regions and are roughly representative of working-age adults in terms of age, gender and social class: samples sizes of 1061 and 1691 were generated in the US and the UK, respectively.

Our survey data include four questions designed to measure variants of experienced utility[12] (Table 18.1). These are related to overall life satisfaction, the level of happiness experienced yesterday, the level of anxiety experienced yesterday and the extent to which individuals feel the things they do in life are worthwhile.[13] Responses are provided on a scale from 0 (= lowest score) to 10 (= highest score); in our main empirical results, we report two sets of analyses, one considers life satisfaction alone and the other is an equally weighted average of all four happiness measures.[14]

---

[10] See Fujiwara, Oroyemi and McKinnon (2013).
[11] We did not analyse data for a third country covered by this survey as there were signs of a slightly different underlying mix of respondents.
[12] See ONS (2014).
[13] These were embedded in the survey instrument following recent research by the Office of National Statistics.
[14] Note that we rescale question 3 such that responses are 0 for high levels of anxiety and 10 for low levels of anxiety.

Table 18.1 *Measures of experienced utility*

ONS4 happiness	Life satisfaction	Question	Responses (N pooled)										
			0 – Lowest	1	2	3	4	5	6	7	8	9	10 – Highest
Yes	Yes	Overall, how satisfied are you with your life nowadays?	72	47	113	209	186	346	368	613	484	194	120
Yes	No	Overall, how happy did you feel yesterday?	62	76	143	180	207	383	367	532	455	203	144
Yes	No	Overall, how anxious did you feel yesterday?	241	226	330	307	279	416	266	278	222	117	70
Yes	No	Overall, to what extent do you feel that the things you do in life are worthwhile?	76	62	111	164	190	360	378	482	441	275	213

The dataset also contains two sets of questions that were designed to capture different elements of social capital. The first set of questions is related to the quality of the social environment of the respondent as highlighted in Maggino (2006), e.g. the extent to which individuals treat each other fairly, engage in community volunteering, trust local government officials, and so forth, which we label 'community social capital'. The second set of questions is more reflective of the social skills of the respondents (e.g. ability to diffuse a difficult situation or negotiate), and will henceforth be referred to as 'individual social capital' – following the term developed or at least advocated by two statistical sociologists: Van Der Gaag and Snijders (2003).[15] Table 18.2 summarises the questions designed to measure both aspects of social capital. Responses are provided on a scale from 0 (= strongly disagree) to 10 (= strongly agree): two social capital indices are constructed by assigning equal weights to all questions.

The income variable included in the data is gross annual household income (i.e. combined income of all earners in the household, including wages, salaries and rent, before taxes or deductions). Respondents are asked to select one of eight income bands.[16] Only 12 respondents (all from the UK) refused to provide an answer for household income, and were dropped from the analysis.[17] As controls, we consider sociodemographic factors that have been found in the literature to have a systematic relationship with happiness, such age, gender and ethnicity. In addition we control for any shocks to utility (including

---

[15] The term may seem puzzling if one thinks of social capital as an external feature of the environment but less so if we focus on the concept of social resources which we believe is more useful in human approaches to human development. Some individuals as a matter of fact have large and active networks whilst others do not – and this makes a difference to who the winners and losers from any development initiative are likely to be.

[16] The intervals are: Up to £10,000; £10,000–£19,999; £20,000–£29,999; £30,000–£39,999; £40,000–£49,999; £50,000–£74,999; £75,000–£99,999; and, £100,000 or more (and equivalent bands in USD).

[17] While providing income data as intervals increases the likelihood of obtaining truthful responses, this study requires a continuous measure of income. Thus, we replace each income band value from 1 to 7 with the midpoint of the interval, and replace the top income band with £100,000. Moreover, we normalise income by the number of equivalent adults in the household to account for economies of scale in household consumption and construct a measure of *equivalised* income.

Table 18.2 *Measures of social resources*

Question	Responses (N pooled)											
	0 – Strongly disagree	1	2	3	4	5	6	7	8	9	10 – Strongly agree	
We can strike up a conversation with most new people I meet	81	49	128	150	156	288	311	420	417	304	448	
We can diffuse a difficult situation	64	40	73	110	176	391	419	522	487	219	251	
We can provide leadership in a group	82	56	74	116	165	329	345	482	504	284	315	
We can take guidance from a group leader	35	19	21	41	91	268	275	542	644	411	405	
We can negotiate effectively	42	24	53	77	135	358	345	532	575	321	290	
We can see things from other people's point of view	17	6	22	34	70	237	239	434	617	523	553	

Individual social capital

(cont.)

Table 18.2 (cont.)

Question	Responses (N pooled)										
	0 – Strongly disagree	1	2	3	4	5	6	7	8	9	10 – Strongly agree
Community social capital People in my community are helpful	85	47	92	129	154	475	345	475	407	226	317
People in my community get along	63	31	72	92	136	420	341	536	480	275	306
People in my community treat each other fairly	70	38	71	96	141	465	305	493	478	293	302
People in my community would help us if someone in the family was ill	155	85	121	165	175	489	285	360	352	260	305
People in my community engage in community volunteering	205	126	162	213	224	670	324	325	222	118	163
People in my community trust local government officials	275	148	197	230	244	723	293	300	187	85	70

These questions are part of a larger survey designed to provide a full and direct operationalisation of the capability approach to welfare economics (Sen, 1999). This is the only tailor-made dataset to do this so far as we are aware though there is a now huge literature that

unemployment, permanent illness, divorce, separation and bereavement), and a generic measure of health status (the EQ5D index).[18]

Given the cross-sectional nature of the data and variables used, there are obvious potential endogeneity effects that could be addressed using, for example, a fixed effects approach applied to panel data. As a partial control for possible simultaneity of income and life satisfaction we therefore include a set of personality variables.[19] These are derived from a set of 10 questions that cover the Big Five[20] Dimensions of personality:[21] (1) extraversion vs introversion; (2) agreeableness vs antagonism; (3) conscientiousness vs lack of direction; (4) neuroticism vs emotional stability; and (5) openness vs closedness to experience. Personality variables can be expected to provide controls for some of the unobserved determinants of life satisfaction given the thermostat theory that holds that people have relatively fixed internal levels of happiness, but equally it should be recognised that this may not offer a complete solution to the problem.

We consider a long list of activities that the respondent was involved in yesterday and, alternatively, whether yesterday was a normal workday, to account for the possibility that the effects on happiness of the daily activities in which someone is involved may depend on whether or not they were working that day. Table 18.3 summarises the key determinants of life satisfaction considered in this work and provides some descriptive statistics from our sample.

The main results present estimates from ordinary least squares regressions in keeping with recent practice which in some areas (economics of happiness and wellbeing for example) has adopted this practice as results using limited dependent models are generally rather

---

[18] This is a health index developed by EuroQol Group on the basis of five standard health questions, widely used in different countries by clinical researchers in a variety of clinical areas. See www.euroqol.org/.

[19] These are in place of fixed effects which would be available if we had panel data – personality is relatively fixed but only partly controls for any endogeneity.

[20] The Big Five are to psychology what the twelve bar blues are to jazz – they are by no means the end of the story but even for many psychologists they are a natural starting point. In its STEPS program, the World Bank develops a measure of non-cognitive skills based on the big five, grit and other measures, see Pierre et al. (2014).

[21] See John and Srivastava (1999).

Table 18.3 *Determinants of life satisfaction*

Categories	Variables	Value
Sociodemographic traits	Age	40.1 years
	Male	50.1%
	White	88.8%
Shocks	Unemployed	9.1%
	Permanently ill or disabled	6.5%
	Divorced/separated/widowed	8.7%
Health issues (moderate or extreme)	Mobility	16.2%
	Self-care	6.4%
	Usual activities	17.0%
	Pain	40.7%
	Anxiety	43.8%
Personality domains	Extraversion	4.6
	Agreeableness	6.5
	Conscientiousness	7.0
	Emotional stability	6.6
	Openness to experience	6.3
Activity involvement yesterday	Normal workday	65.9%
	Attending an evening class	3.1%
	Caring for someone ill or frail	7.1%
	Community	29.1%
	Cooking	47.2%
	DIY	11.1%
	Drinking alcohol	26.5%
	Eating	75.5%
	Exercising	26.6%
	Housework	50.3%
	Internet (for paid employment)	77.9%
	Internet (for personal use)	22.1%
	Intimate relations	17.5%
	Listening to music	51.3%
	Looking after a pet	36.7%

Table 18.3 *(cont.)*

Categories	Variables	Value
	Other outdoor activities	12.9%
	Paid employment	44.8%
	Playing a musical instrument	6.1%
	Praying or meditating	15.2%
	Reading for pleasure	35.8%
	Relaxing or napping	46.2%
	Self-care	29.7%
	Shopping	14.4%
	Smoking tobacco	31.9%
	Socialising	33.1%
	Time with children	28.9%
	Visiting a cinema/concert/gallery/ museum	80.2%
	Visiting a park or the countryside	77.7%
	Volunteering	76.2%
	Watching TV	94.5%

Note: The full sample (N = 2752) responded to all questions relevant to this table, except for 73 UK respondents that did not answer the questions relating to 'normal workday' and 'personality domains' (N = 2679). Personality questions are measured on a scale from 0 (= strongly disagree) to 10 (= strongly agree). Health issues can be either 'none', 'moderate' or 'extreme'.

similar although any single set of coefficients could be misleading as they vary throughout the dataset.

UK and US Estimated Values of Social Capital

Before coming to our main empirical results in the following section, we should briefly examine how sociodemographic characteristics are related to reported happiness and perceptions of the internal and external social resources that we wish to better understand On a scale from 0 to 10, average self-reported life satisfaction is 5.9 and 6.3 in the UK and US, respectively. Average happiness is 5.8 in the UK and

6.2 in the US. Respondents report higher individual social capital than community social capital, on average (6.7–7.2 compared to 5.7–6.1).

Table 18.8 in Appendix 18A shows the average levels of reported happiness and social capital for different sociodemographic groups. Women in the UK tend to report slightly higher levels of happiness and social capital, while the same is not true of the US. Both happiness and social capital are increasing in the level of household income. Moreover, respondents in the US tend to report higher levels of happiness and social capital across income brackets.[22] As expected, individuals who experienced shocks to income and utility report lower average levels of happiness: the lowest levels are observed among the unemployed, followed by the permanently sick or disabled, and then the separated, divorced or widowed. Highest levels of happiness are observed among those in employment and those in retirement. With the exception of retirees, all groups considered report higher average levels of life satisfaction and happiness in the US than the UK.

Levels of reported individual social capital, which are a (self-reported) indicator of the respondent's social skills, range, on average, across all groups, from 5.8 to 7.3 in the UK and 6.5 to 7.7 in the US. Those with lowest self-reported social skills are the permanently sick, while those with the highest tend to be self-employed and married. Community social capital varies less systematically across respondents, perhaps reflecting that the quality of the environment is independent of potential shocks to income, health and general wellbeing. Nevertheless, unemployed individuals score the lowest in terms of community social capital as well.

Empirical Results

This chapter's main results focus on estimates of the value of personal and external social resources capital based on the compensating variation measure. As explained previously, we use self-reported wellbeing as a measure of utility and assume it depends linearly on the social capital based measures employed and household income – see Equation (18.2). Table 18.8 in Appendix 18A shows the estimation results of life satisfaction equations defined according to Equation (18.2). The

---

[22] Income brackets are reported in GBP but respondents were offered equivalents brackets in USD in the US.

first three columns use life satisfaction as a proxy for utility. The last three columns use the ONS4 happiness index as a proxy for utility. Results for each two measures are presented for the whole sample and for the UK and US separately. The sociodemographic indicators used are as previously explained: the estimated models use a gender dummy, a quadratic function of age, and an ethnicity dummy (white, non-white).[23]

Income, social capital and social skills all have a positive and significant impact on happiness. For every £10,000 increase in income, life satisfaction increases by 0.07, which corresponds to 0.7 per cent. For a 10 per cent increase in social capital, happiness increases by around 2.5 per cent. Results are similar, although smaller, with the happiness index. In terms of demographics, men report systematically lower life satisfaction than women; controlling for income, ethnicity has no impact. Happiness appears to have the well-documented U-shaped relationship associated with age. Good health has a strong positive impact on happiness, while shocks to income and utility have a strong negative effect on happiness. Extraversion and emotional stability are the strongest predictors of happiness out of the personality indices and, having controlled for unemployment shocks, yesterday's activities are insignificant in determining happiness. Table 18.6 shows our estimates of the compensating variation of social capital according to Equation (18.4):

$$CV = \frac{\beta_{SC}}{\beta_y} \tag{18.4}$$

The value of social resources is estimated to be over £30,000. This value is as high as £66,000 for the UK using the ONS4 happiness index, although this may in part be explained by the particularly weak relationship observed between the happiness index and household income. Social resources at the individual level are valued less, ranging £18,000–£28,000 in the US and £25,000–£25,000 in the UK. In other

---

[23] To allow for possible the endogeneity of household income, we include health status and a shocks dummy, which should reflect shocks to utility that lead individuals to revise their decisions about generating income. In addition, and as noted above, we include personality variables as a way creating of partial fixed effect factors. Finally, under the assumption that reported happiness may vary on the basis of daily activities we include a dummy that captures whether the day on which activities were reported was a normal workday.

words, social resources seem to matter quite a bit and perhaps these are underestimates if we allow for adaptation. But we should not be surprised – a human approach to development could simply try to take a human perspective on economic growth but we believe that our evidence is pointing to the need to take social resources more explicitly into account when thinking about development planning.

In a second specification we allow for diminishing marginal utility of income, by applying the log transformation to our measure of equivalised household income (Table 18.7). Under this specification, a 10 per cent increase in equivalised household income is associated with 0.14 per cent increase in happiness. As mentioned previously, the calculation for compensating variation becomes slightly more involved, and follows Equation (18.6):

$$CV = \exp\left(-\frac{\beta_{SC}}{\beta_y} + \ln\bar{y}\right) - \bar{y},$$

$$\text{(18.6)}$$

$$CV = \exp\left(-\frac{\beta_{SR}}{\beta_y} + \ln\bar{y}\right) - \bar{y}.$$

Allowing for diminishing marginal utility greatly reduces the magnitude of our estimates and the variations across countries and utility specifications: estimated value of community social capital is in the range £20,000–£26,000 and for individual social capital, in the range £16,000–£21,000.

Because each observation of social capital and subjective wellbeing are reported by the same individual, our models may suffer from shared method variance (spurious correlation between variables that arises due to the measurement method rather than to the constructs the measures are assumed to represent) or endogeneity. To address this potential source of bias, in a third specification we apply objective measures of environmental deprivation and reports of daily involvement in activities as instruments for levels of community and individual social capital, respectively.[24] Specifically, for the UK, we are able

---

[24] Arguably these are more objectively measured than the variables for which they are instruments and correlated with them.

to match income and happiness data to the UK Index of Multiple Deprivation (IMD) based on postcode information. Moreover, the survey provides information on the respondents' involvement in a list of 29 activities yesterday (see Table 18.4).[25] Thus, in the first stage regression of the IV model, we use the IMD to instrument for community social capital and activity involvement yesterday for individual social capital. The instrument for self-reported community social capital is highly significant in the first stage regression in the direction anticipated, and it passes Card's (1995) refutability test. On the other hand, the relationship between activity involvement and self-reported individual social capital is weak: none of the first-stage instruments is significant and jointly they are also insignificant. Thus we consider these unreliable instruments for individual social capital. Nonetheless, instrumenting for community social capital does not vary our results significantly: community social capital is valued £18,500–£22,028 in our preferred specification that excludes individual social capital.

To help interpret these results, Table 18.5 places them in the context of valuations of other experiences and non-market goods, ranging as high as £200,000 for the death of one's partner to £156 for noise pollution from aircrafts. Estimates for social capital in the logarithmic specification fall somewhere between the value of frequent participation in voluntary work (£13,500) and the cost of having ever experienced domestic violence (£27,170).

Conclusion

It is widely recognised that some forms of growth and economic development are more sustainable than others and that the same might be true with respect to life quality. Social resources, through the concept of social capital, has been used extensively across many disciplines to refer to issues that are of social and economic importance but not explicitly reflected in consumption or production. This has become a standard for work in development, sociology and economics for work

---

[25] Activity involvement yesterday is reported via a binary response (yes/no) to specific prompts. Whilst even questions such as these are not immune from person specific reporting effects, the impact of such effects is arguably less than it would be for numerically valued questions of a more perceptual or subjective nature.

Table 18.4 *Happiness equations: Instrumental variables*

	Life satisfaction	ONS4 happiness	Life satisfaction	ONS4 happiness
	UK	UK	UK	UK
Community SC	0.353**	0.259*	0.488***	0.373***
	(0.163)	(0.135)	(0.144)	(0.117)
Individual SC	0.697***	0.589***		
	(0.264)	(0.219)		
Log Equivalised HH Income	0.167	0.009	0.365***	0.176*
	(0.140)	(0.116)	(0.111)	(0.090)
Age	−0.059	−0.086	−0.058	−0.085*
	(0.064)	(0.053)	(0.059)	(0.048)
Age^2	0.001	0.001	0.001	0.001*
	(0.001)	(0.001)	(0.001)	(0.001)
Gender (= Male)	−0.093	0.059	−0.230	−0.057
	(0.180)	(0.149)	(0.160)	(0.130)
Ethnicity (=White)	−0.301	−0.296	−0.467	−0.437*
	(0.326)	(0.271)	(0.299)	(0.243)
Health (EQ5D)	1.538***	1.453***	1.718***	1.604***
	(0.478)	(0.397)	(0.442)	(0.359)
Shocks	−0.652**	−0.295	−0.823***	−0.440**
	(0.255)	(0.211)	(0.230)	(0.187)
Extraversion	−0.077	−0.045	0.081*	0.089**
	(0.077)	(0.063)	(0.044)	(0.036)
Agreeableness	0.045	0.049	0.080	0.078*
	(0.055)	(0.046)	(0.050)	(0.041)
Conscientiousness	−0.111*	−0.090*	−0.003	0.001
	(0.063)	(0.052)	(0.045)	(0.037)
Emotional stability	0.016	0.082*	0.113**	0.163***
	(0.060)	(0.050)	(0.044)	(0.036)
Openness	−0.112	−0.068	0.019	0.043
	(0.070)	(0.058)	(0.046)	(0.037)

Table 18.4 *(cont.)*

	Life satisfaction	ONS4 happiness	Life satisfaction	ONS4 happiness
Normal workday	0.151	0.230	0.104	0.190
	(0.188)	(0.156)	(0.174)	(0.142)
Constant	−0.637	−1.165	−1.652	−2.023
	(1.744)	(1.446)	(1.587)	(1.291)
Observations	522	522	522	522
R-squared	0.320	0.320	0.408	0.431
Value of Community SC	£22,009	£25,033	£18,459	£22,028
Value of individual SC	£24,648	£25,033		

Note: Standard errors of the means are given in parentheses. *10 per cent, **5 per cent, ***1 per cent. Omitted categories are female and non-white. ONS4 constructed as the average of the scores across the questions in Table 18.1. Mean household equivalised income, $\bar{y}$, is £25,033 in the UK and £27,785 ($43,397) in the US.

Table 18.5 *Experience-based methods of valuation in the literature*

Subject	Description	Value/cost (in annual HH income)	Source
Bereavement	Loss of partner	£206,000	Oswald and Powdthavee (2008)
Bereavement	Loss of child	£137,000	Oswald and Powdthavee (2008)
Bereavement	Loss of father	£78,000	Oswald and Powdthavee (2008)
Bereavement	Loss of mother	£61,000	Oswald and Powdthavee (2008)
Domestic violence	Current exposure to domestic violence	£60,123	Santos (2013)

Table 18.5 *(cont.)*

Subject	Description	Value/cost (in annual HH income)	Source
Bereavement	Loss of sibling	£32,000	Oswald and Powdthavee (2008)
Domestic violence	Past experience of domestic violence	£27,170	Santos (2013)
Community social capital	*Social ties and networks*	£20,000–£26,000	This study
Individual social capital	*Social skills*	£16,000–£21,000	This study
Volunteering	Participation in voluntary work at least once a month	£13,500	Fujiwara, Oroyemi and McKinnon (2013)
Urban renewal	Regeneration of private sector housing in neighbourhood	£6,400–£19,000	Dolan and Metcalfe (2008)
Droughts	Spring drought in rural areas	A$18,000 (£6,497)	Carroll, Frijters and Shields (2009)
Terrorism	Reduction in terrorist activity in NI relative to rest of UK and IE	€6,375 (£4,526)	Frey, Luechinger and Stutzer (2004)
Terrorism	Reduction in terrorist activity in London relative to rest of GB	€5,587 (£3,967)	Frey, Luechinger and Stutzer (2004)

Table 18.5 *(cont.)*

Subject	Description	Value/cost (in annual HH income)	Source
Floods	Sure flood disaster in region of residence	$6,505 (£3,669)	Luechinger and Raschky (2009)
Terrorism	Reduction in terrorist activity in Paris relative to rest of FR	€2,521 (£1,789)	Frey, Luechinger and Stutzer (2004)
Commuting time	Commuting 23 minutes to work	€2,904 (£1,770)	Stutzer and Frey (2004)
Air quality	1 μg/m³ increase in particulate matter (PM10)	$459 (£354)	Levinson (2012)
Informal care	Extra hour per week relative to average (49 hours)	€520 (£317)	Van der Berg and Ferrer-i-Carbonell (2007)
Air quality	Reduction in SO_2 concentration of 1 μg/m³	€195–€458 (£117–£274)	Luechinger (2009)
Noise pollution	Increase in aircraft noise from 20 to 30 Ku	$156 (£91)	Van Praag and Baarsma (2001)

Note: Foreign currency values are converted to GBP using historical exchange rates over the period of data collection. Weekly and monthly figures are converted to annual figures.

on social resources and so it has been suggested that it is a natural starting point for capabilities researchers wanting to incorporate such resources into their analysis.

It has also been suggested that social resources can have instrumental benefits for the operation of markets but also improve quality of life though there is no consensus on what its value might be. Three classes of methods are commonly used in valuation exercises of non-marketed goods and services and, whilst all have strengths in particular settings, none are universally applicable. In this chapter, therefore, estimates of the value of personal and community social resources were developed using a fourth, experience-based method, adapted from work on the value of environmental services, which in turn owes much to earlier work by Oswald and colleagues. There is probably limited work regarding the terminology at this stage but we should not let that obscure the value such resources might have both in enabling a person to live a good quality life they have reason to value and to achieve the basic universal outcomes in core areas of life from income through health to education.

More specifically, we made use of unique data for the US and UK in which variables reflect a distinction between community social capital – the quality and nature of the social environment – and individual social capital – the social skills and connections possessed by an individual. If one considers these as being related public and private goods respectively, then theoretically it is plausible that there is underinvestment in the former. Using compensating variation as the basic measure of value, and controlling for personality factors, there are a wide range of values but that, in general, community social capital has a value comparable with the benefits of volunteering or the costs of domestic violence. By way of robustness, the study found that results are somewhat lower in the US than the UK (possibly reflecting differential population densities, levels of social capital or individualism) and that the preferred specification is one in which the marginal utility of community social capital in declining. These variations, whilst noticeable and systematic are not sufficiently material to undermine the general conclusion that social capital is valuable, at least in the two countries for which we have data.

Although for present purposes, a distinction between individual social resources and those found at community level can be drawn and developed by statistically minded sociologists. The measure of individual social resources (capital) used in the study is very closely related to what Heckman and colleagues call 'non-cognitive' skills. Indeed we could have motivated the measures in that language also. These can also be thought of as 'conversion factors' so there are various ways of describing a set of social skills which are not traditionally measured by education and probably not always well predicted it. (Indeed, the kinds of social skills and resources measured in this case could be seen as a subset of a range of non-cognitive skills that should also be measured; see also Anand and Poggi, 2017.) Whether one terms these skills as non-cognitive, individual social capital or conversion factors has implications both for the background research literatures invoked and for suggested research questions to be analysed but we argue here that if we want to understand how valued activities and states are achieved or what a person's overall advantage is (Sen's first and third equations) then one must allow for the fact that some resources can be social. *A priori* we might not expect these to be as important as financial resources but the study's evidence suggests in comparison with other states and activities their impact is non-insignificant and the policy implications are potentially rather important. For example, human development programmes targeting income health and education could still fail if they do not equip individuals with appropriate non-cognitive skills or develop communities that are complementary to such policies. War-torn states are an obvious example but there may be other situations where features of the environment such as high levels of crime or low levels of trust serve to undermine policy-making even where formal rights and equality have been granted. The township of Soweto in post-apartheid South Africa could be considered a good example of such a situation. In short, and whilst there are reasonable complaints about the terminology of social capital and non-cognitive skills, one can see considerable theoretical and policy value in taking social resources serious within capabilities analyses.

ANNEXURE

Table 18.6 Happiness equations: linear specification

Article III.	Life satisfaction			ONS4 happiness			Life satisfaction			ONS4 happiness		
	All	UK	US	All	UK	US	All	UK	US	All	UK	US
Equivalised HH Income (£0,000s)	0.067***	0.071**	0.072**	0.034**	0.029	0.047**	0.071***	0.077***	0.074**	0.036**	0.033	0.047**
	(0.020)	(0.028)	(0.031)	(0.016)	(0.022)	(0.023)	(0.021)	(0.028)	(0.031)	(0.016)	(0.022)	(0.023)
Community SC	0.252***	0.257***	0.238***	0.184***	0.193***	0.168***	0.299***	0.300***	0.288***	0.208***	0.217***	0.189***
	(0.019)	(0.025)	(0.030)	(0.015)	(0.020)	(0.022)	(0.018)	(0.024)	(0.028)	(0.014)	(0.019)	(0.021)
Individual SC	0.193***	0.182***	0.203***	0.097***	0.102***	0.085**						
	(0.027)	(0.034)	(0.047)	(0.021)	(0.027)	(0.034)						
Age	−0.066**	−0.086***	−0.030	−0.050**	−0.075***	−0.006	−0.059**	−0.086***	−0.014	−0.047**	−0.075***	0.000
	(0.026)	(0.033)	(0.043)	(0.020)	(0.026)	(0.032)	(0.026)	(0.033)	(0.044)	(0.020)	(0.026)	(0.032)
Age^2	0.001**	0.001***	0.000	0.001***	0.001***	0.000	0.001**	0.001***	0.000	0.001**	0.001***	−0.000
	(0.000)	(0.000)	(0.001)	(0.000)	(0.000)	(0.000)	(0.000)	(0.000)	(0.001)	(0.000)	(0.000)	(0.000)
Gender (= Male)	−0.224***	−0.231**	−0.198	−0.115**	−0.182**	−0.005	−0.230***	−0.237**	−0.202	−0.118**	−0.185**	−0.007
	(0.076)	(0.095)	(0.127)	(0.058)	(0.076)	(0.092)	(0.076)	(0.095)	(0.128)	(0.059)	(0.076)	(0.093)
Ethnicity (= White)	−0.019	0.204	−0.082	−0.122	−0.017	−0.160	−0.016	0.226	−0.077	−0.121	−0.005	−0.158
	(0.115)	(0.201)	(0.149)	(0.088)	(0.161)	(0.109)	(0.116)	(0.203)	(0.150)	(0.089)	(0.162)	(0.109)
Health (EQ5D)	2.379***	2.395***	2.427***	1.910***	1.896***	1.982***	2.456***	2.475***	2.452***	1.949***	1.942***	1.993***
	(0.173)	(0.197)	(0.367)	(0.133)	(0.158)	(0.268)	(0.174)	(0.198)	(0.370)	(0.133)	(0.158)	(0.268)
Shocks	−0.441***	−0.396***	−0.517***	−0.187**	−0.176*	−0.204*	−0.464***	−0.440***	−0.524***	−0.199***	−0.200*	−0.207*
	(0.096)	(0.128)	(0.147)	(0.074)	(0.103)	(0.107)	(0.097)	(0.129)	(0.149)	(0.074)	(0.103)	(0.108)

Extraversion	0.041**	0.040*	0.045	0.078***	0.066***	0.098***	0.088***	0.082***	0.098***	0.102***	0.090***	0.120***
	(0.019)	(0.024)	(0.030)	(0.014)	(0.019)	(0.022)	(0.018)	(0.023)	(0.028)	(0.014)	(0.018)	(0.020)
Agreeableness	0.007	0.002	0.017	0.006	−0.012	0.030	0.022	0.020	0.031	0.014	−0.002	0.036
	(0.023)	(0.030)	(0.038)	(0.018)	(0.024)	(0.028)	(0.023)	(0.030)	(0.038)	(0.018)	(0.024)	(0.028)
Conscientiousness	0.028	0.014	0.050	0.031*	0.015	0.053**	0.060***	0.048*	0.077**	0.047***	0.034	0.064**
	(0.022)	(0.028)	(0.035)	(0.017)	(0.022)	(0.026)	(0.021)	(0.027)	(0.035)	(0.016)	(0.022)	(0.025)
Emotional stability	0.124***	0.131***	0.104***	0.209***	0.213***	0.200***	0.146***	0.153***	0.127***	0.220***	0.225***	0.209***
	(0.021)	(0.027)	(0.036)	(0.016)	(0.021)	(0.026)	(0.021)	(0.027)	(0.036)	(0.016)	(0.021)	(0.026)
Openness	−0.002	0.011	−0.023	0.025	0.024	0.025	0.031	0.043	0.012	0.042**	0.042*	0.039
	(0.022)	(0.028)	(0.035)	(0.017)	(0.023)	(0.026)	(0.022)	(0.028)	(0.035)	(0.017)	(0.022)	(0.025)
Normal workday	0.056	0.029	0.121	0.069	0.054	0.107	0.035	0.023	0.080	0.058	0.050	0.089
	(0.077)	(0.098)	(0.127)	(0.059)	(0.078)	(0.092)	(0.078)	(0.098)	(0.128)	(0.060)	(0.078)	(0.092)
Constant	1.410**	1.443**	1.013	1.478***	1.995***	0.554	1.392**	1.457**	0.952	1.469***	2.004***	0.529
	(0.557)	(0.722)	(0.913)	(0.429)	(0.577)	(0.665)	(0.562)	(0.729)	(0.920)	(0.431)	(0.580)	(0.667)
Observations	2,679	1,618	1,061	2,679	1,618	1,061	2,679	1,618	1,061	2,679	1,618	1,061
R-squared	0.353	0.383	0.302	0.410	0.414	0.393	0.341	0.371	0.289	0.405	0.409	0.390
Community SC (£)	£37,612	£36,197	£33,056	£54,118	£66,552	£35,745	£42,113	£38,961	£38,919	£57,778	£65,758	£40,213
Individual SC (£)	£28,806	£25,634	£28,194	£28,529	£35,172	£18,085						

Note: Standard errors of the means are given in parentheses. * 10 per cent, ** 5 per cent, *** 1 per cent. Omitted categories: female, non-white. ONS4 is constructed as the average of the scores across the four questions in Table 18.1. Mean household equivalised income, $\bar{y}i$ is £25,033 in the UK and £27,785 ($43,397) in the US.

Table 18.7 *Happiness equations: diminishing marginal utility*

	Life satisfaction			ONS4 happiness			Life satisfaction			ONS4 happiness		
Article IV.	All	UK	US	All	UK	US	All	UK	US	All	UK	US
Log (Equivalised HH Income)	0.151*** (0.0486)	0.199*** (0.0636)	0.116 (0.0774)	0.0703* (0.0375)	0.0926* (0.0508)	0.0588 (0.0564)	0.172*** (0.0490)	0.225*** (0.0639)	0.133* (0.0779)	0.0808** (0.0375)	0.107** (0.0509)	0.0658 (0.0565)
Community SC	0.253*** (0.0192)	0.257*** (0.0249)	0.239*** (0.0305)	0.184*** (0.0148)	0.193*** (0.0199)	0.170*** (0.0222)	0.299*** (0.0182)	0.299*** (0.0238)	0.288*** (0.0285)	0.208*** (0.0139)	0.216*** (0.0190)	0.190*** (0.0206)
Individual SC	0.191*** (0.0273)	0.178*** (0.0338)	0.201*** (0.0467)	0.0963*** (0.0210)	0.100*** (0.0270)	0.0839** (0.0341)						
Age	−0.0701*** (0.0261)	−0.0903*** (0.0329)	−0.0380 (0.0432)	−0.0521*** (0.0201)	−0.0769*** (0.0263)	−0.0122 (0.0315)	−0.0642** (0.0263)	−0.0912*** (0.0331)	−0.0215 (0.0434)	−0.0491** (0.0202)	−0.0775*** (0.0264)	−0.00535 (0.0314)
Age^2	0.000820** (0.000322)	0.00115*** (0.000405)	0.000311 (0.000535)	0.000668*** (0.000248)	0.00103*** (0.000324)	9.14e−05 (0.000390)	0.000754** (0.000325)	0.00117*** (0.000408)	0.000107 (0.000537)	0.000635** (0.000249)	0.00104*** (0.000325)	6.32e−06 (0.000389)
Gender (= Male)	−0.226*** (0.0758)	−0.239** (0.0947)	−0.189 (0.127)	−0.115* (0.0584)	−0.186** (0.0757)	0.00371 (0.0928)	−0.234*** (0.0765)	−0.246*** (0.0954)	−0.197 (0.128)	−0.119** (0.0586)	−0.191** (0.0760)	0.000549 (0.0930)
Ethnicity (= White)	−0.0294 (0.115)	0.198 (0.201)	−0.0820 (0.150)	−0.127 (0.0885)	−0.0178 (0.161)	−0.158 (0.109)	−0.0271 (0.116)	0.220 (0.202)	−0.0794 (0.151)	−0.126 (0.0888)	−0.00553 (0.161)	−0.157 (0.109)
Health (EQ5D)	2.364*** (0.174)	2.363*** (0.198)	2.445*** (0.370)	1.906*** (0.134)	1.879*** (0.158)	2.008*** (0.270)	2.433*** (0.175)	2.436*** (0.199)	2.458*** (0.373)	1.941*** (0.134)	1.920*** (0.158)	2.013*** (0.270)
Shocks	−0.424*** (0.0967)	−0.362*** (0.130)	−0.518*** (0.149)	−0.181** (0.0745)	−0.157 (0.104)	−0.211* (0.109)	−0.442*** (0.0976)	−0.399*** (0.130)	−0.521*** (0.150)	−0.190** (0.0748)	−0.178* (0.104)	−0.212* (0.109)
Extraversion	0.0418** (0.0187)	0.0408* (0.0240)	0.0457 (0.0301)	0.0789*** (0.0144)	0.0664*** (0.0192)	0.0985*** (0.0219)	0.0882*** (0.0176)	0.0817*** (0.0229)	0.0986*** (0.0277)	0.102*** (0.0135)	0.0894*** (0.0182)	0.121*** (0.0201)

	(1)	(2)	(3)	(4)	(5)	(6)	(7)	(8)	(9)	(10)	(11)	(12)
Agreeableness	0.00623	0.00241	0.0154	0.00532	−0.0115	0.0288	0.0216	0.0197	0.0289	0.0131	−0.00176	0.0344
	(0.0234)	(0.0299)	(0.0383)	(0.0180)	(0.0239)	(0.0279)	(0.0235)	(0.0299)	(0.0384)	(0.0180)	(0.0238)	(0.0279)
Conscientiousness	0.0274	0.0122	0.0502	0.0309*	0.0140	0.0533**	0.0583***	0.0446	0.0766**	0.0465***	0.0323	0.0644**
	(0.0218)	(0.0277)	(0.0355)	(0.0168)	(0.0221)	(0.0258)	(0.0215)	(0.0272)	(0.0352)	(0.0165)	(0.0217)	(0.0255)
Emotional stability	0.125***	0.133***	0.103***	0.210***	0.213***	0.199***	0.147***	0.154***	0.126***	0.221***	0.225***	0.208***
	(0.0213)	(0.0266)	(0.0362)	(0.0164)	(0.0213)	(0.0264)	(0.0213)	(0.0265)	(0.0361)	(0.0163)	(0.0211)	(0.0262)
Openness	−0.00137	0.0127	−0.0213	0.0260	0.0250	0.0262	0.0319	0.0442	0.0129	0.0428***	0.0428*	0.0405
	(0.0220)	(0.0284)	(0.0355)	(0.0169)	(0.0227)	(0.0259)	(0.0216)	(0.0280)	(0.0349)	(0.0166)	(0.0223)	(0.0253)
Normal workday	0.0508	0.0262	0.112	0.0661	0.0525	0.101	0.0302	0.0204	0.0713	0.0557	0.0492	0.0843
	(0.0771)	(0.0974)	(0.127)	(0.0594)	(0.0779)	(0.0925)	(0.0777)	(0.0982)	(0.128)	(0.0596)	(0.0782)	(0.0925)
Constant	0.734	0.321	0.722	1.329**	1.628**	0.579	0.618	0.194	0.598	1.271**	1.556**	0.527
	(0.715)	(0.930)	(1.167)	(0.551)	(0.744)	(0.851)	(0.721)	(0.938)	(1.176)	(0.553)	(0.747)	(0.852)
Observations	2,679	1,618	1,061	2,679	1,618	1,061	2,679	1,618	1,061	2,679	1,618	1,061
R−squared	0.353	0.384	0.300	0.409	0.415	0.391	0.341	0.373	0.287	0.405	0.410	0.388
Community SC (£)	£37,612	£36,197	£33,056	£54,118	£66,552	£35,745	£42,113	£38,961	£38,919	£57,778	£65,758	£40,213
Individual SC (£)	£28,806	£25,634	£28,194	£28,529	£35,172	£18,085						

Note: Standard errors of the means are given in parentheses. * 10 per cent, ** 5 per cent, *** 1 per cent. Omitted categories are female and non-white. ONS4 is constructed as the average of the scores across the four questions in Table 18.1. Mean household equivalised income (ȳ) is £25,033 in the UK and £27,785 ($43,397) in the US.

Table 18.8 *Happiness and social resources in the US and UK*

Category	Average life satisfaction score		Average ONS four happiness score		Community social capital		Individual social capital	
	UK	US	UK	US	UK	US	UK	US
Female	5.97	6.33	5.86	6.14	5.81	5.94	6.84	7.24
	(0.08)	(0.10)	(0.07)	(0.08)	(0.07)	(0.11)	(0.07)	(0.08)
Male	5.83	6.33	5.78	6.29	5.68	6.19	6.62	7.23
	(0.08)	(0.10)	(0.06)	(0.07)	(0.07)	(0.09)	(0.06)	(0.08)
Total	5.90	6.33	5.82	6.21	5.75	6.07	6.73	7.23
	(0.06)	(0.07)	(0.05)	(0.06)	(0.05)	(0.07)	(0.05)	(0.06)
Up to £10,000	4.55	5.53	4.85	5.64	5.21	5.24	5.96	6.30
	(0.19)	(0.24)	(0.15)	(0.17)	(0.17)	(0.24)	(0.17)	(0.20)
£10,000–£19,999	5.28	5.65	5.37	5.63	5.30	5.77	6.28	7.12
	(0.14)	(0.19)	(0.11)	(0.14)	(0.13)	(0.18)	(0.12)	(0.15)
£20,000–£29,999	5.83	6.25	5.79	6.17	5.63	5.88	6.59	7.29
	(0.12)	(0.18)	(0.10)	(0.14)	(0.11)	(0.19)	(0.09)	(0.14)
£30,000–£39,999	6.10	6.29	5.93	6.09	5.72	6.00	6.84	7.28
	(0.13)	(0.16)	(0.11)	(0.13)	(0.12)	(0.16)	(0.11)	(0.13)

£40,000–£49,999	6.62	6.45	6.35	6.35	6.23	6.60	7.19	7.45
	(0.14)	(0.20)	(0.13)	(0.17)	(0.14)	(0.17)	(0.11)	(0.17)
£50,000–£74,999	6.58	6.81	6.37	6.60	6.12	6.23	7.30	7.37
	(0.13)	(0.16)	(0.11)	(0.13)	(0.13)	(0.15)	(0.10)	(0.13)
£75,000–£99,999	6.70	7.10	6.22	6.88	6.36	6.77	7.16	7.75
	(0.18)	(0.21)	(0.17)	(0.16)	(0.18)	(0.19)	(0.15)	(0.14)
£100,000 or more	6.47	7.42	6.33	7.09	6.49	6.83	7.05	7.70
	(0.33)	(0.21)	(0.27)	(0.20)	(0.27)	(0.24)	(0.26)	(0.19)
Employed	6.20	6.77	6.03	6.49	5.83	6.32	6.88	7.39
	(0.06)	(0.08)	(0.05)	(0.07)	(0.06)	(0.08)	(0.05)	(0.07)
Self-employed	5.89	6.30	5.97	6.18	5.98	6.42	7.07	7.68
	(0.21)	(0.23)	(0.16)	(0.18)	(0.21)	(0.22)	(0.15)	(0.18)
Unemployed	4.41	4.91	4.80	5.27	5.10	4.95	6.11	6.51
	(0.24)	(0.22)	(0.20)	(0.14)	(0.21)	(0.22)	(0.21)	(0.19)
Retired	6.81	6.62	6.68	6.36	6.46	6.08	7.34	7.51
	(0.31)	(0.46)	(0.26)	(0.36)	(0.26)	(0.40)	(0.23)	(0.28)
Permanently sick or disabled	4.05	5.15	4.33	5.47	5.11	5.48	5.76	6.75
	(0.24)	(0.30)	(0.19)	(0.25)	(0.23)	(0.33)	(0.25)	(0.28)

(cont.)

Table 18.8 (cont.)

Category	Average life satisfaction score		Average ONS four happiness score		Community social capital		Individual social capital	
	UK	US	UK	US	UK	US	UK	US
Looking after home or family	6.03	6.32	5.83	6.30	5.87	6.24	6.62	7.25
	(0.24)	(0.26)	(0.21)	(0.22)	(0.25)	(0.30)	(0.23)	(0.20)
Other	5.52	6.11	5.60	6.05	5.29	5.54	5.90	6.75
	(0.29)	(0.39)	(0.23)	(0.32)	(0.24)	(0.44)	(0.25)	(0.28)
Single (never married)	5.45	5.79	5.47	5.77	5.42	5.67	6.38	6.73
	(0.10)	(0.13)	(0.08)	(0.10)	(0.08)	(0.12)	(0.08)	(0.10)
Married/living with spouse	6.22	6.70	6.05	6.51	5.91	6.33	6.93	7.51
	(0.07)	(0.08)	(0.06)	(0.07)	(0.07)	(0.09)	(0.06)	(0.07)
Separated/divorced/widowed	5.32	5.89	5.48	5.90	5.80	5.81	6.57	7.29
	(0.20)	(0.26)	(0.17)	(0.19)	(0.18)	(0.23)	(0.16)	(0.20)

Note: Standard errors of the means are given in parentheses. ONS4 is constructed as the average of the respondent's scores across the four questions in Table 18.1.

References

Adger, W. N. (2010) 'Social capital, collective action, and adaptation to climate change'. In M. Voss (Ed.) *Der Klimawandel*. Wiesbaden: VS Verlag für Sozialwissenschaften, 327–45.

Anand, P. and Poggi A. (2017) 'Do social resources matter? Social capital, personality traits and the ability to plan ahead'. *Kyklos*, in press.

Anand, P., Hunter, G., Carter, I., Dowding, K., Guala, F. and Van Hees, M. (2009) 'The development of capability indicators'. *Journal of Human Development and Capabilities*, 10(1), 125–52.

Anand, P., Krishnakumar, J. and Tran, N. B. (2011) 'Measuring welfare: Latent variable models for happiness and capabilities in the presence of unobservable heterogeneity'. *Journal of Public Economics*, 95(3), 205–15.

Anand, P., Roope, L. and Gray, A. (2014) 'Multi-dimensional wellbeing in the US and UK: Evidence for the assessment of progress'. Discussion Paper, Open and Oxford Universities.

Atkinson, G., Healey, A. and Mourato, S. (2005) 'Valuing the costs of violent crime: A stated preference approach'. *Oxford Economic Papers*, 57, 559–85.

Baddeley, M.C. (2007) 'Are tourists willing to pay for aesthetic quality?' In T. Huybers (Ed.) *Tourism in Developing Countries*. Cheltenham: Edward Elgar.

Beugelsdijk, S. and Schaik, T. (2005) 'Social capital and growth in European regions: An empirical test'. *European Journal of Political Economy*, 21(2), 301–24. Available at: https://EconPapers.repec.org/RePEc:eee:poleco:v:21:y:2005:i:2:p:301-324.

Brown, S., Taylor, K. and Price, S. W. (2005) 'Debt and distress: Evaluating the psychological cost of credit'. *Journal of Economic Psychology*, 26, 642–63.

Bruni, L., Comim, F. and Pugno, M. (2008) *Capabilities and Happiness*. Oxford: Oxford University Press.

Card, D. (1995) 'Using geographic variation in college proximity to estimate the return to schooling'. In L. N. Christofides, E. K. Grant and R. Swidinsky (Eds.) *Aspects of Labor Market Behaviour: Essays in Honour of John Vanderkamp*. Toronto: University of Toronto Press, 201–22.

Carroll, N., Frijters, P. and Shields, M. A. (2009) 'Quantifying the costs of drought: New evidence from life satisfaction data'. *Journal of Population Economics*, 22, 445–61.

Chiappero-Martinetti, E. and Moroni, S. (2007) 'An analytical framework for conceptualizing poverty and re-examining the capability approach'. *The Journal of Socio-Economics*, 36(3), 360–75.

Chiappero-Martinetti, E., Egdell, V., Hollywood, E. and McQuaid, R. (2015) Operationalisation of the capability approach. In H. -U., Otto, R. Atzmüller, T. Berthet, L. Bifulco, J. -M. Bonvin, E. Chiappero, V.

Egdell, B. Halleroed, C. C. Kjeldsen, M. Kwiek, R. Schröer, J. Vero, and M. Zielenska, (Eds.) *Facing Trajectories from School to Work.* Springer International Publishing, 115–39.

Clark, A., Frijters, P. and Shields, M. A. (2006) Income and happiness: Evidence, explanations and economic implications. Paris-Jourdan Sciences Economiques, Working Paper No. 2006-24.

Clark, A., Frijters, P. and Sheilds, M. A. (2008) 'Relative income, happiness and utility: An explanation for the Easterlin paradox and other puzzles'. *Journal of Economic Literature*, 46, 95–144.

Dasgupta, P. Serageldin, I. (Eds.) (1999) Social Capital: A Multifaceted Perspective (English). Washington, DC: World Bank. Available at: http://documents.worldbank.org/curated/en/663341468174869302/Social-capital-a-multifaceted-perspective.

Di Tella, R., MacCulloch, R. J. and Oswald, A. J. (2001) 'Preferences over inflation and unemployment: Evidence from surveys of happiness'. *American Economic Review*, 91, 335–41.

Diener, E. and Biswas-Diener, R. (2011) *Happiness: Unlocking the Mysteries of Psychological Wealth.* Malden: Wiley-Blackwell.

Dolan, P. and Galizzi, M. M. (2015) Like ripples on a pond: Behavioral spillovers and their implications for research and policy. *Journal of Economic Psychology*, 47, 1–16.

Dolan, P. and Metcalfe, R. (2008) *Valuing Non-market Goods: A Comparison of Preference-Based and Experience-Based Approach.* London: Imperial College London, Tanaka Business School.

Dolan, P., Peasgood, T. and White, M. (2008) 'Do we really know what makes us happy? A review of the economic literature on the factors associated with wellbeing'. *Journal of Economic Psychology*, 29(1), 94–122.

Durkheim, E. (1897/1951) *Suicide: A Study in Sociology* (J. Spaulding & G. Simpson, Trans.) New York: The Free Press.

Frey, B. S. (1994) 'How intrinsic motivation is crowded out and in'. *Rationality and Society*, 6(3), 334–52.

Frey, B. S. and Stutzer, A. (2002) 'What can economists learn from happiness research?' *Journal of Economic Literature*, 40, 402–35.

Frey, B. S., Luechinger, S. and Stutzer, A. (2004) Valuing public goods: The life satisfaction approach. Center for Research in Economics, Management and the Arts. Working Paper No. 2004-11.

Fujiwara, D. and Campbell, R. (2011) *Valuation Techniques for Social Cost-Benefit Analysis: Stated Preference, Revealed Preference and Subjective Well-Being Approaches.* London: Department for Work and Pensions and HM Treasury.

Fujiwara, D., Oroyemi, P. and McKinnon, E. (2013) Wellbeing and civil society: Estimating the value of volunteering using subjective wellbeing data. DWP Working Paper No. 112.

Gibbons, S. and Machin, S. (2008) 'Valuing school quality, better transport, and lower crime: Evidence from house prices'. *Oxford Review of Economic Policy*, 24, 99–119.

Graham, C. (2005) 'The economics of happiness'. *World Economics*, 6(3), 41–55.

Gutiérrez, N., Hilborn, R. and Defeo, O. (2011) 'Leadership, social capital and incentives promote successful fisheries'. *Nature*, 470, 386–89.

Harper, R. (2001) '*Social Capital: A Review of the Literature*.' UK: Social Analysis and Reporting Division, Office for National Statistics.

Heckman, J. J. and Corbin, C. O. (2016) 'Capabilities and skills'. *Journal of Human Development and Capabilities*, 17(3), 342–59.

Huppert, F. A. and So, T. T. (2013) 'Flourishing across Europe: Application of a new conceptual framework for defining well-being'. *Social Indicators Research*, 110(3), 837–61.

Inkpen, A. and Tsang, E. (2005) 'Social capital, networks, and knowledge transfer'. *The Academy of Management Review*, 30(1), 146–65.

John, O. P. and Srivastava, S. (1999) 'The Big-Five trait taxonomy: History, measurement, and theoretical perspectives'. In L. A. Pervin and O. P. John (Eds.) *Handbook of Personality: Theory and Research*, vol. 2. New York: Guilford Press, 102–38.

Karayiannis, A. D. and Hatzis, A. N. (2012) 'Morality, social norms and the rule of law as transaction cost-saving devices: The case of ancient Athens'. *European Journal of Law and Economics*, 33(3), 621–43.

Kim, D., Baum, C. F., Ganz, M., Subramanian, S. V. and Kawachi, I. (2011) 'The contextual effects of social capital on health: A cross-national instrumental variable analysis'. *Social Science & Medicine (1982)*, 73(12), 1689–97.

Knack, S. and Keefer, P. (1997) 'Does social capital have an economic payoff? A cross-country investigation'. *Quarterly Journal of Economics*, November, 1251–88.

Levinson, A. (2012) 'Valuing public goods using happiness data: The case of air quality'. *Journal of Public Economics*, 96, 869–80.

Lucas, R. E., Clark, A. E., Georgellis, Y. and Diener, E. (2003) 'Re-examining adaptation and the set point model of happiness: Reactions to changes in marital status'. *Journal of Personality and Social Psychology*, 84, 527–39.

Luechinger, S. (2009) 'Valuing air quality using the life satisfaction approach'. *Economic Journal*, 119, 482–515.

Luechinger, S. and Raschky, P. A. (2009) 'Valuing flood disasters using the life satisfaction approach'. *Journal of Public Economics*, 93(3–4), 620–33.

Maggino, F. (2006) 'Perception and evaluation of the quality of life in Florence, Italy'. In *Community Quality-of-Life Indicators*. Netherlands: Springer, 75–125.

ONS (2014) Measuring national well-being: Insights across society, the economy and the environment. Available at: www.ons.gov.uk/ons/dcp171766_371427.pdf

Oswald, A. J. and Powdthavee, N. (2008) 'Death, happiness, and the calculation of compensatory damages'. *Journal of Legal Studies*, 37, S217–52.

Pierre, G., Sanchez-Puerta, M. L., Valerio, A. and Rajadel, T. (2014) STEP skills measurement surveys: Innovative tools for assessing skills (English). Social Protection and Labor Discussion Paper No. 1421. Washington, DC: World Bank Group. Available at: http://documents.worldbank.org/curated/en/516741468178736065/STEP-skills-measurement-surveys-innovative-tools-for-assessing-skills

Poggi, A. (2010) 'Job satisfaction, working conditions, and aspirations'. *Journal of Economic Psychology*, 31(6), 936–49.

Portes, A. (1998) 'Social capital: Its origins and applications in modern sociology'. *Annual Review of Sociology*, 24, 1–24.

Powdthavee, N. (2007) 'Putting a price tag on friends, relatives, and neighbours: Using surveys of life satisfaction to value social relationships'. *Journal of Socio-Economics*, 37(4), 1459–80.

Putnam, R. (1995) 'Tuning, tuning out: The strange disappearance of social capital in America P.S.'. *Political Science and Politics*, 28, 1–20.

Rao, V., Gupta, I., Lokshin, M. and Jana, S. (2003) 'Sex workers and the cost of safe sex: The compensating differential for condom use among Calcutta prostitutes'. *Journal of Development Economics*, 71, 585–603.

Rodríguez-Pose, A. and Berlepsch, V. (2014) 'Social capital and individual happiness in Europe'. *Journal of Happiness Studies*, 15(2), 357–86.

Santos, C. (2013)'Costs of domestic violence: A life satisfaction approach'. *Fiscal Studies*, 34(3), 391–409.

Sarracino, F. (2010) 'Social capital and subjective wellbeing trends: Comparing 11 western European countries'. *Journal of Socio-Economics*, 39(4), 482–517.

Schokkaert, E. (2009) *The capabilities approach*. In P. Anand, P. Pattanaik and C. Puppe (Eds.) *The Handbook of Rational and Social Choice*. Oxford: Oxford University Press.

Sen, A. (1985) *Commodities and Capabilities*. Amsterdam: North-Holland.

Stutzer, A. and Frey, B. S. (2004) Stress that doesn't pay: The commuting paradox. IEW Working Papers No. 151. Zurich: Institute for Empirical Research in Economics, University of Zurich.

Van den Berg, B. and Ferrer-i-Carbonell, A. (2007) 'Monetary valuation of informal care: The well-being valuation method'. *Health Economics*, 16, 1227–44.

Van Der Gaag, M. and Snijders, T. A. (2003). A comparison of measures for individual social capital. Paper given to the Creation and Returns of Social Capital, Conference, Amsterdam, October 2003.

Van Praag, B. M. S. and Baarsma, B. E. (2001) The shadow price of aircraft noise nuisance. Discussion Paper No. 2001-010/3, Tinbergen Institute.

Woolcock, M. and Narayan, D. (2000) 'Social capital: Implications for development theory, research, and policy'. *The World Bank Research Observer*, 15(2), 225–49.

PART IV

The Housing and Urban Frontier

Tracking the Transition From 'Basic Needs' to 'Capabilities' for Human-Centred Development

The Role of Housing in Urban Inclusion

SHAILAJA FENNELL, JAIME ROYO-OLID
AND MATTHEW BARAC

Introduction

The capability approach evolved from the basic needs approach by prioritising the identification of development goals that are ultimately meaningful to the people concerned. This is also relevant to inclusion in so far as it is to involve what people value. While inclusion in cities is a widely shared developmental objective, it is understood and interpreted in categorically different and even opposing ways by a variety of disciplines and stakeholders. The challenge that faces us in making urban inclusion a readily understood requirement for human development is hence to clarify what is it that is to be 'included' to ensure the flourishing of human life.

This chapter makes the case for a conceptually integrative approach to urban inclusion by linking the variety of approaches to housing using the core idea of agency that underlies the capabilities literature. It suggests that the identification of valuable or meaningful freedoms for citizens is facilitated by conceptually distinguishing means and ends such as by differentiating the roles of 'habitation' (i.e. the urban built environment) and 'habitare' (i.e. the evolving forms of inhabiting as the 'functioning' mediated and given context by built structures). We propose an agent-driven measure of human habitation, one that emphasises the notion of 'habitare', and is based on a multi-layered understanding. We make the case that making explicit this habitation–habitare nexus will enrich the structuring of inclusive cities in our times through a new, innovative, evidence-based approach bringing the social into the technical. We use the notion of a discriminant between passive notions of shelter to dynamic agent-driven construction of their preferred habitation to show that an innovative way to integrate the approaches to housing is to employ the concerns that lie at the core of the capability approach. We make the case that the capability approach permits us to use the experiential nature of habitation, to understand the values of the residents and to convert these into objective evaluation criteria and thereby improve the participation and agency of residents in informal and other marginalised communities.

Habitat vs Habitare

Human activity – and particularly interactions between individuals – constitutes a key feature in fashioning individual agency in everyday life. Understanding the formats by which people interact as a distinct exercise, prior to any reckoning of individual contributions, can help us understand the relationship between agency and structure (Giddens, 1986).

A decisive emphasis on structure was a major theoretical advance for understanding the conceptual basis for development, but this has not been accompanied by an improvement in the measurement of agency (Clark, Biggeri and Friediani, 2019). The difficulty of relating structure to the genesis of habitat without a qualitative or quantitative description of a housing environment continues to be a particularly compelling challenge in the field of housing and development (Hamdi, 1995). Placing greater emphasis on the range of productive activities and linking them through the networks of social interaction to the habits of individuals, Castells emphasised the primacy of networks as an institutional pathway in order to understand behaviour through an examination of individual habitation patterns (Castells, 1996).

The importance of a habitat as a 'place' within which individuals feel able to express their intentionality through interactions fits closely, as a form of representation, with an institutional theory of a network. This is not in keeping with the logic followed by the real-estate sector, where marketing focuses on the representation of space (i.e. the structure) and in projecting an associated social status that often do not match the reality of their use. While the academic literature has for at least three decades posited that the technical knowledge of built environment professionals and the immanent knowledge of communities are incommensurable to each other, they remain most often set at odds in the practice of development (Satterthwaite and Mitlin, 2004).

A key challenge in the professional field is to move away from the notion that housing is a technical feature of development, one that must be decided by planners alone – either economic or spatial – and to move to the notion that it is local inhabitants, through their interactions, who can demonstrate the most commonly traversed networks that must be addressed by housing and habitation programmes (UN-Habitat, 2017). A problem prevails in so far as people's preferences remain subject to interpretation by the technical stakeholders even when genuinely committed to empower from the bottom up and when engaging in participatory processes.

In the context of housing as a form of inhabited space, using the effectiveness of actions permits us to place the concepts of *habitation* – as structure – and *habitare* – *as agency* – for understanding of the role of housing in advancing capabilities (Royo-Olid, 2006). The idea here is building on this conceptualisation to develop the core of a new, innovative, evidence-based approach to enrich and integrate established technical approaches with more context specific social considerations.

The next section examines how ideas of housing in the UN development tradition, the current shortcomings and the consequent challenges that human development-led thinking faces in regard to putting people and their interactions at the core of the conceptualisation of housing.

Housing and the Evolving Habitat and Urban Agendas Agendas

The New Urban Agenda devised and put forward by the United Nations represents the latest declaration of institutionalised approaches towards cities and housing resulting from the Habitat III conference (United Nations, 2017). The Agenda not only recognises the importance of participation and inclusion but mentions them thirty-one and forty-six times respectively in a twenty-three-page text. While the institutionalisation of participation and inclusion is an unambiguous achievement of protagonists of the bottom up approach, this repetition tells us little about how and what is to be included and participatory. This calls for the need to substantiate the underlying understanding of those terms to ensure their effectiveness in habitat interventions.

The concept of habitat as a notion in international development was institutionalised in the Vancouver Declaration at the first Habitat meeting (Habitat I) organised by the United Nations in 1976. The meeting intended to provide a platform for practitioners whereby there could be a response to the demands for housing through institutionally formalising the notion of habitat as an object of remediation.[1] The Vancouver Declaration emphasised the centrality of the role that needed to be played by planners and the planning process in the creation of cities in developing countries. It anticipated a vision for future cities, particularly in Asia and Africa when these regions were almost entirely composed of rural settlements until the 1970s. The thinking evident in the declaration is that planning would be undertaken in a top-down manner through national housing policies, the use of zoning, land reserves, changing land ownership and property taxes, alongside infrastructure projects for roads and mass transportation, water and waste systems and energy provision (Biau, 2015).

The notion of housing that provided the starting point for Habitat I was to provide shelter from the elements for the poor who were beginning to reside in informal settlements in the new cities of the developing world. This can be regarded as a prelude to the debates on market and rights-based approaches to housing, with the former emphasising the need for finance to provide basic housing for the poor and the latter underlining the fundamental requirement of housing for a decent life.

The Basic Needs Approach

The basic needs approach was the first attempt to distinguish the importance of both means and ends in human development; in that way it is also a break from earlier thinking on economics which focuses primarily, if not solely, on resources, i.e. the means, such as income and food, to achieve development (Sen, 2003). The importance of distinguishing means from ends also allows us to exercise discrimination between negative and positive liberties. In the case of housing this would mean the difference between shelter, which we define as 'protection from the natural elements' and habitation, which we regard as 'the agency to live and fashion one's life in a suitable abode'. Hence, the basic needs approach emphasised the need to provide resources such as housing to improve the freedoms of those individuals who would not otherwise be able to achieve ends such as growth and productivity (Streeten and

---

[1] The Habitat I meeting was followed by the consolidation of the UN-Human Settlements Programme (UN-Habitat) in 1978, with its headquarters in Nairobi.

Shahid, 1981). The second feature of the basic needs approach was that it was to be a nationally specific strategy permitting countries to most effectively use their domestic resources and also to allow international donors to provide targeted financing for development (ODI, 1978). However, the basic needs approach is philosophically vulnerable in tending to impose development templates on communities who might construct their basic needs quite differently – and in that sense it is not dissimilar to prescriptive approaches in top-down modernist architecture that predetermine urban forms regardless of prevailing preferences (Royo-Olid, 2006).

To overcome these two shortcomings of the basic needs approach it is important to push for a bottom-up typology of housing, and emphasise one that incorporates meaningful indicators as to the well-being of their human residents. The range of characteristics and values accorded to housing is clearly wide-ranging, and these measures go beyond requirements of safety and utility within an individual housing unit to that of the social values of a pleasant neighbourhood and source of social life and personal refuge (Coates, Anand and Norris, 2013). The impact of the neighbourhood on the extent to which agency may be exercised by individuals, to live and reach out as householders, is an important aspect of housing and habitation that still remains inadequately recognised when there is a singular focus on individual homes (Turner, 1976).

The World Bank's Political Economy of Affordable Housing

Another distinctly different approach to the provision of housing focuses on the importance of market forces in providing habitation. There is a history to the engagement of the World Bank in this sector, one which can be pinpointed to the 1980s when it was becoming evident that there was not enough public sector housing, and that which was available was unaffordable. The World Bank began, at this time, to create programmes for lending to countries that needed housing finance. It put forward the view that the public sector was not capable of providing housing, and this lack of capacity was illustrated by the State's failure to identify and use interest rates that would sustain a housing sector (Renaud, 1984). This 1980s overture into the Bank's engagement with housing finance was based on the argument that there was need for a market-oriented approach that could be more efficiently provided by a private sector initiative (World Bank, 1993). The selection of a market-based mechanism for the provision of housing for migrants was, at least in part, linked to acknowledgement among international circles that there was a strong 'urban bias' in city planning that gave power to the elites and worked against the interests of the migrants in the city as well as against the rural poor (Lipton, 1977; Satterthwaite, 1997).

The key proposition set up by the World Bank was that the urban poor were overlooked, and it was not their needs but those of the elites that determined urban planning priorities. The invisible poor (Appadurai, 2001), who were unable to get employment and housing in the formal factor sector, were forced to build their informal settlements and find forms of low-paid self-employed service provision in the commercial and domestic sectors, such as errand boys and maids. The World Bank initially advocated the delivery of sites-and-services products that permitted in-situ incremental growth, to be facilitated by market instruments rather than exclusively by technical, top-down, administrative decision-making by urban planners (World Bank, 1993). The rationale for this alternative approach was that market forces would create an 'enabling' environment rather than a 'passive recipient' environment that had been fostered by a planning approach to urban services such as housing (Huchzermayer, 2011).

Evidence about the growth of, and subsequent rise in, poverty in the informal sector posed a growing challenge to planning authorities, indicating that this expanding demography was experiencing increased marginalisation. The early policies of slum dwellers' relocation advocated by the Bank did not appear to be successful in ameliorating the plight of the urban poor in informal settlements; the Global Urbanizing World Report on Human Settlements (1996) highlighted the plight of over 600 million living in such conditions and literature started recognising the importance of social and economic networks inherent to the location of slums.

A key element in 'enabling' people who are living in substandard conditions is facilitating their security of tenure. There was a decided preference during the 1990s and 2000s for adopting de Soto's approach to security, through the provision of individual freehold titles (De Soto, 2000). Despite the widespread acceptance of individual titling as a enabling mechanism, the programme did not realise its objective of lifting households out of poverty, even in the case of Peru (the original country discussed by de Soto) and despite the large titling programme funded by the World Bank (Payne, 2016). While tenure security is unquestionably central to advancing the habitat agenda, Payne advocates not confusing means and ends. He suggests granting due importance to diverse and alternative forms of tenure in so far as they serve the purpose of effective inhabiting (or *habitare*) and is opposed to tenure that focuses exclusively in owning the habitation regardless of the consequences (e.g. ownership at the expense of excess debt compromising the household's livelihood).

The apparent inability of market-oriented approaches to improve the housing conditions of the urban poor posed a further conundrum to the housing literature, as it would appear that neither planned nor market-initiated housing programmes were able to overcome the very inadequacy of housing provision for the urban poor. The failure of both approaches, notwithstanding their contrasting propositions for the type of provision, underlines the limitations of an exclusively supply-sided approach. The proposition that housing challenges can be resolved solely by an increase in housing stock has been shown to be fallacious also in the US and Spain. From a qualitative perspective, supply-driven housing usually falls short of directly engaging through forms of participation (Satterwaite and Mitlin, 2004) hence ignoring specific needs of residents namely the multitude of innovative, low-cost spatial, social and economic arrangements that characterise informal sector housing. From a quantitative standpoint, the global financial crisis that erupted in 2008 has disclosed an underlying paradox in so far as increasing large stocks of empty houses can coexist with increasing financial effort to buy in the same market sector (Royo-Olid et al., 2017). The global financialisation of housing has hence added a layer of complexity to the challenge of making housing affordable as public policy falls short in its ability to compensate the effects of 'walls of money' seeking high quality collateral that displace the social role of housing in favour of its role as financial asset (Aalbers, 2016).

The basic needs and the market-oriented approaches to housing provision do not have an explicit dimension that is able to engage directly, with residents with regard to the manner in which they visualise and see their homes. While they emphasise the importance of housing for residents, they address the provision of housing through prescriptive frameworks. The prescriptive focus adopted by the World Bank approach in the 1980s and 1990s sought to ensure more effective provisioning through the creation of instruments that improve the procedures and processes by which housing programmes are delivered. These instruments have been designed in line with the Bank's good governance policy framework that is built around the core objectives of transparency and accountability. While the focus on improving housing provision does provide a better chance for ensuring that the informal sector residents do get access to more habitable dwellings, the good governance agenda appears to be better suited to ensuring credible working practices on the supply side than any guarantee of closer engagement with a community's perceptions of their own housing needs and aspirations (World Bank, 2002).

The accountability instrument identified in the good governance framework is regarded as a key feature by which the market-friendly approach can increase the power of 'citizen/client' residents to improve the efficiency of service delivery (see Figure 19.1). This was termed the 'short route to accountability', arising from the direct interaction between the clients and the service providers and based on the mechanism of choice exercised by individual consumers. It simultaneously moves away from the longer-route created by the interventions by state institutions and depending on the use of voice, e.g. that of urban planners and municipalities.

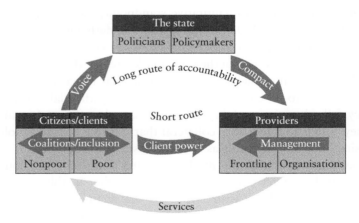

Figure 19.1 Key relationships of power
Source: World Bank (2003: 49)

The shortcoming of this formulation of the relationship between the citizens and the providers is that it does not take account of the importance of the role of direct participation. In the decision-making process, the design, delivery and monitoring of housing is absent from this analysis. Consequently, it focuses only on habitation but does not give any consideration of the *habitare* aspects of housing either having a role in housing conditions, nor of how citizen-directed participation can affect both the provider and the state by claiming a larger share of public action for determining the constitution of decent housing. For example, if informal sector residents deem space outside their residences to be needed for public exchange, then the illumination of local alleys might be a primary concern. On the other hand, if there was a shared consideration that there should be a public meeting place, buildings such as temples or public libraries and community halls might be more immediately in demand.

The more recent Land Governance Assessment Framework (LGAF) developed by the World Bank includes participation at various levels in its considerations and indicators. While owned by national institutions and while local participatory processes are assessed, the LGAF itself remains mainly a technical expert-driven exercise. The short route to accountability does not directly address the set of such stipulations that emerge from consultations driven by rural or urban residents. It is an important approach for developing the consumer features that emerge from a choice based mechanisms, but it is unlikely that the top-down planning approaches which regard the delivery of housing can uncover the larger public dimensions of rather than addressing larger social and public manifestations of inhabiting (habitare) a home that requires bringing other mechanisms to strengthen the voice mechanism in the building of homes.

The Bottom-Up Approach and Participation Agendas

The call to place informal sector residents at the core of the housing and habitation nexus has been advanced by housing sector activists for decades; it has been conceptualised and analysed by inter-disciplinary academic research in development studies and cognate disciplines (Huchzermeyer, 2011). This legacy is explicit in the New Urban Agenda. But it remains important to remind ourselves of the academic

Figure 19.2 Left: Social anthropologist Margot Ehrlich consults tsunami victim about life and housing preferences. Right: Architect Tiago Vier informs and collects choices of end users about different choices of house types
Source: Royo-Olid (2006)

genesis of these ideas. The work of Chambers on the vital requirement for any development policy to place the community at the centre of the design and implementation of development programmes, and to regard their knowledge and understanding of their situation and of their objectives and concerns, has driven the participatory approach to development (Chambers, 1997). Parallel thinking has emerged in the professional disciplines of architecture and town planning (Awan, Schneider and Till, 2011; Watson, 2014) (see Figure 19.2).

It is challenging to extrapolate Chambers' primarily rural account of community participation with its specific power hierarchies to the city-dweller, as it requires an understanding of how urban residents might shape their own habitation agenda based on a set of values and objectives, and which is likely to be oppositional to those of more powerful economic urban interests, typical in countries with a marked 'urban bias'. Thus, squatters in a city may occupy an environmentally-sensitive site or threaten neighbourhood services or connections. On the other hand, a bottom-up approach to housing, such as the one that emerges from Chamber's participatory approach, has the benefit that is allows us to move from a vertical to a horizontal engagement with development policy and practice. It replaces a technical, quantitative approach by a softer, qualitatively-oriented social science approach, and draws on a series of subjective methods such as Participatory Poverty Assessments (PPAs) (Olsen, 2006). The participatory approach moves away from the focus on the supply-side concerns that preoccupy development agencies who naturally focus on good governance and other factors with a view to optimising project outcomes funded by donors (Cleaver, 1999). It places the onus on the moral imperative to work with the poor, using their knowledge, attitudes and practices to improve their lives, and based on understanding their demand for development on their own terms, using their own values and vocabulary (Chambers, 1997). The readiness of the participatory approach to include social dimensions of human life within an economic model of individual advancement is seen to be a vehicle for increasing bottom-up aspects of development policy. In particular, the participatory approach offers a way to incorporate community-level development into poverty analysis within international donor programmes such as the Poverty Reduction Strategy Papers (PRSPs) in the 1990s and 2000s (Cornwall and Brock, 2005).

The prospect of widespread participation by the poor has promised to reduce the asymmetry in power relations emphasised in most international policy thinking (World Bank, 2002) since the early 2000s. It can ensure that design and delivery of development programmes based on bottom-up or horizontal approaches guarantees that policy makers listen to the needs of poor communities. The argument is that this will, in turn, empower participants as they consolidate their gains from participatory processes into more widespread abilities to make positive and life-changing choices in the future (Mosse, 2001), and scale up their arenas of influence (Hamdi, 2004). A change in power relations, so that those with the weakest ability have experienced an improvement in the success associated with making choices (Sen, 1997), is imperative for a more inclusive structuring of habitats. Such a shift in power ensures that it is the values and voices of the community that are used by providers of housing services as well as the regulation of housing provision by the state. Participation also denounces the view that local residents are 'non-experts' and therefore should not be driving the design of the housing process. The result is that it is the recognition of the importance of the experience of inhabiting (i.e. what we posit here as *habitare*) in existing dwelling (i.e. habitation) that provides the baseline of data, both quantitative and qualitative, of the way forward to upgrade settlements rather than a token gesture where there is mere acknowledgement of the needs of informal sector residents (see Hamdi (2004) and Blundell Jones, Till and Petrescu (2005)).

The UN system (UN-Habitat Global Campaign on Urban Governance, 2001) paved the way for a shift from top-down, technically-driven supply side operation to a participatory, bottom-up and socially-constituted demand side approach by linking their five core principles to Amartya Sen's five measures of freedom (Sen, 1999) where each principle may be used to evaluate or assess these freedoms. The UN-Habitat framework (2004) focused on the inclusive idea of capability deprivation and away from an exclusive focus on income poverty (Sen, 1999: 20). The urban governance core principles that correspond to Sen's instrumental freedoms are as follows: effectiveness for economic facilities, equity for social opportunities, participation for political freedom, accountability for transparency guarantees and security for protective security. The UN itself has facilitated this professional mobilisation, from a supply-side to a demand-side emphasis, catalysing housing programmes by hosting an increasing number of initiatives to include civil society and popular discourse into its consultative processes, as well as increasing partnerships and encouraging parallel housing programmes through NGOs and grassroots organisations.

The increasing acceptance of resident participation in the urban informal sector occurs at a key moment in the urbanisation of our world[2]; 50–70 per cent of city-dwellers in low-income countries live in the informal sector. The magnitude and complexity of the housing challenge being addressed by the Habitat Agenda requires urban planners and related professionals – architects, economists, engineers and others – to engage with communities and understand how their experience of their life world gives rise to values regarding spaces and infrastructure. Architectural design and town planning can be used to mediate 'between freedom and structure' (Hamdi, 2004) drawing on Sen's five fundamental freedoms that demand political freedom, economic activity, transparency guarantees, security, and a baseline provision in terms of health and education as fundamental entitlements for all people. Drawing directly on the capability approach, this participatory, horizontal approach of UN-Habitat provides a

---

[2] The so-called 'tipping point' was 2007, when more than 50 per cent of the global population was residing in urban areas.

new blueprint for informal sector communities and residents to act according to individual priorities as they develop their own freedoms (see Hamdi, 2004 and Royo-Olid, 2004). Khosla and Samuels' (2005) redaction of these principles allows for considerable simplification of the Habitat Agenda and the basic needs approaches to urbanisation adopted by other international development agencies by emphasising the link between visualisation by residents in the informal sector and the design principles of technical experts. The consequence of linking housing to capabilities is that it facilitates an exploration of agency arising from inhabiting spaces (*habitare*) in relation to the spatial materialisation of *habitation*.

Habitation, Housing and Capabilities

The importance of habitation has been set out in the field of material culture by Appadurai (1986, 1996) who investigates how the nature and the manner in which we view material objects provides us with the means to understand important aspects of our contemporary culture. The argument is that objects are always in a process of transformation and translation, and that the living in and engaging with things results in the creation of practices and habits. It is this experience of engagement rather than the technical specification that is at the core of habitation:

even though from a theoretical point of view human actors encode things with significance, from a methodological point of view it is the things-in-motion that illuminate their human and social context (Appadurai, 1986: 5)

Gell (1992) uses a similar argument to explain how an individual's engagement with objects generates a form of agency attributable to the object. He coins the term 'technology of enchantment' to indicate how objects have an inherent capacity to elicit meaning, and our encounters with objects are never fixed, but are essentially dynamic and changing. For Daniel Miller, this capacity is an essential aspect of what gives us comfort in our lives (Miller, 2008).

The task of technical experts such as architects and planners is no longer to be solely concerned with improvements to the supply of material resources but to examine and analyse demand factors that could, if translated effectively in spatial terms, promote social arrangements that expand people's freedom to pursue the objectives they value, thereby contributing to improvements in self-worth, well-being, and 'happiness' (De Botton, 2006; Glaeser, 2011; Montgomery, 2013). The pursuit of the objectives that are valued focus on the 'ends' rather than the 'means', so the resources needed to achieve an objective are no longer the focus. Instead it is the ability to use resources, such as income, to 'be' and 'do' and thereby to have a functioning. Capabilities are defined as the combinations of human functionings – the set of 'doings and beings' a person can achieve- and open up the possibility of assessing the opportunity aspect of freedom. The lives that people live and the choices that they make, as in the case of where they live and how they live, also have processual elements that require us to examine the equity aspect of freedom (Sen, 2005: 153-157).

Figure 19.3 illustrates two post-tsunami incremental houses in 2013, which had been reconstructed in 2005 in Veerapakupathy (close to Kanyakumari, Tamil Nadu) with the support of the French NGO *Architecture & Développement* and the Indian architecture office Habitat Technology Group.[3] The home-owners were trained on cost-efficient construction technologies using locally-sourced materials. The houses were designed and located in the individual parcels allocated to each household such as to allow future expansions. In Figure 19.3, the top house remains in 2013 as it was originally built in 2005, whilst the other image shows the same type of house that was expanded vertically and horizontally and beautified. The expansions might reflect improved construction skills or an increase in financial resources in the household. It is noteworthy that bungalows and other similar ground-level houses are more able to accommodate owner-initiated improvements as compared to reconstructed apartments in high-rise buildings. This difference is often neglected and has important consequences for end user's capabilities.

If the goal of development is to expand basic or valuable capabilities, then poverty itself is understood as 'capability deprivation' (Sen, 1999). The capability approach maintains that poverty is a multidimensional state of ill-being that cannot be reduced to simple measurements of household consumption or income. Housing is an important dimension that determines an individual's well-being and it should not be limited to material inputs, but recognised as an important resource that

---

[3] The programme involved the reconstruction of 57 houses and the capacity building of home-owners in appropriate technology. It was mainly funded by Fondation de France and partly by the EU. (Further information is available at: www.fondationdefrance.org/en).

Figure 19.3 Incremental post-tsunami houses by *Architecture & Développement* in Tamil Nadu, India
Source: Royo-Olid (2018)

can, through an individual's agency, be used as 'a verb', to deploy 'conversion factors' to gain new capabilities (Turner and Fichter, 1972). It is this dimension of housing that makes it central to increasing agency and improving freedoms. The variation in the ability of informal settlement residents to successfully use their current habitation to gain such freedoms depends upon how different local and structural 'conversion factors' affect the capacity of individuals to transform commodities into the realisation of valued choices (Frediani, 2010: 176).

The capability approach has begun to address the importance of housing but has not yet accorded sufficient attention to the *habitare* facet of housing. While 'shelter' has been identified as an important dimension, closely mirroring the arguments on the basic needs approach, it has only recently been expanded beyond the criterion of being adequately sheltered, as evidenced in the work on evaluating housing, by examining the instrumental freedoms of human flourishing that emerges from dignified shelter (Frediani, 2007).

The practice of providing for habitat does not often provide appropriate *measures* for *habitation* (Royo-Olid, 2006). The role of politics in the ownership of land, the rights and scope of potential development and associated demarcation of private and public spheres also impacts on the extent and type of measures identified in policy frameworks. Recognition of the importance of spatial experiences of informal sector residents, in informing their assessment of the valuable attributes of their present and proposed habitat, is also lacking (Barac, 2016). Whether people value a shrine or a TV over a structurally sound house, a painting or a family photograph over cleanliness, a prominent façade or an introverted interior over vehicular access, what matters is the extent to which these choices reflect humane forms of differentiation and ordering rather than the materialisation of impositions (likely to result in 'unfreedoms').

A fundamental error of technical planning processes is that much of the 'making' of a city is undertaken without a sufficient understanding of the complex richness imbued, through inhabitation, in the lives of informal sector residents (Barac, 2007). Their expressions of ownership, social relationships and cultural values cannot be pre-empted through design. The suggestion here is that qualitative values identified by residents in informal sector settlements could provide the baseline data on unfreedoms in housing that are crucial for generating quantifiable features of upgrades that would be most effective in increasing resident agency. For example, if public toilets are built to reduce the unfreedom resulting from open defecation, resident agency will not be increased unless they can have access at will to these toilets, without fear of exclusion due to economic or social features (such as women being shamed for being in public spaces during times of the day or night) (see McFarlane and Graham, 2014). It is crucial that these qualitative assessments are undertaken using horizontal methods to be able to generate objective criteria (Comim, 2001), such as distance between the house and toilet, the lighting on the street/journey between the toilet and house, and the other houses that overlook the street/journey between the toilet and house. The ability to generate an appropriately objective assessment tool prior to the roll out of a housing programme will mitigate the problem of 'how the practical nature of context definition influences the objective nature of capabilities' (Comim, 2008: x).

The importance of objective evaluation criteria has been addressed in the design of the Equality Measurement Framework (EMF) used by the United Kingdom Equalities Commission. Its genesis entailed consultation with a range of stakeholders – the government, academic experts, professional and civil society bodies and the national statistical agency – to develop a framework for assessing equality and human rights across a range of domains relevant today. The baseline for these stakeholder engagements was obtained from publicly-available quantitative and qualitative data in which citizens had identified those things in their lives that they value as important to actually be able to do and to be. Table 19.1 provides the criteria for evaluating the housing dimension of capabilities. This domain emphasises the 'comfort' aspect, one that cannot be ascertained accurately without a prior baseline of what citizens value as important for doing and being. It is particularly noteworthy that the personal, social and structural aspects of conversion factors are reflected in the sub-domains, for instance: for an individual who is disabled the definition of what is 'comfortable' in relation to accessing different parts of the home, such as the need for a stair lift to travel between floors; for an individual from a minority group that faces discrimination, 'comfort' entails feeling at peace and secure within their home.

The domain and sub-domains of housing are important but can remain technical requirements imposed on the supply side if they are not based on both survey and qualitative data of how the experience of habitation by residents in an informal settlement creates social meaning regarding what they value for being able to do and be. This requires triangulation with the characteristics identified by the

Table 19.1 *Housing capabilities identified by the Equalities Commission, UK*

Domain: The capability to enjoy a comfortable standard of living, with
   independence and security

Sub-domains:
  A. enjoy an adequate and secure standard of living including nutrition,
      clothing, housing, warmth, social security, social services and utilities,
      and being cared for and supported when necessary;
  B. get around inside and outside the home, and to access transport and
      public places;
  C. live with independence, dignity and self-respect;
  D. have choice and control over where and how you live;
  E. have control over personal spending;
  F. enjoy your home in peace and security;
  G. access green spaces and the natural world; and
  H. share in the benefits of scientific progress including medical advances
      and information and technology.

Source: Equalities Act (2006)

community, particularly the weighting of housing sub-domain dimensions that emerge from the typical informal urban sector resident's
experience of habitation.

  This means that the role of the individual household and its ability
to use of relational and/or contextual conversion factors to choose
existing habitation by exercising their agency is a prerequisite; so that
if they choose a courtyard that becomes a basis for consultation on
why outside space is part of their understanding of their home.[4] These
forms of bottom-up data collection become the basis of devising a sufficiently detailed baseline that shows the richness and complexity of the
relationship between people's experience of habitation. Consequently,
if resident identification points to a dissatisfaction with the present
type of dwelling, such as a building without an open courtyard, then

---

[4] Relational conversion factors arise from the interactions that the individual
   has with social networks (Longshore Smith and Seward, 2009), while contextual conversion factors also include larger social structures such as institutions
   (Chiappero-Martinetti and von Jacobi, 2015).

the design needs to be classified as sub-standard or less than adequate in relation to the particular uses that are undertaken by the household.

This could also be related to forms of utility provision, so that if the original plan was to be able to ensure that services, such as electricity, are to be provided with a central metering facility, and the residents prefer to have an upgrading scheme that has metering facilities that can be easily accessed within every street, so that residents can exercise choice in the extent and timing of use. Then this would require that the providers ensure that they undertake a survey to obtain a base-line of activities that the household undertakes that require the use of electricity. It is in these ways that the capability approach permits us to use the experiential nature of habitation, to understand the values of the residents and to convert these into objective evaluation criteria (see Figure 19.4).

However, accountability based on the notion that citizens and providers can benefit from a choice based model does not take into account the vast asymmetry of information between the technical experts who are designing housing for residents in informal and marginal communities. The capability approach, in contrast, emphasises new routes by which the voices of residents can be heard and become the lever for change in habitation. By focusing on the visualisation and value of the experience of housing, i.e. habitare, it permits an innovative reconfiguration where informal sector citizens provide an account of their habitation, and both providers and the state and are partners in their housing programmes emerging from an iterative process of exchange.

The ability of such innovative horizontal approaches to improve our understanding of the experience of residents has triggered forms of radical architecture and planning, with a number of organisations emphasising the importance of co-locating the training of experts and local residents; examples include Barefoot architects, *Architecture & Développement*, *Architecture Sans Frontieres*, and the Indian Habitat Forum (INHAF). There is also a decided preference for using local construction technologies and methods to have a better match with local skills and ideas, to contribute more to the local economy and increase the ownership of the community with regarding to the housing programmes, e.g. Instituto Torroja, small-scale industrialisation research linked via the CYTED network, CEVE, Development Workshop, Building and Social Housing Foundation and Development Action Group (DAG), CraTerre, COSTFORD, Auroville Earth Institute and many more.

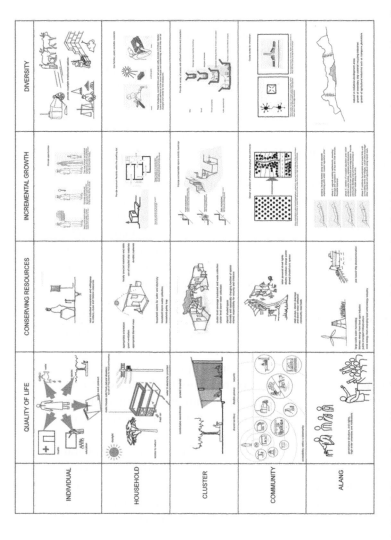

Figure 19.4 Capabilities informed hypothetical design guidelines for bonded-labourers low-cost housing in Alang Ship breaking yards, Gujarat, India

Source: Department of Architecture, University of Cambridge and CEPT University (Joint Design Studio between the Architecture Departments of the University of Cambridge (UK) and the Centre for Environmental Planning and Technology (CEPT) University, (India) run by Himanshu Parihk, Neelkanth Chhaya, Nicholas Ray and Utpal Sharma in 2004)

Figure 19.5 Collage of conventional vs incremental low-cost houses in Gujarat
Source: Jaime Royo-Olid

Figure 19.5 shows how external perceptions, whether obtained from technical analysis within the country or undertaken by international agencies, can provide an erroneous or indeed misleading analysis of the experience of habitation in the urban informal sector context. As poor households are unlikely to afford to build their home in a single period as to ensure outright completion, it is important to create a housing schema that permits sequential home building. On the left of the figure we can see a fragment of a standard two-floor designed building. On the right a proposed incremental housing scheme, showing different forms and stages of expansion of the ground floor building.

A standard policy based on analysis of the official quantitative statistics on the land use, floor coverage and street alignment would indicate a far lower level of housing value to the right side, while a radical, innovative capability imbued approach wherein the experience of habitation would likely indicate that public spaces around the house are important for allowing families to either extend the current premises to add a local shop or have oversight of their family members from the level of the street wall. Housing policies that advocate houses as complete, rigid objects without scope for adaptation end up limiting the possibilities for inhabiting.

A capability-induced housing policy approach, using objective criteria to define the sub-domains of housing capabilities, could push a new partnership. This partnership could be between global agendas, national policy makers, sub-national providers and local informal sector communities, ensuring that housing policy is undergirded by a strong policy of public consultation in which the most relevant expertise is that held by the poor in tackling their reality every day. Laudable efforts made within architectural and urban planning practices to simulate such public consultation is the part of larger agenda to develop spaces for public reasoning, a process by which all stakeholders can exchange information and develop a dialogue of how to create decent and comfortable habitats for the urban informal sector. The importance of the lived experience of residents in informal and marginal communities to signal the distinct possibility of new approach to housing, an approach that regards the act of habitation as the fundamental source of knowledge about the values that informal settlement residents accord to the facets of their everyday lives, is the first step in this important direction.

Conclusion: Taking the Technical into the Social

The principle of abstraction that is the conventional starting point for the professional work of the architect, and the rules and procedures that guide the activities of urban planners, as well as the proliferating pool of experts and administrators involved in housing at any scale – project managers, quantity surveyors, civil and structural engineers, and consultants– are fraught with vertical lines of engagement. There is a risk that this hierarchically constituted protocol will inevitably undermine the experiential dimension of habitation in relation to the technical imperatives of delivery. It is not enough to consult a community through its leaders and develop a schema for a housing programme. Rather, it is imperative to embed a transect approach to the housing problem; in terms of developing a brief, this entails an approach in which every street is explored, every habitation level surveyed, and every spatial attitude embedded in the local community properly appreciated. It is the sense of habitation that is paramount to ensuring that this level of granular data is imbued in the design of the housing programme. Such a procedure should be a primary stipulation of a demand-driving, capability-enhancing housing programme. This would move towards guaranteeing that it is inclusive, guarding against residents being treated fairly because of their particular conversion factors not being taken into account. Individuals can feel overwhelmed or cowed down by a social context if they do not have the conversion factors to use agency.

Habitats created through a mass-production template, one that produces housing as a homogenous market commodity, are rarely inclusive in incorporating features that are socially meaningful to its residents. In contrast, informal settlements, where houses are not identical because they result from the intertwining of factors of the everyday life, tend to be more intricately crafted. This intricacy grows from house owners striving to shape their habitation to allow for the effective enactment of their capabilities out of the scarce resources at hand. Therefore, in contrast to from constructing new homes when upgrading existing habitats, it may be possible to capitalise on pre-existing structures that intimately and meaningfully relate to the lives of inhabitants.

Beyond consultation on urban planning intentions, communities may well value being informed about the implications of living in a tall apartment block detached from public life as opposed to a ground floor house with direct exposure to the street. The latter would allow elderly residents to sit at home yet feel part of the neighbourhood; by the same token, it may cause a resident who is anxious about urban crime to feel insecure. Ideally the design and construction process and its mobilisation through professional activities should incorporate an effort to sensitise inhabitants with regard to their options and engage them in the process. The relationship between the components that structure the experience of housing or being a pedestrian – such as verandas, benches, walls, trees and road traffic – can have an important impact on the experience of the street. By being sensitive to the specificity of a place, the value of a mere channel for transportation can count for more; it can be experientially doubled or tripled, not only as a pleasant place for interaction, and in which good life can occur, but also in terms of how it functions.

Addressing the needs of the poor in developing countries 'requires a re-appraisal of the role of housing' as not a 'welfare burden on economic development' but rather as instrumental 'in stimulating capital formation through domestic savings and investment' (Payne and Majale, 2004). In this vein, a capability-imbued housing policy could be

Figure 19.6 Woman sitting in semi-public verandah in Ahmedabad, India.
Source: Acharya (2008)

a powerful instrument for developing objective evaluation criteria that will feed directly into the economically productive role of housing. In regions of the world where a large informal sector has yet to be connected to the global economy, we would seem to be confronted by the imperative to convert their structure of values to that of the market, with indigenous forms of production not necessarily optimally organised for this impending change. Where such processes of formalisation occur progressively, and housing programmes devised so as to adapt effectively in the design and implementation to resident activities, the localised forms of production would continue to be valued over template-based international commodities. For instance, the use of local doorways or verandas in an agreed building design (see Figure 19.6) would provide cultural and public specificities respectively to upgraded houses. Another important sub-domain particular to the informal sector is the relationship between housing and livelihood, where local craftsman-ship used for construction can be upgraded and provide an improved income stream to residents, thereby increasing resident agency and empowerment with regard to choice in their community sphere.

A capability-imbued housing approach has the advantage of being demand-driven, an approach that does not regard housing as a mass commodity mediated by a market-driven supply side rationale. It no longer regards housing as merely shelter from the elements, and thereby a reduction in negative freedom, but endorses it as an important capa-bility that can catalyse the agency and empowerment of informal sec-tor residents, building upon the participation of residents in the design and implementation of the programme. This approach, being process-sensitive and based on the principle of habitation, would permit the use of local skills and income generation. Low-cost traditional materials, such as earth, as well as innovative low-cost technologies such as solid waste material or agricultural leftovers (such as rice skin)[5] can be used to meet the growing demand for housing in the squatter settlements of cities whose urban populations continue to rise apace: in the cities of India, Kenya, Brazil, Mongolia, South Africa and in much of the world, subject to new patterns of human migration, the demand is set to increase further. There are established examples of urban houses that multiply up to ten times of the value of their original basic dwelling by means of informal and incremental self-building (see Hosagrahar, 2001). The additional capacity to upgrade housing alongside the skills of the residents in the management and maintenance of community assets is a powerful outcome of the capability-based housing approach.

The intellectual advantage of critically exploiting the *habitation–habitare* nexus is that it provides a basis for bringing the social and the spatial realms together in order to devise a powerful demand-driven approach to housing. Furthermore, it offers an advance in operationalising the capability approach as it aims to mobilise acknowledgment of the experience of habitation to generate narra-tive and survey data, using a range of participatory tools to produce objective evaluation criteria regarding context specific conversion

---

[5] Julián Salas has invented a rice-skin mortar with considerable cement-like properties.

factors. The proposed incorporation of the technical domain into the social/spatial nexus promises a more clear-cut procedural schema, one that would allow stakeholders to hold housing service providers accountable by means of their own stipulations as set out in the specific sub-domains that would emerge through consultation. The clear targeting of the context specific sub-domains permits a more direct monitoring of the capacity of a housing programme to be inclusive in its coverage, and to guard against overlooking individuals who might otherwise be unable to benefit because of their particular conversion factors–either on account of personal attributes (age or disability) or social norms (gender or caste), factors that may otherwise prevent them from specifying their values or using their voices to enhance their capabilities.

References

Aalbers, M. B. (2016) *The Financialization of Housing: A Political Economy Approach*. London & New York: Routledge, Taylor & Francis Group.

Acharya, P. (2008) Architectural thresholds welcoming collective affordances: Learning from conventional urban housing in Ahmedabad. Undergraduate Thesis in Architecture, CEPT University, Ahmedabad.

Alkire, S. (2002) *Valuing Freedoms: Sen's Capability Approach and Poverty Reduction*. Oxford: Oxford University Press.

Appadurai, A. (1986) *The Social Life of Things: Commodities in Cultural Perspective*. Cambridge: Cambridge University Press.

  (1996) *Modernity at Large: Cultural Dimensions of Globalization*. Minneapolis: University of Minnesota Press.

Awan, N., Scheneider, T. and Till, J. (2011) *Spatial Agency: Other Way of Doing Architecture*. Oxford: Routledge.

Barac, M. (2007) 'Transit spaces: Thinking urban change in South Africa'. *Home Cultures*, 4(2): 147–76.

  (2016) Spatial misreading: South Africa's urban future seen from within a township shack. In N. Elleh (Ed.) *Reading the Architecture of the Underprivileged Classes*. Farnham: Ashgate.

Biau, D. (2015) *The Bridge and the City: A Universal Love Story*. Plantation, FL: Llumina Press.

Biggeri, M., Ballet, J. and Comim, F. (2011) *Children and the Capability Approach*. Palgrave: Macmillan.

Biggeri, M., D. Clark and A. Friediani, (Eds.) (2019) *The Capability Approach, Empowerment and Participation: Concepts, Methods and Applications*, Basingstoke: Palgrave Macmillan.

Blundell Jones, P., Till, J. and Petrescu, D. (Eds.) (2005) *Architecture & Participation*. Abingdon: Spon Press/Taylor & Francis Group.

Castells, M. (1996) *The Rise of the Network Society*. Malden, MA: Blackwell Publishers, Ltd.

Chiappero-Martinetti, E., and N. von Jacobi, (2015) How can Sen's 'Capabilities Approach@ Contribute to Understanding the Role for Social Innovations for the Marginalised, CRESSI Working Papers, no.3, Creating Economic Space for Social Innovations (CrESSI), Oxford.

Chambers, R. (1997) *Whose Reality Counts? Putting the First Last*. New York: Intermediate Technology Publications.

Clark, D. A., Biggeri, M. and Frediani, A. A. (Eds.) (2018) *Sen's Capability Approach, Empowerment and Participation: Concepts, Methods and Applications*. Basingstoke, New York: Palgrave MacMillan.

Cleaver, Frances (1999) 'Paradoxes of Participation: Questioning Participatory Approaches to Development.' *Journal of International Development*, 11(4). pp. 597–61.

Coates D, Anand P and Norris M. (2013) Housing, Happiness and Capabilities: A Summary of the International Evidence and Models. *International Journal of Energy, Environment and Economics*, 21(3), 181.

Comim, F. (2001) '*Operationalising Sen's Capabilites Approach*' paper prepared for the conference Justice and Poverty: Examining San's Capability Approach. Cambridge, 5-7 June 2001.

(2008) *The Capability Approach: Concepts, Measures and Applications*. Cambridge: Cambridge University Press.

Cornwall, A., & Brock, K. (2005) What do buzzwords do for development policy? A critical look at 'participation', 'empowerment' and 'poverty reduction'. *Third World Quarterly*, 26, 1043–1060.

De Botton, A. (2006) *The Architecture of Happiness*. London: Penguin.

De Soto, H. (2000) *The Mystery of capital: Why Capitalism Triumphs in the West and Fails Everywhere Else*. London: Basic Books.

Equalities Act (2006) https://www.legislation.gov.uk/ukpga/2006/3/contents

Frediani, A. A. (2007) Amartya Sen, the World Bank, and the Redress of Urban Poverty: A Brazilian Case Study. *Journal of Human Development and Capabilities*, 8(1), 133–152.

(2010) 'Sen's capability approach as a framework to the practice of development'. *Development in Practice*, 20(2), 173–87.

Gell, A. (1992) Thetechnology of enchantment and the enchantment of technology. In J. Coote and A. Shelton (Eds.) *Anthropology, Art & Aesthetics*. Oxford: Clarendon Press.

Giddens, A. (1986) *The Constitution of Society: Outline of the Theory of Structuration*. Cambridge: Polity Press.

Glaeser, E. (2011) *The Triumph of the City.* London: Penguin.

Hamdi, N. and Goethert, R. (1995) *Housing Without Houses: Participation, Flexibility, Enablement.* London: ITDG Publishing.

(1997) *Action Planning for Cities.* Chichester: John Wiley.

(2004) *Small Change: About the Art of Practice and Limits of Planning in Cities.* London: Earthscan.

(2005) *Partnerships in Urban Planning: A Guide to Municipalities.* Rugby: Practical Action Publishing.

Hosagrahar, J. (2001) 'Mansions to margins: Modernity and the domestic landscape of historic Delhi, 1847–1910'. *Journal of the Society of Architectural Historians,* 60, 24–45.

Huchzermeyer, M. (2011) *Cities 'with Slums': From Slum Eradication to a Right to the City in Africa.* Cape Town: Juta/UCT Press.

Khosla, R. and Samuels, J. (2005) *Removing Unfreedoms. Citizens as Agents of Urban Development.* London: ITDG Publishing.

Lipton, M. (1977) *Why Poor People Stay Poor: A Study of Urban Bias in World Development.* London: Temple Smith.

Longshore Smith, M., and Seward, C. (2009) The Relational Ontology of Amartya Sen's Capability Approach: Incorporating Social and Individual Causes, *Journal of Human Development and Capabilities,* 10:2, 213–235.

McFarlane, C. and Graham, S. (Eds.) (2014) *Infrastructural Lives: Urban Infrastructure in Context.* London: Routledge.

Miller, D., (2008) *The Comfort of Things,* Cambridge: Polity Press.

Montgomery, C. (2013) *Happy City: Transforming Our Lives Through Urban Design.* London: Penguin Books.

Mosse, David (2001) "People's knowledge', participation and patronage: operations and representations in rural development.' In: Cook, B and Kothari, U, (eds.), *Participation – the new tyranny?* London: Zed Press, pp. 16–35.

National Research Council (2003) *Cities Transformed: Demographic Change and Its Implications in the Developing World.* Washington D.C.: The National Academies Press.

ODI (1978) Basic Needs, Briefing Paper, no. 5, 1978.

Olsen, W. (2006) Pluralism, poverty and sharecropping: Cultivating open-mindedness in development studies. *Journal of Development Studies,* 42, 1130–1157.

Payne, G. (2016) Options for intervention: Increasing tenure security for community development and urban transformation. Paper presented at the United Nations Conference on Housing and Sustainable Urban Development (Habitat III) in Quito, Ecuador, October 2016.

Payne, G. and M. Majale (2004). 'The Urban Housing Manual: Making regulatory frameworks work for the poor' London: Earthscan.

Renaud, B. (1984) *Housing and financial institutions in developing countries: an overview*. Washington, DC: World Bank Staff Working Papers.

Royo-Olid, J. (2004) Urban solidarities: Structures of collective freedom. Dissertation for Diploma in Architecture, Department of Architecture, University of Cambridge.

(2006) Developmental approaches to 'Humane Habitat': From 'basic needs' to 'capabilities'. MPhil Dissertation, Department of Land Economy, University of Cambridge.

Royo-Olid, J., Fennell, S., Boanada-Fuchs, A. and Payne, G. (2017) On the financialisation and affordability of housing in the global south-from political economy to system dynamics: Contrasting cases from cities in India. Presentation to the Royal Geographical Society and Institute of British Geographers Annual Conference 2017, London.

Royo-Olid, J. and Fennell, S. (eds) (2018) *Building, Owning and Belonging: from assisting owner driven housing reconstruction to co-production in Sri Lanka, India and beyond*. European Union and UN-Habitat, Publications Office of the EU.

Rykwert, J. (2000) *The Seduction of Place: The History and Future of the City*. Oxford: Oxford University Press.

Satterthwaite, D. (1997) *Urban Poverty: Reconsidering its Scale and Nature*. IDS Bulletin 28(2): 9–22.

Satterthwaite, D. and Mitlin, D. (2004) *Empowering Squatter Citizens*. London: Earthscan.

Sen, A. (1997) Maximization and the Act of Choice, *Econometrica*, Vol. 65, No. 4 (Jul., 1997), pp. 745–779.

(1999) *Development as Freedom*. Oxford: Oxford University Press.

(2003) Development and Capability Expression, in Fukuda-Parr (et. al.) *Readings in Human Development*, New York and New Delhi: Oxford University Press.

(2005) Human Rights and Capabilities, *Journal of Human Development*, 6, 2, 151–166.

Streeten, P. and Shahid, B. (1981) 'Basic needs: Some issues'. *World Development*, 6(3), 411–21.

Turner, J. F. C. (1976) *Housing by People*. New York: Pantheon Books.

Turner, F. C. and R. Fichter (1972) *Freedom to Build: Dweller Control of the Housing Process*. New York: The Macmillan Company.

UN-Habitat (1996) *An Urbanizing World: Global Report on Human Settlements*. Oxford: Oxford University Press.

(2017) *Building, Owning and Belonging: From Assisting Owner-Driven Home Reconstruction to Co-Production in Sri Lanka*. India and Beyond: EU Publications.

United Nations (2017) New Urban Agenda, Habitat III, http://habitat3.org/
   wp-content/uploads/NUA-English.pdf
Watson, V. (2014) 'Co-production and collaboration in planning: The difference'. *Planning Theory & Practice*, 15(1), 62–76.
World Bank (1993) *Housing: Enabling Markets to Work*. Washington, DC:
   World Bank.
   (2002) *Globalization, growth, and poverty: building an inclusive world
   economy*. Washington, DC: World Bank.
   (2003) *World Bank Development Report 2004: Making Services Work
   for Poor People*. Washington, DC & New York: World Bank & Oxford
   University Press.

20 | Building Regulations through the Capability Lens
A Safer and Inclusive Built Environment?

PRACHI ACHARYA

Introduction

Much of what motivates planners, architects, engineers, builders and others involved in designing, constructing and researching on buildings is the relationship between construction standards and the resulting quality of life of occupants. Building codes play a substantive role in this relationship. While intuitive, this rapport is complex. Yet, it is oversimplified when assuming that high construction standards necessarily contribute to improving wellbeing. This is generally true. For instance, an earthquake-resistant house is safer than one that is not and can facilitate access to insurance. This relationship, however, does not always hold, such as when those who bear the costs (individual, households or the economy) at the expense of excess debt or of other fundamental needs. In contexts of severe poverty, compliance with certain standards might simply be unaffordable. Or, in the absence of technical skill sets, or of functioning supply chains, achieving high standards might be practically unattainable. This raises the question of when and how does increasing standards help, and from which point might it become an impediment for wellbeing? This question is at the heart of the debate put forward by Amartya Sen's capability approach (CA) that considers that resources can be imperfect indicators of human well-being (Sen, 1999).

The above calls for the need to re-examine how building regulatory frameworks can realistically relate to the capabilities of people. That is, how can the relationship be mutually reinforced between what people value and what they can attain with regards to the level of standards. How can this relationship be conceptualised, formulated and communicated for making building regulations effective and efficacious in the context of increasing disaster risks and climate uncertainties. Contextualising this problem with India's largest social housing programme in rural areas (including peri-urban areas), this chapter explores how Sen's CA can offer an alternative way of reconceptualising building regulations, particularly aspects of construction methods and materials.

This chapter has three parts. The first part deliberates the need for building codes for low-income housing in the global south. Next, it discusses the context of India's social housing programme. The final part suggests how viewing building codes for low-income housing through the capability lens may enhance inclusivity and safety in the built environment.

Do We Need Building Codes for Low-Income Housing?

Whether building codes and standards improve or worsen the living conditions of people under high levels of poverty is highly contested. In support of building codes, many argue it as necessary for safety and safeguarding (public) health (Hamza and Zetter, 1998; Bailie and Wayte, 2006; Kumar and Pushplata, 2013). In fact, health implications of housing conditions are highlighted in several public health studies with recurrent references to fire hazards, indoor air pollution from cooking fuels, overcrowding-led infectious diseases, deficiencies in water and sanitary solutions (see Thomson et al., 2001; Bashir, 2002; Krieger and Higgins, 2002; Kumari and Singh, 2007; Rauh et al., 2008; Malaviya et al., 2014; Hernández, 2016; Lam et al., 2016). Beyond chronic health effects, as Coburn and Spence (2002) suggest, building codes can effectively reduce disaster risks. This has emerged as key priority in international and national development agendas, where built environment policies focus on reducing physical and structural vulnerability through stringent and stronger building codes (Theckethil, 2006).

In contrast, prescribed building codes, while differing across countries, are increasingly and often suited to global markets. There are many people in developing nations, however, who cannot afford or access these markets, such those as remote rural communities or severely poor ones closer to urban centres. Turner (1972), in his seminal work on housing standards, built upon two critical points: First, he drew attention to how people living in poverty are penalised for not being able to build or pay for houses that follow high standards, which are set according to views of elite policy makers and professionals. Second, he highlighted that minimum standards are often counterproductive in situations where required investments and the effective demand for it do not match, and subsequently when homeowners cannot cover this gap. Mabogunje et al. (1978) takes an equally strong position and questions whether standards are designed to ensure social stratification rather than actually resolve housing needs.

More objectively, Theckethil (2006) and Yahya et al. (2001) posit that people living in poverty in low- and middle-income countries often find the use of building codes difficult, mainly for three reasons: its techno-legal language makes it difficult to understand; it is usually inflexible to allow innovative solutions; and codes are typically based on construction norms predominant in high-income countries, which are often not suited to local sociocultural requirements. Prompted by similar concerns, the cases of user-led processes for formulating building standards in Sri Lanka and Kenya suggest community-led processes can be advantageous. Community-led processes can provide a basis for bridging experiential and technical knowledge and people are better oriented to effectively utilise them (Theckethil, 2006).

Indian Social Housing and Building Regulatory Framework

To address the problem of how centralised building regulatory tools can become more useful for and usable by end-users by addressing decentralised trade-off processes in housing for people living under high poverty levels, India constitutes an eminent setting. India's rural housing shortage for 2012–17 was estimated to 43.67 million houses (MoRD, 2011). This gap is calculated based on ('acceptable') housing quality, which is determined by 'structural permanence' (Revi, 1990; Singh et al., 2013). Here, the notion of 'permanence' and 'temporal' emerges not from a structure's durability but rather from the construction material that has been used (Revi, 1990; Das et al., 2014). For instance, structures built with fragile cement blocks are considered 'permanent' and rammed earth walls are classified as 'temporary' despite the fact that they can last over 100 years (Revi, 1990).

This understanding of the lifecycle characteristics of rural buildings is reflected in India's largest social housing programme, the *Indira Awas Yojana* (IAY) renamed *Pradhan Mantri Awas Yojana-Gramin* (PMAY-G) in 2016. The IAY/PMAY-G provides housing finance to people living below India's rural poverty line to construct 'permanent' houses with at least $25m^2$ plinth area with long lasting materials.

For this, programme officers tend to encourage engineered materials such as bricks, cement, steel and corrugated sheets (Khanna, 2014). While engineered materials are readily available in urban areas, in rural construction supply chains they are seldom available or affordable. Studies associate such limited prescriptions of accepted materials and an absence of professional training in rural areas as key reasons for poor construction quality, high costs and incomplete houses (Rizvi, 2011; Das et al., 2014).

Given this context and that challenges to building standards compliance in India are not new, the scale and speed required for IAY/PMAY-G to complete 10 million houses between 2016–19 raises few questions: with few masons with training in building with engineered materials in rural India (Chhabra and Chariar, 2014), how can we ensure and scale-up the quality of engineered disaster risk reduction features in such a short duration? With characteristics of local materials varying in each region, how can the performance of the constructed house be consistent? Finally, which of the end-users determines 'performance' – the homeowners, the masons, the project engineers or the policy influencers? These questions ultimately aim at understanding how centralised building regulatory tools – based on linear deterministic approaches – can become more useful for and usable by end-users by addressing decentralised trade-off processes in housing for people living under high poverty levels, and offer flexible and differentiated technical solutions. When suggesting these solutions, however, it is important to clarify usefulness and improved usability for what/whom, to what/whom and of what/whom?

Capabilities-Centered Building Codes: Problem or Solution?

Welfare programmes, such as the social housing programme in India, tend to adopt a basic needs approach (BNA). The BNA focuses on the provision of commodities – basic resources, services and infrastructure – with a particular focus on people severely deprived from these in order to allow for 'opportunities for a full life' (Streeten, 1981: 21 in Clark, 2006). Alkire (2005) argues, however, that the BNA is based on top-down planning that disregards specification of contextual needs. In tailoring welfare planning to contextual needs, she credits Amartya Sen's CA. The CA puts forth the significance of people's values, their choices, the process through which they make choices, and the extent to which these processes are participatory. Emphasising choice processes and their nature, Sen (1997) distinguishes between 'comprehensive outcomes' and 'culmination outcomes'. According to Sen, culmination outcomes limit the focus to the end result only. Instead, he suggests, comprehensive outcomes consider the process and act of choice. The act of choice, includes '... the identity of the chooser, the menu over which choice is being made, and the relation of the particular act to behavioral social norms that constrain particular social actions' (Sen, 1997: 746).

Applying such comprehensive analysis of outcomes in the built environment can allow a better understanding of how people make decisions for building their houses. Indeed, within the built environment literature, people's choice processes has been highlighted by many authors. One of the key prologues to this has been Turner (1976)'s work, where he urged that housing be understood not as a standalone product but as a process. In other words, how does housing and its building process impact or influence peoples' choices and abilities? Turner (1976) strongly argued in favour of decentralising large-scale housing programmes and making households the primary decision-makers. Hamdi and Goethert (1997) take the idea of decentralisation forward for city planning by advocating for handing decision-making powers to communities. More recently, community- and people-centred development has been re-emphasised in scholarship and in practice on post-disaster housing recovery, mainly as owner-driven reconstruction (see for instance Lyons et al., 2010; Bosher and Dainty, 2011; Schilderman and Lyons, 2011; Arlikatti and Andrew, 2012) and on social housing programmes (Majale, 2004; Bradlow et al., 2011; Baquero, 2013; Lizarralde, 2015).

While these studies centre around peoples' processes, they do not explicitly use Sen's CA. Exceptions are the works of (Frediani 2009, 2010) that uses it for evaluating slum upgrading projects, Lewis (2012) in which the public health implications of the built environment are examined, Frediani and Boano (2012) that studies the relationship between participatory processes and resultant products, Hansen (2015) that explores sociospatial processes in urban design, and Sood (2015) who draws parallels between urban design theories and CA. Also, in their work focusing on the built environment, Frediani and Hansen (2015: 3) explain capabilities as 'people's freedoms to achieve the things and experiences they have reason to value'.

Here, they explain, 'freedoms' signifies having 'choices' or strategies available to people to enhance their well-being aspirations; 'abilities' or capacity- and skill-set accessible to people that facilitates realisation of well-being; and 'opportunities' or structural elements, e.g. laws, that allow access to and use of abilities and choices.

Sen's CA is, however, considered too open-ended, notably by Nussbaum (2000). Nussbaum (2000), with her proposition of a 'central human capabilities' set, argues that without a universal list of positive freedoms, it becomes difficult to effectively use the approach. Sen (2005), however, deliberately refrains from suggesting a definite capabilities set, which is prescriptive and prejudged by theorists. This, Sen (2005) suggests, denies the integration of (participatory) consensus from the communities in question. Participative consensus, according to Alkire (2007), allows for a 'give-and-take dialogue', i.e. an iterative process to determine 'dimensions' to appropriately enhance capabilities of a group or community, including understanding long-term valued aspirations and fundamental priorities essential to those aspirations.

To analyse these multiple transactions arising in a participative discourse, Frediani (2010) proposes the use of the capability space – particularly for development planning. He explains that focusing on the capability space will allow development practitioners to understand how resources are transformed into achieved functionings. The capability space illustrates determinants that shape these transformations, i.e. individual, local (e.g. community, traditions, environment) and structural (e.g. laws and regulations) determinants, risks and vulnerabilities that shape peoples' choices, abilities and opportunities that facilitates real capabilities (Frediani, 2010). Frediani (2015: 14) further suggests a 'participatory capabilities' framework to first assess people's 'choice, ability and opportunity to engage in participatory processes' and illustrates 'limitations and opportunities for transformative change'. Taking cue from Frediani (2008, 2010, 2015), this chapter suggests that building standards based on a comprehensive understanding of the capability space of end-users can increase the effective usability of building standards. Ultimately, this effective usability aims to create a safer built environment in rural and peri-urban areas while responding to end-users' vulnerabilities.

For comprehensively understanding the capability space, a participatory inquiry can help unfold the range of trade-offs between aspirations, needs, choices, abilities and opportunities that end-users make in housing construction processes. This approach, however, relies heavily on qualitative evidence. Such evidence, Frediani (2010: 9) points, can be 'compromised by their adverse situations', i.e. participants are found to often lower their aspiration levels in order to accept the worsening living conditions. Elster (1982) coined this as 'adaptive preference'. Frediani (2010) refers to the works of Teschl and Comim (2005) and Clark (2009) that reveal that in communities with scarce accessible resources, adaptations occur and evolve continuously, suggesting that it 'reflects new possibilities' (p. 9). Frediani (2010) also echoes Teschl and Comim (2005)'s reasoning that adaptation does not restrain peoples' ability to self-evaluate and prioritise wellbeing, but resignation does – mainly leading to passivity and 'putting up with fate'. They proceed to argue that in deprived communities, people actively engaged in struggling for improving their living conditions would not be feeling resignation, which according to Clark (2009) makes a strong case for engaging with participatory qualitative inquiries. Teschl and Comim (2005) add that peoples' values and desires cannot be assumed to be static, which thus imparts meaning to study the factors and motivations that induce adaptation, as will be done in this study of a flood-prone rural built environment.

Converging with the arguments presented by Teschl and Comim (2005) and Clark (2009), much of the built environment literature, particularly in the context of climate uncertainties, increasingly sees adaptation and the capacity to adapt as positive attributes in infrastructure and built environment design (see Wamsler, 1999; Moser and Satterthwaite, 2008; Revi, 2008). Adaptability is in fact viewed as imperative to enhance resilience (see Jha et al., 2013; Moullier and Krimgold, 2016).

In scholarship and in practice, as MacAskill and Guthrie (2014) explain, the term 'resilience' has been used in varied ways. For instance, UNISDR (2009: 24) suggest resilience to be '[t]he ability of a system, community or society exposed to hazards to resist, absorb, accommodate to and recover from the effects of a hazard in a timely and efficient manner, including through the preservation and restoration of its essential basic structures and functions'. However, as Béné et al. (2012) highlight, what is required to resist shocks from hazards may differ from what is required to absorb, to adapt and to recover – thus rendering inconsistency in an understanding of a resilient system. Manyena et al. (2011: 423) contend that resilience should be understood as an ability to 'bounce forward' and not bounce back to the

512 The Housing and Urban Frontier

original state. In response to cross-disciplinary and multi-level interpretations of resilience, MacAskill and Guthrie (2014: 667) suggest that 'a strict consensus on the definition of resilience is not practical or perhaps not even possible' and that it needs to be contextualised.

In contextualising resilience in the built environment, structural resilience – i.e. incorporating disaster resilient features – receives significant focus. This, as mentioned earlier, is key in policies geared towards achieving disaster resilience through stringent building standards. In achieving such resilience, however, it may be prudent to acknowledge its undesirable aspects. For instance, communities may increase their capacity to cope with particular structural damages and losses by making adaptations (considered as resilience), but which may come at the cost of other wellbeing dimensions (Béné et al., 2012). An example of this is how in the Indian coastal state of Odisha, the choice of construction materials, methods and house-types specified by the government under India's rural social housing programme – that promoted the use of reinforced cement concrete for structural resilience – often resulted in indebting families in remote rural areas due to high costs of construction material and method, and additional material wastages due to absence of trained masons (Das et al., 2014). Extrapolated into simple terms, a resilient house does not necessarily translate into a resilient home. It is, thus, helpful to work towards resilient homes through an agency-based perspective.

An agency-based perspective to resilience can allow examining what end-users view as resilience, how they take decisions to utilise and strengthen their sources of resilience, and the facilitative and constraining determinants that shape their (understanding of) resilience. This perspective, thus, allows understanding resilience not as a person's intrinsic characteristic, but as the condition(s) that 'enable individuals to beat the odds, or thinking about measures to change the odds by removing obstacles and creating opportunities' (Schoon and Bartley, 2008: 25).

While the building standards are intended to enhance the well-being of end-users, of which increased resilience to disasters is considered important, what is often overlooked in studies on building standards is how it can acknowledge capabilities of different end-users living under high poverty levels. Proceeding from these perspectives, this chapter considers utilising a capabilities-based building standard (see Figure 20.1).

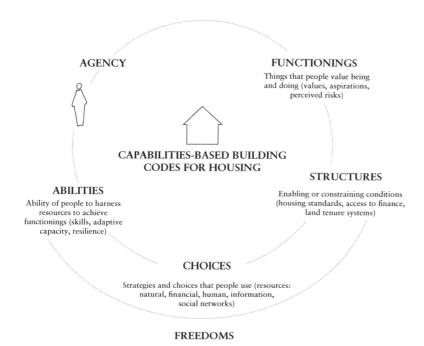

AGENCY

FUNCTIONINGS

Things that people value being
and doing (values, aspirations,
perceived risks)

CAPABILITIES-BASED BUILDING
CODES FOR HOUSING

STRUCTURES

ABILITIES

Enabling or constraining conditions
(housing standards, access to finance,
land tenure systems)

Ability of people to harness
resources to achieve
functionings (skills, adaptive
capacity, resilience)

CHOICES

Strategies and choices that people use (resources:
natural, financial, human, information,
social networks)

FREEDOMS

Figure 20.1 Capabilities framework for building standards

An understanding of the end-user's capability space, that includes an agency-based perspective to resilience, may suggest relevant clues to direct how building standards can be more inclusive and equitable. Its use can suggest differentiated and stratified solutions – ranging from zero damage to life safety – and suggest a roadmap for gradual compliance.

Conclusion

Pro-poor building codes and peoples' processes in housing have been debated over the past five decades. However, literature does not satisfactorily suggest approaches beyond the 'problem-solution' perspective that capitalises on end-users' capabilities to improve the usability and usefulness of building codes. This chapter suggests that utilising Sen's capability framework can provide valuable directions for stratifying building codes and standards that can allow for incremental inclusion of risk reduction elements in the built environment. Such an approach is particularly critical in low- and middle-income countries, where large sections of populations living under high levels of poverty are deprived of access to construction systems suited to global markets, and are concurrently likely to be disproportionately affected by climate uncertainties.

References

Alkire, S. (2005) 'Needs and capabilities'. *Royal Institute of Philosophy Supplement*, 57, 229–52.
  (2007) 'Choosing Dimensions: The Capability Approach and Multidimensional Poverty'. In Kakwani, N. and Silber, J. (Eds.) *The Many Dimensions of Poverty*. London: Palgrave Macmillan.
Arlikatti, S. and Andrew, S. A. (2012) 'Housing design and long-term recovery processes in the aftermath of the 2004 Indian Ocean tsunami'. *Natural Hazards Review*, 13, 34–44.
Bailie, R. S. and Wayte, K. J. (2006) 'Housing and health in Indigenous communities: Key issues for housing and health improvement in remote Aboriginal and Torres Strait Islander communities'. *Australian Journal of Rural Health*, 14, 178–83.
Baquero, I. A. (2013) Organized self-help housing as an enabling shelter and development strategy. Lessons from current practice, institutional approaches and projects in developing countries. Thesis, Lund University.
Bashir, S. A. (2002) 'Home is where the harm is: Inadequate housing as a public health crisis'. *American Journal of Public Health*, 92, 733–8.
Béné, C., Wood, R. G., Newsham, A. and Davies, M. (2012) New Utopia or New Tyranny? Reflection about the potentials and limits of the concept of resilience in relation to vulnerability reduction programmes. IDS Working Paper, Brighton.
Bosher, L. and Dainty, A. (2011) 'Disaster risk reduction and "built-in" resilience: Towards overarching principles for construction practice'. *Disasters*, 35, 1–18.
Bradlow, B., Bolnick, J. and Shearing, C. (2011) 'Housing, institutions, money: The failures and promise of human settlements policy and practice in South Africa'. *Environment & Urbanization*, 23, 267–75.
Chhabra, M. and Chariar, V. (2014) Where are all the masons trained in disaster resilient technologies? Reflections from Indian experiences of capacity building of masons and building artisans. EU–UN Habitat Conference: Restoring Communities through Home-Owner-Driven

Reconstruction: from post-Emergency to Development. Colombo. March 24–25, 2014.

Clark, D. A. (2005) Sen's capability approach and the many spaces of human well-being'. *Journal of Development Studies*, 41, 1339–68.

(2006) Capability Approach. In Clark, D. (Eds.) *The Elgar Companion to Development Studies*. Cheltenham: Edward Elgar Publishing.

(2009) 'Adaptation, poverty and well-being: Some issues and observations with special reference to the capability approach and development studies'. *Journal of Human Development and Capabilities*, 10, 21–42.

Coburn, A. W. and Spence, R. J. S. (2002). *Earthquake Protection*. Hoboken, NJ: John Wiley and Sons.

Das, P. K., Khanna, P. and Mishra, A. U. (2014). *Diagnostic Study on Rural Housing in Odisha*. New Delhi: United Nations Development Programme.

Elster, J. (1982) Sour grapes – utilitarianism and the genesis of wants. In A. K. Sen and B. Williams (Eds.) *Utilitarianism and Beyond*. Cambridge: Cambridge University Press.

Frediani, A. A. (2008) *Planning for Freedoms: The Contribution of Sen's Capability Approach to Development Practice*. Available from: http://discovery.ucl.ac.uk/1317962/1/briefing_ca.pdf [Accessed 30 August 2016].

(2009) The World Bank, Turner and Sen – Freedom in the Urban Arena. DPU Working Paper Development Planning Unit, UCL, London.

(2010) 'Sen's Capability Approach as a framework to the practice of development'. *Development in Practice*, 20, 173–87.

(2015) Participatory Capabilities' in Development Practice. The Capability Approach in Development Planning and Urban Design. Development Planning Unit, UCL, London.

Frediani, A. A and Boano, C. (2012) Processes for just products: The capability space of participatory design. In Oosterlaken, I. and van den, J. (Eds.) *The Capability Approach, Technology and Design*. Dordrecht: Springer.

Frediani, A. A. and Hansen, J. (Eds.) (2015) The Capability Approach in Development Planning and Urban Design. DPU Working Paper Special Issue. Development Planning Unit, UCL, London.

Hamdi, N. and Goethert, R. (1997) *Action Planning for Cities: A Guide to Community Practice*. Chichester: John Wiley.

Hamza, M. and Zetter, R. (1998) 'Structural adjustment, urban systems, and disaster vulnerability in developing countries'. *Cities*, 15, 291–99.

Hansen, J. (2015) Locating capabilities in the built environment: Socio-spatial products and processes and the capability approach. In A. A. Frediani and J. Hansen (Eds.) *The Capability Approach in Development Planning and Urban Design*. London: DPU, UCL.

Hernández, D. (2016) 'Affording housing at the expense of health: Exploring the housing and neighborhood strategies of poor families'. *Journal of Family Issues*, 37, 921–46.

Jha, A. K., Miner, T. W. and Stanton-Geddes, Z. (Eds.) (2013) *Building Urban Resilience*. Washington D.C.: World Bank.

Khanna, P. (2014) Development of state-specific compendium of green technologies for Indira Awas Yojana in Odisha. Draft Report. United Nations Development Programme, India.

Krieger, J. and Higgins, D. L. (2002) 'Housing and Health: Time again for public health action'. *American Journal of Public Health*, 92, 758–68.

Kumar, A. and Pushplata (2013) 'Vernacular practices: As a basis for formulating building regulations for hilly areas'. *International Journal of Sustainable Built Environment*, 2, 183–92.

Kumari, V. and Singh, R. K. P. (2007) 'Rural housing and health condition in North Bihar: A village level study'. *Journal of Rural Development*, 26, 439–53.

Lam, N. L., Pachauri, S., Purohit, P., et al. (2016) 'Kerosene subsidies for household lighting in India: What are the impacts?' *Environmental Research Letters*, 11(4), 044014.

Lewis, F. (2012) 'Auditing capability and active living in the built environment'. *Journal of Human Development and Capabilities*, 13, 295–315.

Lizarralde, G. (2015) *The Invisible Houses: Re-thinking and Designing Low-Cost Housing in Developing Countries*. New York and London: Routledge.

Lyons, M., Schilderman, T. and Boano, C. (Eds.) (2010) *Building Back Better*. Warwickshire, UK: Practical Action Publishing.

MacAskill, K. and Guthrie, P. (2014) 'Multiple interpretations of resilience in disaster risk management'. *Procedia Economics and Finance*, 18, 667–74.

Majale, M. (2004) 'Improving access to adequate and affordable housing for the urban poor through an integrated approach'. International Conference on Adequate & Affordable Housing for All: Research, Policy, Practice, Toronto. June 24 – 27, 2004.

Malaviya, P., Hasker, E., Picado, A., et al. (2014) 'Exposure to phlebotomusargentipes (diptera, psychodidae, phlebotominae) sand flies in rural areas of Bihar, India: The role of housing conditions'. *PLoS ONE*, 9(9), e106771.

Manyena, S. B., O'Brien, G., O'Keefe, P. and Rose, J. (2011) 'Editorial: Disaster resilience: A bounce back or bounce forward ability?' *Local Environment*, 16, 417–24.

Mabogunje, A., Hardoy, J. E. and Misra R. P. (1978) 'The Influence of Standards and Criteria'. In Jackson C. I. (Ed.) *Shelter Provision in Developing Countries: Scope 11*. New York: John Wiley and Sons.

MoRD. (2011) *Working Group on Rural Housing for XII Five Year Plan.* New Delhi: Planning Commission of India.

Moser, C. and Satterthwaite, D. (2008) Towards pro-poor adaptation to climate change in the urban centres of low- and middle-income countries. Climate Change and Cities Discussion, World Bank, Washington DC: IIED.

Moullier, T. and Krimgold, F. (2016) *Building Regulation for Resilience: Managing Risks for Safer Cities.* Washington D.C.: World Bank.

Nussbaum, M. (2000) *Women and Human Development: The Capabilities Approach.* Cambridge: Cambridge University Press.

Rauh, V. A., Landrigan, P. J. and Claudio, L. (2008) 'Housing and health: Intersection of poverty and environmental exposures'. *The Annals of the New York Academic of Sciences*, 1136, 276–88.

Revi, A. (1990) *Shelter in India.* New Delhi: Development Alternatives.
    (2008) 'Climate change risk: An adaptation and mitigation agenda for Indian cities'. *Environment & Urbanization*, 20, 207–29.

Rizvi, F. F. (2011) Housing situation among the poor and marginalised rural households: A study of Indira Awaas Yojana in selected districts of Orissa and Maharashtra. Working Paper. New Delhi: Indian Institute of Dalit Studies.

Schilderman, T. and Lyons, M. (2011) 'Resilient dwellings or resilient people? Towards people-centred reconstruction'. *Environmental Hazards*, 10, 218–31.

Schoon, I. and Bartley, M. (2008) 'Growing up in Poverty: The role of human capability and resilience'. *The Psychologist*, 21, 24–7.

Sen, A. (1997) 'Maximization and the act of choice'. *Econometrica*, 65(4), 745–79.
    (1999) *Development as Freedom.* Oxford: Oxford University Press.
    (2005) 'Human rights and capabilities'. *Journal of Human Development*, 6, 151–66.

Singh, S., Swaminathan, M. and Ramachandran, V. K. (2013) 'Housing shortages in rural India'. *Review of Agrarian Studies*, 3(2), 54–72.

Sood, A. (2015) Design for freedom: A paper examining urban design through the lens of the capability approach. In A. A. Frediani and J. Hansen (Eds.) *The Capability Approach in Development Planning and Urban Design.* London: DPU, UCL.

Teschl, M. and Comim, F. (2005) 'Adaptive preferences and capabilities: Some preliminary conceptual explorations'. *Review of Social Economy*, 63, 229–47.

Theckethil, R. (2006) 'Building codes'. *Journal of Security Education*, 1, 95–106.

Thomson, H., Petticrew, M. and Morrison, D. (2001) 'Health effects of housing improvement: Systematic review of intervention studies'. *BMJ*, 323, 187–90.

Turner, J. F. C. (1972) 'Housing issues and the standards problem'. *Ekistics*, 33, 155–8.
    (1976) *Housing by People: Towards Autonomy in Building Environments.* New York: Pantheon Books.
UNISDR (2009) *Terminology on Disaster Risk Reduction.* New York: United Nations.
Wamsler, C. (1999) 'Managing urban risk: Perceptions of housing and planning as a tool for reducing disaster risk'. *GBER*, 4, 11–28.
Yahya, S., Agevi, E., Lowe, L., Mugova, A., Musandu-Nyamayaor, O. and Schilderman, T. (2001) *Double Standards, Single Purpose: Reforming Housing Regulations to Reduce Poverty.* London: ITDG Publishing.

21 | *Cities and the Capability Approach*

P. B. ANAND

Introduction

This chapter presents an original contribution in applying the capability approach to cities. After critically examining literature at the forefront of the discussion on cities, this chapter develops specific ways in which a capability approach as a theoretical framework can be applied to analyse urban policy challenges especially in the context of development in general and Sustainable Development Goal 11 in particular. Original empirical analysis based on urbanisation and life expectancy in a number of countries identifies what is meant by inclusive urban growth.

The capability approach is about human flourishing. We cannot think of human flourishing without thinking about cities – throughout history from the ancient civilisations through to twenty-first century societies. According to the World Urbanisation Prospects, 54 per cent of people lived in urban areas in 2014 and this proportion is likely to reach 66 per cent by 2050 (UN, 2015). The world urban population is estimated to increase from 3.9 billion in 2014 to over 6.3 billion in 2050. Much of that increase is likely to take place in Asia and Africa. The report also notes that: '... as the world continues to urbanise, sustainable development challenges will be increasingly concentrated in cities, particularly in the lower-middle-income countries where the pace of urbanisation is fastest'. The document also notes that 'in many countries there is a positive relationship between the level of urbanisation and the national per capita income' but the mechanisms are complex and far from straight forward (UN, 2015: 82). Cities can be drivers of structural change and a significant increase in productivity but the prevalence of slums and unorganised sector (in terms of economic activities as well as housing supporting basic survival rather than human flourishing) suggest that the benefits of such structural change do not necessarily reach everyone automatically. Worldwide,

880 million people (about 25 per cent of urban population) live in slums (UN-HABITAT, 2016: 15). The share of the unorganised sector in non-agricultural employment can be as high as 50 per cent (International Labour Organisation, 2013).

Traditional concepts of agglomeration economies suggest that productivity advantage of urban areas is not merely due to economies of scale but due to interactions. Following the work of Bettencourt et al., (2007) and West (2010) and recent work of the MIT's Human Dynamics Lab (Pan et al., 2013), there is now evidence to suggest that the density of human interactions ('super-ties') has a direct impact on innovation and productivity. Much of the recent research on cities (Glaeser, 2011; Batty, 2013; Goldstein and Dyson, 2013; Townsend, 2014; Goldsmith and Crawford, 2014; McLaren and Agyeman, 2015) focuses on cities in the advanced economies with considerable research gaps when it comes to cities in the lower and middle income countries. The Sustainable Development Goal 11 exhorts all those concerned to 'make cities and human settlements inclusive, safe, resilient and sustainable'. What makes a city innovative, inclusive and sustainable? Why are some cities better than others in particular aspects such as innovation, social mobility and equality? What role can city-level analysis and tools play in advancing our understanding of important social issues of our times in an urbanising world?

The capability approach offers some insights in thinking about these issues. However, there is fairly limited literature on applying the capability approach to cities and the issues of urban public policy and urban management. Compared to the vast and emerging literature on the capability approach or its applications to understanding poverty in its multiple dimensions; informing policy on inequalities and theoretical and philosophical perspectives, the extent of literature on cities and capabilities is rather thin. For example, the twenty-four Global Human Development Reports by UNDP so far have focused on important aspects of human development each year but the topic of cities or urban living has not yet merited as the central theme of a global human development report. That is not to say that cities and urban issues are not discussed in the global HDRs but that cities have not yet been seen as warranting the central focus. Even among the national human development reports, cities and urban areas have not been the central focus. One exception is the 2013 National Human Development Report of China.

In this chapter, I shall provide a critical review of the literature on applying the capability approach to cities, with the main aim of identifying a number of potential areas for applying the capability approach in relation to cities as an original contribution. In the third section I shall present some original empirical analysis on specific aspects of cities where we could apply the capability approach and draw some conclusions in the final section.

Cities and the Capability Approach: A Selective Review

There are existing arguments concerning human rights and urban living (HABITAT) and also well-established arguments on the 'right to the city'. Even though the word city or town does not appear even once in the entire text of the Universal Declaration of Human Rights, various aspects of the rights such as right to life and liberty (article 3), equality before law and freedom from discrimination (articles 1, 6 and 7), right to protection of privacy, family and home (article 12), right to freedom of movement (article 13), right to own property (article 17), right to freedom of thought and religion (article 18), right to freedom of opinion and expression (article 19), right to freedom of peaceful assembly (article 20), right to participate in government (article 21), right to work and related choice of employment and leisure (articles 23 and 24), right to a standard of living adequate for health and well-being (article 25), right to education (article 26) and right to participate in the cultural and scientific aspects of society (article 27) are all relevant to cities. In fact, cities may be natural grounds for articles 19 and 20. The International Covenants provide further articulation of many of these rights.

However, while these rights exist on paper and in the minds of constitutional experts, we do know that urban living especially for the poor people and many others involves serious compromises. While it is clear that rights should not be ordered or prioritised (in the sense that all are important), the urban poor households and communities are forced to choose some rights while they lose other rights. The capability approach offers insights to understand these issues from the perspectives of freedoms and what the basis for evaluation should be. These include well-being and agency freedoms, process and opportunity aspects and institutions including deliberative public reasoning and the articulation of duty-bearer institutions whenever any rights are created.

As Sen (1979, 1985, 1992, 2009) pointed out, there are distinct classes of freedoms, and focusing too much on well-being freedoms without adequate consideration of agency freedoms can be misleading. The capability approach encourages us to think deeply about the nature of evaluation of alternative sets of beings and doings and the informational space in which such evaluation is being done. A narrow focus on well-being freedoms may appear to be helpful in producing concrete and clear priorities for policies. However, there are significant challenges about paternalism, public reasoning and how different public resources are prioritised. There is also the importance of agency freedoms and the ability of each individual citizen to focus on things that she values and has reason to value.

New lenses to examine old urban challenges open up new ways of governance. The Mayor of Cali, Columbia in the 1990s pioneered the use of epidemiological approaches to analyse the causes of urban violence. Since this time, the World Health Organization (WHO) has recognised urban violence as a public health problem (Gurrero and Concha Eastman, nd). Another case is of Mayor Mockus of Bogota who used innovative ideas to inform people and used their knowledge to reduce water consumption or improve compliance with traffic laws (Caballero, 2004). More recently, another Mayor of Bogota, Enrique Penalosa challenged received wisdom that transit problems in big cities require rapid rail transit and used rapid bus networks and dedicated cycle lanes to encourage a more sustainable urban transit system. Mahila Milan and SPARC in Mumbai, India promoted innovations by empowering slum-dwellers to work together (Patel and Mitlin, 2001). Lawyers in Delhi used human rights to plead the Supreme Court to intervene to reduce air pollution (Narayan and Bell, 2005). These examples highlight citizen agency (ability to act) and the use of network-based approaches to resolve complex and large scale problems. However, urban violence and riots suggest that we should be cautious about collective action and co-operation (a potential criticism of McLaren and Agyeman, 2015 – see Ellard, 2015).

Removing Unfreedoms

An influential report that aims to apply the capability approach to cities and urban governance is the edited volume titled *Removing Unfreedoms* (Samuels, 2005). This builds on previous work by Khosla (2002).

The cover page and blurb proclaim that this was the first attempt to apply the capability approach to urban development. The various authors of papers propose and use the so called 'five freedoms' framework as proposed by Sen (1999: 10). The five freedoms are: (a) political freedoms including ability to participate in public discussions and in governance through elections; (b) economic 'facilities' including protections related to openness of labour markets, property and access; (c) freedom for social 'opportunities' including good health, basic education, gender equity; (d) transparency guarantees including absence of corruption and access to police protection; and (e) protective security including emergency facilities, shelters and mechanisms to support victims of disasters etc. This is no doubt an interesting framework and the so-called five dimensions cover a 'list' of various important mechanisms related to freedoms.

However, the framework can be criticised for lumping together certain aspects which are causes or determinants and others which are effects or consequences. For example, under political freedoms, the list includes forums for free debate, facilities to scrutinise authorities and ability to participate in public discussions is listed as a distinct aspect from citizen's participation (which can be an effect of there being forums for participation). Similarly, under economics, 'facilities' (rather than freedoms) are mentioned for open labour markets and access to product markets along with stable business ethics. Transparency guarantees underpin both political freedoms and economic security and they cannot exist outside political freedoms. Under transparency guarantees, the list mentions absence of corruption which may be a result of such transparency guarantees (rather than an element of it) and the functioning of political institutions including facilities to scrutinise authorities. The dimension of protective security mainly focuses on the ways to deal with the consequences of vulnerability rather than to reduce vulnerability itself or increase resilience. Thus, the first criticism is that in the framework presented in Samuels (2005), causes and effects are lumped together. Not distinguishing between causes and effects can lead to confusion for public policy purposes.

The second criticism is related to a similar confusion that is also visible in the blurb that explains the framework:

All five *instruments* are interconnected and equally important. They are like the five equally important sides of a box in which urban investments can be contained. Success is measured by the degree to which obstructions are removed and each has to be tackled in the development process. In other words, development will inevitably get distorted if only one or two of these objectives are given a priority by using the argument that some of the freedoms can come afterwards. [emphasis added, from www.removingunfreedoms.org/five_freedoms.htm]

Dimensions have now become instruments in the blurb whereas in the book they are not referred to as instruments (Samuels, 2005: 50). This can also be problematic in applying this framework for policy purposes. Many of the freedoms are intrinsically important (such as freedom to live a life with dignity) while others are instrumental to such healthy and long life. It seems that the authors of the report interpret Sen's arguments against prioritising between various freedoms to mean the lack of necessity to distinguish between instrumental and intrinsic nature of different freedoms.

Also slightly worrying is the concern whether the framework outlined in that report which predates the 2008 financial crisis had a rather benign view of the role of markets (and the importance given to free labour markets and access to product markets). Although the authors of the report do not link freedoms with liberalism, others applying the framework could easily fall in that trap. Thus, while it is not a weakness of the arguments in the report, the third criticism of the report is that it would have been prudent to guard against the possible incorrect application of the framework to justify liberal and neoliberal urban development policies.

While the claim of the authors that it is the first attempt to apply the capability approach to urban development (since 2002) may indeed be valid, previous studies do exist on application to particular aspects of urban inequalities, including my own earlier work on applying entitlements and capabilities framework to the case of inequalities in access to urban water supply (Anand and Perman, 1999; Anand, 2001, 2007). Thus, the fourth criticism is that the report and the framework do not take note of other applications of the capability approach in full flourish by this time with first generation of the Cambridge Capability conferences (2001–5) and other emerging forums.

The fifth criticism is that although the report focuses a lot more on Sen, it appears to have been influenced equally by Martha Nussbaum's capabilities approach of identifying and listing essential freedoms but this is not made evident.

Notwithstanding these criticisms, the report did make some early contributions to the application of the capability approach to urban development issues but these need to be considered in relation to significant advances happening with regard to the capability approach and its applications through the national human development reports.

Cities and Human Development

China's National Human Development Report (UNDP, 2013) is an example of a national report that focuses on urban issues from a human development perspective. The title of the report 'sustainable and liveable cities: towards ecological civilisation' captures the vision of the report which notes that by 2012 already the rate of urbanisation was 52 per cent and some 700 million Chinese citizens lived in cities and urban areas and by 2030 this is likely to increase to urbanisation of 70 per cent by when a billion Chinese citizens will live in cities and urban areas. China's urbanisation was powered by rural to urban migration. The report notes that migrants who by 2010 numbered some 230 million were typically younger in age, had lower income than non-migrants and took up low skilled jobs. While urbanisation and industrialisation absorbed all this labour and produced enormous economic growth that lifted several hundreds of million Chinese citizens out of poverty, concerns about social welfare, environmental impacts including the quality of air and water resource requirements are recognised in the report as important issues. The report notes that air pollution may be the leading cause of death in China now (p. 30). Though the report does not refer to the capability approach, one of the main issues it identifies is about the lack of rights of migrants and not integrating them into the urban institutional arrangements (in terms of specific forums for delivering the rights). The roadmap to liveable cities has four quadrants: equity and adequate infrastructure for all, resource efficiency and sustainability, urban form for quality life and institutions for technological change and innovation. On equity measures the issue of rights for migrants is emphasised: '... To reduce the destabilising impacts of economic disparities, cities need to move from social polarisation to social integration. In particular, the unjust treatment of migrant workers should end, starting with their full integration in the social security system, equal rights to education for their children, and laws and regulations to protect their rights and interests' (UNDP, 2013: 84).

Housing Inequalities

Frediani applies the capability approach to several aspects of urban inequalities especially related to housing and squatter settlements in Brazil. Frediani (2007) compares Sen's capability approach and the multi-dimensional nature of well-being with the World Bank's emphasis on income based measures of poverty. Frediani also notes that the language of freedom has already been used by Turner (1976) with regard to housing as a verb and the freedom of people to build. Housing is certainly an important dimension that affects many other well-being as well as agency freedoms. In the work on slums of Mumbai, it is seen that within a given geographic location, there can be significant differences in access to many basic services depending on whether slum is notified (meaning officially recognised) or non-notified (Subbaraman et al., 2012) and that living in a non-notified slum is associated with significantly increased mental health issues (Subbaraman et al., 2014).

Right to the City and Capabilities

Deneulin (2014) starts with a discussion of the 'right to the city' approach proposed by French philosopher Henri Lefebvre based on Marx's distinction between exchange and use values. While the exchange values dominate, Lefebvre attempts to regain the use value of public spaces and activities using the idea that every citizen – rich or poor – should have the right to the city and be able to participate in its functioning as an equal member. Deneulin goes on to note that after an endorsement of the right to the city by international institutions, the right to the city has been used as a synonym for inclusive cities. For Deneulin the capability approach has four contributions to the right to the city:

... First, it provides tools for wellbeing evaluation, which the right to the city does not. Second, it makes an analysis of inter-linkages between different rights possible. Third, it emphasises the role of institutions and can bring a structural evaluation of wellbeing to match the collective dimension of the right to the city. Fourth, its agency aspect opens up to democratic pluralism within the utopian dimension of the right to the city. (Deneulin, 2014: 7)

Deneulin goes on to combine the rights-based discourses and Susan Fainstain's book title 'The Just City' to frame 'just cities for life' as a way to apply the capability approach.

In my view, the right to the city is primarily a philosophical concept to understand the complexification of the city and the myths and illusions associated with the utopia of urban society. The word 'right' can be misconstrued given the last two decades of 'rights based approaches to development' which focus on individual centred rights whereas right to the city is a kind of collective and aggregate right (Harvey, 2012). Right to the city is a framework to analyse power relations and anticipate and explain why some people win and others lose in the urban phenomenon (unlike in economic models). Holston and Appadurai (1996: 188) remind us that: 'Although one of the essential projects of nation-building has been to dismantle the historic primacy of urban citizenship and to replace it with the national, cities remain the strategic arena for the development of citizenship.' For Appadurai (2002), globalisation is producing new forms of governance relationships (in his words 'governmentalities') where within a city there could be completely different spheres one interconnected with global economy (thus producing enormous opportunities for concentration of wealth) and the other that is not connected with this hyper-marketised system of flows and hence offering little by way of opportunities to escape grinding poverty. For Appadurai, the 40 per cent or so of people in Mumbai living in less than 8 per cent of land in slums and on pavements are 'citizens without a city'.

Let me now summarise some issues from this literature review. My motivation in wanting to use the capability approach to cities and the urban questions are similar to these authors. We can identify below several ways in which the capability approach can help us frame the urban question and find ways to resolve some of the many dilemmas.

(i) Cities in their role as economic engines tend to prioritise and give prominence to economic productivity and thus mainly those who generate economic benefits through industry, services and working. The capability approach encourages us to focus on an expansive view of enhancing substantive freedoms for every single person including children, women, the elderly, the disabled persons, those requiring care and assistance, students, artisans and artists and many other citizens. A challenge for researchers and those applying the capability approach is to demonstrate ways in which the priorities of those currently marginalised or ignored can be centred and emphasised in deliberative public policy.

(ii) In thinking about cities, the capability approach requires us to confront inequality and injustices in every dimension of interpersonal relations including those governed by cultural norms including the norms of reciprocity (in space and time), formal and informal contracts. Here, the capability approach requires us to shine light on injustices that can co-exist with cultural acceptability.

(iii) The capability approach warns against prioritisation of certain aspects of freedoms, and especially the tendency to prioritise more readily visible infrastructure investments that deliver in relation to well-being freedoms while relegating the more complex and less visible agency freedoms. The challenge here is to explore and develop ways in which conflicts between different types or classes of freedoms should be dealt with.

(iv) Using the capability approach we can reframe the relationship between institutions of governance and the citizens where active participation of citizens in all aspects of policy making and implementation should be pursued not merely because it is fashionable or becomes easier due to digital technologies and social media but because the citizens have the right to participate in public reasoning and deliberation.

(v) The capability approach also encourages us to use the informational space for evaluations carefully and to think of pluralistic and multiple dimensions. It is possible to develop indicators for inclusive and sustainable cities focusing on social (gender, youth and ageing, sexual, racial and religious freedoms), economic (employment, financial and enterprise aspects), environmental (housing, quality of life, water and environmental footprint, carbon neutrality) and agency (political participation, institutions and resilience) dimensions. At present only a few such indexes exist. According to an annual index published by *The Economist* (16th August, 2017) the 'most liveable cities' include Melbourne, Vienna and Vancouver at the top, and Damascus, Tripoli, Lagos and Dhaka at the bottom. Top ranked cities tend to be in rich countries, have thriving local government and civil society networks whereas the bottom ranked cities tend to be in post-conflict developing countries where insecurity and conflict may have eroded trust in public institutions. However, such indexes reproduce a wealth ranking of societies and ignore the potential for inclusion and sustainability. An attempt by UN-HABITAT focuses on the so-called city prosperity index (CPI). According to the HABITAT, urban prosperity comprises: 'productivity; infrastructure; quality of life; equity and inclusion; environmental sustainability, and governance and legislation'. The UN-HABITAT website mentions that the CPI framework is 'based' on fundamental principle of human rights'. Presently data has been compiled for some 300 cities worldwide (UN-HABITAT, 2015). Another index worthy of mention is the index of social progress for cities of Colombia (Progreso Social Colombia, 2015; Alidadi et al., 2015). This index combines three dimensions: basic human needs (nutrition, water, sanitation, shelter, and personal safety), foundations of well-being (access to basic knowledge, access to information and communication, health and wellness and ecosystem sustainability) and opportunity (personal rights, personal freedom and choice, tolerance and inclusion and access to advanced education). Compilation of index for ten cities suggested that Manizales and Bucaramanga are at the top while Cali, Cartagena and Valledupar are at the bottom.

While such indexes are constructed with a view to compare cities, in my view it is important to develop indicators of evaluation that are city-specific (and hence may not necessarily be relevant to other cities) and inform public reasoning and deliberations. City-level human development reports such as the Delhi report (Academic Foundation (AF) and Institute for Human Development (IHD), 2013) help to raise discussion and debate on a number of issues relevant to realising freedoms at the city level.

Cities and Urban Issues through the Lens of the Capability Approach: An Exploration

Cities and Living Longer

Among the most basic of freedoms is the freedom to live a long and healthy life with dignity. The capability approach to cities would encourage us to ask the questions such as: do cities help the citizens to live longer, healthier and lead a life of dignity? Evidence for each of those questions is rather mixed. In principle, cities and towns should offer better prospects for health with better infrastructure and access to health care. However, as the UCL Lancet Commission (Rydin et al.,

2012: 1) noted: 'the so called urban advantage ... has to be actively created and maintained through policy interventions'. If people are living longer does this statistic refer to everyone in the city or only those who can afford it? Does this mean that cities, while raising the overall life expectancy, actually hide the significant inequalities in life expectancy?

Data on life expectancy at the level of cities is not available for many cities in the developing countries and emerging economies. National level data is really not appropriate to answer this question. However, just to see if we can find any relationship between the level of urbanisation measured in terms of proportion of population living in urban areas and life expectancy in general, I have used data from the World Development Indicators.

From Figure 21.1a, we can see that urbanisation does not automatically lead to increased life expectancy. There are many countries at the bottom of that scatter diagram where urban population share has increased significantly between 1961 and 2011 with hardly any improvement in life expectancy at all. (Ideally, we should be looking at data over one hundred years or so but we do not have cross-country data earlier than 1961.)

This is a complex relationship so we should be very careful in interpreting or drawing any conclusions from this, but at a first glance from Figure 21.1b there appears to be correlation between level of urbanisation and living longer. However, this can be simply an association and there may be no causality and also both urbanisation and living longer can be endogenously related to other aspects of structural change and development processes that the relationship could be spurious.

In some countries between 1961 and 2011, life expectancy hardly changed at all even when urban population considerably increased (notwithstanding the profound advances in technology and medicine) (Figures 21.2a and 21.2b). These countries include Zimbabwe, Lesotho, Ukraine, Belarus, and the Russian Federation. In the case of southern African countries we know that life expectancy plummeted during the 1980s due to the HIV/AIDS pandemic. The case of former Soviet Union countries is complex and there could be issues related to data quality even when retrospective estimates were made.

On the other hand there are also cases where urbanisation seems to have delivered enormous gains in life expectancy of more than 30 years in the case of countries such as Oman, Nepal, Bhutan, Maldives and Timor-Leste. We do not fully know what is behind this but we can

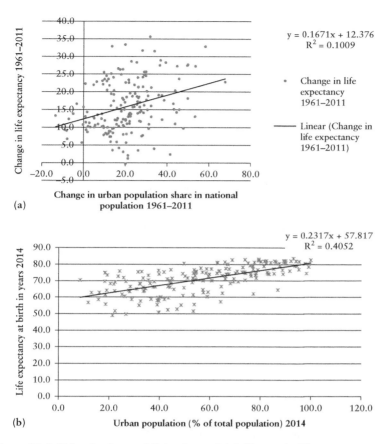

Figure 21.1 Urbanisation and living longer? (a) Change in life expectancy 1961–2011, (b) Cities and long life
Source: Compiled by author using data from the World Development Indicators

surmise that in these countries urbanisation must have taken place alongside significant improvements to public health measures.

The Social Gradient and Social Determinants of Health and Mortality
These national level analyses do not capture (a) any significant differences in sub-national regions such as provinces or states (due to differences in quality of governance, for example); (b) significant differences that can exist between large cities which tend to have better infrastructure and

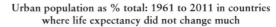

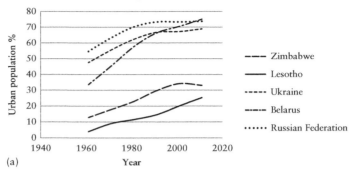

(a)

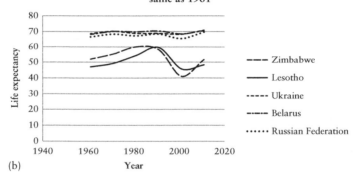

(b)

Figure 21.2 Urbanisation but not living longer? (a) Urban population as per
cent total: 1961 to 2011 in countries where life expectancy did not change
much, (b) Countries where life expectancy in 2011 is almost the same as 1961
Source: Compiled by author using data from the World Development Indicators

health facilities and smaller towns and urban settlements which may
have been classified as urban but do not have the economies of scale and
scope of a large city; and (c) significant differences that can exist within
a city between the wealthier neighbourhoods and the poorer neighbourhoods. In the cities of Great Britain, the concept of social gradient has
been observed whereby within a given city, life expectancy can depend
on where you live. In England the difference in life expectancy between
most deprived and least deprived areas can be up to seven years and for
men in Scotland it could be as high as eleven years. My attempt to examine this in Bradford suggests that there is a gap of almost 14 years in life

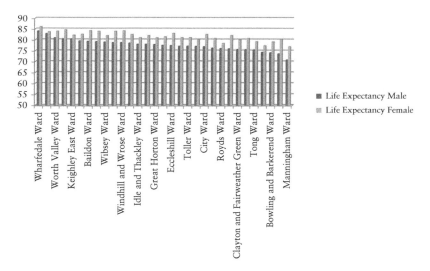

Figure 21.3 Social gradient in Bradford's mortality rates?
Source: Compiled by author using data from the West Yorkshire Observatory

expectancy in the deprived inner city areas ((such as Manningham and Tong wards) compared with life expectancy in the affluent suburbs of Bradford such as Wharfdale, Ilkley, and rural parts of Keighley (Figure 21.3). There is a bus that leaves from the City Centre to Keighley and in that one hour's journey, the passenger will be traversing a geographic area with a gap of 14 years in life expectancy. Such a gap is huge by any scale and is an urgent matter for public policy interventions.

Poor people tend to have a poor diet and lack of opportunities to lead healthy living, including in terms of access to clean water and sanitation, access to basic health care and health and nutrition related information, vaccination programmes and sport and recreational facilities. All of these can have a cumulative effect on life expectancy. However, there is also the so-called 'Glasgow effect' where individual socioeconomic characteristics do not explain lower life expectancy of the city's male population as a whole as compared with other Scottish cities (Hanlon et al., 2005; Department of Health, 2010). Gray (2007) noted:

Elevated rates of acute sickness and potential psychiatric morbidity in men in West Central Scotland, Greater Glasgow, and Glasgow City compared with the rest of Scotland are not explained by socio-economic circumstances. In addition, the higher rates of long standing illness in West Central Scotland remain after adjustment for socio-economic factors.

Since the freedom to live a long and healthy life is an important dimension of freedoms, there is an urgency to focus on these huge differences which are manifestations of institutionalised injustices. As the Marmot Review noted, health inequalities are manifestation of underlying inequalities and unfairness in the society:

Inequalities in health arise because of inequalities in society – in the conditions in which people are born, grow, live, work, and age. So close is the link between particular social and economic features of society and the distribution of health among the population, that the magnitude of health inequalities is a good marker of progress towards creating a fairer society. Taking action to reduce inequalities in health does not require a separate health agenda, but action across the whole of society. (Marmot Review, Department of Health, 2010).

We have a long way to go in understanding and analysing health inequalities in the developing countries. Life expectancy data is not available even at city level for many cities let alone at neighbourhood or sub-city spatial unit level to be able to examine if a similar social gradient exists in cities in Asia and Africa. Social gradient may be a product of spatial segregation of poverty and vulnerability. Some interesting work is being undertaken on slums and health by Ramnath and Deshmukh and we shall briefly discuss this in a subsequent paragraph in this section.

Cities and Social and Economic Inequalities

Cities are engines of economic development and their economic productivity dimension receives prominence in justification for 'urban bias'. However, less recognised is that cities are also social dynamos, in many cases leading to and challenging existing social norms and creating new opportunities. While embedded social hierarchies and stereotypes continue to be reinforced in urban living, cities can also be empowering. In some cases, the scale offered by cities enables collective action possible for individuals who are part of certain vulnerable groups to come together as a group and champion their rights through social movements. As Holston and Appadurai (1996: 198) noted: 'as the social movements of the urban poor create unprecedented claims on and to the city, they expand citizenship to new social bases. In so doing, they create new sources of citizenship rights and corresponding forms of self-rule'.

Theoretically, if urbanisation promotes equality or is a manifestation of pro-poor development, as urbanisation takes place we will expect poverty (in all its dimensions) to decrease significantly. However, from analysis we find that there appears to be several alternative trajectories. Some countries can be examined as cases. This data is based on poverty head count and the limitations of such an approach to measuring poverty are well-known. Income based poverty approaches miss many dimensions of deprivation and thus tend to underestimate the true extent of capability deprivation. If for a moment one suspends judgment and sees income poverty as one of the various dimensions of ill-being, then it can seen that urbanisation is far from pro-poor in many cases (refer to Figure 21.4).

Case 1: Guinea and Honduras, where urban population increased slightly but urban poverty increased faster. This means much of urban population growth is taking place due to migration of poor people to the cities (without the expected growth in income after migration) or that urban growth is resulting in more people in the cities becoming poor.

Case 2: This includes countries where initially urban poverty increases and then it begins to decrease (a type of inverted U curve). Dominican Republic, Ethiopia, Paraguay and Uruguay are good examples of this.

Case 3: With urbanisation poverty decreases steadily and significantly. We can see this in Ecuador, Malawi, Thailand and Kazakhstan.

These cases suggest that urbanisation and the associated economic growth do not automatically result in pro-poor development unless specific policies are taken to make it so. Here, the capability approach can be very useful in challenging urban policies for their impact on poverty and deprivation.

Cities as Disempowering Machines

Cities can be empowering but they can also be systemically disempowering. This is particularly true in the case of four special groups, namely: women, children, the elderly, and the disabled. In each case, cities can systemically disempower each group in different ways and create additional vulnerabilities as the size of the city increases.

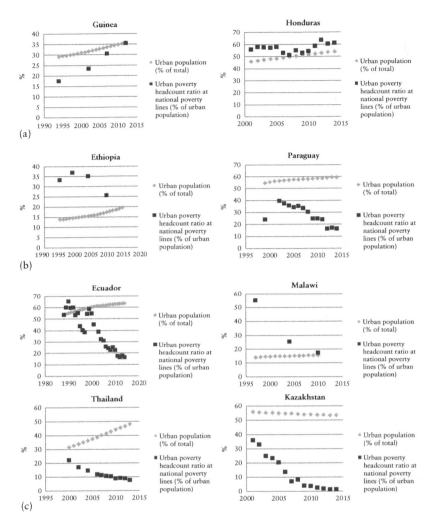

Figure 21.4 Urbanisation and urban poverty: (a) Guinea and Honduras, (b) Ethiopia and Paraguay, (c) Ecuador, Malawi, Thailand and Kazakhstan
Source: Compiled by author using data from the World Development Indicators

Take for example, the simple case of public spaces for the elderly people to be able to walk alone or together with others or to gather to exercise or simply for a conversation. As cities grow, space attracts a premium price and commons such as open or green spaces, parks and pavements become appropriated for private gains, become encroached upon or barriers erected for the exclusive use of the 'powerful'. Pavements become economic spaces rather than social spaces, forcing people to walk on the road and thus risking coming into proximity with moving vehicles. Appropriation of pavements by both organised and unorganised sector economic activities makes walking in cities a very unpleasant and tedious experience. In many cities, pedestrians do not have any rights and in the planning of infrastructure such as inter-sections, road furniture and alignment, they are completely ignored or come at the bottom of the chain if at all. Recently, in a qualita-tive study of road traffic intersections in Chennai, I noticed that many traffic lights did not include lights for pedestrians or even designated crossings. As a result, pedestrians have to wait until enough people have gathered and use collective action to slowly move through traffic and vehicles, indicating for them to slow down. This is a simple mani-festation of a complete denial of the rights of pedestrians and the abil-ity of planning systems to think of the needs of pedestrians and create the necessary safe public spaces and infrastructure for this purpose. It is not a surprise that India has the world's largest number of road traf-fic deaths (some of which may be due to avoidable pedestrian–vehicle collisions). However, we should note that it is not a simple case of resolving the rights of the pedestrians.

The issue is very complex as the right to walk safely clashes with the right to livelihood of many people who depend on unorganised sec-tor jobs. Clearing the pavement of unorganised sectors may solve one problem but it may make people dependent on those livelihoods to go hungry or lose their economic security entirely. What is 'safe' for some may make others 'unsafe' and 'insecure'. This highlights the challenge of defining freedoms, valuing the different freedoms and freedoms of all people.

Smart Cities: Rhetoric versus Freedoms

There is much talk about smart cities. Various definitions exist but a smart city is considered to be one that uses information and communication technologies to define infrastructure that meets the needs of citizens in timely and efficient manner. While many adjectives to describe cities exist, following Hollands (2008), it is perhaps time to ask the real smart, inclusive and sustainable city to 'please stand up'. Whilst discussion on 'smart' cities tends to focus mainly (and for some critics excessively) on digital technologies and information infrastructure, from a capability perspective the real 'smart' cities are those that enhance agency and autonomy of citizens and empower them to lead a healthy and sustainable life and active citizenship. However, the vision of smart citizenship based on big data and open data approaches does not fully reflect the emphasis on freedoms central to the capability approach. Discussions as in the case of Masdar city in Abudhabi, Songdo in the Republic of Korea and the initial phase of the 100 Smart Cities Mission in India can lead to the criticism that these are symptomatic of 'technological determinism' of urban behaviour, which seems to be based on the view that providing infrastructure and digital technologies will lead to sustainable behaviours. Although the underlying models informing these discussions use the so-called 'agent based modelling' approach, their use of the word 'agency' is limited to the way it is used in the context of the capability approach. As Batty (2013: 79) noted, agents in smart cities discourse can include: 'locations, activity types, individuals, or aggregates of populations, all of which have some distinct purpose'. Smartness is usually attributed to the algorithms and the ability of the machines to learn from data and predict human behaviour. It appears that smart cities are ignoring the fact that for millennia real smart cities were those that started by thinking about the citizen first (rather than smartness of technology) and they then developed a better understanding of how both hard and 'soft' infrastructure networks are governed, how individual citizens can shape and influence collective action and how institutions adapt and foster innovative approaches to governance that are by design inclusive, smart and sustainable (Anand, 2019).

Cities and Women: Rapes, Violence, Gendered Nature of Urban Living and the Concept of Safety and Security

While one aspect of cities is that they can bring out the best of creativity and innovation in human mind, they also seem to bring out the basest, meanest and most brutal and bestial parts of human behaviour. It is true that in the digital age, innovation can take place almost anywhere, the agglomeration economies and network externalities offered by cities provide some advantages to the development of an ecosystem of innovation. However, cities also appear to give focus to violence, especially based on identities such as gender, caste, religion or political affiliation. There is spurious correlation if we were to look for a relationship between the level of urbanisation and the level of violence captured by the crime rate but some of this appears to be due to the reporting rates. However, notwithstanding the scope for error in generalising about the level of violence in cities, cities appear to have the ability to degenerate to the lowest levels of human morality in the nature of violence against women, trafficking of women and children and their ability to commodify almost everything. Violence against women and rapes, as often reported from Indian cities such as Delhi in 2013 or Bengaluru in 2017, challenge the very concepts of human decency and naïve views about cities as crucibles of civilisation. In some perspectives, cities seem to be very good at commodification of nature (Bridge and Watson, 2000; Heynen et al., 2006). This seems to extend to commodification of the human body as well whereby rapes (and trafficking as well as trade in human organs) are occasional manifestations of much deeper structural faults which can hide and cover up brutality if not cemented through efforts that nurture moral foundations and critical perspectives of self and society. However, economic incentives and profiteering opportunity through land and real estate appear to be more likely in the case of orchestrated group-based violence such as riots and violence against particular communities.

Notwithstanding the claim of cities about their contribution to social progress, we find no change whatsoever in the proportion of women in non-wage employment when we compare the data for the years 2000 and 2010 in Figure 21.5 (where the horizontal axis shows proportion of population in urban areas and the vertical axis shows proportion of women among non-agricultural wage employment).

This suggests that even though cities and urban areas have slowly (and reluctantly) opened up employment opportunities to both men and women, progress towards equality is indeed very slow. The capability approach would encourage us to challenge deep-seated barriers to equality.

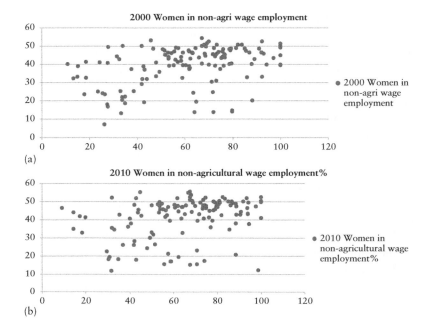

Figure 21.5 Urbanisation and gender inequality in wage employment
(a) in 2000 and (b) in 2010
Source: Compiled by author using data from the World Development
Indicators

Cities and Housing: Slums and Peri-Urban Living

Another intractable issue that a researcher of the capability approach
needs to resolve is about those living in slums and peri-urban locations
with limited infrastructure. As already mentioned some 880 million
people representing approximately one-fifth of all urban residents live
in slums. In many countries, there are numerous barriers to access to
services such as clean water, sanitation and electricity for people living
in slums. Where such services do exist, the quality is often poor, the cost
per unit is often much higher than what non-slum households pay and
the households living in slums appear to have limited legal recognition
and ability to participate in institutions governing urban areas. In general, the more urbanised a country, the proportion of urban residents
in slums appears to decrease. This negative correlation (Figure 21.6)

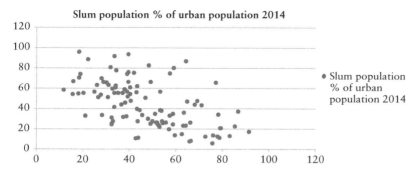

Figure 21.6 Urbanisation and proportion of people living in slums 2014
Source: Compiled by author using data from the World Development
Indicators

is easy to reason: as the country becomes more urbanised, the ability
of urban residents to influence policy and get access to public services
may improve. This may result in reforms to housing and land development and providing adequate funding to address the issues of slum
residents and provide them with decent housing. However, the dis-
persed nature of the scatter diagram suggests there are huge variations.
This suggests that urbanisation is not automatically pro-poor unless
specific social and distributive policies are pursued.

There is some interesting work being undertaken by PUKAR researchers on health impacts of living in slums. Subbaraman et al. (2012) noted
significant differences in health indicators between the 'notified slums'
(meaning legally recognised) and the non-notified slums. This further
highlights the importance of legal recognition and the impact it can
have in the ability of residents to various services which in turn affects
their health indicators including life expectancy and infant mortality.

Conclusion

The aim of this chapter is to take an overview of applying the capability
approach to cities and urban development issues. The literature review
suggested that while there are various islands of exploration, there
is much to be done in applying the capability approach to cities and
urban issues. The exploration included a discussion of some of the freedoms and also the nature of conflicts between different freedoms and

freedoms of different citizens or groups of individuals and how we may be able to use data to examine evidence on some initial conjectures.

Cities do not necessarily and automatically lead to their citizens living a long and healthy life. As the analysis has indicated, the relationship is complex. In some cases, urbanisation does not seem to have any impact on life expectancy at all, whereas in other cases urbanisation coincided with significant increases in life expectancy. The positive gains of urbanisation in terms of access to education and health infrastructure, better access to information, reduced time to respond to health emergencies and seek medical assistance, etc., can be nullified or cancelled by the negative impacts of pollution and urban living on physical and mental health, the lack of opportunities for social interaction and access to urban public spaces by the elderly and the lack of access to water and sanitation by a significant section of urban households living in the slums.

A large city is not merely a scaled-up version of a smaller urban settlement. The small town can be as complex and unfathomable as a large city but there could be additional dimensions of complexity that are more readily visible in the case of larger cities. On the one hand, the scale should offer better possibilities for collective action by minorities, and various vulnerable groups and thus enable them to better organise themselves and articulate their demands for rights. However, the cases of women and slum-dwellers seem to suggest that such collective action does not seem to happen that easily. On the other hand, cities also seem to facilitate collective action by mafia, those who want to sell or consume drugs or various commodities including commodified women and children. Thus the same logic of collective action enables groups of predatory interests to come together and take advantage of proximity.

The issue of pavements and the lack of rights for pedestrians for safe spaces to walk versus the economic livelihood opportunities for the urban informal sector workers bring to the fore the complexity of resolving conflicts between the freedoms of different individuals or different groups of individuals. It is hoped that the explorations in this chapter highlight the enormous possibilities for applying the capability approach to cities to examine various manifestations of urban inequalities and the potential to make a difference to the lives of many whose rights and claims are currently denied in the 'smart city' and other popular rhetorics.

Acknowledgements

This research is part of a three year research programme on inclusive, smart and sustainable cities supported by a British Academy grant under the IPM programme. The ideas in this chapter have been developed over the last eighteen months and some of these were presented at various seminars including at the CCC Conference (June 2016), the ITS Conference at Cambridge (September 2016), the Development Studies Association Conference at Oxford (September 2016), two workshops under the British Academy programme at IIT Madras (March 2016) and the Indian Institute of Science, Bengaluru (November 2016); a Symposium on Smart Cities and Compassionate Cities at Bradford (July 2016); the Healthy Cities Workshop at Bradford (July 2017) and at the seminars given at the University of Florence (April 2016) and Universitas Mohammadiya Yogyakarta (September 2016). I am grateful to participants at these fora for their comments and questions. I alone remain responsible for any flaws and errors.

References

Academic Foundation (AF) and Institute for Human Development (IHD) (2013) *Delhi Human Development Report 2013: Improving Lives, Promoting Inclusion*. Delhi: IHD.

Alidadi, F., Arias, J., Bintrim, R., Miller, M., La Rotta, A. and Tummino, A. (2015) 'The social inclusion index 2015'. *Americas Quarterly*. available from: http://www.americasquarterly.org/charticles/social-inclusion-index-2015/

Anand, P. B. (2001) Water 'scarcity' in Chennai, India: Institutions, entitlements and aspects of inequality in access. UNU-WIDER Discussion Paper 140/2001. Helsinki: UNU-WIDER.

(2007) *Scarcity, Entitlements and the Economics of Water in Developing Countries*. Cheltenham: Edward Elgar.

(2019) *Smart Cities and Stupid People? The Real Challenges of Smart, Inclusive and Sustainable Cities* (forthcoming).

Anand, P. B. and Perman, R. (1999) 'Preferences, inequity and entitlements: Some issues from a CVM study of water supply in Madras, India'. *Journal of International Development*, 11(1), 27–46.

Appadurai, A. (2002) 'Deep democracy: Urban governmentality and the horizon of politics'. *Environment and Urbanisation*, 13(2), 23–44.

Batty, M. (2013) *The New Science of Cities*. Cambridge: MIT Press.

Bettencourt L. and West G. (2010) A unified theory of urban living, *Nature*, 467, 912–13.

Bettencourt, L. et al. (2007) Growth, innovation, scaling and the pace of life in cities'. *PNAS*, 104(17), 7301–6.

Bouteligier, S. (2013) *Cities, Networks and Global Environmental Governance: Spaces of Innovation, Places of Leadership*. New York: Routledge.

Bridge, G. and Watson, S. (Eds.) (2000) *A Companion to the City*. Oxford: Blackwell Publishing.

Caballero, M. (2004) Academic turns city into a social experiment: Mayor Mockus of Bogota and his spectacularly applied theory. Harvard Gazette, March 11, 2004.

Deneulin, S. (2014) Creating more just cities: the right to the city and the capability approach combined. Bath Papers in International Development and Well-being. Working Paper 32, University of Bath.

Department of Health (2010) *Fair society, healthy lives: The Michael Marmot review*. London: DOH.

The Economist (2015) The world's most liveable cities. August 18, 2015.

Ellard C. (2015) Urban studies: Blueprint for a cooperative city, *Nature*, 528, 330–1.

Frediani, A. A. (2007) Amartya Sen, the World Bank, and the redress of urban poverty: A Brazilian case study'. *Journal of Human Development*, 8(1), 133–52.

Glaeser, E. (2011) *Triumph of the City: How Urban Spaces Make Us Human*. London: Pan Books.

Goldsmith, S. and Crawford, S. (2014) *The Responsive City: Engaging Communities Through Data-Smart Governance*. San Francisco, CA: Jossey-Bass/Wiley.

Goldstein, B. and Dyson, L. (Eds.) (2013) *Beyond Transparency: Open Data and the Future of Civic Innovation*. San Francisco, CA: Code for America.

Gray, L. (2007) Comparisons of health related behaviours and health measures between Glasgow and the Rest of Scotland, Briefing Paper 7. Glasgow Centre for Population Health.

Gurrero, R. and Concha Eastman, A. (nd) An epidemiological approach for the prevention of urban violence: The case of Cali, Colombia. World Health and Population, doi:10.12927/whp..17590.

Hanlon, P., Lawder, R., Buchanan, D. et al. (2005) 'Why is mortality higher in Scotland than in England and Wales? Decreasing influence of socio-economic deprivation between 1981 and 2001 supports the existence of a "Scottish Effect"'. *Journal of Public Health*, 27(2)1, 99–204.

Harvey D. (2012) *Rebel Cities: From the Right to the City to the Urban Revolution*, London: Verso.

Heynen, N., Kaika, M. and Swyngedouw, E. (Eds.) (2006) *In the Nature of Cities: Urban Political Ecology and the Politics of Urban Metabolism.* London: Routledge.

Hollands, R. (2008) 'Will the real smart city please stand up? Intelligent, progressive or entrepreneurial?' *City-Analysis of Urban Trends, Culture, Theory, Policy, Action*, 12(3), 303–20.

Holston, J. and Appadurai, A. (1996) 'Cities and citizenship'. *Public Culture*, 8, 187–204.

International Labour Organisation (2013) *Measuring Informality: A Statistical Manual on the Informal Sector and Informal Employment.* Geneva: ILO.

Khosla R. (2002) Removing unfreedoms: citizens as agents of change: Sharing New Policy frameworks for Urban Development, Background Support Project Document, mimeo, London: UCL Development Planning Unit.

McLaren, D. and Agyeman, J. (2015) *Sharing Cities: A Case for Truly Smart and Sustainable Cities.* Cambridge: MIT Press.

Narayan, U. and Bell, R. G. (2005) Who changed Delhi's air? The roles of the court and the executive in environmental policymaking. RFF Discussion Paper 5-48. Washington DC: Resources for the Future.

Pan, W., Ghoshal, G., Krumme, C., Cebrian, M. and Pentland, A. (2013) Urban characteristics attributable to density-driven tie formation, *Nature Communications*, Article 1961 (2013).

Patel, S. and Mitlin, D. (2001) The work of SPARC, the National Slum Dwellers Federation and Mahila Milan. IIED Working Paper 5. London: IIED.

Progreso Social Colombia (2015) Social progress index for cities of Colombia.

Rydin, Y., Bleahu, A., Davies, M. et al. (2012) *Shaping Cities for Health: Complexity and the Panning of Urban Environments in the Twenty-First Century.* London: The Lancet Commissions-UCL.

Samuels, J. (Ed.) (2005) *Removing Unfreedoms: Citizens as Agents of Change in Urban Development.* Rugby: ITDG.

Sen, A. (1979) *Equality of what? Tanner lecture on human values.* Stanford, CA: Stanford University.

   (1985) 'Well-being, agency and freedom: The Dewey Lectures'. *Journal of Philosophy*, 82(4), 169–221.

   (1992) *Inequality Re-examined.* Oxford: Clarendon Press.

   (1999) *Development As Freedom.* New York: Oxford University Press.

   (2009) *The Idea of Justice.* London: Allen Lane.

Subbaraman, R. et al. (2012) 'Off the map: The health and social implications of being a non-notified slum in India'. *Environment and Urbanisation*, 24(2), 643–63.

Subbaraman R. et al. (2014) The psychological toll of slum living—an assessment of mental health, disability, and slum-related adversities in Mumbai, India, *The Lancet Global Health*, 2, S26.

Townsend, A. (2014) *Smart Cities: Big Data, Civic Hackers and the Quest for New Utopia*. New York: W.W. Norton and Co.

Turner J. (1976) *Housing by People: Towards Autonomy in Built Environments*, London: Marion Boyars.

United Nations (UN) (2015) World Urbanisation Prospects: The 2014 Revision, Department of Economic and Social Affairs, New York: United Nations.

UNDP (2013) *China National Human Development Report 2013: Sustainable and Liveable Cities: Toward Ecological Civilization*. Beijing: UNDP.

UN-HABITAT (2015) *The Global Cities Report 2015*. Nairobi: UN-HABITAT.

(2016) *World Cities Report 2016: Urbanisation and Development: Emerging Futures*. Nairobi: UN-HABITAT.

PART V

The Education Frontier

22 Formal Education, Well-Being and Aspirations

A Capability-Based Analysis on High School Pupils from France

ROBIN VOS AND JÉRÔME BALLET

Introduction

Since Gary Becker's work on human capital (1993), an entirely new literature on education has flourished. A focus seems to be placed on variables that attempt to quantify education, such as years of schooling per worker and its impact on wages, measured by GDP per capita. Denison (1972) identifies *formal education* in his classification of sources of macroeconomic growth. Romer (1986) finds a positive link between the growth rate of literacy and per capita income growth. Benos and Zotou (2015), in their metaregression analysis of 57 papers studying the impact of education on growth, show that the identification of a link between education and economic growth is still a topical debate. These studies, amongst many others, consider education from a mere quantitative perspective. One major stake is then the respective effects of family background and school factors on the enrolment and achievement of children in school (Coleman et al., 1966; Peaker, 1971).

Further literature introduces not only the idea that education is important in quantitative terms, but also recognizes the importance of its quality (Barro, 2002). This literature develops further with the addition of several considerations. For instance, Blaug (1985) underlines the importance of the integration of other functions of schooling, such as the function of socialization. Moreover, child well-being has also been given a central role in the formation of capabilities (Conti and Heckman, 2014). The capability approach has contributed, these last years, enhancing the debate on education (for instance, Walker and Unterhalter, 2007; Hinchcliffe and Terzi, 2009; Leßmann et al., 2011; Heckman, 2012; Hart, 2012a,b). Hart (2012b: 276) identifies the ability of this theoretical framework to consider "the potential for individual freedom both in and through education." Moreover, the education viewed by this theory is a "pluralistic approach to research, which accords a central role to children's participation and voice" (Hinchcliffe and Terzi, 2009: 388). This makes the capability approach particularly adaptable for a milieu as changing and diverse as that of adolescents in school.

Nevertheless, the links between education and aspirations are relatively unexplored in the capability approach. Our chapter then deals with aspirations of the youth in a capability-based approach. More precisely, we analyze the effect of formal education on youth pupils' aspirations in France.

In the first part of the chapter, we present a brief overview of the literature on capability, education and aspirations. In the second part, we give a description of the French high school system and the data we collected. In the third part, we present the methodology of our survey. In the fourth part, descriptive statistics are provided. Then, in the fifth part, we present and discuss the results of a multiple correspondence factorial analysis and hierarchical cluster analysis.

The Capability Approach, Education and Aspirations: A Brief Overview

The application of the capability approach when studying children poses several problems. This comes mainly from the implicit, but fundamental, hypothesis of self-determination (see Ballet et al., 2011). Despite the fact that the capability approach focuses on capability informational spaces as evaluative benchmarks, the conversion of these latter is conditioned, among other elements, on the choices made by the individuals. This means that one individual has a notion of what life she or he values. The main criticism that refutes the possibility of applying this theoretical framework to young children is that they are not capable of such a cognitive exercise.

However, such a point of view contradicts with extensive research in psychology on self-determination theory. This theory refers to the degree that individuals experience their autonomy and control over their actions and behaviors. "The child who reads a book for the inherent pleasure of doing so is intrinsically motivated for that activity. Intrinsically motivated behaviors represent the prototype of self-determination – they emanate from the self and are fully endorsed" (Deci et al., 1991: 4). According to these psychologists, children can be self-determinant and are not to be excluded as such from an analysis that involves high subjectivity. Moreover, the applicability of the self-determination theory has been largely discussed by Hirai in this book, specifically the chapter on "Happy Human Development."

Nevertheless, it would seem contradictory at the very least to study future capabilities, intimately related to positive *freedom* of children in the context of *compulsory* education. We may accept that by making a child go to school (compulsory education), one is restricting the child's freedom. This has been noted during the open classes organized with the surveyed children; some noted that going to school now hindered them in undertaking other activities. Saito indicates that in this case *future* freedoms of the child are to be considered (Saito, 2003). In other words, constricting freedom now can contribute to enhanced capabilities in the future. This idea, in educational terms, is supported by psychologists with the marshmallow experiment (Mischel et al., 1989).[1] This study shows how the children who resisted the temptation the longest turned out to be cognitively and socially more competent with better results in school. Restricting current capabilities may therefore enhance opportunities; this seems to favor formal and compulsory education. Following this line of thought, Vaughan (2007) foreshadows a positive impact of education on capabilities, indicating that education enhances the range of skills and, therefore, options for children. More specific cases are to be taken into account, see for example the chapter by Devecchi and Watts elsewhere in this book that explores how education might limit well-being for children with special educational needs.

According to Ibrahim (2011), the capability approach must consider individual aspirations. Her argument is to point out that the focus of the capability approach lies with opportunities an individual *can achieve*. This excludes, according to Ibrahim, all capabilities that

---

[1] This experiment places a child in a room with a marshmallow. The researcher explains to the subject of the experiment that she or he will be given a marshmallow. It will be placed in front of the subject on a table, in a neutral room. The researcher will leave the room for 15 minutes, leaving the child to decide what to do with the marshmallow; either she or he can eat the marshmallow before the researcher comes back or can sit out the 15 minutes and not eat the candy. In the first case, the child eats the marshmallow and the experiment ends for the subject. In the second case, the child waits for 15 minutes and is rewarded with a second marshmallow. The two possible issues of the experiment are clearly exposed beforehand to the subject.

a person *aspires* to gain and eventually transforms into a functioning. *Aspired capabilities* are defined by Ibrahim as "those alternative functioning bundles that the individual values and has reason to value but is unable to achieve due to various structural and institutional constraints" (Ibrahim, 2011: 11).

According to Ray (2006), one may consider that aspirations are, amongst other factors, socially determined. In other words, aspirations do not appear out of the blue, but are the result of social interactions with an individual's social environment. Ray notes, without detailing the consideration, that aspirations can therefore be highly influenced by education. This seems to be linked with another, broader determinant of the aspirations window, which Ray identifies as coming from the "flow of information" (Ray, 2006: 411). Hart (2012a) also emphasizes that education plays a major role in the aspirations of children, and hence the capability approach should carefully consider the relationship between capabilities, education and aspirations.

Several studies confirm that the sociohistorical context, the socioeconomic status of the parents and the level of parental involvement in the education are crucial determinants of children's aspirations (Sewell and Shah, 1968; Kao and Tienda, 1998; Marjoribanks, 1998; Schoon and Parsons, 2002; Heckman, 2011; Croll and Attwood, 2013; among others). Following this literature, we attempt in this chapter to determine to what extent and under which form formal education in French high schools contributes to the formation of aspirations.

The French High School System and Our Data

Specificities of French High Schools

In France, there is no unified secondary education school. The path between primary education – generally children under the age of 11 – and tertiary education is divided into two stages.

A pupil starts off in a "collège," generally at age 11. This first school hosts pupils from the "sixième" (6ème) to "troisième" (3ème), thus counting backwards. The purpose given to these schools by the French government is to provide a unique (no distinction between pupils whatsoever) type of education to every single pupil in France. Compulsory education ends at age 16, this corresponds roughly to the end of "collège," which is finished at age 15 for a pupil who did not repeat any of his classes. This unified education for all is referred to by the Ministry of Education as the "communal knowledge and skill base."[2] This applies to all of the 3,335,200 pupils in collège in 2014.[3]

The second phase of secondary education takes place in a "lycée," from "seconde" (2nde) to "terminale" (Tle). Pupils arrive in these schools around age 15 and it represents the very first time pupils are presented with a choice to make in terms of classes they want to attend. The main feature of this choice resides in the fact that a pupil does not actually chose the specific classes she or he wished to attend, but rather a *package* of classes. This process is generally referred to as "orientation," which we will find to narrow considerably the aspiration window of our surveyed pupils. The term of orientation describes what happens very accurately; it is very often considered as a life determinant decision to make and changing your mind ("ré-orientation") is viewed as a complex process, sometimes unattainable. The first decision to make consists in whether one wants to go to a lycée "general et technologique," "professionnel" or "agricole." Other types of formal education exist, such as 7 lycées "de la Défense" and several lycées "de la mode;" they represent only a few thousand pupils, compared to the total 2,651,600 in lycées in 2014.[4] The second phase of decision-making for a pupil in terms of orientation is the package of subjects she or he wishes to study. In the case of a lycée général, this can be literature, social and economic science or science. In the case of a lycée professionnel or agricole, many more alternatives exist, each relating to a specific type of profession.

The Collected Data

For our study, we used data from one lycée general and one collège. The percentage of students obtaining the diploma at the end of collège, the "Diplôme National du Brevet" was 85.4 percent in 2014 on a national scale which has been relatively stable for the past few years. The surveyed collège has 87 percent of its pupils obtaining the Diplôme National du Brevet. This diploma is not required to continue in a lycée.

[2] www.education.gouv.fr/cid2770/le-socle-commun-de-connaissances-et-de-competences.html [own translation].
[3] www.education.gouv.fr/cid57111/l-education-nationale-en-chiffres.html.
[4] www.education.gouv.fr/cid57111/l-education-nationale-en-chiffres.html.

The national percentage of obtaining the "Baccalauréat" at the end of lycée is 87.9 percent nationally, whereas the studied lycée has 96 percent of its pupils obtaining the Baccalauréat. Note that a Baccalauréat is required to enter a university. This exceptionally high success rate of our studied lycée is intuitively due to the way pupils are "recruited." A regular lycée hosts pupils from its immediate geographical surroundings, which is called the "Carte Scolaire," inducing pupils to the geographically closest lycée. In the case of our lycée, some very specific and rare classes are taught (ancient languages, international sections, specific arts, for example), allowing students to be recruited on the basis of their previous performance in school. The high results at the Baccalauréat are therefore not much of a surprise.

Describing the formation of aspirations by young pupils in developed countries, one would expect the choice of this lycée to bias the selection of our respondents. Pupils with certain academic aptitudes and with intentions to pursue their education would be expected to formulate higher levels of aspirations, especially with regards to their education. We will find that this selection poses no such bias, with the results of our research pointing in the opposite direction.

From both schools, one class per level was chosen, depending on availability and time constraints. Due to the approaching Baccalauréat, no class from the last level of lycée was available. Our panel represents therefore 139 pupils, of which 60 percent were girls, ranging from age 11 to 17, all ages equally represented.

Methodology

The aim here is to identify the formation of aspirations conditioned by formal education. In other words, how and to what extent formal education contributes or hinders the formation of aspirations of pupils in French formal education. This suggests that one measure we want to include in our survey is the pupils' *formal education*. This part of the survey was therefore fixed *ex ante* and invariably in the survey. We will discuss the relative modules in the section on *the survey*.

Second, a link is to be made with the formation of aspirations of the pupils. The multidimensionality of aspirations and their complex elaboration with regards not only to education has been identified by Hart (2012a) amongst others. Methodologies to identify and measure aspirations and their formation within the capability approach are scarce.

Having discussed the ability of young children to be self-determinant in the first section, we will elaborate on previously used participative surveys (Biggeri et al., 2006; Hart, 2009). Both Hart and Biggeri et al. use a highly participative methodology to identify aspirations from young children. Before asking the pupils to respond to the survey, they were invited to participate in its elaboration. This was done through "Open Classes." We will discuss this part of the survey in the section on *Open Classes*.

Finally, to extend the empirical strategy of Hart and Biggeri et al. we use multidimensional statistics. More specifically we use correspondence analysis, which was initially designed to be a statistical method that allows identifying a pattern in multidimensional databases. In other words, Benzécri, who may be considered the founding father of correspondence analysis, argued that "the model has to follow the data, and not the other way around!" (Benzécri, 1973: 6, own translation). This method allows the analysis of our complex data in a highly formalized way, without identifying a preexisting model of any kind. As such, the subjective opinion of the surveyed young children will be rendered in a formalized statistical manner.

The Survey

The first module allowed us to identify the respondent, and corresponding objective information such as gender, age and the number of siblings. This module also comprised questions on respondents' nationality and the education of their parents. These were not considered in further analysis as too few participants came from countries other than France and, surprisingly, very few could precisely name the highest diploma obtained by either of their parents. Some answered with their parent's current employment, whereas others left the answers blank.

The second module on the objective evaluation of the pupil's education comprised questions on their school year, whether they had repeated any classes, if they had any special optional classes they attended, the average grade in previous years, number of hours of class during one week and whether they had a private teacher. Very few of the surveyed pupils had a private teacher at home. The average grade could not be used because the collège had decided not to grade their pupils anymore, but to give sole feedback from the teachers. A high correlation was observed between the rest of the variables in this module and the age of the participants.

A third module was designed to evaluate the subjective view on the quality of education of the participants. This module was also predetermined and asked the participant to evaluate the quality of teacher's and other educational personnel's pedagogy and whether they considered help was given when asked for, for example. This module also attempted to evaluate to what degree the pupils were invested in their education; whether she or he does the homework correctly, and voluntary or involuntary absenteeism, amongst others. Questions concerning the importance of the prepared diploma and educations' role in future life (job, personal knowledge) were asked. Finally the module concludes with questions concerning the impact of relatives and educators in her or his immediate social surrounding on the respondents formal education.

The fourth module was largely inspired by the survey used by Hart in 2009, which evaluates the respondent's well-being and participation in school. The final module, which constitutes the very core of this survey, was determined after the Open Classes. We will discuss these in the next section. The resultant questionnaire brings together therefore subjective measures on different levels relating to schooling; perceived quality of education, well-being in school and aspirations. Moreover, the first modules attempt to obtain objective information about the respondent and achievement in school so far; grades amongst others. The objective of our analysis is therefore to attempt to establish links between these different modules. As mentioned before, we will attempt to do so using multidimensional statistics, thus not requiring a previously established model or hypothesis.

Open Classes

These Open Classes[5] draw on the methods used by Hart (2009) and Biggeri et al. (2006). A double objective was bound to these sessions: first of all, for the researcher to get to know the environment of the schools and the students who would be the future respondents to the survey. The importance of such a preliminary approach is highlighted by Hart (2009), additional to getting to know the pupils through informal

---

[5] All the Open Classes were held between the 10th and the 24th of March 2015.

talking, establishing manners of communication with these latter seemed crucial. Moreover, talking with staff of the school to discuss the specific study revealed to be very informative. Several teachers offered to look at the questionnaire to adapt its language to that used by the pupils, for example. The second objective was for the pupils to identify aspirations they linked to their formal education. This was done during a one-hour discussion, presented very informally to the pupils, mostly without any other adults in the room. Two questions were then asked:

Q1   – Do you think education is important for you and why?
Q2   – Do you think education is going to change your future life and how?

When the pupils were asked to collectively answer these questions, the discussion had no interference. Notes were taken on aspirations that were progressively identified through the discussion that occurred between the pupils. If the discussion stopped, the pupils were asked to identify barriers that school represented to them in aspirational terms.

Q3   – Do you have the impression that school hinders you in attaining things?
Q4   – What are the things you must renounce to by coming to school?

These questions resulted in the identification of aspirations pupils would value, but that they did not feel they could attain. This seems most relevant as to identify which aspirations are inhibited by school. All the identified aspirations were then used to design the last module on aspirations linked to formal education. These dimensions are reported in the following section.

Descriptive Statistics

The distributions of both age and class are relatively homogenous, with a slight exception at age 17. This is due to the absence of a "Terminale" level class, as explained before.

Variable	Modality	Frequency (%)
Age	11	15.83
	12	15.83
	13	12.23

Variable	Modality	Frequency (%)
	14	18.71
	15	17.99
	16	12.23
	17	7.19
Gender	Boys	36.69
	Girls	63.31
Class	Première	12.95
	Seconde	22.30
	Troisième	12.95
	Quatrième	16.55
	Cinquième	13.67
	Sixième	21.58

This survey was to be answered by ticking one out of 5 boxes. It was constituted by questions and propositions which were all answerable with one of 5 modalities, ranging from 1 (indicating a disagreement from the pupil with the question/proposition) to 5 (in which case the pupil agrees with question/proposition). This resulted in 139 individuals for 84 variables corresponding to one question/proposition each. The following figures show the frequency of responses per question and modality. Modalities vary from 1 ("not at all") to 5 ("extremely"). The questions of the first and the second modules are not reported here.

Figure 22.1 reports responses to module 3 and seems to translate major consensuses amongst the pupils. The distributions are much skewed, either to the left or to the right. We may interpret this as many pupils agreeing on the relative "good" quality of their education and the identification of a certain importance that they give to this same formal education. Several exceptions are to be noted nevertheless; almost 67 percent of respondents do not value at all the help they get from their career guidance counsellor, or "other" exterior help in the process of orientation. This can be largely explained because very few of the surveyed pupils ever had a meeting with one of these counsellors. Despite the fact that every collège or lycée in France has at least one career guidance counsellor, during Open Classes many pupils told

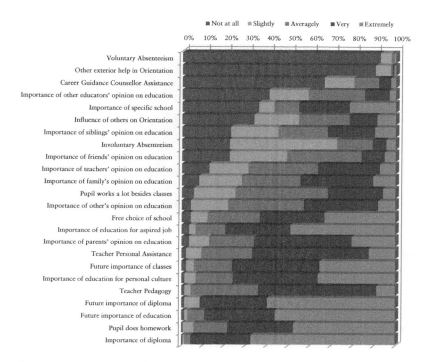

Legend: ■ Not at all ■ Slightly ■ Averagely ■ Very ■ Extremely

Figure 22.1 Frequency of response per modality in module 3: value and quality of education

that they had never thought of consulting one. "Other exterior help" was considered as a career guidance counsellor exterior to the school; even fewer pupils indicated using this help.

Notable responses are also "Influence of others on Orientation" and "Importance of specific school" to which responses cluster also on the lowest modalities, thus indicating a disagreement. In other words, pupils do not feel influenced on their orientation by others and the school they attend is not important as such. This translates a high degree of self-reported autonomy in the formation of aspirations with regards to their schooling. Almost 93 percent of respondents indicate that they have never voluntarily skipped a class, a result that would suggest a high implication of pupils in their formal education.

Figure 22.2 shows modalities that follow a normal distribution, a vast majority of the responses are clustered on modalities 3 and 4,

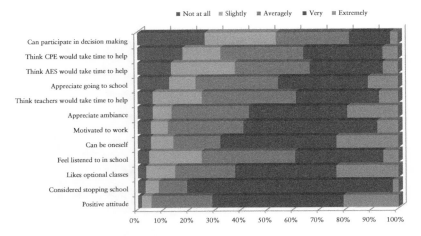

■ Not at all   ■ Slightly   ■ Averagely   ■ Very   ■ Extremely

Can participate in decision making
Think CPE would take time to help
Think AES would take time to help
Appreciate going to school
Think teachers would take time to help
Appreciate ambiance
Motivated to work
Can be oneself
Feel listened to in school
Likes optional classes
Considered stopping school
Positive attitude

0% 10% 20% 30% 40% 50% 60% 70% 80% 90% 100%

Figure 22.2 Frequency of response per modality in module 4: well-being in school

thus oscillating slightly above the average of 3. As this figure attempts to relate well-being in school, we can note that most of the respondents are not in extreme cases. Nor do they express particular distress in terms of well-being, nor does school seem to be the place pupils would feel overly joyful. The only notable exception here is the participation in decision-making; more than 53 percent of respondents answered with modality 1 or 2. This result suggests a feeling of non-representation from a considerable amount of the surveyed pupils.

Figure 22.3 reports responses for the fifth and concluding module of the questionnaire. The presentation is two-fold; the left column displays the 11 dimensions that the respondents identified during the Open Classes. The graph displays the responses to the questions, derived from the identified dimensions.

The Open Classes appear to be a success with regards to the existing literature on the identification of capabilities. 10 out of the 14 dimensions identified by Biggeri et al. (2006) were independently pointed out by the surveyed pupils. These latter did not identify "security and physical integrity," "freedom from economic and non-economic exploitation," "religion" or "time autonomy" as such. This is neither surprising nor a failure of the exercise because of the surveyed population. The children participating in 2006 to the "Children's World Congress on

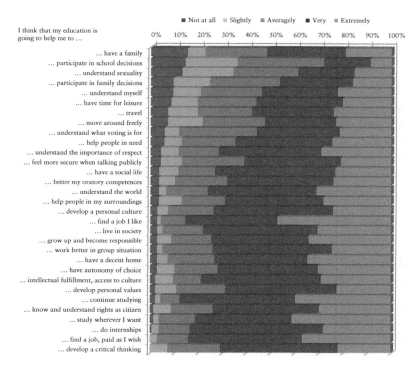

I think that my education is
going to help me to ...

Not at all   Slightly   Averagely   Very   Extremely

... have a family
... participate in school decisions
... understand sexuality
... participate in family decisions
... understand myself
... have time for leisure
... travel
... move around freely
... understand what voting is for
... help people in need
... understand the importance of respect
... feel more secure when talking publicly
... have a social life
... better my oratory competences
... understand the world
... help people in my surroundings
... develop a personal culture
... find a job I like
... live in society
... grow up and become responsible
... work better in group situation
... have a decent home
... have autonomy of choice
... intellectual fulfillment, access to culture
... develop personal values
... continue studying
... know and understand rights as citizen
... study wherever I want
... do internships
... find a job, paid as I wish
... develop a critical thinking

Figure 22.3 Frequency of response per modality in module 5: aspirations, with regard to education

Child Labour" during which Biggeri et al. led their investigation were child delegates from all over the entire world. These children were often personally concerned by child labor, which would explain the identification of dimensions which do not specifically apply to high school children in France. Moreover, an extra dimension was identified, which is not presented in the results by Biggeri et al.; "work and having a job." This dimension of aspirations was one of the most recurring during the Open Classes, almost every class identified "work and having a job" as an aspiration enhanced by formal education. This tends to show how most of the surveyed children consider school as a prerequisite in order to work and find a job.

This last figure presents another major result, at the sole view on the descriptive statistics. The distribution of the modalities appears to be clearly skewed to the right, indicating that a majority of the respondents associate high levels of aspirations with regards to their formal education. This can be viewed as the surveyed pupils expecting high returns of their education on their future capability set; education is considered to contribute to an enhancement of future capabilities. One exception is to be noted nevertheless; the question relating contribution of education to understanding sexuality presents a flat distribution. Surveyed pupils express divergent opinions as to the bettering of their knowledge of sexuality. This seems to be mainly due to the answers of girls; age does not seem to have an impact. For every age group the distribution of the modalities is normally distributed, whereas the distribution for girls is skewed to the left, that of the boys clearly to the right. In other words, girls do not consider that their schooling contributes to their knowledge of sexuality, contrary to the boys.

Multiple Correspondence Factorial Analysis and Hierarchical Cluster Analysis

As we seek links between the previous modules of the questionnaire, *levels of aspiration, levels of well-being in school* and *value and quality of education,* multidimensional statistics will be used. Criteria for the selection of variables pertinent in a multiple correspondence factorial analysis (MCA) exist (see for example Dervin, 1992). Considering the number of initial variables (68) and the relative small group of respondents (139), we cannot adopt a too restrictive criterion of selection. Using the mathematical properties of the MCA, we will rely on the descriptive statistics to select variables carrying the most information. A variable which presents a flat distribution must be eliminated beforehand; it does not present any variance to analyze for the MCA. Variables which appear to be a consensus amongst the respondents are therefore not included in the analysis. In Figures 22.2 and 22.3 we will retain those variables presenting at least four modalities with a minimum of 10 percent of responses each. Figure 22.1 presents several variables representing information that seems intimately related, the variables that differentiate the importance of other's opinion on the surveyed education will not be retained. The information of these six variables will be represented by the global variable "Do you find other's opinion on your education important?" The rest of the retained variables in Figure 22.1 are those presenting at least three modalities with a minimum of 10 percent of the responses each.

The analysis of the responses to the survey has been done in three phases. First of all, we had to select variables that could be used in the MCA; this has been done through the descriptive statistics as exposed in the previous section. Once the variables carrying sufficient information were selected, they were analyzed through a MCA. The resulting information was then clustered into groups using hierarchical cluster analysis (HCA). We will not review here the pertinence or technical details of any of the multidimensional statistic methods used here. Nevertheless, a justification of this method seems in order.

Benzécri states that "when our experience was applied to various types of data, it allows identifying models, not *a priori* but *a posteriori* ... without any restrictive hypotheses" (Benzécri, 1977b: 19, own translation). This allows us to analyze the numerous responses to the survey, without a preexisting model and in a highly formalized manner. In other words, we will be able to identify multiple existing relationships between different dimensions in the survey.

The analysis of results of an MCA is not intuitive and as we will note in this chapter, they are not always clearly conclusive. As stated before, this statistical method does not attempt to conform the data to a preexisting model. It rather allows an attempt to identify underlying relations between the variables. The emergence and identification of these relations is not as clear-cut as counting the stars of significance in inferential statistics. In order to bring out the relations of our date, usage of a HCA on the results of the MCA will provide information on which dimensions seem to be linked to others. Linking these methods we follow a recommendation by Benzécri. According to him, "it is beyond doubt that, in any study using discrimination and based upon multidimensional data, that a factorial analysis must precede a hierarchical cluster analysis" (Benzécri, 1977a: 404, own translation).

To decide the number of clusters, for the MCA and the axis of analysis to retain, we decided to adopt the so-called "elbow criterion." This graphical method looks at the marginal contribution of variance explained by adding one axis. The "elbow" is the point where the supplementary variance drops considerably. In our case, this point arrives at the third axis, we therefore retain the first two axes in our analysis. Following Baccini (2010), the observed values in the case of an MCA are the contributions of each column to the inertia on each retained axis and the coordinates of the columns on the axes. The contributions of the two retained axes are respectively 19.78 percent and 14.99 percent, with a global inertia of 34.78 percent.

The results of the MCA are not conclusive as such, because the number of variables and the number of individuals are too high in order to get a clear geometrical picture. Moreover, not all the modalities of the variables contribute significantly to the elaboration of the two retained axes. The HCA on the other hand, gives a very clear picture of relations between the surveyed dimensions, as described in Table 22.1. The numbers in this table are the modalities of each variable as discussed before, ranging from 1 to 5, from disagreement to agreement with the proposition/question.

This method gives a clear topology of the variables. All the retained variables are listed in Table 22.1 and are deconstructed between their five different modalities (ranging from "not at all" to "extremely"). The HCA clusters the modalities in three groups, represented by the three columns.

The homogeneity of the groups is very clear; the first group is composed of the collège whereas the second represents the respondents from the lycée. The last group does not present any specific class or

Table 22.1 *Distribution of modalities per variable in the hierarchical cluster analysis groups*

	Group 1	Group 2	Group 3	Variable
Teacher Personal Assistance	4, 5	2, 3	1	Educp2
Entourage influence on orientation	1, 3, 5	2, 4	–	Educp4
Importance of specific school	1, 2	3, 4, 5	–	Educp6
Free choice of school	2, 4, 5	1, 3	–	Educp7
Pupil does homework	5	2, 3, 4	1	Educp8
Pupil works a lot besides classes	3, 4, 5	2	1	Educp9
Involuntary absenteeism	2, 4	1, 3, 5	–	Educp10
Future importance of classes	3, 4, 5	–	1, 2	Educp14

Table 22.1 *(cont.)*

	Group 1	Group 2	Group 3	Variable
Importance of entourage opinion on education	3, 4, 5	2	1	Educp15
Future importance of education ...				
... for the aspired job	4, 5	3	1, 2	Educp23
... for personal culture	2, 4, 5	3	1	Educp24
Can participate in decision-making	1, 2, 3, 4, 5	–	–	Bes2
Appreciate going to school	3, 4, 5	1, 2	–	Bes6
Likes optional classes	3, 4, 5	1, 2	–	Bes7
Thinks CPE would take time to help	3, 4, 5	1, 2	–	Bes11
Thinks AED would take time to help	3, 4, 5	1, 2	–	Bes12
I think education is going to contribute to ...				
... do internships	4, 5	1, 2, 3	–	Asp5
... have a family	4, 5	1, 2, 3	–	Asp6
... participate in family decisions	3, 4, 5	1, 2	–	Asp13
... participate in school decisions	3, 4, 5	1, 2	–	Asp14
... have time for leisure	4, 5	1, 2, 3	–	Asp22
... understand myself	3, 4, 5	1, 2	–	Asp25
... travel	3, 4, 5	1, 2	–	Asp28
... move around freely	3, 4, 5	1, 2	–	Asp29
Class	6, 5, 4, 3	2, 1		
Age	11, 12, 13, 14	15, 16, 17	–	

age group; this group may thus be viewed as isolated individuals from different classes. This last group is characterized by the lowest levels of subjective importance of education and these pupils do not consider their formal education of a good quality.

When looking closer at the first group, representing pupils from the collège, we may note the very high values of the modalities representing the different variables. Only 3 modalities in this group are strictly inferior to 3, the other 62 are superior. This may lead us to think that the pupils from collège value their education more than the older pupils from lycée. Moreover these youngest pupils present higher levels of well-being in school on top of higher expectations. These pupils from collège can therefore be viewed as optimists compared to their older homologues.

On the other hand, the pupils from lycée do not have such a high appreciation of their education. They value much less the importance of their education, on top of which some sort of pressure can be identified in "importance of a specific school;" the pupils from lycée consider being in one specific school is very important, more than pupils from collège. This might be due to the phenomenon of orientation we discussed before; pupils from lycée sense the importance of this choice and thus the associated school. The fourth module for group 2 is highly representative of the feeling of aversion that pupils feel towards their school, well-being is extremely low. Moreover, these same pupils associate very low levels of aspiration considering their education. We may consider this last module as the main result of this survey. It seems that the pupils from lycée have the lowest levels of aspirations. This result is very counterintuitive; one would expect that pupils in lycée have higher aspirations because they have been in the formal education system for a longer period of time.

Conclusions

A very clear link between the three modules in this survey appears. Indeed, students who value their education are the same who present the highest levels of well-being in school. On top of this, it is the same pupils who aspire to the highest levels of return of their education. This link identified, we were able to relate it to the age of the pupils, which is highly consistent with the idea of dynamic and evolving capabilities (see for example Ballet et al., 2011).

I think the main argument for compulsory education is that it will give the child when grown up much more freedom and, therefore, the educational argument is a very future oriented argument. (Sen, interviewed by Saito, 2003: 27).

In the light of the capability approach, the results of this survey are worrying. Considering Sen's declaration on compulsory education, we must conclude to a certain inefficiency of the French secondary schooling system. Instead of creating possibilities and thus enhancing freedom, it seems that this system cages the aspirations of its pupils.

We may impute these findings to different elements. First of all, and this has been a recurring remark during open classes, pupils in lycées consider that the process of orientation is experienced as discarding entire sets of possibilities. Many pupils in France take therefore one specific orientation (Scientifique or "S") because it is associated with the most prestige and on top of all, is thought to open most doors at the end of lycée. This leads many pupils to end up in classes they did not particularly want, resulting in a certain difficulty to aspire for a positive outcome. This psychological barrier to aspire, coming from formal education itself, may be a pertinent future inquiry.

Secondly, levels of well-being in lycée seem extremely low. This survey highlights the existing link between well-being in school and aspirations. Specifically, the image of CPEs[6] or AEDs[7] as well as optional classes, contribute to the decreasing well-being in lycée. The entire dimension of "well-being" in school is not part of any policy in France. We may consider this as a major result but further research would be required to deepen our understanding of this phenomenon, such as its origins and precise impacts.

Finally, the third group identified by the HCA should be reflected upon. This group of non-clearly identified and isolated individuals represents a general incomprehension of the very utility of school. These pupils do not feel helped by teachers in school, clearly do not do their

---

[6] CPE: Refers to a "Conseiller Principal d' Éducation," present in every collège or lycée. This person is in charge of every aspect surrounding the pupils' education within school, other than teaching. They take care of administrative matters as well as personal and family problems, amongst others.

[7] AED: Refers to an "Assistant d' Éducation," having similar responsibilities as a CPE, but on an informal level. These positions were created especially for students who want to work during their studies. AEDs thus have a privileged relation with pupils, being only slightly older than these students.

homework and seem to lose interest in school itself. This is underpinned with the feeling that school will not be useful for their future lives. The phenomenon of disinterest in school could also open up a future field of inquiry.

References

Baccini, A. (2010) "Statistique Descriptive Multidimensionnelle." *Publications de l'Institut Mathématique de Toulouse*. Available at: www.math.univ-toulouse.fr/~baccini/zpedago/asdm.pdf

Ballet, J., Biggeri, M. and Comim, F. (2011) "Children's agency and the capability approach: A conceptual framework." In Ballet, J., Biggeri, M. and Comim, F. (Eds.) *Children and the Capability Approach*. Basingstoke: Palgrave Macmillan, 22–45.

Barro, R. J. (2002) "Education as a determinant of economic growth." In Lazear, E. P. (Ed.) *Education in the Twenty-First Century*. Stanford, CA: Hoover Institution Press, 9–24.

Becker, S. G. (1993) *Human Capital: A Theoretical and Empirical Analysis, with Special Reference to Education*. Chicago and London: The University of Chicago Press.

Benos, N. and Zotou, S. (2014). Education and economic growth: A meta-regression analysis. *World Development*, 64, 669–89.

Benzécri, J. P. (1973) "L'Analyse des Données." *L'Analyse des Correspondances*, Vol. 2. Paris: Dunod.

(1977a) "Analyse discriminante et analyse factorielle." *Les Cahiers de l'Analyse des Données*, 2, 4, 369–406.

(1977b) "Histoire et préhistoire de l'analyse des données, Partie V – L'analyse des correspondances." *Les Cahiers de l'Analyse des Données*, 2, 1, 9–40.

Biggeri, M., Libanora, R., Mariani, S. and Menchini, L. (2006) "Children conceptualizing their capabilities: Results of a survey conducted during the first Children's World Congress on Child Labour." *Journal of Human Development*, 7, 1, 59–83.

Blaug, M. (1985) "Where are we now in the economics of education?" *Economics of Education Review*, 4, 1, 17–28.

Coleman, J. S., Campbell, E., Hobson, C., McPartland, J., Mood, A. et al. (1966) *Equality of Educational Opportunity*. Washington, DC: Department of Health, Education, Welfare.

Conti, G. and Heckman, J. J. (2014) *Economics of Child Well-Being*. Dordrecht: Springer, 363–401.

Croll, P. and Attwood, G. (2013) "Participation in higher education: Aspirations, attainment and social background." *British Journal of Educational Studies*, 61, 2, 187–202.

Deci, E. L., Vallerand, R. J., Pelletier, L. G. and Ryan, R. M. (1991) "Motivation and education: The self-determination perspective." *Educational Psychologist*, 26(3–4), 325–46.

Denison, E. F. (1972) "Classification of sources of growth." *Review of Income and Wealth*, 18, 1–25.

Dervin, C. (1992) *Analyse des correspondances : comment interpréter les résultats?* Paris: STAT-ITCF, 41–72.

Hart, C. S. (2009) "Quo vadis? The capability space and new directions for the philosophy of educational research." *Studies in Philosophy and Education*, 28, 5, 391–402.

(2012a) *Aspiration, Education and Social Justice: Applying Sen and Bourdieu*. London: Bloomsbury.

(Ed.) (2012b) "The capability approach and education." *Cambridge Journal of Education*, 42, 3, 275–82.

Heckman, J. J. (2011) *Effective Child Development Strategies. The Pre-K Debates: Current Controversies and Issues*. Baltimore, MD: Paul H. Brookes Publishing Co.

(2012) *The Power of the Early Years: Creating and Measuring Capabilities*. Beijing, China: Human Capital and Economic Opportunity Global Working Group.

Hinchcliffe, G. and Terzi, L. (2009) "Introduction to the special issue 'Capabilities and education'." *Studies in Philosophy and Education*, 28, 5, 387–90.

Ibrahim, S. (2011) Poverty, aspirations and wellbeing: Afraid to aspire and unable to reach a better life – voices from Egypt. Brooks World Poverty Institute Working Paper No. 141.

Kao, G. and Tienda, M. (1998) "Educational aspirations of minority youth." *American Journal of Education*, 106, 3, 349–84.

Leßmann, O., Otto, H.-U. and Ziegler, H. (Eds.) (2011) *Closing the Capabilities Gap: Renegotiating Social Justice for the Young*. Opladen & Farmington Hills, MI: Barbara Budrich Publishers.

Marjoribanks, K. (1998) "Family capital, children's individual attributes, and adolescents' aspirations: A follow-up analysis." *Journal of Psychology*, 132, 3, 328–36.

Mischel, W., Shoda, Y. and Rodriguez, M. L. (1989) "Delay of gratification in children." *Science*, 244, 933–38.

Peaker, G. F. (1971) *The Plowden Children Four Years Later*. London: National Foundation for Educational Research in England and Wales.

Ray, D. (2006) "Aspirations, poverty, and economic change." In Banerjee, A. J., Bénabou, R. and Mookherjee, D. (Eds.) *Understanding Poverty*. New York: Oxford University Press, 409–21.

Romer, P. M. (1986). Increasing returns and long-run growth. *Journal of Political Economy*, 94, 5, 1002–37.

Schoon, I. and Parsons, S. (2002) "Teenage aspirations for future careers and occupational outcomes." *Journal of Vocational Behavior*, 60, 2, 262–88.

Saito, M. (2003) "Amartya Sen's capability approach to education: A critical exploration." *Journal of Philosophy of Education*, 37, 1, 17–33.

Sewell, W. H. and Shah, V. P. (1968) "Social class, parental encouragement, and educational aspirations." *American Journal of Sociology*, 73, 5, 559–72.

Vaughan, R. (2007) "Measuring capabilities: An example from girls' schooling." In Walker, M. and Unterhalter, E. (Eds.) *Amartya Sen's Capability Approach and Social Justice in Education*. New York: Palgrave Macmillan, 109–30.

Walker, M. and Unterhalter, E. (2007) "The capability approach: Its potential for work in education." In Walker, M. and Unterhalter, E. (Eds.) *Amartya Sen's Capability Approach and Social Justice in Education*. New York: Palgrave Macmillan, 1–18.

23 Other People's Adaptations

Teaching Children with Special Educational Needs to Adapt and to Aspire

CRISTINA DEVECCHI AND MICHAEL WATTS

Introduction

Both Sen and Nussbaum view education as a basic capability. It has instrumental and intrinsic value because it can be valuable and can also be an instrument for the development and broadening of other capabilities. It is therefore pivotal to the achievement of socially accepted valuable functionings and functionings that the individual has reason to value. Education, in its instrumental sense, affords the individual both the basic tools of literacy and numeracy, and the higher order skills of making informed decisions through the ability of thinking critically about one's situation. In this latter sense, education forms the basis for self-determination and the fulfilment of what each individual has reason to value in the life they want to lead.

Yet education can also be a barrier to the broadening of capabilities and the achievement of functionings. Barriers can take many forms: they can be of a curricular nature; they can be ingrained in the structure of schooling and the ways in which setting by ability and assessment procedures marginalise students; they can be determined by changes in policy; and finally, through the process of education, students can learn to adapt their preferences and rationalise and justify the very barriers to their own well-being.

The adaptive preference problem is central to the critiques of utilitarian approaches to well-being put forward by Sen and Nussbaum in their justifications of the capability approach (Sen, 1992, 1999; Nussbaum, 2000). They argue that people tend to adapt their preferences under unfavourable circumstances and that the utilitarian concern with preference satisfaction therefore fails to account for the distorted interpretations of well-being framed by deprivation. In this sense, adaptive preferences can be seen as the salience of what people are made to prefer over what they actually prefer. The capability literature typically considers adaptive preferences as self-abnegation

(Sen, 1992, 1999; Nussbaum, 2000) and resignation (Teschl and Comim, 2005) rather than the sour grapes phenomenon described by Elster (1983). Educational structures can generate adaptations, leading young people to accept and internalise external constraints that limit their potential to choose and lead the educational good life (Walker, 2006; Unterhalter and Walker, 2007; Watts, 2007, 2013). The capability approach engages with this problem by addressing not only what individuals value but what they have reason to value. Nevertheless, although education can play a critical part in challenging adaptations, the processes of schooling can discipline students into self-denial and the renunciation of aspirations for a better life.

Respect for human diversity is fundamental to the capability approach and so care must be taken when considering adaptive preferences (Nussbaum, 2000; Watts and Bridges, 2006; Clark, 2009; Watts, 2009). We recognise that many teachers strive to raise the aspirations of their students, often in the face of considerable difficulties (not the least of which may be the indifference of those students to their education). However, the part that teachers can play in producing and reproducing environments in which students adapt their preferences are generally well-recognised. Think, for example, of the teacher who, directly or indirectly, constantly undermines the student, perhaps (using a phrase common in schools in England) by telling her that she, the teacher, has low expectations of her. Under such circumstances, the student may well come to adapt her educational preferences, internalising the restrictive externalities and resigning herself to those structural limitations. In this chapter, we seek to extend this argument by suggesting that such circumstances not only lead to the adaptation of the student's educational preferences but to those of her teachers as well. We presume that raising the aspirations of their students is a central aspect of teachers' professional identities. That is, it is something they should value and have reason to value or, in the language of the capability approach, a professional capability. It follows from this that resignation to circumstances inhibiting that professional capability to encourage the educational flourishing of students constitutes an adaptive preference that detracts from the well-being of the teachers as well.

We consider this argument here in the context of educational provision for children and young people with disabilities and/or special educational needs (SEN) in England. Nussbaum observes that prejudice against children with disabilities can prevent an accurate

understanding of what they can achieve (2006: 189) and is unequiv-
ocal in her defence of human flourishing as the metric for all people,
including – or, perhaps, especially – those with disabilities:

> using a different list of capabilities or even a different threshold of capabil-
> ity as the appropriate social goal for people with impairments is practically
> dangerous, because it is an easy way of getting off the hook, by assuming
> from the start that we cannot or should not meet a goal that would be dif-
> ficult and expensive to meet ... Treatments and programs should indeed be
> individualised, as indeed they ought to be for all children. But for political
> purposes it is generally reasonable to insist that the central capabilities are
> very important for all citizens. (2006: 190)

Elsewhere (2000) she suggests that a certain wariness is required
when dealing with children's capabilities and argues that well-being
assessments should be concerned with the achievement of those
functionings – including educational functionings – that will enable
the mature individual to make her own choices. Nevertheless, it is reasonable to posit a counterfactual question at this point: Would children with disabilities and/or SEN opt for a reduced education if they
had the freedom to choose a more complete one?

Deneulin notes that '*human* freedom and choice cannot be separated from *history* and *community*' and so attention must be paid
to the 'collective and historical processes which underpin all human
choices and affect the conditions in which human well-being can be
promoted' (2006: 209, original emphases). We therefore begin this
chapter with an overview of the SEN agenda, noting that it tends to
reify the distinctions it was intended to negate, and address the part
that pedagogic structures play in producing and reproducing potential
adaptations. We then consider how the construction of SEN provides
a frame of reference for trainee teachers and address the ways in which
they can become resigned to operating within such restrictive structures and so contribute to the adaptive preferences of their students.
The third part of the chapter extends this argument by considering
how the expectations of teachers can inhibit their own capabilities.
That is, we question how the teachers' resignation to the reduced
capabilities of their students can lead to processes of adaptation that
reduces their own quality of life as they come to terms with an impoverished interpretation of teaching.

The Bumpy Road towards Inclusion as Fertile Grounds for Sowing The Seeds of Adaptive Preferences

At the international level, the concept of inclusion is enshrined in the Salamanca Statement which states that 'all children should learn together, whenever possible, regardless of any difficulties or differences that they might have' (UNESCO, 1994: 11). The Statement does not refer specifically to disabilities, special educational needs or any other form of classification and labelling. Instead, it makes a universal appeal to the right of every child to have access *to* and to participate *in* education. However, the validity of the Statement presumes a distinction between those children who have difficulties in learning and who are therefore, for whatever reason, 'different' and those who are not. The underlying discourse – which we argue below is at the heart of how teachers adapt their preferences and rationalise their choices – is one of normal distribution of ability (Gould, 1981) which, as Florian and Rouse argue, 'is informed by a hegemonic belief in bio-determinism' (2009: 595) and which has been supported by professional and medical interests (Tomlinson, 1982; Thomas and Loxley, 2007).

Although critics and supporters alike have pointed out that there is still a lack of agreement on what the practice of inclusion should be like, it is broadly concerned with the idea that all children, regardless of any disabilities or other discriminating factors, have the right *to* education (that is access to educational provision), but they are also entitled to a meaningful and successful participation *in* education. The latter notion of inclusion stresses both the quality of the educational offer and its equity in terms of educational outcomes (Devecchi, 2010). Both principled goals have been factors in the development of the current Sustainable Development Goals (SDGs) (UN, 2015) and in particular Goal 4, that is, 'Ensure inclusive and equitable quality education and promote lifelong learning opportunities for all'.

Yet, the road to inclusion has been, and still is, not a smooth one. Focused on the notion of access, in the 1970s, the movement for inclusion in the UK set itself in opposition to the practice of educating children with disabilities in special schools or other segregated settings. Rather, it was argued, all children had the right to be educated together. In the beginning, then, inclusion was fought on behalf of children with disabilities and the movement argued for the children's right to be educated in mainstream school alongside their peers. Alongside the notion of access, inclusion also challenged the quality of the educational offering by arguing that access to education was necessary but not sufficient because having access to education rested on the notion of integration. While integration assumed that the child had to adjust to the mainstream practices, inclusion supported the idea that it was the responsibility of schools to adjust in order to include the child. As a corollary to inclusion, the two notions of participation and celebration of diversity became part of the conceptual bases of inclusion.

Starting with the Warnock Committee Report (DES, 1978) and following a number of policies and guidelines (DfES, 2001) all the way to the most recent *Special Educational needs and disability code of practice: 0–25 years* (DfE, 2015), the English system has utilised a multi-track approach to the provision of education for children with SEN and disabilities (SEND) which intends to offer a variety of services to bridge the polarised alternatives of the mainstream and the special needs systems. Although this multi-track and multi-agency approach has the appearance of a viable and effective response, in reality it is marred by a strong positional contraposition between those who believe that inclusion offers the best solution to the dilemma and those who, on the other hand, claim that children's special and individual needs are better served in special schools and through specialised pedagogical responses. The polarisation is not a new phenomenon and it can be traced to the Warnock Committee Report which, premised on the common aims of education for all children, introduced the concept of 'special educational needs' (SEN). Radical for its time, the concept aimed to counteract the negative consequences of classification and labelling by asserting that at any point in their educational life any child might have educational needs which are different from those of the majority of other children. The report also used the concept of SEN to argue that children with disabilities were entitled to be educated in mainstream schools and that it was the responsibility of schools to adapt to the needs of every child. Yet, what seemed then a radical move in favour of a social model of disability – that is, a model which shifts the cause of difference from within the child to the way in which social arrangement creates barriers – preserved the status quo by adding two important caveats, reified in the present legislation: children with disabilities and SEN are entitled to mainstream education only if: (i) their education does not prevent the education of other children; and (ii) adequate support and provision is made for the purpose of meeting the children's needs.

Current legislation (DfE, 2011, 2015) not only firmly reasserts the special nature of some children, and therefore the need for specialised education, but it also undermines the project of inclusion by (mis)-appropriating its principles while declaring the end of the 'bias toward inclusion' (DfE, 2011). While such confusing ideological backstepping has been cast as providing more parental choice and better provision, its consequences have been a return to a more medicalised and discriminatory approach. A number of factors have led to the present situation, amongst which the simultaneous and interrelated rise of academies, and the diminishing power of the local authorities. However, one of the most problematic turns has been the major changes to teacher training. First came the decision to allow unqualified teachers into academies and to remove teacher training powers from universities by placing it into schools (DfE, 2010), followed by the decision to remove the need for 'any' teacher to have teacher qualified status (DfE, 2016). The impact a lack of training and opportunities for professional dialogue can have on the quality of the provision and on the inclusion of children can be great.

Thus, the road toward inclusion has been fought along a series of entrenched dichotomies such as ability/disability, mainstream/special education, integration/inclusion and so on. Central to the debate is a series of ideological contradictions and practical obstacles (Terzi, 2005, 2007a; Nussbaum, 2006; Norwich, 2008a). Predicated on the basis of the 'dilemma of difference' (Minow, 1990), inclusion, and the provision which has to be made available to ensure its viability and success, rests upon how conceptions about difference determine the amount, level, quality and, according to Wiebe-Berry (2008), the perceived fairness of the provision. Following Judge's (1981) analysis of dilemmas in education, Norwich summarises the nature of the inclusive dilemma as one in which 'there is no choice between alternatives when neither is favourable' (Norwich, 2008a: 288). Norwich's preoccupation with the dilemma of difference is indicative of more recent questioning of the validity and practicality of inclusion. The dilemma is one which stalls ethical decisions about appropriate pedagogy: if neither inclusion nor special education is a favourable option, how are teachers to decide on the good and right support for all children? On what basis would their decisions be made? We contend that the unavailability of favourable option, as Norwich puts it, challenges the very premise of rational choice theory in which rationally perceived individuals can make choices concerning their self-interest; or, in the case of teachers, what would be the in the interests of the children. We contend, therefore, that the dilemma so conceived is fertile ground for other forms of post-ad-hoc rationalisations that generate adaptive preferences.

One of such form of rationalisation, which can lead to the adaptation of children's and teachers' preferences, is the manner in which their needs are diagnosed, identified, and, ultimately, classified. Much has been written on the issue of classification of disability, the identification of special educational needs and the labelling of students in general (Corbett, 1996; Florian and McLaughlin, 2008; Norwich, 2008b). It is important to note that although the terminology is problematic, especially inasmuch as it can frame a lazy essentialism, and that various terms are at times used interchangeably, the three issues of classification, identification and labelling are closely linked. In various measures, and dependent upon contextual factors such as social, school organisation and individual norms and expectations, all three modes of designating individual ability, cognitive competence and potential to perform can have a bearing on how children and teachers structure their own identities in relation to their expected and assumed roles and responsibilities. However, it is also important to recognise the distinction between how children perform and what they are competent to perform. For example, they may not perform well in examinations but this does not mean they are not competent in other educational contexts.

Moreover, the need to rely on an effective system of identification is predicated on the assumption that equal educational opportunities for all children can be ensured. However, in practice, as Florian et al. (2006) suggest, the system of identification aims to fulfil the following intentions: to diagnose children in order to devise appropriate medical, educational or social intervention programmes; to meet parental expectations; to fulfil children's legal rights; to ensure equity in the fair distribution of limited resources; and to ensure accountability. As conceived by the Warnock Committee Report, the label of SEN was supposed to eliminate the negative connotations of the 1944 Education Act disability categories. Yet, over time, the very label that aimed to eliminate all labels has become a way of separating children between those who have needs and those who do not (Corbett, 1996). The Foucauldian disciplinary power of the SEN label is such that, rather than signifying the acceptance of human diversity as something that is normal, it reifies the assumptions that some children are outside what is expected to be normal, while simultaneously, as Graham and Slee contend, it provides 'the means by which we make judgements about the character, ability and future of different school children' (2008: 280). Labels, thus, define sets of assumptions which have implications for how teachers and children adapt to specific regimes of truth (Foucault, 1977, 1980) which, together with how the National Curriculum is structured and the assumptions about age-related attainment results, regulates beliefs about ability, potential and the capacity to succeed.

Although education has the potential to challenge adaptive preferences, the way education has been systematised and standardised indicates how educational structures can generate and sustain such preferences and lead the individual, without necessarily being aware of it, to accept and even appreciate the limits of a reduced life. As Rose states:

Although an increased understanding of the needs of individual pupils and the characteristics associated with some form of disability can be helpful, where this has led to stereotyping and a lowering of expectations such an approach has done considerable disservice to the very individuals that our education system has identified as being in need of support (Rose, 2010: 2).

The 'considerable disservice' can be construed as the consequence of a process of adaptation which is similar here to the Bourdieusian notion of habitus which is concerned with the internalisation of external circumstances that delimits the individual's worldview. Socialisation processes typically delimit the realisation of particular capabilities as specific functionings – such as valuing one form of education over another (Watts and Bridges, 2006; Watts, 2009, 2013) – and it is important to distinguish between adaptations to a particular form of education and to education altogether. If the aspiration of the capability approach is to enable individuals to lead a truly human life, the danger is that the educational structures within which students with disabilities and/or SEN are located generate an adaptation to the intrinsic and instrumental aspects of education, reducing them, in Sen's phrase, to 'happy slaves' (1999: 62) content with their lot. Moreover, basic capabilities are interrelated so whilst they can lead to mutual enhancement, they can also lead to mutual adaptations. Being different may, for example, cause those with disabilities and/or SEN to adapt to the capability of appearing in public without shame, thereby further restricting their freedom to enhance educational capabilities.

The unintended consequence of SEN policies has been to mark the children out as different; and this highlights the complexities of education and educational systems that Sen (in particular) and Nussbaum tend to gloss over. The capability to be educated (Terzi, 2007b) requires more than the input of educational resources. It requires conditions that enable the conversion of those resources into functionings and so enhance capability. The failure to acknowledge the importance of conversion not only means that the resources may be redundant but that their redundancy reifies the disadvantage of difference (Watts and Ridley, 2012; Ridley and Watts, 2014). The integration argument signals the problem of conversion factors; the inclusion agenda seeks to redress them. The classificatory system leads to separate education (whether in special schools or through additional support in mainstream schools) and/or the mark that these children are different. It offers the potential for enhanced educational capabilities – the freedom to move beyond self-abnegation and to aspire to the better life – by ensuring both the resources and the conditions necessary for their conversion. Appropriate educational structures can enhance aspiration and challenge what Sen terms 'social discipline' (1992: 149). This social discipline may be explicit (for example, the teacher who constantly tells the child that she is no good) but it may also be implicit (as suggested here where the social structures do the 'telling').

There is, then, a dilemma in the classification of disability and SEN. Although intended to promote inclusion, it may simply reproduce the conditions that rendered it necessary. If, as Norwich (2008a) asserts, there is no good option when it comes to educational provision, then the system itself predicates resignation to the reduced educational life: the better options are all out of reach. Furthermore, the very need for additional resourcing may taint those resources with the 'dirty mark' (Schostak, 1993) of their need (Watts, 2011; Watts and Ridley, 2012; Ridley and Watts, 2014). Put another way, the presumption that those with disabilities and/or SEN are second class students may lead to all attempts to do something about it merely reifying the belief; and, with educational structures foreclosing better alternatives, those students may come to accept what they have as the best they are going to get. Yet, even within such limited and limiting structures, individuals can make a difference and teachers can encourage their students to aspire beyond the confines of social discipline.

Teacher Expectations and Training

The capability to be educated is essential in order to avoid disadvantage and implies considerations about the design of social arrangements (Terzi, 2007a: 30). Challenging adaptations may not necessarily lead to greater freedoms because the social structures that generated the adaptations may well remain in place. Nonetheless, the individual's recognition that she has become resigned to her unjust circumstances and her reflection upon those circumstances are typically the first steps towards the enhancement of capabilities; and, given the nature of adaptive preferences, this is likely to require some external prompt. However, Nussbaum (2006) argues that where children are concerned, the focus should be on the achievement of functionings rather than the capability – that is, the substantive freedom – to achieve them. Ensuring that minimum thresholds are met (in the sense of achieved functionings rather than the poor proxy of, in this educational context, examination results) may therefore be sufficient to ensure that adaptations are challenged. This need not require recognition of and reflection on reduced circumstances because of the change in social structures: appropriate change has the potential to disrupt production and reproduction of the social discipline that generates adaptations. Teachers may, therefore, negotiate the adaptive preferences of children with disabilities and/or SEN in their care by enabling the conditions that allow thresholds to be reached – although we contend that teachers should not stop at the threshold as this can become another rationalisation of adaptations signified, for example, by the oft-heard comment about children reaching their potential. This is likely to include the conversion of appropriate resources such as pedagogical, technological and human resources. As those resources may already be in place, albeit tainted with the mark of their need, this requires belief in and respect for the diversity that follows the inclusion (rather than the integration) agenda. It therefore requires engagement with the structural issues that signify the differences that need to be engaged with if they are to be nullified. It touches upon training and, in particular, how teachers are taught to construct and interpret disability and SEN.

Three main models – medical, social and ecological – are interpretative lenses used to describe the nature of disability and/or SEN. The medical model locates disability within the individual and thus promotes rehabilitation as the main intervention. The social model posits that impairment (that is, a departure from human normality) causes disability (a restricted ability to perform tasks) which generates handicap (disadvantage) and so considers disability as the way in which societies create barriers that exclude individuals. The ecological model views the individual as part of a complex structure of relationships between different providers and thus pays more attention to how different stakeholders can work together to prevent exclusion and support inclusion. In practice, all three models are typically used in combination and this gives rise to further complexities and the need to revise old assumptions about the validity of such models. Nonetheless, they still serve as heuristic tools that teachers use to rationalise their decision-making processes when asked to validate their pedagogical interventions (Jordan and Stanovich, 2003).

This state of affairs has led to confusion, misinterpretation and, in some cases, the over-identification of children with SEN (OFSTED, 2010). The present mood has been one of revision and overhaul of the system of identification which has seen the creation of an Education, Health and Care (EHC) Plan for every child identified as having SEN (DfE, 2015). As stated in the Children and Families Act 2014 and in the SEND Code of Practice: 0–25 Years (DfE, 2015), the Plan should simplify the identification of SEN, reduce bureaucracy and empower parents in making better choices for their children. The justification for an overhaul of the system is partly located in the need to reduce costs and partly in the argument that the present system does not seem to be fit for the purpose of establishing effective provision. However, the purpose of the present 'radical' and 'innovative' reform agenda (DfE, 2011) is far from clear: on the one hand, there is the need to ensure the appropriate and justified distribution of resources; on the other, there is the need to devise pedagogical strategies that not only ensure children with SEN are able to access and participate in education but that they are able to use that education to live what Nussbaum calls the 'truly human life' (2000). As Florian et al. note, 'For children who are the recipients of special education, classification can have material consequences in terms of where and how they are educated, which professionals they encounter, and what life courses are mapped out' (2006: 37). Therefore, how teachers make sense of the interplay between classifications of disability and models of disability and how trainee teachers, whether through traditional university routes or directly in schools, are educated to understand the complexity of classifying disabilities and identifying SEN are at the core of how they devise suitable and appropriate provision.

As shown so far, questions about how best to support children with SEN are at the nexus of multiple and complex contexts and paradigms. Although research on inclusion and the efficacy of SEN provision has mainly focused on in-school responses, there is now a growing interest in the role Initial Teacher Education (ITE) plays in preparing new teachers for inclusion. As Norwich (2008a) explains, the 'dilemma of difference' offers two possibilities for action and neither of them is favourable. If we accept this portrayal of what lies at the core of providing all children – and, specifically here, children with disabilities and/or SEN – with equal educational opportunities, how are we to devise training opportunities for would-be-teachers? Related to this, there is the problem of how we are to provide training that will educate would-be-teachers to face the dilemma and to come to terms with it. In both cases, providing such an education requires a shift from the present concern to ensure the accomplishment of top-down regulated targets to an embrace of Peters and Reid's (2009) call for resistance and discursive practice that challenges pre-set assumptions and beliefs about ability and disability.

There are a number of routes by which students can enter the teaching profession in the UK but the predominant model consists of a combination of school placements and lectures at a Higher Education Institution (HEI). This model is the result of a longstanding debate as to whether a university-only based provision truly equips trainee teachers for the complexities of the job. However, it is also important to acknowledge that the debate is also located in the dispute about changing modes of teachers' professional practice and a persistent conservative critical view of the role of higher education in educating teachers. While both sides of this debate stem from the understanding that teaching is not just about theory, but also about experiencing the everyday nuances of practice, the present policy agenda (DfE, 2010, 2011) of making teacher education the sole responsibility of schools is as much about the need to train the school workforce as it to devolve funding from HEIs.

All trainee teachers are required to meet the Professional Standard for Qualified Teacher Status (TDA, 2007) which set benchmarks around three headings: professional attributes; professional knowledge and understanding; and professional skills. While such standards are wide ranging and written in a positive language which reflects the notions of inclusion, McIntyre argues that current ITE provision is:

ill fitted to prepare student teachers to engage with inclusive pedagogy. The English system is obviously inadequate for that purpose, being aimed only at preparing beginning teachers to the *status quo*, and very deliberately being planned to avoid them being encouraged to think critically on that *status quo* (McIntyre, 2009: 603, original emphasis).

Recent interest in the dynamic relationship between what is taught in HE-based courses and what students face and have to come to terms with during their school placements has revealed a number of key issues. Students receive different and, at times, contrasting messages at HE and in-school about inclusion (OFSTED, 2008; Florian and Rouse, 2009). The present focus of standard-based reform on attainment and behaviour management (DfE, 2010) leaves little space in the crammed ITE curriculum to expose students to the complexity of working with children with SEN, although the government has pledged to 'Give a stronger focus on support for children with additional needs, including those with SEN, in the standards for qualified teacher status' (DfE, 2011: 59).

While this is a welcome development, the Green Paper's predominantly medical model of disability does not bode well for inclusion. The messages student presently receive at HE, and the ones they might receive as the result of the proposed changes, might reinforce the idea that some children learn differently because of their disability or SEN. HE lecturers and teachers in schools might explicitly or unconsciously hold the belief that specialist knowledge is required to teach some children, thus unwittingly passing on the message that children with SEN are the class teacher's responsibility.

By far the most interesting area of research has focused on the nature of teachers' and trainee teachers' beliefs, values, assumptions and ideas about disability and SEN and how these can impact on the ways in which they view their professional roles and responsibilities. Yet, there is a certain degree of epistemological confusion and therefore the array of issues above are used interchangeably to define the set of notions used to conceptualise teachers' mental maps. Nevertheless, there is widespread agreement that trainee teachers 'tend to use the information provided in course work to confirm rather than to confront and correct their preexisting beliefs' (Kagan, 1992: 154). In so doing, their pre-existing beliefs form a powerful conceptual map that can lead to the formulation of rational justifications for their future choices as teachers.

So the design of the ITE curriculum in England (which includes pressures of time and the limitations of the tutors) tends towards the reification of the social structures that mark out those with disabilities and/or SEN as different. This can go one of two ways: the orthodox reproduction of the status quo, which tends to inhibit capabilities and generate adaptations; or a heterodox challenge to it which can give students the substantive freedom to achieve the functioning of being educated. Sen and Nussbaum repeatedly emphasise that individuals are influenced by the actions and values of those around them. This is typically not a reflective process (again, it shares much with the Bourdieusian notion of habitus) and leads to what Sen refers to as putting identity before reason (Sen, 1998). That is, to being rather than thinking about being. That being is mediated by social environments and the wider social environments tend to limit opportunities for those with disabilities and/or SEN to lead the truly human life. They may retreat from appearing in public, unable to do so without a sense of shame. The inclusion agenda is intended to challenge this but the classificatory systems tend to act as heuristic short cuts: the label becomes the limitation of the individual, bypassing opportunities to help raise her aspirations beyond her adaptations.

Gasper suggests that aspirations can be 'socially fostered or socially stifled' and so the positive benefits of education can be more effectively realised through a focus on groups rather than individuals (2000: 998). Group aspirations can enhance collective capabilities (Ibrahim, 2006) and collective capabilities generated by social capital can lead to the achievement of functionings that individuals may not be able to reach alone (Ballet et al., 2007: 198). Conversely, however, group adaptations can inhibit collective capabilities and the capabilities of individuals within groups (Watts, 2011). The influence of others on individuals typically presumes a power arrangement whereby those with more power influence those with less; and our concern so far has been with the ways in which the powerful act of labelling can frame the adaptations of children with disabilities and/or SEN. However, we want to take this further and consider the potential adaptations of their teachers and their resigned acceptance of the limitations pressing upon their professional capabilities.

Other People's Adaptations

Mills and Ballantyne (2010) address the concern with preexisting beliefs with reference to the notion of three hierarchical 'dispositional factors': 'openness' in terms of being receptive to other peoples' ideas and diversity; 'self-awareness and reflectiveness' as the ability to be critical and self-critical about belief systems; and 'commitment to social justice'. Their research concludes that preexisting dispositions are hard to shift unless ITE lecturers spend more time and commitment in creating the learning opportunities for students to confront their initial views (although they leave unanswered the question of what impact the dispositional factors of lecturers have on their students). Another way of addressing the conceptual maps of trainee teachers is that of drawing a relationship between attitudes, pedagogical behaviours and value systems. For example, Pearson (2007, 2009) applies a sociocultural model to ITE provision and argues that the language of classification and identification 'allows schools to pathologise students' difficulties thereby reducing the schools' sense of responsibility' (2009: 560). Her findings show that trainee teachers' preexisting beliefs range from a categorical approach to disability to an interactive social model and that, while ITE can have an impact on changing their views, such initial beliefs are hard to challenge. Whilst illuminating, Pearson does not explain what she means by 'value systems' besides reproducing the widely accepted differences between the medical and social models of disability. Yet, what each individual has reason to value is central to how the capability approach evaluates social arrangements. Thus, a discussion about trainee teachers' adaptive preferences requires us to consider what such values might be.

Wiebe-Berry (2008) and Jordan et al. (2009) attempt to do just that. Starting from the principle that 'effective inclusion is akin to effective teaching practices overall, and that enhancing inclusive practices will benefit all students', Jordan et al. (2009: 536) develop their research agenda around the notion of 'epistemological beliefs' (see also Jordan and Stanovich, 2003) and define them as 'beliefs about the nature of ability, of knowing and knowledge, the process of acquiring knowledge, and therefore about the relationship between teaching and learning' (2009: 536). Their research is important inasmuch as it makes explicit the connection between beliefs and the process of learning. While their research focuses on how trainee teachers assume children learn, the same can be applied to how trainee teachers learn about becoming teachers of all children.

This last point is a rejoinder to concerns that trainee teachers might find themselves in different epistemological contexts of learning in HEIs and learning in schools. The point is important because becoming a teacher is not about the acquisition of knowledge but also the application of that knowledge in practice. Such applications do not occur in a vacuum but in the specific and (as far as we know) highly idiosyncratic environment of schools. This is to say that beliefs, value systems and attitudes are based on past and present experiences of and in practice and that that practice shapes not only epistemological beliefs about the nature of knowledge and its acquisition, but shapes also the formation of personal and professional identities.

The notion of 'figured worlds' (Holland et al., 1998; quoted in Naraian, 2010) may be useful here. Premised on the sociocultural principles of activity theory, the 'figured worlds' construct acknowledges that whilst identities are shaped by the cultural environment, they cannot be fully determined by it. Thus, a 'figured world' is a:

socially and culturally created realm of interpretation in which particular characters and actors are recognised, significance is attached to certain acts, and particular outcomes are valued over others (Naraian, 2010: 1678).

In such a world, identities are both *imagined* through the interpretation of the rules of a specific cultural environment and *positional* in that they are actively defined by the lines of powers within the environment. For Naraian, the figured world construct helps the analysis of the collaboration between teachers and special education teachers. More research applied to how trainee teachers might figure their worlds between HE and schools is needed but, in the meantime, Naraian's work shows that we cannot assume an existentialist nature of beliefs. That is, the system of values which underpin the conceptual maps trainee teachers use to negotiate disability, inclusion and SEN is more complex and dynamic than previous research might argue.

However, if this goes to some way in facilitating an understanding of how beliefs are shaped through the interaction of different forms of identity and practice, it does not go far enough in explaining how value systems are constructed. That is to say, that if we leave out of the equation the notion of value, we may fail to recognise the insidious intrusion of adaptive preferences. More specifically, we fail to make a link between adaptive preferences and the pursuit of equality and justice (Sen, 2009). We also run the risk of reifying the notion that teaching is a matter of craftsmanship, of learning 'what works' and forgetting that teaching is about making moral and ethical decisions about what is good and right and is fundamentally concerned with what is fair and just for all children (Devecchi, 2010).

In this respect, the work of Wiebe-Berry (2008) frames the notion of beliefs within a value system based on teachers' conceptions of fairness and how they can use these to rationalise decisions about their educational practice. Wiebe-Berry focuses principally on fairness as a matter of justice; that is, justice in the distribution of resources. She quotes Barrow's definition of fairness according to which: 'it is morally wrong, in itself, to treat individuals differently without providing relevant reasons for so doing' (Barrow, 2001: 1150). One of the rationales for classifying children's needs as 'special' was to determine the amount and distribution of resources so that all children have equal opportunities. Yet once children are classified, the label tends to define teachers' beliefs about children's abilities, learning needs and whether or not teachers feel they can be responsible if they lack the 'special' knowledge required.

For Wiebe-Berry, this complex dynamic can be explained and understood by working out whether teachers (and trainee and newly qualified teachers in her case) believe in a needs-based principle of distributive justice or whether they believe in a 'decent level' of minimum distribution. The decent level argument is necessarily based on a consensus of what is the minimum required to equalise opportunities, beyond which the distribution of surplus resources becomes unfair. The needs-based argument is appropriate when, as she argues, the 'well-being of the individual if of chief concern' (2008: 1150). However, this can lead to teachers becoming frustrated when resources are scarce. Research by Devecchi (2007) shows that the construct of fairness is indeed used by teachers as they make decisions about the distribution of resources, including the attention they give, among all the children in the classroom. However, unlike Wiebe-Berry's findings, Devecchi's inquiry shows that, once again, teachers have to deal with the dilemma of difference and in so doing they are caught in the impossible task of accomplishing justice for each individual child.

Adaptive preferences can become manifest as a delimitation of choice that restricts the opportunities of teachers to think differently and to examine their actions in relation not just to the availability of resources – including training and time – but in relation to how resources can be used differently to develop the well-being of their students. As such, teachers' beliefs about ability, disability and the nature of special educational needs can be barriers not only to the well-being of the student but also to their own professional competences and professional development. Seen thus, they can inhibit the possibility of even envisioning the possibility of better educational lives for students and better professional lives for teachers. This consideration of the adaptive preference problem can offer a new way of looking at teachers' beliefs, attitudes and pedagogical choice making; and that this can open up new ways of preparing teachers to teach all children.

Wiebe-Berry notes that teachers can become frustrated when resources are scarce. Our concern here is with the potential for them to reduce the cognitive dissonance this generates by adaptation. Elster (1983) argues that the tension caused by a mismatch between what the individual wants to do and what she is able to do can be reduced by the adaptation of preferences. This is the sour grapes phenomenon which causes the individual to non-consciously conclude that the object of her initial and unattainable desire is not really worth having and to revise her preferences. Here, this downgrading of the inaccessible may cause teachers to revise their professional preference for the inclusion agenda and focus instead on the more accessible goal of simply getting through the day with what they have. However, Elster's formulation presupposes an initial desire for that which has proven to be inaccessible. The capability approach extends his definition of adaptive preferences to include the self-abnegation that arises from habitual impoverishment and post-hoc rationalisation. Under such circumstances, there may not have been an initial preference to downgrade. The construction of ITE provision in the UK suggests that teachers may be schooled to have low expectations of students with disabilities and/or SEN. Moreover, the classificatory system (intended to promote the inclusion agenda by identifying the special needs of students) provides a heuristic framework that enables the rational-isation of those low expectations. Elster's interpretation of adapta-tion does not necessarily apply to such habitual circumstances but the self-abnegatory definition of adaptive preferences used in the capabil-ity approach is pertinent.

We asked at the outset whether children with disabilities and/or SEN would opt for a reduced education if they had the freedom to choose a more complete one. We now pose that same counterfactual ques-tion of their teachers: would they opt to deliver a reduced education to children with disabilities and/or SEN if they could deliver a more complete one? This frames the issue of teachers' adaptive preferences. We assume that teachers value and have reason to value the delivery of appropriate education to all their students and that this is constitutive of what we might refer to, in capability terms, as their professional well-being. As indicated above, educational and social structures tend to inhibit the inclusion agenda. Several authors (Ibrahim, 2006; Ballet et al., 2007) have tackled the question of collective capabilities, argu-ing that individuals are more likely to bring about social change if they work together for a common cause. The corollary to this is collective adaptations and traces can be seen in the provision of education for children with disabilities and/or SEN: the adaptations of the teachers, generated within the same wider structures that generate adaptations in their students, further limit the aspirations to a better educational life for those students. However, this should not be seen as a collec-tive adaptation as it implies shared responsibility and so contributes to the pathologising of disability and SEN. Significantly, addressing the educational adaptations of any child or young person (whether or not they have disabilities and/or SEN) without acknowledging the potential adaptations of their teachers can contribute to this process of pathologising difference and therefore distort well-being assessments.

It may therefore be considered appropriate to locate this profes-sionalism in what Sen refers to as the agency dimension of capability: that is, doing something for others which is not obviously condu-cive to one's own well-being, doing something extra. For Ballet et al. (2007) this concept of agency is the basis of responsibility for others and collective well-being. Nussbaum refutes Sen's distinction between the well-being and agency dimensions of capability. Whilst acknowl-edging that this distinction can be useful in assessing choices between equally valuable functionings (Watts, 2011, 2013) we side here with

Nussbaum because making appropriate educational provision for children and young people with disabilities and/or SEN should not be seen as something extra for teachers to consider. The 'social discipline' (Sen, 1992: 149) that is the unintended consequence of the classificatory system frames this potential for teachers to become resigned to the socially constructed limitations of their students. Such adaptations may incorporate the frustration at the heart of Elster's interpretation of adaptive preferences but the sour grapes phenomenon does not go far enough in accounting for the resignation to reduced circumstances that can pervade the provision of education for children and young people with disabilities and/or SEN. The internalisation of external circumstances, including the heuristic of labelling, may lead teachers to presume that the better educational life is out of reach for students with disabilities and/or SEN. Accepting this can and should be seen as adaptation of their professional preferences. To do otherwise is to risk the complacent acceptance of the unjust *status quo* and to deny the significance of teachers' professional capabilities.

Conclusion

Adaptive preferences signal the difference between what people prefer and are made to prefer and the part that other people play in generating the circumstances under which individuals adapt their preferences is generally well-recognised. Focusing on the example of children with SEN and/or disabilities, we have shown how students can come to internalise restrictive externalities and accommodate their aspirations to the realities of the structural limitations operating upon them, including those that may be produced and reproduced by their teachers. However, we have sought to extend the debate on adaptive preferences by arguing that these limitations do not only inhibit the well-being of the students but of their teachers as well. We pursued this argument through an examination of the origins of the SEN and inclusivity agendas, initial teacher education (ITE) in the UK and the notion of teachers' professional capabilities. The latter, we suggested, should incorporate a pedagogical commitment to providing the opportunities for their students to flourish educationally. However, ITE provision – or the lack of it – tends to reify the marks of difference the SEN agenda initially sought to erase. Teachers may, therefore, presume their students are incapable of such flourishing and so perpetuate the circumstances under which they adapt their preferences. This, though, denies their professional commitment to the education of all and so leads to the adaptation of their preferences. That is, it can lead to their resignation to an impoverished professional life.

In her defence of universal human values, Nussbaum (2000: 34–110; 2006: 9–95) highlights the importance of 'Being able to use the senses, to imagine, think, and reason – and to do these things in a "truly human" way, a way informed and cultivated by an adequate education' (2006: 76). Teachers can encourage their students – including and especially students with SEN and/or disabilities – to aspire beyond the confines of social discipline. Yet teachers are also taught; and, just as they may teach their students to become resigned to an impoverished educational life (and so, given the interconnectedness of capabilities, to become resigned to the impoverishment of life more broadly) so their ITE may teach them to reproduce these delimiting structures. That the inclusivity agenda has become widely accepted does not detract from this as labelling provides a heuristic shortcut to the pedagogic assumptions and expectations that foreshadow the experiences of teaching and learning. Moreover, as 'there is no choice between alternatives when neither is favourable' (Norwich, 2008a: 288), teachers may be frustrated at the circumstances under which they teach. They may then reduce the cognitive dissonance this generates by adapting their preferences through the sour grapes phenomenon (the less-than-conscious mental adjustment that allows the self-deceptive reassessment of what is perceived as desirable) that Elster describes. They may also rationalise their circumstances and become habituated to them through the broader interpretations of preference adaptation described by Sen and Nussbaum in the capability literature.

Focusing on the education of children with SEN and/or disabilities illustrates the highly social nature of capabilities and adaptive preferences. Viewed through the utilitarian lens of self-reported happiness, education can reduce students to 'happy slaves' (Sen, 1999: 62) who are content with their impoverished lot. It can do the same to their teachers. We tend to think of the adaptive preference problem acting upon less powerful members of society. Whilst teachers are not exactly empowered, they are more powerful than their students. Yet they, too, can adapt their preferences by internalising the socially constructed limitations of their students and downgrading the value of the better educational life which is out of reach. We are not advocating a state of permanent frustration but calling attention to the pervasiveness of adaptive preferences (Bridges, 2006) because it can so easily be overlooked. Our focus on other people's adaptations, particularly as we have constructed it through the distinction of Sen's evaluative spaces, highlights the importance of agency: that one's own well-being extends to a concern for others (especially when, as here, there is a professional commitment to that well-being). Yet if other people's adaptations can reduce one's own well-being, then enhancing other people's capabilities can surely enhance one's own well-being. In the meantime, and following Nussbaum, we do not want to offer the system an easy way of getting off the hook (2006: 190).

References

Ballet, J., Dubois, J.-L. and Mahieu, F.-R. (2007) 'Responsibility for each other's freedom: Agency as the source of collective capability'. *Journal of Human Development*, 8(2), 185–201.

Barrow, R. (2001) 'Inclusion vs. fairness'. *Journal of Moral Education*, 30, 235–42.

Bridges, D. (2006) 'Adaptive preference, justice and identity in the context of widening participation in higher education'. *Ethics and Education*, 1(1), 15–28.

Clark, D. (2009) 'Adaptation, poverty and well-being: Some issues and observations with special reference to the capability approach and development studies'. *Journal of Human Development and Capabilities*, 10(1), 21–42.

Corbett, J. (1996) *Bad-Mouthing: The Language of Special Education*. London: The Falmer Press.

Deneulin, S. (2006) *The Capability Approach and the Praxis of Development*. Basingstoke: Palgrave Macmillan.

Department for Education (DfE) (2016) *Education Excellence Everywhere*. London: The Stationery Office.

   (2015) *Special Educational Needs and Disability Code of Practice: 0–25 Years*. London: The Stationery Office.

   (2011) *Support and Aspiration: A New Approach to Special Educational Needs and Disability*. London: The Stationery Office.

   (2010) *The Importance of Teaching*. London: The Stationery Office.

Department for Education and Skills (DfES) (2001) *Special Educational Need Code of Practice*. London: HMSO.

Department for Education and Science (DES) (1978) Special educational needs. Report of the Committee of enquiry into the education of handicapped children and young people *(The Warnock Report)*. London: HMSO.

Devecchi, M. C. (2007) *Teachers and teaching assistants working together: Inclusion, collaboration, and support in one secondary school*. Unpublished PhD dissertation. Cambridge: Faculty of Education, University of Cambridge.

Devecchi, C. (2010) Which justice for children with special educational needs and disabilities? The application of Sen's capability approach to the analysis of UK school workforce reform policies. Paper presented at the HDCA, Human Rights and Human Development Conference, University of Jordan, Amman, 21–23 September.

Elster, J. (1983) *Sour Grapes: Studies in the Subversion of Rationality*. Cambridge: Cambridge University Press.

Florian, L. and McLaughlin, C. (Eds.) (2008) *Classification in Education: Issues and Perspectives*. Thousands Oaks, CA: Corwin Press.

Florian, L. and Rouse, M. (2009) 'The inclusive practice project in Scotland: Teacher education for inclusive education'. *Teaching and Teacher Education*, 25, 594–601.

Florian, L., Hollenweger, J., Simeonsson, R. J., Wedell, K., Riddell, S., Terzi, L. et al. (2006) 'Cross-cultural perspectives on the classification of children with disabilities: Part I. Issues in the classification of children with disabilities'. *Journal of Special Education*, 40(1), 36–45.

Foucault, M. (1977) *Discipline and Punish*. London: Penguin.

(1980) *Power/Knowledge: Selected Interviews and Other Writings, 1972–1977*. C. Gordon (Ed). New York: Pantheon.

Gasper, D. (2000) 'Development as freedom: Taking economics beyond commodities – the cautious boldness of Amartya Sen'. *Journal of International Development*, 9(7), 989–1001.

Gould, S. J. (1981) *The Mismeasure of Man*. New York: W. W. Norton & Co.

Graham, L. and Slee, R. (2008) 'An illusory interiority: Interrogating the discourse/s of inclusion'. *Educational Philosophy and Theory*, 40(2), 277–93.

Ibrahim, S. (2006) 'From individual to collective capabilities: The capability approach as a conceptual framework for self-help'. *Journal of Human Development*, 7(3), 397–416.

Jordan, A. and Stanovich, P. (2003) 'Teachers' personal epistemological beliefs about students with disabilities as indicators of effective teaching practices'. *Journal of Research on Special Educational Needs*, 3(1), 1–14.

Jordan, A., Schwartz, E. and McGhie-Richmond, D. (2009) 'Preparing teachers for inclusive classrooms'. *Teaching and Teacher Education*, 25, 535–42.

Judge, H. (1981) 'Dilemmas in education'. *Journal of Child Psychology and Psychiatry*, 22, 111–16.

Kagan, D. (1992) 'Implications of research on teacher belief'. *Educational Psychologist*, 27(1), 65–90.

McIntyre, D. (2009) 'The difficulties of inclusive pedagogy for initial teacher education and some thoughts on the way forward'. *Teaching and Teacher Education*, 25, 602–8.

Mills, C. and Ballantyne, J. (2010) 'Pre-service teachers' dispositions towards diversity: Arguing for a developmental hierarchy of change'. Teaching and Teacher Education, 26(3), 447–54.

Minow, M. (1990) *Making All the Difference: Inclusion, Exclusion and the American Law*. Ithaca, NY: Cornell University Press.

Naraian, S. (2010) 'General, special and inclusive: Refiguring professional identities in a collaboratively taught classroom'. *Teaching and Teacher Education*, 26, 1677–86.

Norwich, B. (2008a) 'Dilemmas of difference, inclusion and disability: International perspectives on placement'. *European Journal of Special Needs Education*, 23(4), 287–304.

(2008b) Perspectives and purposes of disability classification systems: Implications for teachers and curriculum and pedagogy. In L. Florian and C. McLaughlin (Eds.) *Classification in Education: Issues and Perspectives*. Thousand Oaks, CA: Corwin Press.

Nussbaum, M. (2000) *Women and Human Development: The Capabilities Approach*. Cambridge: Cambridge University Press.

(2006) *Frontiers of Justice: Disability, Nationality, Species Membership*. Cambridge, MA: Belknap Press.

OFSTED (2008) *How Well New Teachers are Prepared to Teach Pupils with Learning Difficulties and/or Disabilities*. London: OFSTED.

(2010) *The Special Educational Needs and Disability Review. A Statement is not Enough*. London: OFSTED.

Pearson, S. (2007) 'Exploring inclusive education: Early steps for prospective secondary school teachers'. *British Journal of Special Education*, 34(1), 25–32.

(2009) 'Using activity theory to understand prospective teachers' attitudes to and construction of special educational needs and/or disabilities'. *Teaching and Teacher Education*, 25, 559–68.

Peters, S. J. and Reid, D. K. (2009) 'Resistance and discursive practice: Promoting advocacy in teacher undergraduate and graduate programmes'. *Teaching and Teacher Education*, 25, 551–8.

Ridley, B. and Watts, M. (2014) 'Using capability to assess the well-being of adult learners with dis/abilities'. In L. Florian (Ed.) *The Sage Handbook of Special Education*, 2nd edition. London: Sage.

Rose, R. (2010) 'Understanding inclusion: Interpretations, perspectives and cultures'. In R. Rose (Ed.) *Confronting Obstacles to Inclusion: International Responses to Developing Inclusive Education*. London: David Fulton.

Schostak, J. (1993) *Dirty Marks: The Education of Self, Media and Popular Culture*. London: Pluto Press.

Sen, A. (1992) *Inequality Reexamined*. Oxford: Oxford University Press.

(1998) *Reason before Identity: The Romanes Lecture*. Oxford: Oxford University Press.

(1999) *Development as Freedom*. Oxford: Oxford University Press.

(2009) *The Idea of Justice*. London: Allen Lane.

Teacher Development Agency (TDA) (2007) Professional Standard for Qualified Teacher Status. Available at: www.tda.gov.uk/teacher/devel oping-career/professional-standards-guidance.aspx

Terzi, L. (2005) 'Beyond the dilemma of difference: The capability approach to disability and special educational needs'. *Journal of Philosophy of Education*, 39(3), 443–59.

(2007a) 'Capability and educational equality: The just distribution of resources to students with disabilities and special educational needs'. *Journal of Philosophy of Education*, 41(4), 757–73.

(2007b) 'The capability to be educated'. In M. Walker and E. Unterhalter (Eds.) *Amartya Sen's Capability Approach and Social Justice in Education*. New York: Palgrave Macmillan.

Teschl, M. and Comim, F. (2005) 'Adaptive preferences and capabilities: Some preliminary conceptual explorations'. *Review of Social Economy*, 63(2), 229–47.

Thomas, G. and Loxley, A. (2007) *Deconstructing Special Education and Constructing Inclusion*, 2nd edition. Buckingham: Open University Press.

Tomlinson, S. (1982) *A Sociology of Special Education*. London: Routledge and Kegan Paul.

United Nations Educational, Scientific and Cultural Organization (UNESCO) (1994) *The Salamanca Statement and Framework for Action*. Paris: UNESCO.

United Nations (2015) *Sustainable Development Goals*. New York: United Nations (available at https://sustainabledevelopment.un.org/?menu=1300, accessed 5 June 2016).

Unterhalter, E. and Walker, M. (2007) 'Conclusion: Capabilities, social justice, and education'. In M. Walker and E. Unterhalter (Eds.) *Amartya Sen's Capability Approach and Social Justice in Education*. London: Palgrave Macmillan.

Walker, M. (2006) *Higher Education Pedagogies*. Maidenhead: Open University Press.

Watts, M. (2007) 'Capability, identity and access to elite universities'. *Prospero*, 13(3), 22–33.

(2009) 'Sen and the art of motorcycle maintenance: Adaptive preferences and higher education in England'. *Studies in Philosophy and Education*, 28(5), 425–36.

(2011) 'Symbolic capital and the capability gap'. In H.-U. Otto, H. Zeigler and O. Lessmann (Eds.) *Closing the Capability Gap: Renegotiating Social Justice for the Young*. Farmington Hills, MI: Barbara Budrich Publishing.

(2013) 'The complexities of adaptive preferences in post-compulsory education: insights from the fable of The Fox and the Grapes'. *Journal of Human Development and Capabilities*, 14(4), 503–19.

Watts, M. and Bridges, D. (2006) 'The value of non-participation in higher education'. *Journal of Education Policy*, 21(3), 267–90.

Watts, M. and Ridley, B. (2012) 'Identities of dis/ability and music'. *British Educational Research Journal*, 38(3), 353–72.

Wiebe-Berry, R. A. (2008) 'Novice teachers' conceptions of fairness in inclusion classrooms'. *Teaching and Teacher Education*, 24, 1149–59.

24 | *Expanding Children's Capabilities at the Writers' Workshop*

HELENA KIFF

Introduction

This chapter suggests that a twelve-month long ethnographic study of a writers' workshop, at a state primary school in London, provides evidence that the children who attended the club had the opportunity to expand what Martha Nussbaum terms their 'central capabilities' (Nussbaum, 2011: 19). Furthermore, it introduces the concept of 'therapeutic writing for affiliation'.

The grounded theory generated by this research concludes that:

- Through the affordances of the Writers' Workshop, the children have the opportunity to 'find a voice'.
- The environment in the Writers' Workshop provides a fertile environment for the nurturing and expansion of Nussbaum's ten central capabilities.
- 'Therapeutic writing for affiliation', the unique affordance of the workshop, provides significant opportunities for the development of the architectonic central capability, namely, affiliation.

The Writers' Workshop

I would like to open by explaining what the Writers' Workshop is, how I came to be running it and outlining its potential for the expansion of children's capabilities.

By profession I am a primary school teacher and until 2008 I had always worked with children in Key Stage 2. At this juncture, an opportunity arose to join the Early Years Foundation Stage (EYFS) Team as a classroom teacher, for a period of one year. I was eager to experience teaching the children to read and write. I had long been aware that by the time they arrived in my classroom in Years 5 or 6 this had largely been accomplished; and the only real teaching of the initial stages of reading and writing that I had experienced were with ESL learners and 'catch-up' interventions.

One year later, I returned to my niche in the upper echelons of the school with a fresh perspective about learning to read and write and more disturbingly, with a deep sense that something to do with writing was 'missing' in Key Stages 1 and 2. Certainly the children were offered plenty of opportunities to write in the classroom; but there was something different about the sorts of writing that went on in the EYFS and the types of writing that was produced in a teacher-driven environment. What was it and what could I do to breach the hiatus?

After some consideration, I decided to launch a writers' workshop. It was my intention that the weekly club would offer children the opportunity to come together to *write* whatever they wanted. I duly launched the workshop in October 2011. It was free and open to anyone in the school. It lasted for an hour, once a week. The children were undirected, although they were welcome to ask myself or anyone else in the room for assistance. The children had access to a wide variety of writing materials including pens, pencils, paper, a wide range of stationery, an interactive whiteboard, a computer with internet access and a printer.

Over time it became increasingly obvious that whilst the club was located in my school classroom, there was something fundamentally different about the atmosphere, environment, interactions and activities taking place in that space during the workshop. In this chapter, I argue that the club provided a space where children's capability sets could be, and were, expanded.

Rationale for Selecting the Capability Approach by Nussbaum Rather than Sen

Is All Education Good Education?

Amartya Sen does not problematize the role of education in securing capabilities. He appears to conflate all education (by which, in this text, I use to signify schooling) with capability enhancing education. For example, although he recognizes that schooling provision in India is currently inadequate, 'School education in India suffers from two principal deficiencies: firstly, limitation of coverage and secondly poor standards of the education that is offered and received' (Sen, 2014: 120).

Sen does not raise the question of whether all educational experiences are necessarily capability-expanding environments. Indeed, he is glowing in his praise of higher education establishments in the west, 'Since the whole world benefits from the availability of first-rate higher education in the West, non-western nations have no reason to grudge the excellence of the west in this critically important field' (Sen, 2014: 117). This enthusiastic endorsement of the West's education system is not a view shared by all capability scholars, myself included. In contrast, Martha Nussbaum writes with concern about current approaches to American schooling, where the curriculum is narrowed and test scores paramount:

Understandable, and to some extent rightly, the emphasis of these interventions has been on basic literacy and numeracy; and it is surely right to think that when these skills are absent many avenues of opportunity are closed. It is important, however, not to confine the analysis of education and capabilities to those skills. A true education for human development requires much more (Nussbaum, 2011: 155–6).

Nussbaum advocates the nurturing of these central capabilities through education:

One job of a society that wants to promote the most important human capabilities is to support the development of internal capabilities – through education (Nussbaum, 2011: 21).

   Martha Nussbaum's work, while sharing many of the fundamental premises of Sen's original conception of the capability approach, envisages it as the mechanism by which one might set about 'constructing a theory of basic social justice' (Nussbaum, 2011: 19). Central to this approach is her 'specific list of the *Central Capabilities* ... *Life* ... *Bodily health* ... *Bodily integrity* ... *Senses, imagination and thought* ... *Emotions* ... *Practical reason* ... *Affiliation* ... *Other species* ... *Play* ... *Control over one's environment. (A) Political (B) Material*' (Nussbaum, 2011: 19). She argues that all 'citizens be placed above an ample (specified) threshold of capability, in all ten of those areas' (Nussbaum, 2011: 36).
   The list in itself is not without controversy. Sen does not endorse such a list and there are those, such as Melanie Walker, who have noted that the undemocratic nature of the composition of such a list

in itself negates its value and that such an arbitrary list sits at odds with the 'importance of public participation and dialogue in arriving at valued capabilities for specific situations and contexts ... [that Sen] ... has consistently argued for' (Walker, 2006: 47). However, I would concur with Nussbaum when she defends the list by saying, 'The list is a proposal; it may be contested by arguing that one or more of the items is not so central and thus should be left to the ordinary political process rather than being given special protection'(Nussbaum, 2011: 36). Her pragmatic approach to the list is commendable. She opens the discourse and produces a starting point for democratic discussion about what should constitute central capabilities.

Exploring the Evidence of Capability Expansion at the Workshop

Each one of Nussbaum's definitions of the central capabilities was scrutinized to identify which of the actions coded from the data set collected during the twelve-month ethnographic study were present in each definition.

To review, Nussbaum's first three central capabilities are:

1. Life
2. Bodily health
3. Bodily integrity

(Nussbaum, 2011: 33).

The school safeguarding procedures, that are both statutory and regularly checked through OFSTED inspection, must and did ensure that these first three central capabilities are in place for the children in the workshop (and indeed all of the children in the school). It is for this reason that I have not included them in my data scrutiny.

The Fourth Central Capability: Senses, Imagination and Thought

Being able to use the senses, to imagine, think and reason – and to do these things in a 'truly human' way, a way informed and cultivated by an adequate education, including but by no means limited to, literacy and basic mathematical and scientific training. Being able to use imagination and thought in connection with experiencing and producing works and events of one's own choice, religious, literary, musical, and so forth. Being able to use one's mind in ways protected by guarantees of freedom of expression and respect to both political and artistic speech, and freedom of religious exercise. Being able to have pleasurable experiences and to avoid non-beneficial pain (Nussbaum, 2011: 33).

The data analysis revealed that, in total, there were an aggregate of 760 references to the expansion of this central capability in the data set. The nodes under which this data were housed were: choice, creativity, experimentation, imagination and freedom. Drawing on the data coded at choice, freedom, imagination, creativity and experimentation, what does the expansion of the central capability *Senses, imagination and thought* look like in the context of the Writers' Workshop?

Over and above everything else, the children had the luxury of choice. There was more coding at this node that any other in the initial coding stage of the project. The children could choose where to sit, who to sit with, who to work with, what to make, do, talk about or write. They could select whatever medium was available in the classroom to undertake their project. They could work in isolation or collaboration. This amount of freedom is rarely available in any aspect of classroom life. The children repeatedly stated that they enjoyed the high level of freedom they had at the workshop. In this unrestricted environment, the children's creativity blossomed. There is an abundance of evidence that they were able 'to use imagination and thought in connection with experiencing and producing works and events of one's own choice, religious, literary, musical, and so forth' (Nussbaum, 2011: 33). The range and scope of creativity in the workshop was astonishing. The children made a vast array of texts including: 2D and 3D pieces, games, cards, posters, comics, stories, powerpoint presentations, poems and information sheets. The following are a representative selection of the types of texts the children created. I have endeavoured to choose a selection that does justice to the breadth of their works.

Mathusa had been learning about instruction writing in her classroom. She cross-fertilised this with her passion for all things 'fairy' and produced a fantastic instruction leaflet for any budding crafter keen to create their very own Fairy Land.

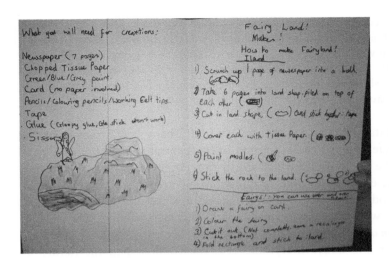

From time to time the children used stories that they were familiar with as a springboard for their own imaginative variations.

E.   Miss, I'm doing about the 3 Billy goats and the big bad wolf

H.   3 Billy goats and the big bad wolf. Have you been reading that story in class?

E.   No, I'm just making it up.

H.   Aaah. What's the big bad wolf going to do to the 3 Billy goats gruff?

E.   He's going to eat 2 of them,

H.   Yes?

E.   But one's still left

H.   Yes?

E.   Erm and he's sleeping erm he's erm and when and he couldn't find the other ones so he went outside to sleep and then the mum comes back cos she went shopping cos they didn't have any food.

H.   Right?

E.   Yes and erm, she saw the wolf

H.   Yeah

E.   And she thought she she went back home and saw that he he ate he that that there's only one child

H.   Oh no!

E.   So so she went back with like a knife

H.   Right?

E. And cut the wolf's belly open
H. Quite right too. And what happened then?
E. And then
B. It's like in ...
E. And then the 2 goats jumped out of the tummy
B. It's like when erm when a story about a deer and um a mother deer goes out shopping and
H. They're always going shopping these animals! It's a bit strange, don't you think?
B. No!

The Fifth Central Capability: Emotions

Being able to have attachments to things and people outside ourselves; to love those who love and care for us, to grieve at their absence; in general to love, to grieve, to experience longing, gratitude and justified anger. Not having one's emotional development blighted by fear and anxiety (Supporting this capability means supporting forms of human association that can be shown to be crucial in their development.) (Nussbaum, 2011: 33).

The data analysis revealed that, in total, there were an aggregate of 292 references to the expansion of this central capability in the data set. The nodes under which this data were housed were affiliation, friendship, self-esteem, empathy, self-image or perception of self, dyslexia and writing as therapy. Drawing on the data coded at affiliation, friendship, self-esteem, empathy, self-image or perception of self, dyslexia and writing as therapy, what does the expansion of the central capability *Emotions* look like in the context of the Writers' Workshop?

Self-Image or Perception of Self

The children are developing their identities. Their self-image and 'who' they perceive themselves to be is being shaped and honed by their surroundings – at school, and at home and by the people that inhabit those spaces with them. For some of the children this is a positive experience. They are happily growing in to young people with a clear sense of their value, agency and identity within their communities. For others, the process is more challenging. Some are brokering unfamiliar territory in a new environment – through a change of home or school location – and are navigating the need to establish their credentials in a new setting. Others are subject to fluctuating stability within the composition of their family, resulting in insecurities about their value or role in the home. They test these identities in the workshop, work with them, by making statements about themselves, drawing pictures of themselves and projecting themselves in to the environment. One such example was Ana, newly arrived in the school. She explained that she went to Reception and Year 1 in the Ukraine and then, when they arrived in England she went straight in to Year 3 at another school. She reads and writes fluently in Russian and Ukrainian. Her written and spoken English was impressive for someone who had been in the country for such a short time and in a family environment where no one spoke English. She explained that Minx is her favourite cartoon character and she watched it on TV in Russian every day. Ana asked me haltingly if she could write in another language – Russian. Yes of course, I replied. She wrote fluently about 'Minx' – a furry/character/ girlie cartoon thing. She read her text to me in Russian and translated it in to English for me, haltingly and with some frustration.

I watched Ana over the course of the year as her language developed and her confidence grew. I am filled with admiration for these children who are forging identities for themselves in foreign lands and in unfamiliar languages.

The Sixth Central Capability: Practical Reason

Being able to form a conception of the good and to engage in critical reflection about the planning of one's own life. This entails protection for the liberty of conscience and religious observance. (Nussbaum, 2011: 34)

The data analysis revealed that, in total, there were an aggregate of 26 references to the expansion of this central capability in the data set. The nodes under which this data was housed were practical reason, disappointment and aspirations. Drawing on the data coded at practical reason, disappointment and aspirations what does the expansion of the central capability *Practical Reason* look like in the context of the Writers' Workshop?

Practical Reason

Mathusa used practical reason in order to overcome challenges in her school environment. She clearly recognized that playtime was difficult so she found a strategy, through imaginative play, to cope. Her text and perhaps more significantly, her concern to share its content with me, point once more to the theme of affiliation so prominent in the interactions of the workshop. Mathusa was able to convey some of her day-to-day difficulties to me through her text. As a result, I came to understand her needs better and was able to share that knowledge with my peers and devise means by which the quality of children's playground time could be improved.

Mathusa Uses Practical Reason and Imagination to Solve Playground Problems

School playgrounds can be overwhelming for some children, particularly in large, urban environments where the number of children in a fairly small, enclosed space can run in to the hundreds. On an ordinary day in Colworth Primary, there would be around 360 children in the playground at each break and lunch time. Mathusa was a quiet, intelligent, thoughtful girl, aged 9 at this time. She found noisy, rambunctious interactions with crowds challenging and I was fascinated to discover some of the mechanisms she employed to combat these challenges through games of the imagination that effectively removed her from the stressful environment and transported her to a safer space. She wrote about one such game in her scrapbook and was keen to share its content with me in our interview.

Ma: We were on the playground and then these magical lockets are actually found on somewhere near the benches so we actually quickly pick them up before anyone else gets them... yea erm ...some of us have got white lockets, red lockets, pink lockets and many other colours erm and we take the magic dust we put it on ourselves.

HK: Mmmm

Ma: We go onto a cloud.

HK: Wow!

Ma: And then there's all these bricks and house making items lying there and then two people ask erm what are these for and then the other two people ask... it's going to, it's a house so so we build a house very quickly we like change to like a human size

HK: Right

Ma: Because it is long work so if we were human size we can do it
      quickly.
HK: Mmm
Ma: And then um then we and then we buy things from different like
      fairy shops that we find and then and then and then we might
      look at the playground and see if and we see if play times ending
      and we just um and we decide erm that erm if everyone is on the
      field and when they um we can still stay up there but if they get
      off the field we have to go down in case we're late.
HK: Right. So it's like a special place to play when playtimes on being
      a fairy
Ma: Yea
HK: That's brilliant and so can you do this everyday if you're a
      fairy – every playtime?
Ma: I might do it some playtimes and not some playtimes
HK: Ok

The Seventh Central Capability: Affiliation

(A) Being able to live with and towards other, to recognize and show concern
for other human beings, to engage in various forms of social interaction;
to be able to imagine the situation of another. (Protecting this capability
means protecting institutions that constitute and nourish such forms of affiliation, and also protecting the freedom of assembly and political speech.)
(B) Having the social bases of self-respect and non-humiliation; being able
to be treated as a dignified being whose worth is equal to that of others. This
entails provisions of non-discrimination on the basis of race, sex, sexual
orientation, ethnicity, caste, religion, national origin (Nussbaum, 2011: 34).

The data analysis revealed that, in total, there were an aggregate of
540 references to the expansion of this central capability in the data
set. The nodes under which this data were housed were imagination,
affiliation, sharing, self esteem, empathy, laughter, respectful/polite
language, self-image or perception of self, mixed age groups, democracy, play and acts of kindness. Drawing on the data coded at imagination, affiliation, sharing, self esteem, empathy, laughter, respectful/
polite language, self-image or perception of self, mixed age groups,
democracy, play and acts of kindness, what does the expansion of the
central capability *Affiliation* look like in the context of the Writers'
Workshop?

Daisy and Her Affiliation with Simin

Daisy was enthusiastic, confident, friendly, hard working and a lover of all things word-related. She was an obvious candidate for a writers' workshop. What made her contribution to the club so special was her generosity of spirit.

In terms of every day survival, Simin spoke English well. Her family had come from Turkey when she was very young and she had ambitious, hard-working parents who both worked full time in semi-professional positions. Her grandparents, who spoke exclusively in Turkish, collected her from the workshop each week. The home language was Turkish and her knowledge of English had been gleaned almost exclusively from school. Fundamentally she wanted to please – her parents, her teachers, everyone. Frustratingly, she had little confidence in her own abilities especially when it came to writing anything of an extended nature in English. Her admiration for Daisy and her writing was plain to see.

Some children (or adults) might have been tempted to laud their superior skills over their peers, and more particularly so over such a gentle natured girl as Simin, but not so Daisy. Noticing that Simin had a habit of emulating whatever she was writing, Daisy made a suggestion that they start a story with the same opening and then they work independently for a while before re-grouping to compare what each had written and then to craft a 'joint' story with components of each text. Simin was clearly delighted and the two of them produced several stories and poems in this manner.

It is doubtful whether Daisy realized how important a contribution she herself made to the friendly environment nor quite how significant for Simin the talking and working together that she mentions really were. Her affiliation with her peer is evident.

The Eighth Central Capability: Other Species

Being able to live with concern for and in relation to animals, plants and the world of nature (Nussbaum, 2011: 34).

The data analysis revealed that, in total, there were an aggregate of 20 references to the expansion of this central capability in the data set. The node under which this data was housed was animals. Drawing on the data coded at animals, what does the expansion of the central capability *Other Species* look like in the context of the Writers' Workshop?

There are not many times and places in the hectic school day for children to take time out to think about their relationships with their pets. I was both moved and surprised by the texts that the writers composed about their animals. The children wrote about real and imaginary animals, pets and comic book characters. They only ever wrote about animals or animal like creatures in a positive way. I was delighted to see lots of evidence of empathy towards the needs of fellow creatures, touched to watch children work through the grief of losing a pet and fascinated to realize that in one instance animals were being used as a conduit through which to mourn the death of family members. Samuel wrote with real tenderness about his hamsters and their needs.

Billy the Hamster Needs...

Billy the hamster needs:
   wheel, food, water, sawdust, ladder, cage, sleeping house, plastic bags, toys, more friends.

When he showed me his list, I was moved by how much thought and care he had given to the needs of the animal and perhaps was most touched by the last two words – more friends. We agreed that everyone always needs more friends.

The Ninth Central Capability: Play

Being able to laugh, to play and to enjoy recreational activities' (Nussbaum, 2011: 34).

The data analysis revealed that, in total, there were an aggregate of 221 references to the expansion of this central capability in the data set. The nodes under which this data were housed were happiness or pleasure in writing, fun, laughter and play. Drawing on the data coded at happiness or pleasure in writing, fun, laughter and play, what does *Play* look like in the context of the Writers' Workshop?

Sometimes the notion of *play* conveys an idea of a robust physical activity. I am delighted that Nussbaum's definition includes the words 'enjoy recreational activity'. Play for some people is a jigsaw puzzle, completed in solitude and tranquillity, play for others might be painting a picture or listening to a story. Writing and activities undertaken by the children at the workshop most certainly, then, classify as *play*. This being so, almost much everything that went on at there would be eligible for inclusion in this section.

The Tenth Central Capability: Control Over One's Environment

(A) Political. Being able to participate effectively in political choices that govern one's own life; having the right of political participation, protection of free speech and association. (B) Material. Being able to hold property (both land and movable goods), and having property rights on an equal basis with other; having the freedom from unwarranted search and seizure. In work, being able to work as a human being exercising practical reason and entering in to meaningful relationships of mutual recognition with other workers (Nussbaum, 2011: 34).

The data analysis revealed that, in total, there were an aggregate of 436 references to the expansion of this central capability in the data set. The nodes under which this data were housed were choice, freedom, self-esteem, self-image or perception of self, practical reason, critical thinking and democracy. Drawing on the data coded under choice, freedom, self-esteem, self-image or perception of self, practical reason, critical thinking and democracy, what does the expansion of the central capability *Control over one's environment* look like in the context of the Writers' Workshop? Although this capability might be considered less relevant to the children – in as much as Nussbaum's definition refers to political and property rights, I would argue that in expanding children's experiences of and confidence with dealing with choice and freedom, as well as nurturing their self-esteem, they are more likely to become engaged democratic citizens who will thus go on to assert their expectations in adulthood that this capability as an entitlement. Therefore, I include evidence of activities that I suggest, will, in the future, support the development of the capability of control over one's environment.

Having said this, the children exhibited both a keen interest in and a maturity towards controlling – by which I mean shaping – their own environment. They felt confident to make suggestions for ways that we might improve the workshop, thus exhibiting the ability to control the environment at the Writers' Workshop.

Laptops

During one of the first pupil interviews I conducted, two year 6 children shared their thoughts about potential enhancements to the workshop.

HK: Now! I know you've got some ideas for improving the work-
     shop. What do you think we could do to make it better?
Ce: I think we should have some laptops out and a group at a time
     to use the laptops.
HK: Mmmmm I think that's a really super idea and we'll put a rota.

Therapeutic Writing for Affiliation: The Unique Affordance of the Workshop

At the Writers' Workshop the children were offered the affordance of 'therapeutic writing for affiliation'. Affiliation, described by Nussbaum as, 'one of the Central Capabilities that play a distinctive *architectonic* role' (Nussbaum, 2011: 39) lay at the heart of the Writers' Workshop. The unique affordance of the Writers' Workshop was that it provided the children with the ability to 'write as therapy' – by which I mean that through their writing the children had the chance to process or work through emotional situations or relationships that they were struggling in some way with. This affordance could not be availed of at any other club offered by Colworth Primary School and this, there-fore, made it very significant.

In every one of the 'therapeutic' texts the child seeks to connect more closely, more securely with the 'someone' referred to either explicitly or implicitly in the text. In the case of Charlie, he used the animals in the text, 'Pets what die' as a metaphor for his deceased siblings. Through the writing of the text he was affiliating more closely with his mother and her suffering. In the case of Barry, he was endeavouring to affiliate more securely with his absent father. Sandra was re-living and savouring the experience of familial affiliation.

A Story of One's Own

Sandra's First Story: Affiliation with Her Family

Of all the children in the workshop probably the most story-impover-ished was Sandra. Although she was born in England and had attended school since nursery, at 9 years of age she struggled academically and had no story repertoire. Her verbal skills were very limited and she had mastered only basic literacy skills. She arrived at the workshop with a single aim: to write about her sister's birthday party. Knowing how poor her spelling was, I suggested that she might like to write it using the laptop, with the aid of spell check. She was thrilled at the prospect and immersed herself in her task for the next hour. This short text was the result of her efforts and her pride in it was enormous.

On the 17th of September my sister had a party at the craft cabin and my dad was there and my mum. There was me. There was face painting and presents for my sister and there were some fries and a crafty bear. Then we danced to the music and we played musical statues. Then we give our presents to my sister. Then after that we sing happy birthday to her then my sister blows out the candles.

Her total delight at having completed this piece of writing was only tempered by her frustration at her partial inability to read it back to me. We 'read' it together and she joined in with the words that she remembered writing.

Sandra rewrote this story with little or no variation almost every week thereafter; sometimes by hand and sometimes on the word-processor. The party was clearly one of the most magical experiences of her childhood and the writing activity gave her the opportunity to re-live the joy she had derived from it on a weekly basis. She was able to connect with her family vicariously through the activity of writing about the party. Once more there is clear evidence of affiliation being developed through the act of writing.

Charlie's Story: Affiliation with Mum, Working through Emotions

Charlie, aged 8, wrote this piece. He was a friendly natured yet slightly reserved boy. Each week he wrote and wrote with intensity and a fierce, quiet focus that was unusual in the group. He would whisper his thoughts and his words whilst he wrote and capturing these whispers inadvertently on the Ipad opened my eyes to his total immersion in his writing and his disconnection from the surrounding chatter and activity.

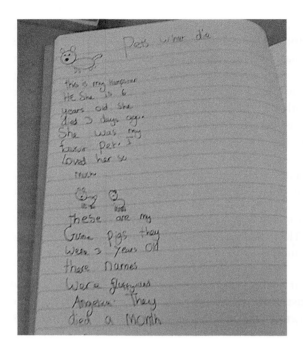

Pets what die

(picture of a hamster)

This is my hamster
　He She is 6
　years old she
　died 3 days ago.
　She was my
　favvrit pet. I
　Loved her so
　much

(pictures of 2 guinea pigs)
　these are my
　gunie pigs they
　were 3 years old
　there names
　were fluffy and

Angelica. They
died a month
ago.

When I saw that he had finished writing this text I approached him and asked if he would like to share his writing with me. He smiled and read it back to me with quiet confidence. Then, when I was expecting to have a conversation about my two cats and pets in general, Charlie told me something quite startling. He used the poem as a precursor to a conversation about other things that die, as well as pets. He told me that he had to really look after his mum at the moment because she was not well. It transpired that mum had lost three babies in the past year, one very recently, all of whom the family had named and buried. The writing was a place to express, to think, to mourn, to connect with mum, to connect with me, a conduit for grief, emotional figuring out, all of which are connected to that core capability; affiliation. There was something about the space of the workshop that permitted, perhaps even nurtured, freedom of speech. There was a capacity for affiliation with peers and teachers in that place that facilitated honesty and discourse such as that that I had previously witnessed in another child, Tayla, and her frank comments about her homeless father. And yet even in this space of freedom, Charlie chose to write not literally about the death of the babies but metaphorically. I wholly concur with the statement by Paul Willis (2000) that:

Metaphorical language is certainly useful to describe things, but it is also and fundamentally useful to think with. It clarifies, or perhaps brings to its only articulation, an abstract idea, or brings our and highlights the abstract quality or essence of something by comparing it to something else, usually concrete, in the world. Where there may be no alternative expression, this is the most condensed thought available. (Willis, 2000: 12)

Barry's Story: Affiliation with His Dad and His Mates

The photograph below is an image of the story by Barry, aged 9, who had written a text about his father, describing him as a famous footballer. It was the longest piece of sustained writing I (or his class teacher) ever saw him produce and he was, rightly, immensely proud of it.

Barry lived with his mother, his stepfather and his two half-brothers. He had very infrequent contact with his biological father. His step-father was not of the same ethnicity as the boy and neither were his two half-brothers. He had no other siblings. Frequently in trouble at school for disruptive behaviour, low level bullying and outbursts of anger, he struggled academically, was dyslexic and had very low self-esteem. At first glance, he might not appear to be the obvious candidate for a writers' workshop and certainly he did not attend voluntarily. Initially he came because his mum thought it would help to improve his writing skills but he enjoyed it, to his own surprise, continued to attend and even persuaded his friends to come along as well. It seems to me that he was using the writing as a means to connect both with his absent father, but also to connect with the boys he had encouraged to come to the workshop. The key theme of affiliation is once more evident here. Looking with particular focus at the text he produced about his father, it is clear that this writing gave him a unique opportunity to work through thoughts and emotions connected with his dad.

Conclusion

The children at the Writers' Workshop exhibited a plethora of 'central capability' (Nussbaum, 2011: 19) actions. The analysis of the data in this grounded theory study provided evidence that the actions engaged in by the children at the workshop developed or expanded Nussbaum's central capabilities.

Furthermore, there is evidence that the children attending the Writers' Workshop were offered the affordance of 'therapeutic writing for affiliation'. Affiliation is described by Nussbaum as, 'one of the Central Capabilities that play a distinctive *architectonic* role' (Nussbaum, 2011: 39) and its development through 'therapeutic writing for affiliation' was a seminal and unique feature of the Writers' Workshop.

During the interviews and in the questionnaires the children repeatedly stated that the workshop was 'different' to the classroom. If the classroom is instantly recognizable to the children as different, the corollary might be that these capability enhancement opportunities are lacking therein. The data is not available to assert this with certainty, but it is offered here as a hypothesis that would merit further exploration.

References

Nussbaum, M. (1998) 'Public philosophy and international feminism'. *Ethics*, 108(4), 762–96.

(2000) 'Aristotle, politics and human capabilities: A response to Anthony, Arneston, Charlesworth and Mulgan'. *Ethics*, 111(1), 102–40.

(2003) Capabilities as fundamental entitlements: Sen and social justice. *Feminist Economics*, 9(2–3), 33–59.

(2005) *Women and Human Development*. New York: Cambridge University Press.

(2006) Education and democratic citizenship: Capabilities and quality education. *Journal of Human Development*, 7(3), 385–95.

Nussbaum, M. C. (2010) *Not for Profit: Why Democracy Needs the Humanities*. Princeton, NJ: Princeton University Press.

(2011) *Creating Capabilities: The Human Development Approach*. Cambridge, MA: The Belknap Press of Harvard University.

Sen, A. (1979) 'Equality of what?' In *The Tanner Lecture on Human Values*. Stanford University, 22 May 1979.

(1985) 'Well-being, agency and freedom. The Dewey Lectures, 1984'. *Journal of Philosophy*, 82(4), 169–221.

(1995) *Inequality Reexamined*. Oxford: Oxford University Press.

(1997) 'Editorial: Human capital and human capability'. *World Development*, 25(12), 1959–61.

(1999a) *Commodities and Capabilities*. New Delhi, India: Oxford University Press.

(1999b) *Development as Freedom*. Oxford: Oxford University Press.

(1999c) 'The possibility of social choice'. *The American Economic Review*, 89(3), 349–78.

(2004) *Rationality and Freedom*. Cambridge, MA: First Harvard University Press.

Unterhalter, E. (2009) Education. In Deneulin, S. and Shahani, L. (Eds.) *An Introduction to the Human Development and Capability Approach: Freedom and Agency*. London: Earthscan.

(2013) 'Educating capabilities'. *Journal of Human Development and Capabilities*, 14(1), 185–88.

Vaughan, R. and Walker, M. (2012) 'Capabilities, values and education policy'. *Journal of Human Development and Capabilities*, 13(3), 495–512.

Walker, M. (2006) *Higher Education Pedagogies*. Maidenhead: Open University Press.

(2010) 'A human development and capabilities "prospective analysis" of Global Higher Education Policy'. *Journal of Education Policy*, 25(4), 485–501.

Walker, M. and Unterhalter, E. (Eds.) (2010) *Amartya Sen's Capability Approach and Social Justice in Education*. Basingstoke: Palgrave Macmillan.

25 | Education, Capabilities and Sustainable Development

CAROLINE SAROJINI HART

Introduction

This chapter aims, first of all, to situate education in relation to the global post-2015 agenda for sustainable development. It argues that educational processes potentially have important roles in contributing to many of the 17 sustainable development goals (SDGs), and not only those specifically related to education (United Nations, 2015a). The discussion goes on to conceptualise the way in which personal goals and wider social and development goals are juxtaposed and the tensions this brings in thinking about personal and social 'trade-offs' in developing and pursuing goals for human development. A new formulation of an individual's capability set is presented to show the way that some capabilities may be expanded and others contracted, due to complex conversion factors. The chapter concludes by arguing that educational processes may contribute significantly towards the development of individual capabilities and sustainable development more broadly, but this cannot be taken for granted due to negative as well as positive outcomes from educational processes, trade-offs and sacrifices along the way.

Sustainable Development: People, Planet, Prosperity, Peace, Partnership[1]

The World Bank, 'has placed education at the forefront of its poverty-fighting mission since 1962, and is the largest external financier of education in the developing world' (World Bank, 2012). In reviewing seven decades of development, Koehler (2015) observes an increasing emphasis on health, education and poverty alleviation and a related shift from a Keynesian-based economic perspective on development to a neoliberal outlook, with a shift from state control and intervention to

---

[1] These five words are used in the 2015 UN resolution (A/RES/70/1) to highlight key targets for sustainable development (United Nations, 2015b).

one of market freedom. In this broad context, key concerns of education development policy have focused on universal access to education and the reduction of gender disparities in educational opportunities (Hart, 2012b). For example, the millennium development goals (MDGs) aimed to ensure, that by 2015, 'children everywhere, boys and girls alike, will be able to complete a full course of primary schooling' and to eliminate, 'gender disparity in primary and secondary education, preferably by 2005, and in all levels by 2015' (Hart, 2012b: 275; United Nations, 2010). In reviewing the progress made on the MDGs in 2015, the UN reported, 'primary school net enrolment rate in the developing regions has reached 91 per cent in 2015, up from 83 per cent in 2000 and the number of out-of-school children of primary school age worldwide has fallen by almost half, to an estimated 57 million in 2015, down from 100 million in 2000. Gender parity in primary school has been achieved in the majority of countries' and for example, 'in Southern Asia, only 74 girls were enrolled in primary school for every 100 boys in 1990. Today, 103 girls are enrolled for every 100 boys' (United Nations, 2015a: 4–5).

The progress on access to education seems very encouraging. However, we cannot assume that all those participating in schooling will benefit in the same way. One of Sen's key observations is that equal resources may not be converted to the same advantage by different individuals. Thus, in relation to our consideration of education we can see that equal access to educational opportunities is not sufficient to constitute justice and fairness because individuals will be more or less able to convert those opportunities into ways of being they have reason to value. The new post-2015 agenda for sustainable development over a fifteen year period to 2030, adopted through a UN Resolution by the General Assembly on 25 September 2015, states:

This agenda is a plan of action for people, planet and prosperity... we recognize that eradicating poverty in all its forms and dimensions, including extreme poverty, is the greatest global challenge and an indispensable requirement for sustainable development...We are resolved to free the human race from the tyranny of poverty and want and to heal and secure our planet (United Nations, 2015b: 1).

Here we see a clear emphasis on eradicating poverty and protecting and securing the sustainability of our planet. This emphasis on

Table 25.1 *Extract from SDG 4, UN, 2015, pp. 17/35*

Extract from Goal 4 of the SDGs which aims to, 'ensure inclusive and equitable quality education and promote lifelong learning for all'

By 2030 ensure:

1. *all girls and boys have <u>access to quality</u> early childhood development, care and pre-primary education*
2. *all boys and girls complete <u>free, equitable and quality</u> primary and secondary education leading to relevant and effective learning outcomes*
3. *<u>equal access</u> for all women and men to affordable and quality technical, vocational and tertiary education, including university*
4. *Ensure all learners <u>acquire the knowledge and skills needed to promote sustainable development</u>*

sustainable development builds on the United Nations Educational, Scientific and Cultural Organization (UNESCO) call for a 'decade of education for sustainable development, to integrate the principles, values, and practices of sustainable development into all aspects of education and learning' with the hope of changing human values and behaviours in sustainable ways (UNESCO, 2005).

Sustainable Development Goal 4: Inclusive and Quality Education

So what is the role of education in this sustainable development agenda? SDG 4 aims to, 'ensure inclusive and quality education for all and promote lifelong learning' (United Nations, 2015a). Table 25.1 outlines highlights from SDG 4. The aims in Table 25.1 place emphases on quality and equitable education as well as access. This focus spans from early years through to tertiary education, including both academic and vocational programmes of study. Significantly, the goal of 'acquiring the knowledge and skills needed to promote sustainable development' is also explicitly stated, marking out educational goals across the life course and with implications for future generations.

However, these are broad goals leaving open to interpretation what might be deemed to constitute sufficient access, quality and equity in education, what is entailed in securing sustainable development, and the knowledge and skills needed by individuals in this regard. The agenda punctuates longstanding debates about development and, in the context of the present discussion, invites reflection on the role and goals of education and in particular how we might conceptualise quality and equity. Tikly and Barrett (2011: 9) have argued that 'education quality can be understood in relation to the extent to which it fosters key capabilities that individuals, communities and society in general have reason to value'. Three inter-related dimensions of quality are identified in their work, in an African context, covering inclusion (access to opportunities to develop capabilities), relevance (for the individual, community and nation) and democracy (public participation in debates about education quality). 'Any understanding of education quality must draw on an appropriate informational base concerning the kinds of capabilities that learners, parents, communities and governments have reason to value. It must also itself be the product of processes of public debate and dialogue at different levels' (Tikly and Barrett, 2011: 9).

Wider Sustainable Development Goals

There are 17 SDGs in total and although SDG Goal 4 is specific to education, other SDGs can also be seen to have significant connections to education, for example, SDG 1 aims to end poverty in all its forms everywhere and SDG 5 aims to achieve gender equality and empower all women and girls (UN, 2015b: 15/35-18/35). In addition, education of mothers in particular, has been linked to improved maternal health and reduced infant mortality (Sen, 1999a), linked to SDG 3 to ensure healthy lives and promote well-being for all ages. Goals to promote peaceful, inclusive societies (SDG 16) could also be supported by educational curricula, teaching practices and building educational institutional cultures supportive of living peacefully in partnership with diverse groups. Education related to sustainable ways of living has potential to contribute towards SDGs 12–15 (covering sustainable consumption, climate change, sustainable use of land and water-based resources). The significance of this potential is underscored by Gore who argues, 'safeguarding Earth's life-support system, on which the welfare of current and future generations depends' (2015: 722) is critical in securing individual capabilities in all aspects of life not only for the present generations but for future generations.

This brief introduction serves to illustrate that arguably there is a role for education in addressing many concerns related to sustainable human development. But can this be equated with expanding individual freedoms? Might there be occasions where education could be called upon to develop values, skills and knowledge that aim to serve humanity more broadly and not (only) the interests of the individuals being educated? In other words, should we guard against individualising the pursuit of freedom to such an extent that it overshadows the pursuit of collective values and action to protect and sustain our planetary home? On the other hand, is it fair to ask individuals, possibly living in extreme poverty, to act in more sustainable ways now, potentially limiting their freedoms, in order to safeguard future generations? We can see there is some tension between personal, social, economic and wider development goals. Some social and economic goals may be in unison with individual goals, others may require some form of sacrifice on the part of the individual for the wider public good, namely, to ensure the preservation of our planet. This theme of personal and public priorities permeates questions about the role of education and what just education may look like.[2] The question of balance and trade-offs between an individual's freedoms and functionings and those of others is returned to later in this chapter.

The Capability Approach and Education

We now turn to address the positioning of education in society through the lens of the capability approach. Sen has argued that, 'what people can positively achieve' is influenced by a number of factors, including 'basic education' (Sen, 1999a: 5). Over the past decade or so, understandings of education within the capability approach have grown substantially and the field has moved on from the time when Sen's capability approach had, 'not yet been examined from an educational perspective' (Saito, 2003: 17). The capabilities approach has been used to theorise diverse dimensions within education, for example, gender justice in education (DeJaeghere, 2012; Walker and Unterhalter, 2007), disability and special educational needs (Terzi, 2007, 2008); children and young people's agency and participation in education (Hart et al., 2014),

[2] Learning is used here to refer generally to the acquisition of knowledge, skills and understanding by an individual and the development of their values, capabilities and functionings; multiple meanings of education are discussed in the chapter, but tending to reflect a more institutional, systematic and teacher-led/designed learning experience.

theorising education (Robeyns, 2006; Vaughan, 2007), quality in education (Tikly and Barrett, 2011) and a number of special issue journals on the capability approach and education.[3] There is also an expanding literature examining the capability approach specifically in relation to further and higher education (Watts and Bridges, 2004; Walker, 2005; Watts, 2006; Garnett 2009; Walker & McClean, 2015; Powell, 2012; Hart, 2012a; Boni & Walker 2013).

So, how does the capability approach invite us to think differently about education and its role in human development? The capability approach offers a unique vocabulary and set of concepts with which to think about and articulate the roles and processes of education in different ways. Sen argues that, 'the evaluation of inequality cannot but be purpose-dependent, and the important need is to provide an appropriate match between (1) the purposes of inequality evaluation, and (2) the choice of informational focus' (Sen, 2002: 71). Using an evaluation framework that takes account of the freedom individuals have for living as well as the ways they actually live significantly expands the space of evaluation of human development (Hart, 2007, 2009, 2012a). Sen argues, 'the plurality of spaces in which equality may be considered reflects a deeper issue, viz. plurality regarding the appropriate notion of individual advantage in social comparisons' (Sen, 1992: 26). In considering what constitutes equity, fairness and advantage, the capability approach provides an alternative rich pluralistic frame of reference compared to other dominant resource-, utility-, preference and rights-based paradigms (Sen, 2009: 231).[4]

Sen comments that, 'my work on the capability approach was initiated by my search for a better perspective on individual advantage than can be found in the Rawlsian focus on primary goods' (2009: 231). Briefly, an individual's capabilities represent the freedom they have to pursue ways of living they have reason to value and 'functionings' represent the actual ways in which people choose to live. 'Conversion factors' refer to the multitude of factors influencing whether commodities

---

[3] See, for example, special journal issues on education and the capability approach including Hinchcliffe (2007), Hinchcliffe and Terzi (2009), Hart (2012b), and Walker (2012).

[4] Locating the capability approach in relation to human capital and human rights approaches has been well-rehearsed elsewhere, see, for example, Robeyns (2006), Flores-Crespo (2007), Lanzi (2007), Unterhalter (2009), and Hart (2012a).

may be converted into capabilities, and capabilities into functionings. In my own work I have also included 'forms of capital' alongside commodities and I look at the development of aspirations as well as capabilities and functionings.[5] The value of education is to be found not merely in the fact of whether an individual is enrolled in a course of study but in whether in and through educational experiences they are able to live in valued ways. Sen has argued there are essentially three roles of capabilities: those directly relevant to individual well-being and freedom; those indirectly involved in influencing social change and those indirectly involved in influencing economic production (Sen, 1999a: 296–97). I propose that education can be seen in the same way, with the *potential* to support individual well-being freedom, with *potential* to influence social change (encouraging social participation and critical agency),[6] and *potential* to influence economic production (developing an educated populace with potential to contribute to and drive economic production).[7]

More specifically, we can think about education from a capability perspective in terms of (i) the acts (functionings) of educating and being educated, (ii) the freedom (capability) to be educated and (iii) the manner in which education acts as a conversion factor to enhance/ diminish existing capabilities and to encourage the development of new ones. The extent to which communities may decide to encourage particular capabilities through, say, public schooling may be influenced by three further dimensions which have emerged in scholarship on the capability approach. The first relates to the idea of 'thresholds' of capabilities, encouraging us to question the minimum level of freedom we may wish to afford members of a society with regard to educational opportunities and experiences within broader sets of capabilities (Nussbaum, 2000, 2005). There is longstanding debate in relation to Nussbaum's list of central human capabilities regarding whether there ought to be a threshold for certain capabilities. For example, if we take the capability to play, what is the minimum acceptable level of functioning an individual should be able to achieve through virtue of their capability for this to be regarded as worthy of

---

[5] See Sen (1992, 1999a, b) and Hart (2012a) for further elaboration.
[6] See Sen (2002) for further elaboration of the concept of critical agency.
[7] As noted elsewhere in this chapter, this potential may or may not be realised and negative as well as positive individual outcomes may arise from educational experiences.

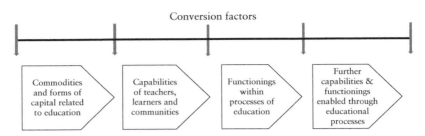

Figure 25.1 Multi-stage process of converting commodities and capitals to capabilities and functionings
Source: www.worldbank.org, retrieved 29 May 2012

a dignified life? Even without answering this question, we can see that the degree of capability a given individual enjoys may vary considerably across time and space and in comparison with others.

The second dimension relats to the idea of generating lists of capabilities, encouraging us to consider how we might prioritise capabilities in a specific context (Nussbaum, 2000, 2005; Sen, 2005; Walker, 2006). Third, Sen's emphasis on democratic deliberation and Robeyns' procedure for developing lists offer ways of thinking about operationalising the capability approach in educational contexts (Sen, 1999a; Robeyns, 2005). However, Clark (2005) draws attention to the potential for abuse of opportunities for public deliberation. Cameron and Ojha also point to an 'idealistic risk' in Sen's emphasis on democratic processes (2007: 66). If the capability approach is to be operationalised in relation to determining context-specific capabilities lists for education, or indeed other areas of personal and social life, then greater consideration of the practicalities and pitfalls of public debate are needed. Hart considers the complexity of democratic deliberation and proposes a theoretical model for reflecting on the way collective judgements are made regarding aspirations and their conversion to capabilities and ways of being individuals have reason to value (Hart, 2016).

Figure 25.1 helps to illustrate the multi-stage process of converting commodities and capitals, in all their forms, into capabilities and functionings, with a focus on educational processes. The ensuing section takes each stage and explores it in further detail, foregrounding the complexities of developing the freedom to live in ways we have reason to value and in choosing which combination of functionings we will realise at a given point in time.

Commodities and Forms of Capital Related to Education

Individuals learn in different ways: some planned, formal and intentional and other unexpected and serendipitous. For example, one may learn by accident, trial and error, observation, modelling, rehearsal, demonstration, collaborative enquiry; by school-, self- or community-led educational activity. Nurseries, schools, colleges and universities can all be positioned as part of the resources that have the potential to support the education of an individual. Digital technologies that can offer access to virtual learning environments can also be considered educational commodities, perhaps in independent ownership, on lease or through public access in libraries, community centres and so forth. Capital may take forms other than an economic form. For example, Bourdieu calls for capital in all its forms to be recognised including cultural, social and symbolic capital (Bourdieu, 1986).[8] These different forms of capital can contribute to the range of resources an individual can draw on in developing their capabilities. There have been huge changes in the possibilities for learning with advent of mobile technology and internet. The United Nations (2015a) reports 43 per cent global access to the internet in 2015 from access to only 6 per cent of the world population in 2000, and mobile phone subscriptions at 7 billion in 2015 from 738 million in 2000. Through virtual platforms, one can find information, share information or build learning networks in extensive new ways. Recently, wishing to learn how to thread a vintage sewing machine, I entered the model details online and was instantly able to watch a step-by-step video showing me how to complete the task. In another example, my daughter, who is learning to play the flute, came home from school anxious because she could not remember the finger positions for a new note she had learned. Again, we searched online and found a video demonstrating the note. These examples illustrate the way that knowledge sources are rapidly dispersing beyond formal institutions of education and that being able to access, navigate, filter and critically evaluate online sources can be an important means to self-led learning. Hence we are seeing a growing bricolage of resources to support learning; albeit that accessibility is still quite variable in different parts of the world. Indeed, inequalities

---

[8] See Hart (2012a: 49–64) for more discussion of 'blending' Sen and Bourdieu's work.

can be significant both between and within countries with variation in relation to educational provision, resources and institutional, community and family-led support for learning. This is often seen most starkly internationally when comparing the global south and the global north and can be seen within individual countries through the urban–rural divide.

Capabilities of Learners, Teachers, Families and Communities

Individuals may be variously able to take advantage of commodities related to education and commodities and capitals may be accrued and activated to different degrees by individuals, based on perceived eligibility, ability, inclination and choice (Laureau and Horvat, 1999). There may be competing interests in the ways in which different individuals in a community wish to activate limited resources and capital in relation to educational purposes. Thus despite having educational resources in a given community, the capability to convert those resources into capabilities may vary from one person to another. Eligibility to apply for a place at a local school may vary, for example, migrant children in China frequently do not meet the household eligibility criteria and so fail to gain access to public education institutions (Chen and Feng, 2013).

The capabilities of learners tend to be the main focus of the existing literature on the capability approach and education. However, this neglects others associated with formal and informal educational practices who may be able to develop or strengthen their capabilities in ways they have reason to value in educational environments and through educational practices. Here, for brevity, we can think about teachers, families of learners, educational leaders and community members. For example, parental well-being may be associated with the capability to enable a child to access what they deem to be a quality education. Kelly (2007) has written about school choice from a capability perspective in this regard. In addition, some of community members' capabilities may have diminished as an effect of the educational participation of others. For example, their job security may be threatened by more educated competitors in their locality.

Assuming resources are available to enable the development of capabilities through education, the challenge then arises regarding which capabilities should be pursued, especially through publicly funded education systems. In a number of cases authors have argued for the importance of particular capabilities that may be developed and expanded through education, either focusing on one or two 'core', 'meta' or 'foundational' capabilities or drawing on Robeyns' theoretical framework to develop lists of capabilities (Robeyns, 2005).

For example, Walker (2005) argues for the importance of developing autonomy through education and she positions 'agency and autonomy' as 'core capabilities' (p. 108). Walker (2005), Garnett (2009) and Nussbaum (2010) have all made proposals for the kinds of capabilities that might be pursued through undergraduate education. In addition, Hart (2012a) argues for the importance of nurturing aspirations and developing capability to aspire as a meta-capability. Nussbaum (2011), Terzi (2007) and Walker (2006) propose lists of capabilities that might be developed through educational processes. Nussbaum's list of central human capabilities (2005) is a frequently used reference point for thinking about lists of capabilities in specific contexts.

Functionings within Processes of Education

Education is often referred to in a monolithic mode where assumptions are made about what a successful or effective or quality education might look like. Metrics used to assess educational quality might look to enrolment, examination achievement (especially in literacy and numeracy) or years of schooling (United Nations, 2015a). One of the principal limitations of measures of development success in education pertains to the (over)use of figures of participation as indicators of progress. There has been a gradual shift from a concentration on aggregate figures to disaggregated statistics (perhaps looking at socioeconomic, gender, age or regional differences) but still this overlooks important differences in the nature of participation in education among different groups and individuals. Whilst for macroeconomic purposes these binary participation/non-participation statistics may be helpful, they obscure the microprocesses associated with individual agency and power differentials in specific contexts. For instance, presence in the classroom for two individuals may yield contrasting experiences of feeling included or excluded, harassed or respected and so forth (Hart, 2012a). As the possibility for generating and accessing different forms of data evolve it will be important to reflect on whether metrics can be improved to reflect capabilities, functionings and nuances in the ways that people are living. The functionings impacted by educational process extend beyond the learners and teachers to include others such as parents, siblings and wider community and employer stakeholders. For example, Reay (2004) writes about the 'emotional labour' of mothers in relation to their children's education.[9]

Agency and Participation

The ways in which learners are able to participate in educational processes may or may not reflect valued functionings. This might depend on the agency afforded to them through participation and here I will explicate this further in three dimensions, (i) being in or out of a certain form of education e.g. enrolled in primary school, (ii) participation in terms of the individual's agency, as seen for example in Hart's (1992) ladder of participation and (iii) participation related to decision-making about educational choices, experiences of participation and related outcomes (Hart, 2012a).

Reay et al. (2005) have argued that individuals engage performative and sociocultural registers of meaning and action in considering whether they plan to apply to participate in higher education. The performative register relates to an individual's tendency to select prospective higher education institutions by self-assessing their past and future performance. The sociocultural register refers to the tendency of individuals to self-classify themselves in terms of the match of sociocultural self-identity and that of a prospective higher education institution (Fuller, 2009; Reay 1998, 2001). Hart (2011, 2012a) has built on this work, identifying a third 'emotional' register of meaning and action, foregrounding the way that educational choices and pathways are influenced by emotions and not only rational or pragmatic factors. Not only is it the case that degrees of meaningful participation may vary but also that the 'cost' may vary across social groups where individuals experience cultural dissonance in educational spaces that do not reflect their cultural habits and preferences (Reay, 2001; Watts, 2006).

Educational endeavours are not neutral and moreover they carry a degree of risk. Nussbaum argues that policies that prioritise economic

---

[9] See also the journal *International Studies in Sociology of Education*, 26(1) which has several papers looking at parent and family involvement in schooling including, for example one by Bates (2017) on managing 'emotional labour' in relation to primary education in England.

growth as the key instrumental role for education provision displace educational provision that might support democratic citizenship, vital for the kinds of public deliberation about capabilities and functionings that so many are keen to propose. In related commentary about the restrictions of programmes of study constrained by economic instrumental priorities for education, Nussbaum warns of a 'silent crisis' (2011: 1). Numerous scholars have warned about the inclusion of political and ideological requirements in state policies about education programmes and how this is detrimental to the expansion of individual freedoms and capabilities (Garnett, 2009). Wang argues that in China, 'education on patriotism, collectivism and socialism is required to be carried out in school to equip students with the virtues necessary to be constructors of socialism. Choice and freedom are substantially confined by the strict requirement on ideology, patriotism and religion' (2014: 317); 'the whole education sector is required to be run in complete separation from religion' (2014: 314).

Thus values may not necessarily be positive for all and may serve the dominant groups in society, e.g. males, a racial or political group. They may be learned through formal and hidden curricula as well as from peers and other individuals and groups (teaching staff, after-school carers). For example, values are played out through family–school interactions, the ways individual instances are dealt with, reactions to personal experiences within educational institutions, e.g. compulsory schooling. How institutions, curricula and teachers privilege different areas of knowledge, history and perspectives may play a significant role in students' value formation. For example, whether colonising and colonised nations reflect one another's positions or whether educational programmes enable participants to critically reflect on human history including practices such as a nation's role in the slave trade, as well as human endeavours that might be judged as positive accomplishments. Different approaches to the organisation and practice of teacher-led education would have varying potential to develop the capability for critical reasoning as well as the formation of values and self-awareness of those values. There has been much debate in the field of education studies regarding the extent to which curricula ought to explicitly address individual values, reflected recently in controversial calls in the UK for schools to include education on 'British values' (Cameron, 2014). McCowan has written on the role of citizenship education in this regard and in the context of developing participatory democracy (2011).

Capabilities and Functionings Enabled (and Disabled) through Processes of Education

Processes of education highlight the significant role that teachers may have in the development and enablement of their students' capabilities through processes of learning. This is in relation to those capabilities an individual has at the outset of their studies as well as in relation to the development of new and emerging capabilities. Walker has written about higher education pedagogies that can support the development of particular capabilities. Others have supported pedagogical practices that encourage collaboration and critical reflection, inclusion and respect for non-dominant forms of knowledge, ways of knowing and communicating ideas. Wallace et al. (2012) have developed a learner-led group task-oriented method to support collaborative learning known as Thinking Actively in a Social Context (TASC). Philosophy for Children has also become popular as a method of developing philosophical enquiry and critical thinking among children in primary education and beyond (Lipman, 2003; Hymer and Sutcliffe, 2012; Fisher, 2013). Santi and di Masi (2014) and Hart (2014) have also written about Philosophy for Children (P4C) as a pedagogy that resonates well with the capability approach.

Open forms of assessment or curricula co-produced with students could offer opportunities for learners to function in educational processes in ways that are meaningful and valuable. For example, instead of being required to write an essay on a set topic for an assessment, a learner could be offered the opportunity to choose different ways of demonstrating their learning e.g. orally, visually, in participatory or multi-modal forms. As mentioned earlier, this expansion of freedom for the learner brings challenges for the teacher/assessor as new ways have to be found to respond to the work students bring. I recently encountered an example of this on a postgraduate programme in my university where one student chose to create a quilt to demonstrate their learning and reflexive thinking and another student presented a small leather suitcase filled with labelled artefacts and annotated notes to represent their learning journey. This expansion of capability for the student in engaging in learning in creative ways required new ways of working for the assessors. Similarly, 'flipped classroom' pedagogy (Roehl et al., 2013) encourages learners to engage with learning resources and stimuli before coming to a learning session with the aim being to maximise the collaborative learning space for critical engagement with knowledge and information rather than teaching sessions being used predominantly to transmit knowledge from teacher to learners. Again, although requiring new ways of working, and commitment from the teacher and learners ahead of the teaching session, an individual's potential to develop practical reasoning (on Nussbaum's list of central human capabilities) may be enhanced by this style of teaching. A session where all participants (teacher and students) are privy to shared knowledge (e.g. having read a paper, listened to a debate) may support more democratic modes of interaction where the teacher is no longer the sole knower of the session content and how arguments will be presented. We need to think about how we can practice education in ways that are enhancing rather than diminishing of individual well-being. Freire calls for a more democratic and symbiotic relationship between teacher and learner claiming, 'education must begin with the solution of the teacher–student contradiction, by reconciling the poles of the contradiction so that both are simultaneously teachers and students' (Freire, 1972: 53). By sharing knowledge and understanding in advance the teacher-learner partnership may be democratised and in a Freirian sense, teachers are also learners and learners are also teachers (Freire, 1972). This could occur from an early age and is not the preserve of higher education.

However, whilst one learner may value the camaraderie of peers and knowing that a teacher is nearby to guide and support learning, another may value independent learning in their home environment. An individual's valued ways of learning may alter over time, in relation to the topic of learning, level of difficulty and so on. In this sense, modes of supported educational opportunities (teachers, learning spaces, equipment and resources) might be enhanced through flexible modes of delivery, but may challenge teachers and parents to act in ways that may diminish their own well-being achievement, requiring more risk, cost, effort or time. What is called into question are the hierarchies of valued knowledge and power between teachers and learners in educational contexts.

There are clearly some tensions here. There are potential threats to traditional institutions of education such as schools, colleges and universities as their longstanding positions as holders of legitimate knowledge and expertise are potentially eroded by the emergence of new digital forms of knowing and understanding. Similarly, individual teachers and academics may feel pressured or threatened by demands to be flexible and adaptable and to become more inclusive with learners in co-constructing curricula, assessments and modes of educational processes and learning activities. Similarly, teachers may feel unprepared to shift teaching from physical to virtual spaces, or to 'blend' physical and virtual learning environments. Consequently, the capabilities of teachers and learners may not elide smoothly.

We can see an organic set of processes, an ecosystem, in the development and practice of education where the capabilities of learners and those around them may expand and contract in mutually and non-mutually beneficial ways. Parents and their offspring may discuss or coerce one another into or out of educational opportunities dependent on different priorities, motivations and values.

Therefore I suggest that in certain cases a learner may develop and expand their capabilities, or exercise certain functionings, only with the sacrifice of a degree of well-being freedom or achievement on the part of others. This way of thinking corresponds with Sen's writing on freedom, agency and well-being where he observes that well-being freedom and well-being achievement, 'can often move in the opposite direction to agency freedom' (Sen, 1992: 60). For example, families may forfeit offspring's support with domestic labour and paid employment outside the home in order that their children are able to participate in schooling. Parents may make adjustments to their household spending to pay for school uniform, school meals or tuition. Teachers may give extra time to ensure that they are able to give students timely comprehensive feedback and that their pedagogical methods are suited to creating inclusive learning environments for diverse classes. Academics in higher education may eat into precious research time to make space to meet the needs of students hampering their promotional prospects based on research income and publications. These 'sacrifices' may be made willingly through commitment to enabling the learner(s) to flourish, however, it should be noted that they may also be made reluctantly. In other words, an individual may willingly reduce their own wellbeing freedom for the sake of others but at other times feel pushed or compelled to do so. At times some negotiation may occur to settle the balance of what might be deemed reasonable in respect of mutual gains and losses in terms of well-being freedom (capabilities) and well-being achievement (functionings).

I propose that there will be other scenarios where learners' capabilities are able to have a positive impact on others. Where schools and colleges are available for public use outside of school hours this might bring a benefit to community members. Living in a society where individuals are able to train to be doctors and nurses can have a health benefit to others living in that community. Children who attend school may be able to use their knowledge and understanding to support family members, for example, teaching siblings to read and so forth.

I now turn to introducing a new formulation in the articulation of capabilities within an individual's capability set in order to represent the points discussed in a more concrete way. When speaking of the capabilities an individual holds prior to a given educational experience, let us represent this as:

$\{LC_1, LC_2, LC_3 \dots LC_n\}$,

where LC represents 'learner capability'.

The learner functionings that may be derived from these capabilities may be denoted:

$\{LF_1, LF_2, LF_3 \dots LF_n\}$,

where LF represents 'learner functioning'.

Educational experiences may offer the opportunity to enhance existing capabilities leading to expanded capabilities which can be represented thus:

$\{ELC_1, ELC_2, ELC_3 \dots ELC_n\}$,

where ELC represents 'expanded learner capability'.

Educational experiences may, however, also have the effect of diminishing existing capabilities leading to 'contracted' capabilities which can be represented thus:

$\{CLC_1, CLC_2, CLC_3 \dots CLC_n\}$,

where CLC represents 'contracted learner capability'.

Some capabilities may stay relatively the same from one point in time, (t_1), prior to a particular educational experience to a later point in time, $(t_1 + x)$, after this particular educational experience, and we can denote capabilities that stay the same as 'stable' capabilities. Let us represent these as:

$\{SLC_1, SLC_2, SLC_3 \dots SLC_n\}$,

where SLC represents 'stable learner capability'

Of course, in addition to enhancing and diminishing existing capabilities, new capabilities may be formed, and let us represent them
thus:

$\{NLC_1, NLC_2, NLC_3 \ldots NLC_n\}$,

where NCL represents 'new learner capability'.

At any point in an individual's educational journey they may hold
a range of expanded, contracted and stable capabilities, together with
new capabilities formed between t_1 and $t_1 + x$ and this can be represented thus:

$\{ELC_1, ELC_2 \ldots ELC_n, CLC_1, CLC_2 \ldots CLC_n, SLC_1, SLC_2 \ldots SLC_n,$
$NLC_1, NLC_2 \ldots NLC_n\}$.

Identifying the start of a new educational experience may, of course,
be easier in some circumstances compared to others. For example,
the beginning of familial and informal educational moments will be
fuzzy compared to, say, starting and completing a new institutional
programme of study, and there may be overlap, but the point here is
to extend and deepen the articulation of the oscillating nature of capabilities, not as fixed freedoms, and often expanding and contracting
in relation to the agency and well-being freedoms and achievements
of the individual and others. We can see that this conceptualisation
of expanded, contracted, stable and new capabilities can be extended
to individuals other than those referred to here as the learners. For
example, a similar notation could be used to represent a teacher or
parent's capabilities set using TC or PC instead of LC respectively,
and so forth.

Conversion Factors

Conversion factors can operate at all stages of the commodity–
capability–functioning cycle, both in ways that enhance or diminish
the conversion of capital and commodities to capabilities; capabilities to functionings and to enable or hinder the evolution of further
capabilities and functionings. Conversion factors may be multiple and
interlinked, cumulative or acting with opposing effects. For example,
civil war may act as a negative environmental conversion factor, preventing an individual from travelling safely to school to access learning resources. Conversely, outreach volunteers in the community may

enable learning to continue, albeit in an alternative and potentially more limited form.

Conversion factors also act on the process of determining which capabilities (freedoms) an individual can realise as functionings. These factors may relate to the individual and their social and environmental circumstances. Although an individual may enjoy a wide capability set, as Sen notes, it is the 'combination of functionings' that is important (1992), and it is likely that a single person will be unable to realise all of the elements of their capability set, such that judgments and choices have to be made, to activate certain capabilities at the expense of others, or to defer the conversion of certain capabilities to functionings until a later point in time.

Trade-Offs and Sacrifices

We are not able to support the infinite expansion of all individuals' capabilities, and even if this were possible, individuals would still need to select combinations of functionings due to time limitations if nothing else. Therefore, judgments will need to be made about which capabilities to grow and how trade-offs will be made within and between different individuals' capability sets. Figure 25.2 illustrates

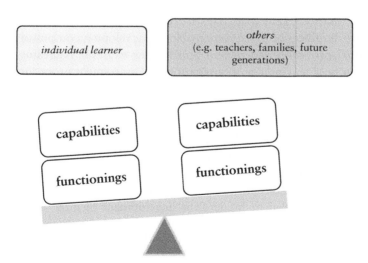

Figure 25.2 Illustration of the trade-off between an individual's capabilities and functionings and those of others

the balancing act between an individual's capabilities and functionings and those of others.

Trade-offs reflect the relationships between individuals and others in society at:

(i)   the macro level in terms of, for example, public spending on schools, development of a national curriculum, tuition fees etc.
(ii) the micro level in terms of the contributions that e.g. parents make to enable their children to access educational opportunities. The contribution may be monetary, in terms of time, emotional support, practical help and so forth.
(iii) at the individual level, where the individual, or their guardians, or the state, may make trade-offs between present and future well-being freedoms and achievements, on behalf of themselves and/or their children. Sen observes, 'when you are considering the child, you have to consider not only the child's freedom now, but also the child's freedom in the future' (Sen quoted in Saito, 2003: 25).

Indeed, 'despite the potential for numerous benefits to accrue to the child or to society from their educational participation, there is also a level of curtailment of liberty inherent in any compulsory schooling process. Most children have limited opportunity to choose the kind of education they can pursue or the place and form in which it takes place' (Hart, 2012b: 278). This foregrounds the moral responsibility on the shoulders of those responsible for developing compulsory educational provision and related policies, for example regarding minimum school leaving age, examination and assessment procedures and child protection within school environments.

It has also been argued that schools may enhance as well as diminish capabilities (Unterhalter, 2003; Walker, 2005). This is echoed in the wider education studies literature in relation to the negative impact school may have (Gillborn and Youdell, 2000; Archer et al., 2003; Power et al., 2003, Reay et al., 2005, Skeggs, 2005). This lack of equity has led Raynor (2007) to call for us to 'identify in what ways the education system helps or hinders the development of girls' capabilities (p. 161). Even where educational practices are predominantly positive for learners, the extent to which the education has undergone will help enable individuals to live in ways they have reason to value will be limited by wider social arrangements and the hierarchies of power between different groups, for example based on race or gender.

Conclusion

I think it is still fair to echo Saito's observation that, 'further work is needed in order to determine the appropriate functionings that best articulate the education needed for one's well-being' (2003: 24). The thematic model presented here directs attention to the multiple dimensions of education that require consideration with regard to expanding and contracting capabilities and functionings formed through individuals' direct and indirect connections to educational processes. This model of capabilities applies not only to learners but to all those involved in the planning, development, practice and evaluation of education. It could also be applied more generically to human development beyond educational concerns, or to other specific areas such as health. It is important to signal the ongoing necessity to democratically debate, within specific contexts, the appropriate capabilities and functionings that might articulate the education needed for one's well-being. Yet this needs to take account of the issues raised earlier in this chapter regarding the challenges of mediating power relations to bring voice and recognition to the widest public in these debates. The difficulties of measuring capabilities should not be an impediment to this goal.

By looking at education from a capability perspective we can identify elements of education that relate to resources, individual capabilities, prior to, during and beyond participation in educational processes. In other words, we can start to look at the freedom an individual has to participate in education, the freedoms enjoyed within the educational process itself and the freedoms enjoyed as an outcome of the education an individual accomplishes, in terms of experience and verification of some of that experience (an individual is likely to learn much more than qualifications will reflect). From a capability perspective our attention is also drawn to functionings enabled in and through educational processes and the future potential for new capabilities and functionings to emerge.

So when we think about the role of education in sustainable human development we benefit from taking an expanded view, beyond the learners themselves, of who stands to gain and lose in terms of capability and functioning expansion and contraction and how trade-offs are negotiated. The ripple effects of educational processes, institutional and otherwise, have far-reaching ramifications.

References

Archer, L., Hutchings, M. and Ross, A. (2003) *Higher Education and Social Class: Issues of Exclusion and Inclusion*. London: Routledge Falmer.

Bates, A. (2017) 'The management of "emotional labour" in the corporate reimagining of primary education in England'. *International Studies in Sociology of Education*, 26(1), 66–81.

Boni, A. and Walker, M. (Eds.) (2013)*Human Development and Capabilities: Re-imagining the University of the Twenty-first-century*. London: Routledge.

Bourdieu, P. (1986) 'The forms of capital'. In A. R. Sadovnik and R. W. Coughlan (2016) *Sociology of Education. A Critical Reader*, 3rd edition. London: Routledge, 83–96.

Cameron, D. (2014) British values. Available at: www.gov.uk/government/news/british-values-article-by-david-cameron. 15 June (Prime Minister's Office, 10 Downing Street, London).

Cameron, J. and Ojha, H. (2007) 'A deliberative ethic for development. A Nepalese journey from Bourdieu through Kant to Dewey and Habermas'. *International Journal of Social Economics*, 34(1/2), 66–87.

Chen, Y. and Feng, S. (2013) 'Access to public schools and the education of migrant children in China'. *China Economic Review*, 26, 75–88.

Clark, D. A. (2005) *The Capability Approach: Its Developments, Critiques and Recent Advances*. Global Poverty Research Group. Available at: www.gprg.org

DeJaeghere, J. (2012) 'Public debate and dialogue from a capabilities approach: Can it foster gender justice in education?' *Journal of Human Development and Capabilities*, 13(3), 353–72.

Fisher, R. (2013) *Teaching Thinking: Philosophical Enquiry in the Classroom*, 3rd edition. London: Bloomsbury.

Flores-Crespo, P. (2007) 'Situating education in the capabilities approach'. In M. Walker and E. Unterhalter (Eds.) *Amartya Sen's Capability Approach and Social Justice in Education*. Basingstoke: Palgrave Macmillan, 45–66.

Freire, P. (1972) *Pedagogy of the Oppressed*. London: Penguin.

Fuller, C. (2009) *Sociology, Gender and Educational Aspirations: Girls and Their Ambitions*. London: Bloomsbury.

Garnett, R. F. (2009) 'Liberal learning as freedom: A capabilities approach to undergraduate education'. *Studies in Philosophy of Education*, 28, 437–47.

Gillborn, D. and Youdell, D. (2000) *Rationing Education: Policy, Practice, Reform and Equity*. Buckingham: Open University Press.

Gore, C. (2015) 'The post-2015 moment: Towards sustainable development goals and a new global development paradigm'. *Journal of International Development*, 27, 717–32.

Hart, C. S. (2007) 'The capability approach as an evaluative and developmental framework for education policy: The example of widening participation in higher education in England'. *Prospero*, 13(3), 34–50.

(2009) 'Quo vadis? The capability space and new directions for the philosophy of educational research'. *Studies in Philosophy & Education*, 28(5), 391–402.

(2011) Thinking, doing, feeling: Capabilities in decision-making and transitions beyond school in the UK. Paper presented at the Children's Capabilities and Human Development Conference, Researching Inside and Outside of Schools, University of Cambridge, 12 April.

(2012a) *Aspirations, Education and Social Justice: Applying Sen and Bourdieu*. London: Bloomsbury.

(Ed.) (2012b) 'The capability approach and education'. *Cambridge Journal of Education*, 42(3), 275–82.

(2014) The capability approach and educational research. In C. S. Hart, M. Biggeri and B. Babic (Eds.) *Agency and Participation in Childhood and Youth – International Applications of the Capability Approach in Schools and Beyond*. London: Bloomsbury.

(2016) 'How do aspirations matter?' *Journal of Human Development and Capabilities*. 17(3), 324–41.

Hart, C. S., Biggeri, M. and Babic, B. (Eds.) (2014) *Agency and Participation in Childhood and Youth – International Applications of the Capability Approach in Schools and Beyond*. London: Bloomsbury.

Hart, R. (1992) Children's Participation – From tokenism to citizenship. *Innocenti Essay No. 4*. Florence: UNICEF.

Hinchcliffe, G. (Ed.) (2007) 'Capability approach and education'. *Prospero*, 13(3), 1–56.

Hinchcliffe, G. and Terzi, L. (Eds.) (2009) 'Capability approach and education'. *Studies in Philosophy and Education*, 28(5), 387–90.

Hymer, B. and Sutcliffe, R. (2012) *P4C Pocketbook*. Alresford: Teachers Pocketbooks.

Kelly, A. (2007) *School Choice and Student Well-Being: Opportunity and Capability in Education*. Basingstoke: Palgrave.

Koehler, G. (2015) 'Seven decades of "development", and now what?' *Journal of International Development*, 27, 733–51.

Lanzi, D. (2007) 'Capabilities, human capital and education'. *The Journal of Socio-Economics*, 36, 424–35.

Laureau, A. and Horvat, E. M. (1999) 'Moments of social inclusion and exclusion, race, class and cultural capital in family school relationships'. *Sociology of Education*, 72, 37–53.

Lipman, M. (2003) *Thinking in Education*, 2nd edition. Cambridge: Cambridge University Press.

McCowan, T. (2011) *Rethinking Citizenship Education: A curriculum for Participatory Democracy*. London: Bloomsbury.

Nussbaum, M. C. (2000) *Women and Human Development: The Capabilities Approach*. Cambridge: Cambridge University Press.

(2005) 'Capabilities as fundamental entitlements: Sen and social justice'. In B. Agarwal, J. Humphries and I. Robeyns (Eds.) *Amartya Sen's Work and Ideas – A Gender Perspective*. London: Routledge, 321–34.

(2010) *Not for Profit*. Princeton, NJ: Princeton University Press.

(2011) *Creating Capabilities*. Cambridge, MA: Harvard University Press.

Powell, L. (2012) 'Reimagining the purpose of VET – expanding the capability to aspire in South African further education and training students'. *International Journal of Educational Development*, 32, 643–53.

Power, S., Edwards, T., Whitty, G. and Wigfall, V. (2003) *Education and the Middle Class*. Buckingham: Open University Press.

Raynor, J. (2007) Education and capabilities in Bangladesh. In M. Walker and E. Unterhalter (Eds.) *Amartya Sen's Capability Approach and Social Justice in Education*. Basingstoke: Palgrave Macmillan.

Reay, D. (1998) '"Always knowing" and "never being sure": Familial and institutional habit uses and higher education choice'. *Journal of Education Policy*, 13(4), 519–29.

(2001) 'Finding or losing yourself: Working class relationships to education'. *Journal of Education Policy*, 16(4), 333–46.

(2004) 'Gendering Bourdieu's concepts of capitals? Emotional capital, women and social class'. *The Sociological Review*, 52(2), 57–74.

Reay, D., David, M. and Ball, S. (2005) *Degrees of Choice: Class, Race, Gender and Higher Education*. Stoke on Trent: Trentham.

Robeyns, I. (2005) 'The capability approach – a theoretical survey'. *Journal of Human Development*, 6(1), 93–114.

(2006) 'Three models of education: Rights, capabilities and human capital'. *Theory and Research in Education*, 4(1), 69–84.

Roehl, A., Reddy, S. L. and Shannon, G. J. (2013) 'The flipped classroom: An opportunity to engage millennial students through active learning strategies'. *Journal of Family and Consumer Sciences*, 105(2), 44–9.

Saito, M. (2003) 'Amartya Sen's capability approach to education: A critical exploration'. *Journal of Philosophy of Education*, 37(1), 17–31.

Santi, M. and di Masi, D. (2014) Pedagogies to develop children's agency in schools. In C. S. Hart, M. Biggeri, and B. Babic (Eds.) *Agency and*

Participation in Childhood and Youth – International Applications of the Capability Approach in Schools and Beyond. London: Bloomsbury, 123–44.

Sen, A. (1992) *Inequality Re-Examined*. Oxford: Clarendon Press.

(1999a) *Development as Freedom*. Oxford: Oxford University Press.

(1999b) *Commodities and Capabilities*. Oxford: Oxford University Press.

(2002) *India: Development and Participation*. Oxford: Oxford University Press.

(2005) 'Capabilities, lists and public reason: Continuing the conversation'. In B. Agarwal, J. Humphries and I. Robeyns (Eds.) *Amartya Sen's Work and Ideas – A Gender Perspective*. London: Routledge, 321–34.

(2009) *The Idea of Justice*. London: Penguin.

Skeggs, B. (2005) 'The making of class and gender through visualizing moral subject formation'. *Sociology*, 39, 965–82.

Terzi, L. (2007) The capability to be educated. In M. Walker and E. Unterhalter (Eds.) *Amartya Sen's Capability Approach and Social Justice in Education*. Basingstoke: Palgrave Macmillan.

(2008) *Justice and Equality in Education: A Capability Perspective on Disability and Special Educational Needs*. London: Continuum.

Tikly, L. and Barrett, A. (2011) 'Social justice, capabilities and the quality of Education in low income countries'. *International Journal of Educational Development*, 31, 3–14.

UNESCO (2005) *Decade of Education for Sustainable Development*. Available at: www.en.unesco.org/themes/education-sustainable-development.

United Nations (2010) The Millennium Development Goals Development Report 2010. Available at: www.un.org.

(2015a) Millennium Development Goals Report 2015.

(2015b) Resolution adopted by the General Assembly on 25 September 2015, Seventieth Session agenda items 15 & 116, A/RES/70/1, 21 October.

Unterhalter, E. (2003) 'The capability approach and gendered education: An examination of South African Complexities'. *Theory and Research in Education*, 1(1), 7–22.

(2009) 'Education'. In S. Deneulin and L. Shahani (Eds.) *An Introduction to the Human Development and Capability Approach*. London: Earthscan, 207–27.

Vaughan, R. (2007) 'Measuring capabilities: An example from girls' schooling'. In M. Walker and E. Unterhalter (Eds.) *Amartya Sen's Capability Approach and Social Justice in Education*. Basingstoke: Palgrave Macmillan.

Walker, M. (2005) 'Amartya Sen's capability approach and education'. *Education Action Research*, 13(1), 103–10.

(2006) *Higher Education Pedagogies. A Capabilities Approach.* Maidenhead: Open University Press/SRHE.

(Ed.) (2012) 'Education and capabilities'. *Journal of Human Development and Capabilities*, 13(3), 331–519.

Walker, M. and Unterhalter, E. (Eds.) (2007) *Amartya Sen's Capability Approach and Social Justice in Education.* Basingstoke: Palgrave Macmillan.

Walker, M. and McLean, M. (2015) *Professional Education, Capabilities and the Public Good – The Role of Universities in Promoting Human Development.* London: Routledge.

Wallace, B., Bernardelli, A., Molyneux, C. and Farrell, C. (2012) 'TASC: Thinking actively in a social context, a universal problem-solving process – A powerful tool to promote differentiated learning experiences'. *Gifted Education International*, 28(1), 58–83.

Wang, L. (2014) 'China's Janus-faced approach to Su Zhi education: a capability perspective'. *Journal of Human Development and Capabilities*, 15(4), 308–19.

Watts, M. and Bridges, D. (2004) *Whose Aspirations? What Achievement? An Investigation of the Life and Lifestyle Aspirations of 16–19 Year Olds Outside the Formal Education System.* Cambridge: Centre for Educational Research and Development, Von Hugel Institute.

Watts, M. (2006) 'Disproportionate sacrifices: Ricoeur's theories of justice and the widening participation agenda for higher education in the UK'. *Journal of Philosophy of Education*, 40(3), 301–12.

World Bank (2012) Homepage. Available at: www.worldbank.org.

Author Index

Aalbers, Manuel, 481
Acharya, Prachi, 8
Adams, James, 117
Addabbo, Tindara, Maria Laura di
  Tommaso and Gisella Facchinetti,
  233, 234, 248
Adelman, Irma and Cynthia Morris,
  411
Adger, Neil, 436
Aiken, William and John Haldane,
  353, 357
Alidadi, Farima, 529
Alkire, Sabina, 98, 167, 198, 200, 203,
  209, 223, 224, 334, 389, 398, 508
Allport, Gordon, 393
Alsop, Ruth Metter Bertelsen and
  Jeremy Holland, 422
Anand, P. B., 8, 9, 524, 538
Anand, Paul, Jaya Krishnakumar Ngoc
  Bric Tran, 247, 248
Anand, Paul and Amra Poggi, 461
Anand, Paula, Graham Hunter, Ian
  Carter, Keith Dowding, Francesco
  Guala, and Martin Van Hess, 442
Anand, Prathivadi and Roger Perman,
  524
Anand, Sudhir and Amartya Sen, 314,
  316, 318, 325
Anand Paul and Martin Van Hees,
  233, 247
Anderson, Benedict, 275
Anderson, Elizabeth, 203
Angrist, Joshua and John-Steffen
  Pischke, 242
Anker, Richard, 355, 371
Anker Richard and Martha Anker,
  354, 356
Appadurai, Arjun, 9, 415, 487, 527
Archer, Louise, Mervyn Hutchings and
  Alastair Ross, 636

Argenton, Carlo and Enzo Rossi,
  218
Aristei David and Bruno Bracalente,
  332, 336
Arlikatti, Sudha and simon Andrew,
  509
Arneson, Richard, 84
Arnold, Denis and Norman Bowie,
  356
Arrow, Kenneth, 183, 186
Athreya, Viijay, 280
Atkinson, Anthony, 259
Austin, Michael, 353
Awan, Nishat, Tatjana Schneider
  and Jeremy Till, 484

Baccini, Alberto, 563
Bailie, Ross and Kayli Wayte, 506
Ballet, Jerome, 9, 82, 87
Ballet, Jerome, Jean-Luc Dubois
  and Francois-Regis Mahieu,
  584, 589
Ballet, Jerome, Mario Biggeri and
  Flavio Comim, 550, 566
Ballet, Jerome and Jean Luc Dubois
  and Francois-Regis Mahieu, 91, 95,
  96, 98, 99, 101, 102
Ballon, Paula, 199, 200, 205, 213
Bandura, Albert, 392
Barac, Matthew, 490
Barac, Matthew, 7, 8, 159
Barclay, Linda, 209
Barr, Abigail and David Clark, 215
Barro, Robert, 549
Barry, Brian, 76
Bartelheimer, Peter Ortrud Leßmann
  and Wenzel Matiaske, 354
Bashir, Samiya, 506
Batty, Michael, 520
Becker, Gary, 262, 549

Bene, Christophe, Rachel Wood, Andrew Newsham and Mark Davies, 512
Ben-Porath, Sigal, 126
Bentham, Jeremy, 120
Benzécri, Jean-Paul, 555, 563
Berlin, Isiah, 54
Bernard, Tanguy, Alemayahu Tafesse and Stefan Dercon, 415
Beugelsdijk, Sjoerd and Ton Schalk, 436
Bharracharjee,Annanya, Sarita Gupta and Stephanie Luce, 366
Biau, Daniel, 478
Biggeri, Mario, 5, 6, 213
Biggeri, Mario, Renato Libanora, Stefano Mariani, Leonardo Menchini, 555
Biggeri, Mario and Andrea Ferrannini, 316
Biggeri, Mario and Renato Libanora, 317
Biko, Steve, 149
Binder, Martin and Tom Broekel, 235, 240
Binelli, Chiara, 331
Birdsall, Nancy, 420
Birtchnell, Thmoas, 287
Bjornskov, Christian, 336
Blagescu, Monica and Robert Lloyd, 368
Blaug, Mark, 549
Blundell Jones, Peter, Jeremy Till and Doina Petrescu, 486
Bohman, James, 218
Boni, Alejandra and Melanie Walker, 622
Bonvin, Jean-Michael, 354, 373
Bonvin, Jean-Michael and Nicolas Farvaque, 82, 84, 85, 86
Bosher, Lee and Andrew Dainty, 509
Bourdieu, Pierre, 7
Bourdieu, Pierre, and Richard Nice
Bourguignon, Francois and Satya Chakravarty, 314, 320
Bovens, Mark, 86, 98, 102, 103, 104
Bradlow, Benjamin, Joel Bolnick and Clifford Shearing, 509
Brandolini, Andrea and Giovanni D'Alessio, 321

Breman, Jan and Arvind Das, 278
Brenner, Mark, 353, 356
Bridge, Gary Sophie Watson, 539
Brock, Gilian, 203, 221, 222, 225
Brown, Kirk and Richard Ryan, 396
Brown, Sarah, Karl Taylor and Stephen Price, 443
Bruno, Luigino, Flavio Comim and Maurizio Pugno, 98
Burchardt, Tania, 34, 39, 203
Burchardt, Tania and Julian Le Grand, 233, 234
Burchardt, Tania and Polly Vizard, 200, 203, 204, 216, 221, 222, 225
Burchardt, Tania and Rob Hick, 333
Burchell, Graham, Colin Gordon and Peter Miller, 173
Burke, Tricia, Alisia Woszidlo and Crhis Segrin, 264
Byskov, Alexander, 199, 206, 220

Calestani, Melania, 142
Callan, Eamonn, 126
Cantril, Hadley, 336
Card, David, 453
Carr, Stuart, Jane Parker, James Arrowsmith, Jarod Watters and Harvey Jones, 354, 357, 376
Carrasco-Songer, Mia, 353
Carroll, Nick, Paul Fritjers and Michael Shields, 443
Carver, Charles and Michael Scheier, 389
Cassen, Robert, 279
Castells, Manuel, 476
Cawthorne Pamela and Gavin Kitching, 356
Chambers, Robert, 213
Chambers, Robert, 484, 485
Chanda, Pranab, 299
Chen, Yuanyuan Shuaizhang and Feng, 626
Chiappero, Enrica, 4, 5, 10
Chiappero-Martinetti, Enrica and Nadia von Jacobi, 492, 510, 511
Chiappero-Martinetti, Enrica and Paola Salardi, 234
Chirkov, Valery, Richard Ryan, Yongmee Kim and Ulas Kaplan, 396, 401

Chouliaraki, Lilie and Norman Fairclough, 160
Claassen, Rutger, 203, 211, 220, 223, 224
Claassen, Rutger and Markus Duwell, 202, 207, 208
Clark, Andrew, Paul Frijters and Michael Shields, 442
Clark, David, 33, 34, 39, 202, 213, 215, 413, 508, 511, 624
Clark, David, Mario Biggeri and Alex Frediani, 476
Clark, David and Mozzafar Qizilbash, 215
Cleaver, Frances, 159, 427, 485
Coakley, Michael and Michael Kates, 356
Coates, Dermot and Paul Anand, 479
Cobb, John, 65
Coburn, Andrew and Robin Spence, 506
Cohen, Gerald, 84
Coleman, James, 549
Comaroff, Jean and John L Comaroff, 141
Comim, Flavio, 3, 4, 10, 188, 203, 246, 251, 491
Comim, Flavio, Mozaffar Qizilbash and Sabina Alkire, 246
Condorcet, Marquis de, 135
Conill Sancho, Jesus, 82, 88, 93
Conradie, Ina, 413
Conradie, Ina and Ingrid Robeyns, 215
Conradie, Ina and Ingrid Robeyns, 415
Conti, Gabriella James Heckman, 549, 621
Cook, Bill and Uma Kothari, 213
Copestake, James and Laura Camfield, 413
Corbett, Jenny, 577
Cord, Robert, 13
Cornwall, Andrea and Karen Brock, 485
Cortina, Adela, 82, 88, 92, 93, 97
Couzens Hoy, David, 158
Crane, Andew and Dirk Matten, 368
Craven, John, 192, 211, 219
Crocker, David, 82, 88, 92, 93, 97, 202
Crocker, David and Ingrid Robeyns, 91

Crossley, Nick, 168
Crow, Ben, Nicole Zlatunich and Brian Fulfrost, 330

Dasgupta, Partha, 15, 17, 274
Davidson, Alastair, 159
De Botton, Alain, 488
De Soto, Hernando, 480
Deaton, Angus, Jane Fortson and Robert Tortora, 443
Decanq, Koen, 330, 331
Deci, Edward, Robert Vallerand, Luc Pelletier, and Richard Ryan, 550
Deci, Edward and Richard Ryan, 95, 396, 397
DeLanda, Manuel, 146, 147
Delaney, Brigid, 144
Deneulin, Severine, 65, 66, 67
Deneulin, Severine, Matthias Nebel and Nicholas Sagovsky, 97, 167
Denison, Edward, 549
Desai, Meghnad, 315
Devecchi, Cristina, 9, 10
di Tommaso, Laura, 247
Diener, Ed, Robert Emmons, Randy Larson and Sharon Griffin, 390
Diener, Ed and Robert Biswas-Diener, 437
DiTella, Rafael, John MacCulloch and Robert McKinnon, 443
Dohmen, Thomas, Armin Falk, David Huffman and Uwe Sunde, 263
Dolan, Paul and Matteo Galizzi, 443
Dolan, Paul and Robert Metcalfe, 443
Dorling, Danny, 418
Douglas, Mary and Stephen Ney, 141
Doyal, Len and Ian Gough, 203
Dreyfus, Hubert and Paul, 158
Dreze, Jean, 5, 33, 202
Dreze, Jean and Amartya Sen, 189, 202, 216, 273, 281, 373, 412, 430, 431
Drydyk, Jan, 203
Dubois, Jean-Luc and Jerome Ballet, 155
Dupont, Veronique and Usha Ramanathan, 431
Durkhelm, Emlie, 440
Dworkin, Ronald, 84

Easterly, William, 411, 417
Elster, John, 510
Erikson, Erik, 400
Escobar, Arturo, 140
Evans, Peter, 73

Fanon, Frantz, 143
Farrell, Paul, 144
Fennell, Shailaja, 7, 8
Fernandez, Leela, 417
Fernandez, Leela and Patrick Heller, 419, 425
Ferracioli, Luara and Rosa Tetazzo, 209
Fisher, Robert, 630
Florian, Lani and Margaret McLaughlin, 577
Florian, Lani and Martyn Rouse, 583
Forster, Edward Morgan, 65
Fredian1, Alexandre Apsan, 9, 202
Frediani, Alexander, 490, 509, 526
Frediani, Alexander and Camillo Boano, 509
Freeman, Gary, 143
Freire, Paulo, 631
Frey, Bruno, 392, 437
Frey, Bruno, Simon Luechinger and Alois Stutzer, 443
Frey Bruno and Alois Stutzer, 442
Fromm, Eric, 390
Fujiwara, Daniel, Paul Oroyemi and Ewan McKinnon, 441, 443, 444
Fukuda-Parr, Sakiko, 210, 315

Gangstead, Steven, 399
Gasper, Des, 5, 6, 7, 10, 33, 37, 40, 41, 246, 247, 274, 275, 282, 285, 306
Gauthier, David, 122
Geary, David, 399
Geertz, Clifford, 57
Geuss, Raymond, 139, 149
Gewirth, Alan, 209
Ghai, Subash, 262
Gibbons, Stephen and Stephen Machin, 441
Giddens, Anthony, 86, 476
Gilbert, Dirk, 368
Gilbert, Dirk and Andreas Rasche, 354
Gillborn, David and Deborah Youdell, 636

Glaeser, Ed, 488, 520
Goldmeier, Gabriel, 2
Goldsmith, Stephen and Susan Crawford, 520
Goldstein, Brett and Lauren Dyson, 520
Gomez, Eduardo, 261
Gould, Stephen Jay, 574
Gramsci, Antonio, 158
Greenberg, Jeff, Sheldon Solomon and Tom Pyszcynski, 399
Grootaert, Christiaan and Thierry Bastelarer, 436
Grosfoguel, Ramon, 143, 149
Grouzet Fredrick, Tim Kasser and Aaron Ahuvia, 395, 399
Guarin, Alejandro and Peter Knorringa, 417
Gullestad, Marriane, 143
Gutirrez, Nicholas, Ray Hilborn and Omar Defeo, 436

Hahn, Frank, 36
Hamdi, Nabeel, 485, 486
Hamza, Mohammed and Roger Zetter, 506
Hanlon, Phil, Richard Lawder and Duncan Buchanan, 533
Hansen, Julia, 509
Hardt, Michael and Antonio Negri, 168, 170
Hare, Richard Mervyn, 63
Harman, Graham, 146
Harper, Rosalyn, 440
Harriss, John, 419
Harriss-White, Barbara, 277
Hart, Caroline, 549, 552, 554, 555, 556, 618, 621, 624, 628, 630, 636
Hart, Caroline Sarojini, 10
Hausman, Daniel, 36
Heckman, James, 549
Heckman, James and Chase Corbin, 436
Heckman, James and Stefano Mosso, 263
Heckman James and Tim Kautz, 265
Hegel, Georg, 122
Herdt, Jennifer, 62
Hernandez, Diana, 506
Heshmati, Almas, 330, 331

Heynen, Nick, Maria Kaika and Eric Swyngedouw, 539
Hinchcliffe, Geoffrey and Lorella Terzi, 549
Hirai, Tadashi, 7, 9
Hobbes, Thomas, 118
Hodgett, Susan and Severine Deneulin, 203, 205, 213, 214
Holland, Breena, 203, 206, 221, 222, 224
Hollenbach, David, 65, 156
Honneth, Axel, 157
Huber, Evelyn, Dietrich Rueschemeyer and John Stephens, 217
Huber, Kristin, 6
Huchzermeyer, Marie, 480
Hume, David, 120
Huppert, Felicia and Tak Yee So, 438
Hurley, Suaan, 86
Hymer, Barry and Roger Sutcliffe, 630
Hyndman, Jennifer and Alison Mountz, 144

Ibrahim, Solava, 215, 415, 551, 584, 589
Ibrahim, Solava and Sabina Alkire, 423, 427
Inkpen, Andrew and Eric Tsang, 436

Jaffrelot, Christophe and Peter van der Veer, 416, 417, 419
Jaggar, Alsion, 206, 219
Jodhka, Surinder and Aseem Prakash, 420
John, Oliver and Sanjay Srivastave, 449
Jonas, Hans, 96
Jones, Steve, 158
Jordan, Paula and Ann Stanovich, 581
Jung, Carl, 400

Karayiannis, Anastassios and Aristides Hatzis, 436
Kasser, Tim, steve Cohn, Alan Kanner, and Richard Ryan, 399
Kasser, Tim and Richard Ryan, 389, 395, 396, 397
Keefer, Philip and Stuti Khemani, 261
Kelly, Anthony, 626, 636

Khader, Serene, 203, 223, 224
Kharas, Homi and Geoffrey Gertz, 417
Khilnani, Sunil, 273, 275
Khosla, Romi, 522
Khosla, Romi and Jane Samuels, 487
Kiff, Helena, 10
Kim, Danier, Christopher Baum, Michael Ganz, S. V. Subramanian and Ichiro Kawachi, 36
Kiugman, Jeni, 315, 319, 320
Klasen, Stefan, 202
Knapp, Michael, Anja Flack and Ercan Ayboga, 146
Koehler, Gabriele, 617
Korten, David, 368
Kreckel, Reinhard, 330, 331
Krieger, James and Donna Higgins, 506
Krishnakumar, Jaya, 4, 5, 203, 237, 247
Krishnakumar, Jaya and Paul Ballon, 233, 247
Krishnakumar, Jaya and Ricardo Nogales, 248, 258, 262
Kuhn, Thomas, 118
Kuklys, Wiebke, 34, 235, 236, 239, 240, 241
Kumar, Sanjay and Pushplata, 506
Kumari, Veena and R K P Singh, 506

Labowitz, Sarahand Dorothy Baumann-Pauly, 366
Laclau, Ernesto, 159, 168
Lake, Christopher, 86
Lam, Nicholas, Shonali Pachauri, and Palav Purohit, 506
Landes, David, 411
Langer, Amim and Graham Brown, 331
Layard, Richard, 392
Leijohhuvud, Alexander, 23
Lelli, Sara, 203, 234, 240, 243
Leßmann, Ortrud, 354, 549
Levinas, Emmanuel, 88, 100
Levinson, Arik, 443
Lewis, David, 161
Liebeg, Klaus, Petra Schmidt and Andreas Stamm, 353, 356, 357
Lipman, Pauline, 630
Lipton, Michael, 480
Lizzarralde, Gonzalo, 509

Locke, John, 118
Longshore Smith, Matthew and
    Ruhiya Seward, 492
Luechinger, Simon, 443
Luechinger, Simon and Paul Raschky,
    443

Mabogunje, Akin, Jorge Hardoy and
    Parameshwar Misra, 507
MacAskill, Kristen and Peter Guthrie,
    511, 512
MacIntyre, Alasdair, 62, 121
Maggino, Filomena, 446
Mahieu, Francois-Regis, 97
Maitland, Ian, 356
Maitra, Sudeshna, 422
Malviya, Paritosh, Albert Hasker and
    Epco Picado, 506
Mamdani, Mahmood, 143
Manyena, Bernard, Geoff O'Brien,
    Phil O'Keefe and Joanne Rose, 511
Marmot, Michael, 534
Maslow, Abraham, 393, 414
Mauro, Vincenzo, 5, 6
May, Todd, 156
Mazumdar, Indrani and Indu
    Agnihotri, 289
Mbembe, Achille, 145
McCowan, Tristan, 129
McFarlane, Colin, 148
McFarlane, Stephen and Colin
    Graham, 491
McGregor, Conor, 148
McKay, Andrew, 331
McLaren, Duncan and Julian
    Agyeman, 520
Meeks, Gay, xiv, xv, 1, 6, 12, 19, 39
Mehrotra, Santosh and Enrique
    Delamonica
Mehrotra, Santosh and Mario Biggeri
Mehrotra, Santosh and Richard Jolly,
    316
Menkiti, Ifeanyi, 141
Mershon, Carol, 261
Mignolo, Walter, 145
Mill, John Stuart, 21, 58, 118
Miller, Daniel, 487
Miller, Doug, 356
Miller, Josh Platzky, 3, 34, 139, 145,
    147, 155
Mills, Charles, 133

Mincer, Jacob, 262
Mischel, Walter, 60
Montgomery, Charles, 488
Moore, Barrington, 411
Moore, George, 63
Morris, Christopher, 154
Moser, Caroline and david
    Satterthwaite, 511
Mosse, David, 485
Mouffe, Chantal, 157, 158
Musiolek, Bettina, 351, 356, 357,
    365, 366, 375

Nair, Rukmini, 299
Naraian,Srikala, 586
Narayan, Deepa, 423
Narayan, Urvashi and Ruth Bell, 522
Nayyar, Deepak, 422
Nebel, Mathias, 2, 94, 99
Nebel, Mathias and Herrera-Nebel,
    Maria-Teresa, 2, 141
Nebel, Matthias and Teresa
    Herrera-Nebel, 82
Neugarten, Bernice, 400
Nilekani, Nandan, 289
Nogales, Ricardo, 4, 5
Norwich, Brahm, 576, 577, 591
Nozick, Robert, 78, 190
Nunez, Javier and Horatio Villegas,
    261
Nussbaum, Martha, xiv, 7, 10, 11, 23,
    55, 61, 70, 91, 99, 119, 122, 127,
    128, 133, 134, 136, 140, 142, 179,
    200, 206, 207, 208, 333, 334, 357,
    384, 386, 389, 397, 401, 402, 424,
    510, 524, 571, 572, 591, 597, 599,
    601, 603, 608, 609, 615, 623, 627

Olsen, Wendy, 484
O'Neill, Onora, 155
Orchard, Macarena, 6
Oswald, Andrew and Nattavudh
    Powdthavee, 443

Panagariya, Arvind, 301
Panet, Sabine and Chantal
    Duray-Soundrun, 155
Paramanand, Benedict, 286
Parfit, Derek, 57
Parker, Jane, 355
Patel, Sheela and Diana Mitlin, 522

Pateman, Carol and and Charles Mills, 132
Payne, Geoffrey, 497
Peaker, Glibert, 549
Pearlin, Leonard and Carmi Schooler, 392
Pelenc, Jerome, Minikeba Lompo, Jerome Ballet and Jean-Luc Dubois, 155
Plato, 62
Poggi, Amra, 443
Portes, Alejandro, 440
Powell, Lesley, 622
Prahalad, C. K., 287
Preiss, Joshua, 356
Putnam, Robert, 17

Qizilbash, Mozzafar, 41, 179, 182, 202

Radin, Tara and Martin Calkins, 356
Ranis, Gustav, Frances Stewart and Emma Samman, 316, 318
Ranis, Gustav and Frances Stewart, 315, 320, 321
Rao, Sachin, 287
Rao, Vijendra, Indrani Gupta, Michael Lokshin and Smarajit Jana, 441
Rasche, Andreas, 368, 369, 371, 373, 374
Rauh, Virginia, Philip Landrigan, and Luz Claudio, 506
Rawls, John, 6, 25, 54, 84, 120, 121, 124, 128, 132, 190, 391
Ray, Debraj, 413, 415, 425, 552
Raynor, Janet
Reay, Diane, 628
Renaud, Bertrand, 479
Revi, Aromar, 507, 511
Riaz, Ali and Mohammad Rahman, 165
Ricouer, Paul, 88
Ridley, Barbara and Michale Watts, 579
Rizvi, Firdaus
Robbins, Lionel, 183
Robeyns, Ingrid, 87, 91, 96, 97, 100, 101, 140, 147, 200, 206, 209, 219, 220, 221, 246, 251, 317, 357, 622, 624, 627

Rodriguez-Pose, Andres and Viola Berlepsch, 436
Roehl, Amy, Shweta Reddy and Gayla Shannon, 630
Roemer, John, 84, 85
Rogers, Carl, 393
Rosseau, Jean-Jacques, 118
Rowling, J. K., 25
Royo-Olid, Jaime, 7, 8, 477, 478, 481, 487, 490
Ryan, John, 372, 389, 510, 572
Ryan, Richard, 389
Ryan, Richard and Edward Deci, 390, 395, 396, 398, 400
Ryan, Richard, Valery Chirkov, Tood Little, Kenneth Sheldon, Elena Timoshina and Edward Deci, 391, 392
Ryan, Richard, Veronica Huta and Edward Deci, 397, 401, 402
Rydin, Yvonne, Ana Bleahu, and Michael Davies, 529
Ryff, Carol, 393, 394
Rffff, Carol and Burton Singer, 393, 394

Sacks, Jonathan, 55
Saito, Madoka, 551, 621
Salardi, Paola, 4, 5, 10
Samuels, Jane, 522, 523
Sandel, Michael, 21, 121
Santi, Marina and Diego di Masi, 630
Santos, Boaventura de Sousa, 129
Satterthwaite, David, 480, 483
Satterthwaite, David and Diane Mitlin, 476, 481
Scanlon, Thomas, 179
Scervini, Francesco, 4, 5, 10
Scheier, Michael and Charles Carver, 389
Scheper, Christian and Jonathan Menge, 356, 375
Schilderman, Theo and Michal Lyons, 509
Schokkaert, Erik, 247
Schokkaert, Erik and Luc Ootegem, 203
Schoon, Ingrid and Mel Bartley, 512
Schostak, John, 579
Schrage, Stephanie, 6

Schwartz, Shalom and Wolfgang
    Bilsky, 390
Schwatrz, Shalom, 390
Sen, Amartya, xiv, xvi, 1, 7, 11, 15,
    16, 17, 18, 19, 20, 21, 22, 23, 24,
    25, 26, 27, 29, 31, 34, 35, 36, 37,
    38, 40, 41, 42, 43, 44, 45, 57, 61,
    63, 71, 82, 84, 87, 89, 90, 124, 125,
    129, 130, 131, 140, 153, 154, 179,
    181, 183, 184, 185, 186, 187, 188,
    189, 190, 191, 192, 193, 194, 216,
    217, 219, 238, 246, 249, 254, 255,
    276, 314, 317, 330, 332, 333, 334,
    337, 352, 353, 357, 358, 363, 372,
    387, 397, 413, 438, 478, 485, 486,
    488, 505, 509, 523, 524, 571, 572,
    598, 622, 624, 632
Sen, Amartya and Thomas Scanlon,
    203, 216
Sengupta, Arjun, 202, 210, 217
Sewell, William, 160, 168
Sheldon, Kennon and Tim Kasser,
    395, 396
Sherer, Mark, James Maddux, Blaise
    Mercandante, Steven Prentice-Dunn,
    Beth Jacobs, and Ronald Rogers,
    392
Sidentop, Larry, 117
Siegfried, Kristy, 44
Singh, Shamsher, Madura
    Swaminathan and V K
    Ramachandran, 507
Skenderovic, Damir, 143
Slottje, Daniel, 202
Smith, Andrew, 217
Snyder, Jeremy, 356
Sollars, Gordon and Fred Englander,
    356
Sood, Amar, 509
Souza, Caroline, 2
Stabile, Donald, 353, 355, 357, 358
Stemplowska, Zofia, 85
Stewart, Francis and Severine
    Deveneulin, 139
Stiglitz, Joseph, 418
Streeten, Paul and Javed Shahid, 479
Stutzer, Alois and Bruno Frey, 443
Stweart, Frances, 74
Subbaraman, Ramanath, 526, 534,
    541

Subramaniam, S. and Barbara
    Harriss-White, 279, 309
Sugden, Robert, 38
Sunstein, Cass, 60
Surin, Kenneth, 157
Suzumura, Kotaro, 184
Swamy, Subramaniam, 302

Taylor, Charles, 120
Tellez, Juan, Jaya Krishnakumar,
    Martine Bungenger and Catherine
    Le Gallas, 248
Terzi, Lorella, 576, 621, 627
Teschl, Miriam and Flavio Comim,
    386
Thachil, Tariq, 305
Thaler, Richard, 60
Theckethil, Reshmi, 506, 507
Therborn, Goran, 330
Thomson, Hilary, Mark Petticrew and
    David Morrison, 506
Tikly, Leon and Barrett, Angeline, 620
Tisdell, Allan and Raj Kumar Sen, 63
Tiwari, Meera, 7, 427
Townsend, Peter, 520
Turner, John, 506, 509, 526
Turner, John and Robert Fichter,
    489

Unterhalter, Elaine, 636
Unterhalter, Elaine and Melanie
    Walker, 572
Upadhya, Carol, 417, 418, 420, 431

van der Berg, Bernard and Ada Ferrer-
    i-Carbonell, 443
van der Gaag, Martin and Tom
    Snijders, 446
van der Veen, Roel, 290
Van Praag, Bernard and
    Ada Ferrer-i-Carbonell, 392
van Praag, Bernard and Alois Stutzer,
    443
van Schendel, William, 161, 162
Vansteenkiste, Maarten, Joke Simmins,
    Willy Lens, Ken Sheldon, Edward
    Deci, 397
Vansteenkiste, Maarten, Richard Ryan
    and Edward Deci, 396
Vaughan, Rosie, 551, 622

Vizard, Polly, 34, 202, 203, 210
Vos, Robin, 9

Wahrman, Dror, 416
Walker, Melanie, 572, 600, 622, 627
Walker, Melanie and Elaine
  Unterhalter, 549
Walker, Melanie and Monica McClean,
  622
Walsh, Vivian, 332
Walzer, Michael, 218
Warner, Jonathan, 2, 141
Waterman, Alan, 389
Watson, Vanessa, 484
Watts, Michael, 9, 10, 572, 578, 584,
  589, 622, 628
Watts, Michael and Barbara Ridley,
  579
Watts, Michael and David Bridges,
  578, 622
Weber, Max, 99
Wendelspiess, Florian, 248

Wiebe-Berry, Ruth,
  576
Willis, Paul, 611
Wolf, Michael, Julie Gazamrarian
  and David Baker, 241
Wolff, Jonathan, 120
Woolcock, Michael and
  Deepa Narayanan, 436

Yahya, Saad, Elijah Agevi, Lucky
  Lowe, Alex Mugova, Oscar
  Musandu-Nyamayaor, and Theo
  Schilderman, 507
Yopo, Martina, 6

Zaidi, Ashghar and Tania Burchardt,
  234, 240
Zhou, Ling, Huazhen Lin and
  Yi-Chen Li, 248
Zimmer, Annette and Mathias Freise,
  155
Zwolinski, Matt, 356

Subject Index

adaptive preferences, 56, 63, 154, 215, 439, 511, 574
affiliation, 606
agency, 53–61, 88n8, 92, 193, 360, 512
  agency freedom, 53, 90n14, 91, 154
  and capabilities, 88–89
  distinction between critical agency and reasoned agency, 155
  and kantian approach, 93
  and meta-capability, 82
  and participation, 628
  strong-agency, 56
Arrow's Impossibility Theorem, 183
Asia Floor Wage, 375
assemblage theory, 145–146
autonomy, 400

basic needs approach, 32, 352–353, 478
big five dimensions of personality, 449
building codes, 506

capabilities, 28–29, 87, 153
  and aspirations, 550
  aspired capabilities, 552
  basic capabilities, 316, 359
  collective agency capabilities, 155
  collective capabilities, 147, 171
  and freedom, 40
  group capabilities, 74
  of learners, teachers, families and communities, 626
  list of, 335
  list of central, 599
  methods for selection, 200, 216–222
  quintile ratio, 342
  social capabilities, 147n24
capabilities approach, 61, 63, 167
  and affiliation, 70

and agency, 82
and Aristotle, 62
list, 200–201, 211, 219, 223
and participatory approach, 214
capability approach, 1, 23, 31, 181–182, 191, 247
  aspirations, 413
  and capabilitarianism, 44
  cities, 519
  comparison with other approaches, 307
  and deliberative democracy, 218
  diagrammatic form, 257
  and education, 621
  eudaimonic measure for, 398
  and inequality, 329
  and operationalisation, 34
  relation with human rights, 210
  and theoretical structure building, 258–260, 262
  work and remuneration in, 362
catholic social teaching, 66
child well-being, 549
cities and human development, 525
cities and women, 538
common good, 65–66, 76–77
  and the New Testament, 72
  and public policy, 68
  and solidarity, 67
community, definition, 71
  and the communities approach, 146–147
comparability, 17, 184
considerable disservice, 578
conversion factors, 27, 232, 238, 250, 360, 634
conversion rates, 233, 238
  and endogeneity issues, 242
  and relation to coversion efficiency, 240

dilemma of difference, 582
disability, 26, 589
disabled, 527, 630
dispositional factors, 585

emotions, 603
equality, 29
  measurement framework, 491
  of opportunities, 85, 259
ethical individualism, 87

figured worlds, 586
flourishing, 70
freedom: instrumental and constitutive, 361
functionings, 28, 249
  effective, 335
  not all conducive to human development, 55
  and opportunities, 29
  that one has reasons to value, 38
  vector, 28
  within processes of education, 627

garment industry, 351
General Capabilities Index, 340
Glasgow effect, 533
groups, definition, 71

habitare, 475
  habitare v habitat, 476–477
habitus, 159
happiness, 384, 488
  and the CA: Nussbaum v Sen, 385–387
  eudaimonia, 387
  self determination theory, 395
happy slaves, 578
hegemony, as defined by Gramsci, 158
Hesse diagram, 194
hierarchical cluster analysis, 562
housing, 475–500, 526, 540
human capital, 549
human development index, 42, 142–144, 194, 205, 315
  arithmetic vs geometric mean, 323
  and the multidimensional human development index, 316, 318

idealistic risk, 624
impartial spectator, 127

impartiality: open vs closed, 125
inclusive built environment, 505
index of multiple deprivation, 455
India, 273–294, 297–298, 300–305, 418–432, 507, 598
individualism
  ethical, 87, 141
  ontological, 140
inequality
  capability approach, 332–334
  multidimensional, 329
informational spaces, 188
instrumental freedoms, 159, 166
internalist essentialism, 206–207
international garment industry
  wages in, 364
international supply chain, 361
intersectionality, 349

justice, 77

labour markets, 321–322
Land Governance Assessment Framework, 483
lazy essentialism, 577
life expectancy, 530
living wage, 352–359
  living wage approaches and the capability approach, 370
  living wage calculation methodology, 357
  living wage debate, 355

maximin, 22
meta-ranking, 36, 180, 187–188, 190
middle classes in India, 411
monotonicity: strict monotonicty, 319
multiple correspondence factorial analysis (MCA) 562
multistakeholder initiatives, 352

objectivity, 17, 19, 27–28
obligations, 85
open classes, 556
open conditionality, 90
opportunity freedom, 316
orderings, 186
  and cardinality, 17
  intersection, 194
  and partial orderings, 27, 90

other species, 607
overlapping consensus, 118, 208–209

Paretian Liberal, 19, 20
parochialism, 127
partial interpersonal comparability, 15,
    17, 21
paternalism, 40
pavements, 537
penalisation, 315
pluralism, 28, 184, 192
political rights, 322
practical reason, 604
primary goods, 20, 21, 84, 85n3

rankings, 179
    complete rankings, 189
    and intersection of shared rankings,
        189
    lexicographic, 190
    partial rankings, 189
rational fools, 35
reasoned scrutiny, 185, 194, 217
resilience, 511
resources, 237
responsibility, 83, 87, 95
    versus agency, 94
    anterior responsibility, 97
    approaches, 86
    areas of responsibility, 96
    individual levels of responsibility,
        108
    natural responsibility, 104
    posterior responsibility, 98–100
    responsibility from and for the other,
        100–101
right to the city, 526

sel determination theory, 395, 551
SEM-MIMIC models, 233–234, 248,
    253–256

Shahbab Moment, 160–166
shelter, 490
smart cities, 537
social capital, 168, 436
social choice, 18, 129–130
social consensus, 364
social contract, 120–123
    and critiques, 123–124
social gradient, 531
social media, 172
socially fostered or socially stifled,
    584
special ecuational needs, 571
strategic nobility, 35
struggle, for Foucault, 158
substitutability, 319–321
Sustainable Development Goals, 314,
    520, 574, 617

teacher expectations and training,
    580
therapeutic writing for affiliation,
    610
tradeoffs and sacrifices, 635
transcendentalism, 32, 128

unfreedoms, 490, 522–525
Universal Declaration of Human
    Rights, 521
urban violence, 522
utilitarianism, 21–23, 28, 119–121

valuation function, 250
valuation methods, 440
value judgments, 17–18
    basic, 18
    nonbasic, 17
virtues, 134

walls of money, 481
writers' workshop, 597